# THE GLOBAL AGENDA:

## ISSUES AND PERSPECTIVES

# THE GLOBAL AGENDA

## ISSUES AND PERSPECTIVES

SIXTH EDITION

EDITED BY

# Charles W. Kegley, Jr.
# Eugene R. Wittkopf

Boston   Burr Ridge, IL   Dubuque, IA   Madison, WI
New York   San Francisco   St. Louis
Bangkok   Bogotá   Caracas   Lisbon   London   Madrid   Mexico City
Milan   New Delhi   Seoul   Singapore   Sydney   Taipei   Toronto

# McGraw-Hill Higher Education

*A Division of The **McGraw-Hill** Companies*

THE GLOBAL AGENDA: ISSUES AND PERSPECTIVES, SIXTH EDITION

Published by McGraw-Hill, an imprint of The McGraw-Hill Companies, Inc., 1221 Avenue of the Americas, New York, NY 10020. Copyright © 2001, 1998, 1995, 1992, 1988, 1984 by The McGraw-Hill Companies, Inc. All rights reserved. No part of this publication may be reproduced or distributed in any form or by any means, or stored in a database or retrieval system, without the prior written consent of The McGraw-Hill Companies, Inc., including, but not limited to, in any network or other electronic storage or transmission, or broadcast for distance learning.

Some ancillaries, including electronic and print components, may not be available to customers outside the United States.

 This book is printed on recycled, acid-free paper containing 10% postconsumer waste.

1 2 3 4 5 6 7 8 9 0 DOC/DOC 0 9 8 7 6 5 4 3 2 1 0

ISBN 0–07–232269–1

Vice president and editor-in-chief: *Thalia Dorwick*
Editorial director: *Jane E. Vaicunas*
Sponsoring editor: *Monica Eckman*
Editorial coordinator: *Hannah Glover*
Marketing manager: *Janise A. Fry*
Project manager: *Mary Lee Harms*
Senior media producer: *Sean Crowley*
Senior production supervisor: *Sandra Hahn*
Coordinator of freelance design: *Michelle D. Whitaker*
Cover designer: *Nathan Bahls*
Cover image: *©PhotoDisc*
Photo research coordinator: *John C. Leland*
Supplement coordinator: *Tammy Juran*
Compositor: *York Graphic Services, Inc.*
Typeface: *10/12 Times Roman*
Printer: *R. R. Donnelley & Sons Company/Crawfordsville, IN*

The credits section for this book begins on page 499 and is considered an extension of the copyright page.

**Library of Congress Cataloging-in-Publication Data**

The global agenda: issues and perspectives / [edited by] Charles W. Kegley, Eugene R. Wittkopf.—6th ed.
    p.  cm.
    ISBN 0–07–232269–1
    1. International relations.  2. International economic relations.  3. Globalization.
    4. World politics—1989–  .  I. Kegley, Charles W.  II. Wittkopf, Eugene R., 1943–  .

JZ1242 .G56  2001
327 .1′01—dc21
                                        00–025531
                                        CIP

www.mhhe.com

For Suzanne and Peter Douglas and
my grandson, Scott
CWK
For Barbara, Debra, and Jonathan
ERW

# ABOUT THE EDITORS

CHARLES W. KEGLEY, JR. earned his Ph.D. in international relations from Syracuse University in 1971. He holds the position of Pearce Professor of International Relations at the University of South Carolina, where he served as chairman of the Department of Government and International Studies from 1981 to 1985 and as director of the James F. Byrnes International Center from 1985 to 1988. President of the International Studies Association (1993–1994), Kegley also has taught at the Georgetown University School of Foreign Service, at the University of Texas, and at Rutgers University as the Moses and Annuta Back Peace Scholar. He has coauthored or coedited, with Eugene R. Wittkopf, *American Foreign Policy: Pattern and Process* (5th ed., 1995); *World Politics: Trend and Transformation* (8th ed., 2001); *The Nuclear Reader: Strategy, Weapons, War* (2nd ed., 1989); and coauthored, with Gregory A. Raymond, *How Nations Make Peace* (1999), *A Multipolar Peace? Great-Power Relations in the Twenty-First Century* (1994), and *When Trust Breaks Down: Alliance Norms and World Politics* (1990); also, he has edited *The Long Postwar Peace: Contending Explanations and Projections* (1991), and *Controversies in International Relations Theory: Realism and Neoliberalism* (1995) and coedited, with Kenneth L. Schwab, *After the Cold War: Questioning the Morality of Nuclear Deterrence* (1991). He has published articles in *International Studies Quarterly, The Journal of Conflict Resolution, The Journal of Peace Research, International Organization, Ethics & International Affairs, Alternatives, The Journal of Politics, The Bulletin of Peace Proposals, USA Today,* the *Harvard International Review,* among others.

EUGENE R. WITTKOPF received his doctorate from Syracuse University. He is currently R. Downs Poindexter Distinguished Professor of Political Science at Louisiana State University. He has also held appointments at the University of Florida and the University of North Carolina at Chapel Hill. Wittkopf is author of *Faces of Internationalism: Public Opinion and American Foreign Policy* (1990) and coeditor, with James M. McCormick, of *The Domestic Sources of American Foreign Policy: Insights and Evidence* (3rd ed., 1999); and coeditor, with Christopher M. Jones, of *The Future of American Foreign Policy* (3rd ed., 1999). With Charles W. Kegley, Jr., he is coauthor of *American Foreign Policy: Pattern and Process* (5th ed., 1996) and *World Politics: Trend and Transformation* (8th ed., 2001); and co-editor of *The Nuclear Reader: Strategy, Weapons, War* (2nd ed., 1989). He has contributed chapters to several books and published articles in the *American Political Science Review, International Journal, International Organization, International Studies Quarterly, Journal of Conflict Resolution, Journal of Politics, Orbis, Polity, Social Science Quarterly,* and the *Washington Quarterly,* among others. In 1997 Professor Wittkopf was named the LSU Distinguished Research Master of Arts, Humanities, and Social Sciences. This is the highest award given by LSU in recognition of contributions to research and scholarship.

# CONTENTS

# PREFACE

There is no scientific antidote [to the atomic bomb], only education. You've got to change the way people think. I am not interested in disarmament talks between nations. . . . What I want to do is to disarm the mind. After that, everything else will automatically follow. The ultimate weapon for such mental disarmament is international education.

—Albert Einstein

Much uncertainty and anxiety characterize the global agenda as we launch a new millennium. Many rapidly unfolding trends, some of recent origin, others long standing, have generated new issues, new cleavages, and a new global landscape. The prospect of revolutionary transformation alongside change and continuity in contemporary world politics obscures our vision of the precise nature of the world in which we live. Perhaps this is why, even as we enter a new century, a consensus has not yet emerged about the defining character of world politics more than a decade after the end of the cold war. Ours is the era of transition from a past epoch that was easily defined and well understood to an era that remains ill defined and not easily characterized. So we find ourselves on the threshold of a new historical era without a concise way to describe it.

Whatever the global system's ultimate nature, the potential for great changes has opened up a Pandora's box of new controversies and unfamiliar developments. Simultaneously, traditional controversies continue to color global political relations. This condition presents an intellectual challenge because the study of contemporary world politics must consider the factors that produce change as well as those that promote continuities in relations among political actors on the global stage.

Because change is endemic to international politics, it is not surprising that many new issues on the global agenda and fresh perspectives on their analysis have emerged since the fifth edition of this book was published in 1998. Our purpose in preparing a sixth edition is to provide a basis for making an informed assessment of world politics by bringing information up to date and by presenting current commentary on the dominant issues in contemporary international politics and the rival analytical perspectives constructed to understand them. But the overarching goals that motivated the first five editions remain: to make available to students what we, as editors, believe to be the best introductions to the issues that underlie contemporary world politics and to introduce the major analytical perspectives and organizing concepts that scholars have fashioned to make these issues comprehensible. It seems to us that, to a greater or lesser degree, coverage of both these elements is missing in standard texts (by design and necessity) and that a supplementary anthology is the logical place for them.

*The Global Agenda: Issues and Perspectives* categorizes essays into four "baskets" that emphasize the politics on peace and security (Parts One and Two) and the politics of non-military issues that tend to emphasize material and nonmaterial well-being (Parts Three and Four). The criteria that guided the selection of particular articles within each part and the rationale that underlies the organization of the book are made explicit in our introductions to each part. These introductions are further designed to help students connect individual essays to common themes.

The organization of the book is intended to capture the diversity of global issues and patterns of interaction that presently dominate the attention of world political actors and precipitate policy responses. This thematic organization allows treatment of the breadth of global issues and of the analytical perspectives that give them meaning, ranging from classical theoretical formulations to the newer analytical foci and concepts that have arisen to account for recent developments in world affairs. In preparing the volume in this manner, we have proceeded from the assumption that there is a need for educational materials that treat description and theoretical exposition in a balanced manner and expose a variety of normative interpretations without advocating any particular one.

Several people have contributed to the development of this book. We wish especially to acknowledge the contributions of David P. Forsythe, Ted Robert Gurr, Ole R. Holsti, Christopher C. Joyner, Jack S. Levy, Bjørn Møller, Donald J. Puchala, Bruce Russett, Marvin Soroos, Linda Y. C. Lim, Greg Mastel, Tim Lang, and Harvey Starr, who provided us with original essays written especially for publication in this book. The helpful suggestions of a number of anonymous reviewers are also gratefully acknowledged, and the commissioned blind reviews by Lev Gonick, California Polytechnic Institute; Vincent Wei-cheng Wang, University of Richmond; Jeanne Jensen, Augusta State University; Tun-Jen Cheng, College of William and Mary; Laura MacDonald, Carlton University; Albert Yee, Georgia State College and University; Gerald Bridgeman, Moorpark College; and John Queen, Arizona State University. We additionally thank Ruth Cooper for her professional assistance in the preparation of this manuscript, and Jamie Pasley, Tahir Cevik, Fahrettin Sümer, Julie Hysong, Se-Woo Pyo, and Jiayin Zhang for their help with proofreading of final copy. At McGraw-Hill we are indebted to Monica Eckman, Hannah Glover, Mary Lee Harmss, and Janise Fry for their support and professional assistance.

Charles W. Kegley, Jr.
Eugene R. Wittkopf

---

# ARMS AND INFLUENCE

---

The contemporary international political system began to acquire its present shape and definition more than three hundred fifty years ago with the emergence of a state system in Europe after the highly destructive Thirty Years War. As the Westphalian treaties in 1648 brought that war to an end and as political, economic, and social intercourse grew among the states of Europe, new legal norms were embraced in an effort to regulate interstate behavior. The doctrine of state sovereignty, according to which no legal authority is higher than the state, emerged supreme. Thus the nascent international system was based on the right of states to control their internal affairs without interference from others and to manage their foreign relations with other states with whom they collaborated or competed as they saw fit. Foremost in this system was the belief, reinforced by the international law created by the Westphalian peace settlement, that the state should possess the right—indeed, the obligation—to take whatever measures it deemed necessary to ensure its preservation.

The international system and the patterns of interaction among its political actors have changed profoundly since the birth of the state system, and rulers' capacity to authoritatively manage their country's domestic and foreign policies has receded as new international norms and institutions, and the pressures of globalization, have curtailed leaders' former sovereign freedom. Nonetheless, contemporary world politics remains significantly colored by its Westphalian legacy: it continues to be conducted in an atmosphere that bears a strong resemblance to anarchy. As in the past, the system remains fragmented and decentralized, with

1

no higher authority of true global governance above nation-states, which, as the principal actors in world politics, can behave toward one another largely as they choose.

This is not meant to imply either that states exercise their freedom with abandon or that they are unconstrained in the choices they make. The political, legal, moral, and circumstantial constraints on states' freedom of choice are today formidable. Moreover, states' national interests are served best when states act in a manner that does not threaten the stability of their relations with others or of the global system that protects their autonomy. Hence, the international system, as the British political scientist Hedley Bull reminds us, may be an anarchical society, but now it is clearly one of "ordered anarchy."

The world has grown increasingly complex, interdependent, and "globalized" as contact, communication, and exchange have increased among the actors in the state system and as the number of nation-states and other nonstate global actors has grown. Expanded interaction enlarges the range of potential mutually beneficial exchanges between and among transnational actors. But just as opportunities for cooperation have expanded, so have the possible sources of disagreement. That we live in an age of conflict is a cliché that contains elements of truth, as differences of opinion and efforts to resolve disputes to one's advantage, often at the expense of others, are part of any long-term relationship. Thus, as distance has disappeared as a factor and the barriers once provided by borders between states have eroded, the mutual dependence of transnational political actors on one another has grown and the number of potential rivalries, antagonisms, and disagreements has increased correspondingly. Friction and tension therefore appear to be endemic to international relations; the image of world politics conveyed in newspaper headlines does not suggest that a shrinking world in the twenty-first century's era of globalization will necessarily become a more peaceful one. Instead, even as memory of the twentieth century's three general wars (World War I, World War II, and the Cold War) fades, competition and conflict persist, as demonstrated by the ubiquitous eruption of ethnic conflicts, civil wars, and religious disputes throughout the world and the inability to prevent their outbreak in many flash points across the globe.

Given the pervasiveness of conflict in contemporary world politics, the number of *issues* that are at any one time in dispute among nation-states and other global actors appears to have increased greatly. The multitude of disagreements and controversies renders the *global agenda*—the list of issues that force their way into consideration and command that they be addressed—more crowded and complex. Because the responses that are made to address the issues on the global agenda shape our lives both today and into the future, it is appropriate that we direct attention to those controversies and major concerns that command the primary attention of decision-makers. At the same time, as different state and nonstate actors view global political issues from widely varying vantage points, it is fitting that we remain sensitive to the various perceptual lenses through which the items on the global agenda are viewed. Accordingly, *The Global Agenda: Issues and Perspectives* seeks to focus on the range of issues that dominates world politics as well as on the multitude of analytical and interpretive perspectives from which those issues are viewed.

The issues and perspectives discussed in *The Global Agenda* are grouped into four broad, somewhat overlapping, but analytically distinct issue areas: (1) arms and influence, (2) discord and collaboration, (3) politics and markets, and (4) ecology and politics. The first two issue areas deal with states' security interests; the latter two deal with the non-military issues on which world political actors also concentrate their attention. In all four issue areas, we seek to convey not only the range of issues now facing those responsible for political choices, but also the many vantage points from which they are typically viewed.

We begin in Part One with consideration of a series of issues appropriately subsumed under the collective rubric *Arms and Influence.* As the term "high politics" suggests, the issues and perspectives treated here focus on the prospects for peace and security in a world of competitive nation-states armed with increasingly diverse arsenals of lethal and "non-lethal" weapons with which to coerce and/or destroy adversaries.

## ARMS AND INFLUENCE

It is often argued that states strive for power, security, and domination in a global environment punctuated by the threat of violence and death This viewpoint flows naturally from the characteristics of the international political system, which continues to be marked by the absence of central institutions empowered to authoritatively manage and resolve conflict. Hence, preoccupation with preparations for defense becomes understandable, for the fear persists that one adversary might use force against another to realize its goals or to vent its frustrations, and the threat of separatist revolts and civil rebellions to sever minority populations from existing sovereign states has become a major trend. In such a threatening environment, arms are widely perceived as useful not only to enhance security at home but also as a means to realize and extend a state's influence abroad. Hence, countries frequently see their interests best served by a search for power, by whatever means necessary. Understandably, therefore, *power* and *influence* remain the core concepts in the study of world politics.

Appropriately, the first essay, "Power, Capability, and Influence in International Politics," by K. J. Holsti, provides a thoughtful discussion of the changing meaning of power, capability, and influence in the foreign policy behavior of states in contemporary world politics. The essay provides important insights not only for evaluating the subsequent essays in this book but also for evaluating the use to which these necessary but ambiguous terms are often incorporated into other interpretations of global issues, because, almost invariably, such discussions make reference, implicitly or explicitly, to the interrelationships among power, capability, and influence.

If the purpose of statecraft is the pursuit of political power, then a critical question is: What are the most appropriate means through which states can effectively exercise influence on the global stage? In addition, are those means changing in fundamental ways at the start of the twenty-first century, departing from the traditional patterns of the past several centuries? In "Power and Interdependence in the Informational Age," Robert O. Keohane and Joseph S. Nye, Jr. provide an interpretation and forecast of the factors that are most likely to enable states to survive, to control their fates, and to increase their power and position in the future global hierarchy. Arguing that a technological revolution in knowledge and technology has produced an "information age," Keohane and Nye contend this revolution has transformed the classical meanings of the nature of power, its sources, and the purposes and functions of the state. Whereas in the past the acquisition of military might (or "hard power") for territorial conquest was habitually seen as the best path to national power and leadership over competitors, today the military struggle for territory no longer holds the payoff that once was widely ascribed to it. Although the struggle for influence through arms clearly continues, this essay predicts that the key to global power in the future will lie primarily in leadership in information and electronic technologies and the prestige and respect that the attainment of such "soft power" provides, rather than in the pursuit of "hard power" through the acquisition of military capability to destroy by force.

Noting that throughout the twentieth century many modernists were in agreement that technology would transform world politics, Keohane and Nye find compelling those futurists' arguments that the information revolution is leading to a new electronic feudalism, with a larger and larger number of overlapping communities in the global arena laying claim to citizens' loyalties. However, they find irony in this development, because this transformation has actually strengthened states, which Keohane and Nye perceive to be very resilient. In fact, in the twenty-first century in which the control and production of information is the most potent source of political power, geographically based states are likely in the "information age" to dominate international politics and shape its direction. What is new, Keohane and Nye predict, is that states will depend less and less on traditional resources of military power to get their way and more and more on their ability to remain credible to a national public with increasingly diverse sources of information. This means the "soft power" will matter more and more and "hard power" will mean less and less; the states that lead the information revolution will lead the world in international politics.

At issue is a basic controversy: how security can best be attained and welfare assured, and how people should most accurately conceive of the sources of global power in the future. Perhaps precisely because the world is rapidly changing, Keohane and Nye's provocative prescriptions about the most viable strategies to both national prosperity and international influence must be given serious attention. These questions deserve a high place on the global agenda because they concern choices regarding policy priorities no policymaker can dare ignore.

The interpretation, predictions, and prescriptions advanced by Keohane and Nye are, of course, subject to theoretical and empirical questioning from other perspectives. In the next selection, "The Role of Military Power in the Third Millennium," Bjørn Møller takes exception to the view that military force no longer plays a decisive role in world politics, and maintains that even with the declining incidence of war between states, it appears likely that military capabilities continue to matter greatly to many states and are perceived by them as useful to exercise international influence. Møller avers that military power continues to play a central, maybe even growing, role in international politics because a number of countries remain committed to developing tools and techniques for waging war in order to gain a competitive advantage over their rivals. Observing that a momentous "revolution in military affairs" (RMA) is underway, Møller emphasizes the growing impact of such revolutionary technologies as satellite imagery, smart bombs, and a variety of so-called "non-lethal weapons" that destroy and incapacitate their targets without killing. This revolution, Møller warns, is transforming the ways military power is currently being pursued to acquire political influence on the world stage.

The traditional military approaches to political power remain popular. Those approaches' popularity stems from the lessons drawn from the recent episodes of armed conflicts that have influenced military planning for future wars. Møller takes as his point of departure two wars in 1999—the U.S.-British war against Iraq and NATO's 78-day war against Yugoslavia—and extrapolates how those war experiences have begun to transform strategies and weapons technologies for the wars perceived likely in the twenty-first century. He finds dangerous the assumptions being made that through the so-called revolution in military technology warfare can be made short, "clean," painless—and therefore attractive as an option in the future. Criticized are four major prevailing "myths" that are driving contemporary military planning. Møller labels these (1) "the myth of success" that encourages victors in wars to rely on those same winning strategies to vanquish their next enemies; (2) the myth that "wars without tears" can be fought; (3) the assumption that invisible and noncontroversial "wars that are not really wars" can be waged through military interventions short of large-scale wars; and (4) the myth that "high-tech smart bombs" and "non-lethal weapons" provide an effective means to war-fighting which rationalizes faith in the aforementioned other "myths" presently dominating military planning. Møller frames the future by showing that "the phenomenon of war is changing shape rather than disappearing," and voices alarm about the possibility that these seductive myths will "weaken the inhibitions against wars of aggression, thereby making wars more likely." The compound effect, Møller concludes, "may be a militarization of world politics." If defense planners get their way, military power and warfare will remain a prominent characteristic of twenty-first century world politics, just as it was throughout the twentieth century. Indeed, technological innovations will make it probable that states will continue to heavily rely on and use "hard power" by military means to exercise political influence on the world stage, and eschew emphasis on "soft power" to win friends, persuade enemies, and gain victories in how people think and act by shaping attitudes in the information age.

Møller's thesis is compelling and sobering, because it foresees the persisting use of armed force throughout the first quarter of the new millennium. To assess the probable accuracy of this prediction, it is useful to step back and consider the factors from which past and future wars originate. The picture and prescriptions Møller presents, he would argue, must be interpreted in light of the changing relationship of arms to decisions regarding war and peace. Indeed, against the backdrop of revolutionary changes in the tools and techniques for waging war, careful consideration needs to be given to the sources or determinants of war, against the backdrop of changing patterns of warfare. Because arms both threaten and protect, a congeries of rival hypotheses can be advanced about the causes of armed conflict and of peace in the twenty-first century. In "War and Its Causes," Jack S. Levy summarizes leading ideas embedded in the assumptions of contending theories to which we might refer to explain the role of force in world politics and the means to preserve peace.

Levy notes that the outbreak of war derives from a wide range of circumstantial and causal factors, some internal to particular states and many external to them, that combine to influence war's occurrence. Levy relies on the well-known "levels-of-analysis" framework to organize inquiry, which separates the roots of war into three major categories: the influence of (1) individuals, (2) national circumstances, and (3) the "systemic" (or "structural") attributes of the international system writ large that affect the outbreak of war. Levy pays special attention to major structural explanations, in the realist theoretical tradition, that stress the potent impact of the global system on states' decisions about war and wars' frequent incidence: (1) international anarchy and the security dilemma it creates; (2) theories of international equilibrium such as the balance of power; (3) "power transition" theories about the rise and fall of great powers and the potentially stabilizing impact of a dominant hegemonic leader; and (4) the liberal economic theory that postulates that free trade promotes peace. This review suggests that, because war clearly has multiple potential causes, it is difficult to control, inasmuch as control depends on a varied combination of tangible and intangible factors. Moreover, Levy warns that the changing distributions of power in international and regional systems that have influenced decisions for war or peace so often in the past will continue to play a central role in such decisions in the future. The reasons for this prediction are elaborated in Levy's concise summary of the "national-level" and "individual-level" theories of war's causes; the former treatment stresses the "democratic peace" proposition, and the latter focuses on the perceptual and psychological factors influencing foreign policy choices about war and peace.

Achieving international security is often confounded by changes in global conditions. One potential change underway that prompts fresh thinking is the growing evidence about a profoundly important long-term global political achievement: Since World War II the great powers have experienced the longest period of uninterrupted peace since the advent of the territorial state system in 1648. In this category of analysis, we can claim that the disappearance of wars between the great powers truly *has* transformed the character of international politics, without risking the accusation that the claim is exaggerated. However, whether weapons produced this remarkable outcome—or whether this long post-World War II peace occurred despite these weapons—deserves consideration.

In "The Obsolescence of Major War," John Mueller explores the policy and moral implications of this accomplishment, in which war between states has passed from a noble institution to one in which it is now widely regarded as illegal, immoral, and counterproductive. The steps to this global awakening are traced in his account, which sees the contribution of nuclear weapons essentially irrelevant to the preservation of the long peace among the great powers that has persisted since World War II. Noting that although "war in the developed world . . . has not become impossible" and war in the Third World remains frequent and increasingly deadly, Mueller nonetheless sees hope for the future in the fact that "peoples and leaders in the developed world—where war was once endemic— have increasingly found war to be disgusting, ridiculous, and unwise." "If war begins in the minds of men, as the UNESCO Charter insists," then, Mueller maintains, "it can end there." That would indeed alter the way the world has conventionally thought about arms, influence, and peace. In such a world (Møller's predictions about the persisting preparations to wage wars through the development of revolutionary military capabilities notwithstanding), the utility of armed force as an instrument of influence would be certain to command far less respect than in the past.

Nuclear weapons are doubtless the most lethal form of power and hence the most threatening instruments of influence. How to avoid their use has dominated strategic thinking ever since the atomic age began in 1945. *Deterrence*—preventing a potential adversary from launching a military attack—has dominated strategic thinking about nuclear weapons since their creation. The failure of deterrence, particularly in a war between nuclear powers, could, of course, ignite a global conflagration culminating in the destruction of humanity, which means that the entire world has a stake in the operation of a successful deterrent strategy.

For many years great faith was placed in the ability of nuclear weapons to keep the peace. Indeed, the most popular theory of the avoidance of general war since 1945 is the claim that nuclear weapons have made general war obsolete. But others endorse John Mueller's thesis that nuclear weapons are "essentially irrelevant" in the prevention of major war. As argued at length in his well-known 1989 book *Retreat from Doomsday,* the growing aversion to war in general, in conjunction with the inhibiting fear of another major *conventional* war in particular, explain the obsolescence of war in the wealthy developed countries in the Global North.

Paul H. Nitze, a realist pioneer in thinking about strategies since the beginning of the nuclear age, evaluates the role that nuclear weapons have played since Hiroshima and can play in the twenty-first century. Whereas he implies that nuclear arsenals may have once served a deterrent purpose in preventing the outbreak of a major great power war in the second half of the twentieth century, Nitze now argues that nuclear weapons today are not only unnecessary but dangerous, and that they should be dismantled because the threat they pose to the survival of the human race is far greater than the safety that nuclear weapons symbolically provide to the seven nuclear-weapons states that presently have a nuclear-weapons capacity. As argued in "Nuclear Weapons Threaten Our Existence," Nitze warns that even if nuclear weapons may have helped to maintain international peace during the Cold War, now nuclear weapons undermine international security instead of enhancing it. Nitze advances the controversial conclusion that nuclear weapons no longer provide the countries which possess them with security at reasonable cost. With nuclear warheads available for use by a growing number of states, Nitze predicts the new millennium world will be less stable. The dangers to the survival of states are increasing, he warns, because following the October 1999 rejection of the Comprehensive Test Ban Treaty by the U.S. Senate, many countries with the capacity to develop nuclear weapons that had formerly pledged not to may now seek to become members of the nuclear-weapons elite, as India and Pakistan did in 1998. In that case, as Nitze warns, nuclear proliferation will increase and the probability that humanity will survive will decrease. Scholars and policymakers have not understood the true strategic implications of nuclear weaponry, Nitze suggests, with the result that the risks posed by nuclear weapons are not fully appreciated.

Without a doubt, the possibility that the number of members of the "nuclear club" could increase dramatically in the future is a critical variable affecting the prospects for peace. As argued by former U.S. Undersecretary of Defense Fred Charles Iklé in 1997, the "second coming of the nuclear age" is on the horizon. This makes worldwide control over weapons of mass destruction at once imperative and at the same time increasingly difficult. Thus managing *nuclear proliferation* is a major political issue.

The risks to international security extend beyond nuclear proliferation, however. In "The New Threat of Mass Destruction," Richard K. Betts argues that although it appears that the risk of a catastrophic exchange of nuclear weapons probably is declining, at the same time the chances that other, non-nuclear uses of weapons of mass destruction are rising. A new arms race is looming on the threshold of the twenty-first century. Despite recent breakthroughs in the negotiated reduction of the major superpowers' nuclear arsenals, many states are actively pursuing development of warfighting capabilities by other means. The proliferation threat has changed, Betts shows, and for the worse. Plans for making weapons of mass destruction, such as biological and chemical weapons, are energetically under way, and although use of these weapons are less a threat to human survival, they are more likely to be used. This ready availability of weaponry raises the stakes; the formidable array of new weapons of destruction puts control over the fate of millions in the possession of lunatics, fanatics, and terrorists throughout the globe who have no qualms about using them for their narrow and evil purposes. As Betts warns, a vial of anthrax dispersed over Washington could kill as many as three million. Traditional deterrence will not stop a disgruntled terrorist group with no identifiable address from striking. How to guard against the threat posed is a major challenge, even for a superpower like the United States, and Betts foresees no assured method of deterrence to safeguard citizens against the new threat. Hence, Betts concludes that the only option is for the United States to withdraw from excessive foreign involvements and begin a program of civil defense to reduce casualties in the event the unthinkable happens.

International security is precarious because new weapons of mass destruction are widespread and growing. Until recently, wishful thinking about the low probability of a calamity inhibited the great powers' ability to create strong international controls of annihilating weapons. Much remains to be accomplished in the area of arms control as an item on the global agenda, because it appears that the strategic mindsets and theories of deterrence of the past half century are still anachronistically being applied to the new threats; defense planning has failed to keep pace with technology, and defense strategies are not equipped to deal with the emergent proliferation threats. Because many deny that a new proliferation threat really exists or consider it a low or remote possibility, the dangers appear to have escalated as crude weapons of mass destruction have become available to a widening group of states and non-state actors. As the risks expand, the control of proliferation is thus destined to remain a growing issue on the twenty-first century global agenda. One consequence of this trend is equally alarming: new forms of violence—often referred to as "low-intensity conflict"—are likely to increase as new instruments of aggression with smaller and deadlier weapons become available through the globalization of the arms trade.

The widespread incidence of low-intensity violence draws attention to perhaps its most conspicuous and threatening form: international terrorism. In "Terror's New Face: The Radicalization and Escalation of Modern Terrorism," Walter Laqueur offers a timely and illuminating discussion of international terrorism, recent trends in its occurrence, its old and new causes, and its probable future impact. Laqueur doubts that this terrifying force can be brought under control in the new millennium; in fact, he foresees terrorism continuing "for years to come as the prevalent mode of conflict" in part because the general lawlessness within collapsing states experiencing civil wars throughout many regions in the world provides an environment conducive to terrorists' use of the threat of violence to achieve political objectives. He contends that efforts to grapple with the terrorism of the future must begin with a sober account of its diverse purposes and changing character as it is likely to be practiced within states and in relations between them. Laqueur warns that fresh thinking about terrorism is required because "the terrorist acts of the past do not necessarily offer a reliable guide for the future." Terrorism is in transition, and displaying a new face, and terror's changing forms must be interpreted in light of prevailing trends.

Laqueur's depiction of the terrorist of the future portrays the new terrorists as different from those of the past: less ideological, more likely to harbor ethnic grievances, perhaps fired by apocalyptic visions, and harder to distinguish from others outside the law. Armed with new weapons and experimenting with others, and willing to use them more indiscriminately, tomorrow's terrorists are likely to operate more freely because of the demise of restraints in future internal wars, which erode the traditional moral inhibitions safeguarding civilians and outlawing acts of brutality. Maintaining that "much of today's terrorist violence is rooted in fanaticism," Laqueur sees terrorism as increasingly difficult to control. In addition, future terrorism is likely to be increasingly violent because terrorists have at their disposal a wider range of weapons and vulnerable targets. He concludes that because the step from fanaticism to barbarism is short, "if present trends continue there is every reason to view the future grimly."

Terrorism is practiced by weak actors in order to attempt to influence strong actors (and, often, through "state terrorism," by powerful governments to repress the powerless within their own country). More commonly, on many occasions states have engaged in another practice by which they hope to change the behavior of a target by methods short of the actual use of force: what in diplomatic practice and international law are termed *sanctions*. Ranging from economic methods of punishment such as trade embargoes to collective international censorship to ostracize the target, the purpose of sanctions is generally the same: to modify the target's conduct so as to persuade it to do something it would not otherwise do (such as ceasing to pursue nuclear armament) or to convince it to stop some action in which it is currently engaging (such as persecution of minorities).

In "The Trouble with Sanctions," Robert A. Sirico evaluates the use of sanctions as a set of methods to attempt to influence another actor's actions. He concentrates his evaluations on the case of the United States, the globe's uncontested military superpower which relies on economic sanctions as a method of coercive diplomacy more than any other state in the global arena. This case illustrates the reasons why sanctions are commonly used and the problems which limit their usefulness for the United States and for other states and international organizations as well. In effect, Sirico's review and critique of U.S. sanctions policy as the most-used weapon in the U.S. government's foreign policy arsenal provides a pointed summary of the substantial body of policy evaluation that examines the effectiveness and failure of economic instruments of non-military coercive diplomacy. Sirico sides with the critics, and concludes that "At a time when the prosperity of Americans increasingly is tied to U.S. trade with the rest of the world, it is a grave mistake to injure economic relations, especially when there is little likelihood sanctions will achieve foreign policy objectives." Needless to say, other policy advisors are likely to take exception to this critique; sanctions would not be so popular as a method for attempting to influence targets if many people did not see in them advantages. After all, sanctions do not require the use of armed force, and under the right conditions have proven to be a strategy that can sometimes work. It is certain that controversies about the use of sanctions will continue to be debated in the early part of the twenty-first century, where, in an era of cascading globalization and interdependence, the temptation to rely on sanctions to reward compliance and/or to punish an uncooperative target will increase.

Finally, Part One concludes with an assessment of power and influence in light of the 1990s' turbulent transformations. In "The Changing Nature of World Power," Joseph S. Nye, Jr. provides us with the tools with which to evaluate how the relationships between arms, influence, and global leadership are likely to change in the new century. Here, Nye comprehensively surveys and critiques current thinking and theorizing about the changing sources of power, the balance of power, and hegemony in modern history. And, in comparing rival models (for example, realist interpretations of hegemonic transitions, the neo-Marxist view of hegemony, and the long-cycle theory of world leadership), Nye provides a theoretical foundation with which to predict the future of American power and evaluate the risks of world war as the twenty-first century unfolds.

The issues discussed in the ten essays in Part One—capabilities and influence, the changing nature of power in the information age, the changing role of military power in the third millennium, the causes of war, the frequency of war, the effects of nuclear weapons, the threat of the proliferation of weapons of mass destruction, terrorism, sanctions as a mode of coercive diplomacy, and the evolving nature of world power—do not exhaust the range of security problems that populate the global agenda. However, in focusing attention on some of the many issues relating to the role of arms and influence in a world of interdependent and often competitive states, these essays offer insight into the complexities of the issues of power politics with which national decisionmakers must grapple. Part Two, in which we shift attention to the nature of discord and collaboration in world politics, will add further insight into the politics of peace and security.

# 1

# POWER, CAPABILITY, AND INFLUENCE IN INTERNATIONAL POLITICS

K. J. Holsti

**In this essay K. J. Holsti clarifies the meaning of three concepts crucial to the conduct of international politics—power, capability, and influence—and examines the complexities of each as it relates to states' efforts to realize their foreign policy objectives. Holsti is Professor of Political Science at the University of British Columbia. His publications include *The State, War, and the State of War* (1996).**

. . . [A foreign policy] act is basically a form of communication intended to change or sustain the behavior of those upon whom the acting government is dependent for achieving its own goals. It can also be viewed as a "signal" sent by one actor to influence the receiver's image of the sender.[1] In international politics, acts and signals take many different forms. The promise of granting foreign aid is an act, as are propaganda appeals, displays of military strength, wielding a veto in the Security Council, walking out of a conference, organizing a conference, issuing a warning in a diplomatic note, sending arms and money to a liberation movement, instituting a boycott on the goods of another state, or declaring war. These types of acts and signals, and the circumstances in which they are likely to succeed, will be discussed. . . . Our organizing principle will be the amount of threat involved in the various techniques of influence. Diplomatic persuasion

---

[1] A comprehensive treatment of how governments "signal" each other is in Robert Jervis, *The Logic of Images in International Relations* (Princeton, N.J.: Princeton University Press, 1970).

seemingly involves the least amount of threat; economic pressures, subversion, intervention, and various forms of warfare involve increasingly great amounts of threat and punishment. To help understand what all these types of action or techniques of influence have in common, however, we will discuss in a more abstract manner the behavior governments show when they turn toward each other to establish orientations, fulfill roles, or achieve and defend objectives.

The international political process commences when any state—let us say state A—seeks through various acts or signals to change or sustain the behavior (for instance, the acts, images, and policies) of other states. Power can thus be defined as the general capacity of a state to control the behavior of others. This definition can be illustrated as follows, where the solid line represents various acts:

A seeks to influence B because it has established certain objectives that cannot be achieved (it is perceived) unless B (and perhaps many other states as well) does X. If this is the basis of all international political processes, the capacity to control behavior can be viewed in several different ways:

**1** Influence (an aspect of power) is essentially a *means* to an end. Some governments or statesmen may seek influence for its own sake, but for most it is instrumental, just like money. They use it primarily for achieving or defending other goals, which may include prestige, territory, . . . raw materials, security, or alliances.

**2** State A, in its acts toward state B, uses or mobilizes certain *resources*. A resource is any physical or mental object or quality available as an instrument of inducement to persuade, reward, threaten, or punish. The concept of resource may be illustrated in the following example. Suppose an unarmed robber walks into a bank and asks the clerk to give up money. The clerk observes clearly that the robber has no weapon and refuses to comply with the order. The robber has sought to influence the behavior of the clerk, but has failed. The next time, however, the robber walks in armed with a pistol and threatens to shoot if the clerk does not give up the money. This time, the clerk complies. In this instance, the robber has mobilized certain resources or capabilities (the gun) and succeeds in influencing the clerk to comply. But other less tangible resources may be involved as well. The appearance of the person, particularly facial expression, may convey determination, threat, or weakness, all of which may subtly influence the behavior of the clerk. In international politics, the diplomatic gestures and words accompanying actions may be as important as the acts themselves. A government that places troops on alert but insists that it is doing so for domestic reasons will have an impact abroad quite different from the government that organizes a similar alert but accompanies it with threats to go to war. "Signals" or diplomatic "body language" may be as important as dramatic actions such as alerts and mobilizations.

**3** The act of influencing B obviously involves a *relationship* between A and B, although, as will be seen later, the relationship may not even involve overt communication. If the relationship covers any period of time, we can also say that it is a *process*.

**4** If A can get B to do something, but B cannot get A to do a similar thing, then we can say that A has more power than B regarding that particular issue. Power, therefore, can also be viewed as a *quantity*, but as a quantity it is only meaningful when compared to the power of others. Power is therefore relative.

To summarize, power may be viewed from several aspects: It is a means; it is based on resources; it is a relationship and a process; and it can be measured, at least crudely.

We can break down the concept of power into three distinct analytic elements: power comprises (1) the *acts* (process, relationship) of influencing other states; (2) the *resources* used to make the wielding of influence successful; and (3) the *responses* to the acts. The three elements must be kept distinct. Since this definition may seem too abstract, we can define the concept in the more operational terms of policy-makers. In formulating policy and the strategy to achieve certain goals, they would explicitly or implicitly ask the five following questions:

**1** Given our goals, what do we wish B to do or not to do? (X)
**2** How shall we get B to do or not to do X? (implies a relationship and process)
**3** What resources are at our disposal so that we can induce B to do or not to do X?
**4** What is B's probable response to our attempts to influence its behavior?
**5** What are the costs of taking actions 1, 2, or 3—as opposed to other alternatives?

Before discussing the problem of resources and responses, we have to fill out our model of the influence act to account for the many patterns of behavior that may be involved in an international relationship. First, the exercise of influence implies more than merely A's ability to *change* the behavior of B. Influence may also be seen when A attempts to get B to *continue* a course of action or policy that is useful to, or in the interests of, A.[2] The exercise of influence does not always cease, therefore, after B does X. It is often a continuing process of reinforcing B's behavior.

---

[2] J. David Singer, "Inter-Nation Influence: A Formal Model," *American Political Science Review* 57 (1963), pp. 420–30. State A might also wish state B to do W, Y, and Z, which may be incompatible with the achievement of X.

Second, it is almost impossible to find a situation where B does not also have some influence over A. Our model has suggested that influence is exercised only in one direction, by A over B. In reality, influence is multilateral. State A, for example, would seldom seek a particular goal unless it has been influenced in a particular direction by the actions of other states in the system. At a minimum, there is the problem of feedback in any relationship: If B complies with A's wishes and does X, that behavior may subsequently prompt A to change its own behavior, perhaps in the interest of B. The phenomenon of feedback may be illustrated as follows:

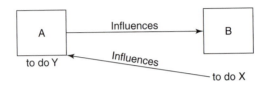

Third, there is the type of relationship that includes "anticipated reaction." [3] This is the situation where B, anticipating rewards or punishments from A, changes his behavior, perhaps even before A makes any "signals" about possible action. Deterrence theory clearly assumes that B—the potential aggressor against A—will not attack (where it might, were there no deterrent), knowing that an unacceptable level of punishment would surely result. A similar situation, but in reverse, is also common in international politics. This is where A might wish B to do X, but does not try to influence B for fear that B will do Y instead, which is an unfavorable response from A's point of view. In a hypothetical situation, the government of India might wish to obtain arms from the United States to build up its own defenses, but does not request such arms because it fears that the United States would insist on certain conditions for the sale of arms that might compromise India's nonalignment. This anticipated reaction may also be multilateral, where A wishes B to do X, but will not try to get B to do it because it fears that C, a third state, will do Y, which is unfavorable to A's interests. India wants to purchase American arms, but does not seek to influence the United States to sell them for fear that Pakistan (C) will then build up its own armaments and thus accelerate the arms race between the two countries. In this situation, Pakistan (C) has influence over the actions of the Indian government even though it has not deliberately sought to influence India on this particular matter or even communicated its position in any way. The Indian government has simply perceived that there is a relatively high probability that if it seeks to influence the United States, Pakistan will react in a manner contrary to India's interests.

---

[3] Herbert A. Simon, "Notes on the Observation and Measurement of Political Power," *Journal of Politics* 15 (1953), pp. 500–16. For further analysis, see David A. Baldwin, "Inter-Nation Influence Revisited," *Journal of Conflict Resolution* 15 (December 1971), pp. 478–79.

Fourth, power and influence may be measured by scholars, but what is important in international politics is the *perceptions* of influence and capabilities held by policymakers and the way they interpret another government's signals. The reason that governments invest millions of dollars for gathering intelligence is to develop a reasonably accurate picture of other states' capabilities and intentions. Where there is a great discrepancy between perceptions and reality, the results to a country's foreign policy may be disastrous. To take our example of the bank robber again, suppose that the person held a harmless toy pistol and threatened the clerk. The clerk perceived the gun to be real and deduced the robber's intention to use it. As a result, the clerk complied with the demand. In this case, the robber's influence was far greater than the "objective" character of the robber's capabilities and intentions; and distorted perception by the clerk led to an act that was unfavorable to the bank.

Finally, as our original model suggests, A may try to influence B *not to do* X. Sometimes this is called negative power, or deterrence, where A acts in a manner to *prevent* a certain action it deems undesirable to its interests. This is a typical relationship in international politics. By signing the Munich treaty, the British and French governments hoped to prevent Germany from invading Czechoslovakia; Israeli attacks on PLO facilities in Lebanon [were] designed to demonstrate that PLO guerrilla operations against Israel [would] be met by vast punishments, the costs of which to the PLO would far outweigh the gains of the terrorist acts. Such a cost-benefit analysis, the Israelis [hoped], would deter the PLO from undertaking further operations. The reader should keep in mind the distinction between compellence and deterrence.

## RESOURCES

The second element of the concept of power consists of those resources that are mobilized in support of the acts taken to influence state B's behavior. It is difficult to assess the general capacity of a state to control the actions and policies of others unless we also have some knowledge of the capabilities involved.[4] Nevertheless, it should be acknowledged that social scientists do not understand all the reasons why some actors—whether people, groups, governments, or states—wield influence successfully, while others do not.

It is clear that, in political relationships, not everyone possesses equal influence. In domestic politics, it is possible to construct a lengthy list of capabilities and attributes that seemingly permit some to wield influence over large numbers of people and important public decisions. Robert Dahl lists such tangibles as money, wealth, information, time, political allies, official position, and control over jobs, and such intangibles as personality and leadership qualities.[5] But not

---

[4] We might assess influence for historical situations solely on the basis of whether A got B to do X, without our having knowledge of either A's or B's capabilities.

[5] Robert A. Dahl, *Who Governs?* (New Haven, Conn.: Yale University Press, 1961).

everyone who possesses these capabilities can command the obedience of other people. What is crucial in relating resources to influence, according to Dahl, is that one *mobilize them for one's political purposes* and possess the skill to mobilize them. One who uses wealth, time, information, friends, and personality for political purposes will probably be able to influence others on public issues. A person, on the other hand, who possesses the same capabilities but uses them to invent a new mousetrap is not apt to be important in politics. The same propositions also hold true in international politics. The amount of influence a state wields over others can be related to the capabilities *mobilized* in support of *specific* foreign-policy objectives. To put this proposition in another way, we can argue that resources do not determine the uses to which they will be put. Nuclear power can be used to provide electricity or to deter and perhaps destroy other nations. The use of resources depends less on their quality and quantity than on the external objectives a government formulates for itself.

The *variety* of foreign-policy instruments available to a nation for influencing others is partly a function of the quantity and quality of capabilities. What a government seeks to do—the type of objectives it formulates—and how it attempts to do it will depend at least partially on the resources it finds available. A country such as Thailand, which possesses relatively few resources, cannot, even if it would desire, construct intercontinental ballistic missiles with which to intimidate others, establish a worldwide propaganda network, or dispense several billion dollars annually for foreign aid to try to influence other countries. We can conclude, therefore, that how states use their resources depends on their external objectives, but the choice of objectives and the instruments to achieve those objectives are limited or influenced by the quality and quantity of available resources.

## THE MEASUREMENT OF RESOURCES

For many years, students of international politics have made meticulous comparisons of the potential capabilities of various nations, assuming that a nation was powerful, or capable of achieving its objectives, to the extent that it possessed certain "elements of power." Comparative data relating to production of iron ore, coal, and hydroelectricity, economic growth rates, educational levels, population growth rates, military resources, transportation systems, and sources of raw materials are presented as indicators of a nation's power. Few have acknowledged that these comparisons do not measure a state's power or influence but only its potential capacity to wage war. Other resources, such as diplomatic or propaganda skills, are seldom measured; but surely they are as important as war-making potential. Measurements and assessments are not particularly useful anyway unless they are related to specific foreign-policy issues. Capability is always the capability to do something; its assessment is most meaningful when carried on within a framework of certain foreign-policy objectives.

The deduction of actual influence from the quantity and quality of potential and mobilized capabilities may, in some cases, give an approximation of reality, but historically there have been too many discrepancies between the basis of power and the amount of influence to warrant adopting this practice as a useful approach to international relations. One could have assumed, for example, on the basis of a comparative study of technological and educational levels and general standards of living in the 1920s and 1930s that the United States would have been one of the most influential states in international politics. A careful comparison of certain resources, called the "great essentials,"[6] revealed the United States to be in an enviable position. In the period 1925 to 1930, it was the only major country in the world that produced from its own resources adequate supplies of food, power, iron, machinery, chemicals, coal, iron ore, and petroleum. If actual diplomatic influence had been deduced from the quantities of "great essentials" possessed by the major nations, the following ranking of states would have resulted: (1) United States, (2) Germany, (3) Great Britain, (4) France, (5) Russia, (6) Italy, (7) Japan. However, the diplomatic history of the world from 1925 to 1930 would suggest that there was little correlation between the resources of these countries and their *actual influence.* If we measure influence by the impact these states made on the system and by the responses they could invoke when they sought to change the behavior of other states, we would find for this period quite a different ranking, such as the following: (1) France, (2) Great Britain, (3) Italy, (4) Germany, (5) Russia, (6) Japan, (7) United States.

Indeed, many contemporary international relationships reveal how often the "strong" states do not achieve their objectives—or at least have to settle for poor substitutes—even when attempting to influence the behavior of "weak" states. How, for instance, did Marshal Tito's Yugoslavia effectively resist all sorts of pressures and threats by the powerful Soviet Union after it was expelled from the Communist bloc? Why, despite its overwhelming superiority in capabilities, was the United States unable in the 1960s to achieve its major objectives against a weak Cuba and North Vietnam? How have "small" states gained trading privileges and all sorts of diplomatic concessions from those nations with great economic wealth and military power? The ability of state A to change the behavior of state B is, we would assume, enhanced if it possesses physical resources to use in the influence act; but B is by no means defenseless or vulnerable to diplomatic, economic, or military pressures because it fails to own a large modern army, raw materials, and money for foreign aid. The successful exercise of influence is also dependent upon such factors as personality, perceptions, friendships, and traditions, and, not being easy to measure, these factors have a way of rendering power calculations and equations difficult. . . .

[6] Frank H. Simonds and Brooks Emeny, *The Great Powers in World Politics* (New York: American Book, 1939).

## VARIABLES AFFECTING THE EXERCISE OF INFLUENCE

One reason that gross quantities of resources cannot be equated with effective influence relates to the distinction between a state's overall capabilities and the *relevance* of resources to a particular diplomatic situation. A nuclear force, for example, is often thought to increase the diplomatic influence of those who possess it. No doubt nuclear weaponry is an important element in a state's general prestige abroad and may be an effective deterrent against a strategic attack on its homeland or "core" interests. Yet the most important aspect of a nuclear capability—or any military capability—is not its possession, but its relevance and the ability to signal one's determination to use it. Other governments must know that the capability is not of mere symbolic significance. The government of North Vietnam possessed a particular advantage over the United States (hence, influence) because it knew that in almost no circumstances would the American government use strategic nuclear weapons against its country. It therefore effectively broke through the significance of the American nuclear capability as far as the Vietnam War was concerned. A resource is useless unless it is both mobilized in support of foreign-policy objectives and made credible. Likewise, nuclear weapons would be irrelevant in negotiations on cultural exchanges, just as the Arab countries' vast oil resources could not be effectively mobilized to influence the outcome of international negotiations on satellite communications. Influence is always specific to a particular issue, and resources must be relevant to that issue.

A second variable that determines the success or failure of acts of influence is the extent to which there are *needs* between the two countries in any influence relationship. In general, a country that needs something from another is vulnerable to its acts of influence. This is the primary reason that states that are "weak" in many capabilities can nevertheless obtain concessions from "strong" countries. Consider the case of France and Germany and some of the "weak" states in the Middle East. Both European countries are highly dependent upon Arab lands for oil supplies. They have an important need, which only the Arab countries can satisfy at a reasonable cost. On the other hand, the Middle Eastern countries that control these oil resources may not be so dependent upon Germany and France, particularly if they can sell their oil easily elsewhere. Because, in this situation, needs are not equal on both sides, the independent states (in terms of needs) can make demands (or resist demands made against them) on the dependent great powers and obtain important concessions. The German and French governments know that if they do not make these concessions or if they press their own demands too hard, the Arab states can threaten to cut off oil supplies. Their dependence thus makes them vulnerable to the demands and influence acts of what would otherwise be considered "weak" states. To the Arab states, oil is much more important as a capability than military forces—at least in their relations with major powers. In the form of a general hypothesis, we can suggest that, regardless of the quantity, quality, and credibility of a state's capabilities, the more state B needs, or is dependent upon, state A, the more likely that state A's acts—threats, promises, rewards, or punishments—will succeed in changing or sustaining B's behavior.

A third variable that has assumed increasing importance in the past several decades, and one that can be considered an important resource, is *level of technical expertise.* An increasing number of issues on the international and foreign-policy agendas are highly technical in nature: law of the sea, satellite broadcasting, international monetary matters, and the like. Many of these issues are discussed in international fora, where leadership often depends more on knowledge of the technical issues than on other types of resources. Those governments that come armed with technical studies, have a full command of the nature of the problem, and are prepared to put forth realistic solutions are more likely to wield influence than are governments that have only rudimentary knowledge of the problem and no scientific studies to back their national positions. A number of recent case studies have demonstrated conclusively that the outcomes of negotiations on technical questions cannot be predicted from the gross power of the participants and that knowledge, among other factors, accounts for more than raw capabilities.[7]

Understanding the dynamics of power relationships at the international level would be relatively easy if resource relevance, credibility, need, and knowledge were the only variables involved. Unfortunately, political actions do not always conform to simple hypotheses, because human characteristics of pride, stubbornness, prestige, and friendship enter into all acts of influence as well. A government may be highly dependent upon some other state and still resist its demands; it may be willing to suffer all sorts of privations, and even physical destruction and loss of independence, simply for the sake of pride. The government of North Vietnam was willing to accept a very high level of destruction of lives and productive facilities by American bombers rather than make diplomatic or military concessions to the United States.

Additional variables affecting the exercise of influence can be observed in the situation where two small states of approximately equal capabilities make similar demands upon a "major" power and neither of the small states is dependent upon the large—or vice versa. Which will achieve its objectives? Will both exercise influence equally? Hypothetically, suppose that the ambassadors of Norway and Albania go to the British Foreign Office the same day and ask the British government to lower tariffs on bicycles, a product that the two countries would like to export to England. Assume that the quality and price of the bicycles are

---

[7] See, for example, the case studies in Robert O. Keohane and Joseph S. Nye, *Power and Interdependence: World Politics in Transition* (Boston: Little, Brown and Company, 1977). See also David Baldwin's strong emphasis on the relevance of resources to particular situations in "Power Analysis and World Politics," *World Politics* 31 (January 1979), pp. 161–94.

approximately the same and that the British government does not wish to allow too many imports for fear of damaging the domestic bicycle industry. Assume further that both the Norwegian and Albanian ambassadors offer roughly equal concessions if the British will lower their tariffs on bicycles. Both claim they will lower their own tariffs on English automobiles. Which ambassador is most likely to succeed—that is, to achieve his government's objectives? Chances are that the British government would favor the request of the Norwegian ambassador and turn down the representation by the diplomat from Tirana. The explanation of this decision can probably not be found in the resources of either of the small countries (both offered approximately equal rewards) or in need, since in this hypothetical situation Britain needs neither of the small countries' automobile markets. Norway would get the favorable decision because British policymakers are more *responsive* to Norwegian interests than to those of . . . a state whose government normally displays through its diplomacy and propaganda strong hostility toward England.

After relevant resources, need, and knowledge, the fourth variable that determines the effectiveness of acts of influence is thus the ephemeral quality of responsiveness.[8] Responsiveness can be seen as a disposition to receive another's requests with sympathy, even to the point where a government is willing to sacrifice some of its own values and interests in order to fulfill those requests; responsiveness is the willingness to be influenced. In one study, it was shown that members of the State Department in the United States may take considerable pains to promote the requests and interests of other governments among their superiors and in other government agencies, provided that the requesting government feels that the issue is important or that the need must be fulfilled.[9] In our hypothetical case, if the quality of responsiveness is present in the case of the Norwegian request, members of the British Foreign Office would probably work for the Norwegians and try to persuade other government agencies concerned with trade and commerce to agree to a lowering of the tariff on bicycles. In the British reaction to the Albanian request, it is not likely that the government would display much responsiveness. Suspicion, traditional animosities, lack of trust, and years of unfavorable diplomatic experience would probably prevent the development of much British sympathy for Albania's needs or interests. . . . When the other variables, such as resources or need, are held constant or made equal, the degree of responsiveness will determine the success or failure of acts taken to influence other states' behavior.

---

[8] The concept of responsiveness is introduced by Karl W. Deutsch et al., *Political Community and the North Atlantic Area* (Princeton, N.J.: Princeton University Press, 1957); developed by Dean G. Pruitt, "National Power and International Responsiveness," *Background* 7 (1964), pp. 165–78. See also Dean G. Pruitt, "Definition of the Situation as a Determinant of International Action," in *International Behavior: A Social-Psychological Analysis,* ed. Herbert C. Kelman (New York: Holt, Rinehart & Winston, 1965), pp. 393–432.

[9] Pruitt, "National Power," pp. 175–76.

If effective influence cannot be deduced solely from the quantity and quality of physical capabilities, how do we proceed to measure influence? If we want to assess a situation that has already occurred, the easiest way to measure influence is to study the *responses* of those in the influence relationship.[10] If A can get B to do X, but C cannot get B to do the same thing, then in that particular issue, A has more influence. If B does X despite the protestations of A, then we can assume that A, in this circumstance, did not enjoy much influence over B. It is meaningless to argue that the Soviet Union [may have been] more powerful than the United States unless we cite how, for what purposes, and in relation to whom the Soviet Union and the United States [were] exerting influence. . . .

## HOW INFLUENCE IS EXERCISED

Social scientists have noted several fundamental techniques that individuals and groups use to influence each other. In a political system that contains no one legitimate center of authority that can command the members of the group or society, bargaining has to be used among the sovereign entities to achieve or defend their objectives. Recalling that A seeks one of three courses of conduct from B (B to do X in the future, B not to do X in the future, or B to continue doing X), it may use six different tactics, involving acts of:

**1 Persuasion**    By persuasion we mean simply initiating or discussing a proposal with another and eliciting a favorable response without explicitly holding out the possibility of rewards or punishments. We cannot assume that the exercise of influence is always *against* the wishes of others and that there are only two possible outcomes of the act, one favoring A, the other favoring B. For example, state A asks B to support it at a coming international conference on the control of narcotics. State B might not originally have any particular interest in the conference or its outcome; but it decides, on the basis of A's initiative. that something positive might be gained, not only by supporting A's proposals, but also by attending the conference. In this case, B might also expect to gain some type of reward in the future, although not necessarily from A. Persuasion would also include protests and denials that do not involve obvious threats.

**2 The Offer of Rewards**    This is the situation where A promises to do something favorable to B if B complies with the wishes of A. Rewards may be of almost any type in international relations. To gain the diplomatic support of B at the narcotics conference, A may offer to increase foreign-aid payments, lower tariffs on goods imported from B, support B at a later conference on communications facilities, or promise to remove a previous punishment. The last tactic is used often by negotiators. After having created an unfavorable situation, they promise to remove it in return for some concessions by their opponents.

---

[10] Robert A. Dahl, "The Concept of Power," *Behavioral Science* 2 (1957), pp. 201–15.

**3 The Granting of Rewards** In some instances, the credibility of a government is not very high, and state B, before complying with A's wishes, may insist that A actually give the reward in advance. Frequently, in armistice negotiations neither side will unilaterally take steps to demilitarize an area or demobilize troops until the other shows evidence of complying with the agreements. One of the cliches of . . . diplomacy holds that deeds, not words, are required for the granting of rewards and concessions.

**4 The Threat of Punishment** Threats of punishment may be further subdivided into two types: (a) positive threats, where, for example, state A threatens to increase tariffs, institute a boycott or embargo against trade with B, or use force; and (b) threats of deprivation, where A threatens to withdraw foreign aid or in other ways withhold rewards or other advantages that it already grants to B.

**5 The Infliction of Nonviolent Punishment** In this situation, threats are carried out in the hope of altering B's behavior, which, in most cases, could not be altered by other means. The problem with this tactic is that it often results in reciprocal measures by the other side, thus inflicting damage on both, and not necessarily bringing about a desired state of affairs. If, for example, A threatens to increase its military capabilities if B does X and then proceeds to implement the threat, it is not often that B will comply with A's wishes, because it, too, can increase its military capabilities. In this type of situation, both sides indulge in the application of punishments that may escalate into more serious forms unless the conflict is resolved. Typical acts of nonviolent punishment include breaking diplomatic relations, raising tariffs, instituting boycotts and embargoes, holding hostages, organizing blockades, closing frontiers, or walking out of a diplomatic conference.

**6 Force** In previous eras, when governments did not possess the variety of foreign-policy instruments available today, they frequently had to rely upon the use of force in the bargaining process. Force and violence were not only the most efficient tactics, but in many cases the only means possible for influencing. Today, the situation is different. As technological levels rise and dependencies develop, other means of inducement become available and can serve as substitutes for force.

## PATTERNS OF INFLUENCE IN THE INTERNATIONAL SYSTEM

Most governments at some time use all their techniques for influencing others, but probably over 90 percent of all relations between states are based on simple persuasion and deal with relatively unimportant technical matters. Since such interactions seldom make the headlines, we often assume that most relations between states involve the making or carrying out of threats. But whether a government is communicating with another over an unimportant technical matter or over a subject of great consequence, it is likely to use a particular type of tactic in its attempts to influence, depending on the past tradition of friendship or hostility between those two governments and the amount of compatibility between their objectives and interests. Allies, for example, seldom threaten each other with force or even make blatant threats of punishment, but governments that disagree over a wide range of policy objectives and hold attitudes of suspicion and hostility toward each other are more likely to resort to threats and imposition of punishments. The methods of exerting influence between Great Britain and the United States are, typically, persuasion and rewards, whereas the methods of exerting influence between the Soviet Union and the United States in the early post–World War II era were typically threatening and inflicting punishments of various types. . . .

To summarize this analysis of power, we can suggest that power is an integral part of all political relationships; but in international politics we are interested primarily in one process: how one state influences the behavior of another in its own interests. The act of influencing becomes a central focus for the study of international politics, and it is from this act that we can best deduce a definition of power. If we observe the act of influencing, we can see that power is a process, a relationship, a means to an end, and even a quantity. Moreover, we can make an analytical distinction among the act of influencing, the basis, or resources, upon which the act relies, and the response to the act. Resources are an important determinant of how successful the wielding of influence will be, but they are by no means the only determinant. The nature of a country's foreign-policy objectives, the skill with which a state mobilizes its capabilities for foreign-policy purposes, its needs, responsiveness, costs, and commitments are equally important. Acts of influencing may take many forms, the most important of which are the offer and granting of rewards, the threat and imposition of punishments, and the application of force. The choice of means used to induce will depend, in turn, upon the general nature of relations between any two given governments, the degree of involvement between them, and the extent of their mutual responsiveness. . . .

# 2

# POWER AND INTERDEPENDENCE IN THE INFORMATION AGE

Robert O. Keohane and Joseph S. Nye, Jr.

Throughout modern history, the usual route that states have followed to acquire power has been through the acquisition of military capabilities and the use of force. This is changing, argue Robert O. Keohane and Joseph S. Nye, Jr., because technology and the information revolution are beginning to transform past patterns of world politics. Indeed, the traditional equation for defining what it means for a state to be powerful is being altered by the coming into being of a new "electronic feudalism" that is affecting how citizens throughout the world see their loyalties. In the information age, it is predicted, the geographically based nation-state will continue to structure global politics, because the state is resilient and because the information on which power increasing depends is generated and desseminated through states. However, in the period of global interdependence a revolution appears to be occurring, because the new age will make it increasingly less useful for states to rely on traditional "hard power" in the form of military resources and correspondingly increasingly more useful for states to depend on "soft power" by seeking influence through credibility to a public with more and more diverse sources of information available. Reviewing numerous trends in the global landscape, this essay paints a broad picture of the factors that are changing the capacity of state and nonstate actors to achieve their political goals and get desired outcomes. Keohane is James B. Duke Professor of Political Science and Co-Director of the Program on Democracy, Institutions, and Political Economy at Duke University, and Nye is Dean of the

**Kennedy School of Government at Harvard University. Both have authored many scholarly publications, and together they have co-authored the influential book *Power and Interdependence* (1977) which this updated essay elaborates in the context of the twenty-first century. In addition, Keohane recently co-edited, with Helga Haftendorn and Jan L. Wallender, *Imperfect Unions: Security Institutions over Time and Space* (1999) and Nye has authored *American Power in the Twenty-First Century* (1999).**

Throughout the twentieth century, modernists have been proclaiming that technology would transform world politics. In 1910 Norman Angell declared that economic interdependence rendered wars irrational and looked forward to the day when they would become obsolete. Modernists in the 1970s saw telecommunications and jet travel as creating a global village, and believed that the territorial state, which has dominated world politics since the feudal age, was being eclipsed by nonterritorial actors such as multinational corporations, transnational social movements, and international organizations. Likewise, prophets such as Peter Drucker, Alvin and Heidi Toffler, and Esther Dyson argue that today's information revolution is ending hierarchical bureaucracies and leading to a new electronic feudalism with overlapping communities and jurisdictions laying claim to multiple layers of citizens' identities and loyalties.

The modernists of past generations were partly right. Angell's understanding of the impact of interdependence on war was insightful: World War I wrought unprecedented destruction, not only on the battlefield but also on the social and political systems that had thrived during the relatively peaceful years since 1815. As the modernists of the 1970s predicted, multinational corporations, nongovernmental organizations (NGOs), and global financial markets have become immensely more significant. But the state has been more resilient than modernists anticipated. States continue to command the loyalties of the vast majority of the world's people, and their control over material resources in most wealthy countries has stayed at a third to half of [gross domestic product] GDP.

The modernists of 1910 and the 1970s were right about the direction of change but simplistic about its consequences. Like pundits on the information revolution, they moved too directly from technology to political consequences without sufficiently considering the continuity of beliefs, the persistence of institutions, or the strategic options available to statesmen. They failed to analyze how holders of power could wield that power to shape or distort patterns of interdependence that cut across national boundaries.

[Nearly twenty-five] years ago, in our book *Power and Interdependence* (1977), we analyzed the politics of such transnational issues as trade, monetary relations, and oceans policy, writing that "modernists point correctly to the fundamental changes now taking place, but they often assume without sufficient analysis that advances in technology and increases in social and economic transactions will lead to a new world in which states, and their control of force, will no longer be important. Traditionalists are adept at showing flaws in the modernist vision by pointing out how military interdependence continues, but find it very difficult accurately to interpret today's multidimensional economic, social, and ecological interdependence." This is still true for the information age in which cyberspace is itself a "place," everywhere and nowhere.

Prophets of a new cyberworld, like modernists before them, often overlook how much the new world overlaps and rests on the traditional world in which power depends on geographically based institutions. In 1998, 100 million people [used] the Internet. Even if this number reaches a billion in 2005, as some experts predict, a large portion of the world's people will not participate. Moreover, globalization is far from universal. Three-quarters of the world's population does not own a telephone, much less a modem and computer. Rules will be necessary to govern cyberspace, not only protecting lawful users from criminals but ensuring intellectual property rights. Rules require authority, whether in the form of public government or private or community governance. Classic issues of politics—who governs and on what terms—are as relevant to cyberspace as to the real world.

## THE EARLY DAYS OF THE REVOLUTION

Interdependence among societies is not new. What is new is the virtual erasing of costs of communicating over distance as a result of the information revolution. The actual transmission costs have become negligible; hence the amount of information that can be transmitted is effectively infinite. Computing power has doubled every eighteen months for the last thirty years. It now costs less than one percent of what it did in the early 1970s. Similarly, growth of the Internet and the World Wide Web has been exponential. Internet traffic doubles every 100 days. Communications bandwidths are expanding rapidly, and communications costs continue to fall. As late as 1980, phone calls over copper wire could carry one page of information per second; today a thin strand of optical fiber can transmit 90,000 volumes in a second. As with steam at the end of the eighteenth century and electricity at the end of the nineteenth, productivity growth has lagged as society learns to utilize the new technologies. Although many industries and firms have undergone rapid structural changes since the 1980s, the economic transformation is far from complete. We are still in the early stages of the information revolution.

That revolution has dramatically changed one feature of what we described in *Power and Interdependence* as "complex interdependence"—a world in which security and force matter less and countries are connected by multiple social and political relationships. Now anyone with a computer can be a desktop publisher, and anyone with a modem can communicate with distant parts of the globe at a trivial cost. Earlier transnational flows were heavily controlled by large bureaucracies like multinational corporations or the Catholic Church. Such

organizations remain important, but the dramatic cheapening of information transmission has opened the field to loosely structured network organizations and even
individuals. These NGOs and networks are particularly effective in penetrating
states without regard to borders and using domestic constituencies to force political leaders to focus on their preferred agendas. The information revolution has
vastly increased the number of channels of contact between societies, one of our
three dimensions of complex interdependence.

However, the information revolution has not made dramatic changes in the
two other conditions of complex interdependence. Military force still plays a significant role in relations between states, and in a crunch, security still outranks
other issues in foreign policy. One reason that the information revolution has not
transformed world politics to a new politics of complete complex interdependence is that information does not flow in a vacuum but in political space that is
already occupied. Another is that outside the democratic zone of peace, the world
of states is not a world of complex interdependence. In many areas, realist assumptions about the dominance of military force and security issues remain valid.
For the last four centuries states have established the political structure within
which information flows across borders. Indeed, the information revolution itself
can be understood only within the context of the globalization of the world economy, which itself was deliberately fostered by U.S. policy and international institutions for half a century after the end of World War II. In the late 1940s the
United States sought to create an open international economy to forestall another
depression and contain communism. The resulting international institutions,
formed on the basis of multilateral principles, put a premium on markets and information and deemphasized military rivalry. It has become increasingly costly
for states to turn away from these patterns of interdependence.

The quantity of information available in cyberspace means little by itself. The
quality of information and distinctions between types of information are probably more important. Information does not just exist; it is created. When one considers the incentives to create information, three different types of information
that are sources of power become apparent.

*Free information* is information that actors are willing to create and distribute without financial compensation. The sender benefits from the receiver believing the information and hence has incentives to produce it. Motives may vary.
Scientific information is a public good, but persuasive messages, such as political ones, are more self-serving. Marketing, broadcasting, and propaganda are all
examples of free information. The explosion in the quantity of free information
is perhaps the most dramatic effect of the information revolution.

*Commercial information* is information that people are willing to create and
send at a price. Senders neither gain nor lose by others believing the information, apart from the compensation they receive. For such information to be available on the Internet, issues of property rights must be resolved so that producers
of information can be compensated by users. Creating commercial information

before one's competitors can—assuming that intellectual property rights can be enforced—generates enormous profits, especially for pioneers, as the history of Microsoft demonstrates. The rapid growth of electronic commerce and the increase in global competition will be other important effects of the information revolution.

*Strategic information,* as old as espionage, confers great advantage on actors only if their competitors do not possess it. One enormous advantage the United States had in World War II was that, unbeknown to Tokyo, the United States had broken the Japanese codes. The quantity of such information is often not particularly important. For example, the strategic information available to the United States about the nuclear weapons programs of North Korea, Pakistan, or Iraq depends more on having reliable satellites or spies than on vast flows of electronic mail.

The information revolution alters patterns of complex interdependence by exponentially increasing the number of channels of communication in world politics—between individuals in networks, not just individuals within bureaucracies. But it exists in the context of an existing political structure, and its effects on the flows of different types of information vary vastly. Free information will flow faster without regulation. Strategic information will be protected as much as possible—for example, by encryption technologies. The flow of commercial information will depend on whether property rights are established in cyberspace. Politics will shape the information revolution as much as vice versa.

## THE NATURE OF POWER

Knowledge is power, but what is power? A basic distinction can be drawn between behavioral power—the ability to obtain outcomes you want—and resource power—the possession of resources that are usually associated with the ability to reach outcomes you want. Behavioral power, in turn, can be divided into hard and soft power. Hard power is the ability to get others to do what they otherwise would not do through threats or rewards. Whether by economic carrots or military sticks, the ability to coax or coerce has long been the central element of power. As we pointed out two decades ago, the ability of the less vulnerable to manipulate or escape the constraints of an interdependent relationship at low cost is an important source of power. For example, in 1971 the United States halted the convertibility of dollars into gold and increased its influence over the international monetary system. In 1973, Arab states temporarily gained power from an oil embargo.

Soft power, on the other hand, is the ability to get desired outcomes because others want what you want. It is the ability to achieve goals through attraction rather than coercion. It works by convincing others to follow or getting them to agree to norms and institutions that produce the desired behavior. Soft power can rest on the appeal of one's ideas or culture or the ability to set the agenda through standards and institutions that shape the preferences of others. It depends largely on the persuasiveness of the free information that an actor seeks to transmit. If a state can make its power legitimate in the eyes of others and establish international institutions that encourage others to define their interests in compatible ways, it may not need to expend as many costly traditional economic or military resources.

Hard and soft power are related, but they are not the same. The political scientist Samuel P. Huntington is correct when he says that material success makes a culture and ideology attractive, and that economic and military failure lead to self-doubt and crises of identity. He is wrong, however, when he argues that soft power rests solely on a foundation of hard power. The soft power of the Vatican did not wane because the size of the papal states diminished. Canada, Sweden, and the Netherlands have more influence than some other states with equivalent economic or military capabilities. The Soviet Union had considerable soft power in Europe after World War II but squandered it by invading Hungary and Czechoslovakia even when Soviet economic and military power continued to grow. Soft power varies over time and different domains. America's popular culture, with its libertarian and egalitarian currents, dominates film, television, and electronic communications. Not all aspects of that culture are attractive to everyone, for example conservative Muslims. Nonetheless, the spread of information and American popular culture has generally increased global awareness of and openness to American ideas and values. To some extent this reflects deliberate policies, but more often soft power is an inadvertent by-product.

The information revolution is also affecting power measured in terms of resources rather than behavior. In the eighteenth-century European balance of power, territory, population, and agriculture provided the basis for infantry, and France was a principal beneficiary. In the nineteenth century, industrial capacity provided the resources that enabled Britain and, later, Germany to gain dominance. By the mid-twentieth century, science and particularly nuclear physics contributed crucial power resources to the United States and the Soviet Union. In the next century, information technology, broadly defined, is likely to be the most important power resource.

## THE SMALL VERSUS THE LARGE

The new conventional wisdom is that the information revolution has a leveling effect. As it reduces costs, economies of scale, and barriers of entry to markets, it should reduce the power of large states and enhance the power of small states and non-state actors. In practice, however, international relations are more complex than the technological determinism this view suggests. Some aspects of the information revolution help the small, but some help the already large and powerful. There are several reasons.

First, important barriers to entry and economies of scale remain in some information-related aspects of power. For example, soft power is strongly affected by the cultural content of movies and television programs. Large, established entertainment industries often enjoy considerable economies of scale in content production and distribution. The dominant American market share in films and television programs in world markets is therefore likely to continue.

Second, even where it is now cheap to disseminate existing information, the collection and production of new information often requires costly investments. In many competitive situations, the newness of information at the margin counts more than the average cost of all information. Intelligence is a good example. States like the United States, Britain, and France have capabilities for collecting intelligence that dwarf those of other nations. In some commercial situations, a fast follower can do better than a first mover, but in terms of power among states, it is usually better to be first.

Third, first movers are often the creators of the standards and architecture of information systems. The use of the English language and the pattern of top-level domain names on the Internet is a case in point. Partly because of the transformation of the American economy in the 1980s and partly because of large investments driven by the Cold War military competition, the United States was often first on the scene and still enjoys a lead in the application of a wide variety of information technologies.

Fourth, military power remains important in some critical domains of international relations. Information technology has some effects on the use of force that benefit the small and some that favor the powerful. The off-the-shelf commercial availability of what used to be costly military technologies benefits small states and non-state actors and increases the vulnerability of large states. Information systems add lucrative targets for terrorist groups. Other trends, however, strengthen the already powerful. Many military analysts refer to a "revolution in military affairs" caused by the application of information technology. Space-based sensors, direct broadcasting, high-speed computers, and complex software provide the ability to gather, sort, process, transfer, and disseminate information about complex events that occur over a wide geographic area. This dominant battlespace awareness combined with precision force produces a powerful advantage. As the Gulf War showed, traditional assessments of balances of weapons platforms such as tanks or planes become irrelevant unless they include the ability to integrate information with those weapons. Many of the relevant technologies are available in commercial markets, and weaker states can be expected to have many of them. The key, however, will not be possession of fancy hardware or advanced systems but the ability to integrate a system of systems. In this dimension, the United States is likely to keep its lead. In information warfare, a small edge makes all the difference. Contrary to the expectations of some theorists, the information revolution has not greatly decentralized or equalized power among states. If anything, it has had the opposite effect.

## THE POLITICS OF CREDIBILITY

What about reducing the role of governments and the power of all states? Here the changes are more likely to be along the lines the modernists predicted. But to understand the effect of free information on power, one must first understand the paradox of plenty. A plenitude of information leads to a poverty of attention. Attention becomes the scarce resource, and those who can distinguish valuable signals from white noise gain power. Editors, filters, interpreters, and cue-givers become more in demand, and this is a source of power. There will be an imperfect market for evaluators. Brand names and the ability to bestow an international seal of approval will become more important.

But power does not necessarily flow to those who can withhold information. Under some circumstances private information can cripple the credibility of those who have it. For instance, economists point out that sellers of used cars know more about their defects than potential buyers. Moreover, owners of bad cars are more likely to sell than owners of good ones. Thus potential buyers discount the price they are willing to pay to adjust for unknown defects. Hence the superior information of sellers does not improve the average price they receive, but instead makes them unable to sell good used cars for their real value. Unlike asymmetrical interdependence in trade, where power goes to those who can afford to hold beck or break trade ties, information power flows to those who can edit and credibly validate information to sort out what is both correct and important.

Hence, among editors and cue-givers, credibility is the crucial resource, and asymmetrical credibility is a key source of power. Establishing credibility means developing a reputation for providing correct information, even when it may reflect badly on the information provider's own country. The BBC, for example, has earned a reputation for credibility, while state-controlled radio stations in Baghdad, Beijing, and Havana have not. Reputation has always mattered in world politics, and it has become even more important because of the paradox of plenty. The low cost of transmitting data means that the ability to transmit it is much less important than it used to be, but the ability to filter information is more so. Political struggles focus less on control over the ability to transmit information than over the creation and destruction of credibility.

Three types of state action illustrate the value of credibility. [First,] much of the traditional conduct of foreign policy occurs through the exchange of promises, which can be valuable only insofar as they are credible. Hence, governments that can credibly assure potential partners that they will not act opportunistically will gain advantages over competitors whose promises are less credible. During the Cold War, for example, the United States was a more credible ally for Western European countries than the Soviet Union because as a democracy the United States could more credibly promise not to seek to exploit or dominate its allies. Second, to borrow from capital markets at competitive interests rates requires credible information about one's financial situation. Finally, the exercise of soft power requires credibility in order to be persuasive. For instance, as long as the United States condoned racial segregation it could not be a credible advocate of universal human rights. But in June 1998, President Clinton could preach human rights to the Chinese—and in answer to a question at Beijing University about American shortcomings, could frankly admit that the United States needed to make further progress to realize its ideal of equality.

One implication of the abundance of free information sources and the role of credibility is that soft power is likely to become less a function of material resources. Hard power may be necessary—for instance, using force to take over a radio station—to generate soft power. Propaganda as a form of free information is not new. Hitler and Stalin used it effectively in the 1930s. Slobodan Milošević's control of television was crucial to his power in Serbia. In Moscow in 1993, a battle for power was fought at a TV station. In Rwanda, Hutu-controlled radio stations encouraged genocide. The power of broadcasting persists but will be increasingly supplemented by the Internet, with its multiple channels of communication controlled by multiple actors who cannot control one another by force. The issue is not only which actors own television networks, radio stations, or web sites—once a plethora of such sources exist—but who pays attention to which fountains of information and misinformation.

In the case of worldwide television, wealth can also lead to soft power. For instance, CNN was based in Atlanta rather than Amman or Cairo because of America's leading position in the industry and technology. When Iraq invaded Kuwait in 1990, the fact that CNN was an American company helped to frame the issue, worldwide, as aggression. Had an Arab company been the world's dominant TV channel, perhaps the issue would have been framed as a justified attempt to reverse colonial humiliation.

Broadcasting is a type of free information that has long had an impact on public opinion. By focusing on certain conflicts and human rights problems, broadcasters have pressed politicians to respond to some foreign conflicts rather than others—say Somalia rather than southern Sudan. Not surprisingly, governments have sought to manipulate television and radio stations and have met considerable success, since a relatively small number of broadcasting sites have been used to reach many people with the same message. However, the shift from broadcasting to narrow-casting has major political implications. Cable television and the Internet enable senders to segment and target audiences. Even more important politically, the Internet not only focuses attention but helps coordinate action across borders. Interactivity at low cost allows for the development of new virtual communities: people who imagine themselves as part of a single group regardless of how far apart they are physically from one another.

These technologies create new opportunities for NGOs. Advocacy networks' potential impact is vastly expanded by the information revolution, since the fax machine and the Internet enable them to send messages from the rain forests of Brazil or the sweatshops of Southeast Asia. The recent Landmine Conference resulted from the activities of a coalition of network organizations working with middle-power governments like Canada, individual politicians like Senator Patrick Leahy (D-Vt.), and celebrities like Princess Diana to capture attention, set the agenda, and put pressure on political leaders. The role of NGOs was also an important channel of communication across delegations in the global warming discussions at Kyoto in December 1997. Environmental groups and industry competed in Kyoto for the attention of the media from major countries, basing their arguments in part on the findings of nongovernmental scientists.

There are substantial opportunities for a flowering of issue advocacy networks and virtual communities, but the credibility of these networks is fragile. Greenpeace, for instance, imposed large costs on Royal Dutch Shell by criticizing its planned disposal of its Brentspar drilling rig in the North Sea, but Greenpeace itself lost credibility when it later had to admit the inaccuracy of some of its claims. Atmospheric scientists' findings about climate change have gained credibility, not just from the prestige of science but from the procedures developed in the Intergovernmental Panel on Climate Change (IPCC) for extensive and careful peer review of scientific papers and intergovernmental vetting of executive summaries. The IPCC is an example of an information-legitimating institution whose major function is to give coherence and credibility to masses of scientific information about climate change.

As the IPCC example shows, the significance of credibility is giving increasing importance to transnational networks of like-minded experts. By framing issues where knowledge is important, such professional communities become important actors in forming coalitions and in bargaining processes. By creating knowledge, they can provide the basis for effective cooperation. But to be effective, the procedures by which this information is produced must appear unbiased. Scientific information is increasingly recognized as in part socially constructed. To be credible, the information must be produced through a process that is in accordance with professional norms and characterized by transparency and procedural fairness.

## THE DEMOCRATIC ADVANTAGE

Not all democracies are leaders in the information revolution, but many are. This is no accident. Their societies are familiar with the free exchange of information, and their institutions of governance are not threatened by it. They can shape information because they can also take it. Authoritarian states, typically among the laggards, have more trouble. Governments such as China's can still limit their citizens' access to the Internet by controlling service providers and monitoring the relatively small number of users. Singapore has thus far been able to reconcile its political controls with an increasing role for the Internet. But as societies like Singapore reach higher levels of development where more citizens want fewer restrictions on access to the Internet, Singapore runs the risk of losing the people who are its key resource for competing in the information economy. Thus Singapore is wrestling with the dilemma of reshaping its educational system to encourage the individual creativity that the information economy will demand while maintaining social controls over the flow of information.

Another reason that closed systems have become more costly is that it is risky for foreigners to invest funds in a country where the key decisions are made in an opaque fashion. Transparency is becoming a key asset for countries seeking investments. The ability to hoard information, which once seemed so valuable to authoritarian states, undermines the credibility and transparency necessary to attract investment on globally competitive terms. Geographical communities still matter most, but governments that want rapid development will have to give up some of the barriers to information flows that protected officials from outside scrutiny. No longer will governments that want high levels of development be able to afford the luxury of keeping their financial and political situations a secret.

From a business standpoint, the information revolution has vastly increased the marketability and value of commercial information by reducing costs of transmission and the transaction costs of charging information users. As Adam Smith would have recognized, the value of information increases when the costs of transmitting it decline, just as the value of a good increases when transportation costs fall, increasing demand by giving its makers a larger market. Politically, however, the most important shift has concerned free information. The ability to disseminate free information increases the potential for persuasion in world politics. NGOs and states can more readily influence the beliefs of people in other jurisdictions. If one actor can persuade others to adopt similar values and policies, whether it possesses hard power and strategic information may become less important. Soft power and free information can, if sufficiently persuasive, change perceptions of self-interest and thereby alter how hard power and strategic information are used. If governments or NGOs are to take advantage of the information revolution, they will have to establish reputations for credibility amid the white noise of the information revolution.

Cheap flows of information have enormously expanded the number and depth of transnational channels of contact. Nongovernmental actors have much greater opportunities to organize and propagate their views. States are more easily penetrated and less like black boxes. As a result, political leaders will find it more difficult to maintain a coherent ordering of foreign policy issues. Yet states are resilient, and some countries, especially large ones with democratic societies, are well-placed to benefit from an information society. Although the coherence of government policies may diminish in these pluralistic and penetrated states, their institutions will be attractive and their pronouncements will be credible. They will therefore be able to wield soft power to achieve many of their objectives. The future lies neither exclusively with the state nor with transnational relations: geographically based states will continue to structure politics in an information age, but they will rely less on material resources and more on their ability to remain credible to a public with increasingly diverse sources of information.

# 3

# THE ROLE OF MILITARY POWER IN THE THIRD MILLENNIUM

Bjørn Møller

This essay questions the hypothesis that military power will decline in importance as a source of state power and a factor in the outbreak of war in the twenty-first century. Taking the two major wars that occurred in the period between August 1998 and August 1999 as examples of the kinds of unlawful uses of military force that are likely to break out in the new millennium, Møller warns that even though such wars were almost total failures they were hailed as victories, and from them lessons are today being drawn that are likely to shape military planning in the coming decades. Hence, in the current period, as in the past, "myths" have grown that increase, through a compound effect, the probability that in the twenty-first century world politics will be dominated by increasing militarization instead of by a new era of peace and disarmament. However, after reviewing four major myths about military power which are driving a new arms race, the essay concludes that the potential range of scenarios for which the traditional methods for fighting wars will be useful in the future is actually narrowing. What is needed are alternative approaches for managing nonviolently the kinds of chaos and aggression likely to occur in the developing countries and/or failed states in the Global South or the Balkans. Møller is Senior Research Fellow and Program Director at the Copenhagen Peace Research Institute and Secretary General of the International Peace Research Association. His publications include *Common Security and Nonoffensive Defense: A Neorealist Perspective* (1992) and *Dictionary of Alternative Defense* (1995).

The year from August 1998 to August 1999 was a veritable *annus horibilis* for world peace, featuring two wars started by the dominant Western powers plus several instances of unlawful use of military force, including cruise missile attacks against Sudan and Afghanistan in August 1998.

Both the United States-British war against Iraq in 1998–99 and NATO's war against Yugoslavia from 24 March to 10 June 1999 were almost total military failures, but both have nevertheless been hailed as victories. Hence, the myths associated with them are likely to influence military planning in the coming decades. The effect is likely to be a growing belief (especially in the United States) in the possibility of short, "clean," and painless high-technology wars. However, not only is the hope for such "wars without tears" illusory, it is also dangerous, as it may weaken the inhibitions against wars of aggression, thereby making wars more likely. The compound effect of this may well be a militarization of world politics.

As an antidote to this militarization, a more sober view of the very phenomenon of war is required. While it would be premature to rule out the use of military means entirely, the range of scenarios for which they remain relevant is narrowing. While war for ends such as territorial conquest make sense almost nowhere (and certainly not in Europe, except for the Balkans), the industrialized countries are entirely unadapted for the much more likely wars in the Third World or the Balkans. What we see here is rather a spread of almost antediluvian (and profoundly violent) chaos for which Western conceptions of war are illsuited.

## THE MYTHS

Military history is replete with mistakes of gargantuan proportions. A frequent element in these mistakes has been that wars have been waged in the manner in which their instigators have believed that their immediate predecessors should have been fought. Hence, if a country won the last war, it has tended to replicate its strategy in the next war, whereas vanquished states have tended towards the opposite extreme.

For instance, World War I was initiated in the belief that it would be swift and decisive, and that the means to this end were maneuvre warfare—as manifested in the German "Schlieffen Plan" and the French "Plan 17."[1] This turned out to be a big mistake, however, as the defensive revealed itself as strong enough to bring the attempted offensives to a complete halt—as had been predicted by a Polish banker (Jan Bloch), but by none of the militaries. World War II, in its turn, was intended to build on this experience by capitalizing on the strength of the defensive (as in the French Maginot line and the British strategy of continental disengagement). Big mistake once again, as the successes of the

---

[1] See Steven E. Miller (ed.), *Military Strategy and the Origins of the First World War* (Princeton: Princeton University Press, 1985).

German blitzkrieg showed, which successfully capatalized on the strength of the offensive.

If it is true that victorious states repeat their strategies while vanquished states reverse them, it was to be expected that the lessons drawn from the victorious 1991 war against Iraq would be applied to all future contingencies bearing the slightest resemblance to it. Instances thereof were the 1998–99 war against Iraq and that against Yugoslavia. While the West failed miserably in both of them, it was not defeated. Hence it has remained able to cling to an illusion about victory that makes repetition seem rational. For analytical purposes, we can disaggregate this delusion into four powerful myths about past and future wars: that victory equals success; that "wars without tears" can be fought; that one can wage "wars that are not really wars"; and that hi-tech war is the best means to these ends.

**The Myth of Success**    To allege that the wars against Iraq and Yugoslavia were failures may seem surprising in view of the fact that the United States and NATO refer to both as victories. What makes the label warranted are the following observations:

• The war against Iraq in December 1998 did *not* weaken (much less dethrone) Saddam Hussein, but rather appears to have strengthened him domestically.

• It did *nothing* to secure access for the United Nations weapons inspectors (which was the offical *casus belli),* but rather resulted in their complete, and probably irreversible, expulsion. Hence, the world now knows less, rather than more, about Iraq's possible clandestine production of weapons of mass destruction.

• The war against Yugoslavia did *not* significantly weaken, much less remove President Milošević, but rather strengthened him domestically. The subsequent peace, on the other hand, seems to have strengthened the opposition in Serbia.

• The war against Yugoslavia did *not* manage to stop the displacement of Kosovar Albanians, but rather contributed to its accelleration and to transforming internally displaced persons into refugees in neighboring countries. According to the U.N. High Commissionar on Refugees (UNHCR), the number of refugees grew from 69,500 by 23 March (the day before NATO's bombing campaign started) to a staggering 792,125 by 14 May.[2]

• The war did *not* stop the killings of the Kosovars which had been labelled "genocidal". On the contrary, the total toll of fatalities before the war was around 2,000, while there are now speculations about mass graves containing as many as 11,000 victims.

In terms of the proclaimed war aims, both wars were thus failures. Indeed, they both appear to have exacerbated the very problems they were intended to solve.

That the myth of success could nevertheless grow may be due to the fact that the two wars were fought quite successfully at the tactical level, in the sense that

---

[2] Quoted from the Danish Foreign Ministry at http://www.um.dk/kosovo/pjece/kosovo2.htm.

most air and missile strikes hit their targets. However, most hits made very little difference in strategic, much less political, terms.[3] Furthermore, both wars were accompanied by intense and quite succesful efforts at controlling the media. The real-time coverage of spectacular hits apparently made such good television that most journalists forgot to ask whether the strikes made any strategic or political difference. What might have caught the medias' attention was body-bags, but while both wars were horrendously expensive in material terms, they were completely without casualties on the Western side.

The decisive factor was probably that the balance of military power was so overwhelmingly in the West's favor that defeat (as opposed to failure) was ruled out from the very start. As set out in Table 3.1, the total "West" (comprising NATO and other formal allies) stands for no less than 87 percent of global military expenditures. However, while this unprecedented military preponderance is a reliable safeguard against defeat, it does not guarantee success.

**TABLE 3.1**
WORLD MILITARY EXPENDITURES (US $MIL., CONSTANT 1995 PRICES)[4]

|  | 1997 | Share | Cumulative |
| --- | --- | --- | --- |
| United States | 258,963 | 36.8% | 36.8% |
| Rest of "old" NATO | 192,037 | 27.3% | 64.1% |
| Hungary, Poland, Czech Republic | 4,345 | 0.6% | 64.7% |
| Israel, Japan, South Korea, Australia, New Zealand | 157,240 | 22.3% | 87.0% |
| Others | 91,415 | 13.0% | n.a. |
| Total | 704,000 | 100.0% | n.a. |

**The Myth of "Wars Without Tears"**   In none of the recent wars in which it has become involved has the West suffered any casualties. As argued by Edward Luttwak, such "post-heroic warfare" may be the paradigm of future wars, as far as the West is concerned.[5] In order to accept his conclusion, one does not even have to accept his (not entirely persuasive) demographic argument that it is the predominance of nuclear families with less than one son that makes parents casualty scared. A sufficient explanation may be that neither the two recent wars nor the most likely future wars are about matters of any great salience (such as

---

[3] A good analysis is Anthony Cordesman's "The Lessons and Non-Lessons of the Air and Missile War in Kosovo," Report to the USAF XP Strategy Forum, 8 July 1999, updated 3 August 1999, and available from www.csis.org/kosovo/lessons.html.

[4] Data from Elisabeth Sköns et al., "Tables of Military Expenditure," SIPRI Yearbook 1998, pp. 222–227.

[5] Edward N. Luttwak, "A Post-Heroic Military Policy," *Foreign Affairs* 75, no. 4 (July-August 1996), pp. 33–44.

national security), but about distinctly less-than-vital interests or concerns. Why risk something as valuable as human lives in order to save Kosovars or East Timorese?

Not only will the West thus not want to fight wars where their own troops may get killed, in most cases they will also go out of their way to avoid killing the opponent—or at least be seen to do so. Wars that are fought over "values" such as human rights are not justifiable if waged against another people unless the ostensible targets are "oppressors" and/or their obedient servants. If wars can be waged only against "dictators," more or less on behalf of their own oppressed citizens, severe constraints are placed on how they can be fought.

Combined with the laws-of-war constraints on such warfare, this factor produced an extreme reluctance on the part of NATO to (be seen to) wage war against civilians during its war against Yugoslavia. In reality, of course, the war was waged almost exclusively against civilian targets such as oil refineries, factories, TV stations, bridges, etc. (with inevitable accidental hits at residential areas or hospitals), but these had to be kept at an absolute minumum (or hushed up) as profoundly illegitimate and incompatible with the stated war aims.

**The Myth of "Non-wars"**   Few of today's wars are called wars, and almost none are declared as they used to be in the past. NATO thus refused to call what it was doing to Yugoslavia through 78 days of bombings a "war," preferring euphemisms such as "action" or "campaign."

The promulgation of this myth of "non-wars" has been aided by the fact that the wars have been fought almost exclusively in the "neutral" and "abstract" aerial domain rather than on the more "concrete" environment on the ground. The fact that nobody fought back made what happened seem even less war-like, to the extent that the French philospher Jean Baudrillard could argue that "The Gulf War did not take place."[6] If the 1991 war was a non-war, then the two wars of 1998–99 were so to an even greater extent. Having thus come to regard such "non-wars" as normal, the United States was apparently caught by surprise when some of the Somali clan leaders and subsequently the Yugoslav army actually did fight back, at least in the sense of "behaving strategically."

**The myth of hi-tech war**   Since the 1991 war against Iraq, the belief has rapidly spread that we are witnessing a true "Revolution in Military Affairs" (nicknamed the "RMA").[7] Of particular impact have been the revolutionary developments in information technologies, for example, with regard to data collection, interpretation, and dissimination, which allow for long-range precision

---

[6] Jean Baudrillard, *The Gulf War Did Not Take Place* (Bloomington: Indiana University Press, 1995).

[7] For a comparison of the various theories see Stephen Biddle, "The Past as Prologue: Assessing Theories of Future Warfare," *Security Studies* 8, no. 1 (Autumn 1998), pp. 1–74.

strikes, realtime battle management, and around the clock combat operations. On this basis, the United States came to believe that air power, information dominance, and technological supremacy will be decisive; that surgical precison will be achievable, hence that collateral damage can be minimized and wars can be waged in full conformity with "just war" criteria of discrimination and noncombatant immunity; and that determined offensives, initiated by air strikes, will be able to break through all defenses.

The United States also came to believe that it would be possibile to wage wars (euphemistically called "campaigns" or "interventions") entirely from the air without any commitment of ground troops. This would presumably allow for the winning of wars without running any significant risks and with an exit route remaining open throughout the "campaign." Even though historical evidence clearly militates against such a strategy, it has nevertheless guided both defense planning and military activities throughout the nineties.

In the following section, I shall contrast the above myths with the "realities." It needs, however, to be acknowledged that most of this reality is socially constructed and thus a product of, *inter alia,* predominant views and attitudes. Some of the above myths may thereby become self-fulfilling. For instance, if everybody comes to believe that the United States is invincible, its actual military strength will never be tested, and the myth may survive indefinitely.

## THE REALITIES

In their 1993 work on *The Real World Order,* Max Singer and Aaron Wildawsky described the world as essentially bifurcated, that is, subdivided into "zones of peace" and "zones of turmoil."[8] The former comprise "the West" (in the broad sense of the term) which is at peace in a very profound sense of the word. Not only do wars not occur between these states, but the states have also ceased planning for them as an eventuality. The "zones of turmoil" are found in the Third World and parts of the "Second World" (former communist countries), where international war remains a serious risk and violent intra-state conflicts are rampant.

**The Zone of Peace**   There is a wealth of explanation of the peace in the "zone of peace." Among the most prominent is that of Francis Fukuyama, according to whom "history" has come to an end with the emergence of a global consensus on basic values and norms such as those of democracy, pluralism, and a market economy.[9] While there is some dispute about which of these values and norms are decisive, there is almost unanimity on the peace-promoting effects of all of them.

---

[8] Max Singer and Aaron Wildawsky, *The Real World Order: Zones of Peace / Zones of Turmoil* (Chatham, N.J.: Chatham House Publishers, 1993).
[9] Francis Fukyama, *The End of History and the Last Man* (New York: The Free Press, 1992).

A further factor pointing in the same direction may be simple war weariness, as argued by John Mueller. In his 1989 work, *Retreat from Doomsday,* he presented a convincing case that major wars had become obsolete among the states of the West, attributing this to an acquired war weariness combined with the absence of traditional *casus belli* such as territorial claims. It is debatable whether such "major wars" are generally obsolete or whether this obsolescence is confined to the aforementioned "zone of peace," within which peace may well be overdetermined, as the same countries happen to be war weary, democratic, and trading states.

Even beyond the narrow confines of "the West," international wars seems to have become a much rarer phenomenon than in the past, as the picture has been dominated by intrastate wars for at least a decade.[10] However, several major international wars remain entirely conceivable, if not likely: between India and Pakistan; between the two Koreas; and between Iraq, Iran, and the members of the Gulf Cooperation Council—in various combinations. Even in Europe, wars between Greece and Turkey (both members of NATO), and between the various states in the Balkans, appear entirely conceivable.

Contrary to the situation during the Cold War, however, none of these wars are likely to escalate much in horizontal terms, as most of the rest of the world would probably seek to contain them by disengaging. The only exception to this may be the hypothetical war between the two Koreas, which might well draw in the United States, Japan, and China. This war would also entail a certain danger of vertical escalation, even to the point of nuclear war, especially if it were to be preceded by a North Korean acquisition of nuclear weapons. The same holds true for the possible war between India and Pakistan which might erupt over Kashmir. As both countries have now abandoned nuclear opacity in favor of full membership of the "nuclear club," one can neither discount the danger that they might bring their nuclear weapons to bear in the final phases of a conventional war, nor that some nuclear weapons might be launched inadvertently or even by accident.

It is thus premature to declare major (and/or nuclear) war to be universally obsolete; hence there is a need to stabilize these remaining conflicts in order to prevent their eruption into war. A defensive restructuring of the armed forces on a regional scale would presumably help a lot in this respect, implying a shift of emphasis from offensive military doctrines and strategies, deployments, and weapon acquisitions towards more strictly defensive ones.[11] This would allow states to improve their national security without making their neighbors less secure.

What is significant about all of the above scenarios, however, is that they only affect the states of the West only to the extent that these states choose to become

---

[10] Peter Wallensteen and Margareta Sollenberg, "Armed Conflict, 1989–98," *Journal of Peace Research* 36, no. 5 (September 1999), pp. 593–606.

[11] Bjørn Møller, *Common Security and Nonoffensive Defense: A Neorealist Perspective* (Boulder: Lynne Rienner, 1992); idem: *Dictionary of Alternative Defense* (Boulder: Lynne Rienner, 1995).

involved. None of the scenarios represent direct (and certainly not existential) threats to the national security of any of these countries, who are thus enjoying a degree of national security without historical precedents. By implication, most of these countries are actually in a position to dismantle most of their military power. That they have so evidently not done so (see Table 3.1) may be attributed both to the "better safe than sorry syndrome," and to their involvement in the armed conflicts of the "zones of turmoil." Unfortunately, however, their military postures and mindsets are almost entirely unadapted for the new tasks arising here.

**The Zone of Turmoil**   Most conflicts in the zones of turmoil fall into the category of what has euphemistically been labelled "small wars," where external participants wage what the United States military calls "operations other than war" (OOTW), for example, peacekeeping or humanitarian assistance. While there have been some success stories with such OOTWs, many (perhaps even most) of them have been partial and complete failures.

The reasons why these "small wars" are so hard to come to grips with is that their dynamics cannot be captured by the paradigm of "modern war," to which the West is accustomed. Whether to call them "postmodern" or "neo-archaic" could be debated, as they in many respects resemble wars as they were fought before the advent of modernity.[12] Their distinguishing features, in comparison with those of premodern and modern wars, are set out in Table 3.2.

Rather than being fought by regular conscripted or professional troops, neo-archaic wars tend to be waged by whoever is around, including women and children. They also tend to be waged in an irregular, sporadic, and spasmodic fashion, where occasional acts of war blend in with everyday life, eroding the distinction between warriors and the productive segments of society. Another reappearing phenomenon is that of various forms of mercenaries, that is, "guns for hire," now sometimes in the form of large firms offering their services to the higest bidder.

While modern war was what Martin Van Creveld calls "trinitarian" (that is, waged by armies on behalf of the trinity of people, army, and government) and profoundly political, neo-archaic wars are waged on behalf of very diverse entities, such as clans, ethnics, religious communities, warlords, or the like—and in some cases on behalf of nobody at all, except the lone warrior himself, operating in a post-apocalyptic "Mad Max" setting.

In contrast with the pre- and early-modern wars, but in analogy with the late-modern ones, most casualties and fatalities in the new "small" wars are civilians. The reason is that the distinction between combatants and civilians becomes blurred or erased with massive collateral damage as the inevitable result. With

---

[12] The best work on this phenomenon is Martin Van Creveld, *The Transformation of War* (New York: The Free Press, 1991).

**TABLE 3.2**
PREMODERN, MODERN, AND NEO-ARCHAIC WAR

|  | Premodern | Modern | Neo-Archaic |
|---|---|---|---|
| Who? | Mercenaries "Amateurs" | Conscripts Professionals | Militias, Terrorists Mercenaries Child Soldiers |
| On whose behalf? | Clan or tribe Feudal rulers Warlords | The state | Nation, ethnic or religious group Warlords |
| Against whom? | Soldiers | Soldiers Civilians | Civilians |
| Why? | Economy ends: booty | Political ends: territory sovereignty | Individual and group ends |
| Where? | Inside/Outside | Outside | Inside/Outside |
| How? | Disorderly | Principles of war | Guerilla warfare Terrorism |
| Limitations? | Low intensity No rules, but chivalry | High intensity Laws of war | High intensity "Anything goes" |
| Means? | Primitive weapons | Conventional weapons WMD | Small arms Computer virus |

the intention of crippling the enemy economically and socially, rather than defeating him militarily, agriculture and/or infrastructure are often targeted, for example, by means of land mines. In some cases, moreover (particularly when ethnicity is involved), war regresses into genocide, ethnic cleansing, or rape.

While modern wars typically have been fought for political ends, the new types of intra-state wars are different. They are not fought for political goals, at least not exclusively, and they can therefore not be adequately captured by the Clausewitzian paradigm of war as "a continuation of politics by other means." War may even cease to be a means and become an end in itself, at least at the level of individual warriors. Having lived the life of a warrior for some time is often tantamount to having lost whatever one owned or cherished before the fighting started: home, land, possessions, family, job, etc. There may thus be no normalcy to return to, and no improvement of one's condition to hope for, unless one's side prevails and can divide the spoils of conquest among themselves.

Contrary to modern wars between states, neo-archaic wars are mostly civil wars that take place within state borders—even though the mismatch between nation and state borders, or the involvement of external actors, may lead to a spread across borders. The very concepts of "front" and "rear" tend to lose their meaning.

One could even argue that the modern distinction between "inside" and "outside" [13] is turned on its head. While in modernity the inside of a state was supposed to be orderly, thanks to the workings of the state as a Hobbesian "Leviathan," the outside remained anarchic. For many states in the Third World, the opposite seems closer to reality—with fairly orderly relations to the outside in the form of diplomatic representations, but total anarchy within.

Modern war is orderly and susceptible to planning, maybe even in a "geometrical fashion." Hence, for instance, the renowned "Principles of War" of Antoine de Jomini which were presumably of perrenial validity. While strategic thinkers such as Carl von Clausewitz allowed room for "the fog of battle," war was basically an activity to plan for, and one that was expected to proceed (largely) according to plan. Neo-anarchic war, however, is profoundly disorderly. At its most orderly, it may be guided by strategies of guerilla war, but sometimes even this is lacking. That conventional (that is, "modern") strategies are to no avail against such adversaries was demonstrated in the Vietnam War, where Robert McNamara's "technowar" failed miserably, simply because the enemy was too intangible and refused to play "by the rules."

Contrary to some readings of Clausewitz, modern war has only very rarely assumed the form of the absolute war with a boundless escalatory momentum that he described in *Vom Kriege*. It is usually limited, by virtue of the strength of the defensive, by the political ends as a means to which war is conceived, and by a set of legal regulations. Neo-archaic warfare, in comparison, is unregulated and it tends to be boundless, if only because of who is waging it. The laws of war are laws for states, whereas there are few, if any, laws regulating the behavior of individuals or bands of mercenaries that are roaming wild.

## CONCLUSION

We have thus seen that the phenomenon of war is changing shape rather than disappearing. In the place of modern international wars over territory and other values, we see a blend of different types of wars fought over such issues as human rights and other values, as well as a resurgence of an almost antediluvian form of "neo-archaic wars." Not only is the West usually unable to get its way when it becomes involved in such conflicts, but also, by intervening the West also creates the impression of unduly exploiting its position of unprecedented strength. By this behavior it weakens the (already fragile) rule of international law, thereby contributing to a militarization of international affairs.

---

[13] The terms come from R.B.J. Walker, *Inside/Outside: International Relations as Political Theory* (Cambridge: Cambridge University Press, 1993).

# 4

# WAR AND ITS CAUSES

Jack S. Levy

**Noting changing patterns in the frequency and character of warfare, Jack S. Levy emphasizes both the sources of continuity and the sources of change in his analysis of some of the leading theories of the causes of international war. He breaks the primary determinants of past and future wars into three "levels of analysis," and reviews the major ideas about the roots of modern warfare stemming from changes in "systemic" or global conditions, from changes in the characteristics of states such as the proportion of countries which are ruled democratically, and from individual leaders' impact on decisions regarding war and peace. This essay sets the stage for interpreting the probability of armed conflicts of various types in the twenty-first century. Levy is Board of Governors' Professor of Political Science at Rutgers University and author of *War in the Modern Great Power System, 1495–1975* (1983).**

The twentieth century was one of the most conflictual in history, with two world wars, the development of nuclear weapons, the acute crises of the Cold War, and an explosion of ethnonational conflict at century's end.[1] At the same time, however, the period since World War II has seen the longest period of great power

---

[1] On historical trends in war, see Jack S. Levy, Thomas C. Walker, and Martin S. Edwards, "Continuity and Change in the Evolution of Warfare," in Zeev Maoz and Azar Gat, eds., *War in a Changing World* (Ann Arbor: University of Michigan Press, forthcoming).

peace in at least five centuries, as well as the end of the Cold War and the collapse of the Soviet Union. This has led many to assert the obsolescence of war among advanced industrial states, based on the stabilizing effects of nuclear weapons, the end of the bipolar Cold War rivalry, the rapid spread of democratic political systems, globalization and economic interdependence, the growth of international institutions, the "end of history," and changing attitudes in the West toward war.[2]

There has indeed been a "long peace" since World War II, but this peace has been confined to advanced industrial states, while war continues to ravage much of the rest of the world. These trends reflect a dramatic shift, beginning in 1945, in the concentration of war from Europe to other regional subsystems and from international wars to internal wars.[3] Many of these wars have been based on ethnonational or religious "identity conflicts" and have been quite bloody as well as intractable, to the point that some have suggested that the wars between states and political ideologies that dominated the last several centuries may give way to a "clash of civilizations" defined in terms of cultural identity.[4]

The areas of the world in which war is most likely to be fought and the types of states which are most likely to fight these wars may have changed, but there is little reason to believe that war itself will soon cease to exist as a regular pattern of behavior in world politics or that the "laws" of international politics have fundamentally changed. Although recent internal conflicts involve some factors that traditional theories of war tend to downplay—such as identity, environmental, and demographic variables,[5] many of the causal patterns leading to these conflicts can be found in countless other wars that have occurred over the past century or past millennium, and often the "new" factors exert their effects through traditional causal pathways. We must understand both the forces of change and enduring patterns if we are to accurately anticipate likely trends in war or to have

---

[2] John Lewis Gaddis, *The Long Peace* (New York: Oxford University Press, 1987); Robert Jervis, *The Meaning of the Nuclear Revolution* (Ithaca, N.Y.: Cornell University Press, 1989); Robert O. Keohane and Lisa L. Martin, "The Promise of Institutionalist Theory," *International Security* 20, no. 1 (Summer 1995), pp. 39–51; Francis Fukuyama, *The End of History and the Last Man* (New York: Free Press, 1992); James Lee Ray, "The Abolition of Slavery and the End of International War," *International Organization* 43, no. 3 (Summer 1989), pp. 405–39; John Mueller, *Quiet Cataclysm: Reflections on the Recent Transformation of World Politics* (New York: HarperCollins, 1995). Other relevant literature is cited below.

[3] J. David Singer, "Peace in the Global System: Displacement, Interregnum, or Transformation?" in Charles W. Kegley, Jr., ed., *The Long Postwar Peace* (New York: HarperCollins, 1991), pp. 56–84.

[4] Samuel P. Huntington, *The Clash of Civilizations and the Remaking of World Order* (New York: Simon & Schuster, 1996). On ethnonational conflict, see Michael E. Brown, Owen R. Cote, Jr., Sean M. Lynn-Jones, and Steven E. Miller, eds., *Nationalism and Ethnic Conflict* (Cambridge, Mass.: MIT Press, 1996–97); David A. Lake and Donald Rothchild, eds., *The International Spread of Ethnic Conflict: Fear, Diffusion, and Escalation* (Princeton, N.J.: Princeton University Press, 1998).

[5] Thomas Homer-Dixon and Jessica Blitt, *Ecoviolence: Links Among Environment, Population, and Security* (Lanham, Md.: Rowman & Littlefield, 1998); Chester Crocker and Fen Hampson with Pamela Aall, eds., *Managing Global Chaos: Sources of and Responses to International Conflict* (Washington, D.C.: United States Institute of Peace, 1996).

any chance of reducing the frequency of war or mitigating its effects. To that end we analyze some of the leading theories of the causes of war.[6]

## THE "LEVELS-OF-ANALYSIS" FRAMEWORK

The first step toward an understanding of the wide variety of causes of war is to classify them into a more manageable framework. Although political scientists disagree profoundly on specific causes of war, they generally agree that the "levels-of-analysis" framework provides a useful way of classifying the causes of war. This framework builds on Kenneth Waltz's three "images" of international conflict and distinguishes among individual, national, and systemic-level variables influencing the foreign policy behavior of states.[7] The individual level focuses primarily on human nature and on individual political leaders and their belief systems, psychological processes, emotional states, and personalities. The national level includes both governmental variables such as the structure of the political system (democratic vs. authoritarian, or presidential vs. parliamentary democracy) and the nature of the policymaking process, and societal factors such as the structure of the economic system, the role of public opinion and interest groups, ethnicity and nationalism, and political culture and ideology. Systemic-level causes include the anarchic structure of the international system, the distribution of military and economic power among the leading states in the system, patterns of military alliances and international trade, and other factors that constitute the external environment common to all states. Some scholars modify the levels-of-analysis framework by disaggregating the nation-state level into distinct governmental and societal-level factors,[8] or by distinguishing, within the systemic level, among system characteristics common to all states, dyadic relationships between pairs of states, and the external environment of individual states.

Although the levels-of-analysis framework is most commonly used as a typology for classifying independent causal variables, it is sometimes used instead to refer to the dependent variable—to the unit of analysis or type of entity (individual, organization, state, or system) whose behavior is to be explained. Here the systemic level of analysis refers to explanations of patterns and outcomes in the international system, the dyadic level to explanations of the strategic interactions between two states, the national level to explanations of state foreign

[6] John A. Vasquez, *The War Puzzle* (New York: Cambridge University Press, 1993); Michael W. Doyle, *Ways of War and Peace* (New York: W.W. Norton, 1997). The following sections build on Jack S. Levy, "Contending Theories of International Conflict: A Levels-of-Analysis Approach," in Crocker and Hampson, eds., *Managing Global Chaos,* pp. 3–24; and Jack S. Levy, "The Causes of War and the Conditions of Peace," *Annual Review of Political Science* 1 (1998), pp. 139–65.

[7] Kenneth N. Waltz, *Man, the State, and War* (New York: Columbia University Press, 1959).

[8] Robert Jervis, *Perception and Misperception in International Politics* (Princeton, N.J.: Princeton University Press, 1976), chap. 1; James N. Rosenau, *The Scientific Study of Foreign Policy* (New York: Nichols, 1980), chap. 6.

policy behavior, and the individual level to explanations of the preferences, beliefs, or choices of individuals.

It is often desirable to combine variables from different levels of analysis in causal explanations. Variables from several levels can be combined in an explanation of a single dependent variable, and indeed scholars have increasingly moved away from explanations based on a single level of analysis to multi-level explanations. Independent variables from one level can be used to explain dependent variables at another level. Systemic or dyadic-level security threats, for example, can shape both the foreign policy preferences of individuals (greater threats may lead to preferences for more hardline policies) and also national-level structures (greater threats may lead to greater concentrations of political power in state institutions in the name of national security).

We have to be careful, however, when we use variables at one level to explain outcomes at a "higher" level of analysis. National or individual-level variables can be the primary causes of systemic or dyadic-level outcomes. Domestic political pressures or the belief systems of individual political leaders, for example, could be the main causes of some wars. A logically complete explanation of such cases, however, requires the analyst to go beyond leaders' beliefs and explain how those beliefs and policy preferences get aggregated into collective foreign policy decisions by the state, for few political leaders can by themselves dictate foreign policy. The analyst must also go beyond national-level foreign policies and explain how the actions of two or more states interact to lead to war as a dyadic or systemic outcome. To the extent that most wars generally involve the mutual and interactive decisions of two or more adversaries, an explanation for the outbreak of war logically requires the inclusion of dyadic or systemic-level variables.

## SYSTEMIC-LEVEL CAUSES OF WAR

The leading systemic-level approach to the study of war is "realist theory." Realist theory focuses on sovereign states who act rationally to advance their security, power, and wealth in an anarchic international system defined by the absence of a higher authority to regulate disputes and enforce agreements between states. In such an "anarchic" system, with nothing comparable to governments in domestic political systems to maintain order, states must rely on themselves or their allies (who are not always reliable) to provide for their security and other interests. Given uncertainties regarding the current and future intentions of the adversary, political leaders often focus on short-term security needs, adopt worst-case thinking, engage in a constant struggle for power, and utilize coercive threats to advance their interests, influence the adversary, and maintain their reputations.[9]

[9] On realist theories of war see Kenneth N. Waltz, "The Origins of War in Neorealist Theory," in Robert I. Rotberg and Theodore K. Rabb, eds., *The Origin and Prevention of Major Wars* (New York: Cambridge University Press, 1988), pp. 39–52; Michael E. Brown, Sean M. Lynn-Jones, and Steven Miller, eds., *The Perils of Anarchy: Contemporary Realism and International Security* (Cambridge, Mass.: MIT Press, 1995).

There are several paths to war in realist theory. In one, a state prefers war to peace and goes to war to take what it wants or to force the adversary to change its policies. It may first attempt to get what it wants through negotiation or threats, but if its adversary is unwilling to meet its demands the aggressor state may simply resort to force. This path is reflected in Thucydides' account of the Athenians' argument to the Melians that "the strong do what they can and the weak suffer what they must."[10] Another path to war in realist theory involves the unintended consequences of actions by those who prefer peace to war and who are driven more by fear than by ambition. Even defensively motivated efforts by states to provide for their own security through armaments, alliances, and deterrent threats are often perceived as threatening by others (the "security dilemma") and lead to counteractions and conflict spirals which become difficult to reverse.[11]

The leading realist theory is balance of power theory, which is less a well-defined theory than a loosely connected set of hypotheses about the security behavior of states, particularly great powers, in anarchic systems. Although there are many variations of balance of power theory, most balance of power theorists agree that the primary goal of states is to prevent any single state from achieving a position of dominance in the system and that the primary instrumental goal is to maintain an equilibrium of power. This leads states to pursue a strategy of balancing power against the strongest states and the greatest threats to their interests, either through the internal mobilization of military power or through the formation of external alliances against potential aggressors.[12]

Balance of power theory predicts that if any single state threatens to achieve a position of "hegemony" from which it could dominate other states in the system, a military coalition of nearly all other great powers will form. This will result in either a retreat by the aspiring hegemon or a "hegemonic war" to restore equilibrium to the system. The theory predicts that this balancing mechanism almost always works successfully to avoid hegemony, either because potential hegemons are deterred by their anticipation of a military coalition against them or because they are defeated in war after deterrence fails. Hegemonic wars have arisen in response to the threats posed by Philip II of Spain in the late sixteenth century, Louis XIV of France in the late seventeenth century, revolutionary and Napoleonic France in the late eighteenth century, and Germany twice in the first half of the twentieth century. Blocking coalitions are also likely to emerge if one state threatens to establish hegemony over a regional system, as illustrated by the coalition against Iraq in 1990–1991.

Because balance of power theory posits that states balance against the strongest military power in the system, and that the international system is most unstable

---

[10] Robert B. Strassler, *The Landmark Thucydides* (New York: Free Press, 1996), V/89, p. 352.

[11] Robert Jervis, "Cooperation Under the Security Dilemma," *World Politics* 30, no. 2 (January 1978), pp. 167–86.

[12] On balance of power theory, see Hans Morgenthau, *Politics Among Nations,* 4th ed. (New York: Knopf, 1967), part IV; Edward Gulick, *Europe's Classical Balance of Power* (New York: W.W. Norton, 1955), part I.

and most likely to be warlike when power is highly concentrated in the hands of a single great power or a coalition of powers, the theory has trouble explaining why blocking coalitions did not form against Britain in the mid-19th century or against the United States in the later twentieth century, or more generally why periods characterized by a dominant global power are often quite peaceful (for example, the *Pax Britannica* of the nineteenth century). One response is that balance of power theory has a Eurocentric bias and focuses on threats to hegemony in the European system (or any land-based system), not the global system. Global powers, whose strength is generally based on seapower and economic wealth, do not threaten others in the same way that land-based powers with large armies threaten their neighbors, so there are fewer incentives to balance against them.[13]

One theory that may provide a better explanation of international behavior in periods of a dominant global power (but which provides a much weaker explanation of behavior within a land-based system such as Europe for most of the last millennium) is "power transition theory," a form of hegemonic theory that shares realist assumptions but that emphasizes the existence of order within a nominally anarchic system.[14] Hegemons commonly arise and use their strength to create a set of political and economic structures and norms of behavior that enhance the stability of the system at the same time that it advances their own security. Some great powers may bandwagon with the hegemon rather than balance against it (contrary to balance of power theory), but other great powers may be dissatisfied with the existing international order. Differential rates of growth lead to the rise and fall of hegemons, and the probability of a major war is greatest near the point when the declining leader is being overtaken by a rising, dissatisfied challenger. Either the challenger initiates a war to bring it benefits from the system into line with its rising military power or the declining leader initiates a "preventive war" to block the rising challenger while the chance is still available.[15] Hegemonic theory includes the dyadic-level "power preponderance" hypothesis, widely confirmed in empirical studies, that war is least likely when one state has a preponderance of power over another and most likely when there is an equality of power.[16]

---

[13] See Levy, "The Causes of War and the Conditions of Peace," pp. 148–49.

[14] A.F.K. Organski and Jacek Kugler, *The War Ledger* (Chicago: University of Chicago Press, 1980), chap. 1; Robert Gilpin, *War and Change in World Politics* (New York: Cambridge University Press, 1981).

[15] Jack S. Levy, "Declining Power and the Preventive Motivation for War," *World Politics* 40, no. 1 (October 1987), pp. 82–107. The Israeli attack against the Iraqi nuclear reactor in 1981 is a classic example of a preventive strike.

[16] Daniel S. Geller, "Power Differentials and War in Rival Dyads," *International Studies Quarterly* 37, no. 2 (June 1993), pp. 173–93. The logic is that under preponderance the strong are satisfied and do not have the incentives for war and the weak, though dissatisfied, lack the capability for war. Note that the stabilizing effects of power preponderance at the dyadic level does not necessarily imply that imbalances of power are stabilizing at the systemic level, where alliances and blocking coalitions become relevant.

Another theory that emphasizes the systemic-level sources of war and peace, but that is associated with a liberal perspective that downplays the conflictual consequences of anarchy and emphasizes the potential for cooperation in the international system, is the liberal economic theory of war.[17] The argument is that free trade is the best guarantor of peace, for several reasons. Trade promotes prosperity and prosperity contributes to peace, because if people are making money they are satisfied and have little reason for war. Moreover, by increasing economic interdependence between states, trade leaves states vulnerable to any disruption through war, and the fear of economic disruption and the loss of the gains from trade deters political leaders from taking actions that are likely to lead to militarized conflict.

Realists reject the idea that trade promotes peace.[18] They question liberals' implicit assumption that trade is always more efficient than military conquest in promoting state wealth, and note that periods of high levels of economic interdependence have been associated with major wars (World War I, for example) as well as peace. They argue that trade and interdependence are usually asymmetrical, that this tempts states to exploit their trading partner's vulnerabilities and use economic coercion to influence the adversary's policies, and that such coercive behavior can lead to retaliatory actions, increased hostility, conflict spirals, and war.

## NATIONAL-LEVEL THEORIES OF WAR

In emphasizing the external forces that shape state decisions for war, systemic-level theories posit that states in similar situations behave in similar ways. The implication is that factors internal to states have little impact on foreign policy decisions or the strategic interaction between states.[19] There is substantial evidence, however, that the internal makeup of states—particularly their democratic or authoritarian character—has a strong influence on their propensity toward war. There is striking evidence, for example, that democratic states rarely if ever go to war with each other. This finding, along with other evidence, has recently led students of war to give more attention to national-level patterns of causation.

---

[17] Richard Rosecrance, *Rise of the Trading State* (New York: Basic Books, 1986); John R. Oneal and Bruce M. Russett, "The Classical Liberals Were Right: Democracy, Interdependence, and Conflict, 1950–1985," *International Studies Quarterly* 41, no. 1 (March 1997), pp. 267–94.

[18] Katherine Barbieri, "Economic Interdependence: A Path to Peace or Source of Interstate Conflict?" *Journal of Peace Research* 33 (February 1996), pp. 29–49; Norrin M. Ripsman and Jean-Marc F. Blanchard, "Commercial Liberalism under Fire: Evidence from 1914 and 1936," *Security Studies,* 6, no. 2 (Winter 1996–97), pp. 4–50.

[19] Realist theories often acknowledge that domestic demographic and economic variables shape the differential rates of national growth that determine the distribution of power in the system, and liberal theories recognize the domestic factors that affect the terms of trade between states, the ideologies that help shape state interests, and parochial domestic interests that constrain state behavior.

The "democratic peace" does not imply that democracies are always peaceful. The evidence tentatively suggests that there is no difference between democracies and non-democracies in terms of their respective frequency of involvement in wars. Moreover, democracies occasionally get involved in crises with other democracies and use limited amounts of force against them. Democracies have frequently fought imperial wars, and once involved in war they often adopt a crusading spirit and fight particularly destructive wars. But using standard definitions of democracy (fair, competitive elections and constitutional transfers of executive power) and war (which is often distinguished from lesser conflicts by the threshold of a minimum of 1,000 battle-related deaths), there are few if any clearcut cases of wars between democracies.[20]

Although scholars have reached a tentative consensus that wars between democracies are extraordinarily rare, they have yet to agree on how best to explain this "law-like" pattern of behavior. The "institutional model" of the democratic peace argues that checks and balances, the dispersion of power, and the need for public debate in democratic states make it easier for various governmental or societal groups to block attempts by political leaders to take the country into war. The "political culture model" suggests that the norms of peaceful conflict resolution that have evolved within democratic societies are extended to relations between democratic states.[21]

Authoritarian leaders face fewer constraints on their power, and authoritarian systems lack the traditions and the norms for the peaceful resolution of internal conflicts. Given these asymmetries, authoritarian leaders often attempt to exploit the conciliatory tendencies of democracies. The anticipation of this undermines democratic political leaders' expectations that their peaceful conflict resolution strategies will be reciprocated, reduces their internal constraints on the use of force, and provides additional incentives for democratic regimes to use force against authoritarian regimes to eliminate their violent tendencies. Thus democracies not only respond to attacks by authoritarian states, but also initiate wars against them.

One assumption underlying the institutional explanation for the democratic peace is that political leaders are more inclined to war than are peoples, but this is not always true. Leaders are sometimes precluded by hard-line public opinion from making the concessions that are necessary to prevent war or establish a durable peace, and occasionally they are forced into wars that they would prefer

---

[20] Michael Doyle, "Liberalism and World Politics." *American Political Science Review* 80, no. 4 (December 1986), pp. 1151–70; Bruce Russett, *Grasping the Democratic Peace* (Princeton: Princeton University Press, 1993), chaps. 1–2; James Lee Ray, *Democracy and International Politics: An Evaluation of the Democratic Peace Proposition* (Columbia: University of South Carolina Press, 1995).

[21] T. Clifton Morgan and Sally Howard Campbell, "Domestic Structure, Decisional Constraints, and War: So Why Can't Democracies Fight?" *Journal of Conflict Resolution* 35, no. 2 (June 1991), pp. 187–211.

to avoid. One example might be the case of the United States in the Spanish-American War of 1898, where a "yellow press" mobilized substantial popular pressure on President McKinley for a war that he did not really favor. In fact, political leaders in most countries, democratic or authoritarian, have found that whenever they use military force against external adversaries they always receive a boost in public support in the form of a "rally 'round the flag" effect, however temporary that may be. Political leaders anticipate this and are sometimes tempted to undertake risky foreign ventures in an attempt to distract attention from domestic problems and increase their political support. Such "diversionary" strategies, or scapegoating, have been commonly used by political leaders for the purposes of ethnic mobilization of their populations against national rivals, as illustrated by Slobodan Milosevic in the wars in Bosnia and Kosovo.[22] These strategies can backfire, however, if they lead to military defeat, as discovered by the Argentine leaders who unsuccessfully attempted to recover the Falkland/Malvinas Islands from Britain in 1982.

## INDIVIDUAL-LEVEL THEORIES OF WAR

National-level theories, like systemic-level ones, imply that individuals have little impact on foreign policy decisions, that in making decisions for war or peace political leaders are driven by social and economic forces that are beyond their control. The implication is that substituting one individual for another in top decision-making roles would not make much of a difference. Individual-level theories, however, emphasize the role of individual political leaders, their beliefs about the world and the adversary, the psychological processes through which they acquire information and make decisions, and their personalities and emotional states.

One of the most important individual-level causes of war, though one that is also shaped by societal factors, is misperceptions. The most important misperceptions leading to war are those that concern the capabilities and intentions of adversaries and third states. If leaders exaggerate the hostility of their adversary's intentions, they may overreact to genuinely defensive actions, which often leads to a conflict spiral and possibly war. On the other hand, if political leaders underestimate the adversary's hostility or its capabilities, they might fail to build up their own capabilities or fail to demonstrate resolve, either of which undermines deterrence and increases the likelihood of war. If they underestimate adversary capabilities relative to their own, they may be overconfident of a rapid military victory involving minimal costs. This overconfidence is often reinforced

---

[22] Jack S. Levy, "The Diversionary Theory of War: A Critique," in Manus I. Midlarsky, ed., *Handbook of War Studies* (Boston: Unwin Hyman, 1989), chap. 11; V.P. Gagnon, Jr. "Ethnic Nationalism and International Conflict: The Case of Serbia," *International Security* 19, no. 3 (Winter 1994–95), pp. 331–67.

by the tendency to exaggerate the likelihood that one's potential friends will intervene on one's behalf and the likelihood that one's potential enemies will stay neutral. The consequence of military overconfidence is an increase in the likelihood of a war or of hardline bargaining tactics that often lead to war.[23]

## CONCLUSION

War has changed in important respects over the last half-century. There has been an unmistakable shift in war from Europe to other regions of the world, and from the great powers to other states. There is substantial consensus that this shift will continue into the future, though some express concern about the implications of the rising power of China and its growing rivalry with the United States. How to explain these patterns is more contentious, as are questions relating to which of the above-mentioned causal factors are most important in the processes leading to war, whether the causes of war have changed over time, and whether current causal patterns are likely to persist into the future. The increasing salience of ethnonational and religious identity in much of the world may help shape who fights most wars, and the rise of information-based technologies and the development of new weapons of mass destruction may shape the manner in which some wars are fought, but it is unlikely that war will disappear from a global system that will continue to consist of independent units engaged in an ongoing struggle for power, wealth, and autonomy.

[23] Jervis, *Perception and Misperception in International Politics;* Jack S. Levy, "Misperception and the Causes of War: Theoretical Linkages and Analytical Problems," *World Politics* 36, no. 1 (October 1983), pp. 76–99.

# 5

# THE OBSOLESCENCE OF MAJOR WAR

John Mueller

**Observing the virtual absence of war between the great powers since World War II (alongside its continuation in the same period among the powerful and the weak in the Third World), John Mueller explores the various reasons why the probability of another major or general world war appears to have receded and the consequences of the end of the Cold War for this "imperfect" but prolonged postwar peace. Mueller is Professor of Political Science at the University of Rochester, where he serves as director of the Watson Center for the Study of International Peace and Cooperation. He is author of** *Quiet Cataclysm: Reflections on the Recent Transformation of World Politics* **(1995).**

In discussing the causes of international war, commentators have often found it useful to group theories into what they term levels of analysis. In his classic work, *Man, the State and War,* Kenneth N. Waltz organizes the theories according to whether the cause of war is found in the nature of man, in the nature of the state, or in the nature of the international state system. More recently Jack Levy, partly setting the issue of human nature to one side, organizes the theories according to whether they stress the systemic level, the nature of state and society, or the decision-making process.[1]

---

[1] Kenneth N. Waltz, *Man, the State and War* (New York: Columbia University Press, 1959): Jack S. Levy, "The Causes of War: A Review of Theories and Evidence," in Philip E. Tetlock, Jo L.

In various ways, these level-of-analysis approaches direct attention away from war itself and toward concerns that may influence the incidence of war. However, war should not be visualized as a sort of recurring outcome that is determined by other conditions, but rather as a phenomenon that has its own qualities and appeals. And over time these appeals can change. In this view, war is merely an idea, an institution, like dueling or slavery, that has been grafted onto human existence. Unlike breathing, eating, or sex, war is not something that is somehow required by the human condition, by the structure of international affairs, or by the forces of history.

Accordingly, war can shrivel up and disappear, and this may come about without any notable change or improvement on any of the level-of-analysis categories. Specifically, war can die out without changing human nature, without modifying the nature of the state or the nation-state, without changing the international system, without creating an effective world government or system of international law, and without improving the competence or moral capacity of political leaders. It can also go away without expanding international trade, interdependence, or communication; without fabricating an effective moral or practical equivalent; without enveloping the earth in democracy or prosperity; without devising ingenious agreements to restrict arms or the arms industry; without reducing the world's considerable store of hate, selfishness, nationalism, and racism; without increasing the amount of love, justice, harmony, cooperation, good will, or inner peace in the world; without establishing security communities; and without doing anything whatever about nuclear weapons.

Not only *can* such a development take place: it *has* been taking place for a century or more, at least within the developed world, once a cauldron of international and civil war. Conflicts of interest are inevitable and continue to persist within the developed world. But the notion that war should be used to resolve them has increasingly been discredited and abandoned there. War is apparently becoming obsolete, at least in the developed world: in an area where war was once often casually seen as beneficial, noble, and glorious, or at least as necessary or inevitable, the conviction has now become widespread that war would be intolerably costly, unwise, futile, and debased.[2]

Some of this may be suggested by the remarkable speed with which the Cold War ended in the late 1980s. The dangers of a major war in the developed world clearly declined remarkably: yet this can hardly be attributed to an improvement

---

Husbands, Robert Jervis, Paul C. Stern, and Charles Tilly, eds., *Behavior, Society and Nuclear War,* vol. 1 (New York: Oxford University Press, 1989), pp. 209–333. See also J. David Singer, "The Levels of Analysis Problem in International Relations," in Klaus Knorr and Sydney Verba, eds., *The International System* (Princeton, N.J.: Princeton University Press, 1961), pp. 77–92; and James N. Rosenau, "Pretheories and Theories of Foreign Policy," in R. B. Farrell, ed., *Approaches to Comparative and International Politics* (Evanston, Ill.: Northwestern University Press, 1966), pp. 27–92.

[2] For a further development of these arguments, see John Mueller, *Retreat from Doomsday: The Obsolescence of Major War* (New York: Basic Books, 1989).

in human nature, to the demise of the nation-state, to the rise of a world government, or to a notable improvement in the competence of political leaders.

## TWO ANALOGIES: DUELING AND SLAVERY

It may not be obvious that an accepted, time-honored institution that serves an urgent social purpose can become obsolescent and then die out because many people come to find it obnoxious. But the argument here is that something like that has indeed been happening to war in the developed world. To illustrate the dynamic, [consider] two analogies: the processes by which the once-perennial institutions of dueling and slavery have all but vanished from the face of the earth.

### Dueling

In some important respects, war in the developed world may be following the example of another violent method for settling disputes, dueling. Up until a century ago dueling was common practice in Europe and the USA among a certain class of young and youngish men who liked to classify themselves as gentlemen.[3] Men of that social set that once dueled still exist, they still get insulted, and they are still concerned about their self-respect and their standing among their peers. But they no longer duel. However, they do not avoid dueling today because they evaluate the option and reject it on cost-benefit grounds. Rather, the option never percolates into their consciousness as something that is available. That is, a form of violence famed and fabled for centuries has now sum; from thought as a viable, conscious possibility.

The Prussian strategist, Carl van Clausewitz, opens his famous 1832 book, *On War,* by observing that "War is nothing but a duel on a larger scale." If war, like dueling, comes to be viewed as a thoroughly undesirable, even ridiculous, policy, and if it can no longer promise gains, or if potential combatants come no longer to value the things it can gain for them, then war can fade away as a coherent possibility even if a truly viable substitute or "moral equivalent" for it were never formulated. Like dueling, it could become unfashionable and then obsolete.

---

[3] For other observations of the analogy between war and dueling, see Bernard Brodie, *War and Politics* (New York: Macmillan, 1973), p. 275; Norman Angell, *The Great Illusion* (London: Heinemann, 1914), pp. 202–03; G. P. Gooch, *History of Our Time, 1885–1911* (London: Williams & Norgate, 1911), p. 249; J. E. Cairnes, "International Law," *Fortnightly Review* 2, no. 1 (November 1865), p. 650n.

## Slavery

From the dawn of prehistory until about 1788 slavery, like war, could be found just about everywhere in one form or another, and it flourished in every age. Around 1788, however, the anti-slavery forces began to argue that the institution was repulsive, immoral, and uncivilized: and this sentiment gradually picked up adherents. . . .

. . . The abolitionists were up against an institution that was viable, profitable, and expanding, and moreover one that had been uncritically accepted for thousands—perhaps millions—of years as a natural and inevitable part of human existence. To counter this powerful and time-honored institution, the abolitionists' principal weapon was a novel argument: it had recently occurred to them, they said, that slavery was no longer the way people ought to do things.

As it happened, this was an idea whose time had come. The abolition of slavery required legislative battles, international pressures, economic travail, and, in the United States, a cataclysmic war (but it did *not* require the fabrication of a functional equivalent or the formation of an effective supranational authority). Within a century slavery, and most similar institutions like serfdom, had been all but eradicated from the face of the globe. Slavery became controversial and then obsolete.

## War

Dueling and slavery no longer exist as effective institutions; they have largely faded from human experience except as something we read about in books. While their reestablishment is not impossible, they show after a century of neglect no signs of revival. Other once-popular, even once-admirable, institutions in the developed world have been, or are being, eliminated because at some point they began to seem repulsive, immoral, and uncivilized: bearbaiting, bareknuckle fighting, freak shows, casual torture, wanton cruelty to animals, burning heretics, flogging, vendettas, deforming corsetting, laughing at the insane, the death penalty for minor crimes, eunuchism, and public cigarette smoking.

War may well be in the process of joining this list of recently discovered sins and vices. War is not, of course, the same as dueling or slavery. Like war, dueling is an institution for settling disputes; but it was something of a social affectation and it usually involved only matters of "honor," not ones of physical gain. Like war, slavery was nearly universal and an apparently inevitable part of human existence, but it could be eliminated area by area: a country that abolished slavery did not have to worry about what other countries were doing, while a country that would like to abolish war must continue to be concerned about those that have kept it in their repertory.

On the other hand, war has against it not only substantial psychic costs, but also obvious and widespread physical ones. Dueling brought death and destruction but, at least in the first instance, only to a few people who had specifically volunteered to participate. And while slavery may have brought moral destruction, it generally was a considerable economic success.

In some respects then, the fact that war has outlived dueling and slavery is curious. But there are signs that, at least in the developed world, it too has begun to succumb to obsolescence.

## TRENDS AGAINST WAR BEFORE 1914

There were a number of trends away from war in the developed world before World War I. Two of these deserve special emphasis.

### The Hollandization Phenomenon

As early as 1800 a few once-warlike countries in Europe, like Holland, Switzerland, and Sweden, quietly began to drop out of the war system. While war was still generally accepted as a natural and inevitable phenomenon, these countries found solace (and prosperity) in policies that stressed peace. People who argue that war is inherent in nature and those who see war as a recurring, cyclic phenomenon need to supply an explanation for these countries. Switzerland, for example, has avoided all international war for nearly 200 years. If war is inherent in human nature or if war is some sort of cyclic inevitability, surely the Swiss ought to be roaring for a fight by now.

### The Rise of an Organized Peace Movement

While there have been individual war opponents throughout history, the existence of organized groups devoted to abolishing war from the human condition is quite new. The institution of war came under truly organized and concentrated attack only after 1815, and this peace movement did not develop real momentum until the end of the century. . . .

Peace advocates were a noisy gadfly minority by 1900, and they had established a sense of momentum. Their arguments were inescapable, but, for the most part they were rejected and derided by the majority, which still held to the traditional view that war was noble, natural, thrilling, progressive, manly, redemptive, and beneficial. Up until 1914, as Michael Howard has observed, war "was almost universally considered an acceptable, perhaps an inevitable and for many people a desirable way of settling international differences."

## THE IMPACT OF WORLD WAR I

The holocaust of World War I fumed peace advocates into a pronounced majority in the developed world and destroyed war romanticism. As Arnold Toynbee points out, this war marked the end of a "span of five thousand years during which war had been one of mankind's master institutions." Or, as Evan Luard observes, "the First World War transformed traditional attitudes toward war. For the first time there was an almost universal sense that the deliberate launching of a war could now no longer be justified."

World War I was, of course, horrible. But horror was not invented in 1914. History had already had its Carthages, its Jerichos, its wars of thirty years, of one hundred years. Seen in historic context, in fact, World War I does not seem to have been all that unusual in its duration, destructiveness, grimness, political pointlessness, economic consequences, breadth, or intensity. However, it does seem to be unique in that it was the first major war to be preceded by substantial, organized antiwar agitation, and in that, for Europeans, it followed an unprecedentedly peaceful century during which Europeans had begun, perhaps unknowingly, to appreciate the virtues of peace.[4]

Obviously, this change of attitude was not enough to prevent the wars that have taken place since 1918. But the notion that the institution of war, particularly war in the developed world, was repulsive, uncivilized, immoral, and futile—voiced only by minorities before 1914—was an idea whose time had come. It is one that has permeated most of the developed world ever since.

## WORLD WAR II

It is possible that enough war spirit still lingered, particularly in Germany, for another war in Europe to be necessary to extinguish it there. But analysis of opinion in the interwar period suggests that war was viewed with about as much horror in Germany as any place on the continent. To a remarkable degree, major war resumed to Europe only because of the astoundingly successful machinations of Adolf Hitler, virtually the last European who was willing to risk major war. As Gerhard Weinberg has put it: "Whether any other German leader would indeed have taken the plunge is surely doubtful, and the very warnings Hitler received from some of his generals can only have reinforced his belief in his personal role as the one man able, willing, and even eager to lead Germany and drag the world into war." That is, after World War I a war in Europe could be brought about only through the maniacally dedicated manipulations of an exceptionally lucky and spectacularly skilled entrepreneur; before World War I, any dimwit—for example, Kaiser Wilhelm—could get into one.

The war in Asia was, of course, developed out of the expansionary policies of distant Japan, a country that neither participated substantially in World War I nor learned its lessons. In World War II, Japan got the message most Europeans had received from World War I.

---

[4] For a further development of this argument, see John Mueller, "Changing Attitudes Toward War: The Impact of World War I," *British Journal of Political Science* 21 (January 1991), pp. 1–28.

## THE COLD WAR, THE LONG PEACE, AND NUCLEAR WEAPONS

Since 1945 major war [was] most likely to develop from the Cold War that . . . dominated postwar international history. The hostility of the era mostly [derived] from the Soviet Union's ideological—even romantic—affection for revolution and for revolutionary war. While this ideology [was] expansionistic in some respects, it . . . never visualized major war in the Hitler mode as a remotely sensible tactic.

East and West [were] never . . . close to major war, and it seems unlikely that nuclear weapons [were] important determinants of this—insofar as a military deterrent [was] necessary, the fear of escalation to a war like World War I or II [supplied] it. Even allowing considerably for stupidity, ineptness, miscalculation, and self-deception, a large war, nuclear or otherwise, has never been remotely in the interest of the essentially contented, risk-averse, escalation-anticipating countries that have dominated world affairs since 1945. This is not to deny that nuclear war is appalling to contemplate and mind-concentratingly dramatic, particularly in the speed with which it could bring about massive destruction. Nor is it to deny that decision-makers, both in times of crisis and in times of noncrisis, are well aware of how cataclysmic a nuclear war could be. It is simply to stress that the horror of repeating World War II is not all that much less impressive or dramatic, and that leaders essentially content with the status quo will strive to avoid anything that they feel could lead to either calamity. A jump from a fiftyith-floor window is probably quite a bit more horrible to contemplate than a jump from a fifth-floor one, but anyone who finds life even minimally satisfying is extremely unlikely to do either.[5]

In general the wars that have involved developed countries since World War II have been of two kinds, both of them declining in frequency and relevance. One of these concerns lingering colonial responsibilities and readjustments. Thus the Dutch got involved in (but did not start) a war in Indonesia, the French in Indochina and Algeria, the British in Malaya and the Falklands.

The other kind [related] to the Cold War contest between East and West. The communists . . . generally sought to avoid major war, not so much because they necessarily [found] such wars to be immoral, repulsive, or uncivilized, but because they [found] them futile—dangerous, potentially counter-productive, wildly and absurdly adventurous. However, for decades after 1945 they retained a dutiful affection for what they came to call wars of national liberation—smaller wars around the world designed to further the progressive cause of world revolution. The West [saw] this threat as visceral and as one that [had to] be countered even at the cost of war if necessary. Wars fought in this context, such as those in

---

[5] For a further development of this argument, see John Mueller, "The Essential Irrelevance of Nuclear Weapons: Stability in the Postwar World," *International Security* 13, no. 2 (Fall 1988), pp. 55–79.

Korea and Vietnam, [were] essentially . . . seen [as] preventive—if communism [was] countered there, it [would] not have to be countered later, on more vital, closer surf.

The lesson learned (perhaps overlearned) from the Hitler experience is that aggressive threats must be dealt with by those who abhor war when the threats are still comparatively small and distant; to allow the aggressive force to succeed only brings nearer the day when a larger war must be fought. Thus some countries that abhor war have felt it necessary to wage them in order to prevent wider wars.

## CONSEQUENCES OF THE END OF THE COLD WAR

Because of economic crisis and persistent ideological failure, . . .the Cold War . . . ended as the Soviet Union, following the lead of its former ideological soulmate, China, [abandoned] its quest for ideological expansion, questing instead after prosperity and a quiet, normal international situation. Unless some new form of conflict emerges, war participation by developed countries is likely to continue its decline.

As tensions have lapsed between the two sides in what used to be known as the Cold War, there is a natural tendency for the arms that backed that tension, and in a sense measured it, to atrophy. Both sides have begun what might be called a negative arms race. . . .

The end of the Cold War should also facilitate further expansion of international trade and interdependence. Trade and interdependence may not lead inexorably to peace, but peace does seem to lead to trade, interdependence, and economic growth—or, at any rate, it facilitates them. That is, peace ought to be seen not as a dependent but rather as an independent variable in such considerations. The economic unity of Europe and the building of a long-envisioned Channel tunnel are the consequences of peace, not its cause.

Left alone, enterprising business people will naturally explore the possibilities of investing in other countries or selling their products there. Averse to disastrous surprises, they are more likely to invest if they are confident that peace will prevail. But for trade to flourish, governments must stay out of the way not only by eschewing war, but also by eschewing measures that unnaturally inhibit trade.

Furthermore, if nations no longer find it sensible to use force or the threat of force in their dealings with one another, it may be neither necessary nor particularly desirable to create an entrenched international government or police force (as opposed to ad hoc arrangements and devices designed to meet specific problems). Indeed, an effective international government could be detrimental to economic growth since, like domestic governments, it could be manipulated to reward the inefficient, coddle the incompetent, and plague the innovative.

## WAR IN THE THIRD WORLD

War has not, of course, become fully obsolete. While major war—war among developed countries—seems to be going out of style, war obviously continues to flourish elsewhere. The end of the Cold War suggests that the United States and [Russia], in particular, are likely to involve themselves less in these wars. Moreover, it is possible that the catastrophic Iran-Iraq war [has sobered] people in the Third World about that kind of war. And it does seem that much of the romance has gone out of the concept of violent revolution as Third World countries increasingly turn to the drab, difficult, and unromantic task of economic development.

Thus it is possible that the developed world's aversion to war may eventually infect the rest of the world as well (international war, in fact, has been quite rare in Latin America for a century). But this development is not certain, nor is its pace predictable. As slavery continued to persist in Brazil even after it had been abolished elsewhere, the existence of war in some parts of the world does not refute the observation that it is vanishing, or has vanished, in other parts.

## IMPERFECT PEACE

War, even war within the developed world, has not become impossible—nor could it ever do so. When it has seemed necessary, even countries like the United States and Britain, which were among the first to become thoroughly disillusioned with war, have been able to fight wars and to use military force—often with high morale and substantial public support, at least at first. The ability to make war and the knowledge about how to do so can never be fully expunged—nor, for that matter, can the ability or knowledge to institute slavery, eunuchism, crucifixion, or human sacrifice. War is declining as an institution not because it has ceased to be possible or fascinating, but because peoples and leaders in the developed world where war was once endemic have increasingly found war to be disgusting, ridiculous, and unwise.

The view presented in this [chapter] is based upon the premise that, in some important respects, war is often taken too seriously. War, it seems, is merely an idea. It is not a trick of fate, a thunderbolt from hell, a natural calamity, or a desperate plot contrivance dreamed up by some sadistic puppeteer on high. If war begins in the minds of men, as the UNESCO charter insists, it can end there as well. Over the centuries, war opponents have been trying to bring this about by discrediting war as an idea; the argument here is that they have been substantially successful at doing so. The long peace since World War II is less a product of recent weaponry than the culmination of a substantial historical process. For the last two or three centuries, major war has gradually moved toward terminal disrepute because of its perceived repulsiveness and futility.

It could also be argued that, to a considerable degree, people have tended to take peace too seriously as well. Peace is merely what emerges when the institution of war is neglected. It does not mean that the world suddenly becomes immersed in those qualities with which the word "peace" is constantly being associated: love, justice, harmony, cooperation, brotherhood, and good will. People still remain contentious and there still remain substantial conflicts of interest. The difference is only that they no longer resort to force to resolve their conflicts, any more than young men today resort to formal dueling to resolve their quarrels. A world at peace would not be perfect, but it would be notably better than the alternative.

# 6

# NUCLEAR WEAPONS THREATEN OUR EXISTENCE

Paul H. Nitze

**In this essay, one of the leading U.S. strategists, who at the beginning of the age of atomic diplomacy, helped devise the great powers deterrence strategies and doctrines governing the use of nuclear weapons, takes a fresh look at the need for nuclear weapons in the twenty-first century. Using as a springboard for fresh thinking the United States Senate's refusal to ratify the Comprehensive Test Ban Treaty in late 1999, Nitze questions the once orthodox view among realist defense planners that nuclear weapons provide a firm foundation for the prevention of a major war. In a forceful argument, Nitze argues instead why he "sees no compelling reason why [the United States] should not get rid of its nuclear weapons," adding that in his view "to maintain them is costly and adds nothing to [American or global] security." Contending that changing times call for changing weapon systems, Nitze maintains that nearly all national political objectives can be obtained with conventional weapons and that there remains "no purpose to be gained through the use of nuclear arsenals." Nitze is a former U.S. arms control negotiator and served as Ambassador-at-Large in the Reagan Administration. His policy advice has been published in the leading journals dealing with international security affairs, such as *Foreign Affairs*.**

The [U.S.] Senate's failure to ratify the Comprehensive Test Ban Treaty in 1999 set off a contentious debate on American leadership and led President Clinton to decry a "new isolationism" in the Republican majority. However, this is purely a discussion of political preferences rather than a debate affecting . . . basic and intrinsic security.

The fact is, I see no compelling reason why we should not unilaterally get rid of our nuclear weapons. To maintain them is costly and adds nothing to our security.

I can think of no circumstances under which it would be wise for the United States to use nuclear weapons, even in retaliation for their prior use against us. What, for example, would our targets be? It is impossible to conceive of a target that could be hit without large-scale destruction of many innocent people.

The technology of our conventional weapons is such that we can achieve accuracies of less than three feet from the expected point of impact. The modern equivalent of a stick of dynamite exploded within three feet of an object on or near the earth's surface is more than enough to destroy the target.

In view of the fact that we can achieve our objectives with conventional weapons, there is no purpose to be gained through the use of . . . nuclear arsenal[s]. To use them would merely guarantee the annihilation of hundreds of thousands of people, none of whom would have been responsible for the decision invoked in bringing about the weapons' use, not to mention incalculable damage to our natural environment.

As for the so-called rogue states that are not inhibited in their actions by the consensus of world opinion, the United States would be wise to eliminate their nuclear capabilities with the preemptive use of our conventional weapons—when necessary, and when [it has] unambiguous indication of these countries' intent to use their nuclear capability for purposes of aggrandizement. The same principle should apply to any threat emanating from unstable states with nuclear arsenals. By simply having . . . intelligence services "read their mail," [any nuclear weapon state] can tell if there is compelling reason to take preemptive action.

Why would someone who spent so many years negotiating with the Soviet Union about the size of [the U.S.] nuclear arsenal now say [it] no longer [needs] it? I know that the simplest and most direct answer to the problem of nuclear weapons has always been their complete elimination. My "walk in the woods" in 1982 with the Soviet arms negotiator Yuli Kvitsinsky at least addressed this possibility on a bilateral basis. Destruction of the arms did not prove feasible then, but there is no good reason why it should not be carried out now.

For now, the rejection of the test-ban treaty will undoubtedly bring up the question of whether the United States should resume testing, and there may be short-term political considerations in favor of forgoing testing or even making a declaration that [the United States does] not intend to test.

But in the long term, the treaty does not address the survival or existence of states. It is the presence of nuclear weapons that threatens our existence.

# 7

# THE NEW THREAT OF MASS DESTRUCTION

Richard K. Betts

Arguing that today the danger of an annihilating war from the launch of nuclear weapons has declined, this essay demonstrates that new weapons of mass destruction have been deployed, and that the chances of their use have increased. The spread of armaments such as chemical and biological weapons throughout the globe has made the proliferation threat more real, because these deadly weapons are easy to transport and to use in a shrinking globalized world, and traditional methods of deterrence are relatively ineffectual against these weapons of mass destruction readily available to rogue states, terrorists, and organized crime networks. The essay, written from the perspective of the United States which as the global superpower is most threatened by the widespread availability of these new non-nuclear weapons, calls for a reevaluation of defense and deterrence strategy and for construction of new programs for civil defense to reduce the number of casualties in the event that such a catastrophe should occur. Betts is Director of National Security Studies at the Council on Foreign Relations and Leo A. Shifrin Professor of War and Peace Studies at Columbia University. Author of many publications in scholarly journals, Betts has recently written *Military Readiness: Concepts, Choices, Consequences* (1995) and edited *Conflict After the Cold War: Arguments on Causes of War and Peace* (1994).

During the Cold War, weapons of mass destruction [WMD] were the centerpiece of foreign policy. Nuclear arms hovered in the background of every major issue in East-West competition and alliance relations. The highest priorities of U.S. policy could almost all be linked in some way to the danger of World War III and the fear of millions of casualties in the American homeland.

Since the Cold War, other matters have displaced strategic concerns on the foreign policy agenda, and that agenda itself is now barely on the public's radar screen. Apart from defense policy professionals, few Americans still lose sleep over weapons of mass destruction. After all, what do normal people feel is the main relief provided by the end of the Cold War? It is that the danger of nuclear war is off their backs.

Yet today, WMD present more and different things to worry about than during the Cold War. For one, nuclear arms are no longer the only concern, as chemical and biological weapons have come to the fore. For another, there is less danger of complete annihilation, but more danger of mass destruction. Since the Cold War is over and American and Russian nuclear inventories are much smaller, there is less chance of an apocalyptic exchange of many thousands of weapons. But the probability is growing that some smaller number of WMD will be used. Many of the standard strategies and ideas for coping with WMD threats are no longer as relevant as they were when Moscow was the main adversary. But new thinking has not yet congealed in as clear a form as the Cold War concepts of nuclear deterrence theory.

The new dangers have not been ignored inside the Beltway. "Counterproliferation" has become a cottage industry in the Pentagon and the intelligence community, and many worthwhile initiatives to cope with threats are under way. Some of the most important implications of the new era, however, have not yet registered on the public agenda. This in turn limits the inclination of politicians to push some appropriate programs. Even the defense establishment has directed its attention mainly toward countering threats WMD pose to U.S. military forces operating abroad rather than to the more worrisome danger that mass destruction will occur in the United States, killing large numbers of civilians.

The points to keep in mind about the new world of mass destruction are the following. First, the roles such weapons play in international conflict are changing. They no longer represent the technological frontier of warfare. Increasingly, they will be weapons of the weak states or groups that militarily are at best second-class. The importance of the different types among them has also shifted. Biological weapons should now be the most serious concern, with nuclear weapons second and chemicals a distant third.

Second, the mainstays of Cold War security policy—deterrence and arms control—are not what they used to be. Some new threats may not be deferrable, and the role of arms control in dealing with WMD has been marginalized. In a few instances, continuing devotion to deterrence and arms control may have side effects that offset the benefits.

Third, some of the responses most likely to cope with the threats in novel ways will not find a warm welcome. The response that should now be the highest priority is one long ignored, opposed, or ridiculed: a serious civil defense program to blunt the effects of WMD if they are unleashed within the United States. Some of the most effective measures to prevent attacks within the United States may also challenge traditional civil liberties if pursued to the maximum. And the most troubling conclusion for foreign policy as a whole is that reducing the odds of attacks in the United States might require pulling back from involvement in some foreign conflicts. American activism to guarantee international stability is, paradoxically, the prime source of American vulnerability.

This was partly true in the Cold War, when the main danger that nuclear weapons might detonate on U.S. soil sprang from strategic engagement in Europe, Asia, and the Middle East to deter attacks on U.S. allies. But engagement then assumed a direct link between regional stability and U.S. survival. The connection is less evident today, when there is no globally threatening superpower or transnational ideology to be contained—only an array of serious but entirely local disruptions. Today, as the only nation acting to police areas outside its own region, the United States makes itself a target for states or groups whose aspirations are frustrated by U.S. power.

## FROM MODERN TO PRIMITIVE

When nuclear weapons were born, they represented the most advanced military applications of science, technology, and engineering. None but the great powers could hope to obtain them. By now, however, nuclear arms have been around for more than half a century, and chemical and biological weapons even longer. They are not just getting old. In the strategic terms most relevant to American security, they have become primitive. Once the military cutting edge of the strong, they have become the only hope for so-called rogue states or terrorists who want to contest American power. Why? Because the United States has developed overwhelming superiority in conventional military force—something it never thought it had against the Soviet Union.

The Persian Gulf War of 1991 demonstrated the American advantage in a manner that stunned many abroad. Although the U.S. defense budget has plunged, other countries are not closing the gap. U.S. military spending remains more than triple that of any potentially hostile power and higher than the combined defense budgets of Russia, China, Iran, Iraq, North Korea, and Cuba.

More to the point, there is no evidence that those countries' level of military professionalism is rising at a rate that would make them competitive even if they were to spend far more on their forces. Rolling along in what some see as a revolution in military affairs, American forces continue to make unmatched use of state-of-the-art weapons, surveillance and information systems, and the organizational and doctrinal flexibility for managing the integration of these complex innovations into "systems of systems" that is the key to modern military effectiveness. More than ever in military history, brains are brawn. Even if hostile countries somehow catch up in an arms race, their military organizations and cultures are unlikely to catch up in the competence race for management, technology assimilation, and combat command skills.

If it is infeasible for hostile states to counter the United States in conventional combat, it is even more daunting for smaller groups such as terrorists. If the United States is lucky, the various violent groups with grievances against the American government and society will continue to think up schemes using conventional explosives. Few terrorist groups have shown an interest in inflicting true mass destruction. Bombings or hostage seizures have generally threatened no more than a few hundred lives. Let us hope that this limitation has been due to a powerful underlying reason, rather than a simple lack of capability, and that the few exceptions do not become more typical.

There is no sure reason to bet on such restraint. Indeed, some have tried to use WMD, only to see them fizzle. The Japanese Aum Shinrikyo cult released sarin nerve gas in Tokyo in 1995 but killed only a few people, and some analysts believe that those who attacked the World Trade Center in 1993 laced their bomb with cyanide, which burned up in the explosion (this was not confirmed, but a large amount of cyanide was found in the perpetrators' possession). Eventually such a group will prove less incompetent. If terrorists decide that they want to stun American policymakers by inflicting enormous damage, WMD become more attractive at the same time that they are becoming more accessible.

Finally, unchallenged military superiority has shifted the attention of the U.S. military establishment away from WMD. During the Cold War, nuclear weapons were the bedrock of American war capabilities. They were the linchpin of defense debate, procurement programs, and arms control because the United States faced another superpower—one that conventional wisdom feared could best it in conventional warfare. Today, no one cares about the MX missile or B-1 bomber, and hardly anyone really cares about the Strategic Arms Reduction Treaty. In a manner that could only have seemed ludicrous during the Cold War, proponents now rationalize the $2 billion B-2 as a weapon for conventional war. Hardly anyone in the Pentagon is still interested in how the United States could use WMD for its own strategic purposes.

What military planners are interested in is how to keep adversaries from using WMD as an "asymmetric" means to counter U.S. conventional power, and how to protect U.S. ground and naval forces abroad from WMD attacks. This concern is all well and good, but it abets a drift of attention away from the main danger. The primary risk is not that enemies might lob some nuclear or chemical weapons at U.S. armored battalions or ships, awful as that would be. Rather, it is that they might attempt to punish the United States by triggering catastrophes in American cities.

## CHOOSE YOUR WEAPONS WELL

Until the past decade, the issue was nuclear arms, period. Chemical weapons received some attention from specialists, but never made the priority list of presidents and cabinets. Biological weapons were almost forgotten after they were banned by the 1972 Biological Weapons Convention. Chemical and biological arms have received more attention in the 1990s. The issues posed by the trio lumped under the umbrella of mass destruction differ, however. Most significantly, biological weapons have received less attention than the others but probably represent the greatest danger.

Chemical weapons have been noticed more in the past decade, especially since they were used by Iraq against Iranian troops in the 1980–1988 Iran-Iraq War and against Kurdish civilians in 1988. Chemicals are far more widely available than nuclear weapons because the technology required to produce them is far simpler, and large numbers of countries have undertaken chemical weapons programs. But chemical weapons are not really in the same class as other weapons of mass destruction, in the sense of ability to inflict a huge number of civilian casualties in a single strike. For the tens of thousands of fatalities as in, say, the biggest strategic bombing raids of World War II, it would be very difficult logistically and operationally to deliver chemical weapons in necessary quantities over wide areas.

Nevertheless, much attention and effort have been lavished on a campaign to eradicate chemical weapons. This may be a good thing, but the side effects are not entirely benign. For one, banning chemicals means that for deterrence, nuclear weapons become even more important than they used to be. That is because a treaty cannot assuredly prevent hostile nations from deploying chemical weapons, while the United States has forsworn the option to retaliate in kind.

In the past, the United States had a no-first-use policy for chemical weapons but reserved the right to strike back with them if an enemy used them first. The 1993 Chemical Weapons Convention (CWC), which entered into force [April 1998], requires the United States to destroy its stockpile, thus ending this option. The United States did the same with biological arms long ago, during the Nixon administration. Eliminating its own chemical and biological weapons practically precludes a no-first-use policy for nuclear weapons, since they become the only WMD available for retaliation.

Would the United States follow through and use nuclear weapons against a country or group that had killed several thousand Americans with deadly chemicals? It is hard to imagine breaking the post-Nagasaki taboo in that situation. But schemes for conventional military retaliation would not suffice without detracting from the force of American deterrent threats. There would be a risk for the United States in setting a precedent that someone could use WMD against Americans without suffering similar destruction in return. Limiting the range of deterrent alternatives available to U.S. strategy will not necessarily cause deterrence to fail, but it will certainly not strengthen it.

The ostensible benefit of the CWC is that it will make chemical arms harder to acquire and every bit as illegal and stigmatized as biological weapons have been for a quarter-century. If it has that benefit, what effect will the ban have on the choices of countries or groups who want some kind of WMD in any case, whether for purposes of deterrence, aggression, or revenge? At the margin, the ban will reduce the disincentives to acquiring biological weapons, since they will be no less illegal, no harder to obtain or conceal, and far more damaging than chemical weapons. If major reductions in the chemical threat produce even minor increases in the biological threat, it will be a bad trade.

One simple fact should worry Americans more about biological than about nuclear or chemical arms: unlike either of the other two, biological weapons combine maximum destructiveness and easy availability. Nuclear arms have great killing capacity but are hard to get; chemical weapons are easy to get but lack such killing capacity; biological agents have both qualities. A 1993 study by the Office of Technology Assessment concluded that a single airplane delivering 100 kilograms of anthrax spores—a dormant phase of a bacillus that multiplies rapidly in the body, producing toxins and rapid hemorrhaging—by aerosol on a clear, calm night over the Washington, D.C., area could kill between one million and three million people, 300 times as many fatalities as if the plane had delivered satin gas in amounts ten times larger.[1]

Like chemical weapons but unlike nuclear weapons, biologicals are relatively easy to make. Innovations in biotechnology have obviated many of the old problems in handling and preserving biological agents, and many have been freely available for scientific research. Nuclear weapons are not likely to be the WMD of choice for non-state terrorist groups. They require huge investments and targetable infrastructure, and are subject to credible threats by the United States. An aggrieved group that decides it wants to kill huge numbers of Americans will find the mission easier to accomplish with anthrax than with a nuclear explosion.

Inside the Pentagon, concern about biological weapons has picked up tremendously in the past couple of years, but there is little serious attention to the problem elsewhere. This could be a good thing if nothing much can be done, since publicity might only give enemies ideas. But it is a bad thing if it impedes efforts to take steps—such as civil defense—that could blunt nuclear, chemical, or biological attacks.

## DETERRENCE AND ARMS CONTROL IN DECLINE

An old vocabulary still dominates policy discussion of WMD. Rhetoric in the defense establishment falls back on the all-purpose strategic buzzword of the

---

[1] U.S. Congress, Office of Technology Assessment, *Proliferation of Weapons of Mass Destruction: Assessing the Risks* (Washington, D.C.: U.S. Government Printing Office, 1993), p. 54.

Cold War: deterrence. But deterrence now covers fewer of the threats the United States faces than it did during the Cold War.

The logic of deterrence is clearest when the issue is preventing unprovoked and unambiguous aggression, when the aggressor recognizes that it is the aggressor rather than the defender. Deterrence is less reliable when both sides in a conflict see each other as the aggressor. When the United States intervenes in messy Third World conflicts, the latter is often true. In such cases, the side that the United States wants to deter may see itself as trying to deter the United States. Such situations are ripe for miscalculation.

For the country that used to be the object of U.S. deterrence—Russia—the strategic burden has been reversed. Based on assumptions of Soviet conventional military superiority, U.S. strategy used to rely on the threat to escalate to be the first to use nuclear weapons during a war to deter attack by Soviet armored divisions. Today the tables have turned. There is no Warsaw Pact, Russia has half or less of the military potential of the Soviet Union, and its current conventional forces are in disarray, while NATO is expanding eastward. It is now Moscow that has the incentive to compensate for conventional weakness by placing heavier reliance on nuclear capabilities. The Russians adopted a nuclear no-first-use policy in the early 1980s, but renounced it after their precipitous post–Cold War decline.

Today Russia needs to be reassured, not deterred. The main danger from Russian WMD is leakage from vast stockpiles to anti-American groups elsewhere—the "loose nukes" problem. So long as the United States has no intention of attacking the Russians, their greater reliance on nuclear forces is not a problem. If the United States has an interest in reducing nuclear stockpiles, however, it is. The traditional American approach—thinking in terms of its own deterrence strategies—provides no guidance. Indeed, noises some Americans still make about deterring the Russians compound the problem by reinforcing Moscow's alarm.

Similarly, U.S. conventional military superiority gives China an incentive to consider more reliance on an escalation strategy. The Chinese have a long-standing no-first-use policy but adopted it when their strategic doctrine was that of "people's war," which relied on mass mobilization and low-tech weaponry. Faith in that doctrine was severely shaken by the American performance in the Persian Gulf War. Again, the United States might assume that there is no problem as long as Beijing only wants to deter and the United States does not want to attack. But how do these assumptions relate to the prospect of a war over Taiwan? That is a conflict that no one wants but that can hardly be ruled out in light of evolving tensions. If the United States decides openly to deter Beijing from attacking Taiwan, the old lore from the Cold War may be relevant. But if Washington continues to leave policy ambiguous, who will know who is deterring whom? Ambiguity is a recipe for confusion and miscalculation in a time of crisis. For all the upsurge of attention in the national security establishment to the prospect of conflict with China, there has been remarkably little discussion of the role of nuclear weapons in a Sino-American collision.

The main problem for deterrence, however, is that it still relies on the corpus of theory that undergirded Cold War policy, dominated by reliance on the threat of second-strike retaliation. But retaliation requires knowledge of who has launched an attack and the address at which they reside. These requirements are not a problem when the threat comes from a government, but they are if the enemy is anonymous. Today some groups may wish to punish the United States without taking credit for the action—mass killing equivalent to the 1988 bombing of Pan Am Flight 103 over Lockerbie, Scotland. Moreover, the options the defense establishment favor have shifted over entirely from deterrence to preemption. The majority of those who dealt with nuclear weapons policy during the Cold War adamantly opposed developing first-strike options. Today, scarcely anyone looks to that old logic when thinking about rogues or terrorists, and most hope to be able to mount a disarming action against any group with WMD.

Finally, eliminating chemical weapons trims some options for deterrence. Arms control restrictions on the instruments that can be used for deterrent threats are not necessarily the wrong policy, but they do work against maximizing deterrence. Overall, however, the problem with arms control is not that it does too much but that it now does relatively little.

From the Limited Test Ban negotiations in the 1960s through the Strategic Arms Limitation Talks, Strategic Arms Reduction Talks (START), and Intermediate-range Nuclear Forces negotiations in the 1970s and 1980s, arms control treaties were central to managing WMD threats. Debates about whether particular agreements with Moscow were in the United States' interest were bitter because everyone believed that the results mattered. Today there is no consensus that treaties regulating armaments matter much. Among national security experts, the corps that pays close attention to START and Conventional Forces in Europe negotiations has shrunk. With the exception of the Chemical Weapons Convention, efforts to control WMD by treaty have become small potatoes. The biggest recent news in arms control has not been any negotiation to regulate WMD, but a campaign to ban land mines.

The United States' Cold War partner in arms control, Russia, has disarmed a great deal voluntarily. But despite standard rhetoric, the United States has not placed a high priority on convincing Moscow to divest itself of more of its nuclear weapons; the Clinton administration has chosen to promote NATO expansion, which pushes the Russians in the opposite direction.

The 1968 Nuclear Nonproliferation Treaty (NPT) remains a hallowed institution, but it has nowhere new to go. It will not convert the problem countries that want to obtain WMD—unless, like Iraq and North Korea in the 1980s, they sign and accept the legal obligation and then simply cheat. The NPT regime will continue to impede access to fissile materials on the open market, but it will not do so in novel or more effective ways. And it does not address the problem of Russian "loose nukes" any better than the Russian and American governments do on their own.

## CIVIL DEFENSE

Despite all the new limitations, deterrence remains an important aspect of strategy. There is not much the United States needs to do to keep up its deterrence capability, however, given the thousands of nuclear weapons and the conventional military superiority it has. Where capabilities are grossly underdeveloped, however, is the area of responses for coping should deterrence fail.

Enthusiasts for defensive capability, mostly proponents of the Strategic Defense Initiative (SDI) from the Reagan years, remain fixated on the least relevant form of it: high-tech active defenses to intercept ballistic missiles. There is still scant interest in what should now be the first priority: civil defense preparations to cope with uses of WMD within the United States. Active defenses against missiles would be expensive investments that might or might not work against a threat the United States probably will not face for years, but would do nothing against the threat it already faces. Civil defense measures are extremely cheap and could prove far more effective than they would have against a large-scale Soviet attack.

During the Cold War, debate about anti-missile defense concerned whether it was technologically feasible or cost-effective and whether it would threaten the Soviets and ignite a spiraling arms race between offensive and defensive weapons. One need not refight the battles over SDI to see that the relevance to current WMD threats is tenuous. Iraq, Iran, or North Korea will not be able to deploy intercontinental missiles for years. Nor, if they are strategically cunning, should they want to. For the limited number of nuclear warheads these countries are likely to have, and especially for biological weapons, other means of delivery are more easily available. Alternatives to ballistic missiles include aircraft, ship-launched cruise missiles, and unconventional means, such as smuggling, at which the intelligence agencies of these countries have excelled. Non-state perpetrators like those who bombed the World Trade Center will choose clandestine means of necessity.

A ballistic missile defense system, whether it costs more or less than the $60 billion the Congressional Budget Office recently estimated would be required for one limited option, will not counter these modes of attack. Indeed, if a larger part of the worry about WMD these days is about their use by terrorist states or groups, the odds are higher that sometime, somewhere in the country, some of these weapons will go off, despite the best efforts to stop them. If that happens, the United States should have in place whatever measures can mitigate the consequences.

By the later phases of the Cold War, it was hard to get people interested in civil defense against an all-out Soviet attack that could detonate thousands of high-yield nuclear weapons in U.S. population centers. To many, the lives that would have been saved seemed less salient than the many millions that would still have been lost. It should be easier to see the value of civil defense, however, in the context of more limited attacks, perhaps with only a few low-yield weapons. A host of minor measures can increase protection or recovery from biological, nuclear, or chemical effects. Examples are stockpiling or distribution of protective masks; equipment and training for decontamination; standby programs for mass vaccinations and emergency treatment with antibiotics; wider and deeper planning of emergency response procedures; and public education about hasty sheltering and emergency actions to reduce individual vulnerability.

Such programs would not make absorbing a WMD attack tolerable. But inadequacy is no excuse for neglecting actions that could reduce death and suffering, even if the difference in casualties is small. Civil defenses are especially worthwhile considering that they are extraordinarily cheap compared with regular military programs or active defense systems. Yet until recently, only half a billion dollars—less than two-tenths of one percent of the defense budget and less than $2 a head for every American—went to chemical and biological defense, while nearly $4 billion was spent annually on ballistic missile defense.[2] Why haven't policymakers attended to first things first—cheap programs that can cushion the effects of a disaster—before undertaking expensive programs that provide no assurance they will be able to prevent it?

One problem is conceptual inertia. The Cold War accustomed strategists to worrying about an enemy with thousands of WMD, rather than foes with a handful. For decades the question of strategic defense was also posed as a debate between those who saw no alternative to relying on deterrence and those who hoped that an astrodome over the United States could replace deterrence with invulnerability. None of these hoary fixations address the most probable WMD threats in the post–Cold War world.

Opposition to Cold War civil defense programs underlies psychological aversion to them now. Opponents used to argue that civil defense was a dangerous illusion because it could do nothing significant to reduce the horror of an attack that would obliterate hundreds of cities, because it would promote a false sense of security, and because it could even be destabilizing and provoke attack in a crisis. Whether or not such arguments were valid then, they are not now. But both then and now, there has been a powerful reason that civil defense efforts have been unpopular: they alarm people. They remind them that their vulnerability to mass destruction is not a bad dream, not something that strategic schemes for deterrence, preemption, or interception are sure to solve.

Civil defense can limit damage but not minimize it. For example, some opponents may be able to develop biological agents that circumvent available vaccines and antibiotics. (Those with marginal technical capabilities, however, might be stopped by blocking the easier options.) Which is worse—the limitations of defenses, or having to answer for failure to try? The moment that WMD are used somewhere in a manner that produces tens of thousands of fatalities, there will

---

[2] John F. Sopko, "The Changing Proliferation Threat," *Foreign Policy* (Spring 1997), pp. 3–20.

be hysterical outbursts of all sorts. One of them will surely be, "Why didn't the government prepare us for this?" It is not in the long-term interest of political leaders to indulge popular aversion. If public resistance under current circumstances prevents widespread distribution, stockpiling, and instruction in the use of defensive equipment or medical services, the least that should be done is to optimize plans and preparations to rapidly implement such activities when the first crisis ignites demand.

As threats of terrorism using WMD are taken more seriously, interest will grow in preemptive defense measures—the most obvious of which is intensified intelligence collection. Where this involves targeting groups within the United States that might seem to be potential breeding grounds for terrorists (for example, supporters of Palestinian militants, home-grown militias or cults, or radicals with ties to Iran, Iraq, or Libya), controversies will arise over constitutional limits on invasion of privacy or search and seizure. So long as the WMD danger remains hypothetical, such controversies will not be easily resolved. They have not come to the fore so far because U.S. law enforcement has been unbelievably lucky in apprehending terrorists. The group arrested in 1993 for planning to bomb the Lincoln Tunnel happened to be infiltrated by an informer, and Timothy McVeigh happened to be picked up in 1995 for driving without a license plate. Those who fear compromising civil liberties with permissive standards for government snooping should consider what is likely to happen once such luck runs out and it proves impossible to identify perpetrators. Suppose a secretive radical Islamic group launches a biological attack, kills 100,000 people, and announces that it will do the same thing again if its terms are not met. (The probability of such a scenario may not be high, but it can no longer be consigned to science fiction.) In that case, it is hardly unthinkable that a panicked legal system would roll over and treat Arab-Americans as it did the Japanese-Americans who were herded into concentration camps after Pearl Harbor. Stretching limits on domestic surveillance to reduce the chances of facing such choices could be the lesser evil.

## IS RETREAT THE BEST DEFENSE?

No programs aimed at controlling adversaries' capabilities can eliminate the dangers. One risk is that in the more fluid politics of the post–Cold War world, the United States could stumble into an unanticipated crisis with Russia or China. There are no well-established rules of the game to brake a spiraling conflict over the Baltic states or Taiwan, as there were in the superpower competition after the Cuban missile crisis. The second danger is that some angry group that blames the United States for its problems may decide to coerce Americans, or simply exact vengeance, by inflicting devastation on them where they live.

If steps to deal with the problem in terms of capabilities are limited, can anything be done to address intentions—the incentives of any foreign power or group to lash out at the United States? There are few answers to this question that do not compromise the fundamental strategic activism and internationalist thrust of U.S. foreign policy over the past half-century. That is because the best way to keep people from believing that the United States is responsible for their problems is to avoid involvement in their conflicts.

Ever since the Munich agreement and Pearl Harbor, with only a brief interruption during the decade after the Tet offensive, there has been a consensus that if Americans did not draw their defense perimeter far forward and confront foreign troubles in their early stages, those troubles would come to them at home. But because the United States is now the only superpower and weapons of mass destruction have become more accessible, American intervention in troubled areas is not so much a way to fend off such threats as it is what stirs them up.

Will U.S. involvement in unstable situations around the former U.S.S.R. head off conflict with Moscow or generate it? Will making NATO bigger and moving it to Russia's doorstep deter Russian pressure on Ukraine and the Baltics or provoke it? With Russia and China, there is less chance that either will set out to conquer Europe or Asia than that they will try to restore old sovereignties and security zones by reincorporating new states of the former Soviet Union or the province of Taiwan. None of this means that NATO expansion or support for Taiwan's autonomy will cause nuclear war. It does mean that to whatever extent American activism increases those countries' incentives to rely on WMD while intensifying political friction between them and Washington, it is counterproductive.

The other main danger is the ire of smaller states or religious and cultural groups that see the United States as an evil force blocking their legitimate aspirations. It is hardly likely that Middle Eastern radicals would be hatching schemes like the destruction of the World Trade Center if the United States had not been identified for so long as the mainstay of Israel, the Shah of Iran, and conservative Arab regimes and the source of a cultural assault on Islam. Cold War triumph magnified the problem. U.S. military and cultural hegemony—the basic threats to radicals seeking to challenge the status quo—are directly linked to the imputation of American responsibility for maintaining world order. Playing Globocop feeds the urge of aggrieved groups to strike back.

Is this a brief for isolationism? No. It is too late to turn off foreign resentments by retreating, even if that were an acceptable course. Alienated groups and governments would not stop blaming Washington for their problems. In addition, there is more to foreign policy than dampening incentives to hurt the United States. It is not automatically sensible to stop pursuing other interests for the sake of uncertain reductions in a threat of uncertain probability. Security is not all of a piece, and survival is only part of security.

But it is no longer prudent to assume that important security interests complement each other as they did during the Cold War. The interest at the very core—protecting the American homeland from attack—may now often be in conflict with security more broadly conceived and with the interests that mandate promoting American political values, economic interdependence, social Westernization, and stability in regions beyond Western Europe and the Americas. The United States should not give up all its broader political interests, but it should tread cautiously in areas—especially the Middle East—where broader interests grate against the core imperative of preventing mass destruction within America's borders.

# 8

# TERROR'S NEW FACE: THE RADICALIZATION AND ESCALATION OF MODERN TERRORISM

Walter Laqueur

In this essay, Walter Laqueur examines the new character of the terrorist menace at the start of the twenty-first century. The emerging global environment, it is argued, provides unprecedented opportunities for terrorist activities, in part because the lawlessness in failed states experiencing civil wars increases the chances for a new generation of radicalized, fanatical terrorists to carry out the old game of terrorism with new weapons and a growing willingness to use them in a climate without the moral and legal restraints that existed during the past three decades. Laqueur is Chairman of the International Research Council at the Center for Strategic and International Studies in Washington, D.C., and has authored many books, including *Guerilla Warfare: A Historical and Critical Study* (**1997**).

Terrorism promises to continue for years to come as the prevalent mode of conflict—sometimes in its "pure" form, sometimes within the framework of civil war or general lawlessness. Nonetheless, much rethinking must occur since the terrorist acts of the past do not necessarily offer a reliable guide for the future. Only an examination of the changing face of terrorism and an analysis of current trends can offer valuable insights into future outbreaks. For a long time, conventional wisdom held that terrorists were idealistic, courageous young patriots and social revolutionaries driven to desperate actions by intolerable conditions, oppression, and tyranny. This assessment was not entirely wrong; it was buttressed by the existence of oppression and social conflicts to which violence seemed the only effective response.

## TERRORISM IN TRANSITION

While some terrorists are still patriots and genuine revolutionaries, this pattern is no longer typical. Any survey of the world map of terrorism—the parts of the world where the most casualties occur—reveals the emergence of other features. It reveals not only growing fanaticism but also the growth of indiscriminate murder, the desire to exercise power, and sheer bloodlust.

For many years, assessments of terrorism overrated the role of ideology as an underlying motive. Once considered the all-important factor in terrorist acts, ideology now takes second billing. Aggressive and militant individuals, not activists, tend to be those most convinced of the righteousness of their cause. For example, the investigation into the 1997 murders of foreign tourists at Luxor, Egypt, established that the six Islamic perpetrators were not poor, desperate, or deeply religious, but merely misanthropic students from middle-class families eager to find an outlet for their aggression. Wordsworth once wrote about the "motive hunting of a motiveless malignity," and the truth of his words has been ignored for too long. In many instances, a leftist terrorist could easily have turned to the extreme right or to some sectarian group, but for some biographical accident or outside influence. Carlos the Jackal was a precursor of this type, as were the Afghani hired guns now involved in terrorism from Algeria and Bosnia to the Philippines.

This emerging pattern of a new breed of terrorism did not fit the stereotypic assumptions of the earlier age, which held that evil was banal, jihad was an Islamic synonym for the Salvation Army, and all criminals were sick people who needed medical attention. Evil and malignancy were used infrequently, and aggression was considered the consequence of an unhappy, deprived childhood or some other unfortunate social circumstance. In this pluralist world, the grievances of terrorists seemed to some as legitimate and as deserving of a hearing as all others. This argument had its seductions, especially if one happened to live thousands of miles away from the site of bloodshed.

More recently, perceptions of human nature have become more pessimistic. Gaining ground are convictions that genes can predispose people to aggressive behavior, that few truly peaceful societies exist, that even primitive man often disemboweled his victims and regarded outsiders as enemies. In effect, evil has become a genetic problem against which civilization has struggled in vain. Human beings have fought an uphill battle to sublimate this insidious instinct and to replace it with the gospel of love, or at least of peaceful coexistence.

Given this orientation, conventional terrorism is becoming increasingly difficult to justify. St. Thomas once asked whether it was always sinful to wage war, and based on earlier authorities, he concluded that it was not, given three preconditions: the authority of the sovereign (for private individuals had no business declaring war); a just cause; and a rightful intention (namely, the advancement of good or the avoidance of evil). Merely possessing a just cause was not sufficient, for all three stipulations were equally important in conducting a just war. Even before St. Thomas, St. Augustine had observed that the passion for inflicting harm, the cruel thirst for vengeance, and an unpacific and relentless spirit were all rightly condemned in war.

Four hundred years after St. Thomas, Hugo Grotius noted that the Christian world condoned a license for fighting at which even barbarous nations might blush. Rulers declared wars on trifling pretexts—or none at all—and carried on these conflicts without any reverence for law. A declaration of war unleashed the worst tendencies of mankind. Grotius's words aptly describe modern terrorism. In most cases, terrorism is not the *ultima ratio* after all other means of negotiation have failed; instead, it is the immediate solution, enacted at the slightest provocation.

Despite their ruthless actions, most terrorists defend their actions by arguing that they are fighters in a just war. They insist on being treated as soldiers, yet refuse to accept responsibility for war crimes and consider themselves entitled to ignore the tenets of international law, including the protection of innocents and the humane treatment of hostages. In their view, international law is merely an invention of the imperialist West and of the exploiting classes; it does not apply to the treatment of infidels or to those who belong to another class, people, or religion.

Unwritten law—or at least certain legal norms—once governed the behavior of terrorists, but today, terrorists scoff at the idea of a code of conduct. As a result, the question arises whether just terrorism is possible, even if the cause is just, even if we ignore the issue of weapons of mass destruction. Bayard, the military leader and the epitome of chivalry, killed all the crossbowmen he captured because he considered their methods cowardly and treacherous. One wonders what Bayard would have thought of the terrorists of the late twentieth century, our contemporary crossbowmen who place bombs in supermarkets and kill babies. Terrorism will continue, and many factors indicate that the struggle will become increasingly bitter.

## THE DEMISE OF RESTRAINT

A great deal of pessimism exists regarding the possibility of restraint in future internal wars and terrorist activities. Over the centuries, brutality in war has certainly increased. While medieval law generally recognized civilian immunity; at least among Christians, this practice often has been disregarded. In 1740, Emmerich de Vattel, one of the fathers of international law, wrote, "Let us never forget that our enemies are men." This fact has been all but forgotten in the twentieth century.

Restraint in warfare once existed in ancient times when combatants acted honorably and followed the rules of conflict. When the Greeks sent emissaries to Troy, Homer noted that they were treated "in accordance to the laws which govern the intercourse between nations." Although Diomedes and Odysseus occasionally attacked and killed sleeping enemies, the laws held that fighting would cease at nightfall, and that the heroes would exchange presents, such as their swords. In the age of chivalry, Orlando (Roland) would never fight at night, and he slept peacefully beside his enemy, the Saracen Nobleman. No fighting occurred in winter, and other written and unwritten laws, such as the obligation to help the shipwrecked, governed warfare. In 1139, the Second Lateran Council not only banned treacherous weapons such as the crossbow and siege machines but also established the Treuga Dei, the Truce of God. The Treuga Dei outlined specific days for fighting and protected whole categories of people, including travelers, pilgrims, merchants, peasants, and even their animals. Admittedly, these rules applied only to conflicts among Christians; however, in most cases Christians behaved honorably toward other religions, as did the Saracens and the Turks.

Interestingly enough, some aspects of the ancient Treuga Dei have survived into the modern age of terrorism, with the Irish Republican Army (IRA) and other terrorist groups announcing truces over holiday periods. However, the IRA, the ETA, and other terrorist groups only declare significant truces when authorities engage in political negotiations. True, both the IRA and the ETA announced in the summer of 1998 that they would cease their terrorist activities, but only the future will tell whether terrorism in Northern Ireland and Spain has indeed come to an end.

In the Middle Ages, European wars (with the exception of the crusades) and conflicts on the Indian subcontinent were usually the sport of kings. Then, during the seventeenth century, an international law of war developed. At the turn of the last century, various conventions established rules for land and sea warfare, and after World War II, the Geneva Conventions of 1949 updated these guidelines. Several subsequent international agreements outlawed biological weapons (London, 1972) as well as the development, production, and stockpiling of chemical weapons (Paris, 1992). The U.N. General Assembly resolutions of 1961–1962 banned the use of nuclear weapons. Other conventions dealt specifically with terrorist attacks: one with crimes against diplomats, another with hostage taking, and a third with aircraft hijackings.

These conventions were not universally welcomed. To justify the production and even the use of nonconventional weapons, some radical Arab states, including Iraq, railed against an agreement that allowed European and North American nations to keep a portion of their arsenal while banning unconventional weapons from "third world" countries. The same spokesmen maintained that rules developed in Europe, where war between two continental countries was unthinkable, were unsuited to the political instability and volatility of the Middle East. Lending credence to their arguments was a 1973 U.N. resolution that condoned the struggle for self-determination and independence among people under colonial domination or racist regimes. Since any ethnic minority in the world could justify violence under claims of "alien domination" and "racist regime," many guerrilla wars and terrorist acts became justified under international law. Ironically, in trying to prevent escalation through weapons conventions, the U.N. inadvertently provided the impetus for increased global militarism.

Over the years, only a scant few of these international conventions have been observed. An analysis of the reasons behind such disregard is of considerable interest but little relevance in the context of terrorism. As stated earlier, terrorists have traditionally ignored international law and conventions. Terrorists argue, with some degree of justification, that to accept humanist rules would condemn them to impotence, since they can only succeed precisely by breaking established norms. Therefore, the idea of introducing a code of behavior for terrorism, to make it more humane, is almost a contradiction in terms. Taking the indiscriminate violence out of terrorism only emasculates it and dilutes its impact.

### GROWING FANATICISM

Much of today's terrorist violence is rooted in fanaticism. Historically, nationalist and religious fanatics have been active everywhere. The Aum were Buddhist, a Jew killed Prime Minister Yitzhak Rabin of Israel, a Sikh assassinated Prime Minister Indira Gandhi of India, and a Tamil her son, Rajiv. Christianity also had its jihad—the Crusades—seven hundred years ago. Today, the scale of fanatical terrorism has increased. Instead of targeting specific individuals, Baruch Goldstein, the "murderer of Hebron," killed thirty Arabs, and the Algerian terrorists have massacred 75,000 of their own people.

To deny the specific virulence of Islamic terrorism in our time is an exercise in political or ecumenical correctness. If we ignore for a moment the tribal violence in Africa, about ninety percent of the present internal wars occur inside or between Muslim countries, or have one Muslim participant. True, in the Middle Ages more tolerance existed in the Islamic world than in Christian Europe. The Koranic message *"La Ikraha fi'l din"* (no coercion in matters of religion) was once enough to stop a pogrom. In the tenth century, Mehrez ibn Khalaf saved the Jews of Tunis and in the twelfth, Emir Abdelkader liberated the Christians of Damascus. Unfortunately, Ibn Khalaf and Abdelkader have been dead for a long time. Nowadays, the literal message of jihad—the sacred duty of a holy war, which permits unlimited violence and the use of all weapons—is the most prominent feature of militant Islam. Although these terrorists may be a minority, few dare to challenge them openly.

Is a decline in Islamic fundamentalist violence at all likely? In some countries, perhaps, but not in others. Any dramatic improvement in the situation seems unlikely in the near future given the miserable political, social, and economic situation in many Islamic countries. Overpopulation and poverty generate new tensions, and access to weapons of mass destruction fuels dreams of power, aggression, and expansion.

Today, fanatical violence exists throughout the world: among Hindus destroying old mosques and slaughtering Muslim and Sikhs, among Israelis plotting to kill Arabs, in Christian Europe and in the Americas. Neither madness nor fanaticism will vanish from the world, even if the fashionable flight from reason gives way to more sober trends. Unfortunately, nothing indicates that fanatical violence in general will decrease in intensity in the years to come. It may even increase in the future because of social or political upheavals or the emergence of new sects preaching their violent messages.

With the dangers of fanaticism increasing, most experts have agonized over the weapons of mass destruction accessible to terrorists. Some will argue that it is pointless to speculate about the unthinkable and will point out that during the 1950s and 1960s, many apocalyptic scenarios referring to nuclear Armageddon were written and discussed but their predictions never proved true.

The state of affairs today is not comparable to that of forty years ago. Then, only a handful of states possessed nuclear weapons, and a notion of "mutually assured destruction" existed—the assumption that neither the Soviet Union nor the United States would choose to commit collective suicide. Those who had access to extremely dangerous weapons were responsible, rational people, at least as far as their own survival was concerned. They were not fanatics bent on world conquest or global destruction. Today, given broader access to nuclear weapons, the concept of mutual assured destruction does not preclude terrorist acts; governments can only manage deterrence to a limited extent. For some states, when war becomes too risky or costly, weapons of mass destruction used by proxies can continue conflicts by other means. However, states are no longer the only actors on the international stage, and the convictions, mental state, and behavior of the new players have proven to be far from predictable.

Given the indiscriminate and capricious nature of terrorist violence, to what extent will the stigma attached to biological and chemical weapons influence terrorist groups? Terrorist groups may still refrain from using certain weapons of mass destruction, if only for pragmatic reasons—the same reasons that chemical weapons were not used on the battlefields of World War II. While radical elements of these groups may be restrained by their own compatriots, it is unrealistic to depend on this hope at a time when even governments are undertaking major efforts to acquire deadly weapons.

Not much ground for optimism exists, even if nationalist passions and religious fanaticism abate and the new violent interpretation of jihad recedes. The baby killers of Algeria are not pious Muslims, for according to Islam, all children are born Muslim and women should be spared during a holy war. The sad truth is that the candidates for the new terrorism may appear on the fringes of any extremist movement at any time. In the future, even if radicals become more moderate, individuals will still embrace Mephisto's credo of *"Alles was entsteht, ist wert, class es zugrunde geht"* (all that comes into being is worthy of destruction). Hopefully, the damage will be limited to one or two countries without triggering a general conflagration, and the devastating punishment of transgressors will deter imitators. But even this hope is improbable because the principles of costs and benefits may no longer guide the perpetrators.

## NEW WEAPONS, NEW TARGETS

The transformation of terrorism, the growth of fanaticism, and the weapons revolution have affected the treatment of terrorists under law. Although "just war" doctrine has never engendered a "just terrorism" counterpart, at least some past terrorist campaigns have been fought for a just cause, against oppressors and tyrants. For this reason, apprehended terrorists were not treated like common criminals, and sometimes, they were even acquitted because of favorable public opinion.

However, such sympathy belongs to a period when terrorist acts targeted specific individuals deemed personally guilty. Since then, terrorism has evolved from limited to total warfare and has become indiscriminate. Thus, the following question arises: can there be a just terrorist campaign that is total in character and aims to destroy a particular enemy? The protagonists of jihad would answer affirmatively, but the philosophers of international law would disagree. Once the number of victims involved in trying to right a wrong is no longer commensurate, such a campaign cannot be justified by any moral standards even if the cause has merit. Terrorists, of course, will not accept this condemnation; all that matters in our context is that the escalation of terrorism will not remain one-sided. To the extent that terrorism becomes a real danger, those engaged in it can no longer count on the protection of the law. Instead, they will treated by those attacked as they see fit, outside the law. The same will apply, *a fortiori,* if terrorists employ non-conventional weapons. Despite one or two notable exceptions, a general escalation of this sort has not yet occurred. However, as Diderot noted, from fanaticism to barbarism there is but one step. If present trends continue there is every reason to view the future grimly.

# 9

# THE TROUBLE WITH SANCTIONS

Robert A. Sirico

The advantages and disadvantages of alternative strategies for using economic and other types of sanctions for purposes of exercising influence over targets has been highly controversial in the twilight of the twentieth century. Now, at the start of the new century, debate about the use and effectiveness of sanctions has intensified. This essay, focusing on the use of sanctions by the United States, seeks to illuminate the problems that this policy instrument presents and to pinpoint the major circumstances under which sanctions are most likely to succeed. Stressing the costs against the documented failure of economic sanctions to work as a policy tool, as well as the questionable morality of using them as a substitute method of aggression, the essay frames the major issues that are likely to continue to divide policymakers as they debate the wisdom of using sanctions as a method of coercive diplomacy to achieve a variety of foreign policy goals. Sirico is President of the Acton Institute for the Study of Religion and Liberty (Grand Rapids, Michigan)—a nonprofit nongovernmental organization that seeks to promote international contact among scholars, students, and civic groups to further peace, prosperity, and religious freedom. He authored *A Moral Basis for Liberty* (1996).

Trade sanctions against foreign countries are the most-used weapon in the United States government's foreign policy arsenal, but do they accomplish their purpose? Who do sanctions really hurt?

Consider this scene from 1998. Alex Hasbany, the manager of a cigar room at the Patroon, a New York restaurant, was minding his business, clipping cigars, and chatting with thoroughly satisfied customers. Suddenly, Federal agents, armed with search warrants, stomped in and confiscated hundreds of boxes of cigars from his walk-in humidor. Then they arrested him and Kenneth Aretsky, the owner of the restaurant, as well as four customers (who subsequently were released on their own recognizance).

All were charged with violating the Trading with the Enemy Act that dates from World War I. What grave enemy had these men traded with to warrant a full-scale crackdown by the Federal government? They were buying and selling Cuban cigars, a felony that can land an individual in jail for ten years and cost him $100,000.

Even so, in the club set, Cuban cigars are not considered contraband, but a status symbol. People pay expensive prices for them, and not only because of their quality. They represent a high status conferred by the sanctions themselves.

Sanctions against Cuba were imposed in 1962. President Fidel Castro has long blamed the sanctions for the miserable poverty that continues to wrack his once-prosperous island. The real cause is socialism and Castro's brutal regime, but the sanctions haven't helped. Millions of Cubans who might be benefiting from commerce with the United States are barely scraping by instead.

This act is hard to justify on any grounds. Economically, it denies Americans products they want and Cubans jobs they need. Morally, sanctions hit the people of poor countries the hardest, while leaving the governments virtually unaffected. If sanctions didn't work to unseat Castro in nearly four decades, they are unlikely to do so in the future.

In 1970, most regimes in Latin America were not democratically elected. Today, all but Cuba are, and that island nation is the only one that consistently has borne the burden of United States sanctions. Even after the Cold War ended, they have been tightened to punish foreign governments that do business with Cuba.

If [the United States] Congress repealed sanctions, Castro would have to take responsibility for his own socialist failures. The Cuban people would have renewed opportunities to be in contact with American citizens and ideals. There would be new access to books, television, and the Internet. In time, as with other Latin American nations, the regime would give in to democracy.

Far from backing away, however, Congress keeps adding to the list of countries with which Americans cannot trade. The Gulf War [in 1990] was . . . years ago, but the U.S. continues to oppose any trade with Iraq other than tiny importations of some food and medicine. President Saddam Hussein doesn't suffer from this policy, but the Iraqi people do.

Americans do, too. Farmers cannot sell their products to those who would buy them if they had the chance. Consumers must pay higher prices for gas and heating oil. The world is a more hostile place without trade, and angry terrorists strike out in the belief that they are retaliating against the United States.

Meanwhile, bills in Congress propose sanctions be imposed on about two dozen additional countries, for reasons that appear plausible at first. Burma violates human rights, as does China. Colombia permits drug trafficking. Iran backs terrorism, and so does Syria. Zaire persecutes political dissidents. The real question, though, is: What, if anything, do sanctions do to relieve the suffering of the people?

For the most part, they cause regimes to hunker down and point their fingers at the United States for domestic problems of their own creation. Factories close, throwing people out of a job. Markets for goods dry up, which makes the workers in them blame America. That is exactly the opposite message the United States should be sending. It should be teaching the world free enterprise, not closing off opportunities to help it succeed.

Some think that imposing sanctions on China would constitute a much-needed rebuke to the Chinese regime and compel the government to chance its policies regarding minority religions. I agree that the political rulers of China are in need of a moral rebuke, but one that is effective and is itself moral.

As a Catholic priest who has visited with members of the underground churches, I feel a strong spiritual bond to the members of the clergy who have been jailed for speaking out against government policies. We all have a moral responsibility to take action whenever religious freedom is hindered, especially when it involves acts of violence and repression against individuals and groups.

However, cutting China off from membership in the world community of trading nations is not going to bolster religious freedom in that country. From past experience, it should be clear that imposing sanctions against China would seriously injure entrepreneurs and consumers, as well as impede the developing networks of civic and religious contacts on all sides. It would hinder, as well, China's technological development, injure standards of living, and quite possibly throw China into a recession.

Free trade is not solely about economic matters of profit for corporations. It also is about freedom and strengthening the civic order around the world. From my conversations with missionaries, Christian businesspeople, and members of the Church hierarchy, it is clear that there is a struggle taking place in China. It is between this growing civil sector—made up of churches, business associations, and local governments—and the state sector bureaucracy still dominated by old ways of thinking.

Economic exchange, within China and with the rest of the world, is helping to strengthen this civil sector. It is creating pockets of independent wealth that allow people to separate themselves from material reliance on the state. This is especially important to churches, which have to depend to a great extent on the charitable sector to flourish.

The dissemination of such technologies as phone systems, computers, and the Internet allow dissident religious groups to be in contact with each other and with various organizations around the world, and thereby draw attention to the plight of those persecuted for their beliefs. Businesses promote this by donating computers to churches, providing communications technologies to civic groups, and getting dissidents access to books they could not otherwise afford. At the Acton Institute, for example, we supply students, clerics, and academics in China through the mail and increasingly by means of our website with materials that promote the ideas of a free and virtuous society.

In the last twenty years, China has achieved a soaring economic expansion, adding eight to 10 percent to its gross domestic product on an annual basis. This is a period in which the U.S. has had good trading relations with the country. It is not uncommon now to see average Chinese carrying cellular phones, drinking American soft drinks, and owning their own homes. This country is being Americanized and developed at a rapid rate.

What about China's one child per family rule? It is a terrible policy and, as a longtime pro-life activist, I find that nation's population control methods immoral. At the same time, rising prosperity has played a role in reducing the number of forced abortions in China.

Free enterprise is giving the Chinese people the strength and means to resist the bureaucrats. In many cases, families are finding that they have enough money to pay the fines and have the extra children. Local officials even are said to encourage larger families as a means of raising revenue.

The way to further the process of reform and liberalization is to increase trading relations, not curb them. That doesn't mean the United States cannot denounce human rights abuses, but it shouldn't punish innocent people in the process.

## IMPACTING THE ECONOMY

American consumers benefit greatly from imports from all over the world: so do U.S. businesses employing American workers. When the government imposes sanctions, these businesses are not able to export their goods abroad. This can damage U.S. industries and the job market.

It is even worse when these sanctions are imposed unilaterally, as they are against Cuba. When U.S. companies are not importing and exporting, other nations step in to pick up the slack. For instance, in the case of Cuban cigars, most American wholesalers get them illegally from Britain, Canada, Germany, or France.

At a time when the prosperity of Americans increasingly is tied to U.S. trade with the rest of the world, it is a grave mistake to injure economic relations, especially when there is little likelihood that sanctions will achieve foreign policy objectives. The use of unilateral sanctions even poses a danger in countries where relations with the United States are peaceful. As former Secretary of Defense Richard Cheney has warned, "Foreign governments will be reluctant to work with U.S. companies since the U.S. government may attempt to use them for leverage when any political differences arise. We will be viewed as unreliable investors."

Commercial relations should not take place in a moral vacuum. Americans doing business abroad are in a better social position to discourage and denounce violations of freedom when they take place. United States firms have a moral obligation to promote freedom and the rule of law in the nations they operate within.

Speaking as a Catholic priest, I can only echo the words of Pope John Paul II, who says that every decision to invest involves a moral choice and implies certain moral obligations. Free enterprise must take place within a strict juridical framework of human rights or its merits become morally and economically dubious and even counterproductive.

The Pope has been an outspoken opponent of the dangerous trend by the United States to use sanctions as a means of imposing its will on the world. He is right to see that as counterproductive at best, and cruel and inhumane at worst.

With economic sanctions, America loses the chance to have any influence on the structure of government. Indeed, sanctions are more than just a foreign policy tool; they are an act of aggression. Some countries regard them as a perpetual war against their people. Certainly, Washington would see it that way if a powerful foreign nation suddenly cut off all trade with the United States.

The crux of the issue involves how Washington is going about its conduct of foreign policy around the world. The United States need not choose between free enterprise and morality. Economic liberty is essential to human rights, and the only way to promote both is through engagement, not acts of hostility and economic abuse.

My point is not merely about material prosperity, but about its potential and actual civil and social effects. It means a smaller role for government in people's lives, which, in turn, means a lessening of power on the part of the state to violate human rights.

With nations where Washington does not approve of the way the regimes treat their people, Americans face a choice. The United States can erect a wall that shuts out American influence, or it can keep the door open, using moral suasion, commerce, and diplomatic ties to encourage and extend the process of reform. A policy of peace and trade promotes a wider range of freedoms, holds out the prospect for making the right kind of difference, and provides a genuine moral center for international political and economic relationships.

# 10

# THE CHANGING NATURE OF WORLD POWER

Joseph S. Nye, Jr.

This essay draws fundamental distinctions among three concepts—power, the balance of power, and hegemony—and evaluates, in light of several theoretical perspectives, how the revolutionary changes sweeping the world are changing the meaning of these concepts. The author, Joseph S. Nye, Jr., is the former Chairman of the National Intelligence Council and Assistant Secretary of Defense for International Affairs in the Clinton administration, and now serves as Dean of the John F. Kennedy School of Government at Harvard University. His many publications include *Understanding International Conflict* (1999).

## THE CHANGING SOURCES OF POWER

. . . Some observers have argued that the sources of power are, in general, moving away from the emphasis on military force and conquest that marked earlier eras. In assessing international power today, factors such as technology, education, and economic growth are becoming more important, whereas geography, population, and raw materials are becoming less important. Kenneth Waltz argues that a 5 percent rate of economic growth in the United States for three years would add more to American strength than does [its] alliance with Britain.[1]

---

[1] Kenneth N. Waltz, *Theory of International Politics* (Reading, Mass.: Addison-Wesley, 1979), p. 172.

Richard Rosecrance argues that since 1945, the world has been poised between a territorial system composed of states that view power in terms of land mass, and a trading system "based in states which recognize that self-sufficiency is an illusion." In the past, says Rosecrance, "it was cheaper to seize another state's territory by force than to develop the sophisticated economic and trading apparatus needed to derive benefit from commercial exchange with it."[2]

If so, perhaps we are in a "Japanese period" in world politics. Japan has certainly done far better with its strategy as a trading state after 1945 than it did with its military strategy to create a Greater East Asian Co-Prosperity sphere in the 1930s. But Japan's security vis-à-vis its large military neighbors—China and [Russia]—depends heavily on U.S. protection. In short, even if we can define power clearly, it still has become more difficult to be clear about the relationship of particular resources to it. Thus, we cannot leap too quickly to the conclusion that all trends favor economic power or countries like Japan.

Like other forms of power, economic power cannot be measured simply in terms of tangible resources. Intangible aspects also matter. For example, outcomes generally depend on bargaining, and bargaining depends on relative costs in particular situations and skill in converting potential power into effects. Relative costs are determined not only by the total amount of measurable economic resources of a country but also by the degree of its interdependence in a relationship. If, for example, the United States and Japan depend on each other but one is less dependent than the other, that asymmetry is a source of power. The United States may be less vulnerable than Japan if the relationship breaks down, and it may use that threat as a source of power.[3] Thus, an assessment of Japanese and American power must look not only at shares of resources but also at the relative vulnerabilities of both countries.

Another consideration is that most large countries today find military force more costly to apply than in previous centuries. This has resulted from the dangers of nuclear escalation, the difficulty of ruling nationalistically awakened populations in otherwise weak states, the danger of rupturing profitable relations on other issues, and the public opposition in Western democracies to prolonged and expensive military conflicts. Even so, the increased cost of military force does not mean that it will be ruled out. To the contrary, in an anarchic system of states where there is no higher government to settle conflicts and where the ultimate recourse is self-help, this could never happen. In some cases, the stakes may justify a costly use of force. And, as . . . episodes in Grenada and Libya [and Kosovo] have shown, not all uses of force by great powers involve high costs.

---

[2] Richard N. Rosecrance, *The Rise of the Trading State* (New York: Basic Books, 1986), pp. 16, 160.

[3] Robert O. Keohane and Joseph S. Nye, Jr., *Power and Interdependence* (Boston: Little, Brown, 1977), chap. 1.

Even if the direct use of force were banned among a group of countries, military force would still play an important political role. For example, the American military role in deterring threats to allies, or of assuring access to a crucial resource such as oil in the Persian Gulf, means that the provision of protective force can be used in bargaining situations. Sometimes the linkage may be direct; more often it is a factor not mentioned openly but present in the back of statesmen's minds.

In addition, there is the consideration that is sometimes called "the second face of power."[4] Getting other states to change might be called the directive or commanding method of exercising power. Command power can rest on inducements ("carrots") or threats ("sticks"). But there is also an indirect way to exercise power. A country may achieve the outcomes it prefers in world politics because other countries want to follow it or have agreed to a system that produces such effects. In this sense, it is just as important to set the agenda and structure the situations in world politics as it is to get others to change in particular situations. This aspect of power—that is, getting others to want what you want—might be called indirect or co-optive power behavior. It is in contrast to the active command power behavior of getting others to do what you want.[5] Co-optive power can rest on the attraction of one's ideas or on the ability to set the political agenda in a way that shapes the preferences that others express. Parents of teenagers know that if they have structured their children's beliefs and preferences, their power will be greater and will last longer than if they had relied only on active control. Similarly, political leaders and philosophers have long understood the power that comes from setting the agenda and determining the framework of a debate. The ability to establish preferences tends to be associated with intangible power resources such as culture, ideology, and institutions. This dimension can be thought of as soft power, in contrast to the hard command power usually associated with tangible resources like military and economic strength.[6]

---

[4] Peter Bachrach and Morton S. Baratz, "Decisions and Nondecisions: An Analytical Framework," *American Political Science Review* 57 (September 1963), pp. 632–42. See also Richard Mansbach and John Vasquez, *In Search of Theory: A New Paradigm for Global Politics* (New York: Columbia University Press, 1981).

[5] Susan Strange uses the term *"structural power,"* which she defines as "power to shape and determine the structures of the global political economy" in *States and Markets* (New York: Basil Blackwell, 1988), p. 24. My term, *"co-optive power,"* is similar in its focus on preferences but is somewhat broader, encompassing all elements of international politics. The term *structural power,* in contrast, tends to be associated with the neorealist theories of Kenneth Waltz.

[6] The distinction between hard and soft power resources is one of degree, both in the nature of the behavior and in the tangibility of the resources. Both types are aspects of the ability to achieve one's purposes by controlling the behavior of others. Command power—the ability to change what others *do*—can rest on coercion or inducement. Co-optive power—the ability to shape what others *want*—can rest on the attractiveness of one's culture and ideology or the ability to manipulate the agenda of political choices in a manner that makes actors fail to express some preferences because they seem to be too unrealistic. The forms of behavior between command and co-optive power range along this continuum:

| Command Power | coercion | inducement | agenda-setting | attraction | Co-optive power |
|---|---|---|---|---|---|

Robert Cox argues that the nineteenth-century *Pax Britannica* and the twentieth-century *Pax Americana* were effective because they created liberal international economic orders, in which certain types of economic relations were privileged over others and liberal international rules and institutions were broadly accepted. Following the insights of the Italian thinker Antonio Gramsci, Cox argues that the most critical feature for a dominant country is the ability to obtain a broad measure of consent on general principles—principles that ensure the supremacy of the leading state and dominant social classes—and at the same time to offer some prospect of satisfaction to the less powerful. Cox identifies Britain from 1845 to 1875 and the United States from 1945 to 1967 as such countries.[7] Although we may not agree with his terminology or dates, Cox has touched a major point: soft co-optive power is just as important as hard command power. If a state can make its power legitimate in the eyes of others, it will encounter less resistance to its wishes. If its culture and ideology are attractive, others will more willingly follow. If it can establish international norms that are consistent with its society, it will be less likely to have to change. If it can help support institutions that encourage other states to channel or limit their activities in ways the dominant state prefers, it may not need as many costly exercises of coercive or hard power in bargaining situations. In short, the universalism of a country's culture and its ability to establish a set of favorable rules and institutions that govern areas of international activity are critical sources of power.[8] These soft sources of power are becoming more important in world politics today.

Such considerations question the conclusion that the world is about to enter a Japanese era in world politics. The nature of power is changing and some of the changes will favor Japan, but some of them may favor the United States even more. In command power, Japan's economic strength is increasing, but it remains vulnerable in terms of raw materials and relatively weak in terms of military force. And in co-optive power, Japan's culture is highly insular and it has yet to develop a major voice in international institutions. The United States, on the other hand, has a universalistic popular culture and a major role in international institutions. Although such factors may change in the future, they raise an important question about the present situation: what resources are the most important sources of power today? A look at the five-century-old modern state system shows that different power resources played critical roles in different periods. (See Table 10.1.) The sources of power are never static and they continue to change in today's world.

---

Further, soft power resources tend to be associated with co-optive power behavior, whereas hard power resources are usually associated with command behavior. But the relationship is imperfect. For example, countries may be attracted to others with command power by myths of invincibility, and command power may sometimes be used to establish institutions that later become regarded as legitimate. But the general association is strong enough to allow the useful shorthand reference to hard and soft power resources.

[7] Robert W. Cox, *Production, Power, and World Order* (New York: Columbia University Press, 1987), chaps. 6, 7.

[8] Stephen D. Krasner, *International Regimes* (Ithaca, N.Y.: Cornell University Press, 1983).

**TABLE 10.1**
LEADING STATES AND MAJOR POWER RESOURCES, 1500s–1900s

| Period | Leading State | Major Resources |
| --- | --- | --- |
| Sixteenth century | Spain | Gold bullion, colonial trade, mercenary armies dynastic ties |
| Seventeenth century | Netherlands | Trade, capital markets, navy |
| Eighteenth century | France | Population, rural industry, public administration, army |
| Nineteenth century | Britain | Industry, political cohesion, finance and credit, navy, liberal norms, island location (easy to defend) |
| Twentieth century | United States | Economic scale, scientific and technical leadership, universalistic culture, military forces and alliances, liberal international regimes, hub of transnational communication |

In an age of information-based economies and transnational interdependence, power is becoming less transferable, less tangible, and less coercive. However, the transformation of power is incomplete. The twenty-first century will certainly see a greater role for informational and institutional power, but military force will remain an important factor. Economic scale, both in markets and in natural resources, will also remain important. As the service sector grows within modern economies, the distinction between services and manufacturing will continue to blur. Information will become more plentiful, and the critical resource will be the organizational capacity for rapid and flexible response. Political cohesion will remain important, as will a universalistic popular culture. On some of these dimensions of power, the United States is well endowed; on others, questions arise. But even larger questions arise for the other major contenders—Europe, Japan, [Russia], and China. But first we need to look at the patterns in the distribution of power—balances and hegemonies, and how they have changed over history. . . .

## BALANCE OF POWER

International relations is far from a precise science. Conditions in various periods always differ in significant details, and human behavior reflects personal choices. Moreover, theorists often suffer from writing in the midst of events, rather than viewing them from a distance. Thus, powerful theories—those that are both simple and accurate—are rare. Yet political leaders (and those who seek to explain behavior) must generalize in order to chart a path through the apparent chaos of changing events. One of the longest-standing and most frequently used concepts is balance of power, which eighteenth-century philosopher David Hume called "a constant rule of prudent politics." For centuries, balance of power has been the starting point for realistic discussions of international politics.

To an extent, balance of power is a useful predictor of how states will behave; that is, states will align in a manner that will prevent any one state from developing a preponderance of power. This is based on two assumptions: that states exist in an anarchic system with no higher government and that political leaders will act first to reduce risks to the independence of their states. The policy of balancing power helps to explain why in modern times a large state cannot grow forever into a world empire. States seek to increase their powers through internal growth and external alliances. Balance of power predicts that if one state appears to grow too strong, others will ally against it so as to avoid threats to their own independence. This behavior, then, will preserve the structure of the system of states.

However, not all balance-of-power predictions are so obvious. For example, this theory implies that professions of ideological faith will be poor predictors of behavior. But despite Britain's criticism of the notorious Stalin-Hitler pact of 1939, it was quick to make an alliance with Stalin's Soviet Union in 1941. As Winston Churchill explained at the time, "If I learned that Hitler had invaded Hell, I would manage to say something good about the Devil in the House of Commons." Further, balance of power does not mean that political leaders must maximize the power of their own states in the short run. Bandwagoning—that is, joining the stronger rather than the weaker side—might produce more immediate spoils. As Mussolini discovered in his ill-fated pact with Hitler, the danger in bandwagoning is that independence may be threatened by the stronger ally in the long term. Thus, to say that states will act to balance power is a strong generalization in international relations, but it is far from being a perfect predictor.

Proximity and perceptions of threat also affect the way in which balancing of power is played out. A small state like Finland, for instance, [could not] afford to try to balance Soviet power. Instead, it [sought] to preserve its independence through neutrality. Balance of power and the proposition that "the enemy of my enemy is my friend" help to explain the larger contours of current world politics, but only when proximity and perceptions are considered. The United States was by far the strongest power after 1945. A mechanical application of power balance might seem to predict an alliance against the United States. In fact, Europe and Japan allied with the United States because the Soviet Union, while weaker in overall power, posed a proximate threat to its neighbors. Geography and psychology are both important factors in geopolitics.

The term *balance of power* is sometimes used not as a prediction of policy but as a description of how power is distributed. In the latter case, it is more accurate to refer to the distribution of power. In other instances, though, the term is used to refer to an evenly balanced distribution of power, like a pair of hanging scales. The problem with this usage is that the ambiguities of measuring power make it difficult to determine when an equal balance exists. In fact, the major concerns in world politics tend to arise from inequalities of power, and particularly from major changes in the unequal distribution of power.

## HEGEMONY IN MODERN HISTORY

No matter how power is measured, an equal distribution of power among major states is relatively rare. More often the processes of uneven growth, which realists consider a basic law of international politics, mean that some states will be rising and others declining. These transitions in the distribution of power stimulate statesmen to form alliances, to build armies, and to take risks that balance or check rising powers. But the balancing of power does not always prevent the emergence of a dominant state. Theories of hegemony and power transition try to explain why some states that become preponderant later lose that preponderance.

As far back as ancient Greece, observers attempting to explain the causes of major world wars have cited the uncertainties associated with the transition of power. Shifts in the international distribution of power create the conditions likely to lead to the most important wars. However, while power transitions provide useful warning about periods of heightened risk, there is no iron law of hegemonic war. If there were, Britain and the United States would have gone to war at the beginning of this century, when the Americans surpassed the British in economic and naval power in the Western Hemisphere. Instead, when the United States backed Venezuela in its boundary dispute with British Guyana in 1895, British leaders appeased the rising American power instead of going to war with it.

When power is distributed unevenly, political leaders and theorists use terms such as *empire* and *hegemony*. Although there have been many empires in history, those in the modern world have not encompassed all major countries. Even the British Empire at the beginning of this century encompassed only a quarter of the world's population, and Britain was just one of a half-dozen major powers in the global balance of power. The term *hegemony* is applied to a variety of situations in which one state appears to have considerably more power than others. For example, for years China accused the Soviet Union of seeking hegemony in Asia. When Soviet leader Mikhail Gorbachev and Chinese leader Deng Xiaoping met in 1989, they pledged that "neither side will seek hegemony in any form anywhere in the world."

Although the word comes from the ancient Greek and refers to the dominance of one state over others in the system, it is used in diverse and confused ways. Part of the problem is that unequal distribution of power is a matter of degree, and there is no general agreement on how much inequality and what types of power constitute hegemony. All too often, hegemony is used to refer to different behaviors and degrees of control, which obscures rather than clarifies that analysis. For example, Charles Doran cites aggressive military power, while Robert Keohane looks at preponderance in economic resources. Robert Gilpin sometimes uses the terms *imperial* and *hegemonic* interchangeably to refer to a situation in which "a single powerful state controls or dominates the lesser states in the system."[9] British hegemony in the nineteenth century is commonly cited even though Britain ranked third behind the United States and Russia in gross national product and third behind Russia and France in military expenditures at the peak of its relative power around 1870. Britain was first in the more limited domains of manufacturing, trade, finance, and naval power.[10] Yet theorists often contend that "full hegemony requires productive, commercial, and financial as well as political and military power."[11]

Joshua Goldstein usefully defines hegemony as "being able to dictate, or at least dominate, the rules and arrangements by which international relations, political and economic, are conducted. . . . Economic hegemony implies the ability to center the world economy around itself. Political hegemony means being able to dominate the world militarily."[12] However, there are still two important questions to be answered with regard to how the term *hegemony* is used. First, what is the scope of the hegemon's control? In the modern world, a situation in which one country can dictate political and economic arrangements has been extremely rare. Most examples have been regional, such as Soviet power in Eastern Europe [during the Cold War], American influence in the Caribbean, and India's control over its small neighbors—Sikkim, Bhutan, and Nepal. In addition, one can find instances in which one country was able to set the rules and arrangements governing specific issues in world politics, such as the American role in money or trade in the early postwar years. But there has been no global, systemwide hegemon during the past two centuries. Contrary to the myths about *Pax Britannica* and *Pax Americana,* British and American hegemonies have been regional and issue-specific rather than general.

Second, we must ask what types of power resources are necessary to produce a hegemonic degree of control. Is military power necessary? Or is it enough to have preponderance in economic resources? How do the two types of power relate to each other? Obviously, the answers to such questions can tell us a great deal about the future world, in which Japan may be an economic giant and a military dwarf while [Russia] may fall into the opposite situation. A careful look at the interplay of military and economic power raises doubt about the degree of American hegemony in the postwar period.

---

[9] Charles F. Doran, *The Politics of Assimilation: Hegemony and Its Aftermath* (Baltimore: Johns Hopkins University Press, 1971), p. 70; Robert O. Keohane, *After Hegemony* (Princeton, N.J.: Princeton University Press, 1984), p. 32; Robert Gilpin, *War and Change in World Politics* (New York: Cambridge University Press, 1981), p. 29.

[10] Bruce M. Russett, "The Mysterious Case of Vanishing Hegemony; or, Is Mark Twain Really Dead?" *International Organization* 39 (Spring 1985), p. 212.

[11] Robert C. North and Julie Strickland, "Power Transition and Hegemonic Succession," Paper delivered at the meeting of the International Studies Association, Anaheim, Calif., (March–April 1986), p. 5.

[12] Joshua S. Goldstein, *Long Cycles: Prosperity and War in the Modern Age* (New Haven, Conn.: Yale University Press, 1988), p. 281.

## THEORIES OF HEGEMONIC TRANSITION AND STABILITY

General hegemony is the concern of theories and analogies about the instability and dangers supposedly caused by hegemonic transitions. Classical concerns about hegemony among leaders and philosophers focus on military power and "conflicts precipitated by the military effort of one dominant actor to expand well beyond the arbitrary security confines set by tradition, historical accident, or coercive pressures."[13] In this approach, hegemonic preponderance arises out of military expansion, such as the efforts of Louis XIV, Napoleon, or Hitler to dominate world politics. The important point is that, except for brief periods, none of the attempted military hegemonies in modern times has succeeded. (See Table 10.2.) No modern state has been able to develop sufficient military power to transform the balance of power into a long-lived hegemony in which one state could dominate the world militarily.

**TABLE 10.2**
MODERN EFFORTS AT MILITARY HEGEMONY

| State Attempting Hegemony | Ensuing Hegemonic War | New Order After War |
|---|---|---|
| Hapsburg, Spain | Thirty Years War, 1618–1648 | Peace of Westphalia, 1648 |
| Louis XIV's France | Wars of Louis XIV | Treaty of Utrecht, 1713 |
| Napoleon's France | 1792–1815 | Congress of Vienna, 1815 |
| Germany (and Japan) | 1914–1945 | United Nations, 1945 |

Source: Charles F. Doran, *The Politics of Assimiliation: Hegemony and Its Aftermath* (Baltimore: John Hopkins University Press, 1971), pp. 19–20.

More recently, many political scientists have focused on economic power as a source of hegemonic control. Some define hegemonic economic power in terms of resources—that is, preponderance in control over raw materials, sources of capital, markets, and production of goods. Others use the behavioral definition in which a hegemon is a state able to set the rules and arrangements for the global economy. Robert Gilpin, a leading theorist of hegemonic transition, sees Britain and America, having created and enforced the rules of a liberal economic order, as the successive hegemons since the Industrial Revolution.[14] Some political economists argue that world economic stability requires a single stabilizer and that periods of such stability have coincided with periods of hegemony. In this view, *Pax Britannica* and *Pax Americana* were the periods when Britain and the United States were strong enough to create and enforce the rules for a

---

[13] Doran, *Politics of Assimilation*, p. 15.
[14] Keohane, *After Hegemony*, p. 32; Gilpin, *War and Change*, p. 144.

liberal international economic order in the nineteenth and twentieth centuries. For example, it is often argued that economic stability "historically has occurred when there has been a sole hegemonic power: Britain from 1815 to World War I and the United States from 1945 to around 1970. . . . With a sole hegemonic power, the rules of the game can be established and enforced. Lesser countries have little choice but to go along. Without a hegemonic power, conflict is the order of the day." [15] Such theories of hegemonic stability and decline are often used to predict that the United States will follow the experience of Great Britain, and that instability will ensue. Goldstein, for example, argues that "we are moving toward the 'weak hegemony' end of the spectrum and . . . this seems to increase the danger of hegemonic war." [16]

I argue, however, that the theory of hegemonic stability and transition will not tell us as much about the future of the United States. Theorists of hegemonic stability generally fail to spell out the causal connections between military and economic power and hegemony. As already noted, nineteenth-century Britain was not militarily dominant nor was it the world's largest economy, and yet Britain is portrayed by Gilpin and others as hegemonic. Did Britain's military weakness at that time allow the United States and Russia, the two larger economies, to remain mostly outside the liberal system of free trade? Or, to take a twentieth-century puzzle, did a liberal international economy depend on postwar American military strength or only its economic power? Are both conditions necessary today, or have modern nations learned to cooperate through international institutions?

One radical school of political economists, the neo-Marxists, has attempted to answer similar questions about the relationship between economic and military hegemony, but their theories are unconvincing. For example, Immanuel Wallerstein defines hegemony as a situation in which power is so unbalanced that

> one power can largely impose its rules and its wishes (at the very least by effective veto power) in the economic, political, military, diplomatic, and even cultural arenas. The material base of such power lies in the ability of enterprises domiciled in that power to operate more efficiently in all three major economic arenas—agro-industrial production, commerce, and finance.[17]

According to Wallerstein, hegemony is rare and "refers to that short interval in which there is simultaneously advantage in all three economic domains." At such times, the other major powers become *"de facto* client states." Wallerstein claims there have been only three modern instances of hegemony—in the Netherlands, 1620–1650; in Britain, 1815–1873; and in the United States, 1945–1967 (see

---

[15] Michael Moffitt, "Shocks, Deadlocks and Scorched Earth: Reaganomics and the Decline of U.S. Hegemony," *World Policy Journal* 4 (Fall 1987), p. 576.

[16] Goldstein, *Long Cycles,* p. 357.

[17] Immanuel M. Wallerstein, *The Politics of the World-Economy: The States, the Movements, and the Civilizations* (New York: Cambridge University Press, 1984), pp. 38, 41.

Table 10.3.) He argues that "in each case, the hegemony was secured by a thirty-year-long world war," after which a new order followed—the Peace of Westphalia after 1648; the Concert of Europe after 1815; and the United Nations–Bretton Woods system after 1945.[18] According to this theory, the United States will follow the Dutch and the British path to decline.

**TABLE 10.3**
A NEO-MARXIST VIEW OF HEGEMONY

| Hegemony | World War Securing Hegemony | Period of Dominance | Decline |
|---|---|---|---|
| Dutch | Thirty Years War, 1618–1648 | 1620–1650 | 1650–1672 |
| British | Napoleonic Wars, 1792–1815 | 1815–1873 | 1873–1896 |
| American | World Wars I and II, 1914–1945 | 1945–1967 | 1967– |

*Source:* Immanuel Wallerstein, *The Politics of the World Econcomy* (New York: Cambridge University Press, 1984), pp. 41–42.

The neo-Marxist view of hegemony is unconvincing and a poor predictor of future events because it superficially links military and economic hegemony and has many loose ends. For example, contrary to Wallerstein's theory, the Thirty Years War *coincided* with Dutch hegemony, and Dutch decline began with the Peace of Westphalia. The Dutch were not militarily strong enough to stand up to the British on the sea and could barely defend themselves against the French on land, "despite their trade-derived wealth."[19] Further, although Wallerstein argues that British hegemony began after the Napoleonic Wars, he is not clear about how the new order in the balance of power—that is, the nineteenth-century Concert of Europe—related to Britain's supposed ability to impose a global free-trade system. For example, Louis XIV's France, which many historians view as the dominant military power in the second half of the seventeenth century, is excluded from Wallerstein's schema altogether. Thus, the neo-Marxist historical analogies seem forced into a Procrustean ideological bed, while other cases are left out of bed altogether.

Others have attempted to organize past periods of hegemony into century-long cycles. In 1919, British geopolitician Sir Halford Mackinder argued that unequal growth among nations tends to produce a hegemonic world war about every hundred years. More recently, political scientist George Modelski proposed a hundred-year cyclical view of changes in world leadership. (See Table 10.4.) In this view, a long cycle begins with a major global war. A single state then emerges as the new world power and legitimizes its preponderance with postwar peace treaties. (Preponderance is defined as having at least half the resources available

---

[18] Ibid.
[19] Goldstein, *Long Cycles*, p. 317.

for global order keeping.) The new leader supplies security and order for the international system. In time, though, the leader loses legitimacy, and deconcentration of power leads to another global war. The new leader that emerges from that war may not be the state that challenged the old leader but one of the more innovative allies in the winning coalition (as, not Germany, but the United States replaced Britain). According to Modelski's theory, the United States began its decline in 1973.[20] If his assumptions are correct, it may be Japan and not [Russia] that will most effectively challenge the United States in the future.

**TABLE 10.4**
LONG CYCLES OF WORLD LEADERSHIP

| Cycle | Global War | Preponderance | Decline |
|-------|-----------|---------------|---------|
| 1495–1580 | 1494–1516 | Portugal, 1516–1540 | 1540–1580 |
| 1580–1688 | 1580–1609 | Netherlands, 1609–1640 | 1640–1688 |
| 1688–1792 | 1688–1713 | Britain, 1714–1740 | 1740–1792 |
| 1792–1914 | 1792–1815 | Britain, 1815–1850 | 1850–1914 |
| 1914– | 1914–1945 | United States, 1945–1973 | 1973– |

*Source:* George Modelski, *Long Cycles in World Politics* (Seattle: University of Washington Press, 1987), pp. 40, 42, 44, 102, 131, 147.

Modelski and his followers suggest that the processes of decline are associated with long waves in the global economy. They associate a period of rising prices and resource scarcities with loss of power, and the concentration of power with falling prices, resource abundance, and economic innovation.[21] However, in linking economic and political cycles, these theorists become enmeshed in the controversy surrounding long cycle theory. Many economists are skeptical about the empirical evidence for alleged long economic waves and about dating historical waves by those who use the concept.[22] . . .

Vague definitions and arbitrary schematizations alert us to the inadequacies of such grand theories of hegemony and decline. Most theorists of hegemonic transition tend to shape history to their own theories by focusing on particular power resources and ignoring others. Examples include the poorly explained relationship between military and political power and the unclear link between

[20] George Modelski, "The Long Cycle of Global Politics and the Nation-State," *Comparative Studies in Society and History* 20 (April 1978), pp. 214–35; George Modelski, *Long Cycles in World Politics* (Seattle: University of Washington Press, 1987).

[21] William R. Thompson, *On Global War: Historical Structural Approaches to World Politics* (Columbia: University of South Carolina Press, 1988), chaps. 3, 8.

[22] Richard N. Rosecrance, "Long Cycle Theory and International Relations," *International Organization* 41 (Spring 1987), pp. 291–5. An interesting but ultimately unconvincing discussion can be found in Goldstein, *Long Cycles.*

decline and major war. Since there have been wars among the great powers during 60 percent of the years from 1500 to the present, there are plenty of candidates to associate with any given scheme.[23] Even if we consider only the nine general wars that have involved nearly all the great powers and produced high levels of casualties, some of them, such as the Seven Years War (1755–1763), are not considered hegemonic in any of the schemes. As sociologist Pitirim Sorokin concludes, "no regular periodicity is noticeable."[24] At best, the various schematizations of hegemony and war are only suggestive. They do not provide a reliable basis for predicting the future of American power or for evaluating the risk of world war as we enter the twenty-first century. Loose historical analogies about decline and falsely deterministic political theories are not merely academic: they may lead to inappropriate policies. The real problems of a post–cold-war world will not be new challenges for hegemony, but the new challenges of transnational interdependence.

---

[23] Jack S. Levy, "Declining Power and the Preventive Motivation for War," *World Politics* 40 (October 1987), pp. 82–107. See also Jack S. Levy, *War in the Modern Great Power System, 1495–1975* (Lexington: University of Kentucky Press, 1983), p. 97.

[24] Pitirim Aleksandrovich Sorokin, *Social and Cultural Dynamics: A Study of Change in Major Systems of Art, Truth, Ethics, Law and Social Relationships* (1957; reprint, Boston: Porter Sargent, 1970), p. 561.

# DISCORD AND COLLABORATION

States necessarily must direct their attention and resources toward the quest for security, for the threat of war is an ever-present danger in an international system that remains largely anarchical. Issues relating to arms and influence therefore occupy a prominent place on states' foreign-policy agendas. Indeed, the pursuit of national security is widely perceived to be the very essence of international politics. Hence the issues examined in Part One of *The Global Agenda* appropriately command central importance.

This perspective, though compelling and at the core of realist theories, is at best a caricature of international politics, because it fails to acknowledge the broad range of issues and objectives that motivate states' behavior, even in their quest for security. World politics entails both issues and strategies that lie beyond arms and war, peace and security, deterrence, and the raw exercise of influence. International politics also includes states' activities that often have little or nothing to do with armaments or the threat of war, and it includes many actions motivated by the desire to collaborate with others so as to derive mutual benefits.

Indeed, contrary to the harsh realist perspective of the English political theorist Thomas Hobbes, international politics is not accurately described as nothing but a "war of all against all." States are not normally straining at the leash to attack one another. Nor do they devote the bulk of their day-to-day activities to planning the use of force against their perceived adversaries or against rebellious minority nationalities within their borders. The texture of world politics is shaped by more varied national interests and activities.

Part Two of *The Global Agenda* directs attention to the non-military methods by which states seek to promote their national interests. Even under normal conditions when peace prevails, conflict as well as cooperation is exhibited in relations among states. Disputes as well as agreements are common because some level of conflict is unavoidable among actors involved in high levels of cooperative political interaction, and not just when their relations are hostile. Nonetheless, we can observe that how states usually respond to conflict does not routinely involve preparations for war and the threat or use of force.

Part Two begins with the assumption that states respond to a perceived need not only for power but also for order. States value a stable international environment. They therefore seek and support not just a strong defense but also institutions and rules that contribute to the creation of a more orderly world. In short, international politics involves both discord and collaboration.

What factors influence whether enmity or amity will dominate the pattern of interaction among states? Clearly, there are many. Underlying all of them, it may be argued, are states' perceptions of reality. Reality is partially subjective—what states perceive it to be, not just what it is. Thus states' behavior is influenced strongly by images of reality as well as by objective facts. Whether states see the world as fearful and hostile or as peaceful and cooperative will influence the postures they assume toward global issues and their reactions to the challenges and options those issues present.

How international politics and the policies of states toward one another are pictured is shaped by our images of the global system's dominant characteristics. To organize perceptions about these subjects, social scientists have developed models that describe and explain various properties of international relations. To assist us in developing a frame of reference, Ole R. Holsti, in "Models of International Relations: Realist and Neoliberal Perspectives on Conflict and Cooperation," describes and summarizes two models that scholars have fashioned to organize research and theorizing on world politics: the classical and modern versions of "realism," and the neoliberal challengers to it who emphasize the interdependent nature of global realities and the prospects for cooperation and change. Holsti elucidates the assumptions and conclusions about international relations suggested by the alternative theoretical orientations. In so doing, he provides a basis for understanding the diverse ways discord and collaboration manifest themselves in world affairs and why the potential for enduring conflict coexists with the potential for cooperation and change.

Models and theories provide a lens through which international realities are interpreted. Their usefulness depends in large part on the accuracy of the assumptions about international realities upon which they are based. Hence, the accuracy of observers' perceptions will matter greatly in determining the ways in which scholars and policymakers respond to the changes occurring as the twenty-first century unfolds. In "Managing the Challenge of Globalization and Institutionalizing Cooperation Through Global Governance," David Held, Anthony

McGrew, David Goldblatt, and Jonathan Perraton combine their research and theoretical expertise to trace and analyze the major changes in international affairs and to uncover the underlying dynamics that are captured by the popular adjective "globalization." Globalization is a phenomenon that is eroding the longstanding patterns of politics among formerly independent states who are now wrestling with the necessity of adjusting to conditions of unprecedented international interdependence. From their insightful survey, the authors provide a vision of global life in its multiple dimensions—a portrait from which we can interpret the sources of prevailing order and disorder. Their picture of contemporary international affairs highlights the divergent trends making for global change and complexity. Identifying and defining the most significant transformations, the essay shows how the growth of interactions across borders has led to the integration of international relations and, in the process, created "globalization"—or what the essay calls the "biggest idea in world politics today."

For the compelling reasons this broad-based survey documents, a new global landscape is being created, leading to the internationalization of peoples' agendas throughout the world because the significance of borders is vanishing, as is the division between domestic and foreign affairs. As boundaries have become porous while territoriality is still a central preoccupation of many people, globalization in its multiple dimensions is precipitating both cooperation and conflict throughout the world. It is likely that in the years ahead we will witness concurrently high levels of harmony in a rising sea of global integration as well as the persistence of many islands of hostile behavior in countries facing disintegration. The essay by Held, McGrew, Goldblatt, and Perraton frames the environment in which world politics will take place in the new millennium, explaining how the major forces and factors will interact and describing the pressures for institutionalizing cooperation through global governance that globalization is causing. This definitive account of the problems and possibilities on the global agenda that globalization is generating concludes on an optimistic note. It suggests that the dynamics of globalization are the dominant catalysts behind the steps being taken to build strengthened global institutions to manage the conditions and challenges that globalization is itself creating.

By looking at the prevailing properties of the contemporary global landscape, we gain perspective on the nature and mixture of discord and collaboration that appear destined to govern the future. Which will dominate will be shaped by long-term secular trends that cannot be fully controlled. Awareness of the existence of major trajectories suggests why myriad issues will occupy the crowded global agenda of the future, and awareness of the fundamental trends unfolding raises consciousness of the possibility that global problems and challenges may overwhelm the capacity of people to successfully manage them.

Of all the factors that will influence the prospects for global collaboration, how the relationships between the great powers evolve is unquestionably paramount. The probable character of their relationships is the subject of considerable controversy because the intentions and foreign-policy priorities of each emerging great power remain ill defined. For more than four decades following World War II, the expectation of superpower discord remained high and the possibilities for lasting cooperation appeared remote, in large measure because of the distrust, ideological rivalry, and misperceptions that fueled the superpowers' animosity during the Cold War. But in 1989 when the Berlin Wall fell, this chronic antagonism also began to crumble. As we look to the future, the likely shape of the great powers' relations with one another inspires hope that accommodation will prevail and at the same time provokes fear that a new cycle of competition, conflict, or even war will commence.

What is pivotal at the beginning of the new century is the current balance of power, which is heavily tilted or out of balance with only one superpower—the United States—sitting atop the global pyramid of power as the uncontested hegemon or leader without a serious challenger. It is a unipolar moment, with a single "pole" or center of power reigning supreme in military capability. For the United States, supremacy creates enormous opportunities *and* responsibilities; for the other great powers and, for that matter the rest of the world, U.S. preponderance and dominance in military spending, weapons technology, war-fighting capabilities, and arms sales is a frightening problem. In "What to Do with American Primacy," Richard N. Haass places the dilemmas presented by the "enormous" U.S. surplus of power in the world into context, in order to anticipate the choices and consequences. Noting that U.S. supremacy is not a policy, that retaining global preeminence cannot be a U.S. purpose, and that U.S. primacy is not likely to remain permanent as the ascendance of rivals leads to a multipolar distribution of power in the twenty-first century, Haass evaluates the fundamental foundations for a peaceful, prosperous, and just global future. Critical, to his way of thinking, are the diverse ways in which an embryonic set of great-power relationships might develop to cement the great powers' future collaboration with one another, because there exists a strong potential for a new wave of rivalry to emerge that will destroy hopes for future great-power harmony.

This assessment takes as its point of departure the growing evidence that the international system is presently undergoing a historic transformation, because military and economic capabilities are becoming increasingly diffused among great powers. As China, Japan, and Germany (within the network of the European Union) increase their power and position relative to the United States and become U.S. rivals (as they have been doing for the past decade), the structure of the international system is clearly moving toward the advent of a new multipolar distribution of power. Systems composed of many roughly equal great powers have been common throughout history. Some of these systems have been relatively stable. The more typical property of multipower systems has been to gradually break into rigid, antagonistic blocs—followed by the outbreak of a destructive global war. Accordingly, to cope with the welter of transnational security threats that will face the global community in the immediate future, Haass argues that it is imperative that the great powers do not once again split into competitive coalitions, facing each other in a new cold war with each alliance seeking to defend itself by preparing for war against the rival bloc.

Three avenues are available to cope with such an emerging security threat: (1) acting alone through unilateralism, (2) cultivating bilateral strategic partnerships, or (3) building multilateral cooperation. To Haass, neither unilateralism nor special bilateral alliances bode well for an orderly future multipolar system. In contrast, multilateralism through collective security offers far better prospects for building on the great powers' common interests and for agreeing on rules to determine when they should jointly intervene with military force for humanitarian purposes to preserve internal stability in failing states and for preventing rogue governments from committing acts of atrocity within their borders. This means, Haass contends, that the United States should use its power to help the global community reach a consensus on how international society should be organized and how it should manage the core issues and problems on the twenty-first century's global agenda.

Haass' claim that it is not as far-fetched as it might appear for American leaders to build a global consensus about cooperation, and his faith that the great powers have it within their capacity to cooperate in order to achieve greater prosperity and build a firmer foundation for peace, is supported by recent experiences. The best illustration of states' capacity to cooperate is provided by the collaborative links that sovereign states in Europe after World War II purposefully built to pool their sovereignty and create a security community in which the prospects of war have disappeared. This successful regional experience illuminates the means and methods by which collaboration among states can supercede discord and curtail attempts to settle disputes by use of armed force.

The remarkable progress evident in inter-European cooperation and integration did not occur steadily or smoothly. Advances on the path to integration were often followed by reversals and periods without movement. However, the current phase began to accelerate when, in 1985, the European Community (EC) adopted the Single European Act. This treaty sought boldly to jump start momentum for the integration of the twelve Western European countries then comprising the EC. The target date then set for the reduction of a single continent-wide European common market was 1992; in 1999 integration moved beyond that goal when the European Union began to use the single "euro" currency and built a series of increasingly powerful European institutions to more effectively manage "Euroland" and its relations with the rest of the world.

In our next reading selection, "Building Peace in Pieces: The Promise of European Unity," Donald J. Puchala examines the expectations that led, step-by-step in a piecemeal integrative process, to the achievement of this goal and, since then, to progress that culminated in the ability of the European Union (EU) to take a bold step toward the political and economic unification of most of the European continent. Necessarily the process of creating a single common market and currency and enlarging the EU's membership involves political decisions designed to remove economic and political barriers among as many as twenty-six European sovereign states in the early twenty-first century. That integrative process will continue if European unity succeeds in the EU's goal to develop a common foreign and defense policy, as envisioned by the 1999 plans to create a European military that is not dependent on NATO under U.S. leadership. Achieving a truly "United States of Europe" will require rather extraordinary commitments of political will and economic resources on the part of EU countries.

The encouraging advance of integration in Europe inspires hope for international cooperation through institution building, but the barriers to deeper unification serve as a reminder of just how difficult it is to engineer sustained integrative progress that is both deeper institutionally and broader geographically. What a unified and enlarged European Union ultimately portends economically and politically for the rest of the world may, however, be the most important, if the most elusive, question.

The fact that throughout the world turmoil and violence plague many regions—and countries within them—provides a sobering antidote to those who optimistically expect permanent peace to be at hand and progress through international cooperation to expand. The European Union may be an exception to the global pattern, because within many countries domestic stability and prosperity are absent. The prevalence of conflict and the means of containing it are the subjects of our next reading selection. In "Managing Conflict in Ethnically Divided Societies: A New Regime Emerges in the 1990s," Ted Robert Gurr puts into perspective the most threatening source of tension in the world today: the rise of "ethnopolitical conflicts" and the violence that civil wars *within* states are inciting, and what steps have been taken to manage and settle these explosive internal wars within countries divided by many, often hostile, ethnic groups.

Ethnic tensions and secession revolts by oppressed minority nationalities have reached epidemic proportions. They now constitute by far the major cause of death and the greatest threat to international order in the world. As a result, the challenge of resolving conflicts within multi-ethnic societies has become perhaps *the* most critical issue on the agenda facing the international community. Based on a survey and comparison of 275 politically active communal groups undertaken in his *Minorities at Risk* project, Gurr identifies the major trends in ethnic wars throughout the globe, the controversial questions about this issue, and recent changes in the ability to reach accommodations—changes that have produced a "pronounced decline in the onset of new ethnic wars and a shift in many ongoing wars from fighting to negotiation." Thus, Gurr heightens awareness of the magnitude of the challenge and points to the ethical and legal dilemmas confronting the global community in its quest to protect minority populations who are now the principal victims of flagrant human rights violations. He concludes with an informed account of how the global community is seeking to cope with this serious threat to international security.

The zone of turmoil in which most civil rebellions and ethnopolitical conflicts occur is located primarily in the less-developed countries of the Third World (although many states in the advanced industrialized countries are also affected by the challenge of accommodating peacefully the demands of indigenous peoples and ethnic groups for a greater voice in national governance). It is in the so-called "Global South" where poverty, persecution, and the flight of refugees from their homelands are most pronounced that the issue has reached crisis proportions. For this reason, how the world's wealthy countries interact with impoverished and unstable states in the Southern Hemisphere will be a decisive influence on whether order or disorder prevail there in the future. Richard Falk examines the future of rich-poor relations from the vantage point of the latter in "The New Interventionism and The Third World." Falk provides a searching overview of the threats posed by the chronic instability of many collapsing Third World countries, and the options available to the prosperous great powers of the Global North. What, if anything, should the great powers do for humanitarian purposes when innocent victims daily confront human rights persecution, indescribable human suffering, and even genocide practiced by corrupt and ruthless Third World governments? Should the powerful intervene with military force to prevent humanitarian catastrophes? Does the traditional legal prohibition against outside interference in the internal affairs of a sovereign state mean that the great powers are powerless and paralyzed, because traditionally international law proclaimed the right for governments to act as they wish within their borders? These are explosive questions on the global agenda today. Falk confronts the dilemma head on, and dissects the obstacles of preventing ethnic cleansing and other crimes against humanity in the turbulent failing states of the Third World, as well as the opportunities and moral imperative for multilateral institutions like the United Nations to intervene when principles of human rights and compassion justify intervention on behalf of human security.

The barriers to intervention for moral purpose are high, but not as insurmountable as many believe, Falk argues, because the doctrine of state sovereignty is eroding under the pressures of globalization. Still, there remains stiff support for the classical concept of the sacred sanctity of state sovereignty, especially in the Third World. The end of the Cold War has had cataclysmic consequences for the poorest Global South countries whose leaders claim that the Global North now regards the Third World not as allies or equals but as objects of antipathy to be manipulated. Intervention thus is a key issue on the North-South agenda today, because in the less-developed Global South the feeling is widespread that it is under siege by the rest of the international community seeking to meddle in the Global South's affairs. By framing the predicaments, problems, and possible policy postures dividing the Global North and Global South, Falk advises that negotiations and compromise be guided by a higher concern for what doctrine of intervention will best protect human security.

Relations between unequal countries comprise but one important dimension of world politics. Another involves the transnational factors that do not define themselves in terms of territorial borders and that influence the global climate writ large. Of these, cultural variables often exert considerable weight, especially when cultures collide.

Throughout the world's history, when distinct cultures have come into contact, the collisions have ignited a combination of communication, cooperation, and conflict. At times, such cultural contact has produced a healthy respect for diversity, as the members of each interacting cultural tradition have learned from each other. On many other occasions, familiarity has bred contempt. When followers have embraced the ethnocentric view that their own group's values are inherently superior, feuds and face-offs have prevailed.

Today, as the ideological contest between communism and capitalism has disappeared, ancient cultural cleavages and hatreds have reappeared. Tribalism, religious fanaticism, and hypernational ethnicity are again rampant. The nasty trends toward violent assaults on immigrants and the rise of racial violence cast an ugly shadow across the world. Thus far the consequences have been lethal. Secessionist revolts and the attempt by threatened governments to subdue them through state-sponsored terrorism and violence are taking the lives of millions of people. "Ethnic cleansing" often has accompanied ethno-cultural conflicts, with the intent being to destroy unprotected subgroups rather than to pursue accommodation and assimilation. Even genocide has resurfaced.

In "The Coming Clash of Civilizations: Or, the West Against the Rest," Samuel P. Huntington argues that world politics is entering a new era, in which cultural conflict will be the fundamental problem. Because cultural conflict derives from cultural divisions, it is neither primarily ideological nor economic. But it will "dominate global politics," according to Huntington, because cultural hostility between civilizations is deeply entrenched. As "the world is becoming smaller," increased globalization through the technological revolution in communications has intensified "civilization consciousness" and the psychological identities that give much of the world meaning. In particular, Huntington predicts that because "the West is at a peak of its power" and engaged in an effort to promote worldwide its values of liberalism and democracy, the hostile resistance of others is likely to grow increasingly intense. Huntington foresees the cultural conflict "along the fault line between Western and Islamic civilizations" as the most likely source of discord in the next millennium. The challenge, he maintains, is learning how to transcend this centuries-old antagonism.

Huntington's prophecies and warnings are controversial. However, even his most skeptical critics are in agreement with him that *values,* and contests between competing sets of values, are a primary catalyst motivating people, states, international organizations, global cultures, and civilizations. Values are potent determinants of behavior. At the global level, the prevailing consensus about particular values is revealed by the kinds of standards the global community sets about what principles it regards as worthy of respect. Human rights provide a prime example of how a particular principle gains acceptance and, by so enjoying widespread support throughout international society, transforms patterns of behavior within and between countries across the globe.

In "Human Rights: From Low to High Politics in International Relations," David P. Forsythe documents the growing importance of human rights on the global agenda, as well as the continuing debates that are dominating discussion about core values and controversies in this issue area. In redefining global standards, a major issue of contention concerns the tension between universal norms of human rights and regional and cultural traditions. Forsythe shows that this struggle—about how principles that aim to apply everywhere to everyone should be balanced against human rights principles that are meant to be relative to particular groups, religions, or cultures—is at the center of debate about the legitimacy of using forceful intervention and diplomacy to defend particular conceptions of human rights. The difficulty of reconciling clashing values and standards regarding human rights is also analyzed in this essay's penetrating discussion of the continuing controversies about whether punitive approaches to the violation of human rights are more, or less, effective than are supportive attempts at "constructive engagement" that reward efforts to uphold human rights standards. Human rights—how they are defined and how they are protected and promoted—are thus politicized; they have become "high politics" because states are actively struggling to assure that their particular version of what values should define human rights standards gain acceptance in the international community.

Assessments such as those of Gurr, Falk, Huntington, and Forsythe suggest that people's identity—their sentiments of loyalty and sense of membership in a particular group—is an important determinant of their preferences and behavior. Another key influence toward discord or collaboration is *institutional*—the ways groups organize themselves for political action. Throughout the past three hundred fifty years, of course, the predominant institution or actor on the international stage has been the independent territorial state, not ethno-national groups, civilizations, or religions. But in the first years of the twenty-first century, it has become conventional to proclaim that the sovereign nation-state created as a legal entity by the Peace of Westphalia in 1648 is losing its power and legitimacy in the eyes of many people, and that other actors are now competing for people's affiliation because those non-state actors give many people their primary identity. The prospects of "vanishing borders" and the erosion of the sovereign authority of the nation-state thus presents to the world an unfamiliar issue: whether nation-states, designed to separate countries and control conflict between them, are dying, and, if so, whether the demise of this institutional pillar of the international system will spawn a new era of chaos and disorder.

The purpose of Harvey Starr's essay, "The Institutional Maintenance of Twenty-First Century World Order" is to confront the issues surrounding the contemporary debate about the survivability of the nation-state, popular speculations about alternatives to it, and the probable prospects for both discord and collaboration in twenty-first century world affairs. Starr approaches the leading questions about the institutional foundations of the global environment from the perspective of the world leaders facing the daunting task of making decisions about the adaptations required by a changing global system.

Seeing the world in a period of transition from the Westphalian system of independent sovereign nation-states to uncharted waters in the new millennium, Starr emphasizes the extent to which future world order will depend on the willingness and capacity of leaders to design a new institutional structure to manage a world that has become globalized and interdependent. Starr first reviews rival theories about the preconditions for global order, interpreted in light of existing evidence regarding how foreign policy choices incorporate a response to both the opportunity and willingness of the agents making policy decisions regarding adaptations to changing global circumstances. His essay then moves beyond theory to policy, and stresses the need "to analyze, study, and understand" the uncertain new global environment's characteristics in order to gauge if and how states and other actors will create new institutions and rules to peacefully manage global change. This essay identifies some of the prominent obstacles to the cooperative regulation of global disorder, such as, under conditions of anarchy, the existence of many "prisoners' dilemma" relationships between actors whose interdependence creates an inherent tension between individual and group interests and generates conflict. Looking at the future, Starr concludes by warning that the disintegration of "international society" could occur in the absence of visionary leadership to forge a new institutional architecture for twenty-first century world politics. "Without an underlying consensus about values, there would be an increasing potential of a twenty-first century collapse of order," he predicts, adding that "failure to adapt can lead to breakdown, violence, and disorder."

Another dimension to the debate about the impact of institutions on international discord and collaboration concerns the influence of the *types* of governments that states create to make decisions about domestic and foreign policy. One of the core assumptions of liberal international relations theory is that the types of regimes or institutional arrangements for governance *within* nation-states are an important determinant of their foreign behavior. That theoretical tradition also is predicated on the belief that the growth of liberal democracy exerts a medicinal and stabilizing impact on global politics. Since the dawn of history, reformers have searched for the path by which peaceful coexistence between contentious actors might be achieved. Until recently, however, few students of international conflict (especially those schooled in the realist theoretical tradition) paid serious attention to the contribution that democracy and other types of institutions might make to the peaceful management of international disputes. This has changed dramatically since 1989 when a new wave of democratization took root at precisely the moment in history when the Cold War conflict began to thaw. For the first time in history, a majority of countries in the world were democratically ruled.

In response to this sea change, researchers and policymakers alike began to explore the proposition advanced by classic liberal theory that democracy and international organization could tie the world in an interdependent global community and could serve as an antidote to warfare. The pacifying influence of democratic institutions inspires faith in this liberal approach to peace. Much evidence supports the belief that democracies are very unlikely to fight wars with each other. Whereas autocracies have historically been more expansionist and, in turn, more war prone, democracies in contrast have been steadfastly pacifistic in their relations with one another. In addition, democratic states are not only constrained in their warfare but also are prone to form overwhelming counter-coalitions against expansionist autocracies. Because democracies frequently police territorial expansionism through concerted cooperation to maintain the status quo, democracies have been more likely to win wars against aggressive tyrannies. This augurs well for neoliberal theorists' hope that a world of many democratic states will become a peaceful world.

Despite the optimism suggested by democratic peace theory, it is apparent that armed conflict remains pervasive in many failing states throughout the world, even in a post-Cold War era populated by many fledgling democratic states. As we look to the future, we must ask: Will the enlarged community of liberal democratic states approach the issues they face on the global agenda in a collaborative manner? Or will conflict become more common? It is to this question that Bruce Russett brings insight in his informed and provocative interpretative essay. Using the primary structural feature of the international system as his point of reference—namely, that world politics takes place in anarchy, without supranational regulation, Russett shows in "How Democracy, Interdependence, and International Organizations Create a System for Peace" that cooperation *can* prevail even under conditions where it might appear most unlikely. In helping us to understand the success of attempts at cooperation in both military-security relations and political-economic relations, Russett highlights the ways in which democratic institutions, the growth of interdependence, and the influence of international organizations have contributed to the development and maintenance of cooperation. Whether discord or collaboration will be greater or lesser ingredients in the future of world politics *will* be influenced considerably, Russett argues, by the extent to which states organize themselves to make foreign policy decisions through democratic processes and procedures which give people a voice in their government's national security policies and limit the freedom of rulers to wage war. The spread of democratic governance, in combination with the rising tide of economic interdependence through free global trade and investment and the expanding clout of international institutions, he concludes, can reduce the frequency of war and increase the prospects for international cooperation, despite the continuous reality of anarchy and discord.

How states are likely to respond to the challenge of managing global discord and promoting collaboration is likely influenced not only by the kinds of institutions and governments that nation-states create, but also by the kind of norms the international legal system supports. In the concluding reading selection of Part Two of *The Global Agenda,* "The Reality and Relevance of International Law in the Twenty-First Century," Christopher C. Joyner examines a wide spectrum of viewpoints regarding the functions of international law in world affairs. He concludes that despite its limitations (many of which are exaggerated by those uninformed about its principles and procedures), international law succeeds in doing what states ask of it. Not the least of its functions is facilitating the maintenance of the order, stability, and predictability that states prize. Joyner also predicts that international law's contribution to world order will grow, and that its impact will continue to expand.

As the twenty-first century unfolds, we can gain intellectual leverage by comparing the issues and theoretical perspectives described by the essays in Part Two. Although they differ in coverage and conclusions, together they provide a basis for understanding the roots of discord and the foundations of collaboration in international affairs. They should be read with an eye to studying not just military-security issues, but also political-economic issues in the realm of global material well-being. We encourage the reader to apply the concepts and lessons introduced in the essays in Part Two to both categories, in order to better interpret the problems on the global agenda.

# 11

# MODELS OF INTERNATIONAL RELATIONS: REALIST AND NEOLIBERAL PERSPECTIVES ON CONFLICT AND COOPERATION

Ole R. Holsti

**Ole R. Holsti describes two models that have been developed to describe and explain different properties of discordant and accommodative relations in world politics: classical and modern "realism" and the so-called neoliberal elaboration of traditional liberal theories. Holsti is George V. Allen Professor of International Affairs at Duke University and has served as a President of the International Studies Association. He is the author of *Public Opinion and American Foreign Policy* (1996), and an editor of *The Encyclopedia of American Foreign Relations* (1997).**

The question of how best to understand international relations has been debated since the advent of the international system. This debate between proponents of alternative theories has customarily grown especially intense in times of profound turmoil and change.

In the twentieth century, the cataclysm of World War I resurfaced and intensified the dialogue between liberals, such as Woodrow Wilson, who sought to create a new world order anchored in the League of Nations and realists, exemplified by Georges Clemenceau, who sought to use more traditional means to ensure their countries' security. World War II renewed that debate, but the events leading up to that conflict and the Cold War that emerged almost immediately after the guns had stopped firing in 1945 seemed to provide ample evidence to tip the balance strongly in favor of the realist vision of international relation. In the meantime, the growth of Soviet power, combined with the disintegration of the great colonial empires that gave rise to the emergence of some one hundred newly independent countries, gave prominence to still another perspective on world affairs, most variants of which drew to some extent upon the writing of Marx and Lenin.

More recent events, including the disintegration of the Soviet Union, the end of the Cold War, the reemergence of inter- and intranational ethnic conflicts that had been suppressed during the Cold War, the Persian Gulf War, the continuing economic integration of Europe, the severe economic problems that have gripped Japan, as well as several of the once fast-growing "Asian tigers" and most of Africa, and the NATO bombing campaign against Yugoslavia, have stimulated new debates about the theories of the international relations that can best contribute to understanding the emerging issues on the global agenda of the late twentieth century. This essay describes two prominent schools of thought on which contemporary theoretical inquiry presently centers. Although different, they speak to each other and place primary explanatory emphasis on features of the international system. These are the variants of realism and the newly revived liberal theories that challenge one or more of the core premises of both classical and modern realism.

Because "classical realism" is the most venerable and persisting model of international relations, it provides a good starting point and baseline for comparison with competing models. Following a discussion of classical realism, an examination of "modern realism" or "neorealism" identifies the continuities and differences between the two approaches. The essay then turns to an examination of the premises underlying neoliberal theories.

## REALISM: CLASSICAL, MODERN, AND ITS NEOREALIST EXTENSION

Robert Gilpin[1] may have been engaging in hyperbole when he questioned whether our understanding of international relations has advanced significantly since Thucydides, but one must acknowledge that the latter's analysis of the Peloponnesian War includes concepts that are not foreign to contemporary students of balance-of-power politics. There have always been Americans such as Alexander Hamilton who viewed international relations from a realist perspective, but its contemporary intellectual roots are largely European. Three important figures probably had the greatest impact on American scholarship: the historian E. H. Carr, the geographer Nicholas Spykman, and the political theorist Hans J. Morgenthau.[2] Other Europeans who have contributed significantly to re-

---

[1] Robert Gilpin, *War and Change in World Politics* (Cambridge: Cambridge University Press, 1981).

[2] E. H. Carr, *Twenty Years Crisis* (London: Macmillan, 1939); Nicholas Spykman, *America's Strategy in World Politics* (New York: Harcourt, Brace, 1942); and Hans Morgenthau, *Politics Among Nations*, 5th ed. (New York: Knopf, 1973).

alist thought include John Herz (1959), Raymond Aron (1966), Hedley Bull (1977), and Martin Wight (1973), while notable Americans of this school include scholars Arnold Wolfers (1962) and Norman Graebner (1984), as well as diplomat George F. Kennan (1951, 1985–86), journalist Walter Lippmann (1943), and theologian Reinhold Niebuhr (1945).[3]

## Classical Realism

Although classical realists do not constitute a homogeneous school—any more than do proponents of any of the other theories discussed in this essay—most of them share at least five core premises about international relations. To begin with, they consider the central questions to be the causes of war and the conditions of peace. They also regard the structure of the system as a necessary if not always sufficient explanation for many aspects of international relations. According to classical realists, "structural anarchy" or the absence of a central authority to settle disputes, is the essential feature of the contemporary system, and it gives rise to the "security dilemma:" in a self-help system one nation's search for security often leaves its current and potential adversaries insecure; any nation that strives for absolute security leaves all others in the system absolutely insecure, and the search for security can provide a powerful incentive for arms races and other types of hostile interactions. Consequently, the question of *relative* capabilities is a crucial factor. Efforts to deal with this central element of the international system constitute the driving force behind the relations of units within the system; those that fail to cope will not survive. Thus, unlike "idealists" or "liberals," classical realists view conflict as a natural state of affairs rather than a consequence that can be attributed to historical circumstances, evil leaders, flawed sociopolitical systems, or inadequate international understanding and education.

A third premise that unites classical realists is their focus on geographically based groups as the central actors in the international system. During other periods the primary entities may have been city-states or empires, but at least since the Treaties of Westphalia (1648), nation-states have been the dominant units. Classical realists also agree that state behavior is rational. The assumption

---

[3] John Herz, *International Politics in the Atomic Age* (New York: Columbia University Press, 1959); Raymond Aron, *Peace and War* (Garden City, N.Y.: Doubleday, 1966); Hedley Bull, *The Anarchical Society: A Study of Order in World Politics* (London: Macmillan, 1977); Martin Wight, "The Balance of Power and International Order," in Alan James, ed., *The Bases of International Order* (London: Oxford University Press, 1973); Arnold Wolfers, *Discord and Collaboration* (Baltimore: Johns Hopkins University Press, 1962); Norman A. Graebner, *America as a World Power: A Realist Appraisal from Wilson to Reagan* (Wilmington, Del.: Scholarly Resources, 1984); George F. Kennan, *American Diplomacy: 1900–1950* (Chicago: University of Chicago Press, 1951): Walter Lippmann, *U.S. Foreign Policy: Shield of the Republic* (Boston: Little, Brown, 1943); and Reinhold Niebuhr, *The Children of Light and the Children of Darkness* (New York: Scribner, 1945). At the age of 95, Kennan continues to be among the most articulate proponents of classical realism. For example, see Kennan, "Morality and Foreign Policy," *Foreign Affairs* 64 (1985–86), pp. 205–18.

behind this fourth premise is that states are guided by the logic of the "national interest," usually defined in terms of survival, security, power, and relative capabilities. To Morgenthau, for example, "rational foreign policy minimizes risks and maximizes benefits."[4] Although the national interest may vary according to specific circumstances, the similarity of motives among nations permits the analyst to reconstruct the logic of policymakers in their pursuit of national interests—what Morgenthau called the "rational hypothesis"—and to avoid the fallacies of "concern with motives and concern with ideological preferences."

Finally, the nation-state can also be conceptualized as a *unitary* actor. Because the central problems for states are starkly defined by the nature of the international system, their actions are primarily a response to external rather than domestic political forces. At best, the latter provide very weak explanations for external policy. According to Stephen Krasner, for example, the state "can be treated as an autonomous actor pursuing goals associated with power and the general interest of the society."[5] However, classical realists sometimes use domestic politics, especially the alleged deficiencies of public opinion, to explain deviations from rational policies.

Realism has been the dominant model of international relations during recent decades, perhaps in part because it seemed to provide a useful framework for understanding the collapse of the post–World War I international order in the face of serial aggressions in the Far East and Europe, World War II, and the Cold War. Nevertheless, the classical versions articulated by Morgenthau and others have received a good deal of critical scrutiny. The critics have included scholars who accept the basic premises of realism but who found that in at least four important respects these theories lacked sufficient precision and rigor.

Classical realism has usually been grounded in a pessimistic theory of human nature, either a theological version (e.g., St. Augustine and Reinhold Niebuhr) or a secular one (e.g., Machiavelli, Hobbes, and Morgenthau). Egoism and self-interested behavior are not limited to a few evil or misguided leaders, as the idealists would have it, but are basic to *homo politicus* and thus are at the core of a realist theory. But because human nature, if it means anything, is a constant rather than a variable, it is an unsatisfactory explanation for the full range of international relations. If human nature explains war and conflict, what accounts for peace and cooperation? In order to avoid this problem, most modern realists have turned their attention from human nature to the structure of the international system to explain state behavior.

In addition, critics have noted a lack of precision and even contradictions in the way classical realists use such concepts as "power," "national interest," and "balance of power." They also see possible contradictions between the central

---

[4] Morgenthau, *Politics Among Nations*, pp. 3, 5.
[5] Stephen Krasner, *Defending the National Interest* (Princeton, N.J.: Princeton University Press, 1978), p 33.

descriptive and prescriptive elements of classical realism. On the one hand, as Hans Morgenthau put it, nations and their leaders "think and act in terms of interests defined as power,"[6] but on the other, diplomats are urged to exercise prudence and self-restraint, as well as to recognize the legitimate interests of other nations. Obviously, then, power plays a central role in classical realism. But the correlation between the relative power balance and political outcomes is often less than compelling, suggesting the need to enrich analyses with other variables. Moreover, the distinction between "power as capabilities" and "usable options" is especially important in the nuclear age, as the United States discovered in Vietnam and the Soviets learned in Afghanistan.

### Modern Realism

While classical realists have typically looked to history, philosophy, and political science for insights and evidence, the search for greater precision has led many modern realists to look elsewhere for appropriate models, analogies, metaphors, and insights. The discipline of choice is often economics, from which modern realists have borrowed such tools and concepts as rational choice, expected utility, theories of firms and markets, bargaining theory, and game theory. Contrary to the assertion of some critics, however, modern realists *share* rather than reject the core premises of their classical predecessors.

The quest for precision has yielded a rich harvest of theories and models, and a somewhat less bountiful crop of supporting empirical applications. Drawing in part on game theory, Morton Kaplan described several types of international systems—for example, balance of power, loose bipolar, tight bipolar, universal, hierarchical, and a unit-veto system in which any action requires the unanimous approval of all its members. He then outlined the essential rules that constitute these systems. For example, the rules for a balance-of-power system are "(1) increase capabilities, but negotiate rather than fight; (2) fight rather than fail to increase capabilities; (3) stop fighting rather than eliminate an essential actor; (4) oppose any coalition or single actor that tends to assume a position of predominance within the system; (5) constrain actors who subscribe to supranational organizational principles; and (6) permit defeated or constrained essential actors to re-enter the system."[7]

### Neorealism

Kenneth Waltz's *Theory of International Politics,*[8] the most prominent effort to develop a rigorous and parsimonious model of "neorealist" or "structural"

---

[6] Morgenthau, *Politics Among Nations,* p. 5.
[7] Morton Kaplan, *System and Process in International Politics* (New York: Wiley, 1957), p. 23.
[8] Kenneth W. Waltz, *Theory of International Politics* (Reading, Mass.: Addison-Wesley, 1979).

realism, has tended to define the terms of recent theoretical debates. It follows and builds upon another enormously influential book in which Waltz developed the *Rousseaunian* position that a theory of war must include the system level (the "third image") and not just first (theories of human nature) or second (state attributes) images.[9] Why war? Because there is nothing in the system to prevent it.

*Theory of International Politics* is grounded in analogies from microeconomics: international politics and foreign policy are analogous to markets and firms. Oligopoly theory is used to illuminate the dynamics of interdependent choice in a self-help anarchical system. Waltz explicitly limits his attention to a structural theory of international systems, eschewing the task of linking it to a theory of foreign policy.[10] Indeed, he doubts that the two can be joined in a single theory and is highly critical of many system-level analysts including Morton Kaplan, Stanley Hoffmann, Richard Rosecrance, Karl Deutsch, J. David Singer, and others, charging them with various errors, including "reductionism," that is, defining the system in terms of the attributes or interactions of the units.

In order to avoid reductionism and to gain rigor and parsimony, Waltz erects his theory on the foundations of three core propositions that define the structure of the international system. The first concentrates on the principles by which the system is ordered. The contemporary system is anarchic and decentralized rather than hierarchical; although they differ in many respects, each unit (state) is formally equal. Because Waltz strives for a universal theory that is not limited to any era, he uses the term "unit" to refer to the constituent members of the system; in the contemporary system these are states, but in order to reflect Waltz's intent more faithfully, the term "unit" is used here. A second defining proposition is the character of the units. An anarchic system is composed of similar sovereign units, and therefore the functions that they perform are also similar rather than different; for example, all have the task of providing for their own security. In contrast, a hierarchical system would be characterized by some type of division of labor, as is the case in domestic politics. Finally, there is the distribution of capabilities among units in the system. Although capabilities are a unit-level attribute, the distribution of capabilities is a system-level concept.

A change in any of these elements constitutes a change in system structure. The first element of structure as defined by Waltz is a quasi-constant because the ordering principle rarely changes, and the second element drops out of the analysis because the functions of units are similar as long as the system remains anarchic. Thus, the last of the three attributes, the distribution of capabilities, plays the central role in Waltz's model.

---

[9] Kenneth W. Waltz, *Man, the State, and War* (New York: Columbia University Press, 1959).

[10] For a debate on whether neorealism may be extended to cover foreign policies as well as international politics, see Colin Elman, "Horses for Courses: Why *Not* Neorealist Theories of Foreign Policy," *Security Studies* 6 (Autumn 1996), pp. 7–53; and a rejoinder by Waltz, "International Politics is Not Foreign Policy," in the same issue of *Security Studies,* pp. 54–57.

Waltz uses his theory to deduce the central characteristics of international relations. These include some nonobvious propositions about the contemporary international system. For example, with respect to system stability (defined as maintenance of its anarchic character and no consequential variation in the number of major actors), he concludes that because the Cold War's bipolar system reduced uncertainty, it was more stable than alternative structures. Furthermore, he contends that because interdependence has declined rather than increased during the twentieth century, this trend has actually contributed to stability, and he argues that the proliferation of nuclear weapons may contribute to, rather than erode, system stability.[11]

Unlike some system-level models, Waltz's effort to bring rigor and parsimony to realism has stimulated a good deal of further research, but it has not escaped controversy and criticism.[12] Leaving aside highly charged polemics—for example, that Waltz and his supporters are guilty of engaging in a "totalitarian project of global proportions"[13]—most of the vigorous debate has centered on four alleged deficiencies relating to interests and preferences, system change, misallocation of variables between the system and unit levels, and an inability to explain outcomes.

Specifically, a sparse structural approach suffers from an inability to identify adequately the nature and sources of interests and preferences because these are unlikely to derive solely from the structure of the system. Ideology or domestic considerations may often be at least as important. Consequently, the model is also unable to specify how interests and preferences may change. The three defining characteristics of system structure are too general, moreover, and thus they are not sufficiently sensitive to specify the sources and dynamics of system change. The critics buttress their claim that the model is too static by pointing to Waltz's assertion that there has been only a single structural change in the international system during the past three centuries.

Another drawback is the restrictive definition of system properties, which leads to the charge that Waltz misplaces and therefore neglects elements of international relations that properly belong at the system level. Critics have focused on

---

[11] Kenneth W. Waltz, "The Myth of National Interdependence," in Charles P. Kindleberger, ed., *The International Corporation* (Cambridge Mass.: M.I.T. Press, 1970), and "The Spread of Nuclear Weapons: More May Be Better," *Adelphi Papers,* no. 171 (1981).

[12] See especially Robert Keohane, ed., *Neorealism and Its Critics* (New York: Columbia University Press. 1986); David A. Baldwin, ed., *Neorealism and Neoliberalism: The Contemporary Debate* (New York: Columbia University Press, 1993); Charles W. Kegley, Jr., ed., *Controversies in International Relations Theory: Realism and the Neoliberal Challenge* (New York: St. Martin's Press, 1995); John A. Vasquez, *The Power of Power Politics* (New Brunswick, N.J.: Rutgers University Press, 1988); and Yale H. Ferguson and Richard W. Mansbach, *The Elusive Quest: Theory and International Politics* (Columbia: University of South Carolina Press, 1988). A useful post-Cold War appraisal of realism may be found in "Realism: Restatements and Renewal," *Security Studies* 5 (Spring 1996) pp. ix–xx, 3–423.

[13] Richard K. Ashley, "The Poverty of Neo-Realism," *International Organization* 38 (1984), pp. 225–86.

his treatment of the destructiveness of nuclear weapons and interdependence. Waltz labels these as unit-level properties, whereas some of his critics assert that they are in fact attributes of the system.

Finally, the distribution of capabilities explains outcomes in international affairs only in the most general way, falling short of answering the questions that are of central interest to many analysts. For example, the distribution of power at the end of World War II would have enabled one to predict the rivalry that emerged between the United States and the Soviet Union (as de Tocqueville did more than a century earlier), but it would have been inadequate for explaining the pattern of relations between these two countries—the Cold War rather than withdrawal into isolationism by either or both, a division of the world into spheres of influence, or World War III. In order to do so, it is necessary to explore political processes *within* states—at minimum within the United States and the USSR—as well as *between* them.

Robert Gilpin shares with Waltz the core assumptions of modern realism, but his study, *War and Change in World Politics,* also attempts to cope with some of the criticism leveled at Waltz's theory by focusing on the dynamics of system change. Drawing upon both economic and sociological theory, his model is based on five core propositions.[14] The first is that the international system is stable—in a state of equilibrium—if no state believes that it is profitable to attempt to change it. Second, a state will attempt to change the status quo of the international system if the expected benefits outweigh the costs; that is, if there is an expected net gain for the revisionist state. Related to this is the proposition that a state will seek change through territorial, political, and economic expansion until the marginal costs of further change equal or exceed the marginal benefits. Moreover, when an equilibrium between the costs and benefits of further change and expansion is reached, the economic costs of maintaining the status quo (expenditures for military forces, support for allies, etc.) tend to rise faster than the resources needed to do so. An equilibrium exists when no powerful state believes that a change in the system would yield additional net benefits. Finally, if the resulting disequilibrium between the existing governance of the international system and the redistribution of power is not resolved, the system will be changed and a new equilibrium reflecting the distribution of relative capabilities will be established.

Unlike Waltz, Gilpin includes state-level processes in order to explain change. Differential economic growth rates among nations—a structural-systemic-level variable—play a vital role in his explanation for the rise and decline of great powers, but his model also includes propositions about the law of diminishing returns on investments, the impact of affluence on martial spirits and on the ratio of consumption to investment, and structural change in the economy. Table 11.1 summarizes some key elements of realism. It also contrasts them to

---

[14] Gilpin, *War and Change in World Politics,* pp. 10–11.

**TABLE 11.1**
TWO MODELS OF THE INTERNATIONAL SYSTEM

|  | Realism | Neoliberalism |
|---|---|---|
| Type of model | Classical: descriptive and normative<br>Modern: deductive | Descriptive and normative |
| Central problems | Causes of war<br>Conditions of peace | Broad agenda of political, social, economic, and environmental issues arising from gap between demands and resources |
| Conception of current international system | Structural anarchy | Global society<br>Complex interdependence (structure varies by issue-area) |
| Key actors | Geographically based units (tribes, city-states, nation-state, etc.) | Highly permeable nation-states *plus* a broad range of non-state actors, including IOs, IGOs, NGOs, and individuals |
| Central motivations | National interest<br>Security<br>Power | Human needs and wants (including security) |
| Loyalties | To geographically based groups (from tribes to nation-states) | Loyalties to nation-state declining to emerging global values and institutions that transcend those of the nation-state and/or to subnational groups. |
| Central processes | Search for security and survival | Aggregate effects of decisions by national and non-national actors<br>How units (not limited to nation-states) cope with a growing agenda of threats and opportunities arising from human wants |
| Likelihood of system transformation | Low (basic structural elements of system have revealed an ability to persist despite many other kinds of changes) | High in the direction of the model (owing to the rapid pace of technological change, etc.) |
| Source of theory, insights, and evidence | Politics<br>History<br>Economics (especially "modern" realists) | Broad range of social sciences<br>Natural and technological sciences |

a rival system-level model of international relations—the neoliberal model, to which we now turn our attention.

## NEOLIBERALISM

Just as there are variants of realism, there are several neoliberal theories, but this discussion focuses on two common denominators: they all challenge the first and third core propositions of realism identified earlier, asserting that inordinate attention to the war/peace issue and the nation-state renders it an increasingly anachronistic model of global relations.[15]

The agenda of critical confronting states has been vastly expanded during the twentieth century. Attention to the issues of war and peace is by no means misdirected according to proponents of a liberal perspective, but concerns for welfare, modernization, the environment, and the like are today no less potent sources of motivation and action. Indeed, many liberals define security in terms that are broader than the geopolitical-military spheres, and they emphasize the potential for cooperative relations among nations. Institution building to reduce uncertainty, information costs, and fears of perfidy; improved international education and communication to ameliorate fears and antagonisms based on misinformation and misperceptions; and the positive-sum possibilities of such activities as trade are but a few of the ways, according to liberals, by which nations may jointly gain and thus mitigate, if not eliminate, the harshest features of international relations emphasized by the realists. Finally, the diffusion of knowledge and technology, combined with the globalization of communications, has vastly increased popular expectations. The resulting demands have outstripped resources and the ability of existing institutions—notably the nation-state—to cope effectively with them. Interdependence arises from an inability of even the most powerful states to cope, or to do so unilaterally or at acceptable levels of cost and risk, with issues ranging from trade to AIDS and immigration to environmental threats.

Paralleling the widening agenda of critical issues is the expansion of actors whose behavior can have a significant impact beyond national boundaries;

15 Robert Keohane and Joseph S. Nye, Jr. *Power and Interdependence* (Boston: Little, Brown, 1977); Edward Morse, *Modernization and the Transformation of International Relations* (New York: Free Press, 1976); James N. Rosenau, *The Study of Global Interdependence* (London: F. Pinter, 1980) and *Turbulence in World Politics* (Princeton, N.J.: Princeton University Press, 1990); Richard Mansbach and John Vasquez, *In Search of Theory: A New Paradigm* (New York: Columbia University Press, 1981); and Andrew M. Scott, *The Dynamics of Interdependence* (Chapel Hill, N.C.: University of North Carolina Press, 1982). Two useful summaries of the common elements as well as variations among neoliberal theories may be found in Charles W. Kegley, Jr., ed., *Controversies in International Relations Theory: Realism and the Neoliberal Challenge* (New York: St. Martin's Press, 1995): Kegley, "The Neoliberal Challenge to Realist Theories of World Politics," pp. 1–14; and Mark W. Zacher and Richard A. Matthews, "Liberal International Theory: Common Threads, Divergent Strands," pp. 107–50.

indeed, the cumulative effects of their actions can have profound consequences for the international system. Thus, although nation-states continue to be important international actors, they possess a declining ability to control their own destinies. The aggregate effect of actions by multitudes of non-state actors can have potent effects that transcend political boundaries. These may include such powerful or highly visible non-state institutions as Exxon, the Organization of Petroleum Exporting Countries, or the Palestine Liberation Organization. On the other hand, the cumulative effects of decisions by less powerful or less visible actors may also have profound international consequences. For example, decisions by thousands of individuals, mutual funds, banks, pension funds, and other financial institutions to sell securities on 19 October 1987 not only resulted in an unprecedented "crash" on Wall Street but within hours its consequences were also felt throughout the entire global financial system. Governments might take such actions as loosening credit or even closing exchanges, but they were largely unable to contain the effects of the panic.

The widening agenda of critical issues, most of which lack a purely national solution, has also led to creation of new actors that transcend political boundaries, for example, international organizations, transnational organizations, nongovernmental organizations, multinational corporations, and the like. Thus, not only does an exclusive focus on the war/peace issue fail to capture the complexities of contemporary international life but it also blinds the analyst to the institutions, processes, and norms that permit cooperation and significantly mitigate some features of an anarchic system. In short, according to emerging new liberal perspectives, an adequate understanding of the proliferating issues in the evolving global system must recognize that no single model is likely to be sufficient for all issues, and that if it restricts attention to the manner in which states deal with traditional security concerns, it is more likely to obfuscate than clarify the realities of contemporary world affairs.

The liberal models have several important virtues. They recognize that international behavior and outcomes arise from a multiplicity of motives, not merely security, at least if security is defined solely in military or strategic terms. They also alert us to the fact that important international processes and conditions originate not only in the actions of nation-states but also in the aggregated behavior of other actors. These models not only enable the analyst to deal with a broader agenda of critical issues but, more importantly, they force one to contemplate a much richer menu of demands, processes, and outcomes than would be derived from power-centered realist models. Stated differently, liberal theories are more sensitive to the possibility that the politics of trade, currencies, immigration, health, the environment, and the like may significantly and systematically differ from those typically associated with security issues.

On the other hand, some liberal analysts underestimate the potency of nationalism and the durability of the nation-state. Three decades ago one of them wrote that "the nation is declining in its importance as a political unit to which allegiances are attached." [16] Objectively, nationalism may be an anachronism, but for better or worse, powerful loyalties are still attached to nation-states. The suggestion that because even some well-established countries have experienced independence movements among ethnic, cultural, or religious minorities, the sovereign territorial state may be in decline is not wholly persuasive. Indeed, that evidence perhaps points to precisely the opposite conclusion: in virtually every region of the world there are groups that seek to create or restore geographically based entities in which its members may enjoy the status and privileges associated with sovereign territorial statehood. Evidence from Poland to Palestine, Serbia to Sri Lanka, Estonia to Eritrea, Armenia to Afghanistan, Bosnia to Chechnya, Quebec to Kosovo and elsewhere seems to indicate that obituaries for nationalism may be somewhat premature.

The notion that such powerful non-national actors as major multinational corporations (MNCs) will soon transcend the nation-state seems equally premature. International drug rings do appear capable of dominating such states as Colombia and Panama. However, the pattern of outcomes in confrontations between MNCs and states, including cases involving major expropriations of corporate properties, indicates that even relatively weak nations are not always the hapless pawns of the MNCs. Case studies by Joseph Grieco and Gary Gereffi, among others, indicate that MNC-state relations yield a wide variety of outcomes. [17]

Underlying the liberal critique of realist models is that the latter are too wedded to the past and are thus incapable of dealing adequately with change. For the present, however, even if global dynamics arise from multiple sources (including non-state actors), the actions of nation-states and their agents would appear to remain the major sources of change in the international system.

## THE REALIST-LIBERAL DIALOGUE AND THE FUTURE

A renowned diplomatic historian has asserted that most theories of international relations flunked a critical test by failing to forecast the end of the Cold War. [18] The end of the Cold War has also led some theorists to look beyond the social sciences for appropriate metaphors and models, but these are beyond the scope

16 James N. Rosenau, "National Interest," *International Encyclopedia of the Social Sciences* (New York: Macmillan, 1968), pp. 34–40. See also Richard Rosecrance, *The Rise of the Trading State* (New York: Basic Books, 1986); John Herz, "The Rise and Demise of the Territorial State," *World Politics* 9 (1957), pp. 473–93 and "The Territorial State Revisited: Reflections on the Future of the Nation-State," *Polity* 1 (1968), pp. 12–34.

17 Joseph Grieco, *Between Dependence and Autonomy* (Berkeley, Calif.: University of California Press, 1984), and Gary Gereffi, *The Pharmaceutical Industry and Dependency in the Third World* (Princeton, N.J.: Princeton University Press, 1983).

18 John Lewis Gaddis, "International Relations Theory and the End of the Cold War," *International Security* 17 (1992–93), pp. 5–58.

of the present essay.[19] This conclusion speculates on the related question of how well the theories discussed above might help us understand conflict and cooperation in the post–Cold War world. Dramatic events since the late 1980s appear to have posed serious challenges for several theories, but one should be wary about writing premature obituaries for any of them. The importance of recent developments notwithstanding, one should avoid "naive (single case) falsification" of major theories. Further, in 2000, eleven short years after the Berlin Wall came down and only nine years after dissolution of the Soviet Union, some caution about declaring that major events and trends are irreversible seems warranted.

Liberal theories have recently regained popularity, especially in efforts to explain relations among the industrial democracies. Progress toward the economic unification of Europe, although not without detours and setbacks, would appear to provide significant support for the liberal view that, even in an anarchic world, major powers may find ways of cooperating and overcoming the constraint of the "relative gains" problem. Moreover, Woodrow Wilson's thesis that a world of democratic nations will be more peaceful has stood the test of time rather well, at least in the sense that democratic nations have not gone to war with each other.[20] Wilson's diagnosis that self-determination also supports peace may be correct in the abstract, but universal application of that principle is neither possible nor desirable, if only because it would result in immense bloodshed; the peaceful divorces of Norway and Sweden in 1905 and of the Czech Republic and Slovakia in 1992 are unfortunately not the norm.[21] Although it appears that economic interests have come to dominate nationalist, ethnic, or religious passions among the industrial democracies, the evidence is far less assuring in other areas, including parts of the former Soviet Union, Central Europe, the Middle East, South Asia, Africa, and elsewhere.

Recent events appear to have created an especially acute challenge to structural realism. Although structural realism provides a parsimonious and elegant theory, its deficiencies are likely to become more rather than less apparent in the post–Cold War world. Its weaknesses in dealing with questions of system change and in specifying policy preferences other than survival and security are likely to be magnified. Moreover, whereas classical realism espouses a number of

---

[19] For example, James N. Rosenau's core concept of "turbulence" is drawn from meteorology, and John Lewis Gaddis finds some compelling parallels between the contemporary international system and "tectonics," a concept drawn from geology. See James N. Rosenau, *Turbulence in World Politics: A Theory of Change and Continuity* (Princeton, N.J.: Princeton University Press, 1990); and John Lewis Gaddis, "Living in Candlestick Park," *Atlantic Monthly* (April 1999), pp. 65–74.

[20] Michael Doyle, "Kant, Liberal Legacies, and Foreign Affairs," *Philosophy and Public Affairs* 12 (1983), pp. 205–35, and "Liberalism and World Politics," *American Political Science Review* 80 (1986), pp. 1151–70. The Doyle articles have spawned a huge literature—far too extensive to summarize here—in which proponents and critics are aligned largely along liberal-realists lines.

[21] Although the concept of self-determination is generally associated with liberals, in the wake of civil wars within the former Yugoslavia, two prominent realists have suggested redrawing the map of the Balkans to reflect ethnic identities: John J. Mearsheimer and Stephen Van Evera, "Redraw the Map, Stop the Killing," *New York Times* (April 19, 1999), p. A27.

attractive prescriptive features (caution, humility, warnings against mistaking one's preferences for the moral laws of the universe), neorealism is an especially weak source of policy-relevant theory.[22] Indeed, some of the prescriptions put forward by neorealists seem reckless, such as the suggestion to let Germany join the nuclear club.[23] In addition to European economic cooperation, specific events that seem inexplicable by structural realism include Soviet acquiescence in the collapse of its empire and peaceful transformation of the system structure. The persistence of NATO, a decade after disappearance of the threat that gave rise to its creation in 1949, has also confounded realist expectations that it would not long survive the end of the Cold War. These developments are especially telling because structural realism is explicitly touted as a theory of major powers.[24] Although proponents of realism are not ready to concede that the end of the Cold War has raised some serious questions about its validity, even as distinguished a realist as Robert Tucker has characterized the structural version of realism as "more questionable than ever."[25]

More importantly, even though the international system remains anarchic, the possibility of war among major powers cannot wholly be dismissed, and proliferation may place nuclear weapons in the hands of leaders with little stake in maintaining the status quo; the constraints imposed by systemic imperatives on foreign policy choices are clearly eroding. National interests and even national security have increasingly come to be defined in ways that transcend the military/strategic concerns that are at the core of realist theory. Well before the disintegration of the Soviet Union, an Americans Talk Security survey in 1988 revealed that the perceived threat to national security from "Soviet aggression around the world" ranked in a seventh place tie with the "greenhouse effect" and well behind a number of post-Cold War, nonmilitary threats. Trade, drug trafficking, immigration, the environment, and AIDS are among the nonmilitary issues that regularly appear on lists of top national security threats as perceived by both mass public and elites.

The expanded agenda of national interests, combined with the trend toward greater democracy in many parts of the world, suggests that we are entering an era in which the balance between the relative potency of systemic and domestic forces in shaping and constraining foreign policies is moving toward the latter. Indeed, the frequency of internal wars that have become international

---

[22] Alexander L. George, *Bridging the Gap: Theory and Practice in Foreign Policy* (Washington: U.S. Institute of Peace, 1993).

[23] John Mearsheimer, "Back to the Future: Instability in Europe After the Cold War," *International Security* 15 (1990), pp. 5–56. Rejoinders by Stanley Hoffmann, Robert O. Keohane, Bruce M. Russett, and Thomas Risse-Kappen, as well as responses by Mearsheimer, may be found in the same journal (Fall 1990), pp. 191–99, and (Winter 1990/91), pp. 216–22.

[24] Waltz, *Theory of International Politics.*

[25] Robert W. Tucker, "Realism and the New Consensus," *National Interest* 30 (1992–93), pp. 33–36. See also Paul Schroeder, "Historical Reality vs. Neo-realist Theory," *International Security* 19 (1994), pp. 108–48.

conflicts—the list includes but is not limited to Somalia, Haiti, Bosnia, Rwanda, Congo and Yugoslavia—suggests that "failed states" may compete with international aggression as the major source of war.[26] Such issues as trade, immigration, and others can be expected to enhance the impact of domestic actors—including public opinion and ethnic, religious, economic, and perhaps even regional pressure groups—while reducing the ability of executives to dominate policy processes on the grounds, so frequently invoked during the Cold War, that the adept pursuit of national security requires secrecy, flexibility, and the ability to act with speed on the basis of classified information. In short, we are likely to see the increasing democratization of foreign policy in the post–Cold War era. And that brings us back to the point at which we started for the relationship between democracy and foreign policy is another of the issues on which realists and liberals are in sharp disagreement. Realists such as de Tocqueville, Morgenthau, Lippmann, Kennan, and many others share a profound skepticism about the impact of democratic political processes, and especially of public opinion, on the quality and continuity of foreign policy.[27] In contrast, liberals in the Kant-Wilson tradition maintain that more democratic foreign policy processes contribute to peace and stability in international politics. Thus, if domestic politics do in fact come to play an increasingly important role in shaping post–Cold War era foreign policies, that development will ensure continuation of the venerable debate between realists and liberals.

[26] Robert Kaplan, "The Coming Anarchy," *Atlantic Monthly* 273 (February 1994), pp. 44–76; K.J. Holsti, *The State, War, and the State of War* (Cambridge: Cambridge University Press, 1996); and Barbara F. Walter and Jack L. Snyder, eds., *Civil War, Insecurity, and Intervention* (New York: Columbia University Press, 1999). Donald L. Horowitz, *Ethnic Groups in Conflict* (Berkeley Calif.: University of California Press, 1985) is a classic study of ethnic conflict.

[27] Some recent studies have argued the contrary thesis that, in the aggregate, public opinion is in fact stable and sensible: Eugene R. Wittkopf, *Faces of Internationalism: Public Opinion and American Foreign Policy* (Durham, N.C.: Duke University Press, 1991); Benjamin I. Page and Robert Shapiro, *The Rational Public* (Chicago: University of Chicago Press, 1992); Miroslav Nincic, *Democracy and Foreign Policy: The Fallacy of Political Realism* (New York: Columbia University Press, 1992); and Ole R. Holsti, *Public Opinion and American Foreign Policy* (Ann Arbor Mich.: University of Michigan Press, 1996).

# 12

# MANAGING THE CHALLENGE OF GLOBALIZATION AND INSTITUTIONALIZING COOPERATION THROUGH GLOBAL GOVERNANCE

David Held and Anthony McGrew,
with David Goldblatt and Jonathan Perraton

The forces of change and continuity are creating unprecedented complexity in world affairs and new challenges to global order. Describing the accelerating pace of change across many dimensions of international affairs, this essay surveys the major diverging trends and underlying dynamics of globalization—in an interdependent world—that are altering the very texture of history and are simultaneously producing integration and disintegration, cooperation and conflict, order and disorder. Placing "globalization" into the contemporary context in order to assess the probable impact that this phenomenon will make, across its multiple dimensions, for the prospects for discord or collaboration in twenty-first century international politics, the essay focuses especially on the potential for strengthened global institutions to manage the major problems on the global agenda, such as the continuing danger of the diffusion of violence across borders in a borderless globalized environment. Held is Professor of Politics and Sociology at the Open University in the United Kingdom, and McGrew holds the position of Senior Lecturer in Government there; Goldblatt is Lecturer in Social Sciences at the Open University, and Perraton is Lecturer in Economics at Sheffield University. The authors have published together a comprehensive analysis about globalization in their recent book, *Global Transformations: Politics, Economics and Culture* (1999).

Although everybody talks about globalization, few people have a clear understanding of it. The "big idea" of the late twentieth century is in danger of turning into the cliché of our times. Can we give it precise meaning and content, or should globalization be consigned to the dustbin of history?

The reason there is so much talk about globalization is that everyone knows that something extraordinary is happening to our world. We can send e-mail across the planet in seconds; we hear that our jobs depend on economic decisions in far-off places; we enjoy films, food, and fashion from all over the world; we worry about an influx of drugs and how we can save the ozone layer. These growing global connections affect all aspects of our lives—but it is still not clear what globalization really means.

There has been a heated debate about whether globalization is occurring at all. The debate rages between those who claim that globalization marks the end of the nation-state and the death of politics and those who dismiss the globalization hype and say that we have seen it all before. This debate has continued for a decade, leading to ever more confusion. It is not that these positions are wholly mistaken. In fact, both capture elements of a complex reality. But it is the wrong debate to have when there is no common ground about what globalization is. Until we know what globalization actually means, we will not be able to understand how it affects our lives, our identities and our politics.

In this essay, we try to go beyond the rhetoric of entrenched positions and produce a richer account of what globalization is, how the world is changing, and what we can do about it. So what does globalization mean? We show that globalization is made up of the accumulation of links across the world's major regions and across many domains of activity. It is not a single process but involves four distinct types of change:

• It stretches social, political, and economic activities across political frontiers, regions, and continents.

• It intensifies our dependence on each other, as flows of trade, investment, finance, migration, and culture increase.

• It speeds up the world. New systems of transport and communication mean that ideas, goods, information, capital, and people move more quickly.

• It means that distant events have a deeper impact on our lives. Even the most local developments may come to have enormous global consequences. The boundaries between domestic matters and global affairs can become increasingly blurred.

In short, globalization is about the connections between different regions of the world—from the cultural to the criminal, the financial to the environmental—and the ways in which they change and increase overtime.

We show that globalization, in this sense, has been going on for centuries. But we also show that globalization today is genuinely different both in scale and in nature. It does not signal the end of the nation-state or the death of politics. But it does mean that politics is no longer, and can no longer be, based simply on nation-states. We cannot predict the future or know what the final outcome of globalization will be. But we can now define the central challenge of the global age—rethinking our values, institutions, and identities so that politics can remain an effective vehicle for human aspirations and needs.

First, we need to understand what is distinctive about globalization today. We can do this only by studying the forms it has taken throughout history in all areas of activity—the environment, the economy, politics, and culture. The thread that ties these things together is people, and so it is with the movements of people that we must start.

## PEOPLE ON THE MOVE

Globalization began with people traveling. For millennia, human beings have migrated—settling new lands, building empires or searching for work. Most migrations in history have not been global. But from the sixteenth century onwards, Europeans traveled the world, conquering the Americas and Oceania before making colonial incursions into Africa and Asia. The first great wave of modern migration was the transatlantic slave trade. Nine to twelve million people were shipped as slaves from Africa to the Americas by the mid-nineteenth century. But this was dwarfed by the extraordinary outpouring of Europe's poor to the New World from the mid-nineteenth century onwards. More than thirty million people moved in this way between 1880 and World War I.

Levels of global migration have fluctuated dramatically with political and economic conditions. During World War I, international migration plummeted. European migration stopped, beyond a few forced migrations like that of Armenians and Greeks from Turkey. North America closed its borders and created the first systematic immigration legislation in the modern era. But the bitter struggles and ethnic violence of World War II led to unprecedented levels of forced migrations, refugees, and asylum movements. Ethnic Germans fled the Soviet Union and Eastern Europe. Jews headed for Israel. Pakistan and India exchanged millions of people. And Koreans flooded south.

In the 1950s and 1960s, millions of people poured into Europe, attracted by the rebirth of Western European economies. After the oil shocks of the 1970s, politicians closed many of these migration programs. But they couldn't stop the foreign population and ethnic mix from continuing to grow. A combination of family reunions, unpoliceable borders, and sheer demand for labor have continued to drive migration from the European peripheries of Turkey and North Africa and from the distant outposts of old European empires in Asia and Africa. There has also been a takeoff in legal and illegal migration to the United States and Australasia, enormous flows to the oil-rich and labor-scarce Middle East, and new patterns of regional migration throughout the world.

Today, we are living with the consequences of centuries of migration and conquest. There is more ethnic diversity than ever before in states of the

Organization for Economic and Community Development (OECD), especially in Europe. The process can never be reversed, particularly when in countries like Sweden more than 10 percent of its population are foreign born. Moreover, the United States is experiencing levels of migration that are comparable to the great transatlantic push of the late nineteenth century. In the mid-1990s, this involved more than a million immigrants per year, mainly from Asia, Latin America, and Central America. And it is not just economic migration. There has also been an astronomical rise in asylum seeking, displaced persons, and refugees from wars as states are created and collapse in the developing world. More than half a million applicants for asylum were received per annum by OECD countries in the 1990s.

International attempts to regulate the flow of people have not succeeded. Some states are highly dependent on migrant labor; others find it difficult to win support for tracking illegal migrants. All states have to reassess what national citizenship is and what it means as an era of diversity transforms identities and cultures. The long history of migration is coming home to roost.

## THE FATE OF NATIONAL CULTURES

When people move, they take their cultures with them. So, the globalization of culture has a long history. The great world religions showed how ideas and beliefs can cross the continents and transform societies. No less important were the great premodern empires that, in the absence of direct military and political control, held their domains together through a common culture of the ruling classes. For long periods of human history, there have been only these global cultures and a vast array of fragmented local cultures. Little stood between the court and the village until the invention of nation-states in the eighteenth century created a powerful new cultural identity that lay between these two extremes.

This rise of nation-states and nationalist projects truncated the process of cultural globalization. Nation-states sought to control education, language, and systems of communication, like the post and the telephone. But as European empires became entrenched in the nineteenth century, new forms of cultural globalization emerged with innovations in transport and communications, notably regularized mechanical transport and the telegraph. These technological advances helped the West to expand and enabled the new ideas that emerged—especially science, liberalism, and socialism—to travel and transform the ruling cultures of almost every society on the planet.

Contemporary popular cultures have certainly not yet had a social impact to match this, but the sheer scale, intensity, speed, and volume of global cultural communications today is unsurpassed. The accelerating diffusion of radio, television, the Internet, and satellite and digital technologies has made instant communication possible. Many national controls over information have become ineffective. Through radio, film, television, and the Internet, people everywhere are exposed to the values of other cultures as never before. Nothing, not even the fact that we all speak different languages, can stop the flow of ideas and cultures. The English language is becoming so dominant that it provides a linguistic infrastructure as powerful as any technological system for transmitting ideas and cultures.

Beyond its scale, what is striking about today's cultural globalization is that it is driven by companies, not countries. Corporations have replaced states and theocracies as the central producers and distributors of cultural globalization. Private international institutions are not new but their mass impact is. News agencies and publishing houses in previous eras had a much more limited impact on local and national cultures than the consumer goods and cultural products of global corporations today.

Although the vast majority of these cultural products come from the United States, this is not a simple case of "cultural imperialism." One of the surprising features of our global age is how robust national and local cultures have proved to be. National institutions remain central to public life and national audiences constantly reinterpret foreign products in novel ways.

These new communication technologies threaten states that pursue rigid closed-door policies on information and culture. For example, China sought to restrict access to the Internet but found this extremely difficult to achieve. In addition, it is likely that the conduct of economic life everywhere will be transformed by the new technologies. The central question is the future impact of cultural flows on our sense of personal identity and national identity. Two competing forces are in evidence: the growth of multicultural politics almost everywhere and, in part as a reaction to this, the assertion of fundamentalist identities (religious, nationalist, and ethnic). Although the balance between these two forces remains highly uncertain, it is clear that only a more open, cosmopolitan outlook can ultimately accommodate itself to a more global era.

## THE TERRITORIAL STATE AND GLOBAL POLITICS

One thousand years ago, a modern political map of the world would have been incomprehensible. It is not just that much of the world was still to be "discovered." People simply did not think of political power as something divided by clear-cut boundaries and unambiguous color patches. But our contemporary maps do not just misrepresent the past. By suggesting that territorial areas contain indivisible, illimitable, and exclusive sovereign states, they may also prove a poor metaphor for the shape of the politics of the future.

Modern politics emerged with and was shaped by the development of political communities tied to a piece of land, the nation-state. This saw political power within Europe centralized, state structures created, and the emergence of a sense of order between states. Forms of democracy were developed within certain states, while at the same time the creation of empires saw this accountability denied to others.

Today, we are living through another political transformation, which could be as important as the creation of the nation-state; the exclusive link between geography and political power has now been broken.

Our new era has seen layers of governance spread within and across political boundaries. New institutions have both linked sovereign states together and pooled sovereignty beyond the nation-state. We have developed a body of regional and international law that underpins an emerging system of global governance, both formal and informal, with many layers.

Our policymakers experience a seemingly endless merry-go-round of international summits. Two or three congresses a year convened one hundred fifty years ago. Today more than 4,000 convene each year. They include summits of the U.N., the Group of Seven, the International Monetary Fund, the World Trade Organization, the European Union (EU), the Asia-Pacific Economic Cooperation bloc, the regional forum of the Association of Southeast Asian Nations, and Mercado Común del Sur (MERCOSUR). These summits and many other official and unofficial meetings lock governments into global, regional, and multilayered systems of governance that they can barely monitor, let alone control.

Attention has tended to focus on the failure of global institutions to live up to the vast hopes that their birth created. But they have significant achievements to their credit. Although the U.N. remains a creature of the interstate system with well documented shortcomings, it does deliver significant international public goods. These range from air traffic control and the management of telecommunications to the control of contagious diseases, humanitarian relief for refugees, and measures to protect our oceans and atmosphere.

However, it is regional institutions that have done most to transform the global political landscape. The EU has transformed Europe from postwar disarray to a situation where member states can pool sovereignty to tackle common problems. Despite the fact that many people still debate its very right to exist, the view from 1945 would be of astonishment at how far the EU has come so quickly. Although regionalism elsewhere is very different from the European model, its acceleration in the Americas, Asia-Pacific, and (somewhat less) in Africa has had significant consequences for political power. Despite fears of Fortress Europe and protectionist blocs, regionalism has been a midwife to political globalization rather than a barrier to it. In fact, many global standards have resulted from negotiations involving regional groupings.

Another feature of the new era is the strengthening and broadening of international law. States no longer have the right to treat their citizens as they think fit. An emerging framework of "cosmopolitan law"—governing war, crimes against humanity, environmental issues, and human rights—has made major inroads into state sovereignty. Even the many states that violate these standards in practice accept general duties to protect their citizens, to provide a basic standard of living, and to respect human rights.

These international standards are monitored and vociferously lobbied for by a growing number of international agencies. In 1996, there were nearly 260 intergovernmental organizations and nearly 5,500 international nongovernmental organizations. In 1909, the former numbered just thirty-seven and the latter a mere 176. There has also been a vast increase in the number of international treaties and regimes, such as the nuclear nonproliferation regime.

The momentum for international cooperation shows no sign of slowing, despite the many vociferous complaints often heard about it. The stuff of global politics already goes far beyond traditional geopolitical concerns and will increase whenever effective action requires international cooperation. Drug smugglers, capital flows, acid rain, and the activities of pedophiles, terrorists, and illegal immigrants do not recognize borders; neither can the policies for their effective resolution.

This transformation of international politics does not mean that the nation-state is dead. The multilateral revolution, rather than replacing the familiar world of nation-states, overlays and complicates it. Many familiar political distinctions and assumptions have been called into question. The context of national politics has been transformed by the diffusion of political authority and the growth of multilayered governance (which we discuss further in the section on governing globalization). But it is not entirely clear which factors will determine how far old institutions can adapt and whether new institutions can be invested with legitimacy.

## THE GLOBALIZATION OF ORGANIZED VIOLENCE

Ironically, war and imperial conquest have been great globalizing forces in history. Countries and peoples have met often on the battlefield. Although we live in an era distinguished by the absence of empires, great-power conflict, and interstate war, military globalization is not a thing of the past. It works very differently now but, in many ways, it is more significant than ever. New threats to our security and our responses to these threats have made countries much more interdependent.

One major change comes from weapons themselves. Military competition has always been about developing more powerful weapons. But the last half-century has not just created the most powerful weapons the world has ever seen—including weapons of mass destruction that can travel across entire continents. It has also seen some of these tools of war fall into the hands of an unprecedented number of countries and regimes. This has "shrunk" the world and made it more dangerous. Although the end of the Cold War has undermined the political logic of the global arms dynamic, the Cold War itself accelerated the diffusion of military-technological innovation across the world. Whereas it took two centuries for the gunpowder revolution to reach Europe from China in the Middle Ages, it took less than five decades for India to acquire its existing nuclear capability.

Meanwhile, the same infrastructures that have facilitated global flows of goods, people, and capital have generated new societal security threats. Cyberwar, international and ecological terrorism, and transnational organized crime cannot be satisfactorily dealt with either by traditional military means or solely within a national framework.

These changes have transformed power relationships in the world military order, creating new global and regional risks that demand multilateral action. Global and regional security institutions have become more important. Most states today have chosen to sign up to a host of multilateral arrangements and institutions in order to enhance their security. Few states now see unilateralism or neutrality as a credible defense strategy.

But it is not just the institutions of defense that have become multinational. The way that we make military hardware has also changed. The age of "national champions" has been superceded by a sharp increase in licensing, coproduction agreements, joint ventures, corporate alliances, and subcontracting. This means that few countries today—not even the United States—can claim to have an autonomous military production capacity. This is especially so as key civil technologies such as electronics, which are vital to advanced weapons systems, are themselves the products of highly globalized industries.

Arms producers have also become increasingly reliant on export markets. This is why, despite the end of the Cold War, global arms sales (in real terms) have remained above the level of the 1960s. In fact, since the mid-1990s, their volume has increased. The number of countries manufacturing arms (forty) or purchasing arms (a hundred) is greater than at any time since the crisis-ridden 1930s.

The paradox and novelty of the globalization of violence today is that national security has become a multilateral affair. For the first time in history, the one thing that did most to give nation-states a focus and a purpose, the thing that has always been at the very heart of what sovereignty is, can now be protected only if nation-states come together and pool resources, technology, intelligence, and sovereignty.

## THE GLOBAL ECONOMY

When people are not fighting, they have always made things and sold them to each other. And indeed when most people think about globalization, they think of economics. So what is happening to trade, production, and finance? How do they relate to each other—and how are they changing our world?

### Trade

The world has never been more open to trade than it is today. The dismantling of trade barriers has allowed global markets to emerge for many goods and services. The major trading blocs created in Europe, North America, and the Asia Pacific are not regional fortresses but remain open to competition from the rest of the world. Developing and transition economies have also opened up and seen their shares of world trade rise as a result. The consequence of these trading networks is not just that trade today is greater than ever before. Trade has changed in a way that links national economies together at a deeper level than in the past.

Competitive pressures have blurred the division between trade and domestic economic activity. Countries not only increasingly consume goods from abroad but depend on components from overseas for their own production processes. The massive growth of intra-industry trade, which now forms the majority of trade in manufactures among developed economies, further intensifies competition across national boundaries. The production process can now easily be sliced up and located in different countries—creating a new global division of labor and new patterns of wealth and inequality.

No economic activity can easily be insulated from global competition. A greater proportion of domestic output is traded than in the past. This does not mean that countries' fortunes are simply determined by their national "competitiveness." The basic rules of economics still apply. Countries still specialize according to comparative advantage; they cannot be competitive in everything or nothing. National economies can still gain, overall, from increased trade.

What has changed is the distribution of these gains from trade. These are highly uneven—and in new ways. There are clear winners and losers, both between and within countries. More trade with developing countries hurts low-skilled workers while simultaneously increasing the incomes of more highly skilled workers. National governments may protect and compensate those who lose out from structural change, but employers in tradeable industries vulnerable to global competition will increasingly resist the costs of welfare provision. The welfare state is under pressure from both within and without.

Despite the creation of global markets, regulation remains largely national. The banana dispute waged between the EU and the United States illustrates the international friction that trade can generate. The weakness of international regulation also means that we cannot easily correct for market failures and externalities in global markets. The World Trade Organization, a powerful advocate of deregulation and trade liberalization, is in its infancy in harmonizing national regulatory regimes. It confronts a legitimation deficit—as the banana dispute shows—that can be effectively removed only by greater transparency and wider participation (of those significantly affected by disputes) in its rule making.

### Production

Global exports may be more important than ever, but transnational production is now worth even more. To sell to another country, increasingly you have to move there; this is the main way to sell goods and services abroad. The multinational corporation has taken economic interdependence to new levels. Today, 53,000 multinational corporations and 450,000 foreign subsidiaries sell $9.5 trillion of goods and services across the globe every year. Multinational corporations account for at least 20 percent of world production and 70 percent of world trade. A quarter to a third of world trade is intrafirm trade between branches of multinationals.

Such impressive figures nevertheless underestimate the importance of multinational corporations to global economic prosperity: multinationals also form relationships that link smaller national firms into transnational production chains. Although multinationals typically account for a minority of national production, they are concentrated in the most technologically advanced economic sectors and in export industries. They also often control the global distribution networks on which independent exporters depend, especially in developing countries, and are of fundamental importance in the generation and international transfer of technology.

Multinationals are concentrated in developed countries and a small number of developing ones, but their impact is felt across the world. Almost all countries have some inward foreign direct investment and compete intensely for more. Investment is spreading out, with an increasing share to developing countries and rapid increases in Central and Eastern Europe and in China.

How powerful are multinational corporations today? They have developed transnational networks that allow them to take advantage of differences in national cost conditions and regulations. Domestic economies are also suffering because multinational companies are becoming genuinely more multinational as they find it increasingly difficult to win competitive advantage from their home base alone. In the past, even large multinational corporations like Sony retained many national characteristics. Technological advantages were largely realized in their country of origin and were shared among various national stakeholders. This is less and less possible due to the significant growth of transnational corporate alliances, mergers, and acquisitions (such as Chrysler-Daimler) and the tendency of multinationals to invest in foreign innovation clusters.

Nevertheless, multinationals are not "footloose." Production has to take place somewhere and the costs of shifting can be high—especially where an area of industrial specialization gives strong reasons to stay. But their exit power, as recent events in Sweden and Germany show, has increased over time. And governments increasingly see multinationals as determining the balance of economic power in the world economy, with the power to play different governments off against each other to win extra subsidies for inward investment or changes to regulatory requirements.

In the short term, governments will continue to respond to this pressure by trimming their national regimes to balance domestic priorities and conditions with the demands of global capital. But we can expect increasing pressure for the transnational harmonization of corporate practices, taxes, and business regimes as an escape route from this Dutch auction.

### Finance

Alongside multinationals, the power of global finance has been most central to economic globalization. World financial flows are so large that the numbers are overwhelming. Every day, $1.5 trillion is traded on the foreign exchange markets—as a few thousand traders seem to determine the economic fate of nations. Most countries today are incorporated into global financial markets, but the nature of their access to these markets is highly uneven. When foreign exchange markets turn over sixty times the value of world trade, this is not just a staggering increase; it is a different type of activity altogether. The instantaneous transactions of the twenty-four-hour global markets are largely speculative, where once most market activity financed trade and long-term investment.

The fact that these global markets determine countries' long-term interest rates and exchange rates does not mean that the financial markets simply determine national economic policy. But they do radically alter both the costs of particular policy options and, crucially, policymakers' perceptions of costs and risk. Speculative activity on this scale brings both unprecedented uncertainty and volatility—and can rapidly undermine financial institutions, currencies and national economic strategies. It is not surprising that policymakers take a distinctly risk-averse approach and therefore adopt a more conservative macroeconomic strategy as a result. Even if there is often more room for maneuver with hindsight, future policy will change only marginally when the risks of getting it wrong appear to be, and are, potentially so catastrophic.

The 1997 East Asian crisis forcibly demonstrated the impact of global financial markets and the shifting balance between public and private power. The global financial disruption triggered by the collapse of the Thai baht demonstrated new levels of economic interconnectedness. The "Asian tiger" economies had benefited from the rapid increase of financial flows to developing countries in the 1990s and were held up as examples to the rest of the world. But these heavy flows of short-term capital, often channeled into speculative activity, could be quickly reversed, causing currencies to fall very heavily and far in excess of any real economic imbalances. The inability of the existing international financial regime to prevent global economic turmoil has created a wide-ranging debate on its future institutional architecture—and the opportunity to promote issues of legitimacy, accountability and effectiveness.

Another important change on the policy making menu arises from the exchange rate cases of the 1990s. Fixed exchange rates are ceasing to be a viable policy option in the face of global capital flows of this scale and intensity. The choice that countries face is increasingly between floating rates and monetary union—shown by the launch of the euro and discussion of dollarization in Latin America.

## GLOBALIZATION AND THE ENVIRONMENT

Environmental change has always been with us. What is new today is that some of the greatest threats are global—and any effective response will have to be global too. For most of human history, the main way in which environmental impacts circulated around the earth was through the unintentional transport of flora, fauna, and microbes. The great plagues showed how devastating the effects could be. The European colonization of the New World within a generation wiped out a substantial proportion of the indigenous populations of the Caribbean, Mexico, and parts of Latin America. Over the following centuries, these societies saw their ecosystems, landscapes, and agricultural systems transformed. Early colonialism also damaged the environment in new ways. The Sumatran and Indian forests were destroyed to meet consumer demand in Europe and America. Seals were overhunted to dangerously low levels. And some species of whale were hunted to extinction.

But most forms of environmental degradation were largely local until the middle of the twentieth century. Since then, the globalization of environmental degradation has accelerated. Fifty years of resource-intensive and high-pollution growth in the OECD and the even dirtier industrialization of Russia, Eastern Europe, and the ex-Soviet states have taken their toll on the environment. The [Global] South is now industrializing at breakneck speed, driven by exponential growth of global population. We also know much more about the dangers and the damage that we have caused.

Humankind is increasingly aware that it faces an unprecedented array of truly global and regional environmental problems, which no national community or single generation can tackle alone. We have reacted to global warming; to ozone depletion; to destruction of global rainforests and loss of biodiversity; to toxic waste; to the pollution of oceans and rivers; and to nuclear risks with a flurry of global and regional initiatives, institutions, regimes, networks, and treaties. Transnational environmental movements are also more politically visible than ever. But there has simply not been the political power, domestic support, or international authority so far on a scale that can do any more than limit the very worst excesses of these global environmental threats.

## GOVERNING GLOBALIZATION

Contemporary globalization represents the beginning of a new epoch in human affairs. In transforming societies and world order it is having as profound an impact as the Industrial Revolution and the global empires of the nineteenth century. We have seen that globalization is transforming our world, but in complex, multifaceted and uneven ways. Although globalization has a long history, it is today genuinely different both in scale and in form from what has gone before. Every new epoch creates new winners and losers. This one will be no different. Globalization to date has already both widened the gap between the richest and poorest countries and further increased divisions within and across societies. It has inevitably become increasingly contested and politicized.

National governments—sandwiched between global forces and local demands—must now reconsider their roles and functions. But to say simply that states have lost power distorts what is happening as does any suggestion that nothing much has changed. The real picture is much more complex. States today are at least as powerful, if not more so, than their predecessors on many fundamental measures of power, from the capacity to raise taxes to the ability to hurl force at enemies. But the demands on states have grown very rapidly as well. They must often work together to pursue the public good—to prevent recession or to protect the environment. And transnational agreements, for example dealing with acid rain, will often force national governments to adopt major changes in domestic policy.

So state power and political authority are shifting. States now deploy their sovereignty and autonomy as bargaining chips in multilateral and transnational negotiations, as they collaborate and coordinate actions in shifting regional and global networks. The right of most states to rule within circumscribed territories—their sovereignty—is not on the edge of collapse, although the practical nature of this entitlement—the actual capacity of states to rule—is changing its shape. The emerging shape of governance means that we need to stop thinking of state power as something that is indivisible and territorially exclusive. It makes more sense to speak about the transformation of state power than the end of the state; the range of government strategies stimulated by globalization are, in many fundamental respects, producing the potential for a more activist state.

But the exercise of political and economic power now frequently escapes effective mechanisms of democratic control. And it will continue to do so while democracy remains rooted in a fixed and bounded territorial conception of political community. Globalization has disrupted the neat correspondence between national territory, sovereignty, political space, and the democratic political community. It allows power to flow across, around, and over territorial boundaries. And so the challenge of globalization today is ultimately political. Just as the Industrial Revolution created new types of class politics, globalization demands that we reform our existing territorially defined democratic institutions and practices so that politics can continue to address human aspirations and needs.

This means rethinking politics. We need to take our established ideas about political equality, social justice, and liberty and refashion these into a coherent political project robust enough for a world where power is exercised on a transnational scale and where risks are shared by peoples across the world. And we need to think about what institutions will allow us to tackle these global problems while responding to the aspirations of the people that they are meant to serve.

This is not a time for pessimism. We are caught between nostalgia for causes defeated and ideas lost, and excitement at the new possibilities that we face. We need to think in new ways. Globalization is not bringing about the death of politics. It is reilluminating and reinvigorating the contemporary political terrain.

# 13

# WHAT TO DO WITH AMERICAN PRIMACY

Richard N. Haass

At the start of the new millennium, the distribution of global power has shifted in the sense that at the moment the United States stands alone as the globe's uncontested superpower in its leadership in weapons technology and military capabilities. This situation may not last for long, as many predict that in the next twenty-five years a new multipolar system will emerge in which military power will be shared equally by three, four, or perhaps five major powers. At the moment, however, the dominance of the United States presents both a problem for the rest of the world and an opportunity for the United States to use its superiority and military capabilities for constructive purposes. In this essay Richard N. Haass reconsiders and reevaluates the dilemmas posed by this situation, and the issues confronting the United States about how to harness American primacy in ways that will advance both U.S. national interests and global interests in constructing an international consensus about the need for cooperation to engineer a peaceful, prosperous, and just twenty-first century. Haass is Vice President, Director of Foreign Policy Studies, and Sydney Stein, Jr. Chair in International Security at the Brookings Institution. He is widely published, and his recent publications include *Economic Sanctions and American Diplomacy* (1998).

We live in an era of contradictions: globalization and fragmentation, peace and conflict, prosperity and poverty. Only when one or more of these tendencies wins out will our era gain a name of its own, displacing the awkward "post–Cold War"

147

tag line. But amid this uncertainty is the stark reality that the United States is the most powerful country in the world—first among unequals. Still, this is a description, not a purpose or a policy. The fundamental question that confronts America today is how to exploit its enormous surplus of power in the world: What to do with American primacy?

It must be said at the outset that America's economic and military advantages, while great, are neither unqualified nor permanent. The country's strength is limited by the amount of resources (money, time, and political capital) it can spend, which in turn reflects a lack of domestic support for some kind of American global empire. De Tocqueville's observation that democracy is ill suited for conducting foreign policy is even more true in a world without a mortal enemy like the Soviet Union against which to rally the public.

Moreover, U.S. superiority will not last. As power diffuses around the world, America's position relative to others will inevitably erode. It may not seem this way at a moment when the American economy is in full bloom and many countries around the world are sclerotic, but the long-term trend is unmistakable. Other nations are rising, and nonstate actors—ranging from Usama bin Ladin to Amnesty International to the International Criminal Court to George Soros—are increasing in number and acquiring power. For all these reasons, an effort to assert or expand U.S. hegemony will fail. Such an action would lack domestic support and stimulate international resistance, which in turn would make the costs of hegemony all the greater and its benefits all the smaller.

Meanwhile, the world is becoming more multipolar. American foreign policy should not resist such multipolarity (which would be futile) but define it. Like unipolarity, multipolarity is simply a description. It tells us about the distribution of power in the world, not about the character or quality of international relations. A multipolar world could be one in which several hostile but roughly equal states confront one another, or one in which a number of states, each possessing significant power, work together in common. The U.S. objective should be to persuade other centers of political, economic, and military power—including but not limited to nation-states—to believe it is in their self-interest to support constructive notions of how international society should be organized and should operate.

The proper goal for American foreign policy, then, is to encourage a multipolarity characterized by cooperation and concert rather than competition and conflict. In such a world, order would not be limited to peace based on a balance of power or a fear of escalation, but would be founded in a broader agreement on global purposes and problems. In his insightful first book, *A World Restored,* Henry A. Kissinger argues that the competitive multipolar world of nineteenth-century Europe managed to avoid great-power war because the great powers forged a consensus on certain core issues of international relations. American leaders must seek to build such an international consensus for the twenty-first century.

This goal is not as far-fetched as it may appear. Even now, significant areas of international life are characterized by substantial cooperation, especially in the economic realm. The World Trade Organization (WTO) is an orderly, rule-based mechanism for resolving trade disputes and opening the world economy; finance ministers meet regularly to coordinate monetary policies; and broadly supported conventions ban bribery and corruption. Economic interaction is also regulated by an international marketplace that puts a premium on government policies and procedures—privatization, reduced government subsidies, accepted accounting practices, bankruptcy proceedings—that encourage investment and a free flow of capital.

Military and political interactions are also regulated, although less deeply and extensively. There are some accepted grounds for using military force, such as self-defense. Norms (along with treaties or other arrangements to back them up) outlaw biological and chemical weapons, prohibit nuclear-bomb testing, and discourage the proliferation of nuclear weapons and ballistic missiles. In the political domain, formal international agreements promote human rights, outlaw genocide and other war crimes, and safeguard refugees. Clearly, though, the political-military area is going to be characterized by greater anarchy and discord than is economics. Important questions remain hotly debated: When is it legitimate to use military force other than in self-defense? What should be done to further limit weapons of mass destruction? What restrictions, if any, ought to exist on the ability of governments to act as they wish within their own borders?

Only when there is consensus among the major powers on these and related issues will a significant degree of order exist. Without great-power agreement, international relations could easily revert to a much more hostile system than the one that exists today. With such cooperation, however, we can ameliorate (though never abolish) some of the dangers of great-power competition and war that have plagued the world for much of its history.

## FOUR FUNDAMENTALS

Ideally, post–Cold War international society will be built on four foundation stones: using less military force to resolve disputes between states, reducing the number of weapons of mass destruction and the number of states and other groups possessing such weapons, accepting a limited doctrine of humanitarian intervention based on a recognition that people—and not just states—enjoy rights, and economic openness. Such a world would be relatively peaceful, prosperous, and just.

The goal of reducing, if not eliminating, the role of force is not foolishly optimistic. Already, the use of force by one major power against another is either politically unthinkable or prohibitively expensive—with costs that include the danger of escalation to unconventional weaponry. The challenge is to make any such use of force between major powers even more unlikely and to forge agreement about when using force is legitimate.

Real progress has been made in the effort to reduce the role of weapons of mass destruction. The world has come a long way since nuclear weapons were the basic unit of account of great-power competition. U.S. and Russian nuclear inventories are slated to decrease to approximately 3,500 weapons apiece under the signed but (in the Russian case) unratified START II accord. The two inventories would shrink further under START III. Biological and chemical weapons are prohibited, as is all nuclear testing. Although India and Pakistan conducted nuclear tests [recently], a number of states, including Ukraine, Belarus, Kazakhstan, South Africa, Brazil, and Argentina, have voluntarily given up nuclear weapons programs in recent years. The remaining items on the agenda include negotiating further reductions in the arsenals of existing nuclear weapons states, principally Russia; methodically introducing defensive antimissile systems; discouraging the proliferation of missile and nuclear capability to additional states or nonstate actors; and enforcing the ban against possessing or using chemical and biological weapons.

The third building block of a post–Cold War world could well prove the most controversial. For three hundred fifty years, international order has been buttressed by the notion of sovereignty: that what goes on within the borders of a nation-state is its business and its business alone. The notion of sovereignty was itself an advancement that promoted order by discouraging the meddling that could all too easily lead to conflict. But over the past half century and especially during the past decade, a new reaction against absolute sovereignty has gained strength. Today, sovereignty is increasingly judged as conditional, linked to how a government treats its citizens. When a government proves unable or unwilling to safeguard its citizens—when the inherent contract between the government and the governed is violated—the leadership forfeits its normal right to expect others to keep their distance. It then falls to the international community to act, either diplomatically (utilizing persuasion, sanctions, or aid) or with force, under the banner of humanitarian intervention. The obvious challenge is to gain broader recognition of this modified view of sovereignty, and acceptance of (if not support for) particular interventions.

The fourth building block of post–Cold War international society is economic openness, which requires not only the easy movement of goods, capital, and services across national lines, but also transparent domestic markets that favor private-sector activities. Such openness is necessary to sustain prosperity and works to buttress civil society and increase linkages and interdependencies—factors that should be a bulwark against military conflict. What is needed is not so much a new international financial architecture or added controls on the movement of money as some interior decorating that would increase the transparency and efficiency of national economies throughout much of the world.

## BRINGING OTHERS ON BOARD

The world described here will not come about solely from its inherent appeal. To the contrary, building and maintaining such an order requires sustained effort by the world's most powerful actor, the United States. Its ultimate success, in turn, demands that Americans properly handle their country's role as sole superpower of the world. American foreign policy must project an imperial dimension, although not in the sense of territorial control or commercial exploitation; such relationships are neither desirable nor sustainable today. Rather, the United States must attempt to organize the world along certain principles affecting both relations between states and conditions within them. The U.S. role should resemble that of nineteenth-century Great Britain, the global leader of that era. U.S. influence would reflect the appeal of American culture, the strength of the American economy, and the attractiveness of the norms being promoted. Coercion and the use of force would normally be a secondary option.

The United States seeks a world based on peaceful relations, non-proliferation, respect for human rights, and economic openness. It must therefore convince other great powers to join with it to promote these ends, thereby constructing a stronger and more durable order that protects the bulk of U.S. interests and reduces the foreign policy burden—in financial and human terms alike—on the United States.

Certain costs will accompany such a cooperative arrangement. The United States will need to relinquish some freedom of action and modulate the tone of its rhetoric. Sanctions should cease to dominate policy; incentives need to be employed instead, or in tandem. Carrying out unilateral preemptive strikes on suspected weapons facilities, as the United States did in Sudan [in] August [1999], would become more difficult. The barrier against intervening in internal conflicts would be higher. The pace and extent of additional NATO enlargement would most likely be restrained. The United States would have to limit the scale of any national missile defenses if Russia and China were to cap their strategic forces. Although the benefits would outweigh such costs, bringing about a world that would justify such restraint will be difficult. In fact, three main obstacles lie in the path toward establishing and maintaining an international society to America's liking.

First and most obvious is the opposition of other power centers, major and minor alike. Some resistance is inevitable, at times from France or other European states or Japan, more often from China and Russia. China in particular will oppose any limit on its ability to use force to resolve the Taiwan issue. China is also determined to increase its strategic arsenal. Both China and Russia will feel threatened by American deployment of defensive systems. In response, they may sell technology that could bolster another state's unconventional weapons program. Russia (to some extent) and China (especially) will view humanitarian intervention as a pretext for unwelcome interference in their internal affairs. Japan holds to a more closed view of the ideal economy. Few if any major powers

would support preventive attacks on the fledgling unconventional weapons programs of what the United States views as rogue states; as a rule, the United States
tends to find itself isolated when emphasizing sanctions and military attacks instead of commerce and other forms of unconditional engagement. A host of
smaller but still considerable powers, including India, Pakistan, Iran, Iraq, North
Korea, and others, are likely to view an American-led world as discriminatory,
threatening, or both.

How, then, might the United States persuade others of the desirability of such
a world? The operative word here is "persuade." Areas of consensus will begin
to emerge only following strategic dialogues—intense conversations with other
governments and opinion leaders in various societies. If *negotiations* were at the
center of Cold War diplomacy, *consultations* must form the core of post–Cold
War foreign policy. The goal is to build or strengthen global institutions that buttress the basic principles of order. Optimally, this would include a revamped U.N.
Security Council willing and able to counter aggression, whether by one state
against another or by a government against its own people; a more comprehensive WTO better able to promote open trade; smaller nuclear arsenals and a reduced chance of nuclear conflict; supplier clubs that restrict the spread of advanced weapons technology; and a stronger International Atomic Energy Agency
to police nuclear proliferation and similar organizations to enforce chemical and
biological weapons bans.

Why would other states go along with U.S. preferences? In some cases, they
will see the same inherent benefits as America. This applies best to Europe, already America's most frequent partner. More generally, economic openness tends
to be its own reward. Most major powers also have a stake in avoiding large-
scale conflicts, slowing the spread of technologies that threaten them, and maintaining a free flow of oil and gas. Cooperation with the United States will bring
benefits in the form of shared technology and capital. At least as important is the
status that the United States can confer on its partners. Both Russia and China
clearly want to be seen as great powers, as members of the inner circle shaping
international relations. Only by working with the United States can they and the
U.N. Security Council avoid being regularly bypassed.

Still, consultations alone—even consultations buttressed by incentives—will
not bring about consensus in every area. Persuasion has its limits. The major
powers may not agree on general rules; even when they do, they may not agree
on how to apply them in a particular situation. In such circumstances, it makes
little sense for the United States to work in vain for the emergence of international consensus, guaranteeing only inaction or a lowest common denominator
and hence ineffective foreign policy.

The other extreme, unilateralism, likewise has little appeal. On its own, the
United States can do little to promote order. Too many of today's challenges—
protectionism, proliferation, genocide—cannot be solved by one nation alone, either because cooperation is necessary to combat the problem, resources are limited, or both. The benefits of multilateralism outweigh its tendency to constrain

American means and dilute American goals. In addition to distributing the burden of promoting order, multilateralism can restrain the impulses of others, reduce opposition to U.S. actions, and increase the chances of policy success.

What, then, are the options that fall between perfect internationalism and unilateralism? One idea, put forward by Samuel P. Huntington and others, is dependence on regional powers, sometimes referred to as "pivotal states." There are serious problems with this idea, however. In several regions, the strongest state is not accepted as a legitimate policeman by its weaker neighbors: consider India, Israel, and China. Worse yet, in the Middle East, for example, it is the dominant states (Iran and Iraq) that require policing.

A better option is regionalism. Regionalism is not to be confused with assigning the task of promoting order to regional hegemons. The former involves building consensus and capacity on a regional scale, the latter the assertion of dominance by a single actor over its neighbors.

The problem with regionalism is that in many regions—Northeast Asia, South Asia, the Levant, the Persian Gulf—the principal states do not agree on what constitutes regional order. In other regions such as Europe, the problem is primarily one of capacity. Europe needs far more military muscle—and the ability to speak with a common voice—to play an effective role on the continent or beyond. The same holds for Latin America. In Africa, disagreement and a lack of consensus limit what the principal regional organization (the Organization of African Unity) can do, although subregional organizations have done some good in limited cases.

The main alternative to promoting political, economic, and military order on either a regional or a global scale would be to organize coalitions—as broad as possible—of the able and willing, normally with the United States in the lead. Such groupings are not ideal—they tend to be *ad hoc* and reactive and lack the legitimacy of U.N. or formal regional undertakings—but they are consistent with a world where the willingness of governments to cooperate varies from crisis to crisis and situation to situation, and where great-power consensus is unreliable. Lord Palmerston's dictum—"We have no eternal allies, and we have no perpetual enemies. Our interests are eternal and perpetual, and those interests it is our duty to follow"—applies in spades to the post–Cold War world.

## INDISCRIMINATE AMERICA

In the end, the creation and maintenance of an American world system will depend as much or more on what Americans and their leaders do as on outside influences. One internal obstacle to properly achieving this goal stems from the desire to do too much, from establishing ends that are overly ambitious. Hegemony, as has already been noted, falls under this rubric. So, too, does democratic enlargement, the only attempt by the Clinton administration to define a post-containment foreign policy doctrine. America simply lacks the means to shape the political culture and system of another country—short of long-term occupation, an option usually unavailable and not guaranteed to work, as demonstrated in Haiti. Moreover, partial success might make countries vulnerable to nationalist fervor. A foreign policy informed by a universal humanitarian impulse would surely qualify as a case of what Paul Kennedy defines as "imperial overstretch." At the same time, not acting entails real costs, not only for the innocent people who lose their homes or lives or both, but also for America's image in the world. Moreover, a narrow foreign policy based solely on self-interest is unlikely to capture the imagination or enjoy the support of the American people, who want a foreign policy with a moral component.

But how can the United States get it right? To address this dilemma, it helps to divide the humanitarian intervention issue into three questions: whether, how, and why to intervene.

What factors should influence the decision to intervene? The first is the scale of the problem: not every repression is a genocide. A second consideration is whether there are other interests, economic or strategic, beyond humanitarianism. Do such interests argue against intervening with military force, as they did in Chechnya, or in favor, as in Bosnia? Third is the matter of partners. How much help can the United States expect from others, militarily and economically? Fourth, what are the likely costs and consequences of intervening? Will action significantly reduce the problem? What larger consequences will acting have for U.S. interests in the region and beyond? Last, what would be the likely results of other policies, including, but not limited to, doing nothing?

Such objective questions are no substitute for situational judgment; there can be no intervention template. But they do provide discipline and, with it, some potential guidance. These considerations would have made the United States less likely to occupy Haiti or expand the Somalia intervention into nation-building, but more likely to act earlier in Bosnia and Rwanda, where a small intervention could have prevented genocide.

It is thus impossible to answer the question of *whether* to intervene without also considering *how* to intervene. The likely costs and benefits of various foreign policy instruments—including diplomacy, political and economic sanctions, incentives, covert action, and military force—need to be weighed. Military options can be further divided to include aiding one side in a conflict, deterring through presence or threats to act, creating safe havens, bombing to weaken or coerce one side, deploying combined armed forces to defeat one or more of the protagonists on the battlefield, nation-building, or sending in forces to keep a peace. Significant interventions that require subsequent long-term occupations cannot be pursued very often.

The third and last question concerns purpose. Humanitarian interventions can be undertaken to prop up a failed state, protect an entire population from danger, or shield part of the populace from the government or another group. If a segment of a society is threatened, when should the United States support the desire of a people for their own state?

A universal bias in favor of self-determination would be destabilizing, so several factors should be weighed. There must be some historical legitimacy. The historical argument can be positive, reflecting a tradition, or negative, resulting from necessity borne of persecution. A second consideration is viability: it makes no sense to encourage independence if the new state would be doomed. A third consideration is internal stability and the likely behavior of the new government toward its citizens. The international community should have done more to condition its support for the independence of parts of the former Yugoslavia on the protection of minorities. A fourth factor is regional stability and the likely reaction of neighboring states. It is for this reason that the United States is correct to oppose a unilateral Palestinian claim for self-determination. Israel has a fundamental stake in this decision. Similarly, Kurdish desires for statehood must be weighed against the claims of Turkey and others. The United States ought not adopt political objectives that are more ambitious than what the humanitarian circumstances warrant.

Inconsistency is unavoidable, but it is also a virtue. Intervening everywhere would exhaust the United States; intervening nowhere would encourage conflict and undermine America's belief in itself and its ability to do good.

What would all this have meant in the case of Kosovo? It is not clear even in retrospect how asking these questions would have influenced the decision to intervene militarily. U.S. interests, while less than vital, went beyond the humanitarian; European allies were prepared to offer significant assistance. At the same time, the scale of the problem was decidedly less than genocide, and strong Russian and Chinese opposition was predictable. The most critical judgment—how to use military force—was one the Clinton administration and NATO got wrong: believing that the threat or use of air power alone would pressure Slobodan Milosevic to cease killing and ethnically cleansing the Kosovars and accept the Rambouillet peace accords. Instead, the bombing turned a humanitarian crisis into something much worse. The fact that eleven weeks of bombing led Milosevic to back down does not alter this judgment. It would have been wiser to continue diplomacy and deal with a limited humanitarian crisis while looking for ways to weaken or topple the Milosevic regime, or to send in ground forces at the outset and prevent the displacement and killing. The administration was correct, however, to avoid making Kosovo's independence an objective, an outcome which would have alienated most European states as well as Russia and led to further regional conflict.

A somewhat restrained approach to humanitarian intervention is unlikely to satisfy either those who wish to place it at the center of American foreign policy or those who wish to relegate it to the periphery. But there must be limits on U.S. military action when a situation is not dire, when partners are scarce, or when other major powers oppose American intervention. Promoting this dimension of world order should not be allowed to undermine the other dimensions. At the end of the day, order is more fundamental than justice; one can have the former without the latter, but not vice versa. Adhering to this precept will take discipline, but discipline is essential in foreign policy if the urgent is not to crowd out the important.

Anyone doubting this assertion need only consider for a moment the costs of a breakdown in any of the other three areas of international order. Major conflict, the spread or use of weapons of mass destruction, or a global financial meltdown would have profound and direct consequences for the United States and American society. Humanitarian abuses simply cannot cause comparable harm on a global scale; as a result, the United States must avoid jeopardizing larger interests when addressing them.

## IMPERIAL UNDERSTRETCH

The third obstacle to expanding international order is the opposite of the second. It is the problem of the United States' doing too little, of underachieving. It may seem odd to suggest that a country that spends more than $300 billion a year on national security (if one includes defense, intelligence, economic and military assistance, and diplomacy), stations hundreds of thousands of troops overseas, maintains hundreds of embassies and diplomatic missions of every sort, and listens in on millions of phone calls may not be doing enough, but this is the case. A decade into the post–Cold War era, the United States risks squandering its primacy.

This judgment reflects more than the fact that what is now spent on national security (in terms of percentage of GDP) constitutes a post–World War II low. Indeed, it is precisely what [the U.S. is] *not* prepared to do for [its] global interests and preferences that is most noteworthy. Examples include an increased unwillingness to commit ground forces and risk casualties; a failure to garner "fast-track" negotiating authority from Congress to expand open trading arrangements beyond NAFTA and the WTO; the low priority given to reducing the U.S. and Russian nuclear arsenals; a half-hearted and arbitrarily limited effort to pressure Iraq into accepting the presence of U.N. weapons inspectors; a lack of time devoted by senior officials to discussing basic international issues with other powers; and a lack of effort to explain to the American people why they ought to support an active leadership role—indeed, an imperial role—for the United States despite the end of the Cold War and the demise of the Soviet Union.

But no idea, no matter how compelling, ever sells itself. Ideas must compete in the political marketplace. Polls suggesting strong domestic support for U.S. leadership in the world are misleading. They reflect inclination but not intensity; Americans, for the most part, are not so much isolationist—which requires strong feelings about foreign affairs—as disinterested. Polls therefore offer little insight into political behavior or public readiness to sustain foreign policy amid considerable human or financial cost.

The Kosovo experience revealed deep cleavages. And whereas President Clinton has often called for a national dialogue about race, the time has come for a national dialogue on this country's role in the world. Such a dialogue is necessary because what is being argued for here—a foreign policy directed toward promoting world order—demands not only substantial resources but also public attention. Any approach to the world that includes large elements of hegemony and unilateralism will require more than the American public and the U.S. political system can sustain, but the greater danger is that even a multilateral policy of promoting world order will prove to be too much. Future presidents will not be able to appeal to fear as they could during the Cold War. Nor will they have the advantage of simplicity or clarity. Ultimately, the United States will intervene in some crises but not others; other countries will be less than allies but also less than adversaries; and the United States will look differently on other nations' becoming nuclear powers. In this complicated, ambiguous world, greater understanding and explanation will be necessary. Only the president can lead a dialogue on what to do with America's primacy, and this will be a priority for Clinton's successor. "It's the world, stupid" should be his or her refrain.

# 14

# BUILDING PEACE IN PIECES: THE PROMISE OF EUROPEAN UNITY

Donald J. Puchala

This essay traces the evolutionary process by which the economic and political consolidation of the formerly independent states of Europe led to the creation of the European Union. Processes of European integration have transformed the old continent from an historic arena of warring states into a contemporary zone of peace among peoples. Most agree that European integration has also contributed to the prosperity and exemplary modernity which today characterize European civilization. Drawing on the expectations and vision that after World War II inspired European leaders to construct a level of governance beyond the nation-state, Puchala evaluates, in light of integration theories, the progress, pitfalls, and promise of achieving even greater European unity through the further pooling of national sovereignty in the twenty-first century. Puchala is Charles L. Jacobson of Professor Public Affairs and Director of the Richard L. Walker Institute of International Studies at the University of South Carolina. His many publications include *Fiscal Harmonization in the European Communities* (1984), *Immigration Into Western Societies* (with Emek Uçarer) (1997), and *Visions of International Relations: Assessing an Academic Field* (2001).

Western Europe's movement toward governance beyond the nation-state during the second half of the twentieth century represents a rather remarkable transformation in intra-European international relations. For more than a thousand years, from the fall of the Roman Empire to the end of World War II, Europe was a zone of incessant warfare. During the last three centuries alone, the major states of Europe fought one another one hundred six times, and, by conservative estimate, these conflicts killed some 150 million people.[1] They also destroyed inestimable amounts of property and wasted immense quantities of resources. Yet, we are now able to say with some confidence that the Second World War was probably the last great intra-European war, because since 1945 the way in which European peoples relate to one another has dramatically changed. Transforming Europe from a zone of war into a zone of peace, and progressively extending this zone in all directions, is both the meaning and the accomplishment of European integration.

Practically speaking, since the early 1950s "European integration" has meant the dampening of national sovereignty, the de-emphasizing of national borders, the establishment of international organizations, and the progressive transferring to them of significant authority. Europe has evolved no central *government* as such, but a significant amount of *governance* in the form of lawmaking that deeply affects people's lives already takes place at supranational levels, that is, beyond the political and legal jurisdictions of national governments. All of these have contributed notably to peace and prosperity.

The story of European integration should be familiar to anyone who keeps abreast of current events. Both the vanquished and the victors in Europe were devastated by World War II, even more horribly than they were devastated one generation before by World War I. From these tragic experiences there emerged an awareness among Europeans that if their system of warring sovereign states were not somehow changed, Europe's future might very well be like its past. For some farsighted European statesmen of the immediate post–World War II generation—Jean Monnet, Robert Schuman, Konrad Adenauer, Alcide de Gasperi, Paul-Henri Spaak, and others—moving Europe beyond a system of squabbling states was imperative. National sovereignty needed to be constrained and national autonomy needed to be limited. Differing interests among countries needed to be bargained and adjudicated rather than fought over, and common interests needed to be elevated and acted upon. A united and peaceful Europe had been the dream of philosophers for centuries. Beginning in the early 1950s, this dream became a project.

Western Europe has been integrating for the last half century, that is, uniting economically and politically in small and large institutional steps, in fits and starts, and in leaps forward followed by slides backward. For those countries involved, the predominant course of their relations has been toward incrementally more international cooperation and supranational authority and incrementally less

---

[1] P.A. Sorokin, *Social and Cultural Dynamics, III* (New York, 1962), pp. 547–75. Sorokin estimates about 34 million military casualties in European wars between 1650 and 1918. The standard estimate for military and civilian casualties in Europe in World War II is about 40 million. To include civilian casualties in historic European wars, including the Thirty Years War, I estimated about 75 million.

national autonomy. Postwar intra-European international economic cooperation began in the late 1940s under the incentives of the American-initiated Marshall Plan.[2] The first supranational experiment was the European Coal and Steel Community, where, in 1952, six countries—France, West Germany, Italy, the Netherlands, Belgium and Luxembourg—turned the regulation of their coal and steel industries over to a European High Authority and simultaneously opened their borders to the free movement of goods, money and labor in these industries. By 1958, the Six were able to form the European Economic Community (EEC), which opened borders to free movement in all economic sectors and established the EEC as a single entity in economic dealings with the outside world.

Institutionally, the European Commission, headquartered in Brussels, was created to design common economic policies for the six member states and to oversee their administration. However, the Council of Ministers, representing the governments of the member states, retained final authority in the European policy making process. The European Parliament, representing public opinion and political parties, functioned from the beginning of the movement toward European unity, though initially, this body was appointed rather than elected and it had very little power. So too from the beginning there was the European Court of Justice charged with adjudicating claims and conflicts among governments and between governments and the newly established institutions. Both the parliament and the court were to grow in prominence as the unity movement progressed.

There were of course problems along the way toward greater Western European unity, since national sovereignty is never easily relinquished and opposition to international cooperation is never entirely absent. Formulating and administering a common agricultural policy affecting all EEC member countries, for example, proved to be a major challenge, as did formulating and administering a common system of indirect taxation, a common policy regarding transport and a common approach toward assisting poorer regions and struggling industries. Tensions persisted, and still do, over how far and how fast Europe ought to move toward government beyond the nation-state, over how large the European Union ought to be, over the balance of initiative and authority among the central institutions (and the balance of responsibility between the central institutions and national authorities) and about how the benefits and burdens of forging greater unity ought to be distributed.

Still, the most pronounced fifty-year trend in intra-European international relations has been the broadening and deepening of cooperation among governments along with the relegation of ever increasing authority to institutions and processes operating at the supranational level. The European Economic Com-

---

[2] M. Margaret Ball, *NATO and the European Union Movement* (New York: Frederick A. Praeger, 1959), pp. 217–52; Jacques Freymond, *Western Europe Since the War: A Short Political History* (New York: Frederick A. Praeger, 1964), p. 41.

munity of the Six—alternatively called the European Community, the European Communities, the Common Market, or simply "Brussels"—is today the European Union (EU) of fifteen countries. A first expansion in the early 1970s brought in the United Kingdom, Ireland and Denmark, followed in the early 1980s by Greece, Spain and Portugal, followed again in the 1990s by the accession of Austria, Sweden and Finland. By the late 1990s the European Union was on the threshold of a bold, new enlargement that may eventually encompass all of the former communist countries of Central Europe. Indeed, by 1999 Poland, Hungary, the Czech Republic, Slovenia and Estonia were already negotiating for accession.

While the union was expanding geographically, the functional breadth of its policy making was also broadening. As it turned out, creating a common market among countries involved a good deal more than simply opening borders and freeing trade. Legislation and regulations pertaining to all aspects of economic intercourse needed to be harmonized across countries. Product standards needed to be standardized. Government contracting needed to be competitively opened to non-nationals. Cartels needed to be similarly constrained from country to country, and so too did countless other liberalizing, standardizing and harmonizing actions need to be taken to guarantee that the European Economic Community would be in fact a common market. A major thrust in the direction of completing the common market, and thus harmonizing much of European economic life, was made between 1985 and 1992, driven by the Single European Act (SEA) and pursued under the slogan "Europe 1992."

Making common foreign economic policies with respect to trade and development had been the prerogative of the central institutions of the EEC since their inception. But during the 1980s, under the rubric of Political Cooperation, European Community members began to seek common positions on a range of political issues on the world agenda, such as Middle Eastern and Central American questions. They also began to coordinate their activities within the United Nations and other world organizations. With the signing of the Maastricht Treaties, which transformed the European Communities into the European Union in 1993, seeking common European foreign and security policies (CFSP) became a constitutional prerogative, and the groundwork was thus laid for the emergence of "Europe" as a world political actor. Maastricht also opened the way for common European policy making in a realm called Justice and Home Affairs, which has to do with transnational coordination in combatting criminal and anti-terrorist activities, and in devising a regime to commonly deal with immigration matters all along the European Union's extensive external frontiers. Maastricht pointed the way too toward the eventual harmonization of social policies, pertaining to working conditions, pensions and benefits, health insurance, and the like, across all member countries.

Most importantly, the Maastricht agreements committed the members of the European Union to entering into the Economic and Monetary Union (EMU), with a common currency, a central bank and monetary policy, by the first decade of the twenty-first century. Preparing for an economic and monetary union initially entailed aligning macro-economic conditions across member countries, especially with respect to rates of inflation and national budgetary discipline, and fixing the exchange rates of national currencies, so that, in effect, the European Union began to approximate a single monetary area. These difficult, and for some countries rather painful, measures were undertaken between 1996 and 1998, with the result that eleven countries were able to adopt the "euro" as a common European currency in January 1999. (The United Kingdom, Denmark and Sweden were technically prepared for EMU by the end of 1998, but opted not to join at that time.) When fully implemented just after the turn of the twenty-first century, the EMU will move all monetary policy making from the member states to central European institutions, all accounting will be conducted in euros, all prices will be denominated in the new currency and euro notes and coins will fully replace national currencies. This represents a dramatic step beyond national sovereignty.

Subtly, but unmistakably, while the European Union broadened geographically and deepened functionally, its institutions began to look and to operate increasingly like an embryonic central government. The European Commission, which had supranational authority from the outset, protected its prerogatives over time, and succeeded in inserting itself into areas of policy, like CFSP, where national governments were loath to surrender sovereignty. The Council of Ministers has remained a bastion of national governments, national sovereignty and national interests. Nevertheless, over time, requirements for decisions by unanimity (giving each member state a veto) have been relaxed, and today many important questions before the Council are decided by majority vote. Meanwhile, the European Parliament, now directly elected, has expanded its consultative role rather dramatically and even gained some genuine legislative authority, particularly regarding budgetary matters. For its part, the European Court of Justice has evolved into a constitutional court for the European Union with a perchant for enforcing the superiority of European law over national laws.

While technical accomplishments in transnational harmonization and the institutional evolution of the European Union have been nothing less than remarkable, particularly when set against Europe's history of divisiveness, it also needs to be acknowledged that European unity rests on a philosophical foundation. The European Union is a club of democracies: only countries with democratic governments may join. And the Union itself, with its majoritarian decision-making, its rule of law and its strengthening Parliament underlines that if central government ever emerges it will be a democractic government. The EU is also a club of market economies: private enterprise, open-market competition and freedom of movement and initiative are the norms. Yet, market activity is moderated by public policies aimed at maintaining a "European" way of life where both the extravagances of extreme wealth and the pains of poverty are tempered. Europeans cherish freedom and individuality, but they also recogize their responsibilities to their communities and to one another. In its goals and policies the European Union has upheld these values. It also seeks to be assured that those countries aspiring to membership share them.

Where the European unity movement may be headed remains an open question that will be considered later in this essay. But what the movement has thus far accomplished is quite clear. In the course of a half century intra-European international relations have been transformed. Western Europe is no longer a system of warring sovereign states. In fact, it is not entirely accurate to describe the European Union as a system of sovereign states at all. There exists today a level of governance within the European Union that functions above constituent states and commands mandatory compliance with supranationally formulated legislation. There are also supranational enforcement procedures of a political, judicial and administrative nature that are continually employed and are reasonably effective. Most importantly, when the original peace-building objectives of the European unity movement are recalled, it is quite evident that Western Europe has become a zone of peace. Any possibility that this situation can or will change for the foreseeable future is remote.

## EXPLAINING EUROPEAN UNITY

Because patterns of intra-European international relations since 1945 are not readily explainable in traditional ways, interpreting the movement toward European unity has posed an intellectual challenge. The early consensus among scholars was to label what was happening in postwar Western Europe "international integration." Though several more precise and technical definitions were offered by scholars studying it, most would agree that international integration fundamentally has to do with the peaceful coming together of states and peoples, and this, in the most general way, is what has been happening in postwar Western Europe. Beginning in the early 1950s those who were closely watching European events made efforts to generalize about the hows and whys of international integration and they embodied their insights and formulations in a variety of so-called integration theories.

There was considerable disagreement among theorists about the nature, causes and conditions of international integration. But, there was among them at least initial agreement about what international integration *is not*. It is not traditional power politics, or anything like the kind of international relations depicted by exponents of political realism.[3] International relations as understood by the political realists is a realm of behavior occupied by sovereign states, where each competes with all others for domain, prestige, greater power, or whatever the ingredients of national security turn out to be in particular cases. In this realm,

---

[3] Hans J. Morgenthau, *Politics Among Nations: The Struggle for Power and Peace* (New York: Alfred A. Knopf, 4th ed.), 1967, pp. 3–14; Edward Hallet Carr, *The Twenty Years' Crisis 1919–1939: An Introduction to the Study of International Relations* (New York: Harper Torchbooks, 1964), pp. 63–95.

power, usually military, makes the crucial difference in bringing about outcomes and thus determines winners and losers. According to the realists' understanding, international issues of significance are those that governments are willing to go to war to settle. Other matters, such as trade issues and similar pursuits after welfare are "low politics" and therefore never of central importance in foreign policy or of great consequence for the fate of nations. War is ever possible; it is always expected; it frequently occurs.[4] What does not occur in the realists' world are meaningful or lasting international cooperation (except possibly in military alliances), autonomous or consequential action by international organizations, relinquished sovereignty, important issues that are non-military-strategic in nature, or international order founded upon anything other than balanced power. It needs to be emphasized that the realists' "power politics" vision of international relations is not inaccurate. Historically it has been highly accurate, and in the emerging Cold War system of the 1950s it explained well the fundamental structure and dynamics of crucial aspects of world affairs. But, it did not explain the fundamental structure and dynamics of what has been happening in Western Europe since 1945.

Analysts studying international integration in Western Europe observed and described a kind of international relations that differed from traditional power politics in a variety of ways. As they looked at postwar Western Europe, these analysts observed that:

**1** Sovereign states are not the only consequential actors in international relations. Indeed, some outcomes in international relations can be understood only in terms of the motives, behavior or impacts of international public organizations and bureaucracies, formal and *ad hoc* coalitions of officials transnationally grouped, organized non-governmental associations, multinational business enterprises, international social classes, and other actors traditionally deemed inconsequential.

**2** Issues of national security and war and peace are not the only kinds of foreign policy concerns that governments deem highly important. In fact, some governments allot their most serious attention and efforts to foreign policies directed toward enhancing national welfare defined in terms of per capita income, employment, human security, and the general well-being of their citizens. The importance which governments attach to such welfare goals and the domestic penalties and rewards surrounding their attainment or sacrifice make economic and social issues into "high politics" concerns.

**3** International relations can be fundamentally collaborative processes played out to positive-sum conclusions where all participants "win." Significant outcomes take the form of realizing and distributing rewards among collaborating actors or coalitions. Cooperation, not competition, is the international mode.

---

[4] Raymond Aron, *Peace and War: A Theory of International Relations,* trans. Richard Howard and Annette Baker Fox (Garden City, N.Y.: Doubleday, 1966), pp. 8–17.

**4** Influence in international relations follows from forging and manipulating bonds of interdependence among actors, and not necessarily from threatening or exerting physical force. Bargaining and persuasion, not compulsion, are the modal means to international influence.

**5** Ordered international relations result as readily from adherence to, or compliance with, norms, rules and laws as from balanced power. International law can be an effective ordering force in international relations.

While students of international integration in Western Europe could agree that they were observing a qualitatively new and different kind of international relations on the Old Continent, they could not agree upon exactly what it was that was driving the states and peoples toward ever broadening and deepening unity. Important, though very different, explanations of European integration followed from the seminal work of the American scholars Karl W. Deutsch and Ernst B. Haas, who, in the late 1950s, laid the intellectual groundwork for the theories of international integration that later came to be called international community formation and neo-functionalism.[5] These theories, elaborated and tested by other scholars, retain considerable explanatory power even today.[6]

**International Community Formation**   In explaining the dynamics of European unity, Karl Deutsch distinguished between the coming together of peoples, which he called "integration," and the merger of states or governments, which he called "amalgamation."[7] For Deutsch, a *community* is a population whose members, because of a host of recognized commonalities, identify with one another and distinguish between themselves and others. Integration is essentially community formation, and when it occurs across nations it becomes international community formation. Community formation (i.e., integration) is essentially a social-psychological process during which people come to trust and value one another, to spontaneously respond to one anothers' needs, to emphasize their similarities and dismiss their differences and ultimately to distinguish between themselves collectively and others whom they perceive as being members of alien communities. In ways too complex to deal with in this short essay, the

---

[5] In the social science literature Karl Deutsch's approach which is here called international community formation is referred to as transactionalism, reflecting the fact that communications or transactions among peoples purportedly caused the social-psychological changes that Deutsch studied. Deutsch, however, never used the term "transactionalism" but rather described what he was analyzing as "community formation."

[6] Some of the more imaginative elaborations on integration theory include Leon N. Linberg and Stuart A. Scheingold, *Europe's Would-Be Polity: Patterns of Chance in the European Community* (Englewood Cliffs, N.J.: Prentice-Hall, 1970); Joseph S. Nye, Jr., *Peace in Parts: Integration and Conflict in Regional Organizations* (Boston: Little, Brown, 1971), pp. 21–107; Bruce M. Russett, *Community and Contention: Britain and America in the Twentieth Century* (Cambridge, Mass.: M.I.T. Press, 1963); Karl W. Deutsch et al., *France, Germany and the Western Alliance: A Study of Elite Attitudes and European Integration* (New York: Charles Scribner's Sons, 1967).

[7] Karl W. Deutsch et al., *Political Community and the North Atlantic Area: International Organization in the Light of Historical Experience* (Princeton, N.J.: Princeton University Press, 1957).

community formation process is driven by quantities and qualities of communications or transactions among peoples, which result in learning experiences, and accumulate, under particular conditions, to the merging of identities.[8]

What turns out to be crucially important for the Deutschian analysis is that at some point in the community formation process, those involved come to recognize and accept that there is no longer any danger that differences and disagreements among them will result in wars. On the contrary there emerge almost universally shared expectations that conflicts can and will be peacefully resolved. When such social-psychological conditions prevail within an emergent international community, Deutsch instructs that a "security community" has come into being.[9]

In the Deutschian scheme, community formation or the coming together of peoples must occur, both logically and practically, before amalgamation or the merger of states or governments. It is the new international community that decides to make itself into a new political entity and to signal and protect its integrity and autonomy by establishing institutions of government. Furthermore, it is the new international community that renders itself governable by alloting legitimacy to the newly established institutions of government.

From the Deutschian perspective, what had to be happening in Western Europe from the 1950s onward was the emergence of an international community, a "supranationality" as it were, whose needs for collective action internally and autonomy vis-à-vis the outside world were both making imperative, and legitimizing, international amalgamation in the form of overarching institutions and common public policies. If community formation came first, political amalgamation could follow. Empirically, there was some evidence that international community formation was occurring in postwar Western Europe.[10] However, the "supranationality" that Deutsch and his colleagues were looking for never fully materialized, and even today, more than fifty years after the launching of the European unity movement, there exists only a very superficial "European" identification and no really strong indication that Frenchmen, Germans, Italians, or any of the others have exchanged their national self-identifications for European ones. Yet, as earlier discussion here made clear, political amalgamation in the form of overarching institutions and expanding supranational prerogative has been progressing rather impressively, so it would appear that there was no apparent linkage between prior community formation and subsequent amalgamation in the Western European experience.

The apparent failure of the causal connection between integration and amalgamation in Deutsch's theory led some to dismiss his formulation as an expla-

---

[8] Donald J. Puchala, "International Transactions and Regional Integration," *International Organization* 24, no. 4 (Autumn 1970), pp. 732–64.

[9] The concept "security community" was introduced by Richard W. Van Wagenen in his *Research in the International Organization Field* (Princeton, N.J.: Center for Research on World Political Institutions, 1952).

[10] See, Deutsch et. al., *France, Germany and the Western Alliance, op. cit.*

nation for Western Europe's movement toward unity. But, this may have been tantamount to intellectually throwing the baby out with the bath water, because what empirical investigations did disclose was that, by the mid-1960s, a *security community* had emerged in Western Europe. This was particularly evident in the changing attitudes of Frenchmen and Germans who eventually stopped looking upon each another as potential enemies and stopped expecting that they would fight again in the future.[11] Other significant changes in attitudes among Western Europeans also occurred during the early postwar decades which suggested generally rising levels of mutual trust, confidence and amity, particularly evident among the educated, professionals and the young.[12] Even though no full-blown international community emerged among Western Europeans, there was nevertheless an emergent social-psychological foundation—or permissive environment—underpinning the cooperative diplomacy and the institution building that marked the amalgamative dimension of the movement toward European unity. This foundation was probably a necessary condition for the initiation of productive international cooperation, especially since the countries involved were democratic and public sentiments therefore counted politically. There is every indication that this supportive attitudinal environment has persisted over time.

**Neo-Functionalism**  Ernst Haas was influenced by the early work of the British scholar David Mitrany, who, in a formulation that he called "functionalism," proposed to the post–World War II world that the path to lasting peace required organization and governance beyond the nation state.[13] Meaningful international cooperation could take place, Mitrany said, if "functions" generally performed by national governments—e.g., providing for the well-being of citizens, regulating commerce, protecting the environment, etc.—were assigned to supranational agencies and treated as universal human interests rather than separate national interests. But, whereas Mitrany's functionalism was a plan for global action, Haas's neo-functionalism was a scheme for analyzing international integration. He was most interested in what happens *after* functions are in fact supranationalized. With specific regard to Western Europe, Haas wanted to know what happened after the regulation and administration of economic sectors were assigned to supranational authorities, and in his first integration study, *The Uniting of Europe,* he closely observed the results of the creation of the European Coal and Steel Community.[14] What Haas discovered, and what became the core of neo-functionalism, is that supranationalizing particular functions or policy

---

[11] Puchala, "International Transactions and Regional Integration," *op. cit.,* pp. 744–46.

[12] Donald J. Puchala, "Integration and Disintegration in Franco-German Relations, 1954–1963, *International Organization* 24, no. 2 (1970), pp. 183–208; Karl W. Deutsch et al., *France, Germany and the Western Alliance, op. cit., passim.*

[13] David Mitrany, *A Working Peace System* (Chicago: Quadrangle Books, 1966).

[14] Ernst B. Haas, *The Uniting of Europe: Political, Social, and Economic Forces* (Stanford: Stanford University Press, 1958); see also, Haas, "International Integration: The European Process and the Universal," *International Organization* 15, no. 3 (Summer 1961), pp. 366–92.

sectors tends to unleash a dynamic that almost makes imperative the supranationalizing of additional ones. International integration builds upon itself step by step; it "spills over" until something like a full-blown government emerges at the international level. This happens because each functional step toward expanded international authority sets in motion political processes that generate demands for further steps. At each step, and in the face of demands for new ones, national governments are forced to choose between surrendering additional automony and diluting sovereignty or refusing to do so and risking the collapse of their initial efforts at sector amalgamation. Neo-functionalism posits that, other things being equal, political pressures mounted at key decision points will cause governments to choose to move toward greater amalgamation.

Spillover follows from several causes, all having to do with the politicization of issues in pluralistic societies. First, because modern industrial societies are internally highly interdependent, it is impossible to internationalize one functional sector, say, steel production, without affecting numerous other sectors, as for example, mining, transport, and labor organization and representation. Because other sectors are affected and because elites within them are organized to exert pressure on national governments, their concerns become subjects of international discussion and questions arise about granting further authority to international agencies to handle matters in affected cognate sectors. At such points governments must decide to either grant the expanded international authority or court failure in the initial sector amalgamation. If the balance of perceived rewards and penalities favors moving toward greater amalgamation, as it frequently does, governments will grant expanded authority to international agencies. Sometimes spillover also follows from failures to appreciate the true magnitude or implications of tasks assigned to international agencies: initial conservative grants of authority prove unfeasible and must be extended. It is frequently discovered, for example, that international authorities are unable to perform their assigned tasks within initially imposed jurisidictional limits, so that either assigned tasks have to be abandoned or jurisidictional limits have to be extended.

The great strength of Haas's work was his accurate portrayal of international integration as an intensely political phenomenon. It has to do with numerous political actors, pursuing their own interests, pressuring governments, or, if they are governments, pressuring one another to negotiate toward international policies that are collectively beneficial because they are individually beneficial for all concerned. Like politics more generally, the politics of international integration is a game of bargaining that eventuates in generally acceptable public policies—e.g. common European policies in the case of the European Union.

The weakness of the neo-functional analysis of international integration is that since it begins by looking at the results of initial efforts at supranationalization, it offers little insight into how or why decisions are made to engage in sectoral integration in the first place. Neo-functionalism as applied to Western European integration also tended to assume too much automaticity in the spillover dynamic and therefore could not account for the intermittent slowing down or halting of the movement toward unity which occurred several times. Still, as a description of what has been happening within, and to, postwar Western Europe, neo-functionalism paints a very reliable picture. It also explains in a candidly political, and empirically accurate way, why the picture has taken the form it has taken. Integration has proceeded from functional sector to functional sector. The logic of spillover, for example, is much in evidence in the political imperatives that drove the movement from the sectoral amalgamation in coal and steel in 1952 to a comprehensive common market in 1958, and then to the completion of the common market in 1992. Similar spillover dynamics also account today for Europe's drive to Economic and Monetary Union, and other pressures for spillover could very well accelerate movement toward single, common European foreign and defense policies.

Some recent studies of European integration have reinforced the findings of earlier neo-functionalist scholars. Designating themselves "new institutionalists," American scholars such as Wayne Sandholtz and Alec Stone Sweet, and Europeans like Kenneth Armstrong and Simon Bulmer, have closely examined the origins of policies formulated by the European Union.[15] Among their main findings are that the European institutions (and of course, the officials who in effect are the institutions) are themselves increasingly powerful motors driving integration forward. While commitment, imagination, initiative, legislation, and implementation are by no means the sole prerogatives of the Brussels institutions, these capacities tend to be found there in increasing abundance. Therefore, the key to "Brussels" success is "Brussels" itself, and the fate of the European Union appears to rest increasingly in the efficacy of the central institutions and the quality of the people who lead them.

Relatedly, current scholarship also shows that the European Court of Justice has been playing a much more consequential part in European integration than heretofore acknowledged.[16] Our tendency often is to discount the importance of international courts, because, historically, such institutions have not been very impressive. Not so regarding the European Court. By asserting the superiority of European law over national law, this court has repeatedly forced the sweeping aside of nationally constructed obstacles to deeper integration. Moreover, because of the Court, and via EU judicial processes, business firms and other organizations are able to bypass national authorities and take their claims and their cases

---

[15] Wayne Sandholtz and Alec Stone Sweet, *European Integration and Supranational Governance* (New York: Oxford University Press, 1998); Kenneth Armstrong and Simon Bulmer, *The Governance of the Single European Market* (Manchester, U.K.: Manchester University Press, 1998).

[16] J.H.H. Weiler, "A Quiet Revolution: The European Court and Its Interlocutors," *Comparative Political Studies* 26 (1994), pp. 510–34; J.H.H. Weiler, "Journey to an Unknown Destination: A Retrospective of the European Court of Justice in the Arena of Political Integration," in S. Bulmer and A. Scott (eds.), *Economic and Political Integration in Europe: Internal Dynamics and Global Context* (Oxford, U.K.: Blackwell Publishers, 1994), pp. 131–60.

directly to the level of the European Union, thereby further reinforcing supranationality and driving integration forward.

By far the most significant new contribution to the study of European integration is that of Harvard University's Andrew Moravcsik who in 1998 published *The Choice for Europe*. This study adds an entirely new dimension to our understanding of the origins and dynamics of European Integration, because Moravcsik focuses on the aims and the influences of the governments of the member countries. In contrast to other explanations, like Karl Deutsch's or Ernst Haas's or those of the new institutionalists, where broader and deeper integration are depicted as happening in spite of national governments, Moravcsik sees integration happening because the national governments want it to happen and doggedly push it forward. At almost every juncture since the early 1950s, major European governments—the French and the German governments in particular—have deemed greater international cooperation and more international organization to be in their national interests. They have consistently acted accordingly, and European integration has been the result. The national governments therefore must not be left out of the explanation of European integration. Their influence has been pivotal and must be factored in.

## EUROPEAN INTEGRATION: RETROSPECT AND PROSPECT

If our understanding of Western European integration were informed only from newspaper accounts, we would have to conclude that the European experiment with unity has been an interminable series of crises. It appears from the newpapers that the union is almost always on the verge of breaking apart, that one member country or another, and more often than not the United Kingdom, is always obstructing cooperation, that the European Commission is always overstepping the bounds of its supranational authority and provoking criticism, or that the next integrative step—be it completing the monetary union, agreeing on a common defense policy or a common immigration policy, or enlarging the union's membership—cannot possibly be taken in the face of opposition and complexities. As noted earlier, there has certainly been no shortage of problems along the way to greater European unity, and there certainly have been major crises that have slowed international cooperation and raised doubts about the future. French President Charles DeGaulle, for example, forced the EEC to a standstill in 1966 over questions of majority voting in the Council of Ministers. The energy crisis and global inflation of the 1970s threw the European Communities into disarray as different member states were differently affected by world economic conditions. Margaret Thatcher held up European movement in the 1980s over budgetary questions. The Danes initially rejected the Maastricht Treaty, and the French very nearly defeated it too. The British brought the European Union to a halt in 1996 by escalating the "Mad Cow Crisis." The European Union is poised in 2000, on the threshold of a new enlargement, which critics say the Union cannot digest. It is preparing to complete the monetary union, and pundits are oscillating between confidence and dismay watching the rise and fall of the euro on international exchanges. Brussels is taking up the rest of the Maastricht agenda, which journalists say is too ambitious. The Union is still contending with British ambivalence, which Europeans in the street say is intolerable and destructive. Europe today is confronted with slow economic growth and high unemployment that persist despite diligent remedial efforts, and some say that these failures are the EU's failures. Europeans are also digesting the implications of the conflict in Kosovo and wondering publicly whether NATO remains the answer to European security. Perhaps the time has arrived, some are saying, for the European Union to see to its own military interests. Others strongly disagree, and another wrenching debate within the EU undoubtedly looms.

Though the movement toward Western European unity may appear perennially precarious when examined close up in any short time frame, the longer-run, and more reliably assessable, European experience looks quite different. Historically, the course of intra-European international relations in the context of the European Community and its institutional progeny is best seen as a series of problems constructively solved and a congeries of crises constructively weathered. To date, almost every crisis in Community affairs has resulted in broadened and/or deepened integration. The characteristic pattern of international interaction during European integration has been dialectical: movements toward greater unity invariably provoke opposition, which generates confrontations, which engender negotiations, which eventuate in compromises, which reaffirm unity. Political phases in the working out of the integrative dialectic are frequently long, drawn out, tension-filled, exhausting to those immediately involved and worrisome to those following the media. But, with each succeeding synthesis unity tends to strengthen. Moreover, almost every major goal (and countless minor ones as well) in the course of European integration to which Community members have committed themselves—e.g. establishing the customs union, formulating the common agricultural policy, enlarging in phases, implementing the value-added tax, completing the common market, introducing direct parliamentary elections, moving to majority voting, empowering the Parliament, establishing monetary union, etc.—has eventually been accomplished. This has not always accorded with optimistic timetables, but eventually, and usually later rather than sooner, the goals get accomplished nonetheless. Though member governments in the European Union have differing images of where European integration is, or should be, heading, they have displayed an almost unremitting political will to always move in the direction of greater unity. In historical context then, the future would appear to favor those who favor greater European unity.

Integration theory likewise points to further integration and amalgamation within the European Union. The permissive social-psychological environment of mitigated alienation, mutual confidence, amity and community that Karl Deutsch sought among Europeans is more in evidence today than it was at the time of Deutsch's studies. There is also rather strong public endorsement for the notion of European unity, and notable public approval for the institutions of the EU. So too are there in everyday evidence the political forces and processes pressing for institutional spillover and further supranationalization that Ernst Haas identified as the dynamics of integration. Monetary Union will be a product of these dynamics; so too will be a common European immigration policy, and eventually the politics of spillover will also yield a common European foreign and security policy. The institutions of the European Union are today far more authoritative, autonomous and proactive than they were at the outset of the integration movement. Not only do they embody strong vested interests in greater unity, but they themselves are increasingly capable of pressing unity forward because they have enhanced powers and greater legitimacy. Member governments remain strongly committed to the Europe Union. The political will is there. Prospective new members in Central and Eastern Europe have invested their hopes for the future in the European Union.

In the autumn of 1972, when Andrew Shonfield, Director of London's Royal Institute of International Affairs, was invited to deliver the prestigious Reith Lectures over the BBC, he chose for his subject *Europe: Journey to an Unknown Destination*.[17] His subject remains as perplexing in 2000 as it was in 1972. It is still unclear when European integration will end and what the end product will look like. Some believe that the European Union will evolve into a federation— a United States of Europe. Others envisage a looser kind of confederation wherein the member states will retain considerable autonomy—*L'Europe des Etats*. Still others foresee that Europe, structurally, will not look much different in the future from how it looks today, though they expect that the central institutions— Commission, Council, Parliament and Court—will become increasingly authoritative, and certainly more tasked with common policy making as times goes on. It is more than likely that the eventual institutional framework for continuing European cooperation will be *sui generis;* it will not resemble traditional models like federation or confederation and it will be tailored for European needs and twenty-first century conditions. Few expect that Europe in the future will be less unified than Europe today.

Admittedly, there is no way to say with any assurance where Europe is heading. To date, European integration has been a process, not a product. This process has yielded peace, and has led, over the span of a half century, to incrementally intensifying cooperation among an expanding group of states and peoples. All of this is continuing.

---

[17] Andrew Shonfield, *Europea: Journey to an Unknown Desitination* (London: Penguin Books, 1973).

# 15

# MANAGING CONFLICT IN ETHNICALLY DIVIDED SOCIETIES: A NEW REGIME EMERGES

Ted Robert Gurr

**The breakup of the international system into warring ethnic statelets, which many feared in the early 1990s, has been checked by more effective international and domestic strategies for managing ethnopolitical conflict. In this essay Ted Robert Gurr reports global findings about trends during the 1990s in ethnic conflict and accommodation from the Minorities at Risk project, which he founded and directs. Gurr is a Distinguished University Professor at the University of Maryland. He has written extensively on the causes and accommodation of civil conflict, including _Why Men Rebel_ (1970) and _Ethnic Conflict in World Politics_ (1994, with Barbara Harff). This essay is excerpted from his latest book, _Peoples versus States: Minorities at Risk in the New Century_ (2000).**

The tidal wave of ethnic and nationalist conflict that swept across large parts of Eurasia and Africa in the early 1990s raised grave doubts about the future of the international system of states and the security of their citizens. The pessimistic tone of scholarly and policy analysis at the time is reflected in book titles like "conflicts unending," "pandemonium" and "clash of civilizations." By the mid-1990s armed conflict within states had abated: there was a pronounced decline in the onset of new ethnic wars and a shift in many ongoing wars from fighting to negotiation.

Comparative evidence summarized below shows that deadly ethnopolitical conflict subsided in most world regions from the mid- through late-1990s and that relatively few new contenders have emerged since the early 1990s. The exceptions to this generalization are found mainly in Central and West Africa and in South and Southeast Asia. Most protagonists in the ethnic wars that continued in the late 1990s were veterans of past episodes of protracted communal conflict, not new contenders. This is true of Hutus and Tutsis in the Great Lakes region, and equally true of the Kosovar Albanians. Their conflicts took dramatic and deadly turns in the mid- to late 1990s but have been serious and intermittently violent since the 1960s, in the case of the Hutus and Tutsis, and since the late 1980s in the case of the Kosovars.

Three general reasons can be suggested for the downward trend in ethnic wars. First, the shocks of state reformation in the former Soviet sphere and Eastern Europe have largely passed. The breakup of old states and the formation of new states and regimes in these regions opened up opportunities for ethnopolitical activism; now windows of opportunity in the post-communist states have closed. Second, civil capacities for responding to ethnopolitical challenges have increased, especially in democratic societies. Democratic elites are less likely to rely on strategies of assimilation and repression, more likely to follow policies of recognition, pluralism, and group autonomy. Third, international efforts at publicizing and preventing violations of group rights increased markedly after the Cold War. States and international organizations, prompted by intense media attention and the activism of nongovernmental organizations, as well as their own security concerns, have been more willing to initiate preventive and remedial action. Public and private pressures also have helped persuade governments in some countries with mixed human rights records to improve their treatment of minorities in ways that vary from cosmetic to substantial.

## THE WORLD OF ETHNOPOLITICAL GROUPS

Ethnic and national identities matter to most people but they do not necessarily lead to open conflict. Ethnic groups, also called communal and identity groups, are peoples who share a distinctive and enduring collective identity based on a belief in common descent, shared experiences, and cultural traits that distinguish them from other groups. The Minorities at Risk project tracks a subset of these identity groups, those whose ethnicity or religion has political consequences. Specifically, the project focuses on 275 *ethnopolitical groups* defined to include groups that are disadvantaged by comparison with other groups in their society, usually because of discriminatory practices; and those that have organized politically to promote or defend their collective interests. More than two-thirds of the 275 groups are both disadvantaged and politically active; the others meet only one criterion. Most are numerical minorities like Kosovar Albanians and Americans of African descent; a few are majorities like the Shi'is in Iraq. Also included are advantaged minorities like the Chinese in Indonesia. Small groups are excluded, as are groups in countries with less than 500,000 population.

**TABLE 15.1**
MINORITIES AT RISK IN THE 1990s BY WORLD REGION

| World Region | Number of Countries with Minorities at Risk | Number of Minorities at Risk | | | Total Group Population as Percent of Regional Population |
| | | National peoples | Minority peoples | Total | |
| --- | --- | --- | --- | --- | --- |
| Western democracies and Japan (21) | 15 | 17 | 13 | 30 | 11.8 |
| Eastern Europe and the NIS (27) | 23 | 49 | 10 | 59 | 13.8 |
| East, Southeast, and South Asia (24) | 20 | 36 | 23 | 59 | 13.3 |
| North Africa and the Middle East (20) | 13 | 15 | 13 | 28 | 27.9 |
| Africa south of the Sahara (45) | 27 | 14 | 53 | 67 | 36.1 |
| Latin America and the Caribbean (24) | 18 | 20 | 12 | 32 | 24.5 |
| **Total countries (161)** | **116** | **151** | **124** | **275** | **17.4** |

*Note:* Politically significant national and minority peoples greater than 100,000 or one percent of country population in countries with 1998 populations greater than 500,000. The list is based on current research by the Minorities at Risk project, Center for International Development and Conflict Management, University of Maryland. Changing political circumstances and new information lead to periodic updates in the inclusion and exclusion of groups under observation. Numbers of countries above the 500,000 threshold in 1998 are shown in parentheses in the *World Region* column. The population estimates for national and minority peoples are approximations. Population percentages are calculated from 1998 estimates for all countries in each region.

The Western democratic region includes Canada, the United States, Australia, New Zealand, and Japan in addition to Western Europe. The Middle East includes North Africa, the Arab states, Turkey, Cyprus, Iran, and Israel. Asia includes Afghanistan, the Indian subcontinent, Southeast Asia, and Pacific Asia. Africa includes South Africa but excludes North Africa. Latin America includes Central America and the Caribbean.

National peoples include ethnonationalists (41), national minorities (44), and indigenous peoples (66). Minority peoples include ethnoclasses (43), communal contenders (68), and religious sects (13).

Information on ethnopolitical groups is summarized in Table 15.1. Nearly three-quarters of the world's larger countries (116 of 161) have politically significant minorities. They make up about one-sixth of the world's population, ranging from a low of 10.8 percent of Western democracies and Japan to a high of nearly 40 percent in Africa south of the Sahara. The Minorities at Risk project distinguishes among types of ethnopolitical groups, most basically between national peoples and minority peoples. *National peoples* are 151 regionally concentrated groups that have lost their autonomy to states dominated by other groups but still preserve some of their cultural and linguistic distinctiveness. Their political movements usually seek to protect or reestablish some degree of politically separate existence. Most ethnic wars arise from demands for autonomy or independence by 41 ethnonationalists and 44 national minorities. Indigenous peoples (66) are more likely to use protest. *Minority peoples* (124 groups) have a defined socioeconomic or political status within a larger society—based on some combination of their race, ethnicity, immigrant origins, economic roles, and religion—and are concerned mainly about protecting or improving that status. They include ethnoclasses, communal contenders—some of whom are advantaged— and religious sects. To make the distinction most sharply, national peoples ordinarily seek separation from or greater autonomy within the states that govern them whereas minority peoples seek greater rights, access, or in some cases control of the state itself.

## TRENDS IN ETHNOPOLITICAL CONFLICT
## AND ACCOMMODATION

The most common political strategy among ethnopolitical groups in the 1990s was not rebellion, it was symbolic and organizational politics. Equally important, the numbers of groups using armed violence is declining after decades of increase. The eruption of ethnic warfare that seized observers' attention in the early 1990s was actually the culmination of a long-term general trend of increasing communal-based protest and rebellion that began in the 1950s and peaked immediately after the end of the Cold War. The breakup of the USSR and Yugoslavia provided opportunities for new ethnonational claims and the eruption of a dozen new ethnic wars between 1988 and 1992. In the Global South more than two dozen ethnic wars began or restarted in roughly the same period, between 1988 and 1994.

By mid-decade a world-wide shift in strategies of ethnopolitical action was taking place. When we compare the early with the late 1990s we observe a modest decline from 115 to 95 groups in open conflicts, those in which the parties included coercion and violence among their tactics. More important is the balance between escalation and de-escalation: when we examined 59 armed ethnic conflicts underway in 1998, de-escalating conflicts outnumbered escalating ones by 23 to 7 and the remaining 29 had no short-term trend.

Another way of documenting trends is to time the onset of new episodes of ethnopolitical conflict. When this is done over the thirteen years from 1986 to 1998 we find that two-thirds of all new campaigns of protest and new armed rebellions began in the five years from 1989 to 1993. Few new ethnopolitical conflicts began after 1994, neither protest movements nor rebellions. The decline in numbers of new protest movements is especially hopeful. We observed that a median of 10 years of nonviolent political action preceded the new rebellions of 1986 to 1998. Since the number of new ethnopolitical protest campaigns is declining—from a global average of 10 per year in the late 1980s to 4 per year since 1995—the pool of potential future rebellions is shrinking.

A third way to look at trends is to examine secessionist wars—ethnonational conflicts whose protagonists aim at establishing a new ethnic state or autonomous

**Figure 15.1: Trends in Outcomes of Ethnonational Wars, 1956-1998**

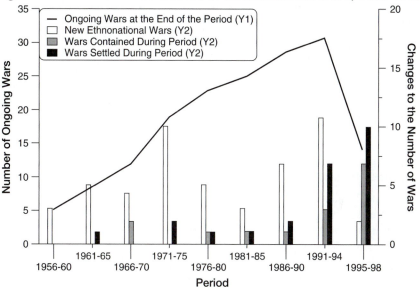

region. These wars are among the most deadly and protracted of all ethnopolitical conflicts and spillovers from them pose serious threats to regional security.
Secessionist wars are in especially steep decline. Between 1991 and 1998 eighteen were settled and ten others were checked by cease-fires and negotiations, as
shown in Figure 15.1. By early 1999 fewer secessionist wars were being fought—
14 by our count—than at any time since 1970. Revolutionary wars that had begun during the Cold War also were being settled, especially in Africa. The trends
help put the rebellion of Kosovar Albanians in perspective. It was the only new
ethnic war in Europe since 1993 and one of only two ethnic wars to begin anywhere in the world in 1997–98.

Less visible than the shift toward settlement of ethnonational wars in the 1990s
is a parallel trend toward accommodation of ethnopolitical conflicts that have not
yet escalated into protracted rebellion. One remarkable and little-noticed achievement of democratic Russia has been the successful negotiation of sub-state autonomy agreements with Tatarstan, Bashkiria, and more than forty other potentially secessionist regions in the Russian Federation. These agreements provide
models that could and should have been employed to head off ethnic wars in
Chechnya and Kosovo. Accommodation failed because of the intransigence of
one or both parties to the disputes.

If political and economic inequalities and cultural restrictions are essential incentives for political action by disadvantaged minorities, which they usually are,
then implementation of international standards of individual and group rights

should reduce the potential for conflict. This is precisely what has happened in the 1990s. Discrimination eased for more than one third of the 275 groups in the Minorities at Risk project between 1990 and 1998, mainly because of shifts in public policies and practices that lifted restrictions on their political and cultural rights. Groups gained most in the new democracies of Europe, Asia, and Latin America. This trend was only partly offset by new restrictions imposed by autocratic governments in the name of exclusive nationalism or in response to security threats. In fact some autocratic governments, especially in Asia, reduced restrictions on their minorities in the 1990s.

## THE EMERGING REGIME OF MANAGED ETHNIC HETEROGENEITY

The global decline in serious ethnic conflict during the 1990s is the result of concerted efforts by a great many people and organizations, including domestic and international peacemakers and some of the protagonists themselves. The term *regime* is used in international politics to refer to a framework of rules, norms, principles, and procedures that facilitate the negotiation of substantive agreements among states. Relations between ethnopolitical groups and governments have changed in the 1990s in ways which suggest that a new regime governing minority-majority relations is under construction. I use the concept in a broader sense to refer to a widely held set of principles about intergroup relations in heterogenous states, a repertoire of strategies for institutionalizing the principles, and agreement on both domestic and international policies for how best to respond to ethnopolitical crises and conflicts.

These are the outlines of the emerging global regime governing the status and rights of national and minority peoples. The first and most basic principle is the recognition and active protection of the rights of minority peoples. This means freedom from discrimination based on race, national origin, language, or religion, complemented by institutional means to protect and promote their collective cultural and political interests. A corollary principle is the right of national peoples to exercise some degree of autonomy within existing states to govern their own affairs. This is a logical consequence of the first principle. That is, it follows that if minority peoples who constitute a majority in one region of a heterogenous democratic state have the right to protect and promote their collective interests, then they should have the right to local or regional self-governance.

Contemporary democracies have been most consistent in articulating, promoting, and implementing such policies. After World War II a human rights regime evolved in the Atlantic democracies that emphasized the protection of individual rights. During the early 1990s the emphasis of Western advocates shifted from individual rights to protection of collective rights of national minorities. The effect of standard-setting texts adopted in 1990–95 by the Organization for Security and Cooperation in Europe and the Council of Europe was to establish what Jennifer Preece calls "an international regime for protection of national minorities in

Europe—however limited . . ."[1] The texts embody several principles. One is prohibition against forced assimilation and population transfer, another is endorsement of autonomy for minority communities within existing states, a third is recognition that national minority questions are legitimate subjects of international relations both at the United Nations and within European regional organizations.

Virtually all European democracies have implemented these principles. In the first stage of democratization in post-communist Europe, at the beginning of the 1990s, some ethnonational leaders manipulated the democratic process to serve nationalist interests at the expense of national minorities like the Russians in the Baltic states, Hungarians in Slovakia and Romania, and Serbs in Croatia. In most of these countries a combination of diplomatic engagement by European institutions and the democratic process led to a reversal of discriminatory policies by the late 1990s.

The principle of sub-state autonomy for national minorities is more difficult to implement than policies of nondiscrimination, for two reasons. One is the resistance of most governing elites to devolution of central authority, the other is the necessity to negotiate situation-specific arrangements that satisfy both parties. The best known models for sub-state autonomy agreements have been reached through negotiated settlements of ethnonational rebellions. Such rebellions usually begin with demands for complete independence—and usually end with negotiated or de facto autonomy for the ethnonationalists. What can be discerned is a growing disposition of parties to these conflicts to work toward accommodation in early stages rather than after prolonged warfare. Nationalist Serbia has become the pariah state and bombing range of Europe precisely because of its blatant violation of principles about group rights that elsewhere are widely accepted.

The recognition and protection of collective rights is one of the three elements of the regime or doctrine of managed ethnic heterogeneity. Political democracy is another. It provides the institutional means by which national peoples and minorities in most societies secure their rights and pursue collective interests. There are other institutional mechanisms for the protection of communal groups' interests, for example the hegemonic exchange system (the term is Donald Rothchild's) found in many nondemocratic African states. Nonetheless democracy, in one of its European variants, is widely regarded as the most reliable guarantee of minority rights. It is inherent in the logic of democratic politics that all peoples in heterogenous societies should have equal civil and political rights. Democratic governance also implies acceptance of peaceful means for resolving civil conflicts.

A third element of the new regime is the principle that disputes between communal groups and states are best settled by negotiation and mutual accommodation. The principle is backed up by the active engagement of major powers, the United Nations, and some regional organizations (especially in Europe and

---

[1] Jennifer Jackson Preece, "National Minority Rights vs. State Sovereignty in Europe: Changing Norms in International Relations?" *Nations and Nationalism* 3, no. 3 (1997), 345–64, quotation p. 359.

Africa) which use various mixes of diplomacy, mediation, inducements, and threats to encourage negotiated settlements of ethnic conflicts. The notion of preventive diplomacy has great current popularity not only because early engagement is potentially cheaper than belated responses to ethnic and other internal disputes, but because it is the preferred instrument of the new regime. Coercive intervention, as in Serbia, is the international system's response of last resort to gross violations of human rights and to ethnic wars whose spillover effects threaten regional security.[2]

Four general, i.e. regional and global, forces reinforce the application of principles of accommodation in heterogeneous societies. First is the active promotion of democratic institutions and practices by the Atlantic democracies. There is near-conclusive evidence that modern democracies rarely fight one another and are tempered in their use of repression against internal opponents. Before-and-after comparisons of national and minority peoples in new democracies, included in the book from which this essay is drawn, show their political and cultural status improves substantially during democratic transitions.[3]

The second source of reinforcement is proactive action on behalf of the rights of national peoples and minorities by the U.N. and its constituent organizations, by regional bodies, and by interested nongovernmental organizations. In a number of instances bodies such as the Organization for Security and Cooperation in Europe, the Council of Europe, the Organization for African Unity, and the Organization of the Islamic Conference have used diplomatic initiatives and mediation to temper the policies of member states toward minorities and to move open conflicts toward agreement.

Third is the virtually universal consensus among the international political class—the global foreign policy elite—about the goal of reestablishing and maintaining global and regional order. Empire building is out of fashion, interstate rivalries in the 1990s focus mainly on increased productivity and competition for markets, wars of any stripe are a threat to regional order and stable economic relations. Thus the U.N., the United States and regional powers, and the regional organizations of Europe, Latin America, and Africa give high priority to containing local conflicts by preventive measures where possible, by mediation and peacekeeping operations where necessary.

Finally, whatever the nature of the political system, the costs of violent ethnopolitical conflict have become evident to both governing elites and the leaders of ethnopolitical movements. The costs of civil war have been acknowledged with deep regret in countries where post-war settlements are taking hold—in

---

[2] Recent works that emphasize international responsibilities for preventing internal conflict include Connie Peck, *The United Nations as a Dispute Settlement System: Improving Mechanisms for the Prevention and Resolution of Conflict* (The Hague: Kluwer Law International, 1996); and Hugh Miall, Oliver Ramsbotham, and Tom Woodhouse, *Contemporary Conflict Resolution: The Prevention, Management, and Transformation of Deadly Conflicts* (Cambridge, U.K.: Polity Press, 1999).

[3] See chap. 5 in Ted Robert Gurr, *Peoples versus States: Minorities at Risk in the New Century* (Washington, D.C.: United States Institute of Peace Press, 2000).

Bosnia, the Philippines, Mozambique, and elsewhere. The lesson drawn by outside observers of the war in Chechyna was the inability of the Russian military—as earlier in Afghanistan—to defeat highly motivated guerrilla opponents. The lesson for the protagonists was that the war was not worth fighting since neither side gained much that could not have been achieved by negotiations before the Russian invasion. Caution about the likely costs of renewed war and the unlikely chances of victory on either side probably have helped check ethnic rebellions elsewhere on the periphery of Russia and in most of the Soviet successor states. NATO's spring 1999 campaign against Serbia conveys a similar message to other states whose leaders have not been willing to compromise with ethnonationalists. The lesson has reached as far as China, where the Kosovo crisis reportedly prompted Communist Party officials to begin drafting alternative policies for dealing with Tibetans and Uighers.[4]

In summary, international doctrines specify the rights of minorities and national peoples within states and stipulate international responsibilities for promoting those rights. These doctrines are invoked by representatives of minorities and nongovernmental organizations as well as public and international officials. Democratic governance, power sharing, and devolution are widely advocated as institutional means for securing group rights. Although the principles and institutions are mainly of Western democratic origins, they are articulated and applied in many other places including Latin America, much of Asia, and some parts of Africa and the Middle East. They underlie two global trends documented above, one the crisscrossing trends of declining ethnic warfare and increasing numbers of negotiated settlements, the second the reduction of political and cultural restrictions on minorities in virtually every world region. Both are sustained and reinforced by the emergence of democratic norms and institutions in heterogenous societies in most post-communist states, in Latin America, in much of Asia, and parts of Africa.

## CHALLENGES TO THE PEACEFUL MANAGEMENT OF HETEROGENEITY

The claim that there is an emerging global regime for managing ethnic heterogenity challenges the conventional wisdom of policy makers and foreign affairs analysts in Western societies. What about communal warfare and genocide in central Africa, ethnic cleansing in Kosovo, Muslim and Hindu fundamentalism, and regional rebellions in Indonesia? The answer is a paradox. Objectively we have shown that there are substantially fewer such conflicts in the mid- to late-1990s than in previous years, but subjectively they get far more public attention—precisely because they challenge the emerging norms of recognition for group rights, peaceful accommodation of communal conflicts, and the comforting assumption that the "international community" is capable of guaranteeing local and regional security.

---

[4] John Pomfret, "Kosovo Hits Close to Home," *Washington Post,* May 7, 1999, A31ff.

The heterogenous world system that is emerging from the settlement of ethnic and regional conflicts is more complex than its Cold War predecessor. It is a multilayered system with three interdependent sets of political actors: states; ethnopolitical movements, some of which are situated within existing states, others of which transcend them; and regional and international organizations that are assuming greater responsibility for managing relations among the other two. States remain the paramount actors in this heterogenous system but are constrained by a growing network of mutual obligations with respect to identity groups and supranational actors.

This heterogenous world system is not fully developed and faces violent challenges from states and ethnopolitical movements that do not accept its principles. Few states in the Islamic world are prepared to grant full political and cultural rights to religious minorities. A number of protracted ethnopolitical conflicts are highly resistant to regional and international influence. Conflicts in Afghanistan and Sudan look to be intractable unless and until one party or coalition wins a decisive victory. Odds are against settlement of protracted conflicts between Kurdish nationalists and governments in Iraq and Turkey or containment of communal conflict between Hutus and Tutsis. Some ethnoconflicts are being held in check by cease-fires and promised reforms that can easily come apart. South Asia has a dozen serious ethnopolitical conflicts whose chances for settlement are highly problematic. Since the 1950s the central government of India has faced a series of secessionist challenges; no sooner has one movement been checked than another emerges. Other problematic conflicts are those that have been "settled" in the traditional way, by overwhelming force, for example by the governments of Burma, Indonesia, and China. Repression without accommodation leads with some regularity to renewed resistance and rebellion, as has happened in Indonesia's Aceh region since the fall of Suharto's government in 1998.

The theory and data of the Minorities at Risk project provide a means for systematically identifying groups at high risk of future rebellion. A risk model is developed along the lines used by medical researchers to assess the risks that individuals will suffer from heart disease. Risk factors are measured for past cases of ethno-rebellion, then the 275 groups in the Minorities study are profiled on these factors in 1998 and statistical models are used to assess each group's probability of new or escalating rebellion. The risk model starts with the premise, based on empirical evidence, that incentives for future conflict are inherent in discriminatory treatment and policies of repressive control. Other major factors in the risk equations are groups' capacity for action, their domestic opportunities—especially regime instability—and international support. About 90 of the 275 groups in the study, including those already fighting ethnic wars, had medium to high predicted risks of future rebellion.[5]

---

[5] The risk models and how they are derived are described in chap. 7 and Appendix B of Gurr, *Peoples versus States.*

**TABLE 15.2**
RISKS OF NEW AND ESCALATING ETHNIC WARS

| Region and Groups | Groups in Ethnic Wars in 1998 and at Future Risk | Highest-Risk Groups and Facilitating Factors in 1998 |
|---|---|---|
| *Western democracies:*<br>31 ethnopolitical groups | No groups in ethnic wars<br>5 groups at medium risk | Basques in France  ++<br>Basques in Spain  + |
| *Eastern Europe and Former USSR:*<br>59 ethnopolitical groups | Two groups in ethnic wars<br>8 groups at high risk<br>7 groups at medium risk | Armenians in Nagorno-<br>  Karabakh  - -<br>Kosovars in Yugoslavia  -<br>Russians in Estonia  -<br>Crimean Tatars  +<br>Crimean Russians  +<br>Bosnian Serbs  + |
| *Southeast and Pacific Asia:*<br>34 ethnopolitical groups | Five groups in ethnic wars<br>3 groups at high risk<br>12 groups in medium risk | Uighers in China  ++<br>Timorese in Indonesia  -<br>Aboriginal Taiwanese  0 |
| West and South Asia:<br>25 ethnopolitical groups | Eleven groups in ethnic wars<br>6 groups at high risk<br>13 groups at medium risk | Hazaras, Tajiks, and Uzbeks<br>  in Afghanistan  0<br>Kashmiris in India  ++<br>Tripuras and Scheduled<br>  tribes in India  + |
| *North Africa and Middle East:*<br>28 ethnopolitical groups | Three groups in ethnic wars<br>6 groups at high risk<br>2 groups at medium risk | Kurds in Turkey  0<br>Shi'a in Iraq  +<br>Shi'a in Lebanon  +<br>Palestinians in Gaza and the<br>  West Bank  0<br>Kurds in Iraq  ++<br>Arabs in Israel  0 |
| *Africa South of the Sahara:*<br>67 ethnopolitical groups | Eleven groups in ethnic wars<br>12 groups at high risk<br>8 groups at medium risk | Ogani in Nigeria  ++<br>Tutsi in Congo-Kinshasa  0<br>Ovimbundu in Angola  +<br>Yoruba in Nigeria  ++<br>Hutu in Burundi  ++<br>Afar in Ethiopia  ++ |
| *Latin America and Caribbean:*<br>32 ethnopolitical groups | No groups in ethnic wars<br>1 group at high risk<br>11 groups at medium risk | Miskitos in Nicaragua  - -<br>Maya in Mexico  0<br>Indigenous highlanders in<br>  Ecuador  - - |

*Note:* Ethnic wars in 1998 are conflicts between rebels and states with rebellion magnitudes of 4 or greater. No more than six highest-risk groups in each region are listed here. For details see Gurr, *Peoples versus States,* chap. 7 and Appendix B.

The Minorities project risk assessments come in two parts. One is a probability estimate for each group generated by a statistical risks model; the numbers of high- and medium-risk groups in each region are shown in the first column of Table 15.2. The second is a data-based set of indicators that show whether domestic and external factors that facilitate rebellion are increasing or decreasing. The highest-risk groups in each region are listed in the second column of Table 15.2; the net escalating and dampening effects for each group are summarized in the pluses and minuses.

The risk assessment approach gives some perspective on the Kosovo conflict. In no sense was it unprecedented; rather, it was the most warned-about crisis in Europe during the 1990s. A group's loss of political autonomy is one of the strong leading indicators of future rebellion: the Yugoslav government led by Slobodan Milosevic dissolved the Kosovo regional government in 1989. A decade of political activism and protest typically precedes the onset of ethnic wars: the Kosovars resisted their loss of autonomy by forming a parallel government but the first terrorist attacks did not begin until 1997 and large-scale rebellion in 1998. Milosevic's ultranationalist policies fundamentally contradict European and international principles about minority rights: no significant concessions were offered to the Kosovars. Preventive international responses to the situation were not carried through: the Bush Administration warned the Yugoslav government against using repression in Kosovo in December 1992 but the issue was not addressed in the Dayton Accords in 1996 (negotiated by the Clinton Administration) and the preparatory steps in the ethnic cleansing campaign in October 1998 elicited no international response.

The 90 medium- to high-risk groups are the most likely protagonists in new and escalating ethnic wars early in the twenty-first century. The largest numbers of at-risk groups are situated the post-communist states, West and South Asia, and Africa south of the Sahara. Risks of ethnic war are minimal in the Western democracies and only slightly greater in Latin America and the Caribbean.

In Europe risks are highest in the Balkans. Spillover from the Kosovo conflict could increase them, especially for groups already at risk like the Sandzak Muslims and Vojvodina Hungarians in Serbia. A new democratic government in Serbia is the best antidote for these risks. Our analysis also points to medium potentials for renewed fighting among Serb, Muslim, and Croat contenders in the Yugoslav successor states. In the Caucasus preventive diplomacy and peacekeeping efforts have paid off in the containment and settlement of most ethnic wars of the early 1990s. Risks remain high, however, for intensification of warfare over the status of Nagorno-Karabakh and armed conflict by the Ingush, who live on Chechnya's western border.

Outside Europe prospects for ethnopolitical peace are best in Latin America. Almost all domestic and external factors indicate a dampening of risks in this region. Most high-risk protagonists are indigenous peoples whose demands for recognition and local autonomy are being substantially addressed by democratic governments. The Nicaraguan and Mexican governments face the greatest risks of rebellion. In Nicaragua this is due mainly to lack of resources for implementing an autonomy agreement for the coastal peoples, in Mexico because of lack of political will to respond with real reforms to political action by indigenous peoples in Chiapas, Oxaca, and elsewhere.

Four other zones of ethnopolitical conflict pose greater present and future challenges. One is the Middle East, where the central issues are the unsatisfied ethnonational aspirations of Palestinians and Kurds. Further east is the West and South Asia zone, characterized by communal contention for power in Afghanistan and Pakistan and by ethnonationalist rebellions by Kashmiris and Sri Lankan Tamils. The largest number of ongoing and prospective ethnic wars anywhere in the world occur in the Central Asian uplands, stretching from the hill country of Bangladesh, Assam, and Burma to Tibet and China's Xinjiang province.

Africa's situation is the most grave. Twenty African groups are at medium to high risk of future rebellion, half of whom live in or on the periphery of the Eastern and Middle African conflict zone (or two zones) ranging from Sudan and Ethiopia through the Great Lakes region to the Congo basin and the Angola highlands. There is also a less threatening West African conflict zone, where revolutionary and ethnic wars have been brought under control in Niger, Mali, and Liberia but continue in Sierra Leone and Chad. The greatest risk in this region has been the possibility of internal war in Nigeria along the north-south, Muslim-Christian divide. The Ogoni minority of the Niger delta and the much larger Yoruba both are high on the factors that elsewhere predict to ethnic war. The prospects of ethnic war in Nigeria are very much dependent on the current transition to democracy. Civil war in Nigeria would have spillover effects far beyond its borders.

The primary purpose of the risk analysis is to highlight situations that should have the highest priority for remedial and preventive action. By whom and how? The answers depend on which actors have the will, the political leverage, and the resources to act. The Kosovo case illustrates that the reach of the new doctrine of managed ethnic heterogeneity depends on whether it is accepted by those whose conflicts are to be managed, and on the willingness of regional and international organizations to enforce it. International and regional organizations are more likely to pursue effective preventive strategies in areas where the Western powers have vital interests, which means Europe, Latin America, and the Middle East. Asian and African conflicts are more remote and resistant to external influence. When preventive strategies fail, or are not made in the first place, the international challenges are different: how to provide humanitarian aid and how to contain the regional dispersion of conflict.

The evidence reviewed above shows decisively that group rights and interests are being protected and promoted more effectively in the decade since the Cold War ended than they were before 1989. The norms, institutions, and practices of managed ethnic heterogeneity have strong international support but their application is ultimately a local matter, the result of decisions taken by societies and governments. Many of the principles are embodied in democratic doctrine, and democracy is in the ascendance in all world regions. However, ultranationalists can impose majoritarian tyranny. Islamist leaders reject the validity of groups' claims based on dispensations of religious doctrine other than their own. Probably the greatest threats to claims of a universal regime of group rights comes from predatory, hegemonic elites who use the state as an instrument to protect and promote the interests of their own people at the expense of others. These and other sources of communal warfare and repression remain in many corners of the world and will continue to cast up challenges to those who would promote human rights and contain ethnic violence.

The zones of ethnopolitical conflict will pose a critical set of tests of whether regional and international actors will act to strengthen the regime of managed ethnic heterogeneity. The regime is most likely to operate in the more developed and democratic regions. Regional powers in Asia can be expected to evolve and promote their own responses to ethnopolitical conflict, especially when and where it threatens economic development and regional stability. The most severe new challenges probably will come in Africa, particularly in the broad middle belt of Africa where resource constraints and economic decline are severe, failures of governance are endemic, and the international will and ability to act has been weakest.

No one strategy is likely to contain deep-rooted communal conflicts in Central Africa or any other high-risk regions. What is needed is coordinated efforts by international actors and major powers to facilitate negotiated settlements, guarantee local and regional security, promote democratic power sharing, and assist economic development. If policies of managed ethnic heterogeneity are to succeed, they have to be devised in partnership with elements of civil society, those local people and organizations who are committed to the nonviolent and democratic reconstruction of their societies. And they require sustained effort. Building civil peace in divided societies depends not just on peace settlements and institutional engineering but on consistent, long-term engagement to ensure that agreements are implemented and institutions work.

# 16

# THE NEW INTERVENTIONISM AND THE THIRD WORLD

Richard Falk

Many issues continue to divide the developing countries of the Global South from the wealthy countries of the Global North. Highly problematic is how the rich countries will pay attention to, interact with, and intervene in the internal affairs of the most unstable failing states in the Third World, where the danger of human rights violations and even genocide most cry for external intervention to alleviate human suffering and prevent innocent and powerless victims from state-sponsored terrorism. In this essay Richard Falk addresses the problems arising from humanitarian catastrophes in these collapsing states, catastrophes that are making for a new world disorder. These problems are seen against the backdrop of the legal barriers prohibiting, in the name of respect for traditional territorial sovereignty, humanitarian intervention (by powerful Global North countries) in the internal affairs of established states. Falk also examines the challenge of preventing, by multilateral institutions such as the United Nations, ethnic cleansing and other crimes against humanity in the Third World. This assessment of the threats to the unity and survival of failing Third World states puts the tragic conditions that afflict many Global South countries into perspective, and shows why it will be difficult, given growing support for human rights and the impact of globalization, to "get the genie of self-determination back into the bottle of state sovereignty" in the twenty-first century. Falk is Albert G. Milbank Professor of International Law and Practice at Princeton University. Among his many books, he has recently published *Law in an Emerging Global*

*Village: A Post-Westphalian Perspective* (**1998**) and *Predatory Globalization: A Critique* (**1999**).

The most vexing problems in the 1990s have arisen from human catastrophes in economically and politically disadvantaged countries. Somalia, Bosnia, Rwanda, Chechnya, Kosovo, Sierra Leone, Liberia, and Sudan are some of the most prominent instances. These countries are either in the geographical South or in two dismantled states, the Soviet Union and Yugoslavia. Their plight is linked to a circumstance of "new world disorder" that emerged after the end of the Cold War and continued through the 1990s.

Because they are no longer of strategic interest to the world power structure or from the perspectives of globalization, leading states have had no incentive to invest heavily in rescue operations. At the same time, however, the global media have highlighted with vivid images the suffering associated with these crises of governance.

Furthermore, there has been a strong buildup of support for international human rights in recent decades, the result of concerted activity by nongovernmental organizations around the world, as well as the success of the anti-apartheid campaign directed at South Africa and the struggle for civil and political rights in Eastern Europe. This recent emphasis on human rights has added poignancy to the tragedy of societies seemingly caught in a deadly downward spiral of events with no serious prospects of a reversal through self-help.

## SUMMONING THE UNITED NATIONS . . .

Pressure to do something about humanitarian catastrophes has mounted, but what to do, and by whom, has proved controversial, with undertakings in response often leading to despair and disappointment. The most obvious approach was to turn for urgent help to the United Nations. After all, cooperation within the Security Council seemed much more feasible than it had during the gridlock of the Cold War era. The U.N. had made major contributions even before the collapse of the Soviet Union, playing useful peacekeeping roles in ending regional conflicts in a series of countries, including Afghanistan, El Salvador, Angola, Mozambique, and Namibia. Such optimism about an expanding U.N. role reached its climax with the 1991 Persian Gulf War, when the Security Council joined together in support of action to restore Kuwaiti sovereignty after Iraq's invasion the previous year.

But relying on the U.N. to address humanitarian crises was not a problem-free solution. First, constitutional problems arose associated with the limitation of U.N. authority. Article 2(7) of the U.N. Charter declared that internal matters were beyond the reach of the organization. This principle had been designed to reassure member states that their sovereign rights would be respected, and that they would not become targets of collective intervention in the future. Beyond this, it was not clear that the U.N. could mobilize the political will or the capabilities to address internal problems in weak states whose destiny seemed unrelated to the strategic interests of those that are rich and powerful. Concerns were also voiced that the U.N. mandate was being appropriated by the United States to disguise the unilateral character of an essentially military undertaking. During the Gulf War, the Security Council did not appear to play a significant role after its initial act of authorization was given, and all decisions about the scope, the tactics, and even the goals of the war were reached in Washington after only limited consultation with coalition partners.

Yet the non-Western world itself is divided as to what is the appropriate U.N. role. It is split between those who advocate a stronger United Nations able and willing to mount effective humanitarian interventions as needed, and those who fear that such action serves as a cover for geopolitics and offers a pretext for new forms of postcolonial intervention by the North in the South. In the background is the tension between protecting the sovereign rights of weaker states, an essential value for recently independent countries, and providing the international capabilities needed to rescue people from extreme ethnic violence and other conditions of life-threatening chaos.

This background had drawn into question two overlapping arenas of action and influence. The first is the United Nations, especially the Security Council. The last three secretaries-general of the U.N. have each called for an expanded peace and security mandate that limits the sovereignty of states by reference to norms of international human rights. Given the experience of the last decade, it is extremely doubtful whether the U.N. can act effectively, independently, and consistently in response to these essentially internal challenges.

The Gulf War is misleading as a model. The main theater of conflict was international, with several major powers acting in collective self-defense on behalf of Kuwait. Furthermore, the preconditions for successful U.N. action were satisfied because the geopolitical interests at stake coincided with the basic U.N. mission to restore Kuwaiti sovereignty. In all subsequent undertakings, the U.N. has been given an uncertain mandate and insufficient capabilities by the U.N. Security Council, reflecting the ambivalence and divisions among the five permanent members of the Security Council. The ideological fervor of the Cold War has happily vanished from U.N. undertakings, but fundamental differences on global policy continue to put Russia and China on one side and the three Western states of France, the United Kingdom, and the United States on the other side of many issues. At bottom, the opposition arises from Russian and Chinese fears of what they regard as a Euro-American effort to exert control over the U.N. and world politics more generally.

The other related arena of potential action is that of the United States government, as the "sole surviving superpower" and the state that provides diplomatic leadership for global peace and security. Its own shifting assessments of the importance and method of responding to internal political turbulence have often undermined the U.N.'s role and created confusion as to the character of its foreign policy.

In the early 1990s, Washington was an enthusiastic advocate of humanitarian activism within a U.N. framework, but it seriously underestimated the potential costs and nature of such rescue operations in the setting of what was then referred to as "failed states." This American ebullience received a rude shock in 1993 when an incident during a peacekeeping operation in Somalia resulted in the death of 18 American soldiers. A sharp political backlash produced an abrupt shift in approach by the Clinton administration that saw the United States use its leadership role in 1994 to minimize the U.N. response to genocide in Rwanda, and generally to favor extremely limited responses to humanitarian catastrophes elsewhere, thereby degrading U.N. credibility.

The failure of the U.N. mission to protect the victims of Serbian ethnic cleansing in Bosnia gave rise to considerable criticism directed at the ineffectuality of the United Nations and contributed to a rethinking of how to address future humanitarian catastrophes, especially if they occurred in Europe. The ordeal of the Bosnian war was finally brought to an end by a combination of NATO bombing missions and a forceful diplomatic initiative spearheaded by the United States that produced the Dayton Accords at the end of 1995. Although the wisdom, justice, and durability of these arrangements are still being debated, they did represent a clear shift away from reliance on the United Nations.

## . . . ONLY TO ABANDON IT

Then came the challenge of ethnic cleansing in Kosovo during the late 1990s. The crimes against humanity attributed to Yugoslav President Slobodan Milosevic's government directly challenged Europe and the United States to protect these new victims of ethnic cleansing before it was too late. Remembering the failures to stop genocidal outbreaks in Rwanda, and especially the mass killings in Bosnia, Western states favored a strong response for Kosovo. Partly for domestic political reasons in the United States, and partly because of the difficulty of gaining the support of Russia and China in the Security Council, a regional approach was adopted. It led to a diplomatic effort to induce Belgrade to accept a NATO peacekeeping force for Kosovo, and when that failed, to launch a 78-day air campaign under NATO auspices. Finally, in mid-1999 Yugoslavia relented, and an occupying international force under a NATO commander, but within a U.N. framework, was agreed upon.

Contrary to stated NATO objectives, Kosovo was then moved closer to a condition of independence under the authority of its Albanian population, a group that previously had been the victim of Serbian oppression but was now apparently engaged in ethnic cleansing of its own. The result seems to be an ethnic Albanian ministate rather than the sort of multiethnic entity being destroyed by Milosevic. It is also noteworthy that NATO and the United States felt obliged to rely on Russian diplomacy to negotiate an end to military operations that lasted much longer than hoped, straining public support and alliance unity. The ironic result of the essentially one-sided war was to allow the Milosevic regime a face-saving way out of Kosovo, almost the very one that had been refused before the war commenced.

Although effective as a show of force and political will, the alliance's approach to Kosovo was exceedingly controversial and unsatisfactory in several respects, producing anxieties in Third World settings and a debate virtually everywhere. The legal authority of the U.N. with respect to the use of force was bypassed, and the explicit U.N. Charter prohibition on unauthorized regional enforcement action was ignored. A threatening precedent under the rubric of humanitarian intervention was established.

The form of intervention was also troublesome. The stark unevenness of the war-fighting capabilities, with no NATO casualties despite thousands of bombing sorties, suggested that an intimidating military predominance was now lodged in the West, specifically under the control of the United States with its mastery of the application of information technology to warfare. The threatening character of this military predominance was abetted by the unilateral use of force by Washington in recent years in response to allegations of complicity with international terrorism or in its struggle against so-called rogue states. Sudan and Afghanistan, for example, were bombed in 1998 without any authorization from the U.N. Yet these bombings were only speculatively and rather remotely connected with the terrorist incidents against American embassies in Kenya and Tanzania that allegedly justified such recourse to force outside the area of self-defense, the sole legal grounds for the use of force by a state under contemporary international law.

Then came East Timor, outside the European sphere and in the immediate aftermath of doubts about the Kosovo approach. Again the U.N. seemed indispensable. The Indonesian military had encouraged a brutal response to a U.N.-sponsored referendum in which 78.5 percent of those voting indicated support for an independent East Timor. In response to Indonesian state-sponsored terror, a combination of geopolitical pressure from the United States on the government of Jakarta, regional responsibility by Australia to supply most of the personnel for a peacekeeping mission, and a formal U.N. mandate have seemed to provide some relief for the East Timorese. However, the future of this long-suffering people remains in doubt.

What emerges from this chronology of events is a wavering sequence of international responses in which several elements are moved back and forth on a case-by-case basis that reflects shifting political moods, foreign policy calculations, and a variety of distinct patterns of humanitarian catastrophe. Of greatest importance seems to be the attitude taken by the United States with regard to the degree of response and under whose auspices.

Three main ideas are woven together in different patterns in each specific instance: unilateral action by the United States; a U.N. undertaking; and reliance on the primacy of regional responsibility. It needs to be realized that often the main priority of potential intervenors is to minimize responses to humanitarian catastrophes so as to avoid being drawn into costly undertakings of uncertain outcome and little strategic value. The common element in these crises is to raise crucial policy choices between preserving the territorial unity of existing sovereign states and upholding the rights of self-determination for oppressed peoples.

## UNITY VERSUS SELF-DETERMINATION

A special section of the July 31 *Economist* was devoted to "The Road to 2050," involving what the editors called "the new geopolitics." It contained an inquiry into whether state-shattering turbulence would reshape the world map of the future, either moving in the direction of adding many new states to the current [207], or cutting back to a small number of regional giants. The humanitarian catastrophe in East Timor, coming so quickly after the Kosovo campaign, provides a vivid reminder of the centrality of political turbulence within states to the quality of world order as . . . the twenty-first century [unfolds].

What makes these challenges so bewildering is that they often appear to arise at the intersection of two conflicting fundamental principles: that of respect for the state's territorial sovereignty and that of the right of self-determination enjoyed by "the peoples" of the world. Throughout the Cold War a modus vivendi between these two principles generally prevailed. It consisted of limiting self-determination claims for political independence to those situations that did not involve the dismemberment of any existing state. The main context of self-determination was associated with the dynamics of decolonization, and both East and West, along with the leadership of the Third World, accepted the idea that colonial borders would be respected during the transition to independence. Challenges along the way have involved Tibet and China, the Ibos and Nigeria, and Kashmir and India, but in each instance the territorial sovereign has successfully resisted secessionist moves. Only Bangladesh, with India's help, was able to shatter the unity of Pakistan after a bloody genocidal ordeal in 1971 that sent as many as ten million refugees temporarily into India.

This pattern of limiting self-determination was accepted as operative international law, and was endorsed unanimously by the U.N. General Assembly's 1970 Declaration of Principles of International Law Concerning Friendly Relations among States. A kind of Faustian bargain, it meant consigning restive minority peoples, in effect, "captive nations," to oppressive regimes that persistently abused their rights in exchange for an agreed principle of order that recognized the primacy of the sovereign state within its own territory. Occasionally, as in South Africa in the apartheid period or in Kosovo, the oppressed group was actually the large majority of the affected population. Such bargains always seem like moral backsliding when one recalls the tragic inaction of the international community toward the plight of the Jews during the Nazi period before and during World War II, persecution ignored because it was occurring within German territory.

Several developments eroded, if not altogether destroyed, the bargain between advocates of self-determination and defenders of sovereignty. The first and foremost was the political current unleashed by the ending of the Cold War. By moving quickly to recognize the recovery of statehood by the Baltic countries, and then the other republics that had composed the Soviet Union, a major precedent seemed to be set: self-determination could be realized under certain conditions in a manner that disrupted the former unity of a state. In the Soviet instance, the process seemed spontaneous, and appeared to be a largely voluntary adjustment to the collapse of the Soviet Union and its internal empire. Subsequent developments in the former Yugoslavia were less reconcilable with the older bias against state-shattering involuntary claims of secession. European diplomacy, led by Germany, quickly moved to recognize Slovenia and Croatia as states, and appeared to deny Belgrade the right to maintain the unity of Yugoslavia.

As had been understood from the moment it was given currency in the days after World War I, the idea of self-determination is a highly combustible concept that can be used in many contradictory ways. Even at its inception, President Woodrow Wilson regarded self-determination as pertaining mainly to the peoples emerging out of the collapsing Austro-Hungarian and Ottoman Empires, while Lenin regarded it as primarily applicable to the overseas colonies of the European powers. More recently, self-determination has been used to assert the claims of indigenous peoples to safeguard their traditional homelands and way of life and by minorities that are targets of ethnic hatred. As international law vests this right in "peoples" rather than either "nations" or "states," there is considerable room for interpretation.

But it is not plausible to explain the turbulence of this period merely by reference to the ambiguities of practice and concept associated with self-determination. Another powerful effect of the ending of the Cold War has been a weakening of what might be called "geopolitical discipline." The Soviet state successfully suppressed ethnic nationalisms within its sphere of influence, but with its collapse, these sentiments erupted in many parts of the former empire. A wide array of Euro-Asian nationalisms smoldered during the ordeal of Soviet rule, but were never extinguished. After the Soviet collapse, these ethnic nationalisms resurfaced as passionate movements for independent statehood.

The West also relaxed its geopolitical grip with the ending of the Cold War. It no longer was as fearful of realignment emerging out of internal political turbulence, or the risks of competitive interventions that had occurred during the Cold War in many countries of the South, especially Vietnam and Afghanistan. It stopped subsidizing friendly artificial or weak states, thereby allowing the strains within civil society to exert themselves more potently. This could be seen in Yugoslavia, where the West had invested heavily in the country's stability during the Cold War years when the anti-Soviet Yugoslav army was seen as important to the defense of Europe. After 1989 such considerations no longer applied, and a sharp reduction in external financial support contributed to the rise of various expressions of anti-Serb nationalism.

This loss of strategic value dramatically affected the stability of sub-Saharan Africa. Whereas both Moscow and Washington had once worked hard to keep particular governments in firm control, the incentives to do so in the post–Cold War years evaporated. These countries were no longer strategic battlegrounds. Additionally, human rights considerations often reinforced this impulse, especially in instances where authoritarian and corrupt regimes had been long kept in power solely because they were geopolitically reliable.

A further set of factors associated with economic globalization has intensified these state-shattering challenges. The worldwide spread of consumerism has threatened traditional identities in many societies, producing a chauvinistic backlash against alleged threats of Westernization or even "McDonaldization." The state often appears to be weak and ineffectual, while many extremist movements are seen to be gaining strength by appealing to particular ethnic or religious identities. The rise of market forces, including the pressures exerted on states by the IMF and World Bank, have further seemed to erode the capacity of the state, shifting loyalty to ethnic and civilizational identities, and often provoking severe conflict.

## PUTTING CONFLICTS INTO CONTEXT

In contrast, East Timor can be viewed as unfinished business from the colonial era. Shortly after Portugal granted independence to East Timor, Indonesia moved in 1975 to annex by brute force the new state in an aggression that more than anything else resembled Iraq's attack on Kuwait. The revealing difference involves the geopolitical climate, which encouraged winking at Indonesia's aggression while mounting a full-scale counterattack in support of Kuwait. Now with moves toward independence for East Timor provoking a bloody repression of horrifying magnitude, the geopolitical climate is different. Indonesia is no longer, as in 1975, seen as a vital Cold War ally. Human rights and self-determination have grown far more important in recent years. The East Timorese have made their case effectively in the global court of public opinion, making it difficult for the world to turn away from their torment, especially since the chaos was created by their reliance on democratic means in the form of a U.N.-monitored referendum on the future of East Timor.

Where does this pattern of ethnic conflict and humanitarian catastrophe lead? Where should it lead? Because each situation presents such a unique set of relevant factors, it is impossible to offer convincing generalizations. The legal framework defining the right of self-determination and respect for territorial sovereignty is in disarray. Deference to the state has weakened in recent years by changes in geopolitics, greater support for human rights, the impact of globalization, and the countervailing emergence of a variety of micro-nationalisms and ethnic causes. Furthermore, the United Nations has been viewed as incapable of addressing these challenges in a consistent or principled manner. It is either unable to produce a consensus among its members or tries to act on the basis of a vague mandate without having access to sufficient financial and military capabilities.

Both Kosovo and East Timor illustrate experiments in forging cooperation between regional actors and the U.N., with a strong orchestrating role being played by the United States. And always, there is need to take account of the strategic calculus and the relation of a given country to the world economy. Thus, it is impossible to do much about Tibet or Chechnya because the political costs of intervention seem too high or to address the plight of ethnic strife and genocidal politics in sub-Saharan Africa because the public concern and geoeconomic stakes seems so small.

So where does this leave us? I would anticipate an ongoing debate in the United States and elsewhere on the broad theme of humanitarian intervention and self-determination that will not be resolved in the next decade. Unfortunately, the best guess is that a series of humanitarian catastrophes will invite response, but that neither Washington nor the U.N. often will be successful.

On the level of international law, it is late in the day to get the genie of self-determination back into the bottle of state sovereignty. The best we can now hope for is compromise. Both Kosovo and East Timor suggest the form it might take: no support for claims of self-determination that would shatter an existing state unless a "people" was being victimized either by genocidal behavior or through repeated crimes against humanity, and in exceptional cases, as a result of severe abuses of basic human rights targeted at a given ethnic community and sustained over a period of years.

A longer-term view would be to rethink the role of the United Nations. It could become a more responsible vehicle for response if it were allowed to form a voluntary professional military and police force on a secure financial basis that ensured a much higher degree of political independence than currently exists. Many cases would still require the collaboration of the United States and regional actors, as can be seen with Australia's leading role in the U.N. operation in East Timor, but the U.N. could bear the burden of political responsibility, and there would not be raised so directly the issue of whether a country should risk the lives of its young citizens in the pursuit of humanitarian goals.

Still, the trend toward further breakdowns in state-society relations seems likely to continue unabated. Perhaps, as seems the case for micronationalisms in Western Europe, the formation of strong regional communities will lessen the insistence on separate statehood. Another promising line of response is to establish various arrangements that maintain the unity of the state but grant substantial rights of autonomy and self-administration, an approach that might finally address the Kurdish challenge afflicting several Middle East countries. Also helpful would be placing greater reliance on preventive diplomacy, heeding early warning signals, as were abundantly present in the settings of both Kosovo and East Timor. The successful deployment of a small deterrent peace force has seemed helpful in preventing the spread of ethnic violence to Macedonia, until it was recently terminated for extraneous reasons because of a Chinese veto at the U.N.

No challenge is more likely to test the maturity and morality of American global leadership in the years ahead than its ability to address these various instances of humanitarian catastrophe that threaten the unity and even survival of the afflicted state.

# 17

# THE COMING CLASH OF CIVILIZATIONS OR, THE WEST AGAINST THE REST

Samuel P. Huntington

Viewing the post-Cold War landscape and its prospects, Samuel P. Huntington predicts that in the future global conflict will be primarily cultural—a clash of civilizations—along the borders where different cultures come into contact. He explains why hypernationalism is on the rise and why the impending clash of cultures will pit Western civilization against the other major world civilizations. Huntington is Albert J. Weatherhead III University Professor at Harvard University, Chairman of the Harvard Academy for International and Area Studies, and Director of the Olin Institute for Strategic Studies at Harvard. His books include *The Clash of Civilizations and the Remaking of World Order* (1996).

World politics is entering a new phase in which the fundamental source of conflict will be neither ideological nor economic. The great divisions among mankind and the dominating source of conflict will be cultural. The principal conflicts of global politics will occur between nations, and groups of different civilizations. The clash of civilizations will dominate global politics.

During the Cold War, the world was divided into the first, second, and third worlds. Those divisions are no longer relevant. It is far more meaningful to group countries not in terms of their political or economic systems or their level of economic development but in terms of their culture and civilization.

A civilization is the highest cultural grouping of people and the broadest level of cultural identity people have, short of that which distinguishes humans from other species.

Civilizations obviously blend and overlap and may include subcivilizations. Western civilization has two major variants, European and North American, and Islam has its Arab, Turkic, and Malay subdivisions. But while the lines between them are seldom sharp, civilizations are real. They rise and fall; they divide and merge. And as any student of history knows, civilizations disappear.

Westerners tend to think of nation-states as the principal actors in global affairs. They have been that for only a few centuries. The broader reaches of history have been the history of civilizations. It is to this pattern that the world returns.

Civilization identity will be increasingly important and the world will be shaped in large measure by the interactions among seven or eight major civilizations. These include the Western, Confucian, Japanese, Islamic, Hindu, Slavic-Orthodox, Latin American, and possibly African civilizations. The most important and bloody conflicts will occur along the borders separating these cultures. The fault lines between civilizations will be the battle lines of the future.

Why? First, differences among civilizations are basic, involving history, language, culture, tradition and, most importantly, religion. Different civilizations have different views on the relations between God and man, the citizen and the state, parents and children, liberty and authority, equality and hierarchy. These differences are the product of centuries. They will not soon disappear.

Second, the world is becoming smaller. The interactions between peoples of different civilizations are increasing. These interactions intensify civilization consciousness: awareness of differences between civilizations and commonalities within civilizations. For example, Americans react far more negatively to Japanese investment than to larger investments from Canada and European countries.

Third, economic and social changes are separating people from long-standing local identities. In much of the world, religion has moved in to fill this gap, often in the form of movements labeled fundamentalist. Such movements are found in Western Christianity, Judaism, Buddhism, Hinduism, and Islam. The "unsecularization of the world," the social [philosopher] George Weigel has remarked, "is one of the dominant social facts of life in the late twentieth century."

Fourth, the growth of civilization consciousness is enhanced by the fact that, at the moment that the West is at the peak of its power, a return-to-the-roots phenomenon is occurring among non-Western civilizations—the "Asianization" in Japan, the end of the Nehru legacy and the "Hinduization" of India, the failure of Western ideas of socialism and nationalism and, hence, the "re-Islamization" of the Middle East, and now a debate over Westernization versus Russianization in [Vladimir Putin's Moscow].

More importantly, the efforts of the West to promote its values of democracy and liberalism as universal values, to maintain its military predominance, and to advance its economic interests engender countering responses from other civilizations.

The central axis of world politics is likely to be the conflict between "the West and the rest" and the responses of non-Western civilizations to Western power and values. The most prominent example of anti-Western cooperation is the connection between Confucian and Islamic states that are challenging Western values and power.

Fifth, cultural characteristics and differences are less mutable and hence less easily compromised and resolved than political and economic ones. In the former Soviet Union, Communists can become democrats, the rich can become poor and the poor rich, but Russians cannot become Estonians. A person can be half-French and half-Arab and even a citizen of two countries. It is more difficult to be half-Catholic and half-Muslim.

Finally, economic regionalism is increasing. Successful economic regionalism will reinforce civilization consciousness. On the other hand, economic regionalism may succeed only when it is rooted in a common civilization. The European [Union] rests on the shared foundation of European culture and Western Christianity. Japan, in contrast, faces difficulties in creating a comparable economic entity in East Asia because it is a society and civilization unique to itself.

As the ideological division of Europe has disappeared, the cultural division of Europe between Western Christianity and Orthodox Christianity and Islam has reemerged. Conflict along the fault line between Western and Islamic civilizations has been going on for 1,300 years. This centuries-old military interaction is unlikely to decline. Historically, the other great antagonistic interaction of Arab Islamic civilization has been with the pagan, animist and now, increasingly, Christian black peoples to the south. On the northern border of Islam, conflict has increasingly erupted between Orthodox and Muslim peoples, including the carnage of Bosnia and Sarajevo, the simmering violence between Serbs and Albanians, the tenuous relations between Bulgarians and their Turkish minority, the violence between Ossetians and Ingush, the unremitting slaughter of each other by Armenians and Azeris and the tense relations between Russians and Muslims in Central Asia.

The historic clash between Muslims and Hindus in the subcontinent manifests itself not only in the rivalry between Pakistan and India but also in intensifying religious strife in India between increasingly militant Hindu groups and the substantial Muslim minority.

Groups or states belonging to one civilization that become involved in war with people from a different civilization naturally try to rally support from other members of their own civilization. Decreasingly able to mobilize support and form coalitions on the basis of ideology, governments and groups will increasingly attempt to mobilize support by appealing to common religion and civilization identity. As the conflicts in the Persian Gulf, the Caucasus, and Bosnia continued, the positions of nations and the cleavages between them increasingly were along civilizational lines. Populist politicians, religious leaders, and the media have found it a potent means of arousing mass support and of pressuring hesitant governments. In the coming years, the local conflicts most likely to escalate into major wars will be those, as in Bosnia and the Caucasus, along the fault lines between civilizations. The next world war, if there is one, will be a war between civilizations.

If these hypotheses are plausible, it is necessary to consider their implications for Western policy. These implications should be divided between short-term advantage and long-term accommodation. In the short term, it is clearly in the interest of the West to promote greater cooperation and unity in its own civilization, particularly between its European and North American components; to incorporate into the West those societies in Eastern Europe and Latin America whose cultures are close to those of the West; to maintain close relations with Russia and Japan; to support in other civilizations groups sympathetic to Western values and interests; and to strengthen international institutions that reflect and legitimate Western interests and values. The West must also limit the expansion of the military strength of potentially hostile civilizations, principally Confucian and Islamic civilizations, and exploit differences and conflicts among Confucian and Islamic states. This will require a moderation in the reduction of Western military capabilities, and, in particular, the maintenance of American military superiority in East and Southwest Asia.

In the longer term, other measures would be called for. Western civilization is modern. Non-Western civilizations have attempted to become modern without becoming Western. To date, only Japan has fully succeeded in this quest. Non-Western civilizations will continue to attempt to acquire the wealth, technology, skills, machines, and weapons that are part of being modern. They will attempt to reconcile this modernity with their traditional culture and values. Their economic and military strength relative to the West will increase.

Hence, the West will increasingly have to accommodate these non-Western modern civilizations, whose power approaches that of the West but whose values and interests differ significantly from those of the West. This will require the West to develop a much more profound understanding of the basic religious and philosophical assumptions underlying other civilizations and the ways in which people in those civilizations see their interests. It will require an effort to identify elements of commonality among Western and other civilizations. For the relevant future, there will be no universal civilization but instead a world of different civilizations, each of which will have to learn to coexist with others.

# 18

# HUMAN RIGHTS: FROM LOW TO HIGH POLITICS IN INTERNATIONAL RELATIONS

David P. Forsythe

**The growing importance of human rights in international context is analyzed by David P. Forsythe, who emphasizes the continuing debates in this issue area. He analyzes the debates over universality versus cultural relativism in the setting of standards, protection by forceful intervention versus diplomacy, and protection by negative acts versus constructive engagement. Forsythe is the Charles J. Mach Distinguished Professor at the University of Nebraska in Lincoln. He is the author of *Human Rights in International Relations: Liberalism in a Realist World* (2000); and the editor of *Human Rights and Comparative Foreign Policy* (1999) and *The United States and Human Rights: Looking Inward and Outward* (1999).**

Human rights became an established part of international relations only from 1945. The United Nations Charter made the advancement of human rights one of the principle goals of the organization, and that treaty obligated states to co-operate on matters of human rights Before then human rights was mostly a national matter, thought to be within the bounds of state sovereignty and domestic jurisdiction. But the U.N. Charter, the 1948 Universal Declaration of Human Rights, the Nuremberg and Tokyo War Crimes Tribunals, and the 1948 Genocide Convention firmly established human rights as a legitimate part of international relations. Even so, human rights remained a matter of low politics for about a quarter of a century after that. Human rights did not receive a great deal of specific and high-level attention from the major states until approximately 1970. From then until the present, human rights has become more often a matter of high politics. Major states, prodded by the media and nongovernmental organizations, often direct specific and high-level attention to various human rights issues. On occasion, as in Bosnia, Somalia, and Kosovo, they even expend treasure, and some blood, in behalf of internationally recognized human rights. This essay analyzes the changing nature of human rights in international relations, the forces that account for that change, and the continuing debates that plague this issue area.

## BACKGROUND

Human rights is correctly associated with liberal political philosophy. While most cultures evolved principles mandating respect for human beings,[1] it was Western liberalism that developed the idea that individuals had inherent moral rights that the state could not abridge. It was Western liberal states like the United States and France, building on notions of constitutionalism in the United Kingdom—that is, limited government—that first created broad-based politics centering on the notion of individual human rights. Thus in the West, human rights were progressively written into national constitutions and bills of rights as the most fundamental personal rights that were necessary for a minimal conception of human dignity. Human rights were widely accepted as the essential means to minimal social justice or human dignity.

Classical political liberals like John Locke or Thomas Jefferson might have written that all men were created equal and possessed equal rights. But they and their liberal colleagues meant *certain* men—white, property owning, otherwise qualified. They did not mean to include women, slaves, Native Americans, colonialized peoples, and other "outsiders." Jefferson and Benjamin Franklin, among others, owned slaves at the time they were writing of moral and legal equality. From one perspective the evolution of international human rights reflects the effort to make behavior match semantics: to make the notion of human rights truly international and universal—as the U.N. Charter suggests, without negative discrimination on the basis of gender, race, ethnicity, or opinion.

As we all know, persons are not equal in many material and moral ways. Some are physically stronger, some more wealthy, some more intelligent, some of greater moral virtue as best we can determine it. But liberalism takes the myth of equality, the fiction of equal status, the aspiration of equal opportunity from equal rights, and tries to create human dignity or social justice or the just society.

---

[1] Paul Gordon Lauren, *The Evolution of International Human Rights: Visions Seen* (Philadelphia: University of Pennsylvania Press, 1998).

Surprisingly enough, Western liberal states did not push for human rights in international relations until the 1940s.[2] These Western states dominated international relations in the modern era—that is, from the mid-seventeenth century. But they were content to leave human rights to the optional judgment of states. In the rhetoric of liberalism, all persons were created equal and possessed certain inalienable rights, but it was up to each state to recognize this "universal truth" or not. Liberalism endorses both universal standards of rights and tolerance for diversity. Persons, or states for that matter, should not be coerced into accepting truth. Reason will lead to the recognition of this truth.

In addition to liberal logic, concrete history played its role in determining the status of human rights in international relations prior to 1945. The European religious wars had been ended around 1648 via the Treaties of Westphalia by letting each territorial ruler adopt whatever religion he deemed best. Out of this practical politics arose both the notion of state sovereignty and the system of international relations built on state sovereignty. This was the Westphalian state system. The central proposition of this system was the notion of nonintervention by outside states into the domestic or internal affairs of another state. This orientation helped produce peace in Europe for a time, at least concerning religion, but it gave a free hand to the territorial ruler to treat "his" subjects as he saw fit in other ways as well.

There were periodic attacks on the ideas of state sovereignty and nonintervention. The French sought to rationalize a broad empire on the basis of equality, fraternity, and solidarity. Others sought to make democracy a universal standard. Marxists sought to rationalize their international movement in the name of perfect equality and a classless society. Still others campaigned across borders against the African slave trade and eventually slavery itself, or to protect "blue collar" labor, or for aid to the sick and wounded in war. Thus there were international or transnational efforts to create a more ethical international order.

The League of Nations was the scene of several debates about universal human rights. But the fundamental fact remained that through the first half of 1945 no general treaty obligated states to respect human rights. This legal fact reflected the basic underlying psychology: states were not expected to respect human rights; it was a matter of national choice. The League of Nations Covenant was silent on human rights, particularly since the United States and Britain had given up their effort to have the principle of religious freedom written into the covenant. These Anglo-Saxon states were unwilling to accept a companion Japanese proposal endorsing racial equality.[3]

---

[2] Jan Herman Burgers, "The Road to San Francisco: The Revival of the Human Rights Idea in the Twentieth Century," *Human Rights Quarterly* 14, no. 4 (November 1992), pp. 447–77.

[3] Paul Gordon Lauren, *Power and Principle: The Politics and Diplomacy of Racial Discrimination,* 2nd ed. (Boulder Colo.: Westview, 1996).

What altered matters was World War II and its horrors—particularly the brutal aggressiveness of the Axis powers. Key policy makers such as Franklin D. Roosevelt and Harry Truman accepted the notion in the early and mid-1940s that human rights were related to international peace and security. They accepted the Wilsonian notion (taken from Immanuel Kant) that the liberal democratic states that respected a broad range of human rights not only did good things for their people, but also were less aggressive in their foreign policies. The United States had produced drafts of a U.N. charter containing human rights language long before the United States had full knowledge of the horrors of the Nazi holocaust—and certainly long before the gruesome concentration camps were liberated in the spring of 1945. The United States, prodded by nongovernmental organizations and certain Latin American states, took the lead in writing human rights language into the U.N. Charter, which put human rights on every state's policy agenda—at least in theory. Security concerns had not a little to do with this development.

San Francisco greatly modified Westphalia. The San Francisco conference of 1945 that adopted the U.N. Charter, with its references to international human rights, greatly modified the principle of state sovereignty (nonintervention less so) that had been established in the two peace treaties (Munster and Onasbruck) in 1648. Whereas in the middle of the seventeenth century it was thought peace depended on deferring to national choice in religious matters, in the twentieth century it was thought peace depended, at least in part, on establishing certain fundamental personal rights in all states.

While the United States took the lead in writing human rights language into the U.N. Charter, it also took the lead in insisting that this language be general. A few states and many nongovernmental organizations wanted much more precise language that might be enforceable through court action. They lobbied hard for, in effect, a legally precise bill of rights. But the Truman Administration, knowing that the United States was still a racially segregated society in the 1940s, and fearful that particularly powerful senators from the U.S. south might scuttle consent to the U.N. Charter as had happened to the League Covenant, refused to be moved toward accepting more-binding language. Likewise, when the United States championed the adoption in the U.N. General Assembly of the 1948 Universal Declaration of Human Rights, Washington stressed that this was a nonbinding General Assembly resolution and thus a statement of aspirations. From one perspective the evolution of international human rights since the 1940s has been about the struggle to make international standards precise and enforceable. It was important to get human rights principles widely endorsed in 1945 and 1948, but that endorsement was bought at the price of generality. The United States was largely responsible for both.

## BASIC NORMS AND PROCESSES

1945 presented a strange situation. The U.N. Charter obligated states to respect human rights, but there was no *international* list or definition of them. So states negotiated the 1948 Universal Declaration of Human Rights, comprised of thirty normative statements. This U.N. General Assembly resolution was the product of a broad negotiating process, not just of the ideas of a few Western states, although Africa and Asia were underrepresented.[4] The result, approved without negative vote but with eight abstentions (the then-communist states, South Africa, and Saudi Arabia), embodied a broad range of rights. There were the civil and political rights well known to the West, such as freedom of speech and association, freedom from torture and arbitrary detention, right to political participation, and freedom of religion, among others. Then there were social and economic rights, such as the rights to adequate food, clothing, shelter, medical care, and education. These were more the product of Latin American social democrats than of Soviet-style Leninists. There was also a vague right to a system of international relations within which these other rights could be realized. This latter right has been interpreted by some to mean a right to economic development, a right to peace, and a right to a healthy environment.

For reasons noted above, the United States insisted that the Universal Declaration was a statement of aspirations, not immediately binding law. The Soviet Union and certain other states were only too happy to fall in line with this argument. These states knew only too well that an enforceable international law of human rights restricted freedom of policy making at home as well as abroad. In federal states like the United States, there was already a vigorous debate about whether the federal or central government wielded too much power relative to the state or provincial governments. Creating international legal norms and the means to enforce them added great complexity to this long-standing controversy.

In the same year as the Universal Declaration, the U.N. General Assembly approved the Genocide Convention, making it an international crime to destroy in whole or part a social group. Under this treaty, which was a direct reaction to the German holocaust and its attempt to exterminate Jews, Roma (Gypsies), homosexuals, and others, the World Court—or International Court of Justice—was given authority to handle disputes among states. Nevertheless, by the 1990s states had sought to involve this court in very few allegations about genocide. (Bosnia brought genocide petitions to the court, but this tribunal did not play a significant role in subsequent developments.)

Also in the second half of the 1940s, the victors in World War II put on trial top German leaders at Nuremberg, and top Japanese leaders at Tokyo, for war crimes, crimes against humanity, and crimes against peace. There was a

---

[4] Johannes Morsink, *The Universal Declaration of Human Rights: Origins, Drafting, and Intent* (Philadelphia: University of Pennsylvania Press, 1999).

considerable amount of victor's justice at work in these international trials, and a number of legal principles pertaining to procedure were violated. The Tokyo Tribunal was especially deficient regarding standards of due process and errors of substantive judgment. Nevertheless, both courts contributed to the evolving notion that individual policy makers should be held accountable for violations of international criminal law through international proceedings. As we shall see, this idea had a renaissance in the 1990s.

In 1966, after protracted negotiations, the General Assembly approved two basic, general human rights treaties: one on civil and political rights, and one on economic, social, and cultural rights. Thus the principles found in the Universal Declaration were eventually turned into more precise legal standards. There came to be an international bill of rights, made up of the Declaration, the International Covenant on Civil and Political Rights, and the International Covenant on Economic, Social, and Cultural Rights—against the background of the U.N. Charter. However, no human rights court was created. Rather, a supervising committee was eventually created for each covenant. This meant that rather than judicial enforcement, one had to rely on diplomatic persuasion for implementation. The "monitoring mechanisms" created had the ultimate authority only to issue some public criticism regarding offending states. States had to report on implementation, and they had to respond to committee questions. The committee could make general comments. But in the last analysis states retained the legal authority to have the last say as to what was a violation of the treaties and what was not. Most states wanted to be associated with the idea of human rights, and about 140 of them (out of a U.N. membership of 185) formally accepted each covenant. But states still resisted creating a strong international legal regime that would clearly supercede state sovereignty. States wanted to have it both ways, or to have their cake and eat it too.

Many other human rights treaties were negotiated during the first fifty years of the United Nations. They covered such subjects as the rights of women, the crime of apartheid, the rights of the child, labor rights, refugees, slavery, stateless persons, racial discrimination, torture, and more. Human rights are designed primarily to protect the vulnerable and marginalized, and the treaties focus on these persons—or situations encompassing such persons. If one has power and/or wealth, one needs legal protection of rights much less.[5]

Many of these treaties were linked to a specific supervising agency, which eventually led to a very fragmented or dispersed implementation process for international human rights in general. For example, there was the Committee on the Elimination of Discrimination Against Women, as well as the Committee Against Torture. Moreover, there were parts of the United Nations system that focused on human rights as mentioned in the charter, rather than under specific

[5] For one thorough overview see Henry J. Steiner and Philip Alston, *International Human Rights in Context: Law, Politics, Morals* (New York: Oxford University Press, 1996).

treaty provisions. This added even more complexity. For example, there was the U.N. Human Rights Commission, the U.N. Human Rights Sub-Commission, and the U.N. Commission on the Status of Women, among other agencies. In 1993 the U.N. voted to create the High Commissioner (a sort of permanent roving ambassador) for Human Rights. It was clear that human rights had become a fixture in international relations. Some states might try to avoid judicial scrutiny of their own policies, but at the same time all states acknowledged the legitimacy or permissibility of diplomatic discussion about human rights. International human rights presented a half-way house or incomplete picture: states were expected to respect international human rights, which were more and more specified. The *United Nations Yearbook* devoted more pages to human rights than any other subject. But there were few international court cases on the subject—at least on a global basis through the United Nations.

Regional developments should also be mentioned. The Council of Europe produced the European Convention on Human Rights, covering civil and political rights. By 1999 forty-one states not only became a party to this treaty but also accepted the supranational authority of the European Court on Human Rights. By the 1990s this court had developed such a heavy caseload, even when dealing with mostly liberal democracies, that it had to expedite its procedures. The keys to development were twofold. Individuals were allowed to bring complaints that their treaty rights had been violated (even European states do not like to sue each other about human rights, fearing the workings of reciprocity in the future). And states have been so committed to protecting human rights on a regional basis that they have been willing to sacrifice some national independence or autonomy in the process. Likewise, the Europe Economic Community and the European Union manifest the European Court of Justice which also makes supranational judgments about certain human rights. This integrated process, along with the weaker European Social Charter that covers mostly labor rights, constitutes the most impressive international system for the protection of human rights that exists to date.

The inter-American system, centering on the Organization of American States (OAS), also seeks the regional protection of human rights. On paper this regional protection of human rights in the Western Hemisphere looks much like the European system. There is the Inter-American Convention on Human Rights, which covers mostly civil and political rights, with brief mention of social and economic rights. And there is the supranational Inter-American Court of Human Rights. Historically, however, the functioning of the two regional systems has been quite different for several reasons. In the Western Hemisphere, while there has been much lip service to human rights, many ruling elites have not been seriously interested in advancing human rights for indigenous Indians, women, the laboring classes, and other "outsiders." The commitment to broad human rights is much more genuine in Europe. Furthermore, despite articulations of democratic theory, the military has played a large role in much of hemispheric history.

The military plays a much weaker role in the daily politics of Europe, Turkey aside. Moreover, the regional hegemon, the United States, has often elevated strategic and economic interests over the protection of human rights in the hemisphere. The United States is not a party to the Inter-American Convention, and does not accept the jurisdiction and authority of the related court. The major states of Europe all accept the European Human Rights Convention and associated court.

For all of these reasons and more, the OAS protection of human rights is much weaker than the regional system in Europe, although by the 1990s some improvement was underway in the Western Hemisphere. More liberal democracies in the region meant a greater commitment to human rights. This resulted in more adherences to the regional treaty and court, and more cooperation with the Inter-American Commission on Human Rights. Military rule had been discredited after the excesses of the 1970s and 1980s. But the court still handled far fewer cases than its counterpart in Europe. And the United States continued to refuse to give full support to, and participation in, hemispheric human rights arrangements.

There was also a regional human rights treaty and human rights commission in Africa, associated with the Organization of African Unity. The African Charter on Human and People's Rights, however, played a distinctly marginal role in African affairs, and the African Human Rights Commission was generally weak. There was no regional human rights court in Africa, although discussions about creating one were held from time to time. Given the large number of failed states in Africa, where central authority had collapsed or nearly so, and given the large number of authoritarian states, despite a certain wave of democratization, it was difficult to see how regional human rights norms and processes could make much difference in Africa in the near future. Asia manifests no regional intergovernmental organization for human rights, although subregional political organizations like ASEAN (the Association of South East Asian Nations) discuss human rights from time to time.

The European experience indicated that it took a genuine commitment to liberal political philosophy and liberal democracy at the national level before one could build effective regional regimes for human rights. Even in Europe, when one had strong illiberal forces in Greece from 1967 to 1974, and in Turkey periodically, the European regional mechanisms faced great difficulty in preventing or punishing human rights violations. The same could be said of the Western Hemisphere. Moreover, in the latter region, the recent history of the United States showed the additional point that even a state committed to liberal democracy at home did not necessarily make it a real priority in its policy toward regional arrangements.

Finally in this section, we should note international humanitarian law and what the U.N. calls "complex emergencies." Most of our human rights discussion thus far pertains to situations of peace, insofar as these can be distinguished from situations of violence (meaning there is much violence even in "peaceful" international relations, via terrorists, low-level unrest, etc.). Most of the human rights treaties, aside from the Genocide Convention, are predicated on assumptions of peaceful international relations. A number of human rights treaties, both regional and global, allow many protections of rights to be suspended in war or national emergency threatening the life of the nation, and thus leaving only a small number of rights such as freedom from political murder and torture to be absolutely respected.

For war, international or civil, there is international humanitarian law—that part of the international laws of war devoted to helping victims of war. Thus the 1949 Geneva Conventions and 1997 Protocols (additional treaties) seek to limit hostilities for the benefit of sick or wounded or detained combatants, civilians in distress or in occupied territory, and all those caught up in civil or internal wars. To be legally precise, human rights law and humanitarian law are different, with different rules intended for different situations. Yet both center on international legal standards intended to advance minimal human dignity and social justice.

In many situations like Bosnia (1992–1995), Kosovo (1999), Somalia (1992–1994), and the Great Lakes region of Africa (1994–2000), it was difficult to say if the situation was one of international war, internal (civil) war, or some type of national emergency (for example, riots and rebellion) falling short of war. Whatever the factual situation, various types of persons were in dire straits. National authority was contested. Outside parties felt an obligation to act, at least to relieve human suffering. Thus the distinctions between human rights and humanitarian law were blurred. Whether one was acting for human rights or for humanitarian affairs became less important than that one act to help persons in distress. Lawyers and academics might argue over whether persons had a right to humanitarian assistance under humanitarian law, or a right to adequate food, clothing, shelter, and medical care under the International Covenant on Economic, Social, and Cultural Rights. But this was a distinction without a difference for practical action in the field.

International law, both in peace and war, offered certain protections and assistance to persons in need. It was less important that legal categories became blurred in the serum of international relations, and more important that international action be taken in fact—regardless of the precise legal basis. But it remained important that international humanitarian law existed. War and complex emergencies did not provide a license to mayhem. Responsible authorities were still under legal limits regarding the treatment of individuals. Humanitarian law was the first cousin to human rights law, and shared a number of fundamental values with it.

The United Nations started calling some situations "complex emergencies." This semantical development was intended to bypass sterile debates about whether one faced peace or war, whether it was the law of human rights in peace or international humanitarian law for war that should be applied. Instead, one developed nonbinding codes of conduct for humanitarian action in complex emergencies. The fundamental point was that the international community was taking more interest in such situations. It was trying to help persons in need, particularly where national authority had collapsed or was contested.

In sum to this point, international relations at the turn of this century was not what it once was. Extensive human rights and humanitarian standards had been negotiated and widely accepted—at least in theory, which is to say in the abstract. At the same time, many violations of internationally recognized human rights and humanitarian law existed, leading to many efforts at international action. This action occurred through global actors such as the U.N., regional actors such as the Council of Europe and the OAS, states via their foreign and domestic policies, and transnational actors like Amnesty International and Human Rights Watch or the International Red Cross and the Red Crescent Movement. Even transnational corporations like Nike, Reebok, or Heinekin developed human rights policies and sometimes based production and marketing decisions on human rights factors.

## CONTINUING CONTROVERSIES

The relationship between citizen and state, between the individual and community, has been controversial since the beginnings of recorded history. Since 1945 another layer—the international—has been added to this debate.

**Universalism versus relativism**   The central debate in the setting of international human rights standards is whether there can be universal human rights leading to universal conceptions of human dignity and social justice, or whether what is good for humans varies from one culture and society and situation to the next. Since at least the European Enlightenment, much of the West has believed that through reason one can arrive at universal truths. Global human rights are linked to this intellectual and philosophical tradition. A modern defense of universal human rights holds that the individual everywhere is threatened by the power of the modern state and contemporary corporations acting under capitalism. Thus individuals everywhere need the protections offered by international human rights (and humanitarian law). Just as it does not matter where the bicycle was invented, so it is argued that it does not matter that human rights were "invented" in the West. Just as the bicycle (or telephone, or computer, etc.) is useful everywhere, so it is said that human rights have universal applicability. Universal principles may have to be adapted to particular situations, but many persons, not just in the West, believe in universal human rights.

Strong cultural relativists take exception to this argument. For example, there are a number of anthropologists in particular who endorse the preservation of the societies of indigenous peoples even though such societies may lack gender equality, courts, modern education, and a number of other values associated with internationally recognized human rights. Should outsiders seek to change these societies if the greatest number of such persons are happy with their existence and want to see it continue as is? Closely related to this debate is the subject of female genital mutilation in a number of societies, mostly in Africa. Given that a number of *women* endorse this practice as a gateway to social acceptability, should others seek to bring about change according to modern notions of adequate health and freedom from abuse?

During the 1990s there was considerable attention to the debate about "Asian values."[6] A number of Asian states, all of them authoritarian, argued publicly that the modern version of international human rights was nothing more than Western cultural imperialism. They argued that the West, with its individualist rather than communitarian tradition, was fostering a particular conception of international human rights that was ill suited to Asian societies. (Some non-Asian authoritarians like Cuba and Syria, among others, were only too happy to support this Asian argument.) Some Asian authors argued that there was a small core of generally universal human rights standards: freedom from murder, torture, genocide, etc. But these persons argued that the West had taken other individualist values and tried to project them as universal, even though such values had undermined a sense of community and done great damage to the West. Leaders of Singapore in particular pointed to their stability and economic growth since independence from Britain, while noting such things as youth misbehavior, drug abuse, crime, and poverty in the West—and especially in the United States, the most individualistic of the Western societies.[7]

The United States manifested a most interesting position in this debate. It presented itself as the champion of universal human rights at the 1993 U.N. Conference on Human Rights at Vienna. But at the same time, it rejected the notion of economic and social rights, saying that human rights were only civil and political. It rejected the Inter-American Convention on Human Rights and the associated Inter-American Court, saying that the U.S. Constitution could not be superceded by international human rights law. It attached so many reservations, understandings, and declarations to its formal acceptance of the International Covenant on Civil and Political Rights that its acceptance was legally meaningless. And in other ways, too, the United States practiced a type of national particularism, if not cultural relativism, in rejecting many international human rights standards as inapplicable to itself. It wanted its version of human rights to be applied to others, but it did not want others' version of human rights to be applied to itself.

---

[6] See further Joanne R. Bauer and Daniel A. Bell, eds., *The East Asian Challenge for Human Rights* (New York: Cambridge University Press, 1999).

[7] See especially Bilahari Kausikan, "Asia's Different Standard," *Foreign Policy,* no. 92 (Fall 1992), pp. 24–41.

**Forceful intervention versus diplomacy**   Global international human rights law by and large seeks implementation through diplomacy, such as through the diplomatic review of monitoring mechanisms noted above. This is consistent with the U.N. Charter, which calls for the peaceful resolution of disputes and seems to forbid the threat or use of military force. The Charter authorizes the use of force primarily for individual or collective self-defense against armed attack. The 1999 situation in Kosovo, when NATO used military force in defense of ethnic Albanians inside Yugoslavia, nicely demonstrates the debate over whether humanitarian intervention is legitimate. Is the use of force by outsiders to protect the rights of others permissible in modern international relations? Should the international community override claims to state sovereignty when the latter is used to engage in gross violations of internationally recognized human rights?

Given the U.N. Charter, not to mention the sensitivities of weaker states fearing the actions of stronger states, there is no treaty law on humanitarian intervention. It is doubtful if there is any customary international law on this subject either.[8] Yet in 1999 the North Atlantic Treaty Organization used military force in behalf of ethnic Albanians in Kosovo, who were being brutally repressed, and increasingly expelled, by the government of Slobodan Milosevic in Belgrade. NATO members claimed they had the right to use force because of the implied meaning of previous resolutions of the U.N. Security Council. Yugoslavia claimed that NATO was engaging in aggression, since NATO was clearly not acting in self-defense against any cross-border attacks by Belgrade. To a number of observers it seemed clear that NATO was engaging in humanitarian intervention, even though the Western military alliance avoided legal claims that would have undermined the U.N. Charter's stand against force—and might have opened the door to possible misuse in the future by other states looking for a pretext to use force.

The fact that nineteen NATO members, supported by considerable domestic public opinion, held together during the controversial bombing of Yugoslavia indicates that as a practical matter the powerful West may support at least some forms of humanitarian intervention. They did so at times during the Bosnian war of 1992–1995, and they also supported the use of force for a brief time in Somalia during 1992–1994 (although there, military operations were not directed against a state, but rather against private armed elements, and initially had the consent of many local clan leaders). In the Kosovo case, President Clinton and others could make a strong argument that the European neighborhood was basically a liberal democracy, Yugoslavia should conform to that proper regional standard, the repression ordered by Milosevic was truly a gross violation of minimal standards of decency and if left unchecked those violations could destabilize a broader area.

---

[8] Customary international law is explained in the chapter by Professor Christopher Joyner in this book.

Still, many states remained fearful about leaving the use of force to a Western military alliance that might act without authorization or review by the U.N. Security Council. Broad repression, ethnic cleansing, and perhaps even genocide were occurring in Kosovo. But would the next case of Western use of force be as morally compelling?

**Punishment versus constructive engagement** In archaic international relations without a central government or a reliable court system, it is not always clear when one should respond to human rights violations with sanctions, including criminal justice, and when one should respond with continued diplomacy over time in search of progressive evolution. This debate overlaps with the previous one but is broader.

To stop the brutal war in Bosnia during 1995, which had produced many gross violations of human rights and humanitarian law, the West negotiated with Milosevic in order to get him to reduce his support for the Bosnian Serbs and to get him to support a peace treaty. Likewise in Sierra Leone in 1999, the U.N. brokered a peace agreement between the government and the rebel side (which had been chopping off the limbs of civilians), promising to overlook at least some violations of human rights and humanitarian law. The quest for peace sometimes supercedes some aspects of (criminal) justice—meaning punishment for gross violators of human rights. On the other hand, Milosevic was indicted by the International Criminal Tribunal for Former Yugoslavia (which sits at the Hague) for violations of international criminal law in Kosovo. Impunity (lack of punishment) for human rights violations is, in general, a bad thing, but so is the continuation of murderous conflict.

Beyond the issue of criminal justice, the United States in particular and the West in general faced the same dilemma with authoritarian China that they had faced with white-ruled South Africa. There were clear, systematic, and major violations of human rights in communist China, just as there had been in apartheid South Africa. A considerable controversy occurred about how to deal with China at the turn of the century, just as a long-running dispute had plagued the West in its dealing with the South Africa of the past.

Whereas the Clinton administration began by threatening to link U.S. trade with China to its human rights performance, eventually Clinton delinked these two subjects. The Clinton team opted for constructive engagement—meaning the continuation of most business as usual while continuing to discuss such subjects as the detention of pro-democracy advocates, prison conditions, and similar human rights subjects. The central argument was that encouraging capitalism under the rule of law would lead to more personal freedom over time, and eventually a spillover effect from freedom in economics to freedom in politics. On the other hand, there were calls in Congress for a tougher approach to China, and most human rights nongovernmental organizations supported these calls. But many academic specialists on China supported constructive engagement. All of this was reminiscent of the debates about South Africa, at least until the mid-1980s when Congress overrode a presidential veto and voted general economic sanctions on white-ruled South Africa.

It is frequently not clear whether carrots or sticks comprise the better approach to human rights violations. We know that unilateral economic sanctions are not often effective, although they may have symbolic value. We know that multilateral economic sanctions can do some damage, but usually do not bring quick results—if only because some parties don't cooperate in the sanctioning effort. We know that states are reluctant to expend blood and treasure for the rights of others; Kosovo is the partial exception that proves the more general rule (NATO used high-altitude bombing and no ground troops to minimize Western casualties). And we know that different parties have responded in different ways to past human rights violations—sometimes with international trials, sometimes with national trials, sometimes with truth commissions or other nonpenal measures, and sometimes doing nothing in particular (with sometimes good effects as in the transition from dictatorship to liberal democracy in Spain and Portugal).[9] In 1999 Spain wanted General Augusto Pinochet extradited from Britain to stand trial for human rights abuses in Chile, but the elected government of Chile opposed the move as destabilizing to Chilean democracy.

## CONCLUSIONS

Human rights is now one of the big four issue-areas in international relations, along with security, economics, and ecology—but it remains one of the most perplexing. The abstract notion of internationally recognized human rights is now widely accepted, but this acceptance is a mile wide and sometimes an inch deep. We do not lack for human rights treaties, supposedly making up hard law. And we have numerous human rights declarations and other nonbinding documents making up considerable soft law. We even see extensive routine diplomacy, both multilateral and bilateral, in behalf of human rights. Human rights matters much more in the U.N. era than during the League of Nations. The difference is one between night and day.

And yet. Outside of Europe with its European Court of Human Rights and European Court of Justice, most states are reluctant to take international human rights fully seriously. They show great difficulty in managing the contradictions inherent in trying to combine an interest in human rights with other interests in security, economics, and ecology. After all, human rights is only one part of foreign policy.[10] Other parts are equally legitimate. Sometimes ad hoc international

---

[9] For an argument in favor of criminal justice, see Aryeh Neier, *War Crimes: Brutality. Genocide, Terror, and the Struggle for Justice* (New York: Times Books, 1998). But see Martha Minow, *Between Vengeance and Forgiveness: Facing History After Genocide and Mass Violence* (Boston: Beacon Press, 1998) for a more balanced survey.

[10] Joseph S. Nye, Jr., "Redefining the National Interest," *Foreign Affairs* 78, no. 4 (Summer 1999), pp. 22–35.

courts are created to deal with human rights issues, as in the former Yugoslavia and also Rwanda. A statute was approved in 1998 for a standing or permanent international criminal court, although it will not function for a considerable number of years and may not obtain the support of the major states—above all the United States. Its jurisdiction will center on war crimes, crimes against humanity, and genocide. But international relations still does not show consistent and firm and reliable measures for preventing or controlling human rights violations. Much is left up to the vagaries of decentralized foreign policy, and to the pressures generated by the communications media and private human rights groups.

# 19

# THE INSTITUTIONAL MAINTENANCE OF TWENTY-FIRST CENTURY WORLD ORDER

Harvey Starr

This essay argues that, in the new millennium, states and other international actors will continue to exist in an interdependent global environment whose changing character will confront them with many opportunities and constraints. Today, as in the past, decision-makers are continually faced with the necessity of making difficult policy choices as they try to adapt to a changing environment. As the end of the twentieth century is a period of transition, moving from the Westphalian system into something not yet clearly defined, this chapter analyzes how the evolving global environment tests states' capacity to adapt to the challenges of managing discord and cementing collaboration in the evolving twenty-first century world. Its author, Harvey Starr, is Dag Hammarskjold Professor in International Affairs at the University of South Carolina. His most recent book is the edited volume, *The Understanding and Management of Global Violence* (1999).

States, as all other actors in world politics, must react to a changing global environment which confronts them with many opportunities and constraints. The decision-makers who steer these states through the muddy, often treacherous, but potentially harmonious and rewarding waters of world politics are continually faced with the necessity of making difficult policy choices about behavior—to act cooperatively or conflictually; to oppose or appease; to look for common interests or treat potential opponents as enemies in a zero-sum world of dog-eat-dog realism; to employ diplomacy or use force; to choose among economic, political, legal, environmental, or military tools in the implementation of foreign policy; and a host of other decisions. For any behavior to occur, decision-makers must be *willing* to choose among the possible options. These options define the *opportunities* made available to them by the prevailing global environment or context. These opportunities both constrain decision-makers in their choices about policies and enable them to do things previously not possible.

## OPPORTUNITY AND CHANGE IN THE WORLD SYSTEM

What is known by scholars of international politics as the "agent-structure" perspective underlines specifically the feature surrounding international decision-makers just introduced, namely the fact that all foreign policy choices incorporate a response to both the opportunity and willingness of the agent making choices. Those choices are shaped by the willingness and motivations to act, and they, in turn, are shaped by the structure of the environment at the point of decision. This perspective draws the attention of the analyst of world politics to those properties of the international system which have changed (and how), and those which have remained constant. In trying to help us understand the world of the policy maker, the analyst can look at the structure of the system in terms of a number of important dimensions, such as the number and types of international actors (for example, states, international organizations, nongovernmental organizations, and a panoply of other non-state actors), the number and types of relations that characterize the actors' behavior towards one another, the various ways in which these actors can be compared (according to their relative military power, size of economy, or trade, for example), and the degree and nature of the interdependence that exists for the actors within the system.

*Interdependence* is another characteristic of all systems. Systems involve units of interaction and how they interact with one another. Interdependence is a measure of the degree to which interactions or behaviors in one part of a system effect the interactions and behaviors of the other units all across the system. Nation-states as we know them since the emergence of the Westphalian state-system in 1648 after the Thirty Years War have continuously existed within a system of states and non-state actors. Thus, states have always been sensitive and vulnerable to the behavior of the other actors in the system. Interdependence within international systems has affected the opportunity and willingness of policy makers. Policy makers must understand how they have been affected and thus must understand this concept. Analysts must use this idea to study policy makers.

At the same time, the degree to which the actors are interdependent on one another for welfare or security has varied over time and, indeed, has greatly expanded in the era of globalization that characterizes the integration of states and erosion of distance in the late twentieth century. In addition, many other aspects of the interstate system structure have also continually changed, in ways that have transformed many other dimensions of the international or global environment. These dimensions include the ideologies or types of government that exist at any point in time. Just as important is the technological dimension of the environment. This dimension can change very rapidly, and in so doing can radically affect the opportunities or possibilities available to the actors in the interstate system (and thus affect the willingness of decision-makers to make certain choices). Technology can override the effects of geography and distance, of time and space. Technology can change the meaning of geography and geopolitical factors, and can contribute to the globalization of interstate politics that is eroding the ability of sovereign states to control their national destiny.[1]

Analysts and policy makers must be concerned with how international actors *adapt* to changing conditions in the system, and how they have attempted to manage interdependence under different conditions. This perspective is crucial to clear thinking about the prospects for order and/or disorder in twenty-first century world politics because, while it recognizes the importance of the environment or context provided by the global system it also recognizes that this importance ranges far beyond the continuing debate between advocates of structural-realism and proponents of various "liberal" or pluralist models of world politics.[2]

Sovereign states exist in an "anarchic order," that is, one where there is no higher, formal authority above states. However, focusing on systemic "anarchy" as the primary explanatory factor or cause of global politics is fatally flawed. The argument presented in this chapter is that while the "environment" is important, this importance does not derive from the formally anarchic nature of the system. Actors must adapt to the opportunities provided to them by their environments. (This is what we mean when we discuss "agents" influenced by, and acting within, "structures.") Anarchy is only one part of the global environment, and one which has been relatively unchanged for three hundred and fifty years.

A simple reality faces any analyst of twenty-first century world politics. While the "anarchy" condition has remained unchanged, across history there have been periods of varying conflict and cooperation; individual states have experienced long periods of aggression and conflict followed by "long peaces" or periods in which pacific relations have prevailed without warfare. Moreover, many different kinds of economic arrangements have thrived and declined; for example, the past three centuries have witnessed periods of rapid economic growth and periods of disastrous decline. Consider also that throughout most of the history of the international system few democracies have been in existence, but in today's world there is now an approximate majority of democracies. Thus, while the an-

---

[1] A discussion of global trends that are altering the nature of state sovereignty—both the growing interdependence of the global system along with its fragmentation—is presented by James N. Rosenau. See, in particular, *Turbulence in World Politics* (Princeton, N.J.: Princeton University Press, 1990), and *Along the Domestic-Foreign Frontier* (Cambridge: Cambridge University Press, 1997).

[2] See Ole Holsti's chapter in this book, which summarizes these theoretical orientations.

archic nature of the system has remained constant, just about everything else has changed. To state the case boldly: it is impossible to explain such variation in behavior or ways of organizing with a constant (a system that has always been anarchic).[3]

At the end of the twentieth century we find ourselves in a period of *transition,* moving from the Westphalian system into something not yet clearly defined or understood. We need to analyze, study and understand this evolving new environment in order to gauge how states and other actors can adapt to the environment of the twenty-first century. Successful adaptation means a greater chance of cooperation and order in the global system; failure to adapt can lead to breakdown, violence, and disorder.

The argument presented here is that there is more change and dynamism in the phenomenon of the "environment" or "context" than can possibly be captured by the idea of anarchy, or, the lack of authority above states. The concept of opportunity rests on a changing set of environmental possibilities. These possibilities change through major events that alter the nature of the international system, such as war. However, change also comes about through the dynamic of technology and the infinite inventiveness and creativity of humans. These possibilities change with every new ideological system (religious and/or political). They change with every innovation in how humans organize themselves for economic or political purposes—including administrative and bureaucratic forms, types of government, as well as the broader issue of the relationship between individuals and governmental authority. They change with every innovation in how economic, social and political exchange can take place; in forms of finance; in the creation of new types of organization (from the multinational corporation to different forms of international organizations, or IGOs).

Policy makers must recognize such changes, and understand how their opportunities are affected by change. Analysts must recognize such changes in their attempts to discover how the world works. Both policy makers and analysts need concepts and theories to guide them. We are in the midst of a sea change at the dawn of a new millennium that requires a reassessment of our theoretical compass if we are to visualize accurately our future and find a way of managing global order to preserve peace with prosperity.

## ADAPTATION TO CHANGE IN THE TWENTY-FIRST CENTURY WORLD SYSTEM

Maintenance of world order in the twenty-first century will require states to recognize just how the global systemic environment has changed, and then

---

[3] This is like trying to explain behavior with the constant of "human nature." If some people are good, selfless, and cooperative, while others are evil, selfish, and warlike, and yet others are somewhere in between, we cannot explain their behavior by using "human nature." All these people are "human"—thus, human nature as a constant cannot explain the variability in behavior.

understand what they must do to adapt to the changed set of interdependencies in that system. From the end of the Second World War in 1945 until the late 1980s, world politics was dominated by the "Cold War" between two military superpowers: the United States and the Soviet Union. With large arsenals of nuclear weapons and a global military presence, these countries led large blocs of allies in a global confrontation between Western democratic capitalism and Soviet-style centrally planned economic management under the rubric of communism. In many ways, world politics was simplified by this ideological confrontation. The problems undermining world order such as the collapse of failed states and the advent of ethnic conflicts and civil wars that have been experienced since the end of the Cold War, symbolized by the fall of the Berlin Wall in 1989, derive from the failure of policy makers and analysts alike to appreciate the character of the transformed global environment and to recognize the dilemmas of adapting to a more complex new system which is not dominated by the U.S.-U.S.S.R. conflict.

To understand such historic and massive change at the birth of the new millennium, it is helpful to return to the idea of "opportunity" in foreign policy decision-making. Opportunity has two broad characteristics. The first is the possibility of undertaking adaptive action in the international system. The second is the extent to which the available options are influenced by the distribution of the resources and capabilities among actors in the system, especially resources which would allow the actors to take advantage of the possibilities that exist. New opportunities or possibilities in the system, then, have both universal and particular effects. For example, today's emergent technologies will affect all the units, because the development of new treatments for victims of AIDS means that this possibility for dealing with a terrible disease exists in the environment of all global actors. However, not all states can afford the large costs of providing such treatments to their citizens, and are not able to exploit this new possibility. Another example illustrates the same principle: thermonuclear weapons and intercontinental delivery systems, which are indeed possible tools for foreign policy makers, are beyond the reach of most states due to their cost and high technology requirements.

It is important to remember that anarchy is fundamentally a permissive characteristic of the system. The lack of an authoritative hierarchy, the absence of legitimate authority above states, permits a range of behavior to occur that otherwise would be prohibited by the existence of supranational institutions capable of regulating the conduct of states and transnational actors. The persistence of conditions of international anarchy is largely responsible for creating the existence of a global prisoners' dilemma. The *prisoners' dilemma* is the name for a social situation that occurs in many different areas of human interaction. It is a situation with a special set of incentives for choice. It belongs to a class of situations (or games) which are called "variable sum" as opposed to the zero-sum situation which characterizes much of realist analysis. Zero-sum situations are those where whatever one player wins, the other must lose. In variable sum situations such as the prisoners' dilemma both players may win, both may lose, or one may win while the other loses. If policy makers or policy analysts fail to grasp that a situation is a prisoners' dilemma, and therefore *not* zero-sum, then they may make choices (or advise choices) that are very wrong—choices that will make the policy maker worse off rather than helping to move towards achieving the policy makers' goals.

This sort of situation prevails across many global issues today, which explains why it is so popular for interpreting the difficult choices about world order that must be made by actors in interaction whose relationships combine conflict and cooperation. The prisoners' dilemma is endemic to the frequent tension between trust and temptation in the conflict between individual and group interests (the interest of both players collectively). A typical prisoners' dilemma situation means that two players have the choice either to cooperate with each other, or to defect from the other. The payoffs of a prisoners' dilemma create an incentive structure where the best payoff comes from defecting while the other player cooperates; the second best payoff is from the rewards of mutual cooperation; the next best payoff is from the mutual punishment when both players defect; but the *worst* outcome is being caught as the "sucker"—cooperating while the other party to the interaction defects.

Many examples illustrate the pervasive nature of prisoners' dilemma situations across global issues. For example, an arms race is a prisoners' dilemma: each player can "cooperate" and refrain from building more or new weapons, or can "defect" and increase arms in some way. Arms control is also a prisoners' dilemma: each player can "cooperate" by complying with an arms control treaty, or "defect" by breaking the treaty. Ecological issues are often prisoners' dilemmas: "cooperate" by not hunting whales (or harvesting some other fish species into extinction), "defect" by continuing to hunt whales (or catch other fish). Similarly, one can "cooperate" by not polluting some body of water (such as the Rhine River or the Mediterranean Sea), or "defect" by continuing to pollute. In all these cases, a positive outcome cannot occur without group or collective action. The temptation to defect (because of the incentive structure) makes each situation a prisoners' dilemma.

Thus, while the group (both players collectively) does best when they both cooperate, the incentives for a rational player tempt the player to defect, either as protection from the other player's defection (to avoid being the sucker), or as an exploitative attempt to catch the other as a sucker. Since both players must make the same calculation, the incentive structure of this kind of situation drives them to double defection even though each would be better off if both parties had been cooperators.

Scholars across a number of disciplines, from psychology to economics to sociology to political science, have analyzed the nature of the prisoners' dilemma and how interdependence may affect actors. Their investigations illuminate the multiplicity of ways humans may, and have at times, been able to organize to overcome the chronic self-defeating selfishness within situations resembling the prisoners' dilemma, so as to manage this particular negative consequence of interdependence. Neither the concept nor phenomenon of anarchy can help to explain when groups of humans are able to solve prisoners' dilemma situations and when they are not; under what conditions the prisoners' dilemma is most manageable; and what forms or human organization are most or least able to deal with collective action problems.

To approach the prisoners' dilemma, it is useful to look at how the environment of international actors can and has changed, and how state actors have dealt with that change. "Opportunity" is useful here, because the global environment must be perceived by human policy makers (agents), who then react to the images they hold of that environment. The environment of perceived opportunities thus provides an incentive structure that will affect the willingness of policy makers to choose among the assorted options available to them. The realist fixation on anarchy assumes certain static preferences and uniform perceptions across actors; to that theoretical tradition, actors in a prisoners' dilemma will *always* defect, creating more conflict rather than cooperation. The structures of opportunity discussed here bring into view a wider range of possibilities, including the recognition of common interests and ways to solve the prisoners' dilemma. If these opportunities or possibilities are seized, the twenty-first century can be far more orderly than was the twentieth.

A basic cause of the dynamism of world politics since 1648 has been the interdependent system within which states (and an ever growing cast of other actors) have had to exist. Interdependence makes actors ever more sensitive and vulnerable to one another. States can adapt through "defection" or "cooperation." Because of sensitivity and vulnerability, even those new elements of environmental opportunity that might *appear* to be minor (such as the beginnings of integration in Western Europe in the mid-1950s with the creation of the European Coal and Steel Community, the emergence in the late 1940s of new norms about human rights in the global system beginning with the creation of the United Nations, or the dramatic increase in the number of democracies in the global system since the 1970s), and through cooperative exchanges would certainly appear to be minor to traditional realist analysts, have had an extraordinary impact on the global system in which states now interact.

If we are to grasp the potential for either twenty-first century order or disorder, both opportunity and willingness in the transformed globe must be considered. They must be considered to comprehend how entities adapt to their changing environments in their attempts to cope (that is, to survive) and to prosper (that is, to get what they want in order to develop, grow, become wealthier, more powerful, more secure). All attempts across history by states to cope have had to consider and accommodate the interdependence which has always existed in the state system (and which characterizes the prisoners' dilemma), and that analytic perspective remains as instructive as ever for interpreting twenty-first century world politics.

## SYSTEM "REGULATORS," WAR, AND INTERNATIONAL "ORDER"

It follows that while the anarchic structure of the Westphalian system has been static, "order" within that system has not. Let us conceive of order as being about security against violence, assurance that agreements will be kept, and the stability of possession or ownership.[4] In realist or traditional geopolitical thought, centered on European history, the only critical or important challenge to such order would be the rise of a state or a coalition of states powerful enough to dominate the system militarily and subordinate all other states before it. Thus, the primary mechanism—and for realist statesmen or analysts, in actuality, the *only* mechanism—which could possibly cope with such miltary challenges to international order was the deterrent threat of the balance of power.

However, any number of other conditions could arise to challenge order as defined above. These conditions affect the "menu for choice" that confronts any policy maker. They include technological innovations and the often related differential growth of military capabilities and/or economic wealth among states. They also include new types of governments and/or distributions of countries with different governments or ideologies. In addition, they include new forms of international organizations. Even more importantly, changing conditions could include the breakdown of norms which could lead to the disintegration of "international society." Without an underlying consensus about values there would be an increasing potential for a twenty-first century collapse of order.[5]

World order can be threatened in various ways. In this transitional period into the twenty-first century, policy makers and analysts must address a set of disintegrative "isms," such as separatism, nationalism, fundamentalism. These "atavistic forces"[6] all threaten order in different ways for different subsets of states. Thus, there can be varying levels and types of order for different actors under different conditions. Given this range of possible variation, there can exist a variety of potential mechanisms by which states and international organizations may adapt to challenges to order. This idea is captured by thinking about the existence of system "regulators," or, mechanisms created by states to deal with systemic disturbances and to manage interdependence.[7]

One significant type of regulator is international law. International law is based on the idea of "expectations." International law, as any system of law, requires mutual expectations of "normal" behavior—that is, behavior which is rule-bound,

---

[4] This idea of order is developed by Hedley Bull, in chapter six of his book, *The Anarchical Society* (London: Macmillan, 1977).

[5] This pessimistic forecast is one of the themes in Samuel Huntington's book, *The Clash of Civilizations and the Remaking of World Order* (New York: Simon and Schuster, 1996).

[6] This term was introduced by Donald Puchala in discussions about theories of world politics.

[7] The classic treatment of system regulators is presented by Richard Rosecrance, *Action and Reaction in World Politics* (Boston: Little, Brown, 1963).

and which can be broadly characterized by the "Golden Rule." This reciprocity and acceptance of rules is a necessary component of "order." The actors in a system must share expectations (perceptions) that there will not be random violence, that there is some safety in possession, and that treaties will be honored. Any "society" must exhibit these shared norms of behavior if there is to be order.

Such norms are fragile and reversible, but when they exist they take on characteristics of what economists and political scientists call a "collective good." If there is a general expectation of certain kinds of behavior, especially cooperation rather than defection, then the "order" created can be jointly supplied to all actors once created for some. A good—or some consequence of activity—is considered to be jointly supplied when, if it is provided to any of the members of a group, *all* of the members of the group receive the good also. If a good is jointly supplied, then additional consumers of the good do not diminish its availability to other consumers. Examples of jointly supplied goods are clean air, or homeland deterrence against external aggression, or the light from a lighthouse. The jointly supplied good of order is fragile in that even a small number of defections (or a set of minor defections) might be enough to threaten such an order.

Order as jointly supplied may be particularly relevant to the current transitional world, both post–Cold War and post–Gulf War. The international system was changed by the end of the Cold War between the U.S. and U.S.S.R. as thoroughly as those systems which existed before and after the great general wars of the past two centuries: the Napoleonic Wars, World War I, and World War II. The view of most realist analysts, that war is the primary or only mechanism of system change, is illustrated by George Modelski: "The systems of world order we have known each originated in a great outburst of activity that was both creative and destructive and that was closely linked to conditions of global conflict and large-scale violence."[8]

It is instructive that the sort of enormous structural and normative change that took place with the break-up of the Soviet Union, the collapse of the "Eastern bloc" and the re-integration of the East European states into a broader European system, the disappearance of the Warsaw Pact alliance structure, and the end of a "bi-polar" international system, could all occur *without* some great system-change war. To realist policy makers and analysts, this should not have happened. Yet, as John Mueller has observed about the end of the Cold War, "the quiet cataclysm suggests that, in fact, no war or important war threat is required at all: the *system can be transformed by a mere change of ideas*"[9] (emphasis added).

---

[8] George Modelski, "The Long Cycle of Global Politics and the Nation-State,' *Comparative Studies in Society and History* 20 (1978), pp.214–35; quotation from p. 226.

[9] John Mueller, *Quiet Cataclysm: Reflections on the Recent Transformation of World Politics* (New York: HarperCollins, 1995), p.33.

It is also instructive that the changes in regulatory mechanisms that have accompanied the conclusion of these great wars appear to be missing in the post–Cold War era. As convincingly demonstrated by Charles Kegley and Gregory Raymond, great power conflicts tend to generate significant increases in the forging of cooperative norms and institutions—in the writing and signing of new treaties and in the creation of new international organizations.[10] That is, after periods of substantially higher levels of instability such as those generated by major wars, the leaders of states are prone to pay greater attention to the development of rules to regulate the use of force. This is consistent with the need for any society—even an "anarchic" international society—to develop norms, rules, and mechanisms to manage conflict.

The great wars of the past led to major peace conferences at Vienna, Versailles and, analogously, San Francisco. From them came the Concert of Europe, the League of Nations, and the United Nations. These periods of hot war—general in participation, massive in destruction, and of long duration—set in motion inventive thinking about what the world was to look like when the war was over. The natural forum of a post-war peace conference provided the setting for the creation (or reinvigoration) of regulatory mechanisms which might be robust enough to deal with the sorts of disturbances that were seen as leading to the war just ended. Great general wars change systems. Conditions are changed. Actors disappear and new actors appear. Some states fail. The geopolitical landscape is rearranged. (New technologies are being tested and disseminated.) Changing conditions call for a serious review and revision of regulatory mechanisms.

However, most wars provide not only time, but also *warning signals* which indicate that the war will soon be coming to an end. Such signals indicate that the moment for dealing with the changed system is at hand. This *was not* the case for the end of the Cold War in the early 1990s. In distinction from the great global wars, the end of the Cold War had few such warnings. In essence, policy makers and analysts were caught short. No broad-based post-war peace conference was convened. In the last decade of the twentieth century, neither policy makers nor analysts have yet succeeded in reaching agreements about the regulatory mechanisms which are needed to deal with the issues of order and the changing conditions of interdependence that followed the conclusion of the Cold War. This has been amply demonstrated by policy (or failure thereof) towards the conflicts among former-Yugoslavian states throughout the 1990s, first in Bosnia and then in Kosovo.

We have entered an uncertain period of transition not simply because the Cold War is over, but because the world system and its regulatory needs have since changed. There is a clear need to adapt, but the international community is

---

[10] See, Charles W. Kegley, Jr. and Gregory A. Raymond, *When Trust Breaks Down* (Columbia: University of South Carolina Press, 1990), and *How Nations Make Peace* (New York: Bedford/ St. Martin's Press, 1999).

having to do so without the prodding warnings of a general system-change war, and without the general peace settlement where such regulatory mechanisms historically have been created. As former U.S. Secretary of State Henry Kissinger has observed:

> . . . none of the most important countries which must build a new world order have had any experience with the multistate system that is emerging . . . Nor has any previous order had to combine attributes of the historic balance-of-power systems with global democratic opinion and the exploding technology of the contemporary period.[11]

### A "NEW" WORLD ORDER?

It is within these contexts that we should try to make sense of the vast, and growing, commentary on a "new world order." After leading the United States and its U.N.-based coalition in the Gulf War, President George Bush called for a "new world order." Putting aside the question of how much he really understood the message he was espousing, Bush's post–Gulf War assertion of a "new world order" can be interpreted as advocating the renewed use of collective security as the primary systemic regulatory mechanism. With the end of the Cold War, and the demonstration that the great powers could cooperate in regional conflicts large and small (as in the Gulf War, or even in Bosnia), both Bush and later President Clinton were asking the international community to return to the original vision of a United Nations, led by "five policemen," managing systemic conflict through collective security mechanisms.

During the last half of the twentieth century the balance of terror threat of mutual destruction was the primary systemic regulator. This version of the balance of power had acted as a much more broad-based system regulator than many observers realized. Not only did it constrain the two superpowers but their allies as well. Because nuclear capabilities were essentially bi-polar, it meant that the adversarial competition between the United States and the Soviet Union was global. Through interdependence, all other international actors were caught up in this global face-off. The bi-polar balance of terror—including the fear that any conflict could escalate to the point of nuclear exchange between the superpowers—constrained not only the U.S., the U.S.S.R., and their respective allies, but also most other states whose local or internal conflicts could easily become part of the global superpower face-off.

In addition, the 1950–1990 period severely limited the utility of United Nations peacekeeping activities. International organizations were of little use in most conflicts in the latter half of the twentieth century. Only after superpower agreement could IGOs become involved. Balancing regulators not only served as central regulatory mechanisms, but the security-oriented environment of the second

---

[11] Henry A. Kissinger, *Diplomacy* (New York: Touchstone Books, 1994), p.26. See also the last chapter in his final volume of memoirs, *Years of Renewal* (New York: Simon and Schuster, 1999).

half of the twentieth century also blocked the application of other regulators in any situation that affected the vital interests of the superpowers. Thus, we find that with the end of the twentieth century, and the growth in the number of democracies in the system, IGOs appear to be emerging as much more significant system regulators.

With the end of the millennium, and increasing demonstrations that the two former superpower antagonists could work together—as well as with the cooperation of China, Japan, Germany, and the other European powers—it made sense to fumble toward a U.N.-based collective security. The peace enforcement activities of the U.N. coalition during the Gulf War, were as *ad hoc* as those during the Korean War (the only other example of U.N.-based peace enforcement).[12] While the U.N. Charter contains a set of articles which formalize U.N. collective security operations, they have been ignored. Instead, policy makers have experimented (that is, groped and stumbled) toward new, diplomacy-based ways to provide collective security. The U.N.—and other international organizations, such as NATO in Kosovo during 1999—have become more than forums for discussion and the articulation of norms. They have become arenas of *action* for the implementation of collective security actions to restore order (especially as based on the principles of the liberal democracies).

In addition, a careful analysis of international law reveals the rather substantial growth of norms against the use of force over the last fifty years. These norms also restrict the threat of the use of force, as well as restricting force to an ever more narrowly defined notion of self-defense. The U.N. has been an important participant in the evolution of these norms.

## A RECIPE FOR MANAGING WORLD ORDER

The U.N. is uniquely positioned to operate as the primary engine to develop and implement a collective security regulatory mechanism for the twenty-first century. The opportunities are available now because states have already become enmeshed in sets of "regimes" which generate order in specific functional and geographic areas (such as the Antarctic regime, a trade regime, an ozone regime). Such regimes reflect the full network of rules, norms, and institutions that have been created by states, IGOs, and non-state actors to regulate or provide governance over some issue or geographic area. As part of the shift in the contemporary world towards the management of interdependence over the desire for sovereignty and autonomy, states (through regimes) have developed norms of coordination and cooperation, and have relied on decentralized enforcement, or sanctioning mechanisms. The political will is needed to continue building on these opportunities to govern international issue areas and manage international problems.

---

[12] See Bruce Russett and James S. Sutterlin, "The U.N. in a New World Order," *Foreign Affairs* 70 (1991), pp. 69–83.

These other regimes of cooperation and coordination also help to provide us with explanations for the difficulties which face the development of a collective security mechanism. Sometimes regimes can be created relatively quickly, as with the regime to protect the ozone layer. But many regimes, such as those on the Law of the Sea or those managing international trade or monetary policies, may take a very long time to be established. Some regimes, such as that for the non-proliferation of nuclear weapons, constantly threaten to break down. Many regimes are difficult to create and maintain. "Governance" by regimes is messy. It is messy in part because groups of democratic states which have abandoned the military option in their relations with each other still have to work out complex solutions to complex collective action problems under conditions of growing interdependencies. For some analysts and policy makers, particularly those with realist sympathies, this is far too messy when applied to regulatory mechanisms for dealing with security issues. Realists are unconvinced and worried; such regulatory mechanisms lack the clarity, and simplicity, of the nuclear balance of terror between superpowers (based on force and the threat of force).

Claims that this transitional system into the twenty-first century is more dangerous and unstable than that of the twentieth are exaggerated. Such claims, however, reflect a lack of understanding about systemic disturbances, and the appropriate regulators to deal with them. The existing regulators did moderately well with many (clearly not all) of the disturbances characteristic of the global system from the end of the Second World War to the early 1990s. With the end of superpower confrontation, other disturbances (some new and different, some old but reemerging such as ethnic conflict) have been able to come to the fore. Many observers have ignored the regulators centered on international law and regimes which have been developed over the years to take care of these disturbances, and which now must also be moved to the forefront of policy makers' menus.

Collective security appears, now, in the transformation to the twenty-first century to be a relevant, plausible, and useful regulator for conflict within a system which still continues to be anarchic and populated by sovereign states, and yet is characterized by high levels of interdependence and growing zones of peace. Max Singer and Aaron Wildavsky depict zones of "peace, wealth, and democracy," which are distinct from zones of "turmoil, war, and development." They are impressed with the fact that the zones of peace and democracy are growing, and that the major democracies ("if not 'the good guys,' at least 'the less-worse guys' ") now have "a near monopoly on the most effective military force." [13]

The newly found dominance of democratic zones of peace presents international actors with different challenges, disturbances, and problems than in past systems. The term "the democratic peace" has been used to refer to an important historical regularity now fully recognized by analysts and policy makers

---

[13] Max Singer and Aaron Wildavsky, *The Real World Order* (Chatham, N.J.: Chatham House, 1993), p.xiv.

alike: that two clearly and fully democratic states have never fought a war against each other.[14] Democratic states have needed to discover other ways and means to solve their problems than the threat or use of military force. Again, this can be "messy." While new, complex, and challenging to the states which must adapt, there is good news. Based on liberal norms of society and democratic zones of peace, the nature of this environment is one in which many opportunities for cooperative management of global issues can take place, in which regimes can work, in which the expectations of coordination and cooperation through rules can have great effect, and in which an IGO-based collective security does indeed have the capacity to work successfully.

Allusion to a "new world order" deserves careful attention, not derision. It is incorrect to point to a newly dangerous or incomprehensible world, only a more complex one where the previous regulator has disappeared, and where conditions call for mechanisms of regulation that slowly have been developing throughout the global system. While members of the international community have been somewhat tardy in recognizing the change in systems, and the opportunities provided by change, they now must cultivate a shared willingness to deal with that change so as to manage interdependence in the twenty-first century.

---

[14] See, for example, Bruce Russett, *Grasping the Democratic Peace* (Princeton, N.J.: Princeton University Press, 1993).

# 20

---

# HOW DEMOCRACY, INTERDEPENDENCE, AND INTERNATIONAL ORGANIZATIONS CREATE A SYSTEM FOR PEACE

---

Bruce Russett

Disputes invariably arise among states in an anarchical international system, but when they do, democracies cooperate by bargaining for compromises at the negotiating table. More than that, democracies almost never go to war with one another. This essay traces three principles embedded in "liberal democratic international theory"—free governments, free markets and economic interdependence, and international organizations—that explain why and how they contribute to international cooperation and security and can fundamentally change the past patterns of conflict among nations. Its author, Bruce Russett, is Dean Acheson Professor of International Relations and Director of United Nations Studies at Yale University. He edits the *Journal of Conflict Resolution* and is the author most recently of *Grasping the Democratic Peace: Principles for a Post–Cold War World* (1993), and *The Once and Future Security Council* (1997).

For nearly half a century the United States and its allies carried out a policy of containment during the Cold War, to prevent the spread of communist ideology and Soviet power. That policy succeeded, spectacularly. Now it must be replaced by another policy, one designed to consolidate the new acceptability of free institutions around the world. The new century presents more than just the passing of a particular adversarial relationship; it offers a chance for fundamentally changed relations among nations.

## THREE PRINCIPLES FOR A PEACEFUL
## INTERNATIONAL ORDER

Containment meant far more than just building a strong military establishment; it used trade, economic assistance, foreign investment, and cultural instruments like the BBC and Radio Free Europe. A key feature of containment was that it was not a unilateralist policy, but multilateralist. Its multilateral instruments ranged far beyond NATO and the rest of the alliance system, to depend heavily on regional trade arrangements like the OECD, the Bretton Woods financial institutions (the World Bank and the International Monetary Fund), GATT, and many U.N. specialized agencies. Central U.N. institutions were also vital, such as the Security Council, for endorsing peace enforcement action in Korea and for managing dangerous confrontations like the 1956 Suez War or keeping the Soviet-U.S. rivalry at arms length from some regional conflicts.

Contemporary policy needs a similar central organizing principle. That principle should build on the principles which underlay the rhetoric and much of the practice of containment, rooted in beliefs about the success of free political and economic systems. Those principles are democracy, free markets—especially on the argument that economic interdependence promotes peace as well as prosperity—and international law and organization. Each makes a contribution to peace, and in many instances they reinforce each other (and are themselves reinforced by peace) in "virtuous circles" or feedback loops.

Consider a puzzle about the end of the Cold War. The question is not simply why did the Cold War end, but rather, why did it end before the drastic change in the bipolar distribution of power, and why did it end peacefully? In November 1988 Margaret Thatcher proclaimed, as did other Europeans, that "the Cold War is over." By spring 1989 the U.S. State Department stopped making official reference to the Soviet Union as the enemy. The fundamental patterns of East-West behavior had changed, on both sides, beginning even before the circumvention of the Berlin Wall and then its destruction in October 1989. All of this preceded the unification of Germany (October 1990) and the dissolution of the Warsaw Pact (July 1991). Even after these latter events, the military power of the Soviet Union itself remained intact until the dissolution of the U.S.S.R. at the end of December 1991. None of these events was resisted militarily.

Any understanding of the change in the Soviet Union's international behavior, before its political fragmentation, and in time reciprocated by the West, demands attention to the operation of the three principles.

**1** Substantial political liberalization and movement toward democracy in the Soviet Union, with consequent improvements in free expression and the treatment of dissidents at home, in the East European satellites, and in behavior toward Western Europe and the United States.

**2** The desire for economic interdependence with the West, impelled by the impending collapse of the Soviet economy and the consequent perceived need for access to Western markets, goods, technology, and capital, which in turn required a change in Soviet military and diplomatic policy.

3 The influence of international law and organizations, as manifested in the Organization for Security and Cooperation in Europe (OSCE) and the human rights basket of the Helsinki accords and their legitimation and support of dissent in the communist states. Also important were the various international nongovernmental organizations (NGOs) devoted to human rights.

A vision of a peace among democratically governed states has long been invoked as part of a larger structure of institutions and practices to promote peace. In 1795 Immanuel Kant spoke of perpetual peace based partially upon states sharing "republican constitutions," which is essentially what we now mean by democracy. As the elements of such a constitution he identified freedom, with legal equality of subjects, representative government, and separation of powers. The other key elements of his perpetual peace were "cosmopolitan law" embodying ties of international commerce and free trade, and a "pacific union" established by treaty in international law among republics.

Woodrow Wilson expressed the same vision for the twentieth century. His Fourteen Points sound as though Kant were guiding Wilson's writing hand. They included Kant's cosmopolitan law and pacific union. Point three demanded removal "of all economic barriers and the establishment of an equality of trade conditions among all the nations consenting to the peace and associating themselves for its maintenance." The fourteenth point was, "A general association of nations must be formed under specific covenants for the purpose of affording mutual guarantees of political independence and territorial integrity to great and small states alike." He did not explicitly invoke the need for universal democracy, since not all of America's war allies were democratic. But his meaning is clear if one considers the domestic political conditions necessary for his first point: "Open covenants of peace, openly arrived at, after which there shall be no private international understandings of any kind but diplomacy shall proceed always frankly and in the public view." His 1917 war message to Congress asserted that "a steadfast concert of peace can never be maintained except by a partnership of democratic nations." This vision emerged again after World War II, animating the founders of what became the European Union. It has since been taken up among countries of South America. At the beginning of a new century, it is newly plausible.

## DEMOCRACIES RARELY FIGHT EACH OTHER

Democratization is key to this vision for two reasons. First, democracy is a desirable form of government on its own merit. It both recognizes and promotes human dignity. Democracy is not perfect, and should not be forced upon peoples who do not wish it. But for many countries it is better than the alternatives under which they have suffered.

Second, we now have solid evidence that democracies do not make war on each other. Some of it can be found in my book, *Grasping the Democratic Peace: Principles for a Post–Cold War World,* and in many more recent works.[1] In the contemporary era, "democracy" denotes a country in which nearly everyone can vote, elections are freely contested, the chief executive is chosen by popular vote or by an elected parliament, and civil rights and civil liberties are substantially guaranteed. Democracies are not always peaceful—we all know the history of democracies in colonialism, covert intervention, and other excesses of power. Democracies frequently resort to violence in their relations with authoritarian states. But the relations between stable democracies are qualitatively different.

Democracies are unlikely to engage in any kind of militarized disputes *with each other* or to let any such disputes escalate into war. They rarely even skirmish. Pairs of democratic states have been only one-eighth as likely as other kinds of states to threaten to use force against each other, and only one-tenth as likely actually to do so. Established democracies fought *no wars* against one another during the entire twentieth century. (Although Finland, for example, took the Axis side against the Soviet Union in World War II, it engaged in no combat with the democracies.)

The more democratic each state is, the more peaceful their relations are likely to be. Democracies are more likely to employ "democratic" means of peaceful conflict resolution. They are readier to reciprocate each other's behavior, to accept third-party mediation or good offices in settling disputes, and to accept binding third-party arbitration and adjudication.[2] Careful statistical analyses of countries' behavior have shown that democracies' relatively peaceful relations toward each other are not spuriously caused by some other influence such as sharing high levels of wealth, or rapid growth, or ties of alliance. The phenomenon of peace between democracies is not limited just to the rich industrialized states of the Global North. It was not maintained simply by pressure from a common adversary in the Cold War, and it has outlasted that threat.

The phenomenon of democratic peace can be explained by the pervasiveness of normative restraints on conflict between democracies. That explanation extends to the international arena the cultural norms of live-and-let-live and peaceful conflict resolution that operate within democracies. The phenomenon of

---

[1] (Princeton, N.J.: Princeton University Press, 1993). There is an enormous body of more recent scholarship on this matter, largely confirming or extending the principle, but some of it critical. See especially James Lee Ray, *Democracy and International Conflict* (Columbia: University of South Carolina Press, 1995; Spencer Weart, *Never at War: Why Democracies Will Not Fight One Another* (New Haven, Conn: Yale University Press, 1998); Bruce Russett and Harvey Starr, "From Democratic Peace to Kantian Peace: Democracy and Conflict in the International System," in Manus Midlarsky, ed., *Handbook of War Studies* (Ann Arbor, Mich.: University of Michigan Press, 2000, 2nd ed.).

[2] Russell Leng, "Reciprocating Influence Strategies and Success in Interstate Bargaining," *Journal of Conflict Resolution* 37, no. 1 (March 1993), pp. 3–41; William Dixon, "Democracy and the Peaceful Settlement of International Disputes," *American Political Science Review* 88, no. 1, (March 1994), pp. 14–32; Gregory Raymond, "Democracies, Disputes, and Third-Party Intermediaries," *Journal of Conflict Resolution* 38, no. 1 (March 1994), pp. 24–42.

democratic peace can also be explained by the role of institutional restraints on democracies' decisions to go to war. Those restraints insure that any state in a conflict of interest with another democracy can expect ample time for conflict-resolution processes to be effective, and democracies' political decision-making processes are relatively transparent. These two influences reinforce each other. The spread of democratic norms and practices in the world, if consolidated, should reduce the frequency of violent conflict and war. Where normative restraints are weak, democratic institutions may provide the necessary additional restraints on the use of violence against other democratic states.

To the degree that countries once ruled by autocratic systems become democratic, the absence of war among democracies comes to bear on any discussion of the future of international relations. The statement that in the modern international system democracies have almost never fought each other represents a complex phenomenon (a) Democracies rarely fight each other (an empirical statement) because (b) they have other means of resolving conflicts between them and therefore don't need to fight each other (a prudential cost-benefit statement), and (c) they perceive that democracies should not fight each other (a normative statement about principles of right behavior), which reinforces the empirical statement. By this reasoning, the more democracies there are in the world, the fewer potential adversaries we and other democracies will have and the wider the zone of peace will be.

The *possibility* of a widespread zone of democratic peace in the world exists. To turn that possibility into a policy two fundamental problems must be addressed: the problem of consolidating democratic stability, and the prospects for changing basic patterns of international behavior.

## STRENGTHENING DEMOCRACY AND ITS NORMS

Samuel Huntington's book, *The Third Wave: Democratization in the Late Twentieth Century*[3] synthesizes much of the literature on the prerequisites of democracy. Among developments in the world that played significant parts in *producing* the latest wave of recent transitions to democracy he identifies changes in the policies of other states and international organizations—to promote human rights and democracy, and "snowballing" or demonstration effects, enhanced by international communication, as transitions to democracy in some states served as models for their neighbors. Among conditions that favor the *consolidation* of new democracies he lists a favorable international political environment, with outside assistance.

Probably most of the conditions affecting the success of democratization arise from circumstances internal to any particular state. But this list of possible conditions from outside is impressive also. Favorable international conditions may

---

[3] (Norman, Okla.: University of Oklahoma Press, 1991).

not be essential in every case, but they can make a difference, and sometimes a crucial one when the internal influences are mixed.

With economic conditions so grim in much of the developing world, eastern Europe, and the former Soviet Union, and the consequent dangers to the legitimacy of new democratic governments, external assistance—technical and financial—is especially important. New democracies will not survive without some material improvement in their citizens' lives. As a stick, aid can surely be denied to governments that regularly violate human rights, for example of ethnic minorities. A military coup or an aborted election can be punished by suspending aid. As to the carrot of extending aid on a conditional basis, broader goals of developing democratic institutions require creation of a civil society. Recipients may see multilateral aid, with conditions of democratic reform attached, as a less blatant invasion of their sovereignty than aid from a single country.

It would be a terrible loss if the richer and older democracies did not make serious efforts—a loss to themselves as well as to the peoples of the struggling democracies. Any solution requires external assistance and protection to aid and speed transitions to democracy. It also requires devising institutions, and nurturing norms and practices, of democratic government with respect for minority rights. The creation of institutions, norms, and practices to protect minorities has never been easy. But it presents the fundamental challenge of world political development in this era. It is worth remembering that the most terrible acts of genocide in this century (from Turkey's slaughter of the Armenians through Hitler, Stalin, Pol Pot, and others) have been carried out by authoritarian or totalitarian governments, not democratic ones.[4]

Understanding that democracies rarely fight each other, and why, has great consequence for policy in the contemporary world. It should affect the kinds of military preparations believed to be necessary, and the costs one would be willing to pay to make them. It should encourage peaceful efforts to assist the emergence and consolidation of democracy. But a misunderstanding of it could encourage war-making against authoritarian regimes, and efforts to overturn them—with all the costly implications such a policy might imply.

Recollection of the post-1945 success with defeated adversaries can be both instructive and misleading. It is instructive in showing that democracy could supplant a thoroughly discredited totalitarian regime. It can be misleading if one forgets how expensive it (Marshall Plan aid for Germany and Italy, and important economic concessions to Japan) was, and especially if one misinterprets the political conditions of military defeat. The allies utterly defeated the Axis coalition. Then, to solidify democratic government they conducted vast (if incomplete) efforts to remove the former elites from positions of authority. But they had something to build on, in the form of individuals and institutions from previous

---

[4] R. J. Rummel, *Death by Government: Genocide and Mass Murder in the Twentieth Century* (New Brunswick, N.J.: Transaction, 1994).

experiences with democracy. The model of "fight them, beat them, and then make them democratic" is no model for contemporary action. It probably would not work anyway, and no one is prepared to make the kind of effort that would be required. Not all authoritarian states are inherently aggressive. Indeed, at any particular time the majority are not. A militarized crusade for democracy is not in order.

Sometimes external military intervention against the most odious dictators may make sense. With a cautious cost-benefit analysis and with the certainty of substantial and legitimate internal support, it might be worthwhile—that is, under conditions when rapid military success is likely *and* the will of the people at issue is clear. Even so, any time an outside power supplants any existing government the problem of legitimacy is paramount. The very democratic norms to be instilled may be compromised. At the least, intervention cannot be unilateral. It should be approved, publicly and willingly, by an international body like the U.N. or the Organization of American States. When an election has been held under U.N. auspices and certified as fair—as happened in Haiti—the U.N. has a special responsibility, even a duty, to see that the democratic government it helped create is not destroyed.

Under most circumstances, international bodies are best used to promote democratic processes when the relevant domestic parties are ready. Peacekeeping operations to help provide the conditions for free elections, monitor those elections, and advise on the building of democratic institutions are far more promising and less costly for all concerned than is military intervention. The U.N. experienced highly publicized troubles in Somalia and the former Yugoslavia as it tried to cope with a range of challenges not previously part of its mandate. Nonetheless, its successes, though receiving less attention, outnumber the failures. It was a major facilitator of peaceful transitions and democratic elections in places like Cambodia, El Salvador, Mozambique, and Namibia. Its Electoral Assistance Unit has provided election monitoring, technical assistance, or other aid to free electoral processes in over seventy states.[5]

## ECONOMIC INTERDEPENDENCE AND INTERNATIONAL ORGANIZATIONS

Ties of economic interdependence—international trade and investment—form an important supplement to shared democracy in promoting peace. Analyses that show how rarely democracies used or threatened to use military force against each other also show a similarly strong peaceful effect when states trade heavily with each other. The effect of economic interdependence does not supplant, but supplements, the effect of democracy, and like democracy its effect remains

---

[5] The scope of these efforts is evident in Boutros Boutros-Ghali, *An Agenda for Democratization* (New York: United Nations, 1996).

even when alliance, wealth, and economic growth rates are controlled for in the analysis.[6]

Here then is the second element of the Kantian/Wilsonian vision, representing the role of free trade and a high level of commercial exchange. Economic interdependence gives countries a stake in each others' well-being. War would mean destruction, in the other country, of one's own markets, industrial plants, and sources of imports. If my investments are in your country, bombing your industry means, in effect, bombing my own factories. Even the threat of violent conflict is likely to inhibit traders and raise their costs. Economic interdependence also serves as a means of obtaining information about each other's perspectives, interests, and desires on a broad range of matters not the subject of the economic exchange. These communications form an important channel for conflict management. Interdependence, however, is the key word—mutual dependence, not one-sided dominance.

The end of the Cold War represents a surrender to the force of values of economic as well as political freedom. Democracies trade more heavily with each other than do other kinds of states, even after taking into account the standard kinds of economically driven market calculations.[7] Moreover, trade and peace form a mutually reinforcing relationship. Not only does trade promote peace, peace in turn promotes trade, and traders and governments develop greater confidence in the stability of political relationships. International organizations promoting free trade and stable economic conditions (for example, the IMF, the World Trade Organization, and the United Nations Development Programme) thus make an indirect contribution to peace, as well as to development.

The role of international law and institutions, and the need for strengthening them, constitutes the third element of the Kantian/Wilsonian vision. As expressed by former U.N. Secretary-General Boutros Ghali, the U.N. has a new mission of "peace-building," attending to democratization, development, and the protection of human rights.[8] It is newly strengthened and, paradoxically, also newly and enormously burdened. The U.N. and other international organizations promote democratization and peace directly as well as indirectly. As noted above, democracies are much more likely to use international institutions for peacefully resolving disputes among themselves than are dictatorships.

Large-scale statistical analyses of the effect of international organization memberships have also been carried out. For example, the more intergovernmental organizations (IGOs) that any pair of states belongs to, the less likely they are to use or threaten violence in their relations with each other. Again, this effect is in

---

[6] John Oneal and Bruce Russett, "The Classical Liberals Were Right: Democracy, Interdependence, and Conflict, 1950–1985," *International Studies Quarterly* 41, no. 2 (June 1997), pp. 267–94.

[7] Harry Bliss and Bruce Russett, "Democratic Trading Partners: the Liberal Connection," *Journal of Politics* 60, no. 4 (November 1998), pp. 1126–47.

[8] *An Agenda for Peace* (New York: United Nations, 1993), paragraph 81.

addition to that of democracy and economic interdependence, and holds even when alliances, wealth, etc. are controlled for. International organizations promote the flow of information to help settle conflicts, provide institutions to mediate disagreements, help establish norms for behavior, and promote some sense of common identity among peoples and countries. In turn, democracies and economically interdependent states are more likely to join with each other in international organizations.[9] Democracy, interdependence, and IGOs thus form a system, with feedback loops whereby each strengthens the other, contributes to peaceful relations, and in turn is nurtured by continued peace.[10]

The effects of these three Kantian influences can be found throughout most of the twentieth century—both before the Cold War era and in the first few years after it. Two kinds of pairs of countries are especially likely to have reasons for violent conflict, and the ability to fight each other: geographically contiguous countries, and pairs of states in which at least one is a major power, with long-range military capability. Among these pairs during the past century, high levels of shared democracy and of economic interdependence both reduced the chances of a militarized dispute by about a third, and shared IGO memberships did so by roughly 12 percent. And in periods when levels of democracy and interdependence are generally high throughout the international system, the norms and institutions that go with them seem to have some restraining effect even on countries that are not very democratic or interdependent.[11] Common perceptions can be misleading: actually, the number of international wars worldwide has dropped precipitously since 1987.[12]

Another generalization applies to fears raised by Samuel Huntington's book, *The Clash of Civilizations and the Remaking of World Order.*[13] He contends that in recent years the most pervasive and dangerous international conflicts have been, and will be, across the fault-lines of great civilizations, notably between Western civilization and all others, and particularly the West and Islam. But the evidence is that, once the effects of democracy and trade have been taken into account, military conflicts between countries in different civilization groupings have, in recent decades, been no more common than within civilizations. The specter of clashes between civilizations essentially dissolves.

---

[9] Bruce Russett, John Oneal, and David Davis, "The Third Leg of the Kantian Tripod for Peace: International Organizations and Militarized Disputes, 1950–1985," *International Organization* 52, no. 3 (Summer 1998), pp. 441–67.

[10] Bruce Russett, "A Neo-Kantian Perspective: Democracy, Interdependence and International Organizations in Building Security Communities," in Emanuel Adler and Michael Barnett, eds., *Security Communities* (New York: Cambridge University Press, 1998).

[11] John R. Oneal and Bruce Russett, "The Kantian Peace: The Pacific Benefits of Democracy, Interdependence, and International Organizations, 1895–1992," *World Politics* 52, no. 1 (October 1999):

[12] Monty Marshall, *Third World War* (Lanham, Md.: Rowman, Littlefield, 1999).

[13] (New York: Simon & Schuster, 1996). Evidence against this argument is in Bruce Russett and John R. Oneal, *Triangulating Peace: Democracy, Interdependence, and International Organization* (New York: W.W. Norton, 2000), ch. 7.

## CAN A WIDER PEACE BE BUILT?

New democracies should be supported financially, politically, militarily, and morally. Successful transitions to democracy in some countries can supply a model for others. A stable and less menacing international system can permit the emergence and consolidation of democratic governments. International threats—real or only perceived—strengthen the forces of secrecy and authoritarianism in the domestic politics of states involved in protracted conflict. Relaxation of international threats to peace and security reduces the need, and the excuse, for repressing democratic dissent.

Democracy and the expectation of international peace can feed on each other. An evolutionary process may be at work. Because of the visible nature and public costs of breaking commitments, democratic leaders may be better able to persuade leaders of other states that they will keep the agreements they do enter into. Democratic states are able to signal their intentions in bargaining with greater credibility than autocratic states. Democracies more often win their wars than do authoritarian states (eighty percent of the time; remember that the coin-flip odds would be only fifty-fifty). They are more prudent about what wars they get into. In war they seem to be superior in organizational effectiveness and leadership, and with free speech and debate they are more accurate and efficient information processors. Authoritarian governments who lose wars are often overthrown, and may be replaced by democratic regimes. States with competitive elections generally have lower military expenditures, which in relations with other democracies promotes cooperation; as democracies' politically relevant international environment becomes composed of more democratic and internally stable states, democracies tend to reduce their military allocations and conflict involvement.[14]

The modern international system is commonly traced to the Treaty of Westphalia and the principles of sovereignty affirmed by it. In doing so it affirmed the anarchy of the system, without a superior authority to ensure order. It also was a treaty among princes who ruled as autocrats. Our understanding of the modern anarchic state system risks conflating the effects of anarchy with those stemming from the political organization of its component units. When most states are ruled autocratically—as in 1648 and throughout virtually all of history since—playing by the rules of autocracy may be the only way for any state, democracy or not, to survive in Hobbesian anarchy.

---

[14] James Fearon, "Domestic Political Audiences and the Escalation of International Disputes," *American Political Science Review* 88, no. 3 (September 1994), pp. 577–92; Kenneth Schultz, "Do Democratic Institutions Constrain or Inform?" *International Organization* 53, no. 2 (Spring 1999), pp. 24–37; Bruce Bueno de Mesquita, Randolph Siverson, and Garry Woller, "War and the Fate of Regimes: A Comparative Survey," *American Political Science Review* 86, no. 3 (1992), pp. 639–46; Allan C. Stam, *Win, Lose, or Draw* (Ann Arbor: University of Michigan Press, 1996); Michelle Garfinkel, "Domestic Politics and International Conflict," *American Economic Review* 84, no. 5 (December 1984), pp. 1294–1309; Zeev Maoz, *Domestic Sources of Global Chance* (Ann Arbor: University of Michigan Press, 1996).

The anarchic security dilemma of threat and counterthreat drove the pessimism of "realists" like Hans Morgenthau. But the emergence of new democracies with the end of the Cold War presents an opening for change in the international system more fundamental even than at the end of other big wars—World Wars I and II and the Napoleonic Wars. For the first time in world history, by the mid-1990s a solid majority of states approximated the standards for electoral democracy that I listed above. This proportion has subsequently been quite stable (117 out of 194 as of early 1998). Slightly over half of the world's population lived in democracies.[15] And some big countries made a precarious transition toward democracy in 1999, notably Indonesia and Nigeria. Democracy in many of these countries is far from complete, and it may not be stable. This global democratic wave may crest and fall back, as earlier ones have done. Even so, this is a huge achievement. States probably can become democratic faster than they can become rich. If further enlargement of the zone of democracy now sounds too ambitious, consolidation is the very least we should settle for. If the chance for wide democratization can be grasped and held, world politics might be transformed.

A Kantian peace would be sustained by an interacting and mutually supporting combination of democratic government, economic interdependence, and international law and organization. Such an international system—an international society as well as a collection of sovereign states—might reflect very different behavior than did the previous one composed predominantly of autocracies. The West won the Cold War, at immense cost. If we should now let slip this marvelous but brief window of opportunity to solidify basic change in the international order at much lower cost, our children will wonder why. Some autocratically governed states will surely remain in the system. In their relations with states where democracy is unstable, or where democratization is not begun at all, democracies must continue to be vigilant and concerned with the need for military deterrence. But if enough states do become stable democracies in the twenty-first century, then we will have a chance to reconstruct the norms and rules of the international order. A system created by autocracies centuries ago might now be re-created by a critical mass of democratic states, economically interdependent with peaceful relations facilitated by international institutions.

---

[15] Freedom House, *Freedom in the World: The Annual Survey of Political Rights and Civil Liberties, 1997–1998* (Piscataway, N.J.: Transaction Books, 1998).

# 21

# THE REALITY AND RELEVANCE OF INTERNATIONAL LAW IN THE TWENTY-FIRST CENTURY

Christopher C. Joyner

International law reflects the need for order, predictability, and stability in international relations. The functions and impact of international law are analyzed by Christopher C. Joyner, who emphasizes both the strengths and limitations of legal norms as instruments for managing conflicts and promoting collaboration in world politics. Recently, the growth of human rights law and the establishment of a permanent war crimes court to hold rulers' accountable for their policies toward citizens has built confidence that a true world of law will emerge with greater institutional support than in the past. This essay provides a basis for evaluating whether international law can begin to even more effectively in the future contribute to global stability with justice in the ways reformers have sought since Hugo Gratius first founded modern international law in the seventeenth century. Joyner is Professor of Government at Georgetown University. He is the author of *Governing the Frozen Commons: The Antarctica Regime and Environmental Protection* (1998) and editor of *The United Nations and International Law* (1997).

The dawn of the new millennium brings greater recognition of the reality and relevance of international law than ever before. New challenges during the late 1990s underscored the essential need for legal solutions for problems affecting interstate relations. Resort to military force by a NATO coalition on humanitarian grounds to halt "ethnic cleansing" by Serb paramilitary forces of Albanians in Kosovo; revival of the Middle East peace process between a new Israeli government and the Palestinian Authority; humanitarian intervention to stop gross human rights abuses by Indonesian militia in East Timor; taking policy action on the Rio "Earth Summit's" agenda for global environmental and development issues; entry into force of a new regime for governing the world's oceans, as well as the General Agreement on Tariffs and Trade/World Trade Organization arrangement for regulating international commerce; peacekeeping actions by the United Nations to end violence in Kosovo, Bosnia, Georgia, Angola, Cambodia, and Haiti; the decision of a British court to proceed with the extradition to Spain of former Chilean dictator General Augusto Pinochet to face charges of torture and other human rights abuses during his rule; establishment of international tribunals to try persons accused of genocidal atrocities and crimes against humanity in the former Yugoslavia and Rwanda and creation of a like-minded International Criminal Court for the world community; and, ongoing multilateral efforts to manage massive refugee crises affecting Bosnia, Rwanda, Burundi, the Democratic Republic of the Congo, Sierra Leone, and Kosovo—these recent events among many others are manifestly anchored in international legal implications.

Yet, students of international relations rightly continue to ask certain fundamental questions about the nature and purpose of international law. Is international law really "law"? Or is it nothing more than "positive morality"? How can international law work in a modern state system dictated by considerations of national interests and power politics? Is international law more of a restraint on national policy, or is it merely a policy instrument wielded by governments to further their own ad hoc purposes to gain legitimacy? In sum, what is the reality and relevance of international law to contemporary world politics? This essay seeks to address these inquiries and in the process to explore the role of international law in international affairs as we enter the twenty-first century.

## THE CONCEPTUAL FOUNDATIONS OF INTERNATIONAL LAW

International law, often described as public international law or the law of nations, refers to the system of law that governs relations between states. States traditionally were the only subjects with rights and duties under international law. In the modern era, however, the ambit of international law has been greatly expanded to where it now encompasses many actors other than states, among them international organizations, multinational corporations, and even individual persons. Nevertheless, states remain the primary concern and focus of international law in world politics.[1]

---

[1] See generally Alan James, *Sovereign Statehood: The Basis of International Society* (London: Allen and Unwin, 1986); Gene Lyons and Michael Mastanduno, eds., *Beyond Westphalia? State Sovereignty and International Intervention* (Baltimore: Johns Hopkins University Press, 1995); and Hendrik Spruyt, *The Sovereign State and Its Competitors* (Princeton, N.J.: Princeton University Press, 1995).

It is important at the outset to note that the initial reaction of many students and laypeople alike to the notion of international law is one of skepticism. A prevalent view holds that national governments have scant respect for international law, and therefore they have little or no incentive to obey it, given the absence of a supranational system armed with sanctions capable of being enforced against a lawbreaker. In short, a popular belief is that international law is not really law.

However, the reality as demonstrated through their behavior is that states do accept international law as law and, even more significant, in the vast majority of instances they usually obey it. Though it is certainly true that international law is sometimes disobeyed with impunity, the same observation is equally true of any domestic legal system. For example, do local laws prevent traffic violations from occurring? Do municipal (i.e., domestic) laws against murder, rape, burglary, or assault and battery prevent those crimes from being committed? Put simply, does the presence of "enforced" law *ipso facto* ensure compliance or even apprehension and prosecution? Clearly, in the real world, the answer is no. Richard Falk put it well when he observed that:

> The success of domestic law does not rest in its capacity to solicit the respect of its subjects; the incidence of homicide and civil violence, and even of rebellion, is high. International law is a weak legal system not because it is often or easily flouted by powerful states, but because certain violations, however infrequent, are highly destructive and far-reaching in their implications.[2]

International law is not violated more often, or to a higher degree, than the law of other legal systems. Yet why does the contrary misconception persist? Two general reasons may offer much of the explanation. First, there is sensationalism; people tend to hear about international law only when blatant violations make the news. When states attack each other (or, for that matter, when a person is murdered), it becomes a newsworthy event. If the law is obeyed, and international relations between states proceed uninterrupted by violence, those affairs usually go unreported. The second reason for the misimpression that international law is frequently violated is the tendency of many people to presume that the mere existence of a transnational dispute automatically signifies that some law has been breached. This, of course, is not true; the fact that a dispute between states has arisen ought not to be taken to mean that a breach of international law has occurred, just as a civil dispute involving two individuals is not necessarily indicative of a breach in municipal law. Disputes between states may arise over many concerns, none of which may involve violations of law. For example, there may exist a genuine uncertainty about the facts of a case or uncertainty about the law itself; there may be need for new law to meet changing

---

[2] Richard A. Falk, *The Status of Law in International Society* (Princeton. N.J.: Princeton University Press, 1970), p. 29.

international conditions; or there may even occur the resort to unfriendly but legal acts (called retorsion) by one state against another. While these situations may be unfortunate and perhaps in some instances regrettable, they do not perforce constitute violations of the law.

Most criticism about international law can be generally categorized. First, there are those who view the law of nations as something that can never work and is therefore ignored by states, groups, or individuals. Law, in effect, becomes an "orphan" within the international community. On the other hand, there is the group that sees international law as an instrument of purpose, a "harlot" as it were, to be used, abused, or discounted in accord with one's own moment of convenience, interest, or capability. Still other critics perceive the law as not having any "teeth" or power of enforcement. The absence of an executive authority or international policeman thereby renders all values, norms, and rules subject to mere voluntary accession. International law in this instance becomes a "jailer." Perhaps more cynical is the view that international law does not exist and that it cannot exist until either all states agree to cooperate and coordinate the creation of mutually acceptable legal codes or this condition is imposed upon them. In this scenario, international law must assume the role of a "magician." Prevalent in the hard-line realist school of international politics, this perception suggests that international law provides nothing more than a utopian dream. That is, governments that place heavy emphasis upon inserting morality in foreign policy considerations live in a world of idealism, naively hoping for the mythical attainment in international affairs where law will govern supremely and people will be saved from a system of international anarchy. For these critics, proponents of international law thus represent a "never-never land" school of thought.[3]

The reality of international law does not fit either neatly or aptly into any of these perceptions. John Austin, who dominated jurisprudential thinking in Great Britain during the nineteenth century, contributed much in the way of theory suggesting the frailties of international law. Austin reasoned that for a legal system to exist in fact, three indispensable elements were essential: (1) There had to exist a clearly identifiable superior, or sovereign, who was capable of issuing (2) orders or commands for managing society, and (3) there had to be punitive sanctions capable of enforcing those commands. For Austin, law thus was defined as the general command emanating from a sovereign, supported by the threat of real sanctions. Since international law had neither a sovereign nor the requisite enforcement authority, Austin concluded that it was not really "law;" international law, he believed, ought to be considered merely as "positive morality."[4] The Austinian concept involves the relatively uncomplicated contention that genuine law has its rules laid down by a superior power (the executive), and that they are en-

---

[3] These schools critical of international law are proposed in John H. E. Fried, "International Law—Neither Orphan Nor Harlot, Neither Jailer Nor Never-Never Land," in Karl Deutsch and Stanley Hoffmann, eds., *The Relevance of International Law* (New York: Doubleday, 1971), pp. 124–76.

[4] John Austin, *The Province of Jurisprudence Determined and the Uses of the Study of Jurisprudence* (London: Weidenfeld and Nicolson, 1954), pp. 121–26, 137–44.

forced by another superior power (the police). At first blush, this line of thinking may seem logically attractive. However, in the real world, it becomes intellectually simplistic to assume that law exists only when and where formal structures exist; moreover, it is likewise faulty to confuse characteristics of a legal system as being those prerequisites necessary to define law's existence. The remainder of this essay addresses these contentions.

## THE NATURE OF INTERNATIONAL LAW

Generally speaking, the function of law is to preserve order. That is, law embodies a system of sanctioned regularity, a certain order in itself, which conveys the notion of expectations. Law provides for the regularity of activities that can be discerned, forecast, and anticipated in a society. Through law, the attempt is made to regulate behavior in order to insure harmony and maintain a society's values and institutions.[5]

In this connection, a system of law should have three basic characteristics. First, a statement of a prescribed pattern of behavior must be evident. Second, an obligational basis approved by the society must be present. And third, some process for punishing unlawful conduct in the society must be available. As essential facets, the measure of how well these elements interact will in large part determine the effectiveness of the legal system as a whole as well as the extent of its actual existence and performance.

Given these general observations, what significance can be attached to the nature of international law? Expressed in an Austinian sense, can a bona fide legal system that fulfills these objectives exist in the absence of a formal government structure, that is, without a centralized system of law creation, law application, and law enforcement? The answer clearly is yes. International law does qualify as a legal system, albeit a somewhat primitive and imperfect one. International law consists of a set of norms that prescribe international behavior, although those patterns may at times seem vaguely defined. International law furnishes a principled foundation for policy decisions, albeit adherence to principle often becomes justifiable if it can be shown to be practical. Relatedly, reasons do exist for states to obey international law; in other words, an obligatory basis does in fact exist to support international law's operation in world affairs. Finally, a system of sanctions is available in international law, and it contributes to coercive enforcement of the law. To appreciate these observations more fully, it is worthwhile to examine the evolutionary nature and sources of international law, the obligational basis for its operation, and the enforcement process available for punishing illegal behavior in the international community.

---

[5] For a thoughtful compendium on the evolution of law in international society, see Robert J. Beck, Anthony Clark Arend, and Robert D. Vander Lugt, eds., *International Rules: Approaches from International Law and International Relations* (Oxford: Oxford University Press, 1996).

## THE SOURCES OF INTERNATIONAL LAW

No legal system flashes into existence fully panoplied. All orders of law, from the most primitive to the most sophisticated, have their roots in the society they govern. International law is no different. The modern law of nations has undergone a process of evolution as old as the nation-state system itself, owing its direct origins to the Treaty of Westphalia in 1648. Importantly in this regard, over the past three centuries, specific sources for the creation of new international law have become widely acknowledged in and accepted by the international community.[6]

Foremost among the sources of international law are international conventions and treaties.[7] When ratified by a substantial number of states some multilateral conventions may be deemed tantamount to an international legal statute and are aptly labeled "lawmaking" treaties. Examples of these types of treaties include the four 1949 Geneva Conventions on the Law of War, the 1961 Vienna Convention on Diplomatic Relations, the 1967 Outer Space Treaty, the 1982 U.N. Convention on the Law of the Sea, the 1989 U.N. Convention on the Rights of the Child, and the 1992 U.N. Conventions on Biodiversity and Climate Change. Also, general multilateral treaties can create the organizational machinery through which new international law can be developed. For example specialized agencies of the United Nations, such as the World Health Organization, International Civil Aviation Organization, Universal Postal Union, and International Telecommunication Union—all of which were created by specific international treaties—have themselves become sources of rules and regulations throughout the international community. Thus international organizations that were created by international law contribute to the growth of additional law through the purpose of their functional operation.[8]

The second major source of international law is custom. In the eighteenth and nineteenth centuries, when interaction among states was relatively sporadic and less complex than today, certain habitual patterns of behavior often emerged to

---

[6] See generally Clive Parry, *The Sources and Evidences of International Law* (Dobbs Ferry, N.Y.: Oceana, 1965). The following enumeration of sources is based upon the priority set out in Article 38 of the Statute of the International Court of Justice, appended to the Charter of the United Nations.

[7] T. O. Elias, *The Modern Law of Treaties* (Leiden, Neth.: Sijhoff, 1974); I. M. Sinclair, *The Vienna Convention on the Law of Treaties,* 2nd ed. (Dobbs Ferry. N.Y.: Oceana, 1984); Shabati Rosenne. *The Law of Treaties: A Guide to the Legislative History of the Vienna Convention* (Dobbs Ferry, N.Y.: Oceana, 1971); and Paul Reuter, *Introduction to the Law of Treaties* (New York: Columbia University Press, 1989).

[8] See generally Oscar Schachter and Christopher C. Joyner, eds., *United Nations Legal Order* (Cambridge: Cambridge University Press, 1995) and Rosalyn Higgins, *The Development of International Law through the Political Organs of the United Nations* (London: Oxford University Press, 1963). Significantly, however, resolutions adopted by the United Nations General Assembly are deemed to be only recommendations and are not lawfully binding upon the membership. See Christopher C. Joyner, "The U.N. General Assembly Resolutions anal International Law: Rethinking the Contemporary Dynamics of Norm-Creation," *California Western International Law Journal* 11, no. 3 (Summer 1981), pp. 445–78.

form obligatory rules. That is, through widespread adherence and repeated use certain customary practices by governments became accepted as law, with normatively binding constraints.[9] Prominent among laws evolving from customary state practice were those pertaining to the law of the sea, in particular those regulations establishing the three-mile territorial limit, the definition of piracy, and proper division of the spoils of war. Today, however, due to the increasing interdependence and complexity of modern international relations coupled with the spread of the traditional Eurocentric legal system beyond the borders of the Western world, custom as a body of unwritten though clearly recognized norms seems to be diminishing as a source of international law. Much of customary international law developed in the era of nineteenth century colonialism. Largely for this reason, it is now viewed with suspicion or held in disrepute by many of the newly independent states in the Third World. Another critical weakness of custom as a contemporary source of law is couched in the traditional requirement that customary law must grow into acceptance slowly, through a gradual, evolutionary process over many decades, perhaps even hundreds of years. This requisite for gradual evolution and slow acceptance of an emergent customary norm leaves that rule vulnerable to becoming archaic or anachronistic even before it can become accepted as law. This likelihood undoubtedly is at work today as rapid advances in technology play havoc with traditional legal parameters and jurisdictional designs—a reality that makes imperative the constant need for international law to keep pace with technological developments.

The third primary source of international law is the general principles of law recognized by civilized nations.[10] Often general principles are associated with the Roman notion of *jus gentium,* the law of peoples. These principles of law, derived largely from municipal experience, hold relevant legal connotations for the international realm; consequently, they have been assimilated into the corpus of international law. General principles of law—which include notions such as "equity" (justice by right), "comity" (voluntary courtesy), and *pacta sunt servanda* ("pacts made in good faith are binding," the underpinning precept for treaty agreement)—serve as sources by analogy for the creation and perfection of international legal norms. Yet general principles of international law are encumbered by the difficulty of being framed as sources of law in terms of morality and justice. "Morality" and "justice" remain highly subjective concepts, susceptible to disparate interpretations; thus, in their application, general principles may

---

[9] See Anthony A. D'Amato, *The Concept of Custom in International Law* (Ithaca, N.Y.: Cornell University Press, 1971); H. W. A. Thirlway, *International Customary Law and Codification* (Leiden, Neth.: Sijhoff, 1972) and Karol Wolfke, *Custom in Present International Law,* 2nd ed. (Dordrecht, Neth.: Martius Nyhoff, 1993).

[10] See generally Wolfgang Friedmann, "The Uses of 'General Principles' in the Development of International Law," *American Journal of International Law* 57 (April 1963), pp. 279–99; Arnold McNair, "The General Principles of Law Recognized by Civilized Nations," *British Yearbook of International Law* 33 (1957), pp. 1–19; and Georg Schwarzenberger, *The Dynamics of International Law* (South Hackensack, N.J.: Rothman, 1976).

be vulnerable to vagaries perceived in the situation or the particular context in which they are set.

The final source of modern international law is twofold and deemed to be secondary and indirect as compared to treaties, custom, and general principles. This source, first, encompasses judicial decisions of courts—both national and international—and, second, teachings and writings of the most qualified jurists and publicists. Two important points merit mention here. The first is that for international law, court decisions are principally employed as guidelines; they cannot set precedents. There is no *stare decisis* in the law of nations; accordingly, a decision by any court or tribunal, inclusive of the International Court of Justice, cannot be held as binding authority for subsequent judicial decisions. The second point is that while writings by scholars and jurists supply a rich seedbed for opinions on the law, they too carry no binding legal authority. Text writers by themselves cannot create or codify international law; however, their importance as sources of the law may become amplified to the extent that governments may adopt suggestions and interpretations in the application of international law to foreign policy.[11]

International law is broad in scope and far-reaching in content; for convenience, it may be divided into laws of peace and laws of war. Under the realm of peace, international law provides norms for stipulating its subjects and sets out the process of recognition for states and governments: the rights and duties of states, how title to territory is acquired, how national boundaries are determined, and various regulations for use of ocean, air, and outer space. Also in this respect is the international law pertinent to individuals. It not only encompasses rules affecting nationality, diplomatic agents, resident aliens, and extradition but also more recent norms pertaining to international criminal law, refugees, and the protection of human rights. Within the ambit of laws relating to war, much ground is likewise covered. Included here are those laws and procedures promoting peaceful settlement of disputes; techniques available for self-help short of war; the legal nature of and requirements for belligerency; the laws of armed conflict on land, on sea, and in the air; conditions for neutrality; and the treatment and definition of war crimes.[12] Important to remember here is that these international

---

[11] See, e.g., *Restatement (Third) of the Foreign Relations Law of the United States* (St. Paul, Minn.: American Law Institute Publications, 1987).

[12] The texts on international law are manifold. For representative examples, see Barry E. Carter and Phillip R. Trimble, *International Law,* 2nd ed. (Boston: Little, Brown, 1995); Rebecca M. M. Wallace, *International Law,* 3rd ed. (London: Sweet & Maxwell, 1997); Peter Malanczuk, *Akehurst's Modern Introduction to International Law,* 7th rev. ed. (London: Routledge, 1997); Mark W. Janis and John E. Noyes, *Cases and Commentary on International Law* (St. Paul, Minn.: West Publishing Co., 1997); Mark W. Janis, *Introduction to International Law,* 3rd ed. (New York: Aspen Publishing, 1999); Gerhard von Glahn, *Law Among Nations: An Introduction to Public International Law,* 7th ed. (New York: Allyn & Bacon, 1996); Malcolm M. Shaw, *International Law,* 3rd ed. (Cambridge: Cambridge University Press, 1998); William R. Slomanson, *Fundamental Perspectives on International Law,* 3rd ed. (Belmont, Calif.: Wadsworth, 1999); The classic modern treatise on international law is Robert Jennings and Arthur Watts, eds., *Oppenheim's International Law,* 9th ed. (London: Longmans, 1996).

legal considerations have been integrated into states' national laws, usually by treaty but also through specific legislation, judicial decisions, or executive fiat. This realization, however, should not imply that international law is thus rendered subservient to domestic laws. It is not, either in theory or in factual application.[13]

Though made up of a wide-ranging body of norms, international law has no specific codes or statutes. The closest approximations to municipal legal codes are called digests in international law. These digests, each of which usually entails a series of several volumes, are compendia containing selections from court decisions, international treaties, foreign policy statements, government memoranda, juridical opinions, scholarly publications, and other like materials that furnish detailed views on international legal matters. While held as important comments on the law, digests are not regarded in and of themselves to be definitively authoritative or legally binding in their contents.[14]

Notwithstanding doubts and skepticism, then, the unmistakable fact remains that international law has definite sources and exists as a body, a reality that mirrors the fundamental conviction by states that such law is necessary. The law of nations has evolved over nearly four centuries into a body of treaty-based and customary rules, undergirded by general principles of law and explicated through judicial decisions as well as in the writings of prominent jurists and publicists. Intimately connected to this are the attendant realizations that an obligatory basis exists for international law and that, in substantial measure, the law is obeyed.

## THE BASIS OF OBLIGATION IN INTERNATIONAL LAW

Perhaps the archfiction of international law is the notion of absolute sovereignty. Such sovereignty embodies the idea of totality and completeness; as a legal creation, sovereignty consequently becomes a paradox, if not an impossibility, when placed into the interdependent complexities of the modern state system. More significantly, unlimited sovereignty has become unacceptable today as the preeminent attribute of states, a fact which national governments have increasingly recognized as more and more of their sovereignty has been relinquished to international commitments. For example, traditionally in international law, absolute, unfettered sovereignty allowed for states to exercise free national will in deciding whether or not to resort to war. Given the incredible power of military capability today, the costs of this license could literally lead to destruction of the

---

[13] At least one prominent scholar of international law has cogently argued to the contrary, namely that the law of nations in fact represents a higher order than domestic or national law. See Hans Kelsen, *Principles of International Law,* 2nd ed. (New York: Holt, Rinehart and Winston, 1996).

[14] For examples, see the following: Green H. Hackworth, *Digest of International Law,* 8 vols. (Washington, D.C.: U.S. Government Printing Office, 1940–1944); John Bassett Moore, *A Digest of International Law,* 8 vols. (Washington, D.C.: U.S. Government Printing Office, 1906); Marjorie M. Whiteman, *Digest of International Law,* 15 vols. (Washington. D.C.: U.S. Government Printing Office, 1963–1973), Marian Nash, ed., *Cumulative Digest of U.S. Practice in International Law (1981–88)* (Washington, D.C.: U.S. Government Printing Office, 1990).

entire international community; as a consequence, through international legal instruments promoting arms control and national restraint, such sovereignty has been diminished by states themselves for the sake of international security. Recent examples clearly demonstrating this trend include the 1991 and 1993 Strategic Arms Reduction Talks Treaties (START I and II) between the United States and former Soviet Republics, the 1993 Convention on the Prohibition of Chemical Weapons, the renewal in 1995 of the Nuclear Nonproliferation Treaty, agreement in 1996 on a Comprehensive Test Ban Treaty and entry into force in 1999 of the Ottawa Landmine Ban Treaty.

The above observations prompt the obvious question concerning why states should obey international law. That is, what is the obligatory basis upon which the rule of law is founded in contemporary world affairs? The answer is plain and undeniable: It is in the states' fundamental interest to do so. States are the lawgivers in the international community. Agreement upon a legal norm and the effectiveness of its application clearly rest in how it affects each state's own national interests. Consent therefore remains the keystone to international law's efficacy because it appeases the desire of states to maintain their relative freedom of action in the name of national sovereignty. In short, states obey international law because they agree to do so. But why should they? Several plausible reasons may be proffered: National governments recognize the utility of the law; they prefer some degree of order and expectation over unpredictable anarchy; obedience is less costly than disobedience; a certain sense of justice may motivate their willingness to obey; or, habit and customary practice in international dealings over many years have operated to promote obedience.

More significant than any of these explanations, however, is the recognition that reciprocity contributes to the efficacy of international law and, correspondingly, to more regularized patterns of behavior in the international system. Put simply, states accept and obey international law because governments find it in their national interest to do so. It serves a state's national interest to accept international legal norms if other states also accept these norms, and this reciprocal process can give rise to predictive patterns of interstate conduct in international relations. States, like individual persons, have discovered that consent to be bound by and obligated to certain rules can serve to facilitate, promote, and enhance their welfare and opportunities in the society. Contemporary international law consequently has come to embody a consensus of common interests— a consensus that plainly indicates that international law works efficiently and most often when it is in the national interest of states to make it work.[15]

---

[15] See generally Thomas M. Franck, *The Power of Legitimacy Among Nations* (Oxford: Oxford University Press, 1991); Rosalyn Higgins, *Problems and Process: International Law and How We Use It* (Oxford: Clarendon Press, 1994); Fernando R. Tesón, *A Philosophy of International Law* (Boulder Colo.: Westview Press, 1998); and Anthony C. Arend, *International Rules* (Oxford: Oxford University Press, 1999).

## ENFORCEMENT OF INTERNATIONAL LAW

The third critical consideration in determining the effectiveness of international law—the quality of its enforcement—is still left hanging: What happens when states fail to obey the law, when they violate the agreed-upon norms? How is the law to be enforced or, put differently, how are violators of international law to be punished? International law does supply means for both sanction and enforcement, although, to be sure, these means are primitive in comparison to municipal procedures. Despite development over the past eighty years of relatively sophisticated, universalistic, sanctions-equipped international organizations—namely, the League of Nations [16] and the United Nations [17]—the world community still relies primarily upon the principle of self-help to enforce international legal sanctions.

The principle of self-help permits sanctions to be applied by one party in reaction to perceived illegal conduct committed by another party. Self-help has emerged as the major means for effecting sanctions in the international community.[18] Not only must states perceive when their rights have been violated; they must also confront the state that allegedly has committed that illegal act and must compel the state to make restitution for its wrongdoing. Techniques for applying self-help range from diplomatic protest to economic boycott to embargo to war. Consequently, in international law, states literally *must* take the law into their own hands to protect their legal rights and to get the law enforced. It is not surprising, then, that international law is often characterized as being primitive.

In assessing the sanctions process in international law, it is fair to conclude that as international disputes become more serious and are viewed by governments as placing national prestige or survival increasingly at risk, the principle of limited self-help as a sanctioning process is likely to make the legal system

[16] The League of Nations Covenant, which was incorporated as Part I of the Treaty of Versailles (1919), contained in Article 16 sanction provisions that would subject a member "who committed an act of war" against another member to "the severance of all trade or financial relations, the prohibition of all intercourse between their nationals and the nationals of the Covenant-breaking State, and the prevention of all financial, commercial or personal intercourse between the nationals of the Covenant-breaking State and the nationals of any other State, whether members of the League or not."

[17] After determining "the existence of any threat to the peace, breach of the peace or act of aggression" as authorized in Article 39 of the United Nations Charter, the Security Council is empowered under Article 42 to "take such action by air, sea, or land forces as may be necessary to maintain or restore international peace and security. Such action may include demonstrations, blockade, and other operations by air, sea, or land forces of Members of the United Nations."

[18] Even so, specific legal limitations have been set on the use of force, that is, the degree and kind of "self-help" exercised. See, for example, Anthony C. Arend and Robert J. Beck, *International Law and the Use of Force* (New York: Routledge, 1993); Charles W. Kegley, Jr. and Gregory A. Raymond, *A Multipolar Peace? Great-Power Politics in the Twenty-First Century* (New York: St. Martin's Press, 1994); and Louis Henkin, Stanley Hoffmann, Jeane J. Kirkpatrick and Allan Gerson, William D. Rogers, David J. Scheffer, *Might v. Right: International Law and the Use of Force,* 2nd ed. (New York: Council on Foreign Relations, 1991); and *Ethics & International Affairs* 10 (1996).

correspondingly less effective. Absent a centralized agency for approving and supervising the sanctioning action, self-help may be rendered subject to prevalent conditions in the environment. In sum, self-help's prominent role in international law places a major limitation upon that legal system's effectiveness. As revealed in the international legal order, resort to self-help for law enforcement represents a necessary but limiting compromise between a sanctioning process required by international law and the desires by states to retain their independence, that is, their sovereignty. Self-help thus highlights the observation that international law is a relatively weak, decentralized, and primitive legal system. The fact remains, however, that international law still enjoys the status of being a legal system— one that works effectively nearly all the time and for nearly all situations when its participant member states want it to do so.

On balance, the performance of international law is hampered by disabilities within those very elements that generally contribute to the effectiveness of legal systems. First, there is a lack of international institutions for clarifying and communicating legal norms; that is, modern international law is still characterized by an imperfect process of norm creation. Second, there is no central, generally recognized belief system to serve as an obligatory authority for international law. The obligatory basis for international law lies with the states themselves. Third, and perhaps most debilitating, international law is without an efficient, corporate process for perceiving and punishing illegal behavior in the world community. Resort by states to self-help remains the principal means for sanctioning international wrongdoing.

Yet, what appears really faulty with international law does not stem from these weaknesses in the international legal process. Rather, it derives from the decentralized international community that the law is attempting to regulate. In short, that the operation of contemporary international law may be less than wholly effective can be attributed mainly to the condition that there does not presently exist sufficient international consensus among states to demand that the law be made more effective in its application.

All this should not be inferred to mean that international law is either surrealistic or irrelevant in the contemporary world. It certainly is neither. To rush to the conclusion that international law's frailties leave it with little real function in international relations today would be not only superficial but also short-sighted. It would overlook the hundreds of decisions made by national and international tribunals aimed at settling claims and setting arbitration awards. It ignores the thousands of international law cases affecting contractual relations between corporations and governments. It fails to account for the constant, pervasive process of international intercourse that goes on involving states, organizations, and individual persons. In a modern age of satellite telecommunications, worldwide transportation, and interdependent global commerce, international law has become indispensable. Setting frequencies for telecommunication broadcasts, flight routes for aircraft, conditions for international postage and media communication, monetary exchange rates, navigation transit by ocean vessels carrying goods in trade—all these activities and myriad others are made possible only through the channels afforded by international legal agreement, that is, through international law. International law codifies ongoing solutions for persistent international problems. The law of nations has become in effect the lubricant that permits transnational commerce, communication, transportation, and travel to operate smoothly and on course in the global community.[19]

## CONCLUSION

Law prescribes the conduct of a society's members and makes coexistence and the survival of that society possible. Not surprisingly, then, the law of nations is pervasive and fundamental. It not only seeks to regulate or lessen possibilities for conflict but also works to promote international exchange and cooperation on a broad, multifaceted scale. International law is man-made; governments of states in the international society can in large part determine the nature of that society and formulate laws to meet those ends. Hence, the ingredients of international law are neither preordained nor immutable.

International law is law. It is not some form of diplomatic maneuvering or rhetorical camouflage. International law has form and substance: there exists a clearly identifiable corpus of rules and regulations that have been generally accepted by states in their dealings with one another. International law has specific sources from which legal norms can be derived, and self-imposed sanctions are available to states to punish illegal behavior. Yet international law should not be construed as being pure law; in other words, it is not apolitical, nor is it wholly comprised of normativism or legalism. International law cannot be so because the very components of that legal system—states—are highly politicized actors in their own right.[20]

International law is crafted not accidentally or capriciously but carefully and intentionally by the states themselves. The law of nations is a product of the times and of the national governments that operate in the international milieu. It can change, adapt, and evolve. International law is not static; it is a dynamic and evolutionary process that is shaped by events and influences events. Contemporary international law reflects the nature of the changing world because it must be responsive to that evolving reality. Flexibility therefore remains one of international

---

[19] Importantly in this regard, the United Nations since 1945 has generated a tremendous volume of international law to meet new global needs and facilitate international intercourse. See Christopher C. Joyner, "Conclusion: The United Nations as International Law-Giver," in Christopher C. Joyner, ed., *The United Nations and International Law* (Cambridge: Cambridge University Press, 1997), pp. 433–56.

[20] On this theme, see Francis Anthony Boyle, *World Politics and International Law* (Durham, N.C.: Duke University Press, 1985) and Anne-Marie Slaughter Burley, "International Law and International Relations Theory: A Dual Agenda," *American Journal of International Law* 87 (April 1993), pp. 205–39.

law's chief strengths. Even so, ironically, it is sometimes blamed for fostering one of the law's greatest weaknesses: namely, the lack of a centralized, formal structure for codifying international norms, an omission that invites distortions in legal interpretation as well as self-serving policy positions.

International law must not be regarded as a panacea for prohibiting unlawful international conduct or as a brake on incorrigible governments. It does, however, provide internationally acceptable ways and means of dealing with these situations. Modern international law may not satisfy all national governments all of the time; nor can it supply every answer for all the international community's ills. Nevertheless, it remains far preferable to the alternative of no law at all and, similarly, it is far wiser for national governments to appreciate the existence and function of this international legal system than to overlook the mutual advantages it affords. International law remains the best touchstone and only consistent guide for state conduct in a complex, multicultural world.[21]

At the dawn of the twenty-first century, grave global problems have emerged as foci for serious international concern. The Third World development crisis, the disintegration of states through ethnoseparatism, forced migrations and millions of displaced refugees, transnational terrorism, overpopulation, air and water transboundary pollution, global warming, AIDS, depletion of the ozone layer, drug trafficking, proliferation of weapons of mass destruction—none of these issues are amenable to domestic or unilateral resolution. If politically viable solutions are to be reached, international cooperation is essential. The law of nations supplies proven ways and means to facilitate these collaborative international efforts. Indeed, in the search for global solutions to global problems, international law supplies the best opportunities for accommodating national interests with international priorities.

In the final analysis, international law does not fail in contemporary world society. Instead, it is the states themselves that fail the law whenever they choose not to adhere to its basic norms. Thus the need to surmount this fundamental obstacle of self-serving, sovereign-state interests must remain as the preeminent challenge on international law's global agenda in this new century. To be sure, given the profound lessons of state conduct in the past, it will not be an easy task.

---

[21] For discussion on this point, see Christopher C. Joyner and John C. Dettling, "Bridging the Cultural Chasm: Cultural Relativism and the Future of International Law," *California Western International Law Journal* 20, no. 2 (1989–1990), pp. 275–314.

# PART THREE

# POLITICS AND MARKETS

Today's global agenda embraces a broad array of international economic issues, ranging from monetary instability to deflationary pressures and from debt relief to trade protectionism. These have been matched by comparable issues on the domestic agendas of many states as they struggle with economic stagnation, unemployment, budget deficits, and productivity imperatives. The two sets of issues are not unrelated. Under conditions of global interdependence, defined as a condition of *mutual sensitivity* and *mutual vulnerability,* decisions made in one state often have important implications and consequences for other states. Thus politics—the exercise of power and influence—and economics—the distribution of material wealth—are often tightly interconnected.

The term *political economy* highlights the intersection of politics and economics, whose importance in world politics enjoys a long heritage. A combination of political and economic considerations gave rise to the state system more than three centuries ago and has shaped patterns of dominance and dependence ever since. Today the term highlights the extensive interdependent relationships between states that knit national and global welfare into a single tapestry. Political economy thus comprises an analytical perspective that accommodates the complex realities of the contemporary global system.

Controversies over the distribution of wealth and the processes and institutions that govern it now affect everyone, thus often commanding the utmost attention of policy making elites. Indeed, in the immediate wake of the Cold War it became commonplace to argue that geo-economics would rival geopolitics as the motive force behind states' struggle for preeminence in the world political system. Competition for market share, not political-military allies, would animate relations among nations. And commercial advantage, not military might, would determine who exercises influence over whom and who would feel threatened and who secure.

In some respects these predictions have been borne out, but in other ways they have been overtaken by the rapid *globalization* of the world political economy during the past decade. Globalization has so intensified interdependence that that term, long popular among analysts, has largely been replaced by a new vocabulary. Symbolized by the Internet and fueled by the revolution in computers and telecommunications, globalization's most visible manifestations are found in the global reach of Coca-Cola and McDonald's, of shopping centers that look the same whether they are in London or Hong Kong, Chicago or Rio de Janeiro, of rock music and designer jeans that know no political boundaries, contributing to the development of a global culture in which national identities are often submerged. As states, economies, and societies are increasingly integrated with one another, the state system itself is being challenged, since policy makers often find they cannot control the forces that affect their destinies. As one analyst put it, "we are witnessing the dawn of multiple overlapping sovereignties." Hence "the core dilemma of the global economy is interdependence without political influence."[1]

As these brief remarks suggest, insights from political economy are necessary to answer the classic question of politics: Who gets what, when, and how? Robert Gilpin points us in the direction of important answers in the first essay in Part Three. He summarizes and critically analyzes "Three Ideologies of Political Economy": the liberal, nationalist (sometimes called mercantilist), and Marxist paradigms. The three are regarded as ideologies, as they purport "to provide scientific descriptions of how the world *does* work while they also constitute normative positions regarding how the world *should* work." Their importance derives from their impact on both scholarship and domestic and international affairs for centuries.

The differences among the three ideologies turn on their "conceptions of the relationships among society, state, and market." Liberalism directs attention to "the market and the price mechanism as the most efficacious means for organizing domestic and international economic relations." Thus economics and politics should be completely separated into distinct spheres. This viewpoint has long dominated policy thinking throughout the Global North, that is, the industrial world in which market-oriented democratic capitalism is the preferred form of domestic political economy. It also was the guiding principle underlying the international economic system created after World War II under U.S. hegemony

---

[1] Rosabeth Moss Kanter, "Global Competitiveness Revisited," *Washington Quarterly* 22 (Spring 1999), pp. 53, 55.

(leadership), whose interests liberalism served. Today liberalism is the ideology of globalization.

Unlike liberalism, the central idea in the nationalist (mercantilist) ideology "is that economic activities are and should be subordinate to the goal of state building and the interests of the state. All nationalists ascribe to the primacy of the state, of national security, and of military power in the organization and functioning of the international system." Because they see interdependence as a source of conflict and insecurity, economic nationalists are concerned not only with *absolute gains* in their material well-being but also with how they fare in comparison with others, their *relative gains*. Thus economic nationalism as an ideology of political economy bears a striking resemblance to the doctrine of political realism as applied to international politics.

The 1990s witnessed a surge of privatization and other efforts to unleash market forces throughout the world, as democratic capitalism emerged as the preferred pattern of domestic political economy nearly everywhere. Moreover, the liberal principle of nondiscrimination and free trade continues to dominate thinking internationally. Still, economic nationalism is a potent force in the world. It underlies much of the protectionist sentiment toward trade issues rife throughout the Global North and South (the developing countries). It also rationalizes the appeal of *strategic trade theory,* a form of industrial policy that seeks to create comparative advantages by targeting government subsidies toward particular industries. Thus, as Gilpin notes, whatever the shortcomings of economic nationalism, it "is likely to be a significant influence in international relations as long as the state system exists."

The appeal of Marxism, on the other hand, is much diminished. Marxism-Leninism has been repudiated in the former Soviet Union and throughout Eastern Europe, and it is on the wane in Cuba and Vietnam. Although Marxism-Leninism (communism) remains the official ideology in China, even here the forces of liberalism are evident as Chinese leaders not only accept but actively encourage the development of private enterprise. Nonetheless, in the history of ideas that have animated world politics during the past two centuries Marxism and Marxism-Leninism still command attention.

Like economic nationalism, Marxism places economic issues at the center of political life. But whereas nationalists are concerned primarily with the international distribution of wealth, Marxism focuses on both the domestic and international forces that affect the distribution of wealth. The ideology also focuses on international political change. "Whereas neither liberalism nor nationalism has a comprehensive theory of social change," Gilpin observes, "Marxism emphasizes the role of economic and technological developments in explaining the dynamics of the international system."

Lenin's reformulation of Marxist doctrine in his famous treatise *Imperialism* directs particular attention to the role that differential rates of growth in power play in promoting international conflict and political change. For Marx, class struggle over the distribution of wealth was the central force of political change. For Lenin, international political relations among capitalist states was more important. He argued that "intensification of economic and political competition between declining and rising capitalist powers leads to economic conflict, imperial rivalries, and eventually war. He asserted that this had been the fate of the British-centered liberal world economy of the nineteenth century." Gilpin conjectures that "today [Lenin] would undoubtedly argue that . . . a similar fate threatens the . . . liberal world economy, centered on the United States."

Gilpin assesses the strengths and limitations of the three political economy perspectives. Because of the ideological character of each it is impossible to determine which one is "right." Nonetheless, all continue to make important contributions to political economy theory and practice. Liberalism and nationalism/mercantilism in particular continue to compete for the attention of policy makers and analysts.

As noted, the liberal vision guided policy makers during and after World War II as they sought to create trade and monetary systems that would avoid repetition of the economic collapse of the 1930s, to which aggressive economic nationalism was believed to have contributed measurably. The tremendous growth in international trade since the 1940s, which has fueled an unprecedented expansion of global welfare, is a measure of the success of liberalism. Now, however, the globalization of the world political economy through trade, global finance, and transnational investment is threatening the political autonomy and decision-making authority of the world's preeminent capitalist centers and the ability of the international institutions they created and support to cope with the challenges.

The susceptibility of states to global financial shocks became painfully obvious when exchange-rate crises in Central and South American, in East Asia, and in Russia at various times during the 1990s buffeted the entire world economy, destabilizing the economies of the immediately affected countries and sending shock waves throughout the world political economy. Indeed, the crises that pummeled East Asia, Latin America, and Russia toward the end of the decade were often cited as posing the most serious challenge to global economic stability since the Great Depression of the 1930s. Inevitably, then, these events rekindled centuries-old debates about which ideology of political economy best fits our rapidly globalized and globalizing world. The utility of the international institutions created after World War II has now also come under close scrutiny. These and related issues punctuate the analyses in many of the chapters that follow in Part Three of *The Global Agenda.*

Linda Y.C. Lim opens the debate by asking "Whose 'Model' Failed?" Focusing attention on the Asian currency crises, she notes that some policy analysts had concluded the embrace of liberal principles in once statist (mercantilist) countries explained their remarkable economic success during the past several decades. Others, however, conclude that statist and strategic trade policies underlie the "Asian economic miracle."

Lim urges that a full understanding of Asia's economic success—and failure—must include a consideration of cultural factors ("Asian values"). "Crony capitalism" figures prominently in such discussions. The term refers to the tightly knit relationships among corporate and other economic agents in Asian societies, including government officials, that often dictate their economic decisions, regardless of market imperatives. Although Lim acknowledges the impact of crony capitalism on Asia's economic problems, she concludes "it is certainly not the whole story."

Discerning the "whole story" may prove to be an elusive, perhaps impossible exercise. Meanwhile, Lim cogently argues that the "lessons" of the recent economic crises reinforce the view that the classic "ideologies" of political economy discussed by Gilpin often fail to match the realities of contemporary challenges. She concludes that *both* the competing statist (mercantilist) and open (liberal) models of political economy in some sense failed. In her words: "The Asian crisis . . . exposed the futility of applying simplistic and essentially ideological models to the messy practical business of public and private sector economic management in developing countries whose political, economic, and business systems are not only diverse and complexly intertwined, but also still evolving."

The rapid spread of the Asian crisis, sometimes referred to as the "Asian Contagion," showed clearly how tightly interconnected the world political economy had become in the new, post–Cold War era. Indeed, Thomas L. Friedman, foreign correspondent for the *New York Times,* suggests in the title to our next chapter that "The World Is Ten Years Old." In a fast-paced yet penetrating analysis, he contrasts the new era of globalization with the Cold War world that preceded it.

Friedman begins by noting that the early twentieth century was also a period of globalization, which ultimately fell victim to World War I, the Bolshevik revolution, and the Great Depression of the 1930s. The new era of globalization can be differentiated from its pre-1914 counterpart along two dimensions: "the sheer number of people and countries able to partake of this process and be affected by it"; and by "falling telecommunications costs," which have given rise to new technologies "able to weave the world together even tighter."

"Free-market capitalism"—the ideology of liberalism—is the driving force behind contemporary globalization. "Globalization," writes Friedman, "means the spread of free-market capitalism to virtually every country in the world." It also has a dominant culture: "Culturally speaking, globalization is largely . . . the spread of Americanization—from Big Macs to iMacs to Mickey Mouse—on a global scale." And the defining technologies of the information age give globalization a "defining perspective," namely "integration," with the World Wide Web its defining symbol.

In contrast, a wall—the Berlin Wall—was the defining symbol of the Cold War era. Division, not integration, was its hallmark; competition between the United States and the Soviet Union its driving force; missile throw weight its "defining measurement"; and nuclear annihilation its "defining anxiety." Citing political scientist Michael Mandelbaum's apt metaphor, Friedman notes that if the Cold War were a sport, "it would be sumo wrestling." But if globalization were a sport, he adds, "it would be the 100-meter dash, over and over and over."

The globalization portrait Friedman paints is decidedly more optimistic than many of our images of a half century of Cold War competition between nuclear giants. Still, Friedman takes care to note that globalization "is also producing a powerful backlash from those brutalized or left behind by this new system." Many of the world's workers are among them.

Kathleen Newland pursues this theme in Chapter 25, titled "Workers of the World, Now What?" Her introduction sets the stage for the analysis that follows. "There is an empty seat at the banquet of economic globalization," she writes. "While international capital, trade, and business feast on open markets, heightened efficiency, and vanishing barriers in the new global marketplace, labor is nowhere to be found." Structural, institutional, and political factors explain why labor has been kept on a globalization diet.

Organizing labor is the traditional approach to protecting workers from the hazards of the marketplace, but, as Newland shows, labor unions have been ineffective in the face of globalization. She notes, for example, that while capital is highly mobile in today's world political economy, barriers to immigration limit workers' ability to move, even if they want to. The size of the global workforce has also increased measurably, particularly with the influx of large numbers of female workers. A surplus of workers at the low end of the wage scale inhibits efforts to unionize, while those at the high end of the scale generally spurn organized efforts to protect against the hazards of globalization as well as enjoy its fruits.

Meanwhile, no global institution effectively promotes labor's mobility or its interests. Among the many extant international organizations, the International Labor Organization (ILO) is charged with protecting the interests of workers, but "the ILO today is seen by many as an anachronism, too closely tied to trade union organizations that are having trouble keeping up in the new global economy." Today, newer, issue-based coalitions created to protect the rights of powerless employees, like sweatshop workers in developing countries' shoe and apparel industries, offer greater promise than the ILO in dealing with the issues that labor now faces.

Newland vividly summarizes labor's plight this way: "Workers worldwide have been slow to reap globalization's rewards and have instead watched it shrink their social safety nets, squeeze wages, erode working conditions, and degrade public services." If political leaders and the business community turn "a blind eye to these developments," she writes, they risk undermining the liberal precepts on which the promise and prosperity of globalization rest. Newland cites Kofi Annan, Secretary-General of the United Nations, who put it this way: "We may find it increasingly difficult to make a persuasive case for the open global market."

It has often been suggested that workers frequently find themselves victims of a "race to the bottom" in terms of wages and working conditions as states seek to promote their competitiveness in the global marketplace. Whether the drive to be competitive explains workers' plight, and, indeed, whether "competitiveness" is an appropriate objective of states' economic policies is questioned by the prominent trade theorist Paul Krugman, who characterizes policy makers' concern with competitiveness an "unwarranted obsession."

Concern with competitiveness was especially acute in the United States in the early 1990s, as the country found itself mired in recession at home and challenged by Japan and others abroad. Krugman became a vocal critic of the proposition that income growth in the United States had lagged because of many U.S. firms' inability to sell in world markets. He supports his arguments with evidence that a decline in domestic productivity explains almost all of the decline in U.S. living standards between 1973 and 1990. The same was true in Europe and Japan: "In each case, the growth rate of living standards essentially equals the growth rate of domestic productivity—not productivity relative to competitors, but simply domestic productivity." Thus, even as world trade grows, "as a practical, empirical matter the major nations of the world are not to any significant degree in economic competition with each other. Of course, there is always a rivalry for status and power—countries that grow faster will see their political rank rise. So it is always interesting to *compare* countries. But asserting that Japanese growth diminishes U.S. status is very different from saying that it reduces the U.S. standard of living—and it is the latter that the rhetoric of competitiveness asserts." Hence "competitiveness is a meaningless word when applied to national economies" and can lead to policies that are "both wrong and dangerous."

If Krugman is correct that a concern for competitiveness, which relates primarily to international trade domestic industrialization policies, is misplaced, are policy proposals designed to cope with monetary instability also misplaced? In particular, is the widely discussed proposal to "dollarize" the currencies of developing economies to achieve stability in their currencies warranted or not?

"Dollarization" proposes that other countries abandon their own currencies and adopt the U.S. dollar for all of their financial transactions. In our next selection, "Dollarization: More Straightjacket Than Salvation," by Jeffrey Sachs and Felipe Larrain, the authors argue that "dollarization is an extreme solution to market instability, applicable in only the most extreme cases. The opposite approach—a flexible exchange rate between the national currency and the dollar—is much more prudent for most developing countries."

Flexible exchange rates have been used to link states' currencies since the early 1970s, when the Bretton Woods system of fixed exchange rates was abandoned. There are two arguments in favor of fixed exchange rates, according to Sachs and Larrain. "The main argument for a pegged exchange rate system is that it enforces discipline. If an irresponsible central bank is given freedom to issue pesos without worrying about the consequences for the exchange rate, it will simply print pesos to its heart's content to fund a large budget deficit or to provide cheap credits to the banking system. These will be popular moves in the short run, but they will soon lead to inflation and a collapsing exchange rate."

The second argument in favor of fixed exchanged rates is that they reduce business transaction costs. "There is no risk in changing currencies if the exchange rate remains stable, and costs of switching between the peso and the dollar . . . are also likely to be very low."

The case for flexible rates also comes in two flavors. "The first argument for flexibility is that an exchange rate depreciation (or appreciation) can act like a shock absorber for the economy." That is, as demand for a particular commodity, such as oil, declines, changing the exchange rate becomes a relatively easy way to effect adjustments throughout the economy that otherwise might prove more painful economically and politically.

The second argument in favor of flexible exchange rates is that "what is good for the United States is not necessarily good for other countries." This, Sachs and Larrain argue, is a principal reason to reject dollarization as a solution to monetary instability. "A country that pegs its currency to the dollar is, in effect, tying its monetary policy wholly to U.S. monetary policy. That decision makes sense only if U.S. monetary policy is wholly appropriate for its national economy, which is rarely the case." Sachs and Larrain concede that "fixed exchange rates may be appropriate under some conditions and flexible rates under others," but they quickly add that "recent practical experience suggests that most emerging markets are better off with the latter."

Dollarization speaks to monetary reform at the state level. Others focus on "Global Rules for Global Finance," the title of Chapter 28 written by Ethan B. Kapstein, a former international banker and official at the Organization for Economic Cooperation and Development.

Kapstein notes that the economic malaise of the 1990s has stimulated the search for global economic reforms at both the national and international levels, including calls for abolition of the International Monetary Fund (IMF), which was created at the 1944 Bretton Woods conference as an institutional mechanism to ensure stability and predictability in international monetary relations. Since then it has become a major—and controversial—actor in assisting states facing economic travails, typically by insisting that they follow the now popular precepts of economic liberalism sometimes described as the "Washington consensus." The term refers to the convergence of policy prescriptions emanating from the IMF, the World Bank, and the U.S. government that emphasizes free trade, reduction of barriers to foreign investment, deregulation of national economies, and privatization. Thus economic reforms were promoted throughout the Global South and elsewhere, as in Russia and Eastern Europe, that reflected free-market strategies designed to achieve export-led economic growth.

Despite the controversy that has engulfed the IMF as a principal advocate and enforcer of the Washington consensus, Kapstein is doubtful that its role can be minimized. "Should the IMF fade into irrelevance," he writes, "new institutions to stabilize the world economy will be needed."

Part of the controversy surrounding the IMF concerns what Kapstein and others describe as the "moral hazard" problem. The term refers to private investors' decisions to make risky choices when investing in emerging markets based on their expectation that the IMF or someone else (the United States?) will bail them out if the countries in which they invest face economic instability or, worse, collapse. In short, if private investors are protected from failure by public authorities, they are likely to take higher risks (with other people's money) than would otherwise be warranted. In the end, the public (taxpayers) foot the bill for the failed choices of private investors, who in effect bear none of the costs of failure.

Kapstein puts the moral hazard problem in a larger context, noting that "the international financial system is dominated by money-center and investment banks that have failed to master the assessment of risk in a world economy characterized by floating exchange rates, differing political economies, and a diversity of business practices. . . . As a result, the international financial system is a reckless place in which accidents inevitably happen."

Is there a cure for the disease? Kapstein reviews proposals that have been made to deal with the problems plaguing global finance, including those that seek elimination of the IMF, and concludes that "the best we can expect for the foreseeable future is a muddle-through strategy based on existing cooperative frameworks."

Another problem facing the world political economy is how to integrate the former communist countries into an economic order based on the principles of free-market capitalism. Greg Mastel addresses this issue in "The WTO and Nonmarket Economies." China's bid for entry into the World Trade Organization (WTO) stimulates Mastel's concern, but the issues he raises extend more broadly.

Mastel worries that because most of the "reforming nonmarket economies are neither rule-based nor fully market-oriented," they fail to meet the test for membership in the WTO, "the ultimate rule-based, market-oriented economic institution." He notes that state-owned enterprises are still commonplace in China and Russia, that economic planning by state agencies continues, and that, particularly in the case of China, the market "remains protected by a web of trade barriers." He also is concerned about the absence of the rule of law. "In China, contracts are not secure, bribery is rampant, and regulation promulgation a mystery. Russia may be even worse—the Mafia may actually control much of the economy."

Despite these problems, Washington and Beijing in late 1999 reached an agreement designed to bring China into the WTO. The agreement was consistent with the U.S. policy of "constructive engagement" with China, but it raised the ire of critics who viewed it as a reward to a mercantilist state with a long history of human rights abuses. It also does not assuage Mastel's long-term concerns. As he puts it, "The claim that the Cold War is over has been repeated so often that it is accepted without much debate. The reality, however, is that many of the issues raised by the decades-long struggle between communism and capitalism remain unresolved. The most important problem remaining is how to integrate these former communists into a global, market-based economy."

The "Network"—the global system of interconnected computers—is the epicenter of the global, market-based economy into which the former communist states have yet to be fully integrated. Daniel F. Burton argues in the next chapter, "The Brave New Wired World," that the United States, because of its commanding position at the forefront of the networked economy, will play a critical role in shaping the world political economy of the future. Its structure, he warns, "will come as a complete surprise to most politicians and pundits. It will not be the cold peace of mercantilism that was pioneered by Japan and other Asian nations during the 1980s. Nor will it consist of the different brands of regionalism that have proliferated in Europe, the Pacific, and the Americas in recent years. Instead, the new international order will be built around the brave new worldwide web of computers and communications."

After tracing the development and evolution of the Network, Burton offers a glimpse of what a networked economy will look like. Among other things, it will be heterogeneous, decentralized, and open, and will offer an abundance of choice.

Because of its characteristics, a networked economy will have an important impact on states' pursuit of security, wealth, and preservation of their cultures. Definitions of security and security threats will change as individuals demand protection from intrusions on their private lives. Meanwhile, governments "that are adept at building partnerships with the private sector will enhance their ability to access and manage strategic information, thereby gaining extraordinary advantages over those that are not." In terms of wealth, the explosion of high-tech industries offers new employment opportunities but will change traditional industries as well. "As commerce is increasingly comprised of the exchange of electrons, business notions about economies of scale, sales, distribution, marketing, and advertising will change, as will ideas about the economic significance of national borders and the nature of international trade."

Finally, the Network promises to change culture. "The Internet is already home to a kind of Wild West ethos that is often associated with new frontiers. It is anti-authoritarian, vehement in its defense of individualism and free speech, radical in its concern with privacy, and, for the most part, extremely antigovernment." What are the implications of these developments for international politics? "The Internet has already overrun geographic borders, making possible the creation of virtual communities of shared interests that transcend national boundaries."

Not all have participated in the networked world or shared the benefits of globalization. This theme is explored in detail in the last chapter in Part Three titled "Life Is Unfair: Inequality in the World," written by Nancy Birdsall, a vice president of the InterAmerican Development Bank. Her theme is simple yet stark and poignant. "Inequality looms large on the global agenda," she writes, adding that "the old saw is still correct: The rich get richer and the poor get children." It may be a wired world, but some seem to have been short-circuited.

Inequality is evident even in the United States, the primary node in the networked, market-based global economy. Elaborating on the theme Paul Krugman introduces in Chapter 26, Birdsall notes that "the income of the poorest 20 percent of [American] households has declined steadily since the early 1970s. Meanwhile, the income of the richest 20 percent has increased." And that pattern has been replicated around the world.

What explains inequality and its persistence? The question has plagued economists and policy makers for decades, even centuries. What makes it so troubling today is that "inequality is growing at a time when the triumph of democracy and open markets was supposed to usher in a new age of freedom and opportunity." For many around the world, that simply has not happened.

Birdsall offers no definitive answers to this long-standing question, but she does point us toward an understanding of the causes of inequality. After briefly reviewing the facts nationally and globally, Birdsall suggests that history, people's rational choices, prosperity, and bad economic policy all contribute to inequality. Historically, the simple fact is that "inequality begets inequality," as "economic and institutional arrangements" perpetuate the concentration of wealth after it first develops. "Rational differences in human behavior also add to inequality. In many countries, the poor are members of ethnic or racial groups. If they suffer discrimination in the labor market, their gains from schooling and job skills are small, prompting them to respond by investing little in these income-producing assets. But by handicapping their children economically, the sum of these parents' sensible decisions can lock society as a whole into another generation of inequality." Moreover, for good economic reasons, poor people tend to have more children than rich people, so the number of those at the bottom end of the economic ladder is likely to grow.

Ironically, prosperity itself tends to perpetuate inequality. "The market reforms that bring prosperity also may not give all players an equal shot at the prize." Information technologies likewise contribute to inequality, as they are more accessible to some groups in society than to others. Finally, economic policies "that hamper economic growth and fuel inflation" take a toll. Birdsall cautions that "most populist programs designed to attract the political support of the working class hurt workers in the long run." And she defends IMF-style reforms, "often attacked for hurting the poor majority," as the key to ending corrupt practices that usually benefit only a few.

Open markets and political freedom have been promoted since World War II on the expectation that "convergence" would eventually occur; that is, both within and between countries, the differences between rich and poor would narrow, not widen. That has not happened. Nor is it likely to happen in the near future. Birdsall notes, for example, that China and India experienced growth rates for a decade and a half that exceeded rates in the rich countries, "yet it would take them almost a century of constant growth at rates higher than those in today's industrialized countries just to reach current U.S. income levels." Hence inequality "cannot be fixed in our lifetime."

Despite that pessimistic conclusion—and government policies that are often self-defeating—Birdsall does note that, with time and patience, inequality can be addressed. Investing in education is a key: "In the increasingly service-oriented global economy, education and skills represent a kind of wealth. They are key assets—and once acquired cannot be taken away, even from those who are otherwise powerless."

# 22

# THREE IDEOLOGIES OF
# POLITICAL ECONOMY

Robert Gilpin

**Robert Gilpin summarizes and critically analyzes three "ideologies" of political economy: liberalism, nationalism (mercantilism), and Marxism. Each ideology alleges "to provide scientific descriptions of how the world *does* work, while they also constitute normative positions regarding how the world *should* work." Together the three ideologies have had a profound impact on world affairs. Gilpin is Dwight D. Eisenhower Professor of International Affairs, Emeritus, at Princeton University. His books include *The Challenge of Global Capitalism* (2000).**

Over the past century and a half, the ideologies of liberalism, nationalism, and Marxism have divided humanity. . . . The conflict among these three moral and intellectual positions has revolved around the role and significance of the market in the organization of society and economic affairs. . . .

These three ideologies are fundamentally different in their conceptions of the relationships among society, state, and market, and it may not be an exaggeration to say that every controversy in the field of international political economy is ultimately reducible to differing conceptions of these relationships. . . .

It is important to understand the nature and content of these contrasting "ideologies" of political economy. The term "ideology" is used rather than "theory" because each position entails a total belief system concerning the nature of human beings and society. . . . These commitments or ideologies allege to provide scientific descriptions of how the world *does* work while they also constitute normative positions regarding how the world *should* work.

Although scholars have produced a number of "theories" to explain the relationship of economics and politics, these three stand out and have had a profound influence on scholarship and political affairs. In highly oversimplified terms, economic nationalism (or, as it was originally called, mercantilism), which developed from the practice of statesmen in the early modern period, assumes and advocates the primacy of politics over economics. It is essentially a doctrine of state building and asserts that the market should be subordinate to the pursuit of state interests. It argues that political factors do, or at least should, determine economic relations. Liberalism, which emerged from the Enlightenment in the writings of Adam Smith and others, was a reaction to mercantilism and has become embodied in orthodox economics. It assumes that politics and economics exist, at least ideally, in separate spheres; it argues that markets—in the interest of efficiency, growth, and consumer choice—should be free from political interference. Marxism, which appeared in the mid-nineteenth century as a reaction against liberalism and classical economics, holds that economics drives politics. Political conflict arises from struggle among classes over the distribution of wealth. Hence, political conflict will cease with the elimination of the market and of a society of classes. . . . Both nationalism and Marxism in the modern era . . . developed largely in reaction to the tenets of liberal economics. . . .

## THE LIBERAL PERSPECTIVE

Some scholars assert that there is no such thing as a liberal theory of political economy because liberalism separates economics and politics from one another and assumes that each sphere operates according to particular rules and a logic of its own.[1] This view is itself, however, an ideological position and liberal theorists do in fact concern themselves with both political and economic affairs. Whether it is made explicit in their writings or is merely implicit, one can speak of a liberal theory of political economy.

There is a set of values from which liberal theories of economics and of politics arise; in the modern world these political and economic values have tended to appear together. . . . Liberal economic theory is committed to free markets and minimal state intervention, although . . . the relative emphasis on one or the other may differ. Liberal political theory is committed to individual equality and liberty, although again the emphasis may differ. . . .

The liberal perspective on political economy is embodied in the discipline of economics as it has developed in Great Britain, the United States, and Western Europe. From Adam Smith to its contemporary proponents, liberal thinkers . . . are committed to the market and the price mechanism as the most efficacious

---

[1] The term "liberal" is used . . . in its European connotation, that is, a commitment to individualism, free market, and private property This is the dominant perspective of most American economists and of economics as taught in American universities. . . .

means for organizing domestic and international economic relations. Liberalism may, in fact, be defined as a doctrine and set of principles for organizing and managing a market economy in order to achieve maximum efficiency, economic growth, and individual welfare.

Economic liberalism assumes that a market arises spontaneously in order to satisfy human needs and that, once it is in operation, it functions in accordance with its own internal logic. Human beings are by nature economic animals, and therefore markets evolve naturally without central direction. As Adam Smith put it, it is inherent in mankind to "truck, barter, and exchange." To facilitate exchange and improve their well-being, people create markets, money, and economic institutions. . . .

The rationale for a market system is that it increases economic efficiency, maximizes economic growth, and thereby improves human welfare. Although liberals believe that economic activity also enhances the power and security of the state, they argue that the primary objective of economic activity is to benefit individual consumers. Their ultimate defense of free trade and open markets is that they increase the range of goods and services available to the consumer.

The fundamental premise of liberalism is that the individual consumer, firm, or household is the basis of society. Individuals behave rationally and attempt to maximize or satisfy certain values at the lowest possible cost to themselves. Rationality applies only to endeavor, not to outcome. Thus, failure to achieve an objective due to ignorance or some other cause does not, according to liberals, invalidate their premise that individuals act on the basis of a cost/benefit or means/ends calculus. Finally, liberalism argues that an individual will seek to acquire an objective until a market equilibrium is reached, that is, until the costs associated with achieving the objective are equal to the benefits. Liberal economists attempt to explain economic and, in some cases, all human behavior on the basis of these individualistic and rationalistic assumptions. . . .

Liberalism also assumes that a market exists in which individuals have complete information and are thus enabled to select the most beneficial course of action. Individual producers and consumers will be highly responsive to price signals, and this will create a flexible economy in which any change in relative prices will elicit a corresponding change in patterns of production, consumption, and economic institutions; the latter are conceived ultimately to be the product rather than the cause of economic behavior. . . . Further, in a truly competitive market, the terms of exchange are determined solely by considerations of supply and demand rather than by the exercise of power and coercion. If exchange is voluntary, both parties benefit. In colloquial terms, a "free exchange is no robbery."

Economics, or rather the economics taught in most American universities (what Marxists call orthodox or bourgeois economics), is assumed to be an empirical science of maximizing behavior. Behavior is believed to be governed by a set of economic "laws" that are impersonal and politically neutral; therefore, economics and politics should and can be separated into distinct spheres. Governments should not intervene in the market except where a "market failure" exists . . . or in order to provide a so-called public or collective good. . . .

A market economy is governed principally by the law of demand. . . . This "law" (or, if one prefers, assumption) holds that people will buy more of a good if the relative price falls and less if it rises; people will also tend to buy more of a good as their relative income rises and less as it falls. Any development that changes the relative price of a good or the relative income of an actor will create an incentive or disincentive to acquire (or produce) more or less of the good; this law in turn has profound ramifications throughout the society. Although certain exceptions to this simple concept exist, it is fundamental to the operation and success of a market system of economic exchange.

On the supply side of the economy, liberal economics assumes that individuals pursue their interests in a world of scarcity and resource constraints. This is a fundamental and inescapable condition of human existence. Every decision involves an opportunity cost, a trade-off among alternative uses of available resources. . . . The basic lesson of liberal economics is that "there is no such thing as a free lunch"; to get something one must be willing to give up something else.

Liberalism also assumes that a market economy exhibits a powerful tendency toward equilibrium and inherent stability, at least over the long term. This "concept of a self-operating and self-correcting equilibrium achieved by a balance of forces in a rational universe" is a crucial one for the economists' belief in the operation of markets and the laws that are believed to govern them.[2] If a market is thrown into a state of disequilibrium due to some external (exogenous) factor such as a change in consumer tastes or productive technology, the operation of the price mechanism will eventually return it to a new state of equilibrium. . . .

An additional liberal assumption is that a basic long-term harmony of interests underlies the market competition of producers and consumers, a harmony that will supercede any temporary conflict of interest. Individual pursuit of self-interest in the market increases social well-being because it leads to the maximization of efficiency, and the resulting economic growth eventually benefits all. Consequently, everyone will gain in accordance with his or her contribution to the whole, but, it should be added, not everyone will gain equally because individual productivities differ. Under free exchange, society as a whole will be more wealthy, but individuals will be rewarded in terms of their marginal productivity and relative contribution to the overall social product.

Finally, most present-day liberal economists believe in progress, defined most frequently as an increase in wealth per capita. They assert that the growth of a properly functioning economy is linear, gradual, and continuous. . . . Although political or other events—wars, revolution, or natural disasters—can dramatically

---

[2] J.B. Condliffe, *The Commerce of Nations* (New York: W.W. Norton, 1950), p. 112.

disrupt this growth path, the economy will return eventually to a stable pattern of growth that is determined principally by increases in population, resources, and productivity. Moreover, liberals see no necessary connection between the process of economic growth and political developments such as war and imperialism; these political evils affect and may be affected by economic activities, but they are essentially caused by political and not by economic factors. For example, liberals do not believe that any causal relationship existed between the advance of capitalism in the late nineteenth century and the upheavals of imperialism after 1870 and the outbreak of the First World War. Liberals believe economics is progressive and politics is retrogressive. Thus they conceive of progress as divorced from politics and based on the evolution of the market.

. . . Today, the conditions necessary for the operation of a market economy exist, and the normative commitment to the market has spread from its birthplace in Western civilization to embrace an increasingly large portion of the globe. Despite setbacks, the modern world has moved in the direction of the market economy and of increasing global economic interdependence precisely because markets *are* more efficient than other forms of economic organization. . . .

In essence, liberals believe that trade and economic intercourse are a source of peaceful relations among nations because the mutual benefits of trade and expanding interdependence among national economies will tend to foster cooperative relations. Whereas politics tends to divide, economics tends to unite peoples. A liberal international economy will have a moderating influence on international politics as it creates bonds of mutual interests and a commitment to the status quo. However, it is important to emphasize again that although everyone will, or at least can, be better off in "absolute" terms under free exchange, the "relative" gains will differ. It is precisely this issue of relative gains and the distribution of the wealth generated by the market system that has given rise to economic nationalism and Marxism as rival doctrines.

## THE NATIONALIST PERSPECTIVE

Economic nationalism, like economic liberalism, has undergone several metamorphoses over the past several centuries. Its labels have also changed: mercantilism, statism, protectionism, the German Historical School, and, recently, New Protectionism. Throughout all these manifestations, however, runs a set of themes or attitudes rather than a coherent and systematic body of economic or political theory. Its central idea is that economic activities are and should be subordinate to the goal of state building and the interests of the state. All nationalists ascribe to the primacy of the state, of national security, and of military power in the organization and functioning of the international system. . . .

Although economic nationalism should be viewed as a general commitment to state building, the precise objectives pursued and the policies advocated have differed in different times and in different places. Yet, as Jacob Viner has cogently argued in an often-quoted passage, economic nationalist (or what he calls mercantilist) writers share convictions concerning the relationship of wealth and power:

> I believe that practically all mercantilists, whatever the period, country, or status of the particular individual, would have subscribed to all of the following propositions: (1) wealth is an absolutely essential means to power, whether for security or for aggression; (2) power is essential or valuable as a means to the acquisition or retention of wealth; (3) wealth and power are each proper ultimate ends of national policy; (4) there is long-run harmony between these ends, although in particular circumstances it may be necessary for a time to make economic sacrifices in the interest of military security and therefore also of long-run prosperity.[3]

Whereas liberal writers generally view the pursuit of power and wealth, that is, the choice between "guns and butter," as involving a trade-off, nationalists tend to regard the two goals as being complementary. . . .

Economic nationalists stress the role of economic factors in international relations and view the struggle among states—capitalist, socialist, or whatever—for economic resources as pervasive and indeed inherent in the nature of the international system itself. As one writer has put it, since economic resources are necessary for national power, every conflict is at once both economic and political.[4] States, at least over the long run, simultaneously pursue wealth and national power.

As it evolved in the early modern era, economic nationalism responded to and reflected the political, economic, and military developments of the sixteenth, seventeenth, and eighteenth centuries: the emergence of strong national states in constant competition, the rise of a middle class devoted at first to commerce and increasingly to manufacturing, and the quickening pace of economic activities due to changes within Europe and the discovery of the New World and its resources. The evolution of a monetarized market economy and the wide range of changes in the nature of warfare that have been characterized as the "Military Revolution" were also critically important.[5] Nationalists (or "mercantilists," as they were then called) had good cause to identify a favorable balance of trade with national security.

For several reasons, the foremost objective of nationalists is industrialization. . . . In the first place, nationalists believe that industry has spillover effects (externalities) throughout the economy and leads to its overall development. Second, they associate the possession of industry with economic self-sufficiency and political autonomy. Third, and most important, industry is prized because it is the basis of military power and central to national security in the modern world.

---

[3] Jacob Viner, *The Long View and the Short: Studies in Economic Theory and Policy* (New York: Free Press, 1958), p. 286.

[4] Ralph G. Hawtrey, *Economic Aspects of Sovereignty* (London: Longmans, 1952).

[5] Michael Roberts, *The Military Revolution, 1560–1600* (Belfast: Boyd, 1956).

In almost every society, including liberal ones, governments pursue policies favorable to industrial development. As the mercantilist theorist of American economic development, Alexander Hamilton, wrote: "not only the wealth but the independence and security of a country appear to be materially connected to the prosperity of manufactures"; . . . no contemporary dependency theorist has put it better. This nationalist objective of industrialization . . . is itself a major source of economic conflict.

Economic nationalism, both in the early modern era and today, arises in part from the tendency of markets to concentrate wealth and to establish dependency or power relations between the strong and the weak economies. . . .

In a world of competing states, the nationalist considers relative gain to be more important than mutual gain. Thus nations continually try to change the rules or regimes governing international economic relations in order to benefit themselves disproportionately with respect to other economic powers. As Adam Smith shrewdly pointed out, everyone wants to be a monopolist and will attempt to be one unless prevented by competitors. Therefore, a liberal international economy cannot develop unless it is supported by the dominant economic states whose own interests are consistent with its preservation.

Whereas liberals stress the mutual benefits of international commerce, nationalists as well as Marxists regard these relations as basically conflictual. Although this does not rule out international economic cooperation and the pursuit of liberal policies, economic interdependence is never symmetrical; indeed, it constitutes a source of continuous conflict and insecurity. Nationalist writers from Alexander Hamilton to contemporary dependency theorists thus emphasize national self-sufficiency rather than economic interdependence. The desire for power and independence have been the overriding concern of economic nationalists.

Whatever its relative strengths and weaknesses as an ideology or theory of international political economy, the nationalist emphasis on the geographic location and the distribution of economic activities provides it with powerful appeal. Throughout modern history, states have pursued policies promoting the development of industry, advanced technology, and those economic activities with the highest profitability and generation of employment within their own borders. As far as they can, states try to create an international division of labor favorable to their political and economic interests. Indeed, economic nationalism is likely to be a significant influence in international relations as long as the state system exists.

## THE MARXIST PERSPECTIVE

Like liberalism and nationalists, Marxism has evolved in significant ways since its basic ideas were set forth by Karl Marx and Friedrich Engels in the middle of the nineteenth century. Marx's own thinking changed during his lifetime, and his theories have always been subject to conflicting interpretations. Although Marx viewed capitalism as a global economy, he did not develop a systematic set of ideas on international relations; this responsibility fell upon the succeeding generation of Marxist writers. The Soviet Union and China, furthermore, having adopted Marxism as their official ideology, . . .reshaped it when necessary to serve their own national interests. . . .

Marxism characterizes capitalism as the private ownership of the means of production and the existence of wage labor. It believes that capitalism is driven by capitalists striving for profits and capital accumulation in a competitive market economy. Labor has been dispossessed and has become a commodity that is subject to the price mechanism. In Marx's view these two key characteristics of capitalism are responsible for its dynamic nature and make it the most productive economic mechanism yet. Although its historic mission is to develop and unify the globe, the very success of capitalism will hasten its passing. The origin, evolution, and eventual demise of the capitalist mode of production are, according to Marx, governed by three inevitable economic laws.

The first law, the law of disproportionality, entails a denial of Say's law, which (in oversimplified terms) holds that supply creates its own demand so that supply and demand will always be, except for brief moments, in balance. . . . Say's law maintains that an equilibrating process makes overproduction impossible in a capitalist or market economy. Marx, like John Maynard Keynes, denied that this tendency toward equilibrium existed and argued that capitalist economies tend to overproduce particular types of goods. There is, Marx argued, an inherent contradiction in capitalism between its capacity to produce goods and the capacity of consumers (wage earners) to purchase those goods, so that the constantly recurring disproportionality between production and consumption due to the "anarchy" of the market causes periodic depressions and economic fluctuations. He predicted that these recurring economic crises would become increasingly severe and in time would impel the suffering proletariat to rebel against the system.

The second law propelling the development of a capitalist system, according to Marxism, is the law of the concentration (or accumulation) of capital. The motive of capitalism is the drive for profits and the consequent necessity for the individual capitalist to accumulate and invest. Competition forces the capitalists to increase their efficiency and capital investment or risk extinction. As a result, the evolution of capitalism is toward increasing concentrations of wealth in the hands of the efficient few and the growing impoverishment of the many. With the petite bourgeoisie being pushed down into the swelling ranks of the impoverished proletariat, the reserve army of the unemployed increases, labor's wages decline, and the capitalist society becomes ripe for social revolution.

The third law of capitalism is that of the falling rate of profit. As capital accumulates and becomes more abundant, the rate of return declines, thereby decreasing the incentive to invest. Although classical liberal economists had recognized this possibility, they believed that a solution could be found through such countervailing devices as the export of capital and manufactured goods and the import of cheap food. . . . Marx, on the other hand, believed that the tendency for profits to decline was inescapable. As the pressure of competition forces capitalists to increase efficiency and productivity through investment in new labor-saving and more productive technology, the level of unemployment will increase and the rate of profit or surplus value will decrease. Capitalists will thereby lose their incentive to invest in productive ventures and to create employment. This will result in economic stagnation, increasing unemployment, and the "immiserization" of the proletariat. In time, the ever-increasing intensity and depth of the business cycle will cause the workers to rebel and destroy the capitalist economic system.

The core of the Marxist critique of capitalism is that although the individual capitalist is rational (as liberals assume), the capitalist system itself is irrational. The competitive market necessitates that the individual capitalist must save, invest, and accumulate. If the desire for profits is the fuel of capitalism, then investment is the motor and accumulation is the result. In the aggregate, however, this accumulating capital of individual capitalists leads to the periodic overproduction of goods, surplus capital, and the disappearance of investment incentives. In time, the increasing severity of the downturns in the business cycle and the long-term trend toward economic stagnation will cause the proletariat to overthrow the system through revolutionary violence. Thus, the inherent contradiction of capitalism is that, with capital accumulation, capitalism sows the seeds of its own destruction and is replaced by the socialist economic system.

Marx believed that in the mid-nineteenth century, the maturing of capitalism in Europe and the drawing of the global periphery into the market economy had set the stage for the proletarian revolution and the end of the capitalist economy. When this did not happen, Marx's followers, such as Rudolf Hilferding and Rosa Luxemburg, became concerned over the continuing vitality of capitalism and its refusal to disappear. The strength of nationalism, the economic successes of capitalism, and the advent of imperialism led to a metamorphosis of Marxist thought that culminated in Lenin's *Imperialism,* first published in 1917.[6] Written against the backdrop of the First World War and drawing heavily upon the writings of other Marxists, *Imperialism* was both a polemic against his ideological enemies and a synthesis of Marxist critiques of a capitalist world economy. In staking out his own position, Lenin in effect converted Marxism from essentially a theory of domestic economy to a theory of international political relations among capitalist states. . . .

In the years between Marx and Lenin, capitalism had experienced a profound transformation. Marx had written about a capitalism largely confined to Western

---

[6] V. I. Lenin, *Imperialism: The Highest Stage of Capitalism* (New York: International Publishers, 1939 [1917]).

Europe, a closed economy in which the growth impulse would one day cease as it collided with various constraints. Between 1870 and 1914, however, capitalism had become a vibrant, technological, and increasingly global and open system. In Marx's day, the primary nexus of the slowly developing world economy was trade. After 1870, however, the massive export of capital by Great Britain and subsequently by other developed economies had significantly changed the world economy—foreign investment and international finance had profoundly altered the economic and political relations among societies. Furthermore, Marx's capitalism had been composed mainly of small, competitive, industrial firms. By the time of Lenin, however, capitalist economies were dominated by immense industrial combines that in turn, according to Lenin, were controlled by the great banking houses *(haut finance)*. For Lenin, the control of capital by capital, that is, of industrial capital by financial capital, represented the pristine and highest stage of capitalist development.

Capitalism, he argued, had escaped its three laws of motion through overseas imperialism. The acquisition of colonies had enabled the capitalist economies to dispose of their unconsumed goods, to acquire cheap resources, and to vent their surplus capital. The exploitation of these colonies further provided an economic surplus with which the capitalists could buy off the leadership ("labor aristocracy") of their own proletariat. Colonial imperialism, he argued, had become a necessary feature of advanced capitalism. As its productive forces developed and matured, a capitalist economy had to expand abroad, capture colonies, or else suffer economic stagnation and internal revolution. Lenin identified this necessary expansion as the cause of the eventual destruction of the international capitalist system.

The essence of Lenin's argument is that a capitalist international economy does develop the world, but does not develop it evenly. Individual capitalist economies grow at different rates and this differential growth of national power is ultimately responsible for imperialism, war, and international political change. Responding to Kautsky's argument that capitalists were too rational to fight over colonies and would ally themselves in the joint exploitation of colonial peoples (the doctrine of "ultra-imperialism"), Lenin stated that this was impossible because of what has become known as the "law of uneven development." . . .

In effect, . . . Lenin added a fourth law to the original three Marxist laws of capitalism. The law is that, as capitalist economies mature, as capital accumulates, and as profit rates fall, the capitalist economies are compelled to seize colonies and create dependencies to serve as markets, investment outlets, and sources of food and raw materials. In competition with one another, they divide up the colonial world in accordance with their relative strengths. Thus, the most advanced capitalist economy, namely Great Britain, had appropriated the largest share of colonies. As other capitalist economies advanced, however, they sought a redivision of colonies. This imperialist conflict inevitably led to armed conflict among the rising and declining imperial powers. The First World War, according to this analysis, was a war of territorial redivision between a declining Great Britain and other rising capitalist powers. Such wars of colonial division and redivision would continue, he argued, until the industrializing colonies and the proletariat of the capitalist countries revolted against the system.

In more general terms, Lenin reasoned that because capitalist economies grow and accumulate capital at differential rates, a capitalist international system can never be stable for longer than very short periods of time. In opposition to Kautsky's doctrine of ultra-imperialism, Lenin argued that all capitalist alliances were temporary and reflected momentary balances of power among the capitalist states that would inevitably be undermined by the process of uneven development. As this occurred, it would lead to intracapitalist conflicts over colonial territories. . . .

Lenin's internationalization of Marxist theory represented a subtle but significant reformulation. In Marx's critique of capitalism, the causes of its downfall were economic; capitalism would fail for economic reasons as the proletariat revolted against its impoverishment. Furthermore, Marx had defined the actors in this drama as social classes. Lenin, however, substituted a political critique of capitalism in which the principal actors in effect became competing mercantilistic nation-states driven by economic necessity. Although international capitalism was economically successful, Lenin argued that it was politically unstable and constituted a war-system. The workers or the labor aristocracy in the developed capitalist countries temporarily shared in the exploitation of colonial peoples but ultimately would pay for these economic gains on the battlefield. Lenin believed that the inherent contradiction of capitalism resided in the consequent struggle of nations rather than in the class struggle. Capitalism would end due to a revolt against its inherent bellicosity and political consequences.

In summary, Lenin argued that the inherent contradiction of capitalism is that it develops the world and plants the political seeds of its own destruction as it diffuses technology, industry, and military power. It creates foreign competitors with lower wages and standards of living who can outcompete the previously dominant economy on the battlefield of world markets. Intensification of economic and political competition between declining and rising capitalist powers leads to economic conflicts, imperial rivalries, and eventually war. He asserted that this had been the fate of the British-centered liberal world economy of the nineteenth century. Today he would undoubtedly argue that, as the U.S. economy declines, a similar fate threatens the twentieth-century liberal world economy, centered in the United States. . . .

## A CRITIQUE OF THE PERSPECTIVES

As we have seen, liberalism, nationalism, and Marxism make different assumptions and reach conflicting conclusions regarding the nature and consequences of a world market economy or (as Marxists prefer) a world capitalist economy. . . .

Each of the three perspectives has strengths and weaknesses, to be further explored below. Although no perspective provides a complete and satisfactory understanding of the nature and dynamism of the international political economy, together they provide useful insights. . . .

### Critique of Economic Liberalism

Liberalism embodies a set of analytical tools and policy prescriptions that enable a society to maximize its return from scarce resources; its commitment to efficiency and the maximization of total wealth provides much of its strength. The market constitutes the most effective means for organizing economic relations, and the price mechanism operates to ensure that mutual gain and hence aggregate social benefit tend to result from economic exchange. In effect, liberal economics says to a society, whether domestic or international, "if you wish to be wealthy, this is what you must do." . . .

. . . Liberal economics can be criticized in several important respects. As a means to understand society and especially its dynamics, economics is limited; it cannot serve as a comprehensive approach to political economy. Yet liberal economists have tended to forget this inherent limitation, to regard economics as the master social science, and to permit economics to become imperialistic. When this occurs, the nature and basic assumptions of the discipline can lead the economist astray and limit its utility as a theory of political economy.

The first of these limitations is that economics artificially separates the economy from other aspects of society and accepts the existing sociopolitical framework as a given, including the distribution of power and property rights; the resource and other endowments of individuals, groups, and national societies; and the framework of social, political, and cultural institutions. The liberal world is viewed as one of homogeneous, rational, and equal individuals living in a world free from political boundaries and social constraints. Its "laws" prescribe a set of maximizing rules for economic actors regardless of where and with what they start; yet in real life, one's starting point most frequently determines where one finishes. . . .

Another limitation of liberal economics as a theory is a tendency to disregard the justice or equity of the outcome of economic activities. Despite heroic efforts to fashion an "objective" welfare economics, the distribution of wealth within and among societies lies outside the primary concern of liberal economics. . . .

Liberalism is also limited by its assumption that exchange is always free and occurs in a competitive market between equals who possess full information and are thus enabled to gain mutually if they choose to exchange one value for another. Unfortunately, as Charles Lindblom has argued, exchange is seldom free and equal.[7] Instead, the terms of an exchange can be profoundly affected by co-

---

[7] Charles E. Lindblom, *Politics and Markets: The World's Political-Economic Systems* (New York: Basic Books, 1977), pp. 40–50.

ercion, differences in bargaining power (monopoly or monopsony), and other essentially political factors. In effect, because it neglects both the effects of noneconomic factors on exchange and the effects of exchange on politics, liberalism lacks a true "political economy."

A further limitation of liberal economics is that its analysis tends to be static. At least in the short run, the array of consumer demands, the institutional framework, and the technological environment are accepted as constants. They are regarded as a set of constraints and opportunities within which economic decisions and trade-offs are made. . . . Liberal economists are incrementalists who believe that social structures tend to change slowly in response to price signals. Although liberal economists have attempted to develop theories of economic and technological change, the crucial social, political, and technological variables affecting change are considered to be exogenous and beyond the realm of economic analysis. As Marxists charge, liberalism lacks a theory of the dynamics of international political economy and tends to assume the stability and the virtues of the economic status quo.

Liberal economics, with its laws for maximizing behavior, is based on a set of highly restrictive assumptions. No society has ever or could ever be composed of the true "economic man" of liberal theory. A functioning society requires affective ties and the subordination of individual self-interest to larger social values; if this were not the case the society would fly apart. . . . Yet Western society has gone far in harnessing for social and economic betterment a basic tendency in human beings toward self-aggrandizement. . . . Through release of the market mechanism from social and political constraints, Western civilization has reached a level of unprecedented affluence and has set an example that other civilizations wish to emulate. It has done so, however, at the cost of other values. As liberal economics teaches, nothing is ever achieved without a cost.

### Critique of Economic Nationalism

The foremost strength of economic nationalism is its focus on the state as the predominant actor in international relations and as an instrument of economic development. Although many have argued that modern economic and technological developments have made the nation-state an anachronism, at the end of the twentieth century the system of nation-states is actually expanding: societies throughout the world are seeking to create strong states capable of organizing and managing national economies, and the number of states in the world is increasing. Even in older states, the spirit of nationalist sentiments can easily be inflamed. . . . Although other actors such as transnational and international organizations do exist and do influence international relations, the economic and military efficiency of the state makes it preeminent over all these other actors.

The second strength of nationalism is its stress on the importance of security and political interests in the organization and conduct of international economic relations. One need not accept the nationalist emphasis on the primacy of security considerations to appreciate that the security of the state is a necessary precondition for its economic and political well-being in an anarchic and competitive state system. A state that fails to provide for its own security ceases to be independent. . . .

The third strength of nationalism is its emphasis on the political framework of economic activities, its recognition that markets must function in a world of competitive groups and states. The political relations among these political actors affect the operation of markets just as markets affect the political relations. In fact, the international political system constitutes one of the most important constraints on and determinants of markets. Since states seek to influence markets to their own individual advantage, the role of power is crucial in creating and sustaining market relations; even Ricardo's classic example of the exchange of British woolens for Portuguese wine was not free from the exercise of state power. . . . Indeed, as Carr has argued, every economic system must rest on a secure political base.[8]

One weakness of nationalism is its tendency to believe that international economic relations constitute solely and at all times a zero-sum game, that is, that one state's gain must of necessity be another's loss. Trade, investment, and all other economic relations are viewed by the nationalist primarily in conflictual and distributive terms. Yet, if cooperation occurs, markets *can* bring mutual (albeit not necessarily equal) gain, as the liberal insists. The possibility of benefit for all is the basis of the international market economy. Another weakness of nationalism is due to the fact that the pursuit of power and the pursuit of wealth usually do conflict, at least in the short run. The amassing and exercising of military and other forms of power entail costs to the society, costs that can undercut its economic efficiency. Thus, as Adam Smith argued, the mercantilist policies of the eighteenth-century states that identified money with wealth were detrimental to the growth of the real wealth created by productivity increases; he demonstrated that the wealth of nations would have been better served by policies of free trade. Similarly, the tendency today to identify industry with power can weaken the economy of a state. Development of industries without regard to market considerations or comparative advantage can weaken a society economically. Although states in a situation of conflict must on occasion pursue mercantilistic goals and policies, over the long term, pursuit of these policies can be self-defeating.

In addition, nationalism lacks a satisfactory theory of domestic society, the state, and foreign policy. It tends to assume that society and state form a unitary entity and that foreign policy is determined by an objective national interest. Yet, as liberals correctly stress, society is pluralistic and consists of individuals and groups (coalitions of individuals) that try to capture the apparatus of the state and

[8] Edward Hallett Carr, *The Twenty Years' Crisis, 1919–1939.* 2d ed. (London: Macmillan, 1951 [1939]).

make it serve their own political and economic interests. Although states possess varying degrees of social autonomy and independence in the making of policy, foreign policy (including foreign economic policy) is in large measure the outcome of the conflicts among dominant groups within each society. Trade protectionism and most other nationalist policies result from attempts by one factor of production or another (capital, labor, or land) to acquire a monopoly position and thereby to increase its share of the economic rents. Nationalist policies are most frequently designed to redistribute income from consumers and society as a whole to producer interests.

Nationalism can thus be interpreted as either a theory of state building or a cloak for the interests of particular producer groups that are in a position to influence national policy. In their failure to appreciate fully or distinguish between the two possible meanings of economic nationalism, nationalists can be faulted for not applying, both to the domestic level and to the determination of foreign policy, their assumption that the political framework influences economic outcomes. They fail to take sufficient account of the fact that domestic political groups frequently use a nationalist rationale, especially that of national security, to promote their own interests. . . .

The validity of nationalists' emphasis on protectionism and industrialization is more difficult to ascertain. It is true that all great industrial powers have had strong states that protected and promoted their industries in the early stages of industrialization and that without such protectionism, the "infant" industries of developing economies probably would not have survived the competition of powerful firms in more advanced economies. Yet it is also the case that high levels of protectionism in many countries have led to the establishment of inefficient industries and even retarded economic development. . . . In the final quarter of the twentieth century, economies like those of Taiwan and South Korea, which have limited protectionism while favoring competitive export industries, . . . performed better than those less developed countries that . . . attempted to industrialize behind high tariff walls while pursuing a strategy of import substitution.

The nationalist's bias toward industry over agriculture also must get a mixed review. It is true that industry can have certain advantages over agriculture and that the introduction of industrial technology into a society has spillover effects that tend to transform and modernize all aspects of the economy as it upgrades the quality of the labor force and increases the profitability of capital. Yet one must remember that few societies have developed without a prior agricultural revolution and a high level of agricultural productivity. . . . In fact, certain of the most prosperous economies of the world, for example, Denmark, the American farm belt, and western Canada, are based on efficient agriculture. . . . In all these societies, moreover, the state has promoted agricultural development.

One may conclude that the nationalists are essentially correct in their belief that the state must play an important role in economic development. A strong state is required to promote and, in some cases, to protect industry as well as to foster an efficient agriculture. Yet this active role of the state, though a necessary condition, is not a sufficient condition. A strong and interventionist state does not guarantee economic development; indeed, it might retard it. The sufficient condition for economic development is an efficient economic organization of agriculture and industry, and in most cases this is achieved through the operation of the market. Both of these political and economic conditions have characterized the developed economies and the rapidly industrializing countries of the contemporary international system.

It is important to realize that, whatever its relative merits or deficiencies, economic nationalism has a persistent appeal. Throughout modern history, the international location of economic activities has been a leading concern of states. From the seventeenth century on, states have pursued conscious policies of industrial and technological development. Both to achieve stable military power and in the belief that industry provides a higher "value added" . . . than agriculture, the modern nation-state has had as one of its major objectives the establishment and protection of industrial power. As long as a conflictual international system exists, economic nationalism will retain its strong attraction.

### Critique of Marxist Theory

Marxism correctly places the economic problem—the production and distribution of material wealth—where it belongs, at or near the center of political life. Whereas liberals tend to ignore the issue of distribution and nationalists are concerned primarily with the *international* distribution of wealth, Marxists focus on both the domestic and the international effects of a market economy on the distribution of wealth. They call attention to the ways in which the rules or regimes governing trade, investment, and other international economic relations affect the distribution of wealth among groups and states. . . .

Another contribution of Marxism is its emphasis on the nature and structure of the division of labor at both the domestic and international levels. As Marx and Engels correctly pointed out in *The German Ideology,* every division of labor implies dependence and therefore a political relationship. . . . In a market economy the economic nexus among groups and states becomes of critical importance in determining their welfare and their political relations. The Marxist analysis, however, is too limited, because economic interdependence is not the only or even the most important set of interstate relations. The political and strategic relations among political actors are of equal or greater significance and cannot be reduced to merely economic considerations, at least not as Marxists define economics.

The Marxist theory of international political economy is also valuable in its focus on international political change. Whereas neither liberalism nor nationalism has a comprehensive theory of social change, Marxism emphasizes the role of economic and technological developments in explaining the dynamics of the international system. As embodied in Lenin's law of uneven development, the differential growth of power among states constitutes an underlying cause of international political change. Lenin was at least partially correct in attributing the First World War to the uneven economic growth of power among industrial states and to conflict over the division of territory. There can be little doubt that the uneven growth of the several European powers and the consequent effects on the balance of power contributed to their collective insecurity. Competition for markets and empires did aggravate interstate relations. Furthermore, the average person's growing awareness of the effects on personal welfare and security of the vicissitudes of the world market and the economic behavior of other states also became a significant element in the arousal of nationalistic antagonisms. For nations and citizens alike, the growth of economic interdependence brought with it a new sense of insecurity, vulnerability, and resentment against foreign political and economic rivals.

Marxists are no doubt also correct in attributing to capitalist economies, at least as we have known them historically, a powerful impulse to expand through trade and especially through the export of capital. . . . Capitalists desire access to foreign economies for export of goods and capital; exports have a Keynesian demand effect in stimulating economic activity in capitalist economies, and capital exports serve to raise the overall rate of profit. Closure of foreign markets and capital outlets would be detrimental to capitalism, and a closed capitalist economy would probably result in a dramatic decline in economic growth. There is reason to believe that the capitalist system (certainly as we have known it) could not survive in the absence of an open world economy. The essential character of capitalism, as Marx pointed out, is cosmopolitan; the capitalist's ideology is international. Capitalism in just one state would undoubtedly be an impossibility.

In the nineteenth and twentieth centuries the dominant capitalist states, Great Britain and the United States, employed their power to promote and maintain an open world economy. They used their influence to remove the barriers to the free flow of goods and capital. Where necessary, in the words of Simon Kuznets, "the greater power of the developed nations imposed upon the reluctant partners the opportunities of international trade and division of labor."[9] In pursuit of their own interests, they created international law to protect the property rights of private traders and investors. . . . And when the great trading nations became unable or unwilling to enforce the rules of free trade, the liberal system began its steady retreat. Up to this point, therefore, the Marxists are correct in their identification of capitalism and modern imperialism.

The principal weakness of Marxism as a theory of international political economy results from its failure to appreciate the role of political and strategic factors in international relations. . . . Although competition for markets and for

---

[9] Simon Kuznets, *Modern Economic Growth: Rate, Structure, and Spread* (New Haven: Yale University Press, 1966), p. 335.

capital outlets can certainly be a cause of tension and one factor causing impe-rialism and war, this does not provide an adequate explanation for the foreign policy behavior of capitalist states.

The historical evidence, for example, does not support Lenin's attribution of the First World War to the logic of capitalism and the market system. The most important territorial disputes among the European powers, which precipitated the war, were not those about overseas colonies, as Lenin argued, but lay within Eu-rope itself. The principal conflict leading to the war involved redistribution of the Balkan territories of the decaying Ottoman Empire. And insofar as the source of this conflict was economic, it lay in the desire of the Russian state for access to the Mediterranean. . . . Marxism cannot explain the fact that the three major im-perial rivals—Great Britain, France, and Russia—were in fact on the same side in the ensuing conflict and that they fought against a Germany that had few for-eign policy interests outside Europe itself.

In addition, Lenin was wrong in tracing the basic motive force of imperial-ism to the internal workings of the capitalist system. As Benjamin J. Cohen has pointed out in his analysis of the Marxist theory of imperialism, the political and strategic conflicts of the European powers were more important; it was at least in part the stalemate on the Continent among the Great Powers that forced their interstate competition into the colonial world.[10] Every one of these colonial con-flicts (if one excludes the Boer War) was in fact settled through diplomatic means. And, finally, the overseas colonies of the European powers were simply of little economic consequence. As Lenin's own data show, almost all European overseas investment was directed to the "lands of recent settlement" (the United States, Canada, Australia, South Africa, Argentina, and the like) rather than to the de-pendent colonies in what today we call the Third World.[11] In fact, contrary to Lenin's view that politics follows investment, international finance during this period was largely a servant of foreign policy, as was also the case with French loans to Czarist Russia. Thus, despite its proper focus on political change, Marx-ism is seriously flawed as a theory of political economy.

---

[10] Benjamin J. Cohen, *The Question of Imperialism: The Political Economy of Dominance and Dependence* (New York: Basic Books, 1973).

[11] Lenin, *Imperialism,* p. 64.

# 23

# WHOSE "MODEL" FAILED? IMPLICATIONS OF THE ASIAN ECONOMIC CRISIS

LINDA Y.C. LIM

The Asian financial crisis of 1997–1999 raised serious questions about the validity of both "Asian models" of economic development based on the strong roles of states and cultures and "Western models" based on open markets, free trade, and capital flows, since the countries affected by the crisis had been touted as models of both paths to development. Linda Y.C. Lim argues that both statism and openness contributed to the Asian growth miracle which preceded the crisis and to the crisis itself. Openness without the support of appropriate state policies and institutions can lead to trouble, as can the abuse or an excess of inappropriate state interventions. Lim is professor in the department of Corporate Strategy and International Business at the University of Michigan. She has published widely in books and journals on trade, investment, and business in Southeast Asia and, with Pang Eng Fong, is coauthor of *Foreign Direct Investment and Industrialization in Malaysia, Singapore, Taiwan, and Thailand* (1989).

After three decades of nearly uninterrupted rapid economic growth and industrial development popularly characterized as "the Asian miracle," several East and Southeast Asian countries unexpectedly fell victim to severe financial crisis and ensuing deep recession in 1997 and 1998. The collapse of the Thai baht in July 1997 was quickly followed by similar currency declines against the U.S. dollar of between 35 percent and 85 percent in the Philippines, Malaysia, Indonesia and South Korea, as capital fled out of these countries, leaving in its

wake a "liquidity crunch" and sharp economic contraction which averaged minus 7 percent of GDP in 1998. Contagion from these five most seriously crisis-
hit economies also adversely affected their neighbors Hong Kong, Singapore, Taiwan and China, through regional trade and investment linkages. The crisis
eventually spread to Latin America and Russia in 1998, as the Asian downturn
both reduced global demand for exports, and increased import competition in domestic markets from now cheaper Asian products, and as worried international
investors withdrew their funds from all emerging markets, now deemed to be
much more risky than previously thought.

Although the Asian economies began recovering by 1999, the crisis has become cause for rethinking the long-established consensus, among mostly Western and Western-trained economists, about the causes of the region's "miracle"
economic growth and industrial development. Most recently restated in the Asian
Development Bank's 1997 study on *Emerging Asia: Changes and Challenges,*
essentially an update of the World Bank's 1993 study on *The East Asian Miracle,* this consensus interpretation among mainstream economists goes as follows.

Asian economic success before the crisis was the product simply of the application of orthodox Western textbook economic principles—external "openness" to trade and foreign investment on the one hand, and domestic "good government" with small, balanced or surplus government budgets and conservative
monetary policy leading to low inflation and high savings rates on the other. For
these reasons, Asian countries typically rank relatively high on the "Economic
Freedom" indices annually produced by think tanks like the Fraser Institute in
Canada and the Heritage Foundation in Washington DC. Of the most badly hit
crisis countries, South Korea, had been less open than Southeast Asia, but
nonetheless had subjected its firms to the discipline of the international marketplace through export manufacturing.

But mainstream economists are not the only Western or Western-trained scholars who have sought to dissect the Asian economic miracle through the lens of
their particular discipline. Political scientists and political economists have also
had their play with the subject, usually concluding that the "developmental state"
(focused on promoting economic development in the national interest) and statist industrial policy (government protection and subsidies targeted at developing
specific "strategic" industrial sectors) have been key to the rapid industrialization of the East Asian newly-industrialized economies.[1] South Korea is the

---

[1] Frederic C. Deyo, *The Political Economy of the New Asian Industrialism* (Ithaca, N.Y.: Cornell
University Press, 1987); Alice Amsden, *Asia's Next Giant: South Korea and Late Industrialization*
(New York: Oxford University Press, 1989); Stephan Haggard, *Pathways from the Periphery: The
Politics of Growth in Newly Industrialized Countries* (Ithaca, N.Y.: Cornell University Press, 1990);
Robert Wade, *Governing the Market: Economic Theory and the Role of Government in East Asian
Industrialization* (Princeton, N.J.: Princeton University Press, 1990); Karl Fields, "Strong States
and Business Organization in Korea and Taiwan," in Sylvia Maxfield and Ben Ross Schneider, eds.,
*Business and the State in Developing Countries* (Ithaca, N.Y.: Cornell University Press, 1997),
pp. 122–151.

classic case here, but it is harder to identify "developmental states" and successful industrial policy in Southeast Asia outside of Malaysia and Singapore. Rather, state development policy in Thailand, Indonesia and the Philippines is more likely to be viewed as having been captured by crony capitalists with close personal relations with governments, thereby violating the developmental state principle of state autonomy from special interests.[2]

Notwithstanding this, and despite the contradiction between the economist and the political scientist/political economist views, the Southeast Asian countries are always included as part of the so-called Asian economic miracle or "Asian model" that has been promoted by advocates of free market economics. These include both conservative Western think tanks like the Heritage Foundation and more liberal multilateral institutions like the World Bank and the International Monetary Fund, whose "Washington consensus" of liberal economic policies has been foisted on emerging economies around the world.

Although economists like these generally did not care for the industrial policies and microeconomic state interventions pursued by Asian governments, they did praise the latter's practice of conventional macroeconomic policy embracing both openness and fiscal and monetary conservatism. It is not an exaggeration to say that the Asian economies became showcases for the success of a policy prescription that has been peddled to other newly-liberalizing emerging economies in Latin America, East Central Europe, Central Asia and Africa.

When the Philippines, Taiwan, South Korea and Thailand became politically democratic as well in the late 1980s, this completed the picture of triumph for the Western liberal model of free-markets-with-democracy which Francis Fukuyama in 1992 proclaimed ushered in *The End of History,* or the end of the ideological political-economic conflict between East and West which defined the Cold War. In Asia, for example, it was proclaimed that the United States "lost the Vietnam War (against communism) but won the peace," as reflected in the economic prosperity and political stability enjoyed by its capitalist allies in the region, and the subsequent embarkation of their socialist neighbors, particularly China and Vietnam, on the path of market-oriented economic reform. About the only sour note in this triumph was sounded by Samuel Huntington's 1996 *Clash of Civilizations,* which warned that the cessation of the Cold War's ideological conflicts would usher in an era of mounting cultural conflict between the West on one side and the competing civilizations of Islam and Confucianism on the other.

Culture as an element in the Asian economic miracle has largely been neglected or dismissed by both Western economists and political scientists, though the former might occasionally acknowledge that the highly entrepreneurial, economically responsive populations in the region, themselves the product of market

---

[2] Andrew MacIntyre, ed., *Business and Government in Industrializing Asia* (Ithaca, N.Y.: Cornell University Press, 1994); K. S. Jomo, ed., *Southeast Asia's Misunderstood Miracle* (Boulder, Colo.: Westview Press, 1997).

forces, might have spurred the development of essentially private-enterprise economies. The latter sometimes noted that Confucian cultures may have lent moral authority and political legitimacy to interventionist developmental states. Western and some Asian anthropologists and sociologists, on the other hand, have identified kin and ethnic networks, or "culturally embedded network capitalisms," as locally efficient means of mobilizing capital and industrial growth in the Asian miracle economies.[3]

Culture has also played a much larger role in explanations for the Asian miracle offered by Asian intellectuals who hail mostly from the political establishment in patriarchal-authoritarian and semi-authoritarian states like Singapore, Malaysia, China and Indonesia, who argued that "Asian values" emphasizing the primacy of order over freedom, family and community interests over individual choice, and economic progress over political expression, together with thrift, ambition and hard work, were largely responsible for the fortunate public sector policies and private sector actions which resulted in the Asian miracle.

## WHOSE MODEL FAILED?

The "Asian values" school was unpopular among many Western commentators for suggesting, among other things, that capitalism and democracy need not go hand-in-hand. So it was predictable that when the Asian economic crisis hit during a period of unprecedented economic strength in the United States and economic recovery in Western Europe, opponents of the "Asian values" school were out in full swing (chiefly in the editorial pages of *The Wall Street Journal),* crowing over its assumed demise and the concomitant assumed triumph of the "American way."

The Asian miracle was particularly attacked for its reliance on industrial policy and cronyism, or relationships between big business and government, both of which contributed to moral hazard in the inefficient financial sector and the resultant over-investment in a classic asset bubble. Paul Krugman—the MIT economist whose 1994 *Foreign Affairs* article, "The Myth of Asia's Miracle," had pronounced the Asian miracle a "myth" based on low total factor productivity growth—was one of those who initially favored the moral hazard argument that "crony capitalism" or Asian reliance on *guanxi* (relationships) caused the crisis, which in this view was essentially a crisis of bad investments in both the public and private sectors. This line of argument directly challenges both the praise of statist industrial policy by mostly Western political scientists and

---

[3] S. Gordon Redding, *The Spirit of Chinese Capitalism* (Berlin: Walter de Gruyter, 1990); Gary G. Hamilton, ed., *Business Networks and Economic Development in East and Southeast Asia* (Hong Kong: Center of Asian Studies, University of Hong Kong, 1991); Richard Whitley, *Business Systems in East Asia: Firms, Markets and Societies* (London: Sage Publications, 1992); Robert W. Hefner, ed., *Market Cultures: Society and Morality in the New Asian Capitalisms* (Boulder, Colo.: Westview, 1998).

of "culturally-embedded networks" favored by mostly Western anthropologists and sociologists.

There is no question that crony capitalism did play a role in the over-inflation and subsequent deflation of economic growth and asset prices in Asia. But this is far from the only or most plausible interpretation for the crisis, and it is certainly not the whole story. Indeed, in the affected Asian countries and other emerging economies around the world, another interpretation quickly became popular, one that is much less favorable to the liberal orthodoxy favored by Western economists. In this view, it is the Western model of free-markets-with-democracy that has failed with the collapse of its prime success stories in Asia—or a case of "the west won the Cold War, only to lose the peace."

## THE PERILS OF OPENNESS

First, if openness was a key ingredient of the Asian economic miracle, too much openness too fast was responsible for its downfall. In particular, rapid and sweeping (although not yet complete) capital market liberalization beginning in the late 1980s led to a massive influx of foreign capital, especially short-term loan and equity capital, which contributed to the boom economy and over-investment bubble of the 1990s. Without this influx of foreign funds—which in some cases amounted to as much as 75 percent of the equity capital on local stockmarkets— domestic crony capitalism alone could not have fed a boom and bubble of such proportions. Even without crony capitalism, high growth and the expectation of continued uninterrupted high growth, fed in large part by foreign capital, might have led to excessive risk-taking and over-leveraging of local businesses believing their economies immune from the business cycle.

High domestic growth and investment in turn contributed to ballooning current account deficits, with imports (mostly of machinery and equipment required by the flood of new investments) constantly exceeding exports by a wide margin. This was further fueled by overvalued exchange rates, the result both of more or less fixed exchange-rate regimes established to attract foreign capital by removing currency risk, and of large inflows of capital. Open capital markets and capital-account convertibility also increased these economies' vulnerability to currency speculation which could, at the appropriate moment, trigger a sudden massive exit of foreign funds as easily as these funds had previously entered.

Financial market liberalization in Asia also proceeded in advance of the appropriate state or collective institutions necessary to monitor and regulate financial institutions, and in advance of local expertise to manage them. The region's much-vaunted entrepreneurialism led to establishment of a horde of new banks and finance companies—Indonesia alone came to have over 200 banks—within a short space of time and with inadequate expertise and experience in the management of money. Even without crony capitalism, excess capacity in the financial sector and intense competition to lend and invest among these neophyte institutions would have led to a fair proportion of "bad investments." It was aggravated by the easy availability of cheap capital from abroad, in many cases pressed on local borrowers by overeager foreign lenders who should have known better, but faced intense competition among themselves and were attracted by the returns presented by higher interest rates and by rosy projections of continued rapid growth.

With or without the moral hazard presented by local crony capitalism, the resultant excess supply of capital was bound to lead to some bad investments as capital started flowing to more and more marginal projects. Unlike their local borrowers, foreign lenders and investors from advanced countries possessed the requisite expertise and experience in risk assessment and credit evaluation. But they apparently chose not to apply this knowledge, yielding instead to herd instinct and, as Alan Greenspan characterized the sentiments toward the booming U.S. stockmarket, "irrational exuberance." This contributed first to the overvaluation of assets, then reversed course and with "irrational pessimism" led to the subsequent undervaluation, as the following quotes from early 1998 indicate:[4]

> "All banks are under certain competitive pressure. If the market is attractive you go with the herd. Even if you have doubts you don't stop lending."
>
> —*Ernst-Mortiz Lipp, member of the Board of Managing Directors of Dresdner Bank AG*

> "There was a huge euphoria about Asia and Southeast Asia. It was the place to be."
>
> —*Dennis Phillips, Commerzbank*

> "All the banks would be standing in line—J.P. Morgan, Deutsche Bank, Dresdner. We were all standing in line trying to help these countries borrow money. We would all see each other at the same places. We all knew each other."
>
> —*Klaus Friedrich, Chief Economist, Dresdner Bank AG*

> "There are problems in Asia now because investors and bankers were overly optimistic about the Asian economies, and then they panicked."
>
> —*Anonymous American banker*

Openness and the dominance of private enterprise in the Asian economies also severely limited their governments' ability to intervene to control these flows. Given domestic excess demand and external imbalance (huge current account deficits), governments should have allowed their currencies to depreciate and/or

---

[4] The Lipp quote is from Nayan Chanda, "Rebuilding Asia," *Far Eastern Economic Review,* February 12, 1998, pp. 46–50; other quotes are from Timothy O'Brien, "Covering Asia with Cash, Banks Poured Money into Region Despite Warning Signs," *New York Times,* January 28, 1998, p. D1.

raised taxes and interest rates and cut government spending, to reduce domestic demand and correct the external imbalance. But in very open economies such as these, with high import shares of GDP, currency depreciation would increase costs, including offshore loan-servicing costs, and cause much inflation from higher import prices, while higher domestic interest rates would be ineffective so long as businesses could resort to cheaper borrowing in accessible offshore markets—that is, they may well have *increased* rather than reduced external borrowing.

> "We could have borrowed locally, something like 14 percent per annum, or borrowed overseas, where we could get (dollar) loans for 8 percent or 9 percent. If I had borrowed locally, the analysts would be saying that we were being foolish for not taking advantage of lower rates overseas. . . . We could have bought insurance, but that would only be adding to the cost. Our government, our bankers, economists, even foreigners were telling us that the baht was stable. . . . We never imagined that the baht would be devalued."
> —*Chumpol Nalamlieng, CEO of Siam Cement, a blue-chip Thai company, quoted in* Asiaweek *October 24, 1997, on their $4.2 billion debt*

At the same time, public sectors were small (at around 10 percent of GDP) and mostly in balance, and governments had little control over overborrowing in the private sector. This reduced the effectiveness of raising taxes and cutting expenditures, as typically required, for example, in IMF programs usually applied in countries with large fiscal deficits and loose money policies. In short, the dominance of private enterprise reduced the influence that governments had over the macroeconomy.

## THE PERILS OF DEMOCRACY

The nascent democracies that since the late 1980s had taken hold in Korea, Thailand and the Philippines also caused a loss of government control over the macroeconomy. Whereas previous authoritarian regimes could impose higher interest and taxation costs on local business communities almost at will, and had done so to maintain currency stability for decades prior, this had become difficult with the increased political influence of business over elected legislatures whose members were either business persons themselves, or required business support to get and stay elected. As editor George Melloan commented on the *American* political process in *The Wall Street Journal* on February 17, 1998.

> Practicing politics costs money, and all politicians, unless they are fabulously wealthy, depend on campaign contributions. The more generous donors usually would like a favor or two. Quid pro quo, dating back at least to the steps of the Roman Forum, is alive and well in the U.S., as in most other corners of the world.

Thailand's short-lived coalition governments (five in six years), frequent
|general elections, and extensive vote buying ($1.1 billion in the November 1996
general election alone) made it particularly vulnerable to vested interest opposition to the fiscal and monetary contraction necessary to correct an external
imbalance—as suggested by the parade of four finance ministers and three central bank governors in the twelve months before the July 2, 1997 devaluation of
the baht. Democracy has also contributed to the expansion of crony capitalism,
as exemplified by the favoring of businesses with ruling political party connections in Malaysia's joint public-private sector infrastructure projects, who naturally would oppose both interest rate increases and cuts in public expenditures
from which they benefit.

In contrast, Hong Kong—which does not have an elected government—and
Singapore—which has a single-party-dominated parliament—did relatively well
through the economic crisis. Like the authoritarian governments of the past in
Korea and Thailand, both administrations maintained strong central economic
control and could impose economic hardship on their populations or take politically unpopular measures when necessary for economic stabilization. Thus the
Singapore government acted to cool off the domestic property market when it
was still booming in 1996, and the Hong Kong authorities were initially able to
ignore domestic business leaders' complaints about the currency peg hurting their
businesses, and to raise local interest rates to beat back an attack by currency
speculators in 1997. In the terminology of political scientists, both states had an
autonomy from business interests that governments in their newly democratic
neighbors did not have.[5]

## IN DEFENSE OF THE WESTERN MODEL

Proponents of the Western liberal model do not, of course, see things this way.
Instead, they assert that open markets and democracy have worked, and that it is
the "Asian" parts of the Asian economic model which have failed—particularly
statist industrial policy in Korea (beloved though it has been by some Western
political scientists); crony capitalism in Thailand, Malaysia and Indonesia (a re-
flection of both statist industrial policy and culturally embedded networks); and
political mismanagement everywhere—from the virtual absence of government
in Thailand before the crisis, to authoritarianism in Indonesia (before the crisis
exacted the downfall of President Suharto in May 1998), and an idiosyncratic
strong leader in Malaysia. They further argue that the excess lending and investment by domestic and foreign financial institutions resulted from informa-

---

[5] Note, however, that Hong Kong suffered much more than Singapore did because of its adherence to a currency peg, and that as the government's autonomy from local business interests waned,
its economic policies also changed, in late 1998. See Linda Y.C. Lim, "Free Market Fancies: Hong
Kong, Singapore and the Asian Financial Crisis," in T.J. Pempel, ed., *The Politics of the Asian Economic Crisis* (Ithaca, N.Y.: Cornell University Press, 1999), pp. 101–115.

tion gaps caused by inadequate local government prudential regulation, monitoring and disclosure requirements, not from mistakes made by financial market actors. They believe that financial restructuring along Western lines and the takeover of troubled local financial institutions by more experienced and expert foreign counterparts would increase efficiency in the channeling of local savings to investments, reduce the risk of bad investments and forestall the recurrence of crisis.

The IMF occupies a peculiar position in the Western economic policy canon. On the one hand, the multilateral agency is seen and has operated as an instrument of Western policy orthodoxy advocating free trade and capital flows together with fiscal austerity and monetary conservatism. The IMF typically requires policy deregulation and liberal economic reforms, including financial sector liberalization and restructuring, in exchange for low-interest emergency loans of foreign exchange for client countries facing balance of payments difficulties and inability to meet their external liabilities. At the same time, it is recognized that the availability of IMF "bailouts" creates another moral hazard problem, by encouraging governments and private borrowers, lenders and investors to take excessive risks in emerging markets, secure in the expectation that their risk is minimized by the likelihood of an IMF rescue should things go really bad. The result is periodic over-investment and over-lending bubbles such as characterized Mexico in 1994 and Southeast Asia and Korea in 1997.

## THE ASIAN RESPONSE

For Asians, the economic crisis led to disillusionment with market openness. At worst, many saw themselves as the victims of a massive conspiracy of Western governments, the IMF, financial markets and industrial corporations to first deliberately inflate and then deflate the asset values of Asian banks and corporations, and then to subsequently take control of them at post-crisis "fire sale" prices and under forced liberalization by the IMF. At best, Asians viewed the crisis as a case of massive market failure, particularly on the part of globally unregulated foreign financial market actors who, despite their greater expertise and global experience, still indulged in excess lending and investment to Asian markets, and so cannot be trusted to better manage the local financial institutions that they may take over.

One of Thailand's most respected economists, Ammar Siamwalla, former President of the Thailand Development Research Institute, was very critical of his own government's errors which led to the crisis, but still expressed extreme doubts about the policy of financial liberalization, as quoted in *The Wall Street Journal* on January 20, 1998:

> The currency market is really crazy. . . . we are receiving all the punishment because we have opened our currency markets to the forces of globalization (which) in retrospect has been far too rapid.

Others shared his views. Park Yung Chul, President of the Korea Institute of Finance, said in *Business Week* on January 26, 1998:

> The West has pushed us to open our markets, but what are we getting in return? Through globalization we have created a monster.

China and Vietnam postponed capital market liberalization that would expose their currencies to speculation, and calls for more regional and global cooperation in the monitoring and possibly regulation of international capital flows have become de rigeur in international for on the crisis. This idea was first raised by Malaysian Prime Minister Mahathir and supported by his nemesis, currency trader George Soros, who said in the *Atlantic Monthly* in January 1998:

> Financial markets are inherently unstable, and international financial markets are especially so. International capital movements are notorious for their boom-bust pattern. . . . The recent turmoil in Asian markets raises difficult questions about currency pegs, asset bubbles, inadequate banking supervision, and the lack of financial information which cannot be ignored. Markets cannot be left to correct their own mistakes, because they are likely to overreact and to behave in an indiscriminate fashion.

Today, even the World Bank has lent its support to some forms of capital controls for small open economies which can be severely disrupted by massive inflows and outflows of foreign capital. Both the World Bank and the IMF have acknowledged that Malaysia's controversial imposition of capital controls in September 1998 did not appear to do any damage to its economy, and may have even contributed to its economic recovery in 1999. There is a growing consensus that, at a minimum, more international monitoring, standards and information sharing are necessary to minimize the damage caused by currently largely unregulated cross-border capital flows.

At the same time, the crisis raised the possibility that some Asians could also lose their enthusiasm for the chaos, corruption and weak and unstable government that political democracy ushered in, to different degrees, in Korea, Thailand, the Philippines and (after the crisis began) Indonesia, which contributed to the severity of the crisis both by weakening government macroeconomic control in some cases, and by increasing financial markets' perception and punishment of political risk in these countries.

## CONCLUSION

Clearly, both the Western economists' and Western political scientists' competing open and statist models, respectively, have, in some sense, failed with the crisis in their showcase economies in Asia. On the one hand, market openness without the requisite institutional infrastructure and expertise—including political infrastructure and managerial expertise—to manage it can be a recipe for economic disaster. Even the normal workings of global financial markets themselves can be disruptive to small open economies. On the other hand, statist industrial policy can lead to crony capitalism, excess capacity, over-leverage and bad investments (as can Western sociologists' "culturally embedded networks" of ethnic business relationships or *guanxi)*. Both openness and statism have contributed not only to the Asian miracle, but also to the Asian meltdown.

What about "Asian values"? At first glance, the indictment of openness and democracy in the crisis, and the need that all see for more state-led institution building, state monitoring if not control of private sector financial transactions, and state autonomy from private interests in the political sphere, might seem to be a confirmation of the wisdom of the Asian values school. Too much freedom too fast in both markets and politics can lead to downfall, suggesting a continued need for strong, benevolent central state authority.

But at the same time Asian government involvement in industrial policy and Asian cultural networks may also be indicted for fostering the crony capitalism which led to over-investment in bad projects—ranging from Indonesia's Timor "national car" project (of then President Suharto's son), to Malaysia's privatization of huge public infrastructure projects favoring politically well-connected businesses and individuals, and the over-extension of credit by overseas Chinese-owned banks to overseas Chinese industrial conglomerates with the presumed security of "relationships" substituting for modern risk assessment. The fact that policy errors committed by the authoritarian regime in Indonesia before its downfall in 1998 compounded both the economic crisis and its adverse social and political consequences in that country also undermines the belief of some Asian values advocates that authoritarianism might be superior to democracy in economic policy management. The Indonesian experience of massive economic and political collapse under authoritarianism contrasts vividly with the market confidence inspired by the policy statements and actions of democratically elected President Kim Dae Jung of Korea, and the Korean economy's own spectacular recovery from the crisis in 1999, while Indonesia still languished.

In short, the Asian economic crisis does not provide unqualified support for *either* the Western open-markets-and-democracy model *or* the Asian strong-government-and-cultural-values model. Both need some adjustment for global and national capitalisms to work smoothly. Certainly the paths to capital market liberalization and democracy should be carefully planned, and perhaps staged to occur only in line with the concomitant development of supportive state and civil institutions. At the same time, governments need to resist the pressures of would-be crony capitalists to interfere with their fiscal, monetary and regulatory autonomy, while private sector business networks need to be adjusted to adequately account for risk and to reduce purely rent-seeking behavior.

The Asian crisis has exposed the futility of applying simplistic and essentially ideological models to the messy practical business of public and private sector economic management in developing countries whose political, economic and business systems are not only diverse and complexly intertwined, but also still evolving. Far from yet another presaging of the end of history—in this case the presumed triumph of "Western" over "Asian" models—the crisis suggests that it is time to *return* to history, that is, to each country's particular configuration of economic, political, social and cultural forces, to discern both the complex, multi-faceted causes of the crisis, and its eventual solutions. This is a task too important to allow to be jeopardized by those who would approach it only through the limited lenses of partial, monocausal theories and models of one or the other cultural-ideological predilection.

# 24

# THE WORLD IS TEN YEARS OLD: THE NEW ERA OF GLOBALIZATION

## THOMAS L. FRIEDMAN

"Globalization" is widely used to describe the rapid integration of the world's societies and especially its economies during the past decade. Thomas L. Friedman tells us what globalization means, contrasting it with its early twentieth-century counterpart and with the Cold War world. "The globalization system, which replaced the Cold War system," he argues, is a "dynamic ongoing process" that "involves the inexorable integration of markets, nation-states and technologies to a degree never before witnessed." Friedman is foreign affairs columnist for the *New York Times*. A Pulitzer Prize winner, he is author of *From Beirut to Jerusalem* (1989) and *The Lexus and the Olive Tree* (1999), from which this chapter is extracted.

On the morning of December 8, 1997, the government of Thailand announced that it was closing fifty-six of the country's fifty-eight top finance houses. Almost overnight, these private banks had been bankrupted by the crash of the Thai currency, the baht. The finance houses had borrowed heavily in U.S. dollars and lent those dollars out to Thai businesses for the building of hotels, office blocks, luxury apartments and factories. The finance houses all thought they were safe because the Thai government was committed to keeping the Thai baht at a fixed rate against the dollar. But when the government failed to do so, in the wake of massive global speculation against the baht—triggered by a daring awareness that the Thai economy was not as strong as previously believed—the Thai currency plummeted by 30 percent. This meant that businesses that had borrowed dollars had to come up with 30 percent more Thai baht to pay back each one dollar of loans. Many businesses couldn't pay the finance houses back, many finance houses couldn't repay their foreign lenders and the whole system went into gridlock, putting twenty thousand white-collar employees out of work. The next day, I happened to be driving to an appointment in Bangkok down Asoke Street, Thailand's equivalent of Wall Street, where most of the bankrupt finance houses were located. As we slowly passed each one of these fallen firms, my cabdriver pointed them out, pronouncing at each one: "Dead! . . . dead! . . . dead! . . . dead! . . . dead!"

I did not know it at the time—no one did—but these Thai investment houses were the first dominoes in what would prove to be the first global financial crisis of the new era of globalization—the era that followed the Cold War. The Thai crisis triggered a general flight of capital out of virtually all the Southeast Asian emerging markets, driving down the value of currencies in South Korea, Malaysia and Indonesia. Both global and local investors started scrutinizing these economies more closely, found them wanting, and either moved their cash out to safer havens or demanded higher interest rates to compensate for the higher risk.

\*\*\*

[*USA*] *Today* aptly summed up the global marketplace at the end of 1998: "The trouble spread to one continent after another like a virus," the paper noted. "U.S. markets reacted instantaneously . . . People in barbershops actually talked about the Thai baht."

\*\*\*

[The] slow, stable, chopped-up Cold War system that had dominated international affairs since 1945 [has] been firmly replaced by a new, very greased, interconnected system called globalization. We are all one river. If we didn't fully understand that in 1989, when the Berlin Wall came down, we sure understood it a decade later. Indeed, on October 11, 1998, at the height of the global economic crisis, Merrill Lynch ran full-page ads in major newspapers throughout America to drive this point home. The ads read:

### The World Is 10 Years Old

It was born when the Wall fell in 1989. It's no surprise that the world's youngest economy—the global economy—is still finding its bearings. The intricate checks and balances that stabilize economies are only incorporated with time. Many world markets are only recently freed, governed for the first time by the emotions of the people rather than the fists of the state. From where we sit, none of this diminishes the promise offered a decade ago by the demise of the walled-off world . . . The spread of free markets and democracy around the world is permitting more people everywhere to turn their aspirations into achievements. And technology, properly harnessed and liberally distributed, has the power to erase not just geographical borders but also human ones. It seems to us that, for a 10-year-old, the world continues to hold great promise. In the meantime, no one ever said growing up was easy.

Actually, the Merrill Lynch ad would have been a little more correct to say that *this* era of globalization is ten years old. Because from the mid-1800s to the late 1920s the world experienced a similar era of globalization. If you compared the volumes of trade and capital flows across borders, relative to GNPs, and the flow of labor across borders, relative to populations, the period of globalization preceding World War I was quite similar to the one we are living through today. Great Britain, which was then the dominant global power, was a huge investor in emerging markets, and fat cats in England, Europe and America were often buffeted by financial crises, triggered by something that happened in Argentine railroad bonds, Latvian government bonds or German government bonds. There were no currency controls, so no sooner was the transatlantic cable connected in 1866 than banking and financial crises in New York were quickly being transmitted to London or Paris. I was on a panel once with John Monks, the head of the British Trades Union Congress, the AFL-CIO of Britain, who remarked that the agenda for the TUC's first Congress in Manchester, England, in 1868, listed among the items that needed to be discussed: "The need to deal with competition from the Asian colonies" and "The need to match the educational and training standards of the United States and Germany." In those days, people also migrated more than we remember, and, other than in wartime, countries did not require passports for travel before 1914. All those immigrants who flooded America's shores came without visas. When you put all of these factors together, along with the inventions of the steamship, telegraph, railroad and eventually telephone, it is safe to say that this first era of globalization before World War I shrank the world from a size "large" to a size "medium."

\*\*\*

This first era of globalization and global finance capitalism was broken apart by the successive hammer blows of World War I, the Russian Revolution and the Great Depression, which combined to fracture the world both physically and ideologically. The formally divided world that emerged after World War II was then frozen in place by the Cold War. The Cold War was also an international system. It lasted roughly from 1945 to 1989, when, with the fall of the Berlin Wall, it was replaced by another system: the new era of globalization we are now in. Call it "Globalization Round II." It turns out that the roughly seventy-five-year period from the start of World War I to the end of the Cold War was just a long time-out between one era of globalization and another.

While there are a lot of similarities in kind between the previous era of globalization and the one we are now in, what is new today is the degree and intensity with which the world is being tied together into a single globalized marketplace. What is also new is the sheer number of people and countries able to partake of this process and be affected by it. The pre-1914 era of globalization may have been intense, but many developing countries in that era were left out of it. The pre-1914 era may have been large in scale relative to its time, but it was minuscule in absolute terms compared to today. Daily foreign exchange trading in 1900 was measured in the millions of dollars. In 1992, it was $820 billion a day, according to the New York Federal Reserve, and by April 1998 it was up to $1.5 trillion a day, and still rising. In the last decade alone total cross-border lending by banks around the world has doubled. Around 1900, private capital flows from developed countries to developing ones could be measured in the hundreds of millions of dollars and relatively few countries were involved. According to the IMF, in 1997 alone, private capital flows from the developed world to all emerging markets totaled $215 billion. This new era of globalization, compared to the one before World War I, is turbocharged.

But today's era of globalization is not only different in degree; in some very important ways it is also different in kind. As the *Economist* once noted, the previous era of globalization was built around falling transportation costs. Thanks to the invention of the railroad, the steamship and the automobile, people could get to a lot more places faster and cheaper and they could trade with a lot more places faster and cheaper. Today's era of globalization is built around falling telecommunications costs—thanks to microchips, satellites, fiber optics and the Internet. These new technologies are able to weave the world together even tighter. These technologies mean that developing countries don't just have to trade their raw materials to the West and get finished products in return; they mean that developing countries can become big-time producers as well. These technologies also allowed companies to locate different parts of their production, research and marketing in different countries, but still tie them together through computers and teleconferencing as though they were in one place. Also, thanks to the combination of computers and cheap telecommunications, people can now offer and trade services globally—from medical advice to software writing to data processing—that could never really be traded before. And why not? According to the *Economist,* a three-minute call (in 1996 dollars) between New York and London cost $300 in 1930. Today it is almost free through the Internet.

But what also makes this era of globalization unique is not just the fact that these technologies are making it possible for traditional nation-states and corporations to reach farther, faster, cheaper and deeper around the world than ever before. It is the fact that it is allowing individuals to do so. I was reminded of this point one day in the summer of 1998 when my then seventy-nine-year-old mother, Margaret Friedman, who lives in Minneapolis, called me sounding very upset. "What's wrong, Mom?" I asked. "Well," she said, "I've been playing bridge on the Internet with three Frenchmen and they keep speaking French to each other and I can't understand them." When I chuckled at the thought of my card shark mom playing bridge with three Frenchmen on the Net, she took a little umbrage. "Don't laugh," she said, "I was playing bridge with someone in Siberia the other day."

To all those who say that this era of globalization is no different from the previous one, I would simply ask: Was your great-grandmother playing bridge with Frenchmen on the Internet in 1900? I don't think so. There are some things about this era of globalization that we've seen before, and some things that we've never seen before and some things that are so new we don't even understand them yet. For all these reasons, I would sum up the differences between the two eras of globalization this way: If the first era of globalization shrank the world from a size "large" to a size "medium," this era of globalization is shrinking the world from a size "medium" to a size "small."

\*\*\*

[I] believe that if you want to understand the post–Cold War world you have to start by understanding that a new international system has succeeded it— globalization. That is "The One Big Thing" people should focus on. Globalization is not the only thing influencing events in the world today, but to the extent that there is a North Star and a worldwide shaping force, it is this system. What is new is the system; what is old is power politics, chaos, clashing civilizations and liberalism. And what is the drama of the post–Cold War world is the interaction between this new system and these old passions. It is a complex drama, with the final act still not written. That is why under the globalization system you will find both clashes of civilization and the homogenization of civilizations, both environmental disasters and amazing environmental rescues, both the triumph of liberal, free-market capitalism and a backlash against it, both the durability of nation-states and the rise of enormously powerful nonstate actors.

\*\*\*

When I speak of the "the Cold War system" and "the globalization system," what do I mean?

I mean that, as an international system, the Cold War had its own structure of power: the balance between the United States and the U.S.S.R. The Cold War had its own rules: in foreign affairs, neither superpower would encroach on the other's sphere of influence; in economics, less developed countries would focus on nurturing their own national industries, developing countries on export-led growth, communist countries on autarky and Western economies on regulated trade. The Cold War had its own dominant ideas: the clash between communism and capitalism, as well as detente, nonalignment and perestroika. The Cold War had its own demographic trends the movement of peoples from east to west was largely frozen by the Iron Curtain, but the movement from south to north was a more steady flow. The Cold War had its own perspective on the globe: the world was a space divided into the communist camp, the Western camp, and the neutral camp, and everyone's country was in one of them. The Cold War had its own defining technologies: nuclear weapons and the second Industrial Revolution were dominant, but for many people in developing countries the hammer and sickle were still relevant tools. The Cold War had its own defining measurement: the throw weight of nuclear missiles. And lastly, the Cold War had its own defining anxiety: nuclear annihilation. When taken all together the elements of this Cold War system influenced the domestic politics and foreign relations of virtually every country in the world. The Cold War system didn't shape everything, but it shaped many things.

Today's era of globalization, which replaced the Cold War, is a similar international system, with its own unique attributes.

To begin with, the globalization system, unlike the Cold War system, is not static, but a dynamic ongoing process: globalization involves the inexorable integration of markets, nation-states and technologies to a degree never witnessed before—in a way that is enabling individuals, corporations and nation-states to reach around the world farther, faster, deeper and cheaper than ever before, and in a way that is also producing a powerful backlash from those brutalized or left behind by this new system.

The driving idea behind globalization is free-market capitalism—the more you let market forces rule and the more you open your economy to free trade and competition, the more efficient and flourishing your economy will be. Globalization means the spread of free-market capitalism to virtually every country in the world. Globalization also has its own set of economic rules—rules that revolve around opening, deregulating and privatizing your economy.

Unlike the Cold War system, globalization has its own dominant culture, which is why it tends to be homogenizing. In previous eras this sort of cultural homogenization happened on a regional scale—the Hellenization of the Near East and the Mediterranean world under the Greeks, the Turkification of Central Asia, North Africa, Europe and the Middle East by the Ottomans, or the Russification of Eastern and Central Europe and parts of Eurasia under the Soviets. Culturally speaking, globalization is largely, though not entirely, the spread of Americanization—from Big Macs to iMacs to Mickey Mouse—on a global scale.

Globalization has its own defining technologies: computerization, miniaturization, digitization, satellite communications, fiber optics and the Internet. And these technologies helped to create the defining perspective of globalization. If the defining perspective of the Cold War world was "division," the defining perspective of globalization is "integration." The symbol of the Cold War system was a wall which divided everyone. The symbol of the globalization system is a World Wide Web, which unites everyone. The defining document of the Cold War system was "The Treaty." The defining document of the globalization system is "The Deal."

Once a country makes the leap into the system of globalization, its elites begin to internalize this perspective of integration, and always try to locate themselves in a global context. I was visiting Amman, Jordan, in the summer of 1998 and having coffee at the Inter-Continental Hotel with my friend Rami Khouri, the leading political columnist in Jordan. We sat down and I asked him what was new. The first thing he said to me was: "Jordan was just added to CNN's worldwide weather highlights." What Rami was saying was that it is important for Jordan to know that those institutions which think globally believe it is now worth knowing: what the weather is like in Amman. It makes Jordanians feel more important and holds out the hope that they will be enriched by having more tourists or global investors visiting. The day after seeing Rami I happened to go to

Israel and meet with Jacob Frenkel, governor of Israel's Central Bank and a University of Chicago-trained economist. Frenkel remarked that he too was going through a perspective change: "Before, when we talked about macroeconomics, we started by looking at the local markets, local financial system and the interrelationship between them, and then, as an afterthought, we looked at the international economy. There was a feeling that what we do is primarily our own business and then there are some outlets where we will sell abroad. Now we reverse the perspective. Let's not ask what markets we should export to, after having decided what to produce; rather let's first study the global framework within which we operate and then decide what to produce. It changes your whole perspective."

While the defining measurement of the Cold War was weight—particularly the throw weight of missiles—the defining measurement of the globalization system is speed—speed of commerce, travel, communication and innovation. The Cold War was about Einstein's mass-energy equation, $e = mc^2$. Globalization is about Moore's law, which states that the computing power of silicon chips will double every eighteen to twenty-four months. In the Cold War, the most frequently asked question was: "How big is your missile?" In globalization, the most frequently asked question is: "How fast is your modem?"

If the defining economists of the Cold War system were Karl Marx and John Maynard Keynes, who each in his own way wanted to tame capitalism, the defining economists of the globalization system are Joseph Schumpeter and Intel chairman Andy Grove, who prefer to unleash capitalism. Schumpeter, a former Austrian Minister of Finance and Harvard Business School professor, expressed the view in his classic work *Capitalism, Socialism and Democracy* that the essence of capitalism is the process of "creative destruction"—the perpetual cycle of destroying the old and less efficient product or service and replacing it with near, more efficient ones. Andy Grove took Schumpeter's insight that "only the paranoid survive" for the title of his book on life in Silicon Valley, and made it in many ways the business model of globalization capitalism Grove helped to popularize the view that dramatic, industry-transforming innovations are taking place today faster and faster. Thanks to these technological breakthroughs, the speed by which your latest invention can be made obsolete or turned into a commodity is now lightning quick. Therefore, only the paranoid, only those who are constantly looking over their shoulders to see who is creating something new that will destroy them and then staying just one step ahead of them, will survive. Those countries that are most willing to let capitalism quickly destroy inefficient companies, so that money can be freed up and directed to more innovative ones, will thrive in the era of globalization. Those which rely on their governments to protect them from such creative destruction will fall behind in this era.

James Surowiecki, the business columnist for *Slate* magazine, reviewing Grove's book, neatly summarized what Schumpeter and Grove have in common, which is the essence of globalization economics. It is the notion that: "Innovation replaces tradition. The present—or perhaps the future—replaces the past.

Nothing matters so much as what will come next and what will come next can only arrive if what is here now gets overturned. While this makes the system a terrific place for innovation, it makes it a difficult place to live, since most people prefer some measure of security about the future to a life lived in almost constant uncertainty . . . We are not forced to re-create our relationships with those closest to us on a regular basis. And yet that's precisely what Schumpeter, and Grove after him, suggest is necessary to prosper [today]."

Indeed, if the Cold War were a sport, it would be sumo wrestling, says Johns Hopkins University foreign affairs professor Michael Mandelbaum. "It would be two big fat guys in a ring, with all sorts of posturing and rituals and stomping of feet, but actually very little contact, until the end of the match, when there is a brief moment of shoving and the loser gets pushed out of the ring, but nobody gets killed."

By contrast, if globalization were a sport, it would be the 100-meter dash, over and over and over. And no matter how many times you win, you have to race again the next day. And if you lose by just one-hundredth of a second it can be as if you lost by an hour. (Just ask French multinationals. In 1999, French labor laws were changed, requiring—*requiring*—every employer to implement a four-hour reduction in the legal workweek, from 39 hours to 35 hours, with no cut in pay. Many French firms were fighting the move because of the impact it would have on their productivity in a global market. Henri Thierry, human resources director for Thomson-CSF Communications, a high-tech firm in the suburbs of Paris, told the *Washington Post:* "We are in a worldwide competition. If we lose one point of productivity, we lose orders. If we're obliged to go to 35 hours it would be like requiring French athletes to run the 100 meters wearing flippers. They wouldn't have much of a chance winning a medal.")

To paraphrase German political theorist Carl Schmitt, the Cold War was a world of "friends" and "enemies." The globalization world, by contrast, tends to turn all friends and enemies into "competitors."

If the defining anxiety of the Cold War was fear of annihilation from an enemy you knew all too well in a world struggle that was fixed and stable, the defining anxiety in globalization is fear of rapid change from an enemy you can't see, touch or feel—a sense that your job, community or workplace can be changed at any moment by anonymous economic and technological forces that are anything but stable.

In the Cold War we reached for the hot line between the White House and the Kremlin—a symbol that we were all divided but at least someone, the two superpowers, was in charge. In the era of globalization we reach for the Internet—a symbol that we are all connected but nobody is in charge. The defining defense system of the Cold War was radar—to expose the threats coming from the other side of the wall. The defining defense system of the globalization era is the X-ray machine—to expose the threats coming from within.

Globalization also has its own demographic pattern—a rapid acceleration of the movement of people from rural areas and agricultural lifestyles to urban areas and urban lifestyles more intimately linked with global fashion, food, markets and entertainment trends.

Last, and most important, globalization has its own defining structure of power, which is much more complex than the Cold War structure. The Cold War system was built exclusively around nation-states, and it was balanced at the center by two superpowers: the United States and the Soviet Union.

The globalization system, by contrast, is built around three balances, which overlap and affect one another. The first is the traditional balance between nation-states. In the globalization system, the United States is now the sole and dominant superpower and all other nations are subordinate to it to one degree or another. The balance of power between the United States and the other states still matters for the stability of this system. And it can still explain a lot of the news you read on the front page of the papers, whether it is the containment of Iraq in the Middle East or the expansion of NATO against Russia in Central Europe.

The second balance in the globalization system is between nation-states and global markets. These global markets are made up of millions of investors moving money around the world with the click of a mouse. I call them "the Electronic Herd," and this herd gathers in key global financial centers, such as Wall Street, Hong Kong, London and Frankfurt, which I call "the Supermarkets." The attitudes and actions of the Electronic Herd and the Supermarkets can have a huge impact on nation-states today, even to the point of triggering the downfall of governments. You will not understand the front page of newspapers today—whether it is the story of the toppling of Suharto in Indonesia, the internal collapse in Russia or the monetary policy of the United States—unless you bring the Supermarkets into your analysis.

The United States can destroy you by dropping bombs and the Supermarkets can destroy you by downgrading your bonds. The United States is the dominant player in maintaining the globalization gameboard, but it is not alone in influencing the moves on that gameboard. This globalization gameboard today is a lot like a Ouija board—sometimes pieces are moved around by the obvious hand of the superpower, and sometimes they are moved around by hidden hands of the Supermarkets.

The third balance that you have to pay attention to in the globalization system—the one that is really the newest of all—is the balance between individuals and nation-states. Because globalization has brought down many of the walls that limited the movement and reach of people, and because it has simultaneously wired the world into networks, it gives more power to individuals to influence both markets and nation-states than at any time in history. So you have today not only a superpower, not only Supermarkets, but, as I will also demonstrate later in the book, you have Super-empowered individuals. Some of these Super-empowered individuals are quite angry, some of them quite wonderful—but all of them are now able to act directly on the world stage without the traditional mediation of governments, corporations or any other public or private institutions.

Without the knowledge of the U.S. government, Long-Term Capital Management—a few guys in Greenwich, Connecticut—amassed more financial bets around the world than all the foreign reserves of China. Osama bin Laden, a Saudi millionaire with his own global network, declared war on the United States in the late 1990s, and the U.S. Air Force had to launch a cruise missile attack on him as though he were another nation-state. We fired cruise missiles at an individual! Jody Williams won the Nobel Peace Prize in 1997 for her contribution to the international ban on landmines. She achieved that ban not only without much government help, but in the face of opposition from the Big Five major powers. And what did she say was her secret weapon for organizing one thousand different human rights and arms control groups on six continents? "E-mail."

Nation-states, and the American superpower in particular, are still hugely important today, but so too now are Supermarkets and Super-empowered individuals. You will never understand the globalization system, or the front page of the morning paper, unless you see it as a complex interaction between all three of these actors: states bumping up against states, states bumping up against Supermarkets, and Supermarkets and states bumping up against Super-empowered individuals.

\*\*\*

# 25

# WORKERS OF THE WORLD, NOW WHAT?

KATHLEEN NEWLAND

**In the fast-paced world of globalization, the world's workers often find themselves left behind. Kathleen Newland asks why labor has been left out of the "banquet" while "international capital, trade, and business feast on open markets, heightened efficiency, and vanishing barriers in the new global marketplace." She explains why the answer "is partly structural, partly institutional, and entirely political." Newland is senior associate at the Carnegie Endowment for International Peace, where she directs its International Migration Policy Program, and author of *Strangers in Their Own Land: Migration in Post-Soviet Russia* (2000).**

There is an empty seat at the banquet of economic globalization. While international capital, trade, and business feast on open markets, heightened efficiency, and vanishing barriers in the new global marketplace, labor is nowhere to be found. Why has labor been left out? The explanation is partly structural, partly institutional, and entirely political.

At some point in the 1980s, the balance of power shifted markedly against labor. Some place the defining moment in 1981, when then–U.S. president Ronald Reagan forced an end to the bitter air traffic controllers' strike. Others point to the 1985 victory of then–British prime minister Margaret Thatcher over striking coal miners.

Labor's long downward slide, however, actually began much earlier. The 1970s saw the rise of manufacturing centers outside the industrialized North. Multina-

307

tional corporations began to take advantage of liberalized trade and capital flows to move production to the most advantageous locations—often those with lower labor costs. The deep recessions of the 1970s slashed production. Despite economic recovery in the 1980s and 1990s, the share of total wages as part of the gross domestic product has fallen in almost every member country of the Organization for Economic Cooperation and Development. The supply-and-demand equation further tilted against labor as the global work force ballooned from 1.3 billion in 1965 to 2.5 billion in 1995, owing to rapid population growth in the developing countries and the unprecedented rate at which women entered the labor market.

In the older manufacturing centers of the industrialized countries, organized labor found itself on unfamiliar terrain. High unemployment and the looming threat of plant relocation weakened some of labor's traditional bargaining chips: The prospect of a union walkout became far less devastating when substitute workers were so readily available both at home and abroad. Meanwhile, the majority of new jobs were being generated in the service sector, where unions were traditionally weak. And in many European countries, most notably Britain, trade unions took part of the blame for the rigidity that inhibited quick response to changing conditions and kept national economies mired in recession—a syndrome that the press christened "Eurosclerosis."

By the time center-right electoral victories swept much of Europe and North America in the 1980s, the stage was set for a neoliberal consensus, backed by real political muscle, that frowned on almost all attempts to constrain the operation of free markets, whether in goods, services, labor, or commodities. Most initiatives on behalf of labor—such as the regulation of wages and benefits, the protection of job security, the enforcement of a minimum age of employment, or the promotion of safety standards—were seen as unwelcome distortions of the workings of competitive labor markets.

But the recent financial crises in Asia, Latin America, and Russia and the political unrest that has come in their wake have challenged the neoliberal consensus and seriously eroded confidence in global economic restructuring. Even the so-called Asian tiger economies that embraced restructuring most ardently have watched its rewards evaporate. The International Labour Organization (ILO) estimates that 10 million workers were added to the ranks of the world's unemployed in 1998, in large part due to the Asian economic meltdown. The consequences of these crises—growing poverty, shredded safety nets, and a higher cost of living—are borne mostly by ordinary working men and women.

Clearly, a better balance needs to be struck between pursuing globalization's benefits and protecting against its hazards. Organized labor must strive to exert itself more forcefully in that equation. However, it remains to be seen whether it can overcome the structural and institutional constraints that have weakened unions in the past two decades. Additional, less-institutionalized ways of promoting the interests of working people may need to be developed.

## THE BRAVE NEW WORKING WORLD

In recent years, the world of work has changed enormously, but organized labor has been slow to adapt. Economic globalization has brought about huge increases in international capital flows, a rapid expansion of cross-border trade in goods and services, a rise in foreign direct investment, and explosions in cheap technology, international travel, and communications. And while labor mobility at both the high and low ends of the job market has increased as well, it still pales in comparison with the almost frictionless movement of capital across international borders. At a time when over 22 percent of the world's output is traded internationally, a mere 2 percent of the world's people live outside their countries of origin. And only some of them have migrated for employment purposes.

Although capital is subject to very little political control as it travels in search of the highest return, workers—particularly the unskilled and the poor—are often prevented from following suit. Even as capital controls have virtually disappeared and trade barriers have fallen, marry countries have raised barriers to immigration. This trend is particularly manifest in Western Europe, where a decade of slow growth and high unemployment has prompted governments to clamp down on the intake of foreign labor. In the European Union (EU), the commitment to freedom of movement among member states has been accompanied by stringent measures to defend the external borders against unauthorized entry.

Immigration restrictions, however, are not the only forces that impede the mobility of labor. Some social and economic advantages, such as access to welfare or pension benefits, rights to political participation, or recognition of professional qualifications, are dependent on residence in a certain country or community. And workers often have linguistic, sentimental, or other attachments to their native countries that outweigh the desire to find work elsewhere. In the EU, for example, only about 2 percent of the population have taken advantage of their new-found freedom of movement.

Alongside the relative immobility of workers, organized labor's weakened influence can also be traced to the changing face of the work force in a globalized economy. Low-end labor in globalized industries such as apparel and toy manufacturing is younger, more female, more dispersed, and less enfranchised—all traits that traditional union membership does not have. High-end workers in the knowledge and technology sectors have generally remained unconvinced that their interests are served by collective bargaining. Even more significantly, most of the growth in the job market is taking place outside the established union base of stable, full-time, blue-collar manufacturing work in long-industrialized countries. These new, low-wage, service-sector jobs are often with small companies in marginally competitive industries that have high turnover rates, such as food preparation or janitorial services. Much of the work is part-time, short-term, sporadic, contractual, or home-based.

In low-income countries, only 15 percent of the work force is in the formal sector. Although these factors render traditional union outreach strategies almost useless, most unions have been slow to adopt new strategies or offer new services. To complicate matters further, these "irregular" workers are often pitted against unionized labor as employers seek to lower their costs.

Some labor unions also suffer from the perception that they are little more than special-interest groups whose first priority is to defend the privileges and status of their members—who account for an ever-smaller portion of the work force. This view makes it difficult not only for organized labor to attract and retain members but also to be considered a legitimate representative of the general interests of workers in the dialogue on economic restructuring. Unions tend to benefit when they take an expansive view of their role—seeking to represent not only the concerns of their members but those of working people in general (or indeed of society at large) against the special interests of capital. European unions, which are often affiliated with broad-based political parties, have routinely adopted this stance. When a union such as Solidarity in Poland or the United Mine Workers in South Africa stands at the forefront of a popular social struggle, it both enhances the labor movement's popular esteem and boosts union membership. (Although even Solidarity's stature declined precipitously when it became identified with unpopular government policies in postcommunist Poland.)

Such broad social representation, however, is far easier to achieve at the national level than at the international one. Workers in poorer and less-developed nations often view unions based in the advanced industrial countries as defenders of privilege. Their suspicions persist that such unions' insistence on increased wages, conformity with labor standards, and environmental safeguards for Third World workers is simply a disguised form of protectionism, designed to undercut the developing world's main source of comparative advantage: low labor costs. . . .

The macroeconomic climate has been as inhospitable to unions as the microeconomy of individual firms. Widespread government deregulation in the 1980s, combined with high levels of government debt in the 1990s, increased governments' reliance on international financial markets and gave those markets increased leverage over the economic policies adopted by individual nations. But global financial markets tend to shy away from precisely the kinds of policies that unions have traditionally advocated—full employment, high growth, and a tendency to lower interest rates and increase public spending when employment rates flag. The threat of capital flight (and the ensuing currency devaluations and higher inflation) and the desire to attract international capital to finance deficits and spur economic growth have prompted even center-left governments to turn a deaf ear to union preferences.

The markets instead favored neoliberal reforms that have only spelled trouble for labor. Tighter fiscal controls prompted governments to downsize public-sector payrolls and pensions. Stabilization policies aimed at reducing inflation and controlling prices in some cases included wage freezes. Liberal trade policies have led to increased competition, which often means that inefficient industries must shed labor and, in some cases, may be forced out of business entirely. In this climate, unions in many countries have had increasing difficulty delivering tangible results to their members. In the United States, for example, labor-organizing drives in the 1980s produced lower gains in wages and benefits and less employment growth than had earlier unionization efforts.

Perversely, at a time when circumstances cry out for strong union representation, organized labor makes up a smaller and smaller proportion of the global labor force. Over the last 10 years [1989–1999], the rate of unionization [fell] by more than 20 percent in 35 of the 66 countries for which comparable data are available. The sharpest declines were seen in Argentina, Australia, Costa Rica, France, Israel, Mexico, New Zealand, Portugal, the United States, and Venezuela. The former Eastern bloc countries also experienced dramatic declines due to the end of compulsory membership in officially sanctioned unions. In most of these countries, independent trade unions have not yet established themselves. Only Hong Kong (prior to the resumption of Chinese control in 1997) and the Philippines have seen union membership increase significantly.

## WHO SPEAKS FOR LABOR?

In the debate over economic globalization and its attendant reforms, the interests of governments, businesses, and financial capital are all well represented at the institutional level. Powerful international organizations have arisen to promote the global mobility of capital on the one hand (the International Monetary Fund) and goods and services on the other (the General Agreement on Tariffs and Trade and its successor, the WTO).

But it remains unclear who looks out for the workers at the sharp end of global restructuring. Certainly no international organization actively promotes the mobility of labor—that responsibility is still considered to be firmly within the ambit of national sovereignty. The one international organization charged with promoting the interests of workers, the ILO, has been all but invisible in the global debate.

Founded in 1919, the ILO today is seen by many as an anachronism, too closely tied to trade union organizations that are having trouble keeping up in the new global economy. The ILO's headquarters, which sit like a massive gray supertanker run aground in the green hills of Geneva, seem a metaphor for the organization's detachment and inflexibility.

At the time of the ILO's creation, the Bolshevik Revolution still loomed large in policy makers' minds. Giving labor a role in setting the rules of the international economic game was seen as the price to be paid for social peace. The ILO was established accordingly, with a remarkably innovative three-part structure in which workers and employers were officially represented in the governing body along with governments themselves. Its primary mechanism for achieving "social justice" in the world of work was regulatory. The ILO oversaw the creation of internationally agreed-upon labor standards covering everything from hours of work and minimum wage to the prohibition of forced labor, and became the primary vehicle for articulating, negotiating, and supervising these standards.

---

UNIONS PLUS

The past 10 years have seen a resurgence of creative actions to defend the rights of the traditionally powerless: sweatshop employees, informal-sector workers, child laborers, and immigrant workers. These initiatives range from the campaign against harsh conditions and low wages in the overseas factories that produce Nike shoes, to the drive for self-regulation in the form of voluntary codes of conduct by apparel makers, to the massive lobbying effort by immigrant workers that led to the adoption of a tough wage enforcement law in New York State in 1997. The driving force behind these campaigns has been a diverse coalition composed of organized labor, nonunion workers, activist lawyers, human rights groups, foundations, academics, and even celebrities.

By relying on a combination of legal action, media exposure of abuses, consumer boycotts, legislation, and negotiation, these coalitions have demonstrated a power far beyond what unions alone were able to achieve in the 1980s and 1990s with more traditional tactics. In today's labor-abundant world, conventional strikes pose much less of a threat to mobile industries, but advocates have learned to apply pressure elsewhere.

One particularly noteworthy effort began in January 1999, when apparel workers on Saipan—part of the Northern Marianas Islands, a U.S. commonwealth in the South Pacific—filed a massive lawsuit against 18 prominent American clothing manufacturers and retailers, charging them with conspiracy to hold workers in involuntary servitude in sweatshop conditions. The action [sought] more than $1 billion in damages on behalf of as many as 50,000 workers. It [alleged] that many of the predominantly young immigrant women employed in the garment factories [were] forced to work 12 hours a day, seven days a week, and sometimes [were] denied pay if they [fell] behind on production quotas.

The lawsuit . . . is unusual not only in its size and scope but also in the number and kind of plaintiffs involved. The plaintiffs [included] nonunion apparel workers; the U.S. Union of Needletrades, Industrial, and Textile Employees; human rights organizations such as Global Exchange and Sweatshop Watch; and a group of private law firms. Reports from the U.S. Labor and Interior Departments [formed] part of the brief. The apparel firms [were] not only charged with violating wage and hours laws but also with violating international human rights law, local Marianas laws, U.S. anti-racketeering laws, and their own voluntary codes of conduct.

The apparel companies targeted by the lawsuit have more to lose than just money. The Marianas case is another in a series of public-relations blows to an industry eager to shed the image of its factories as sweatshops—an image that consumers increasingly do not tolerate. More creative and broader-based actions appear to be putting some muscle back into demands for workers' rights, and unions are finding that the scope for solidarity goes beyond the labor movement alone.

—K.N.

---

In the aftermath of World War II, the architects of the new international economic framework were still reeling from the rise of communism, fascism, and the devastation of the war itself. Wary that ignoring labor could lead to further social upheaval and increase the appeal of communism, the framers once again took steps to ensure that workers' interests were factored into the new economic equation. At the domestic level, governments drafted economic compacts, established social safety nets, encouraged the growth of trade unions, and ensured distribution of the benefits of growth through investment in public education, housing, and other social infrastructure. The Governing Body of the ILO sought to reinforce the concept of partnership; in 1944, the ILO constitution was revised to include a declaration that "labour is not a commodity."

In recent years, however, the ILO has struggled to find ways to accommodate labor's changing needs in a globalized economy. It has produced some powerful analyses of globalization and its discontents but has not found a wide audience for these findings or translated them into effective action. The ILO's emphasis on regulation stands in stark contrast to the mobility and flexibility that are the hallmarks of globalized production. The organization relies on moral suasion and voluntary compliance with standards but cannot really sanction violators. Moreover, the innovative tripartite structure of 1919 is now more a source of impasse than of dynamism: Locked into channels of representation through employers' organizations and national trade union confederations, the organization is one step removed from actual unions and enterprises, not to mention from actual workers.

In today's complex environment, it may be unrealistic to expect the ILO—or any one institution—to represent the concerns of everyone from blue-collar industrial workers to civil servants to street vendors. Some of the newer voices speaking up for workers are alliances between multiple institutions: umbrella groups that encompass labor unions, progressive governments, international organization, activist lawyers, and a wide range of nongovernmental organizations (NGOs), including churches, foundations, academic institutions, human rights advocates, media organizations, consumer groups, issue-specific campaigners, and even some businesses. [See box on page 314.] Although such activism is by its very nature ad hoc and limited in scope, these flexible, issue-based coalitions have nonetheless shown enormous promise in articulating and advancing the interests of workers whom unions have not reached.

Aided largely by some of the same forces driving economic globalization, particularly the revolution in information technology, these transnational networks have the potential for enormous reach and impact. Consumer pressure, for example, persuaded the American Apparel Manufacturers Association, whose members represent 85 percent of the $100 billion worth of wholesale clothing manufactured annually in the United States, to devise a strict but voluntary code of conduct requiring that their factories and suppliers will neither use child labor nor subject their adult workers to sweatshop conditions.

Moreover, despite its long-standing resistance to forming alliances with such coalitions (some members of the Governing Body and the ILO bureaucracy argue that the NGOs and some of the other parties involved suffer from a democratic deficit and cannot truly claim to represent anyone but themselves), the ILO has recently displayed a greater openness to coalition building. The International Program on the Elimination of Child Labor, which has made progress toward minimizing child labor in industries such as soccer ball manufacturing in Pakistan, is ILO-based but involves many other international organizations, businesses, and NGOs and receives support from several governments. The ILO's cautious embrace of these new alliances signals an important movement in the right direction. But until it is seen to be dynamic and inclusive, the organization will not be treated as a full partner by financial institutions as they shape the new international economic framework.

## IS THE PENDULUM SWINGING?

Although the late 1990s [offered] no lesson as dramatic as that of the Bolshevik Revolution, there are some warning signs that point to the urgency of addressing labor's needs. Political and social turmoil has followed in the wake of financial crises in East Asia and Russia; economic reform efforts have been rolled back in Zambia and Venezuela; attempts at economic restructuring threaten political stability in Brazil and Mexico. Workers worldwide have been slow to reap globalization's rewards and have instead watched it shrink their social safety nets, squeeze wages, erode working conditions, and degrade public services. Kofi Annan, the U.N. secretary-general, bluntly laid out the consequences of turning a blind eye to these developments, warning that unless businesses worldwide strive to uphold labor standards and adopt codes of conduct, "we may find it increasingly difficult to make a persuasive case for the open global market."

Governments find themselves trying to navigate between the financial markets—which will punish them if they do not cut wages, public spending, and measures to guarantee job protection—and their own citizens, who will punish them if they do. This dilemma, however, may not be quite as intractable as it first appears. Citizens may actually tolerate harsh economic reforms if they feel that their interests have been taken into account in devising them, and if the reforms themselves are perceived as fair and effective. Stringent reform programs with severe social consequences have nonetheless enjoyed strong public support in Argentina (the Cavallo Plan), Brazil (the Cardoso Plan), Peru (Fujimori's economic program), and Poland (the Balcerowicz plan).

A strong labor movement can play an important role in building that kind of public confidence and can provide channels through which conflict over reforms can be addressed. There are encouraging signs that the pendulum that brought the labor movement low in the 1980s may be starting to swing in the opposite direction. In industrialized countries such as Britain, Canada, France, Germany, and Italy, center-left governments with labor roots have replaced center-right governments. If not entirely at one with organized labor, these new governments seem to recognize that those left behind by globalization pose a threat to open markets and liberal institutions; at the very least, they are not openly hostile to labor's interests. . . .

. . . If labor hopes to experience a true renaissance in the brave new world of globalization, it cannot model itself on its past. In the [new] century, unions will not work alone but rather with allies in human rights organizations and civil society, with progressively minded politicians, with international organizations, and with companies that have learned that they can benefit from a socially responsible labor policy.

Unions cannot respond to the challenges of globalization with little more than attempts to hold it back. Increased international competition and pressure to keep costs low are facts of life, but they need not lead to lower wages and fewer social benefits. Investment in skills, infrastructure, research and development, and better management can yield higher productivity and, in turn, justifiably higher wages. Increasingly, organized labor's role must be to forge—and in some cases to lead—alliances that empower workers to take advantage of flexible labor markets, ensure labor is not exploited in the name of greater production efficiency, and bring previously unrepresented workers into the social compact. Labor will find willing partners in government, civil society, and the private sector if it fills that role and will finally be able to claim its seat at the banquet table.

# 26

# COMPETITIVENESS: A DANGEROUS OBSESSION

PAUL KRUGMAN

Policymakers often worry about their states' competitiveness in the global marketplace and embrace domestic and foreign economic policies they believe will enhance their national fortunes. Economic trade theorist Paul Krugman chastises those seemingly obsessed with competitiveness, arguing that it "is a meaningless word when applied to national economies." Krugman is professor of economics at the Massachusetts Institute of Technology. His numerous books include *The Accidental Theorist and Other Dispatches from the Dismal Science* (**1999**).

## THE HYPOTHESIS IS WRONG

In June 1993, Jacques Delors made a special presentation to the leaders of the nations of the European Community, meeting in Copenhagen, on the growing problem of European unemployment. Economists who study the European situation were curious to see what Delors, president of the EC Commission, would say. Most of them share more or less the same diagnosis of the European problem: the taxes and regulations imposed by Europe's elaborate welfare states have made employers reluctant to create new jobs. While the relatively generous level of unemployment benefits has made worriers unwilling to accept the kinds of low-wage jobs that help keep unemployment comparatively low in the United States. The monetary difficulties associated with preserving the European

Monetary System in the face of the costs of German reunification have reinforced this structural problem.

It is a persuasive diagnosis, but a politically explosive one, and everyone wanted to see how Delors would handle it. Would he dare tell European leaders that their efforts to pursue economic justice have produced unemployment as an unintended by-product? Would he admit that the EMS could be sustained only at the cost of a recession and face the implications of that admission for European monetary union?

Guess what? Delors didn't confront the problems of either the welfare state or the EMS. He explained that the root cause of European unemployment was a lack of competitiveness with the United States and Japan and that the solution was a program of investment in infrastructure and high technology.

It was a disappointing evasion but not a surprising one. After all, the rhetoric of competitiveness—the view that, in the words of President Clinton, each nation is "like a big corporation competing in the global marketplace"—has become pervasive among opinion leaders throughout the world. People who believe themselves to be sophisticated about the subject take it for granted that the economic problem facing any modern nation is essentially one of competing on world markets—that the United States and Japan are competitors in the same sense that Coca-Cola competes with Pepsi—and are unaware that anyone might seriously question that proposition. Every few months a new best-seller warns the American public of the dire consequences of losing the "race" for the twenty-first century. A whole industry of councils on competitiveness, "geoeconomists," and managed trade theorists has sprung up in Washington. Many of these people, having diagnosed America's economic problems in much the same terms as Delors did Europe's, are now . . . formulating economic and trade policy for the United States. So Delors was using a language that was not only convenient but comfortable for him and a wide audience on both sides of the Atlantic.

Unfortunately, his diagnosis was deeply misleading as a guide to what ails Europe, and similar diagnoses in the United States are equally misleading. The idea that a country's economic fortunes are largely determined by its success on world markets is a hypothesis, not a necessary truth; and as a practical, empirical matter, that hypothesis is flatly wrong. That is, it is simply not the case that the world's leading nations are to any important degree in economic competition with each other, or that any of their major economic problems can be attributed to failures to compete on world markets. The growing obsession in most advanced nations with international competitiveness should be seen, not as a well-founded concern, but as a view held in the face of overwhelming contrary evidence. . . . Thinking in terms of competitiveness leads, directly and indirectly, to bad economic policies on a wide range of issues, domestic and foreign, whether it be in health care or trade.

## MINDLESS COMPETITION

Most people who use the term "competitiveness" do so without a second thought. It seems obvious to them that the analogy between a country and a corporation is reasonable and that to ask whether the United States is competitive in the world market is no different in principle from asking whether General Motors is competitive in the North American minivan market.

In fact, however, trying to define the competitiveness of a nation is much more problematic than defining that of a corporation. The bottom line for a corporation is literally its bottom line: if a corporation cannot afford to pay its workers, suppliers, and bondholders, it will go out of business. So when we say that a corporation is uncompetitive, we mean that its market position is unsustainable—that unless it improves its performance, it will cease to exist. Countries, on the other hand, do not go out of business. They may be happy or unhappy with their economic performance, but they have no well-defined bottom line. As a result, the concept of national competitiveness is elusive.

One might suppose, naively, that the bottom line of a national economy is simply its trade balance, that competitiveness can be measured by the ability of a country to sell more abroad than it buys. But in both theory and practice a trade surplus may be a sign of national weakness, a deficit a sign of strength. For example, Mexico was forced to run huge trade surpluses in the 1980s in order to pay the interest on its foreign debt since international investors refused to lend it any more money; it began to run large trade deficits after 1990 as foreign investors recovered confidence and began to pour in new funds. Would anyone want to describe Mexico as a highly competitive nation during the debt crisis era or describe what has happened since 1990 as a loss in competitiveness?

Most writers who worry about the issue at all have therefore tried to define competitiveness as the combination of favorable trade performance and something else. In particular, the most popular definition of competitiveness nowadays runs along the lines of the one given in [former U.S.] Council of Economic Advisors Chairman Laura D'Andrea Tyson's *Who's Bashing Whom?*: competitiveness is "our ability to produce goods and services that meet the test of international competition while our citizens enjoy a standard of living that is both rising and sustainable." This sounds reasonable. If you think about it, however, and test your thoughts against the facts, you will find out that there is much less to this definition than meets the eye.

Consider, for a moment, what the definition would mean for an economy that conducted very little international trade, like the United States in the 1950s. For such an economy, the ability to balance its trade is mostly a matter of getting the exchange rate right. But because trade is such a small factor in the economy, the level of the exchange rate is a minor influence on the standard of living. So in an economy with very little international trade, the growth in living standards—and thus "competitiveness" according to Tyson's definition—would be determined almost entirely by domestic factors, primarily the rate of productivity growth. That's domestic productivity growth, period—not productivity growth relative to other countries. In other words, for an economy with very little international trade, "competitiveness" would turn out to be a funny way of saying "productivity" and would have nothing to do with international competition.

But surely this changes when trade becomes more important, as indeed it has for all major economies? It certainly could change. Suppose that a country finds that although its productivity is steadily rising, it can succeed in exporting only if it repeatedly devalues its currency, selling its exports ever more cheaply on world markets. Then its standard of living, which depends on its purchasing power over imports as well as domestically produced goods, might actually decline. In the jargon of economists, domestic growth might be outweighed by deteriorating terms of trade. So "competitiveness" could turn out really to be about international competition after all.

There is no reason, however, to leave this as a pure speculation; it can easily be checked against the data. Have deteriorating terms of trade in fact been a major drag on the U.S. standard of living? Or has the rate of growth of U.S. real income continued essentially to equal the rate of domestic productivity growth, even though trade is a larger share of income than it used to be?

To answer this question, one need only look at the national income accounts data the [U.S.] Commerce Department publishes regularly in the *Survey of Current Business.* The standard measure of economic growth in the United States is, of course, real GNP—a measure that divides the value of goods and services produced in the United States by appropriate price indexes to come up with an estimate of real national output. The Commerce Department also, however, publishes something called "command GNP." This is similar to real GNP except that it divides U.S. exports not by the export price index, but by the price index for U.S. imports. That is, exports are valued by what Americans can buy with the money exports bring. Command GNP therefore measures the volume of goods and services the U.S. economy can "command"—the nation's purchasing power—rather than the volume it produces. And as we have just seen, "competitiveness" means something different from "productivity" if and only if purchasing power grows significantly more slowly than output.

Well, here are the numbers. Over the period 1959–73, a period of vigorous growth in U.S. living standards and few concerns about international competition, real GNP per worker-hour grew 1.85 percent annually, while command GNP per hour grew a bit faster, 1.87 percent. From 1973 to 1990, a period of stagnating living standards, command GNP growth per hour slowed to 0.65 percent. Almost all (91 percent) of that slowdown, however, was explained by a decline in domestic productivity growth: real GNP per hour grew only 0.73 percent.

Similar calculations for the European Community and Japan yield similar results. In each case, the growth rate of living standards essentially equals the growth rate of domestic productivity—not productivity relative to competitors, but simply domestic productivity. Even though world trade is larger than ever before, national living standards are overwhelmingly determined by domestic factors rather than by some competition for world markets.

How can this be in our interdependent world? Part of the answer is that the world is not as interdependent as you might think: countries are nothing at all like corporations. Even today, U.S. exports are only 10 percent of the value-added in the economy (which is equal to GNP). That is, the United States is still almost 90 percent an economy that produces goods and services for its own use. By contrast, even the largest corporation sells hardly any of its output to its own workers; the "exports" of General Motors—its sales to people who do not work there—are virtually all of its sales, which are more than two and a half times the corporation's value-added.

Moreover, countries do not compete with each other the way corporations do. Coke and Pepsi are almost purely rivals: only a negligible fraction of Coca-Cola's sales go to Pepsi workers, only a negligible fraction of the goods Coca-Cola workers buy are Pepsi products. So if Pepsi is successful, it tends to be at Coke's expense. But the major industrial countries, while they sell products that compete with each other, are also each other's main export markets and each other's main suppliers of useful imports. If the European economy does well, it need not be at U.S. expense; indeed, if anything a successful European economy is likely to help the U.S. economy by providing it with larger markets and selling its goods of superior quality at lower prices.

International trade, then, is not a zero-sum game. When productivity rises in Japan, the main result is a rise in Japanese real wages; American or European wages are in principle at least as likely to rise as to fall, and in practice seem to be virtually unaffected.

It would be possible to belabor the point, but the moral is clear: while competitive problems could arise in principle, as a practical, empirical matter the major nations of the world are not to any significant degree in economic competition with each other. Of course, there is always a rivalry for status and power—countries that grow faster will see their political rank rise. So it is always interesting to *compare* countries. But asserting that Japanese growth diminishes U.S. status is very different from saying that it reduces the U.S. standard of living—and it is the latter that the rhetoric of competitiveness asserts. . . .

## THE THRILL OF COMPETITION

The competitive metaphor—the image of countries competing with each other in world markets in the same way that corporations do—derives much of its attractiveness from its seeming comprehensibility. Tell a group of businessmen that a country is like a corporation writ large, and you give them the comfort of feeling that they already understand the basics. Try to tell them about economic concepts like comparative advantage, and you are asking them to learn something new. It should not be surprising if many prefer a doctrine that offers the gain of apparent sophistication without the pain of hard thinking. The rhetoric of competitiveness has become so widespread, however, for three deeper reasons.

First, competitive images are exciting, and thrills sell tickets. The subtitle of Lester Thurow's huge best-seller, *Head to Head,* is "The Coming Economic Battle among Japan, Europe, and America"; the jacket proclaims that the decisive war of the [twentieth] century has begun . . . and America may already have decided to lose." Suppose that the subtitle had described the real situation: "The coming struggle in which each big economy will succeed or fail based on its own efforts, pretty much independently of how well the others do." Would Thurow have sold a tenth as many books?

Second, the idea that U.S. economic difficulties hinge crucially on [its] failures in international competition somewhat paradoxically makes those difficulties seem easier to solve. The productivity of the average American worker is determined by a complex array of factors, most of them unreachable by any likely government policy. So if you accept the reality that our "competitive" problem is really a domestic productivity problem pure and simple, you are unlikely to be optimistic about any dramatic turnaround. But if you can convince yourself that the problem is really one of failures in international competition—that imports are pushing workers out of high-wage jobs, or subsidized foreign competition is driving the United States out of the high value-added sectors—then the answers to economic malaise may seem to you to involve simple things like subsidizing high technology and being tough on Japan.

Finally, many of the world's leaders have found the competitive metaphor extremely useful as a political device. The rhetoric of competitiveness turns out to provide a good way either to justify hard choices or to avoid them. . . .

Many people who know that "competitiveness" is a largely meaningless concept have been willing to indulge competitive rhetoric precisely because they believe they can harness it in the service of good policies. An overblown fear of the Soviet Union was used in the 1950s to justify the building of the interstate highway system and the expansion of math and science education. Cannot the unjustified fears about foreign competition similarly be turned to good, used to justify serious efforts to reduce the budget deficit, rebuild infrastructure, and so on?

A few years ago this was a reasonable hope. At this point, however, the obsession with competitiveness has reached the point where it has already begun dangerously to distort economic policies.

## THE DANGERS OF OBSESSION

Thinking and speaking in terms of competitiveness poses three real dangers. First, it could result in the wasteful spending of government money supposedly to enhance [national] competitiveness. Second, it could lead to protectionism and trade wars. Finally, and most important, it could result in bad public policy on a spectrum of important issues.

During the 1950s, fear of the Soviet Union induced the U.S. government to spend money on useful things like highways and science education. It also, however, led to considerable spending on more doubtful items like bomb shelters. The most obvious if least worrisome danger of the growing obsession with competitiveness is that it might lead to a similar misallocation of resources. To take an example, recent guidelines for government research funding have stressed the importance of supporting research that can improve U.S. international competitiveness. This exerts at least some bias toward inventions that can help manufacturing firms, which generally compete on international markets, rather than service producers, which generally do not. Yet most [U.S.] employment and value-added is now in services, and lagging productivity in services rather than manufactures has been the single most important factor in the stagnation of U.S. living standards.

A much more serious risk is that the obsession with competitiveness will lead to trade conflict, perhaps even to a world trade war. Most of those who have preached the doctrine of competitiveness have not been old-fashioned protectionists. They want their countries to win the global trade game, not drop out. But what if, despite its best efforts, a country does not seem to be winning, or lacks confidence that it can? Then the competitive diagnosis inevitably suggests that to close the borders is better than to risk having foreigners take away high-wage jobs and high-value sectors. At the very least, the focus on the supposedly competitive nature of international economic relations greases the rails for those who want confrontational if not frankly protectionist policies.

We can already see this process at work, in both the United States and Europe. In the United States, it was remarkable how quickly the sophisticated interventionist arguments advanced by Laura Tyson in her published work gave way to the simple-minded claim by U.S. Trade Representative Mickey Kantor that Japan's bilateral trade surplus was costing the United States millions of jobs. And the trade rhetoric of President Clinton, who [stressed] the supposed creation of high-wage jobs rather than the gains from specialization, left his administration in a weak position when it tried to argue with the claims of NAFTA foes that competition from cheap Mexican labor will destroy the U.S. manufacturing base.

Perhaps the most serious risk from the obsession with competitiveness, however, is its subtle indirect effect on the quality of economic discussion and policy making. If top government officials are strongly committed to a particular economic doctrine, their commitment inevitably sets the tone for policy making on all issues, even those that may seem to have nothing to do with that doctrine. And if an economic doctrine is flatly, completely, and demonstrably wrong, the insistence that discussion adhere to that doctrine inevitably blurs the focus and diminishes the quality of policy discussion across a broad range of issues, including some that are very far from trade policy per se. . . .

To make a harsh but not entirely unjustified analogy, a government wedded to the ideology of competitiveness is as unlikely to make good economic policy as a government committed to creationism is to make good science policy, even in areas that have no direct relationship to the theory of evolution. . . .

So let's start telling the truth: competitiveness is a meaningless word when applied to national economies. And the obsession with competitiveness is both wrong and dangerous.

# 27

# DOLLARIZATION: MORE STRAIGHTJACKET THAN SALVATION

JEFFREY SACHS AND FELIPE LARRAIN

**The spate of financial crises in the 1990s led to a variety of recommendations on ways to avert future instability. "Dollarization"—which calls for developing countries to abandon their own currencies and adopt instead the U.S. dollar—has been proposed by some experts to cope with market instability in the face of globalization. Jeffrey Sachs and Felipe Larrain challenge that recommendation. They argue that for most countries "a flexible exchange rate between the national currency and the dollar" is "much more prudent." Sachs is Gallen L. Stone Professor of International Trade at Harvard University; Larrain in Robert F. Kennedy Visiting Professor of Latin American studies at Harvard University.**

The recent wave of financial crises has prompted some observers to argue that developing countries should abandon their own currencies and instead adopt the U.S. dollar (or perhaps the euro or yen, depending on their location). This conclusion is unwarranted, even reckless. Dollarization is an extreme solution to market instability, applicable in only the most extreme cases. The opposite approach—a flexible exchange rate between the national currency and the dollar—is much more prudent for most developing countries, including those hardest hit by recent crises.

There are two main arguments in favor of flexible exchange rates and two main arguments in favor of fixed ones [see box pp. 328–329]. The first argument for flexibility is that an exchange rate depreciation (or appreciation) can act like a shock absorber for an economy. Take the case of an oil exporter, faced with declining prices. The drop in oil revenues would lead to weaker demand for a range of domestic goods and services, an overall slowing of the economy, and a rise in unemployment. Under a fixed exchange rate system (e.g., dollar-peso) one solution would be for wages to decline, so that non-oil industries would be able to cut prices in world markets and thereby increase sales. But as economist John Maynard Keynes famously pointed out over seventy years ago to Winston Churchill, then chancellor of the exchequer, that would be a messy business. It would require the renegotiations of thousands of separate wage contracts, and any such wholesale drop in wages would likely be accompanied by severe social stress. A much simpler solution would be to allow the peso to depreciate vis-à-vis the dollar. By changing just this one price (the number of pesos per dollar), all of the country's export products would suddenly become cheaper in world markets and therefore more attractive to foreign buyers. Increased demand for the country's non-oil exports would compensate for the fall in oil earnings, the shock would be absorbed, and the economy would continue to hum.

The second argument for flexible exchange rates is that what is good for the United States is not necessarily good for other countries. For legitimate reasons of its own (perhaps to lend pesos to the government to cover a budgetary short-fall, or perhaps to spur the domestic economy), country X may need a monetary expansion even if the United States does not. Under a fixed exchange rate system, this policy will lead immediately to a decline in reserves and eventually to a reversal of the monetary expansion itself (since the central bank has to reabsorb the public's increased holdings of pesos, as the counterpart to the sale of its dollar reserves). A country that pegs its currency to the dollar is, in effect, tying its monetary policy wholly to U.S. monetary policy. That decision makes sense only if U.S. monetary policy is wholly appropriate for its national economy, which is rarely the case.

The main argument for a pegged exchange rate system, by contrast, is that it enforces discipline. If an irresponsible central bank is given freedom to issue pesos without worrying about the consequences for the exchange rate, it will simply print pesos to its heart's content to fund a large budget deficit or to provide cheap credits to the banking system. These will be popular moves in the short run, but they will soon lead to inflation and a collapsing exchange rate. All prices, including the price of dollars in terms of pesos, will soar. In this light, a fixed exchange rate system forces the central bank to avoid issuing excessive pesos, since doing so will deplete its reserves. A currency board is an even tighter form of pegged-rate discipline, since the central bank is not allowed to issue credits to the government or to the private sector.

The second argument for a fixed exchange rate system is equally straightforward: A stable exchange rate reduces business transactions costs. There is no risk in changing currencies if the exchange rate remains stable, and the costs of switching between the peso and the dollar (measured by the difference between the

A GUIDE TO EXCHANGE RATE REGIMES

Economists often use words such as fixed, flexible, pegged, and floating to describe the way one nation's currency is exchanged—how it is bought or sold and at what price—for another nation's currency. But they just as often fail to explain exactly what these terms mean.

Take the example of a country where the peso is the national currency. A fixed or pegged exchange rate between the peso and the dollar, say at a rate of one-to-one as in the case of Argentina, is a promise of the central bank to exchange one U.S. dollar to any holder of one Argentine peso that wants to make the trade or to exchange one peso for any holder of one dollar that wants to convert the dollar to pesos. In practice, of course, the central bank is not a party to every transaction. Rather it is a buyer or seller of "last resort": If there is an excess demand in the foreign exchange (or "forex") market for dollars at the one-to-one exchange rate, the central bank must sell dollars and buy pesos. If there is an excess demand for pesos, it must sell pesos and buy dollars.

In a flexible exchange rate system, by contrast, the central bank does not commit to supply dollars or pesos at a predetermined price. Swings in forex market supply and demand may therefore shift the price of the peso in terms of the dollar. If there is an excess demand for dollars, the number of pesos needed to buy one dollar ("the cost of foreign exchange" from the point of view of peso holders) goes up. If there is an excess demand for pesos, the cost of foreign exchange (pesos per dollar) goes down. A rise in the price of foreign exchange is known as a currency depreciation, and a fall in the price is a currency appreciation.

In a pegged exchange rate system, the central bank uses its foreign exchange reserves to make the intervention in the market. Herein lies the rub. If there is a persistent excess demand for dollars, the central bank must sell dollars. Its forex reserves therefore fall. If the central bank's reserves run low, and it is not able to secure financing from private markets, it may have to let the exchange rate depreciate, even if it has promised to defend the national currency. Thus, a fixed or pegged exchange rate is really a conditional promise, not an unconditional commitment. It says that the central bank will use its foreign exchange reserves to defend the currency (that is,

buying and selling price in the currency market) are also likely to be very low. Business executives like the certainty they associate with a pegged rate.

Thus, in theory at least, flexible rates are appropriate in some conditions and fixed rates in others. A flexible rate is probably better if a country is often hit by shocks to its exports—for instance, by sharp price fluctuations. A fixed rate is probably better if shocks to the economy are rare or relatively small, or if the central bank or government either is politically irresponsible or lacks strong institutional controls.

Where you stand on flexible versus fixed rates may depend on where you sit. Businesspeople naturally tend to prefer the predictability promised by stable exchange rates, and it is true that some elements of the Mexican business commu-

*continued*

to keep the rate from depreciating), but it will do so only so long as it has foreign exchange reserves to use for this purpose. If it runs out of reserves, the currency will collapse whether it has been pegged or not. The term "fixed," therefore, is rather optimistic; many fixed rates end up in collapse. The alternative usage of "pegged" exchange rate is probably more accurate in the final analysis, as it seems less definitive.

Some monetary arrangements aim to bolster the commitment to a pegged rate. In a currency board, the central bank may not issue domestic credit to its own banking system or to the government. It may only exchange domestic currency for international currencies at the pegged exchange rate. Moreover, the value of the exchange rate is often set by law. The combination of no credit expansion plus a legally bound exchange rate often strengthens market confidence in the currency peg. It may, however, severely limit the flexibility of economic management.

Under a managed float, governments and central banks intervene in the market with the aim of achieving a specific exchange rate without making any public commitment to a desired target (which would constitute a peg). This system is currently favored by Great Britain and Japan. But when Japan intervened in the currency markets in the 1980s to keep down the value of the yen—thus boosting Japanese exports and making imports more expensive—it was described as a dirty float. Many governments try to have it both ways: to run a monetary policy aimed at domestic economic conditions while intervening in the forex market to influence the exchange rate. These two goals are often at odds or even mutually incompatible.

Virtually every conceivable variant between fixed and floating has been tried. Some currencies operate in a band—the central bank does not commit to a single price for foreign exchange, but rather to a range of upper and lower prices for the currency. Sometimes the pegged rate changes on a preset scale, in which case there is a crawling peg; sometimes an entire band moves over time, in which case the system is a crawling band. The peg may be to a basket of currencies—not to a single counterpart—so that the national currency keeps its value relative to an average of the dollar, the euro, and the yen. Floats may be clean or dirty. In the end, the only thing truly fixed about exchange rates has been the capacity of nations to innovate and to improvise them.

nity have come out in favor of dollarization. But businesspeople may underestimate the indirect costs, such as higher unemployment, which can result when the central bank pursues exchange rate stability to the exclusion of other goals. They also tend to forget that a pegged exchange rate is a conditional promise, not an unconditional guarantee: The exchange rate might still collapse, even if the central bank does everything in its power to prevent that from happening. If enough households and businesses try to convert their pesos to dollars, for example, the central bank will almost surely run out of reserves, since the number of pesos in circulation plus bank deposits is almost always higher than the dollar reserves held at the central bank. If bank depositors and currency holders try to shift out of pesos and into dollars en masse, only one of two things can happen Either the banks will become illiquid, unable to provide the pesos to households that want to remove their funds, or the central bank will run out of reserves as it sells dollars in return for the public's mass flight from pesos. Of course, both a banking crisis and a currency collapse can occur together. That, indeed, is what has happened in many countries in the last three years [1997–1999]. A currency board can help prevent this scenario, but it cannot stave it off altogether if households and businesses are determined to convert their holdings into dollars.

## EXPERIENCE FAVORS FLEXIBLE RATES

The arguments against fixed exchange rates were vividly demonstrated seventy years ago by the problems that the nearly universal gold standard created for countries at the onset of the Great Depression. Countries that needed to increase their money supplies in 1929–1933 to fight the growing depression—but that found themselves strapped into a gold straitjacket—tightened monetary policy rather than loosening it, despite surging unemployment. Only as countries left the gold standard one by one in the 1930s did their economies begin to recover from the global crash.

Seventy years later, we have again seen many countries bound to the dollar standard undertake extremely contractionary policies to preserve the pegged exchange rate at the cost of high unemployment and falling domestic output. Although in theory fixed exchange rates may be appropriate under some conditions and flexible rates under others, recent practical experience suggests that most emerging markets are better off with the latter.

First, many countries in the last several years have been unable to resist the pressure that builds up when markets come to expect that their exchange rates will depreciate. Mexico in 1994, Thailand and South Korea in 1997, and Russia and Brazil in 1998–1999 all experienced the collapse of pegged exchange rates, even though the governments and central banks were committed to defending them to the bitter end of reserve holdings. Expectations of a currency collapse can become a self-fulfilling prophecy. As rumors of a currency depreciation circulate, money holders convert their pesos into dollars, since they do not want to be caught holding pesos that are going to fall in value. The rush out of pesos is often greater than the reserves held by the central bank; the central bank is then unable to mount an effective defense.

Second, a failed defense can be very costly. A country will find itself in serious trouble if its central bank runs out of reserves trying to defend the national currency. In such scenarios, foreign banks often flee, knowing that they will no longer be protected if something goes wrong. If a domestic bank collapses, for example, the central bank will not have the dollars to help that bank meet its foreign obligations. In Mexico in 1994, and in Thailand and South Korea in 1997, the collapse of the pegged exchange rate was followed by a financial panic, in which foreign banks abruptly demanded repayment of loans. Domestic banks could not meet the demands and had to default.

Third, U.S. monetary policy is seldom appropriate for countries whose currencies are pegged to the dollar. For several years, the U.S. economy has been booming. With high rates of return in the United States and the excitement of the information technology (IT) revolution leading to a surge of new IT investments, capital has flowed into the United States from the rest of the world, and the dollar has surged in value relative to the euro and the yen. Therefore, developing countries that pegged their currencies to the U.S. dollar (such as Thailand until July 1997 or Brazil until January 1999) have also seen their currencies soar in value relative to the euro and the yen. But what was good for America was not so good for these other economies. They needed weaker currencies to maintain their export competitiveness. To keep their currencies linked to the dollar, they had to tighten their monetary policies, even though that was not called for by their economic conditions. The defense of rates pegged to the dollar helped bring on recessionary conditions in a number of countries, including Brazil, Russia, South Korea, and Thailand.

Fourth, many emerging markets have experienced sharp declines in world prices for their commodity exports. Especially after the start of the Asian Crisis in 1997, countries selling oil, timber, gold, copper, and many other primary commodities experienced a sharp loss of income. They needed either a currency depreciation or a fall in wage levels. The first is typically easier to achieve, but during the Asian Crisis it was often blocked by commitments to maintain a pegged exchange rate. Commodity exporters such as Argentina and Venezuela, which suffered terms-of-trade losses on world markets but whose currencies were pegged to the dollar, ended up with sharp rises in unemployment and sharp declines in real economic output. The case for exchange rate flexibility is even stronger if we look at Australia and New Zealand, which depend to a large extent on commodity exports. When these economies were hit by sharp declines in commodity prices in the wake of the Asian Crisis, their floating exchange rates helped them absorb the shocks without significant damage to domestic output and employment.

A fifth point seals the practical case against fixed exchange rates in most countries. One vigorous argument has been that central banks cannot be trusted with floating exchange rates—that they will simply print too much money if given the chance. Pegged rates, or even dollarization, are seen as the remedy to chronic, irremediable irresponsibility. Although many developing-country governments or central banks are certainly not blameless, their actual practices are much less irresponsible and irremediable than often claimed. Countries with significant degrees of exchange rate flexibility, such as Chile, or Mexico since 1995, have actually behaved responsibly, keeping money growth low and inflation under control, even without the straitjacket of a pegged rate or dollarization.

## WHAT MAKES DOLLARIZATION DIFFERENT?

If a country abandons its national currency in favor of the U.S. dollar, the result is very much like a pegged exchange rate, only with less room to maneuver. First, of course, there is no longer the "shock absorber" of exchange rate depreciation. The only alternative is a cut in wage levels, which is likely to be a long, drawn-out affair, with lots of interim unemployment. Second, there is no scope for independent monetary policy. Monetary policy would be determined in Washington, by the U.S. Federal Reserve Board. Having the Fed make such decisions is a good thing if the national central bank involved is highly irresponsible. But it is a bad thing if the country needs a more expansionary monetary policy than the Fed wants to provide. (It hardly needs emphasizing that the Fed will choose monetary policies based on U.S. conditions, not on the conditions of the dollarizing country.)

There are, however, some important differences, both positive and negative. One sharp minus to dollarization is its cost. In opting to dollarize, a country would be forgoing its seignorage, the income it receives when the value of its currency exceeds the cost of producing the currency. Instead of making a profit from its national currency, the dollarizing country would be faced with the expense of buying dollars to swap for its national pesos. It would have to pay for these dollars either with its foreign reserves or with money from a large dollar-denominated loan. Either way, the cost in terms of forgone interest payments on its reserves, or new interest payments on its borrowings, would be significant. Argentina, for example, would have to spend $15 billion initially to swap its peso currency notes for U.S. dollars. As the economy grows and needs more greenbacks, there would be a continuing price to pay. In theory, these costs could be offset if the United States agreed to share its seignorage with dollarizers, but this seems a particularly distant political prospect.

Another sharp minus is the absence of a lender of last resort to the banking sector. Suppose that households in a country do decide to take their money out of the banks en masse, perhaps because of rumors about the banking sector's lack of safety. When a country has its own currency, the central bank can lend domestic banks the money needed to satisfy the sudden increase in withdrawals by depositors. The depositors can therefore be confident that the banks will have their deposits available for withdrawal. When a country has dollarized, however, there is no longer a national central bank that can make dollars available in the event of a sudden withdrawal of bank deposits. And there is no reason to expect the U.S. Federal Reserve Board to be the lender of last resort for banks in another country, even if that country has adopted the dollar as its currency. Dollarizing countries could try to establish contingent lines of credit, but producing adequate collateral could prove difficult.

A final sharp difference (one that is a plus, but also a significant minus) between dollarization and a pegged exchange rate is that dollarization is nearly irreversible. This factor is good in that it allays any fears of a possible collapse of a pegged rate or even of a currency board. However, it can be equally bad if a country gets hit by a rare but extreme shock and desperately needs a currency depreciation. With a pegged exchange rate, a depreciation would be possible. The government would tell the public that it has to renege on its promise to keep the exchange rate stable, given the extreme circumstances facing the country. If the country has abandoned its own currency, however, this extreme step (meant for extreme emergencies) might not be available. Dollarization does result in certainty—the lack of worry about exchange rate changes—but that certainty comes from strapping the economy into a monetary straitjacket.

## IS DOLLARIZATION EVER WARRANTED?

Dollarization only makes sense under the following circumstances:

• A country's economy is very tightly integrated with that of the United States and thus would experience very similar shocks. In such a case, U.S. monetary policy might be a good fit. Commodity exporters whose products are subject to sharp swings in world prices rarely fit this criterion.

• A country has a very small economy in which most prices are set in dollars and most goods are used in international trade. In fact, there are only four independent countries that are currently dollarized: the Marshall Islands, Micronesia, Palau, and Panama. Of these, only Panama is of a significant size in terms of population (2.7 million) and gross domestic product (GDP) ($8.7 billion). The other three are islands with populations between 17,000 and 120,000 and GDPs of between $100 million and $200 million.

• A country has very flexible labor markets. If domestic wages have to decline, they can do so without high levels of labor market strife and without a prolonged period of unemployment.

• A country's central bank cannot be trusted to run its own currency in a stable way, perhaps because local politics is too populist or because social demands are too high to resist pressures for money-financed budget deficits.

Very few countries fit this profile; Mexico and Argentina certainly do not. Both countries have relatively inflexible economies and heavy commodity dependence. They face shocks quite different from those that hit the United States and therefore might need monetary policies quite distinct from those of the United States. Argentina has been on a kind of dollar standard since April 1991, when the Argentine peso was pegged one-to-one with the dollar. In spite of some significant achievements, Argentina experienced a sharp recession in 1995 following the Mexican peso crisis and is currently [1999] enduring another one. The objective conditions call for monetary ease, but Argentina's pegged rate will not allow it. Mexico had a pegged rate until December 1994, when the rate was destabilized by a combination of economic shocks and inconsistent monetary policies, which caused the country to run out of foreign exchange reserves. Since 1995, Mexico has operated a floating exchange rate system. In 1999, it was able to absorb shocks in world markets by allowing its currency to depreciate rather than by tightening monetary policy (as Argentina did). The result is that Mexico [continued] to enjoy economic growth in 1999, even as Argentina [sunk] deeper into recession.

Halfway around the world, a similar comparison between Hong Kong and Singapore also puts in relief the risks of a dollarized system. When the Asian Crisis hit in 1997, both Hong Kong and Singapore experienced a sharp fall in demand for their exports in the rest of the region. Singapore countered this external shock by allowing its currency to depreciate. Hong Kong, by contrast, maintained a fixed exchange rate with the U.S. dollar, a rate that has been stable since 1984. Singapore, therefore, escaped recession in 1998 and 1999, while Hong Kong . . . experienced the sharpest decline in its output in recent history (about an 8 percent drop in real GDP from the peak until mid-1999).

## ARE REGIONAL CURRENCIES THE ANSWER?

There may be a golden mean for some countries between the gains from a common currency (reduced transactions costs, depoliticized monetary management) and the gains from flexibility—a shock absorber for terms-of-trade fluctuations or other shifts in world trade patterns. That is the regionalization, rather than dollarization, of national currencies, as in the case of the euro. Suppose countries that are close neighbors have approximately the same economic structure, face the same international shocks, and do a lot of business with one another. They might want to adopt a common currency within the neighborhood, but one that remains flexible vis-à-vis other major currencies such as the U.S. dollar. Many members of the European Union made precisely that choice. Several additional candidate regions around the world come immediately to mind, and two in Latin America especially: MERCOSUR countries in South America and the Central American countries other than Panama (which is already dollarized).

The gains from regionalization of currencies could be quite large. First, there would be the reduction of transactions costs for doing business within the neighborhood. Second, there would be the creation of a supranational central bank run by designated representatives from each of the participating countries, which would take monetary policy out of the domain of populist national politics, while still preserving accountability of the monetary authorities to the political process of the member countries. Third, there would be the great savings of such a scheme compared with dollarization, because the seignorage problem would not be a factor. Suppose the Central American countries, for example, adopted a common currency. Since they would be the issuers, the countries could print the money at low cost and swap it for the outstanding currencies already in circulation. If the countries were to dollarize, by contrast, they would have to sell interest-earning dollar reserves or borrow new dollars at high interest rates in order to swap dollars for the existing currencies.

The obstacles to regionalization of national currencies would of course be significant, even where regionalization might be warranted by underlying economic realities. Take the case of MERCOSUR, for example. Argentina and Brazil would seem to have a common monetary stake: The depreciation of the Brazilian real early in 1999 threw Argentina into a very deep recession. And yet, Argentina apparently remains wedded to fixed parity with the U.S. dollar, if not outright dollarization. Brazil seems to many Argentines to be an unlikely, and unworthy, monetary partner. The probable result is a floating real in Brazil, an overvalued peso in Argentina, and little movement toward either dollarization or regionalization of the national currencies. In Central America, the situation is similar. Each country looks with doubt at its neighbors as plausible monetary partners. There would need to be considerable economic coordination among the countries to prepare for a common currency. The distinct lack of movement in this direction makes such a currency a distant prospect.

## REDUCING THE RISKS OF GLOBALIZATION

The world financial system has become treacherous in recent years, especially since many players have not yet learned the ins and outs of globalization. Emerging markets are whipsawed by huge swings in lending from international banks: Sometimes money floods in; other times it floods out. All countries need to learn how to manage financial risks, and a good exchange rate system is part of good risk management. Under these circumstances, the following three principles can be recommended.

First, except in the extreme cases outlined earlier, flexible exchange rates (either at a national or regional level) are a useful absorber for external shocks. It is not good enough to have a pegged rate that is right most of the time. Countries have to plan for eventualities—natural disasters, collapses in world market prices, abrupt shifts in international capital—that might require the shock absorber role of the exchange rate.

Second, countries should attempt to limit inflows of hot money, especially very short-term loans from international banks. Money that pours into a country can just as easily pour out. Highly volatile short-run capital, often moved by self-fulfilling waves of euphoria or panic, can disrupt economies and cause massive swings in exchange rates. Such flows can be limited through appropriate regulation of the banking system or through some restriction on inflows of short-term capital (once the foreign money has come in, however, it is not a good idea to limit its exit). Countries should also pay close attention to the ratio of short-term foreign debt to international reserves. Most countries that have recently endured currency crises had more short-term debt than international reserves on the eve of the crisis. Under these conditions, it is rational for foreign investors to try to be first to the door, and a speculative attack against the currency can easily happen.

Finally, countries should strengthen the operating capacity of their central banks and give such banks sufficient independence, so that they can resist political pressures for excessive monetary expansion. Advocates of dollarization are wrong to think that developing countries are congenitally incapable of managing a noninflationary currency. There are many developing countries that maintain good internal discipline without the straitjacket of dollarization. These advocates are correct, however, to warn of the risks and to emphasize the importance of institutional design to ensure the central bank has the professionalism and protection from daily politics that it needs to do a responsible job.

# 28

---

# GLOBAL RULES FOR
# GLOBAL FINANCE

---

## ETHAN B. KAPSTEIN

**Ethan B. Kapstein surveys the problems that have plagued the global financial system in recent years and the range of proposed reforms. Noting that misunderstandings often characterize relations between national and international financial authorities, on the one hand, and private sector economic agents, on the other, Kapstein cautions that "the best we can expect for the foreseeable future is a muddle-through strategy based on existing cooperative frameworks." Kapstein is Stassen Professor of International Peace at the University of Minnesota and author of *Governing the Global Economy: International Finance and the State* (1996).**

With the collapse of the Soviet Union in 1991 scholars and public officials in the West began to crow about the triumph of global capitalism. Trade and capital flows were increasing at a faster rate than world product, stock markets were booming, and investors were scurrying to place their funds in the so-called emerging markets. Around the world, countries were liberalizing, privatizing, and deregulating at the urging of public and private international financial institutions.

These developments have, however, been accompanied by a series of financial crises. Beginning with the exchange rate shocks that rocked Western Europe in 1992 and 1993, the world has experienced banking and currency crises in Mexico in 1994–1995, East Asia in 1997–1998, and Russia and Latin America in August 1998. By the early fall of 1998, stock markets around the world had tumbled to levels not seen in a year, and the emerging markets in particular were suffering from the sudden flight of speculative capital, with investors writing off billions of dollars in losses. At the same time, the long-standing banking crisis in Japan remained far from a solution, with the government engaged in half-hearted measures that were doing little to reignite the country's economy. Far from being the decade of global capitalism, the 1990s may well be remembered as the decade of financial instability.

Like earlier periods of sustained financial crisis—such as the Great Depression and the Latin American debt crisis of the 1980s—the current malaise has prompted policy makers and analysts to draw lessons that could provide the basis for future efforts at systemic and national reform. A wide array of policy options has been placed on the table, ranging from abolition of the International Monetary Fund (IMF) to the renewal of capital controls. This suggests that the debate over international financial policy will become increasingly politicized in the years ahead, and will no longer remain the exclusive province of the "experts." ... For the international system as a whole, the best we can expect for the foreseeable future is a muddle-through strategy based on existing cooperative frameworks. ...

## THE PROBLEM

The international financial system, like all financial markets, exists to connect borrowers with savers. Because it involves transactions across different countries and currencies, linking a financial institution in country A with a borrower in country B, it raises special problems that do not occur in domestic financial markets. Because information about the economic policies of foreign governments, the business practices of foreign companies, and exchange rate movements is generally more difficult for financial intermediaries to obtain, international transactions may not necessarily be assigned the appropriate degree of risk. This failure of financial intermediaries to account fully for the risks associated with conducting overseas transactions must be considered among the major issues facing those who seek to stabilize the global economy.

Ironically, that failure has been heightened by the profound misunderstanding that seems to characterize relations between financial authorities (national and international) and private sector economic agents. The misunderstanding concerns the role the authorities may be expected to play during periods of economic crisis. Witnessing the swift response of the United States Treasury to Mexico's financial crisis in December 1994, when billions of dollars flowed across the Rio Grande in an effort to stabilize the peso, financial agents apparently concluded that they would be bailed out by Washington or the IMF in the event of a national financial collapse in an important country.

This belief undoubtedly provided these agents with some comfort in dealing with corrupt and opaque regimes such as in Russia, a country that [had] amassed $120 billion in external debt and another $40 billion in domestic debt (a significant percentage of which [was] held by foreigners). Now, having suffered the default of Russian debt in the late summer of 1998, and with no bailout forthcoming, investors may finally have learned a hard lesson. Still, it is a lesson that . . . cost the world economy billions of dollars. Finding less costly ways of dealing with this "moral hazard" problem is at the core of many contemporary reform programs.

## RISKY BUSINESS

Banking is a risky business in even the most stable economic environment. But in nearly every country the challenge of running an international bank has grown increasingly complex since the abandonment of the Bretton Woods system of fixed exchange rates in 1971. Exchange rates now fluctuate widely, creating the potential for huge losses by speculators who bet incorrectly on the direction of change. At the same time, the liberalization of capital flows has made it easier than ever for investors to find new ways of placing—and losing—their cash. And while banks have developed an array of instruments aimed at limiting an agent's downside risk—derivatives, options, forward contracts, and the like—they have proved to be weak reeds.

Given the ease and imagination with which banks manage to lose their depositors' money, these entities face a generally similar set of regulations, even if their application varies widely. Basically, banks are regulated to protect both depositors and the process of money creation. When banks fail, citizens are threatened with the loss of their savings, while the effects of a contraction in the money supply may reverberate throughout the entire economy. Accordingly, a set of regulations exists that includes prudential measures to maintain bank solvency; prudential measures to protect bank liquidity; official assurances such as deposit insurance to prevent panic runs on banks; mechanisms for resolving the problems of failing banks; and lender of last resort facilities to permit solvent institutions to keep functioning. These regulations also carry with them the moral hazard problem, for if bank managers are convinced that public authorities will not permit them to fail, they may take significant risks with depositors' funds.

Regulatory problems and solutions are compounded in the context of an international system with close to 200 nation-states and nearly as many different financial regimes. The fundamental issue is that while banks cross borders, regulators do not. Strengthening the international bank supervisory regime has been an important agenda item for central bankers for a generation now, and the Basel Committee of Bank Supervisors, based at the Bank for International Settlements (the central bank of central banks) in Basel, Switzerland, is the most prominent organization to perform that role. But as important as that group has become, its recommendations are still informal and must be set into national law by domestic regulators.

## ON A COLLISION COURSE

It is at the intersection of the international monetary system, national economic policy making, and financial intermediation that the global pileup of bad loans has occurred. And sprawled at this intersection are the institutions known as banks. Financial crises usually involve banking crises at some stage, and most banking crises begin with incorrect managerial analysis of credit, currency, and country risk. Further, in many countries these are failures of commission rather than omission, dosed as they are with a good measure of corruption involving government officials, for whom banks exist mainly to facilitate embezzlement of public funds and capital flight.

In sum, the international financial system is dominated by money-center and investment banks that have failed to master the assessment of risk in a world economy characterized by floating exchange rates, differing political economies, and a diversity of business practices. And to the extent that international supervision of the financial system exists, it has often sent perverse signals to bankers and investors, and probably governments as well, about the existence of lender of last resort facilities. As a result, the international financial system is a reckless place in which accidents inevitably happen. If that is the general diagnosis, what is the cure?

## IN SEARCH OF STABILITY

At bottom, almost every proposal for financial reform represents a search for stability. In confronting the recent rash of crises, public officials and mainstream economists have generally advanced an agenda that includes the following three proposals: first, the publication of better economic and financial information; second, the development of sound, sustainable national economic policies and financial regulations; and third, international financial and regulatory reform. Let us treat each of these in turn before examining some of the more radical solutions now being touted.

In a recent speech, [then] United States Treasury Secretary Robert Rubin made the case for "better information." He claimed that "when investors are well informed, use that information wisely, and expect to bear the consequences of their actions, they will make better decisions." He then asserted that in the case of East Asia there were "obstacles to getting good information about economic and financial matters"—obstacles that stood in the way of banks, governments, and international institutions alike. Rubin went on to encourage governments, financial firms, and the IMF to substantially expand "the types of economic and financial data made available."

It is hard to argue against a public call for better information. Still, Rubin's claims lack credibility. Few investors have blamed their analytical failures on a lack of data. It is all the more disingenuous coming from an American official who [had] the massive resources of the government at his disposal. Does . . . anyone . . . in the financial community really believe that additional data could be effectively processed?

The problem is not simply a lack of numbers but the quality of our understanding about financial risk. Good country risk assessment, for example, requires more than data about the balance of payments, monetary policy, or the banking system. It requires a deep knowledge of domestic politics.

Consider Albania, which had great numbers in the mid-1990s. What the data did not reveal was the involvement of organized crime in arms sales to Serbia and Montenegro in breach of a United Nations embargo. Financial pyramid schemes were built to siphon off the country's savings into these illicit activities; the ending could only be (and was) an unhappy one.

A second and much more prominent example comes from Asia. Until the financial crisis of 1997, most countries in the region seemed to enjoy sustained export-led growth coupled with sound macroeconomic management. But what did these numbers tell us about "crony capitalism," that familial and old boy network that lay at the center of most of these economies? Cronyism should have provided the starting point for our analysis.

And even Russia, for all its economic problems, did not have such bad numbers coming into 1998. Its current account balance was certainly weakening with the fall in oil prices, but its external debt burden as a percentage of exports was low compared to other emerging economies, and its central bank had effectively throttled inflation. Again, the numbers told us nothing about the corruption and criminality that had remained untouched by a decade of economic reform.

These lessons suggest that better economic and financial information will do nothing to help stabilize the world economy if it is not coupled to a deeper understanding of domestic political economics. And that information certainly exists within the universities, foreign ministries, and intelligence agencies of the leading industrial nations. This is the information that needs better dissemination, and the best message we could possibly send to economies everywhere is simply that we are watching you and are prepared to publicize your misdeeds. Only in that way can we hope to eliminate the political rot that lies at the core of so many financial crises.

The second policy recommendation concerns the adoption of sound and sustainable macroeconomic policies along with strong systems of financial regulation. Again, to cite [former] Secretary Rubin, "a common element amongst all the countries involved in the crisis in Asia—and, for that matter, in virtually all countries experiencing financial crises—is a badly flawed domestic financial sector." As was mentioned, weakness in the banking system may derive from external forces, especially the perverse incentives sent to financial intermediaries by poor government policy making, and from forces that are internal to the banks themselves, namely poor risk assessment. Macroeconomic management and financial regulation thus go hand in hand.

Unfortunately, this has not been the case in most emerging markets. The failure to maintain credible monetary, fiscal, and international economic policies has brought countries into a vicious circle with global currency traders. Honing in on such weaknesses as large current account deficits, an inability to collect taxes, or failure to control the money supply, speculators bet against currencies, often leading to devaluations, problems in the exposed banking sector, further economic instability as citizens panic, and, in the Russian case, a default on the outstanding debt.

How would better financial regulation lessen the probability or at least the effects of a crisis? The answer is found in the key role banks play in the process of financial intermediation, especially in emerging markets where alternative sources of finance are generally less developed. A shock to the banking system in these countries is likely to have especially severe effects on the real economy, since few other sources of credit exist. For this reason, creating a solid, well-regulated banking system is now viewed as an integral part of a successful development strategy.

But few developing countries have the internal institutional resources needed to develop independent regulatory authorities; even in the industrial countries, a long tradition in economic research argues that regulators are inevitably captured by the industries they supervise. This points to a larger and more general problem with respect to the relationship between states and markets. To the extent that markets need strong governments that can enact and enforce the rule of law, economic liberalization must be accompanied by a process of state building. In the absence of state institutions that create a level playing field for market participants, it is difficult to see how either government or market can become legitimate in the eyes of citizens and consumers. Here the international system has a role to play, and any discussion of national economic and financial policy reform necessarily relates to the third topic on the reform agenda, global financial supervision.

## THE IMF AND ITS DISCONTENTS

Many proposals now being aired with respect to the international financial system focus on the role of the IMF. These proposals range from abolishing the fund to breaking it up into several regional institutions. The mainstream view tends toward rejection of these alternatives, and instead focuses on IMF reform. This means making the institution more transparent and accountable, suggestions that have already been made in years past. The IMF's more immediate problem, however, is that it is dying on the vine, running out of funds and without the domestic political support—especially in the United States Congress—needed to refill its coffers.

The IMF has long been a target (or scapegoat) for those seeking international financial reform, but since the Asian crisis erupted a growing chorus of voices has found fault with its policies and management. Led by the unlikely team of former Secretary of State George Shultz, former Treasury Secretary William Simon, and former Citicorp chairman Walter Wriston, the IMF's critics call the organization "ineffective, unnecessary, and obsolete." They claim that "it is the IMF's promise of massive intervention that has spurred a global meltdown of financial markets." Naturally, they call for its closure.

The three argue that "the promise of an IMF bailout insulates financiers and politicians from the consequences of bad economic and financial practices, and encourages investments that would not otherwise have been made." This, in essence, is the moral hazard problem stated earlier. But such an analysis raises the question: If we do not need an IMF for the international system, why do we need lenders of last resort domestically?

The answer is that we need both, for reasons that have to do with externality effects. In economic terminology, we may say that the social costs of a banking collapse are greater than the private costs. Since people and industries that are not customers of bank A will suffer when it fails, some entity, usually a central bank, must act to contain the financial damage.

In the international system, the analogous problem is known as contagion. When a financial crisis arises in country A, investors and creditors in country B may fear that it will spread. This may lead them to exit country B, sell its currency, equities, and bonds, and take other actions that result in a self-fulfilling prophecy. Because investors and creditors usually act in herds—no one wants to be taken for the "sucker"—country B may feel the full wrath of the marketplace even if it has done nothing to bring about this turn of events. Again, the social costs of an economic crisis in country A—that is, the costs that spread to "innocent" country B—are greater than the private costs, or those borne by "irresponsible" country A alone. To the extent that a lender of last resort can contain the financial damage caused by the crisis in A, it should do so for the good of the entire international system.

The problem is one of balancing lender of last resort obligations against moral hazard effects. Mainstream reformers are urging that the IMF's conditional lending programs be made into more of a burden-sharing exercise in which private sector lenders also "feel the pain." This has certainly been the case with Russia, where creditors and investors . . . suffered large losses. But the flip side is that the IMF seems to lack the clout to keep crises from spreading, and the innocents have indeed been hurt. Should the IMF fade into irrelevance, new institutions to stabilize the world economy will be needed.

## THE RULES OF THE GAME

Policy attention has also focused on the role of the main international regulatory bodies for global finance, the Basel Committee of Bank Supervisors and the International Organization of Securities Commissions (IOSCO). The Basel Committee, which formulated the December 1987 Basel capital adequacy accord that strengthened the capital requirements of international banks, is now being urged to examine the international lending practices of banks and to draw up additional prudential guidelines with respect to their foreign currency and foreign loan exposures. The committee is also playing a larger role in providing technical advice to regulators in emerging markets, ensuring that they possess the tools needed for supervising domestic financial institutions. The IOSCO is working along a parallel track when it comes to stock exchanges around the world, and it is also trying to develop new prudential rules for global investment firms.

These efforts at reform provide useful starting points, but they may well prove too timid. . . . This possibility has opened the door to more radical policy ideas that range from a return to capital controls to the imposition of quantitative limits on cross-border lending by banks. There is also renewed attention being paid to the idea, first articulated by Nobel Prize winner James Tobin, of placing a tax (the "Tobin tax") on all short-term international financial transactions in the hope of limiting speculation in favor of long-term investment. A possible model here is provided by Chile, which imposes a heavy tax on investors who withdraw their funds from the country after less than twelve months.

Perhaps a better approach, however, is to return to the basic governing principles of the global economy, and ensure that these are respected by all parties. The major industrial countries must state clearly the rules of the game and penalize those who do not follow them. Countries that cannot abide by the current set of rules should receive the technical assistance they need to become full participants, or they should stay out of the game. These rules should include the following:

• Banks in the industrial countries will not be permitted to conduct any financial activity with banks in emerging markets that do not adopt the regulatory standards provided by the Basel Committee of Bank Supervisors. Further, they will not make any loans to companies that do not adopt international accounting standards.

• Investors in the industrial countries will be permitted to invest their funds only in stock exchanges that are supervised by regulatory bodies that are members of the IOSCO. They will not invest in companies that have not adopted international accounting standards.

• Following the IMF charter, no country will obtain an IMF loan that has unilaterally devalued its currency and defaulted on its external debt obligations without prior IMF consultation and agreement.

Other points could be added, but the aim of this approach is hopefully clear: to establish that the world economy has rules, and that all players must abide by them in the interests of global stability and fairness. This approach actually does the governments of emerging markets a favor, for it allows them to turn to private sector actors—many of whom are cronies—with a simple choice: either join the global system, or opt out. By opting in, they agree to take these steps, and in the process "normalize" their political economy. By opting out, they remain isolated, with the freedom to do as they wish, but at the likely price of extreme poverty. The alternatives are clear, and the choice is theirs to make.

This approach could be perceived by some as insensitive to local cultures and their economic practices. It is, and that is now required in the interest of system stability. The world economy needs rules and institutions that must be made clear to all market participants. And at no time does the need for guideposts become more compelling than during periods of financial crisis.

# 29

# THE WTO AND NONMARKET ECONOMIES

GREG MASTEL

How to integrate the former communist countries into the global, market-based economic system has bedeviled policy makers during the past decade. Greg Mastel is especially cautious about integrating China into the World Trade Organization (WTO), the mainstay of institutional efforts to develop and maintain rules governing international trade. While the WTO promotes trade liberalization, "the Chinese market remains protected by a web of trade barriers" and its political system lacks "a rule of law." Analogous problems plague other former communist states. Mastel is Director of the Global Economic Policy Project at the New America Foundation and author of *The Rise of the Chinese Economy* (1997).

One of the little-discussed challenges created by the end of the Cold War is integrating former communist economies into the global economic system they once shunned. Though these countries generally have recognized the need for economic and political reform, most are far from being Jeffersonian democracies with free-market economies. Most do not even aspire to such a goal; they seek much more modest change.

Nonetheless, most of these reforming nonmarket economies are now seeking to join international economic institutions, some of which presuppose the existence of a functioning market economy. The most immediate challenge is posed by the entry of several of these, led by China and Russia, into the World Trade Organization (WTO).

344

It has been clear for many years that communism is a failure as an economic system. Its one-time adherents have long been experimenting with reform. Now China is one of the five largest economies in the world and, if growth continues, could soon be the world's largest economy. Russia, Vietnam, and several other former or current communist countries are also significant forces in the world economy. The reforming communist countries are also becoming a force in global commerce: China is one of the world's top 10 exporters; Vietnam is attempting with some success to emulate China; Russia lags behind, but its foreign trade is now increasing.

World trade is policed by a world trading system. The first incarnation of this system, the General Agreement on Tariffs and Trade (GATT), had limited coverage and a weak dispute settlement procedure. Over the years, frustration over the GATT's inadequacies mounted and in 1986 a new round of multilateral negotiations known as the Uruguay Round was launched to remedy these failings. In addition to creating the WTO, the Uruguay Round succeeded in extending trading rules to services, agriculture, textiles, investment, and intellectual property, and improving dispute settlement procedures. As a result, the WTO became the ultimate rule-based, market-oriented economic institution.

Unfortunately for the WTO, most of the reforming nonmarket economies are neither rule-based nor fully market-oriented. Nonetheless, China sought membership in the trading system since the mid-1980s and finally won support for its application from the United States in late 1999. Despite numerous problems, Russia is also likely to become a WTO member in the near future. The arrangements struck with these two will establish the template for WTO membership for other former nonmarket countries—more than a dozen of which now seek membership.

A critical examination of existing economic structures in China and Russia demonstrates many troubling holdovers from the communist system. State-owned enterprises (SOEs) still play a prominent role in both countries. Despite several waves of reform rhetoric, China's SOEs account for about 30 percent of the economy. Most are poorly run and require heavy state subsidies far in excess of WTO-prescribed limits to survive, but Beijing is unwilling to reduce these subsidies quickly. Beijing's reluctance is understandable; SOEs employ more than 100 million Chinese and appear to provide the majority of jobs in several major Chinese cities. Recently, Russia seems to be inclined to move toward more state ownership, with the government speaking of renationalizing industries such as aluminum production.

Economic planning also continues. China manages its economy through communist-style five-year plans. Chinese ministries are busy drafting industrial plans for many sectors, which rely upon WTO-prohibited policies like subsidies, investment requirements, trade barriers, and technology transfer requirements.

The Chinese market remains protected by a web of trade barriers. Import demand in many sectors is still set by consultations between government ministries, not the marketplace, and the government must approve of all imports and exports. None of these policies are permitted under the WTO.

Under pressure from the International Monetary Fund, Russia has taken some steps towards trade liberalization. In 1998 and 1999, however, the Yeltsin government reversed course by instituting a "buy Russian" campaign, launching broadsides at foreign investment, and erecting new nontariff barriers. In an almost humorous move, the lead Russian negotiator on WTO accession demanded that Russia be allowed to raise tariffs upon entry to the WTO.

Piracy of intellectual property is also a widespread problem, which some trace back to communism's refusal to recognize ideas as property. The U.S.-China disputes over protection of computer programs and music recordings are well known. Less well known is that Russia and several of its former Eastern European satellites appear to be nearly as tolerant of piracy as China.

As thorny as these trade barriers will be to address, there is a still more difficult problem: the lack of a rule of law. In China, contracts are not secure, bribery is rampant, and regulation promulgation a mystery. Russia may be even worse—the Mafia may actually control much of the economy.

In 1992, after a heated dispute with the United States, China implemented sweeping legal changes that brought its intellectual property protection laws up to a world standard. The laws simply were not enforced, however, and the piracy industry actually continued to grow. Worse, the People's Liberation Army and government officials appear to be directly involved in the piracy.

Just as troubling, the WTO's quasi-judicial process is not equipped to enforce rules on a lawless country. In both China and Russia, policy often is not set through clearly established laws and procedures. Informal ministry decisions, the practices of corrupt officials, and even Mafia decisions have a more direct impact on business and commerce. Lacking a "paper trail," these practices probably could not be proven before a WTO panel and, even if a case is won, the government could well be powerless or unwilling to enforce the decision. If China's recent behavior is any guide, it could well respond to any effort to force its hand through trade sanctions with the threat of counter sanctions.

The WTO could gain in power and influence by integrating former nonmarket economies into its membership. If the WTO could discipline these countries' trade practices and related industrial policies, membership would be a boon to the WTO and its member countries. If, on the other hand, these countries were allowed to join the WTO with liberal waivers or long phase-ins, the reforming nonmarket world could become free riders on the trading system. These free riders could break the system. Other WTO members would justifiably complain about being held to standards from which China and Russia are effectively exempt; the consensus in support of the WTO and mutual free trade would likely suffer. And if the WTO proved unable to police international trade with these countries, its credibility could suffer still more.

In the longer term there are other serious worries. China has made it clear that it wants to join the WTO to have a role in writing the rules for the future. Given that China and other former nonmarket economies do not seem to share Western assumptions about the desirability of the market and free trade, they are likely to oppose stronger trading rules on investment, services, or the other areas where the WTO hopes to make further progress. History has demonstrated that individual countries that wish to slow progress can halt trade liberalization for years. Injecting another dozen or so potential footdraggers could indefinitely stymie the WTO. Attempting to integrate a group of countries into the WTO that does not aspire to free trade and that the WTO is ill equipped to deal with would, at best, multiply existing problems and, at worst, erase much of the hard-won trade progress.

The choice, however, need not be so stark. It may be possible to integrate the one-time communist world into the WTO in a way that will strengthen, not weaken, the WTO. This would require an innovative accession process rather than a simple phase-in or a set of waivers.

There are some precedents for such an innovative process. At the height of the Cold War the GATT attempted to integrate several nonmarket economies— Poland, Romania, and Hungary—into its membership, but faced many of the same seeming incompatibilities discussed above. The problem was addressed through special measures enabling other countries to protect against subsidized competition, guarantees of increased market access, and a provision to allow the withdrawal of trade benefits if the nonmarket economies failed to reform.

Many of these same provisions could appropriately be applied to China, Russia, and other reforming economies while they reformed SOEs and took other steps to make their economies fully consistent with the WTO. These countries' participation in ongoing negotiations also would be limited until economic reform was completed. Except for the just listed limitations, the transitional economies would gain all other benefits of membership. This approach would strike a balance between compliance and benefit levels and would encourage further reform to gain further benefits. Hopefully, once economic reforms were fully adopted, these countries would also become more open to further trade liberalization.

The claim that the Cold War is over has been repeated so often that it is accepted without much debate. The reality, however, is that many of the issues raised by the decades-long struggle between communism and capitalism remain unresolved. The most important problem remaining is how to integrate these former communists into a global, market-based economy. Under even the best of circumstances, the road to full integration will be bumpy.

# 30

# THE BRAVE NEW WIRED WORLD

DANIEL F. BURTON, JR.

The global system of interconnected computers—the "Network"—is the nerve center of the information age and a driving force behind globalization. Daniel F. Burton describes the evolution of the Network and explores its implications for private-sector actors and for states' foreign policies in the security, economic, and cultural domains. He concludes that the post–Cold War world order "will be a networked world comprised of electronic communities of commerce and culture—a world that ironically will strengthen the position of the United States as a nation among nations, even as it disrupts the system of nation-states." At the time this essay was written, Burton was Vice President of Government Relations at Novell.

Mention of the Internet brings to mind thoughts of cool technology, expanding markets, and pitched battles between high-tech companies. Missing from the picture are the huge implications for foreign policy. A driving force behind the foreign policy debate is the emergence of the networked economy—an economy in which computing and communications converge to create an electronic marketplace that is utterly dependent on powerful information networks. As the pioneer of this economy, the United States will play a defining role in how it develops. No other country combines the diverse set of assets necessary to drive its evolution—a towering software presence, a world-class hardware business, a dynamic content industry, a telecommunications sector that is rapidly being deregulated, a strong venture capital base, flexible labor markets, and an unparalleled university system.

Because of its commanding position, the United States is poised not only to create the domestic policies necessary to make the networked economy tick, but also to reshape the face of foreign policy. In doing so, it will answer the enduring question of what kind of international regime will replace the bipolar order of the Cold War. Though we are already well down the path toward this new regime, its structure will come as a complete surprise to most politicians and pundits. It will not be the cold peace of mercantilism that was pioneered by Japan and other Asian nations during the 1980s. Nor will it consist of the different brands of regionalism that have proliferated in Europe, the Pacific, and the Americas in recent years. Instead, the new international order will be built around the brave new worldwide web of computers and communications.

Other nations are looking to the United States, as the inventor of the Internet and the world's foremost technological superpower, to take the lead in creating the policy framework for this new world. How [the United States responds] to this summons will inspire the prospects for democracy and international economic prosperity in the twenty-first century. In order to fathom the forces driving this new world, we must understand the evolution of computer networks. In order to take advantage of it, we must grasp the trends that propel the networked economy. And in order to determine where America stands, we must measure [the United States] against a new set of benchmarks that indicate the extent of infrastructure and usage. Only then will we be able to begin defining the necessary policies.

## THE EVOLUTION OF THE NETWORK

The worldwide system of interconnected computers—call it the "Network"—is comprised of computing power, software, and telecommunications infrastructure. Its evolution has been so rapid that it caught even leaders of the computing scene, such as Bill Gates, offguard.

The Internet is often viewed as synonymous with the Network but in fact is only one component of it. The Internet is best understood as a set of standards or protocols that enables thousands of independent computer networks to communicate. A protocol called TCP/IP makes it possible for Internet users to communicate with each other easily even though they may use different kinds of computers that are attached to different kinds of networks and that communicate over different mediums. It is this ability to link together diverse platforms and systems that makes the Internet such a powerful tool.

The Internet is an outgrowth of a 1960s Department of Defense network, the Advanced Research Projects Agency network (ARPAnet), which was established to maintain communications in the event of a nuclear attack. During the 1980s, the National Science Foundation (NSF) established ARPAnet's successor NSFnet, and expanded its reach to include many universities and government agencies. In 1989, the U.S. government decided to stop funding ARPAnet. By 1995, the

NSF had shut down NSFnet and turned its operations over primarily to seven private companies. Even when it became a commercial service, however, the Internet's first customers were mostly scientists at universities and high-tech companies who used it to exchange research results and electronic mail (e-mail).

The real explosion of the Internet has come . . . as massive communications capabilities have been coupled with powerful computers and sophisticated software. The overall effect of two decades of steady increases in the capacity of microprocessors has been to drive down prices and put tremendous computing power in the hands of the average citizen. Today's desktop computers, for example, are a hundred times more powerful than the first mainframe and have several thousand times more memory. And we are still in the early stages of this technological evolution.

Despite these hardware advances, the Internet did not achieve star status until the World Wide Web was created. The Web makes it easy for someone using a computer connected to the Internet to grasp information across the Network merely by clicking on little symbols displayed on the computer screen. The basic Web software was created by Tim Berners-Lee at CERN, the European Particle Physics Laboratory in Switzerland. Berners-Lee developed the standards for addressing, linking language, and transferring multimedia documents over the Internet. With the advent of the World Wide Web, the Internet was suddenly easy to use for anyone with a computer, a modem (the device that connects phone lines to personal computers), a browser (the software application that lets users easily access information on the Internet), and some time on their hands. It was no longer the province of scientists and researchers but was open to everyone from students and business executives to retirees. As a result, usage soared. . . .

To grasp how far technology has come and how fast the world of computing is changing, it is instructive to review the evolution of the computer. First came the mainframe. The Electronic Numerical Integrator and Calculator (ENIAC), first demonstrated in 1946, is commonly thought of as the first modern computer. It was designed to calculate firing trajectories for artillery shells and could execute the then astonishing number of 5,000 arithmetic operations per second. It weighed 30 tons, filled an enormous room at the University of Pennsylvania, consumed 150,000 watts of power, and used 18,000 vacuum tubes. The mainframe launched the computer industry with its promise of dramatic gains in businesses productivity. With the mainframe, businesses could automate their payroll, billing, inventory controls, and a host of other activities, thereby significantly boosting their efficiency. . . .

The second phase of the computing revolution began with the stand-alone personal computer (PC), which offered to increase dramatically personal productivity. With a PC, individuals could enhance their performance using word processors, spreadsheets, and personal databases. This shift from the mainframe to the PC during the 1980s was made possible by awesome advances in technology. For example, Intel's Pentium microprocessor is built on a piece of silicon the size of a thumbnail and can execute more than 200 million instructions per second—a long way from the days of ENIAC. As a result of this increase in computing power, terminals emerged as power centers in their own right, and for millions of PC users the computing center shifted from the mainframe to the desktop. . . .

Today we stand at the edge of a third major shift in computing—the rise of the Network. Driving this shift is the desire of individual users to make connections with the outside world. Businesses are striving to connect with their partners, their vendors, and their customers, and individuals are striving to connect with each other and the information they need.

The Network is not just the Internet, as many people believe. It started off with LANS (local area networks) that linked different groups of computers together, like those in a company or small office, so that they could perform common functions like filing and printing. LANS soon grew to WANS (wide area networks) and ultimately to intranets, the Internet, and the World Wide Web. Companies . . . now foresee a new phase of the Network, in which inexpensive "network computers" will replace expensive PCs and plug directly into the Internet, where specific applications, or "applets," will be available "for rent" from the Internet as needed. For example, if someone wants a French lesson for restaurant conversation, they would not have to buy the entire software package for French language and civilization—they would simply download the necessary applet from the Internet.

One of the most important lessons in the evolution of computing is that each transition has been compounding, not serial. The PC did not really replace the mainframe: IBM still sells mainframes. Similarly, it is doubtful that the network computer will really replace the PC. Instead, network computers will continue to exist side by side with millions of PCs, just as private networks and LANS will continue to exist alongside the Internet.

This lesson from the computer industry holds true for the worlds of commerce and politics. Electronic commerce will not destroy traditional markets for physical goods but will coexist with and transform them. Similarly, in the realm of international relations, the networked world will not replace the nation-state but will exist alongside it and exercise a profound influence over its evolution.

## THE FACE OF THE NETWORKED ECONOMY

To grasp the changes before us, we need only look at trends in the private sector. The information revolution has already transformed traditional manufacturing and service industries; what we are about to witness is the creation of entire new electronic markets. Ten trends drive the evolution of the networked economy, and policy makers will have to come to terms with each.

**1. The networked economy will be connected.** By providing a portal to the outside world, the Network connects people with each other and the information they need, enabling them to act on it at any time and from any place. In doing so, it changes what computing and communication are about. The Network is not just about productivity or typing, but it is about the value that comes from connecting to a wide world of people and interesting information. One of the central tenets of the networked economy is that the value of computing devices increases dramatically as they are connected to resources on the Network. These connections allow for a degree of access to people and information that was unimaginable even 10 years ago. This access, in turn, will foster the creation of electronic communities and lead to a wholesale restructuring of markets.

2. **The networked economy will be heterogeneous.** No single company, carrier, or technology will rule this complex economic web. Instead, it will consist of a multiplicity of agents. Again, the analog of the computing industry is instructive. When one thinks of a computer today, a keyboard, a screen, and a processing unit come to mind. In fact, computers are found everywhere—in missiles, telephones, cars, microwave ovens, washing machines, and even wall switches. These computers consist of many different types of devices and operating systems linked together via diverse modes of transmission. Similarly, a heterogeneous group of organizations will provide the hardware, software, services, and content necessary to drive the networked economy.

3. **The networked economy will be decentralized.** It will consist of a broad base of people, organizations, markets, hardware, and software. There will be no Fort Knox of computing that holds the keys to the Network in reserve. Instead, assets and information will be dispersed. The Internet exemplifies this trend. It has no central bank of computers, no central database, and no centralized management. Instead, the Internet is a web of computers, software, databases, protocols, and transmission channels that link organizations and individuals around the world.

4. **The networked economy will be open.** The intrinsic openness of the Internet has driven its phenomenal growth. During the 1970s and 1980s, the Internet was the privileged playground of defense analysts and research scientists. Not until the 1990s did the general public begin to realize that they, too, could gain easy access to the communication abilities and wealth of information on the Web. When they did, usage soared. Entrepreneurs have seized upon this openness to build electronic communities and establish the means to conduct worldwide electronic commerce on the Web. . . . Companies—or countries—that try to manage this new medium too closely or that restrict access to it too severely will find not only that their efforts are frustrated but also that they hamper their own economic performance.

5. **The networked economy will crave content.** The creation of a powerful pipeline that allows for the instant delivery of electronic information and entertainment in all its forms is the promise of the digital revolution. But if the pipeline leaks—if there are inadequate intellectual property safeguards—the flow of rich content will slow to a trickle. America's copyright industries—which include

movies, television programs, home videos, books, music, sound recordings, and computer software—account for 5 percent of U.S. gross domestic product and employ more than 3 million workers. During the [latter half of the 1990s] these industries [grew] much more rapidly and created jobs much more quickly than the overall U.S. economy, and this trend will accelerate. Countries with strong intellectual property protection regimes that encourage the creation and distribution of electronic content will attract investments and see their involvement in the networked economy grow. Those that do not will find that investment will slow and that progress toward the electronic marketplace will halt.

**6. The networked economy will be secure.** Digital markets cannot exist in an insecure environment. Unless commercial transactions and exchanges of sensitive information are protected, no one will risk them over the Web. . . . Electronic commerce, telemedicine, and corporate communications all require extreme levels of security. But while the first two markets do not provide adequate security and have been slow to mature, the market for intranets is exploding. Intranets are private networks that offer the functionality of the Internet but have firewalls that assure security, thus allowing for sophisticated corporate communications. A big reason for their popularity is their ability to prevent unwanted outside access.

**7. The networked economy will be extremely sensitive to market fluctuations.** The digital revolution is still in its early stages, and markets are sure to go in startling, unexpected directions. It is essential that they have time to develop, yet, daring periods of transition, economic and political anxiety make it hard for governments to be patient. . . . Unfortunately, there are no quick solutions. Policy makers should be cautious about implementing elaborate regulations, since they could stifle markets that are still in their infancy, exacerbating the very problems they are meant to solve.

**8. The networked economy will offer an abundance of choice.** This is the real lesson of the 1996 [U.S.] telecommunications bill, which opened the U.S. telecommunications market to greater competition. The future will bring an abundance of technologies, providers, services, information, and consumer choices. During much of the twentieth century, there was only one major telephone company (AT&T), which provided a standard telephone (for many years, a black rotary dial) and a homogenous service (local or long distance) over one path (twisted-pair copper wires). Today, there are hundreds of telephone companies that provide many communications devices (including cellular phones and pagers) and offer a wide range of services (such as voice mail, call-waiting, and conference calling) that can be delivered over numerous channels (like fiber optic cable, ISDN, satellite, and even the Internet). This proliferation of choices will be reflected in a host of products. And, as countries like China are discovering, greater economic choice creates tremendous pressure for more open political systems.

**9. The networked economy will place a premium on soft assets.** During the Cold War, the world was obsessed with hardware. Careful count was kept of nuclear warheads, armored divisions, and military personnel. In the economy, the manufacturing sector reigned supreme. The Dow Jones industrials dominated the stock market, and analysts looked at such statistics as durable goods purchases and machine tool orders to gauge economic trends. The networked economy will marry the traditional reliance on hard assets with a new premium on soft ones. The skills of people, the management of R&D enterprises and information, and the vitality of intellectual property will drive economic performance.

**10. The networked economy will be lean.** The information revolution has already resulted in massive realignments in corporate America. Its real potential, however, is not the heightened productivity that it affords individual companies but its ability to restructure entire markets. The networked economy promises to create an electronic marketplace in which consumers can communicate their needs directly to vendors, thereby minimizing costs and facilitating product customization. As these markets emerge, many jobs will be created, but many traditional ones will vanish. The resulting dislocation will lead to calls to protect the status quo, which will test the resolve of governments.

Many of the characteristics listed above—heterogeneous, decentralized, open, and market driven—are textbook descriptions of U.S. society. Because the United States created the Network, this similarity should come as no surprise. These elements were necessary to give birth to the Network, and they will be essential to its evolution. Indeed, the United States finds itself in a strong position to lead the networked economy.

## WHERE DO WE STAND?

Almost any assessment of the U.S. economy begins with a look at macroeconomic indicators. In recent years, these have reflected a sustained U.S. recovery. American gross national product growth, productivity, employment, inflation, and even investment rates have all been strong, especially when compared with the indicators for the other Group of Seven countries. These rosy numbers, however, mask some fundamental problems. [The U.S.] national savings rate is abysmal, and [its] education system faces fundamental challenges. Chronic trade imbalances . . . and a widening disparity between the rich and the poor compound the gloom.

Usually the debate stops here, with analysts selecting their indicators, going into minute detail, and arguing at length over whether the glass is half full or half empty. Underneath these macroeconomic statistics, however, lies another set of indicators that reveal a very different picture. These indicators are technology related and show just how far the United States is along the path to a networked economy—and how much more rapidly it is moving than other nations.

The data that would allow for a systematic, technology-related comparison of the United States with many other countries are not yet available. It is possible, however, to make some direct comparisons with Japan. Viewed through the lens of the 1980s, Japan was an awesome competitor. Five years ago [the early 1900s], conventional wisdom held that Japan's version of developmental capitalism was far superior to the American laissez-faire model. Japan's combination of flexible wages, lifetime job security, megabanks, incremental innovation, and industrial policy were said to produce an unbeatable work force, financial system, and industrial base.

Technological indicators that signal a nation's readiness to participate in the networked economy, however, paint a different picture of the strength of the U.S. economy relative to that of Japan:

- In 1995, the United States had 365 computers per 1,000 people, compared with 145 in Japan.
- In 1996, 66 percent of U.S. homes subscribed to cable television, compared with only 29 percent in Japan.
- In 1994, there were over 5,500 domestic commercial databases in the United States, compared with only 1,050 in Japan.
- In 1995, 23 per cent of U.S. workers used a network-connected PC, compared with only 1.3 per cent in Japan.

Other indicators also highlight America's strong position in the networked economy. The U.S. software industry accounts for three-fourths of the world market, and nine of the world's ten biggest software companies are located in the United States, as are most of the major computer-related companies. PC penetration of the business market in the United States has reached nearly 90 percent, and more than one-third of American families have them in their homes. In 1995, for the first time, the amount of money spent on PCs exceeded that spent on televisions.

Moreover, America's Internet usage is soaring. Of the estimated 64 million Internet users worldwide, 41 million are in the United States. [These numbers have increased dramatically since this article was first published in 1997—eds.] The rate of growth is breathtaking. In 1995, the number of powerful computers that serve as Internet hosts increased by 95 percent. The United States has the greatest number of Internet hosts. North America as a whole accounts for 68 percent of the total, Europe for 23 percent, and the rest of the world for only 9 percent. These indicators show that the United States is blazing the trail to the networked economy.

In short, no other country has moved as far toward the networked economy as fast as the United States. It has a robust computer hardware industry, the world's leading software industry, a telecommunications sector that is being rapidly deregulated, and strong consumer demand. Japan, by contrast, has a strong computer hardware industry but is weak in software and has not yet begun seriously to deregulate its telecommunications sector. Europe is in an even worse position, lagging in hardware, software, and telecommunications deregulation.

## POLICY IMPLICATIONS

During the 1980s, many Asian and European nations looked at Japan's runaway economic success and concluded that the corporate state was the wave of the future. Japan's centralized decision-making and government-industry collaboration—and its emphasis on producer interests—seemed like the winning combination in world markets. This is no longer the case. Although the corporate state may work well when the trajectory of the economy and the scope of industrial competition are fairly predictable, it does not work well in times of transition. In such times, qualities that are anathema to the corporate state—such as decentralized decision-making, entrepreneurial risk taking, and open markets—are most prized. These characteristics are at the core of the networked economy and endow it with a flexibility and a dynamism that are lacking in more closed, centralized states.

The Internet is a tangible expression of the world coming together. If regionalism was the intermediate step toward a true global community, the World Wide Web is its consummation. As borders become more porous and the role of nation-states more tenuous, the distinction between domestic and foreign policy will fade. Perhaps the best way to assess the foreign policy debate in this new environment is to think of the Internet's implications for the three traditional foreign policy interests of security, treasure, and culture.

When it comes to security, the impact of the Internet is already apparent. Increasingly, security is defined not by the number of weapons in place or the number of troops that can be deployed at a moment's notice but by the ability to gain or deny access to critical information. The raging debate in the United States about encryption reflects the clash between global electronic markets and national governments. On one side are Internet users and the U.S. private sector; on the other is the U.S. government. The Internet community claims that unbreakable encryption is part of its First Amendment rights. The U.S. private sector points out that industrial-strength encryption is essential to electronic commerce and that if American companies cannot supply it, foreign vendors will. Government agencies counter that unless they can gain real-time access to the information flowing across computer networks—much as they tap telephones—the country will face unacceptable law enforcement and security risks.

Stripping away all the rhetoric, two facts shine through. The first is that there is an inexorable demand for security on the Web. Individuals, companies, and governments all insist upon it. The second, is that governments that are adept at building partnerships with the private sector will enhance their ability to access and manage strategic information, thereby gaining extraordinary advantages over those that are not.

Just as the concept of security is changing, so is the definition of threats. Because the Network puts extraordinary power in the hands of individuals and small groups, its existence inevitably heightens concerns about terrorism. Hackers have occasionally broken into the Pentagon's network and [in 1996] defaced the CIA's home page. As more and more business activity takes place on the Web, the specter of economic terrorism will also rise. For example, the existence of the Network makes it possible for malicious hackers to crash the New York Stock Exchange, to siphon billions of dollars of "digital cash" from banks, or to seize control of computers that manage electric powergrids.

When it comes to the Internet's impact on a nation's economy, however, most people focus not on security, but on the extraordinary opportunities to increase national treasure. In the United States, the sheer growth of the computing and software industry is astonishing. From 1987 to 1994, the U.S. software industry grew 117 percent in real terms, while the rest of the economy grew only 17 percent. Moreover, employment in this sector has grown about 10 percent each year over the past decade. . . .

The economic impact of the Internet is not limited to the explosive growth of the high-technology sector. The rise of powerful computing and information networks promises to transform traditional industries as well. As commerce is increasingly comprised of the exchange of electrons, business notions about economies of scale, sales, distribution, marketing, and advertising will change, as will ideas about the economic significance of national borders and the nature of international trade. All this will leave its imprint not only on the fabric of the U.S. economy but also on the nature of the policy making process. Indeed, the technology policy debate is becoming the economic policy debate. This point was driven home in the fall of 1996 in a speech by Federal Reserve chairman Alan Greenspan that focused exclusively on the extraordinary impact of technology on world markets.

As more and more value is created and exchanged in the digital world, issues such as the protection of intellectual property and the establishment of technical standards—once considered arcane—will move to the front and center of the economic policy debate. Others, such as antitrust enforcement, which was thought to be moribund as a result of global competition, will be given new life. . . . Perhaps the most important test for economic policy makers, then, will be whether they can look at issues with a fresh eye—not in the context of existing industries and markets but in the context of emerging ones.

Many of the trends that we see in the economy will have a major cultural impact. The Internet is already home to a kind of Wild West ethos that is often associated with new frontiers. It is antiauthoritarian, vehement in its defense of individualism and free speech, radical in its concern with privacy, and, for the most part, extremely antigovernment. True believers will even go so far as to assert that the Internet is a strong moral force that allows individuals to take absolute responsibility for their lives. Although this kind of sentiment is sure to leave its mark on [the U.S.] national identity, the Internet's greatest cultural legacy will stem from its ability to occasion the creation of electronic communities.

The Internet has already overrun geographic borders, making possible the creation of virtual communities of shared interests that transcend national boundaries. The next big barrier is language, and here too the walls are coming down.

Machine translation software companies . . . have developed programs that can translate Web pages from other languages into English, and vice versa. . . . These technologies promise to . . . further loosen culture from its geographic moorings, thereby contributing to the creation of a free-floating cosmopolitan class that is not restricted by national identity. In fact, this trend is already evident in the proliferation of corporate intranets. By allowing employees to collaborate and share information, while restricting outside access, they provide a powerful means of exchanging the values that undergird corporate culture.

Like security concerns, cultural issues are inextricably tied to the networked economy. This linkage generates both tremendous advantages and vulnerabilities for the United States. America's chief advantage is the seemingly insatiable international appetite for its movies, music, books, and entertainment. This content provides the fuel for global electronic markets and will pay significant dividends to the U.S. economy. As [the United States reaps] more value from digital content, however, [it] will also become more vulnerable to electronic piracy. This dynamic is already evident in [its] relationship with the People's Republic of China, where the piracy of U.S. software, movies, and music remains a significant problem.

Ultimately, all nations will have to subject their notions of blood, treasure, and culture to this digital filter. While some will do everything they can to resist the dictates of the new networked world, others will reluctantly adjust to it. But only the United States has the assets, the economic momentum, and the vision necessary to lead the transformation. In doing so, it will embark on the painstaking task of building the post–Cold War international order. This new world order will not be the cold peace of mercantilism that Asia and many developing countries are counting on. Nor will it be the cultural divide that others have predicted. It will not consist of the regional blocs that Europe, the Americas, and parts of Asia have labored to build. Instead, it will be a networked world comprised of electronic communities of commerce and culture—a world that ironically will strengthen the position of the United States as a nation among nations, even as it disrupts the system of nation-states.

# 31

---

# LIFE IS UNFAIR: INEQUALITY IN THE WORLD

## NANCY BIRDSALL

Nancy Birdsall notes that "[income] inequality looms large on the global agenda," adding that, "ironically, inequality is growing at a time when the triumph of democracy and open markets was supposed to usher in a new age of freedom and opportunity." She explores the multiple causes of inequality within and between states and examines remedies that often have the unintended effect of worsening rather than alleviating inequality. She concludes rather pessimistically that "inequality is nobody's fault and cannot be fixed in our lifetime." At the time this essay was written, Birdsall was Executive Vice President of the Inter-American Development Bank.

. . . One hundred and fifty years after publication of the *Communist Manifesto,* inequality looms large on the global agenda. In the United States, the income of the poorest 20 percent of households has declined steadily since the early 1970s. Meanwhile, the income of the richest 20 percent has increased by 15 percent and that of the top 1 percent by more than 100 percent. In Asia, the high concentrations of wealth and power produced by strong growth have been given a new label: crony capitalism. In Russia and Eastern Europe, the end of communism has brought huge income gaps. In Latin America, wealth and income gaps—already the highest in the world in the 1970s—widened dramatically in the 1980s, a decade of no growth and high inflation, and have continued to increase even with the resumption of growth in the 1990s.

At the global level, it seems that the old saw is still correct: The rich get richer and the poor get children. The ratio of average income of the richest country in the world to that of the poorest has risen from about 9 to 1 at the end of the nineteenth century to at least sixty to one today. That is, the average family in the United States is sixty times richer than the average family in Ethiopia. Since 1950, the portion of the world's population living in poor countries grew by about 250 percent, while in rich countries the population increased by less than 50 percent. Today, 80 percent of the world's population lives in countries that generate only 20 percent of the world's total income (see charts on page 363).

Ironically, inequality is growing at a time when the triumph of democracy and open markets was supposed to usher in a new age of freedom and opportunity. In fact, both developments seem to be having the opposite effect. At the end of the twentieth century, Karl Marx's screed against capitalism has metamorphosed into post-Marxist angst about an integrated global market that creates a new divide between well-educated elite workers and their vulnerable unskilled counterparts, gives capital an apparent whip hand over labor, and pushes governments to unravel social safety nets. Meanwhile, the spread of democracy has made more visible the problem of income gaps, which can no longer be blamed on poor politics—not on communism in Eastern Europe and the former Soviet Union nor on military authoritarianism in Latin America. Regularly invoked as the handmaiden of open markets, democracy looks more and more like their accomplice in a vicious circle of inequality and injustice.

Technology plays a central role in the drama of inequality, and it seems to be making the situation worse, not better. The television and the airplane made income gaps more visible, but at least the falling costs and increasing accessibility of communication and transportation reduced actual differences in living standards. The computer, however, represents a whole new production process and creates a world in which the scarce commodities commanding the highest economic returns are information and skills. As information technology spreads . . . will some fundamental transformation take place that permanently favors an agile and educated minority? Or are we simply in the midst of a prolonged transition, analogous to the one that fooled Marx, to a postindustrial world with an expanded information age middle class?

In fact, postwar progress toward free trade and free politics has been dominated by the expectation of "convergence"—that those now lagging behind, whether nations or groups within nations, will inevitably catch up. But what happens if that expectation fails to materialize? How would the end of convergence affect conduct among nations? Can open and democratic societies endure the strains of high inequality? Will inequality become a lightning rod for dangerous populist rhetoric and self-defeating isolation? Even as we talk of disappearing national borders, is the worldwide phenomenon of inequality creating instead a new set of global rifts?

# While Rich Nations Get Richer...
**Estimated GDP (in 1980 dollars)**

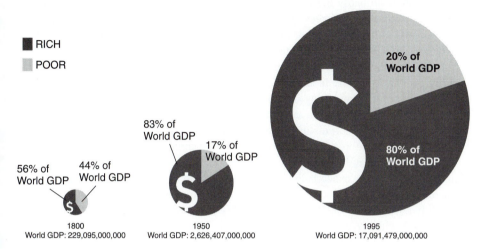

■ RICH

▒ POOR

56% of
World GDP

44% of
World GDP

1800
World GDP: 229,095,000,000

83% of
World GDP

17% of
World GDP

1950
World GDP: 2,626,407,000,000

20% of
World GDP

80% of
World GDP

1995
World GDP: 17,091,479,000,000

# the Poor Population Continues to Grow
**World Population**

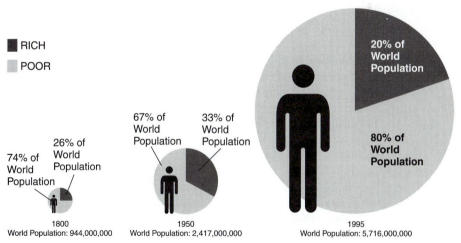

■ RICH

▒ POOR

74% of
World
Population

26% of
World
Population

1800
World Population: 944,000,000

67% of
World
Population

33% of
World
Population

1950
World Population: 2,417,000,000

20% of
World
Population

80% of
World
Population

1995
World Population: 5,716,000,000

**Sources:** *1984 World Development Report* (Washington: World Bank, 1984), *U.N. World Population Prospects, The 1994 Revision* (New York: United Nations, 1994), and author's calculations.

## WHAT ARE THE FACTS?

In the United States, where the impact of global integration and the information revolution is probably the most widespread, the facts are sobering. Income inequality in the United States is increasing, not only because of gains at the top, but more disturbingly, because of losses at the bottom. . . . The average wage of white male high-school graduates fell 15 percent from 1973 to 1993, and the number of men aged 25 to 54 years earning less than $10,000 a year grew. Possibly for the first time in the nation's history, educational gains may be reinforcing rather than offsetting income inequality: Higher education has become a prerequisite for economic success, but because access to it depends on family income, the poor are at a distinct disadvantage.

Elsewhere, the forces of change—whether the spread of capitalism and global integration, or simply the march of technological progress—have at best reinforced, or at worst exacerbated, high inequality. In Latin America, the ratio of income of the top 20 percent of earners to the bottom is about sixteen to one (almost twenty-nine to one in Brazil, probably the world's most unequal country, compared with about ten to one in the United States and about five to one in Western Europe). The wage gap between the skilled and the unskilled increased in [the 1990s] by more than 30 percent in Peru, 20 percent in Colombia, and nearly 25 percent in Mexico. Ironically, these were the countries with the greatest wage increases.

The situation is less clear but no more heartening in other parts of the world. In China, the liberalization of agricultural and other markets has spurred growth, yet large segments of the population have been left behind. In the affluent countries of northern Europe, increases in poor immigrant populations, growing unemployment, and the stricter fiscal demands of the Maastricht Treaty are undermining the historic commitment of these nations to address inequality.

Economic growth (and for that matter lack of growth) in the postwar era has seemed everywhere to be accompanied by persistent, often high, and sometimes worsening, inequality within countries. The few exceptions include Hong Kong, Korea, Malaysia, Singapore, Taiwan, and Thailand in East Asia—where several decades of extraordinarily high growth saw low and even declining levels of inequality. Even when income distribution does improve, it does so painfully slowly. A study that examined income distribution in forty-five countries found that only eight, including Japan and three European nations, showed any improvement in income distribution over any time period, and this progress was minimal.

The idea of convergence of income across countries—that poor countries will ultimately catch up to the rich—has also gone by the wayside. China and India illustrate the difficulties of arguing for the eventual convergence in income of poor and rich countries. For the last fifteen years, these two nations have experienced faster income growth than the rich countries, yet it would take them almost a century of constant growth at rates higher than those in today's industrialized countries just to reach current U.S. income levels.

## WHAT MAKES THE WORLD UNFAIR?

Inequality is nobody's fault and cannot be fixed in our lifetime. Understanding its causes helps us determine what can be done about it and what might actually make it worse. But what are the causes of inequality, across and within countries?

### History

Inequality begets inequality. Therefore, history matters. Consider Latin America. The combination of mineral wealth, soils and climate suitable for sugar production, and imported slave labor, or conquered indigenous labor, helped produce two castes: large landowners and politically unarmed workers. In 1950, just 1.5 percent of farm owners in Latin America accounted for 65 percent of all agricultural land; unequal land distribution, then the highest in the world, has risen since. Wealth in natural resources invited concentration of income. History and politics subsequently conspired to produce economic and institutional arrangements that have perpetuated that concentration.

### The Poor's Rational Decisions

A source of some inequality lies in predictable human behavior. Because the rich and educated marry each other, as do the poor and uneducated, family income gaps widen. Rational differences in human behavior between the rich and the poor also add to inequality. In many countries, the poor are members of ethnic or racial groups. If they suffer discrimination in the labor market, their gains from schooling and job skills are small, prompting them to respond by investing little in these income-producing assets. But by handicapping their children economically, the sum of these parents' sensible decisions can lock society as a whole into another generation of inequality.

The same happens with fertility. For good reasons, the poor and the less educated tend to have more children. As is to be expected in these poor households, spending per child on nutrition, health, and education declines with the number of children. Less spending on the children of the poor creates a new generation in which the number of unskilled workers grows faster than skilled workers, bringing down wages for the former and thus perpetuating the cycle. In societies with high population growth (Africa, for example), the education levels of mothers are a major determinant of fertility rates. As poorly educated mothers have many more children than their well-educated sisters, the cycle of high fertility and poor opportunities for their children continues, helping perpetuate inequality in their societies.

East Asia provides an example of how fertility change can break this vicious cycle. A dramatic decline in infant mortality in the region after World War II was followed in the early 1960s by an equally dramatic, and very rapid, decline in fertility—which spread quickly to the poor and less educated. These changes had major demographic consequences: In Korea, for example, the percent of the population in the prime working ages of twenty-five to fifty-nine rose from less than 35 percent to close to 50 percent between 1965 and 1990, while the percent of children between ages zero and fourteen fell. With this demographic growth in the work force came dramatic increases in savings and investment (from about 15 to 35 percent in Korea and Indonesia) that helped fuel growth. Compared with those of other regions, East Asia's private and household savings and investment rates were especially high—including among poor households that invested heavily in the more affordable education of their fewer children.

## Prosperity

Prosperity can produce inequality—an outcome that, within limits, may be economically justifiable. After all, some inequality may encourage innovation and hard work. Newfound inequality in China and in the economies of Eastern Europe may simply mean that new economic incentives are not only inducing growth but also creating opportunities for some individuals to excel and profit.

But the market reforms that bring prosperity also may not give all players an equal shot at the prize. In the short run, privatization and public-sector downsizing will penalize some workers; and open trade, because it hurts formerly protected industries and makes their inefficiencies unsustainable, can lead to wage reductions and higher unemployment. If corruption infects the privatization process, as in Russia, such reforms will provide windfalls to insiders. More insidious for the poor over the long run are the effects of reforms on the value of assets. During the Latin American debt crisis of the 1980s, many high-income citizens of indebted countries were able to store most of their financial assets abroad, even as their governments (and thus, their fellow taxpayers) assumed the bad debts incurred by enterprises either owned or controlled by the rich. Today's lower inflation and more realistic exchange rates mean dollar accounts held abroad can now buy more at home. Similarly, well-connected individuals in emerging markets who had previously profited from cheap credit, subsidized prices for hard foreign currency, or government regulatory exceptions (say, on the use of urban land) benefited again, as economic reforms raised the market value of assets that they had been able to acquire at low cost.

## Bad Economic Policy

The most avoidable and thus most disappointing source of inequality are policies that hamper economic growth and fuel inflation—the most devastating outcome of all for the poor. Most populist programs designed to attract the political support of the working class hurt workers in the long run. When financed by unsustainable fiscal largesse, they bring the inflation or high interest rates that exacerbate inequality. Inflation worsens inequality because the poor are forced to hold money and cannot acquire the debts that inflation devalues. High interest rates, driven by unsustainable public debt, crowd out investments and jobs in small and medium enterprises, while encouraging easy gains in government bonds for those with plenty of money. Price controls, usually imposed on the products most consumed by the poor, often lead to their disappearance from stores, as they are hoarded and resold at higher prices. The imposition of a minimum wage temporarily benefits those who have formal jobs but makes it harder for the unemployed to find work. Finally, regulatory privileges, trade protection, and special access to cheap credit and foreign exchange—all bad economic policies—will inevitably increase the profits of a wealthy minority. For all these reasons, IMF-style reforms, often attacked for hurting the poor majority, are key to ending corrupt practices that usually benefit only a few.

Bad policy also includes what governments fail to do. Failure to invest in the education and skills of the poor is a fundamental cause of inequality. When adequate education does not reach enough of any population, educated workers become scarce, and employers compete for them by offering higher wages. The widening wage gap between college graduates and others in the United States indicates that the demand for graduates still exceeds the supply, feeding inequality. In Brazil, during the 1970s, the salaries of scarce university graduates rose rapidly, worsening wage inequality. In contrast, wage differences in Korea between those with university education and their less-educated colleagues fell, as more and more students completed secondary school and attended universities. In fact, above-average spending on education characterizes each of the few countries that have managed high growth with low inequality in the postwar period.

## TEMPTING AND DANGEROUS REMEDIES

Paradoxically, the rhetoric of fairness can encourage policies that worsen global and local inequalities. Some examples of these self-defeating policies include:

### Protectionism

Protection from global competition is a dangerous nonremedy, whether it involves import barriers, high import tariffs, or currency controls. Developing countries that have been most open to trade have had the fastest growth, reducing global inequality; those least integrated into global markets, such as many African economies, have remained among the world's poorest. Historically, the same pattern holds. Those countries that aggressively sought commercial links to the outside world—Japan, beginning in the Meiji Era, and the East Asian countries after World War II—whether via technology licensing, openness to foreign investment or an export push, have had the fastest growth. Trade (along with mass migration) explains most of the convergence in income among the countries of

Europe and between them and the United States in the late nineteenth century. Convergence of incomes in Europe stalled as economic links disintegrated from 1914 to 1950 and then resumed in force in the postwar period, when European economies became more integrated.

But does global integration create worsening inequality within countries, rich and poor alike? The growing wage gap in the United States coincides with increasing imports from developing countries that have large pools of unskilled labor. But most research shows that technology is more to blame than trade for most of the U.S. wage gap: Few U.S. workers (probably less than 5 percent) are in industries competing with low-wage goods from developing countries, and the wages of workers without a high-school diploma have fallen as much if not more in nontrade as in trade industries. True, more subtle forces are also at play—for example, the ability of firms to threaten to move jobs overseas may be undermining American unions. But a recourse to protectionism would almost surely hurt poor consumers more than it would help low-skilled workers.

Growing wage inequality is associated with increased trade and integration into global markets even in developing countries. One reason: Foreign capital inflows and higher domestic capital investment create new jobs for skilled workers, and skilled workers' wages then rise faster than average wages. But the bottom line is that international trade and open markets are less of a problem than worldwide changes in the technology of production that favor skilled workers everywhere.

Indeed, increases in trade and economic integration in poor countries, though associated with high wage inequality, may actually reduce inequality of income and consumption. There are two possible reasons: First, as obstacles to imports fall and price competition intensifies, prices drop—a boon for the poor, who use most of their income for consumption. Second, trade liberalization and open markets in general weaken the unfair advantages enjoyed by the rich and connected, undermining the economic privileges and monopolies (reflected in wealth not wage gaps) that otherwise perpetuate high inequality.

### Special Worker Entitlements

[U.S.] President Franklin Roosevelt's New Deal legislation set countrywide wage rates and labor standards for U.S. workers during the 1930s depression. Could a global minimum wage and global labor standards force up wages of the unskilled in poor countries, reducing in-country and worldwide wage gaps?

Advocates of a global New Deal have a point: Property rights remain elaborately protected in the complex codes of international trade agreements, while labor rights remain unacknowledged. Almost all countries can agree on some standards of behavior: the prohibition of slavery and debt bondage, assurance of a reasonable measure of safety in the workplace, a guarantee of rights to collective bargaining The problem is that in developing countries, even standards that look noncontroversial (the prohibition of child labor, for example) may hurt those they are meant to protect (see box on page 369). Most standards, including collective bargaining rights, which might increase wages in some firms, would affect only the usually small proportion of workers in the formal urban sector, thus increasing the gap between them and the majority of workers in rural and informal jobs. This result might do little harm if it helped a few without hurting others. But harm to many is likely because higher labor costs would then induce employers to invest in labor-saving technologies. The loss of new jobs would hurt mostly the poor and unskilled, whose main asset, after all, is their own labor.

---

SOME CHILD LABOR WORKS

At first glance, abolition of child labor looks like one of the few labor standards on which everyone could agree. An estimated 250 million children under the age of fourteen work. Some 60 million of these are under the age of ten; of those who are older, one-half work nine or more hours a day—enough to interfere with their normal development.

These statistics and the horror stories often behind them have inspired worldwide action, from the creation of new NGOs, such as Free the Children, to [the 1998] Global March Against Child Labor, a five-month demonstration [that spanned] Africa, the Americas, Asia, and Europe. Meanwhile, consumer outrage has prompted multinational corporations such as Nike and the Gap to adopt codes of conduct (which prohibit child labor in their factories abroad) and attach "child labor-free" labels to the products they sell.

But do these initiatives make poor children in developing countries better off? Probably not. In many cases, a child's income defines the difference between destitution and mere "poverty" for a struggling family. Without it, indigence (earnings per capita of less than one dollar a day) would more than double among many of these households; in urban Latin America, for example, the incidence of poverty in low-income households would rise 10 to 20 percent without the earnings contributed by working children.

When children work because they must, banning their labor can actually make them worse off. Legally invisible, they may end up working anyway—unprotected by laws that prohibit long hours, abusive treatment, and hazardous conditions. Business codes of conduct are just slightly better. They affect only a small percentage of child workers in organized export industries and may simply drive children into lower paying, and more dangerous, work in the streets. Labeling programs do have one advantage: The levies that participating firms pay can be used to educate child workers, subsidize parents who send their working children to school, or create local partnerships between employers and community groups that monitor working conditions.

Unfortunately, these efforts to deal with child labor may also blind people to a more troubling bottom line: The real solution to the exploitation of child workers involves the complex business of economic growth and development in poor countries.

—N.B.

Weaker infrastructure, unreliable judicial and regulatory regimes, and less education mean workers in developing countries produce less—even in well-equipped export firms. A global New Deal will only work when it is no longer needed: that is, when development progress in poor countries brings worker productivity—now as low as one-third the U.S. level—much closer to rich country levels. Only with convergence of worker productivity (and worker pay) across and within nations—as was the case across the United States in Roosevelt's time—could global rules on workers' rights help rather than hurt those now worse off.

### Underpricing Public Services

For decades, governments have monopolized delivery of such public services as water, sanitation, electricity, and health care. They have also charged industries and households much less for these services than they actually cost—all in the name of helping the poor. Mountains of evidence demonstrate two virtually universal results:

First, in the face of any scarcity at all, prices that are too low reduce public supply of the underpriced service. India's public resources will never be sufficient to cover hospital care for its entire population. Short of privatization and adequate meter-based customer charges, electricity services in cities such as Lagos and Karachi will never catch up to demand, and "brownouts" (scheduled times without electricity) will continue.

Second, in the face of any kind of rationing, the poor will be last in line. The guarantee of free university education in Egypt and France, for example, is a false entitlement: Low-income families cannot afford the secondary schooling and tutoring needed to pass the university admissions test. In the Philippines, cheap electricity and water are available to powerful industrial interests, while the poor in the slums rely on jerrybuilt connections and buy bottled water at high prices from private trucks. In Mexico, for decades, general food subsidies benefited the urban middle class and created the incentives for food producers to bribe the politicians and government officials who controlled allocation of these subsidies. Meanwhile, the poor in rural areas and indigenous communities received little if any benefit.

### Laissez-Faire Economics

Because trade protection, worker rights, and cheap public services can in fact hurt the poor does not mean the inequality problem can be left to the market. It is one mistake for government to restrict and distort market activity, reducing competition and perpetuating privileges; it is another to assume that market forces will automatically create opportunities for those at the margin.

Every society has some interest in avoiding the worst forms of inequality and injustice. That means in every society there is a role for government—not only to avoid the creation of unfair advantages for the rich and powerful, but to guarantee equal opportunities that market forces will naturally neglect, especially for those individuals who will otherwise be left on the sidelines. But this brings us to the question of what does work.

## WHAT DOES WORK

The false remedies have short-run political appeal. Unfortunately, what does work takes time and patience.

### Worker-Based Growth

Economic growth that is based on the intensive use of labor reduces income inequality—within as well as across countries. Oil-rich countries such as Venezuela and Nigeria have grown quickly at times, but the advantages of oil, bauxite, copper, and other mineral wealth can be short-lived. An abundance of natural resources invites concentration of income and discourages reliance on people, technology, and skills. Lack of natural resources, meanwhile, can be a hidden blessing, as the sustained and equitable growth of Switzerland and Hong Kong show. The labor-using growth of Taiwan and Singapore has reduced income gaps in those economies and propelled their convergence toward industrial-country income levels over the last three decades.

Worker-based growth is best encouraged by avoiding the wrong policies—those that directly or indirectly raise employers' cost of labor. In countries such as Costa Rica and Ghana, where agriculture is labor-using and generates exports, the correction of overvalued exchange rates (which make imports cheaper for urban consumers) . . . increased rural jobs and income. In England, and . . . Venezuela, relaxation of onerous severance pay rules . . . encouraged hiring, inducing employers to substitute people and skills for energy and environmentally costly production inputs. The United States could also encourage more hiring of unskilled workers by reducing payroll tax rates and raising the threshold at which these rates are applied.

### Education: The People's Asset

In the increasingly service-oriented global economy, education and skills represent a kind of wealth. They are key assets—and once acquired cannot be taken away, even from those who are otherwise powerless. Moreover, as education is shared more broadly, other assets such as land, stocks, or money will become less important.

It should be no surprise that the best predictor of a child's education is her parents' education and income. The poor, especially in developing countries, are last in line for education, as well as other publicly financed services. (Among thirteen industrialized countries studied, only in Sweden and the Netherlands have educational opportunities become less stratified by socioeconomic class during this century.) So without a jump-start from public policy, the rich will become educated and stay rich, and the poor will not, perpetuating the inequality of assets and income across generations. In the United States, Europe, and in today's poor developing countries, the single best weapon against income inequality is educating the poor.

Other mechanisms to distribute and redistribute assets, including land reform and microcredit programs, can also improve the pattern by which income is distributed. Pension reforms in Chile, Mexico, Peru, and elsewhere in Latin America have the potential to reduce the disequalizing characteristics of traditional pay-as-you-go systems and to create stakeholders in a market economy among those once excluded from its benefits. In the United States, the . . . arguments against "privatizing" social security reflect in part the myth that traditional systems are highly redistributive. Much evidence suggests that this is not necessarily true.

## Democracy

Relatively low levels of income inequality in China, Cuba, and the former Soviet Union seem to suggest that authoritarian politics can at least produce equality. But in fact, it is the Western democracies that have over time generated sustained and equalizing economic growth. In economically unequal societies, the one-person, one-vote system can offset the ability of the economically powerful to perpetuate their privileges by buying political power. Perhaps this is why the market today sees greater risk of social disorder fed by political privilege in Indonesia than in its more democratic neighbors, such as Thailand and Korea. In today's global market, good politics is good for equalizing growth.

## Opportunities, Not Transfers

Although transfers and income subsidies to help the poor or reduce inequality make sense on paper, they are not long-run solutions. As declining spending on income-tied welfare programs in the United States shows, transfers and subsidies tied to low income are politically difficult to sustain. In fact, because the poor tend to be less organized and politically effective, redistributive programs often respond to more vocal entrenched interests, transforming these initiatives into a regressive tax rather than a safety net. For example, Senegal's program to cushion the effects of its economic reforms channeled state money to privileged groups within the system (civil servants and university graduates), while doing nothing to protect the urban and rural poor from rising consumer prices and unemployment. Often, even those subsidies originally meant for the poor are quickly captured by the middle class and the rich, as ample public spending on university education in [the U.S. state of] California suggests. Finally, the taxes that pay for large transfer programs are increasingly regressive. Because global competition puts pressure on governments to reduce taxes on footloose capital and highly mobile skilled labor, workers and consumers must bear more of the tax burden associated with redistributive transfers, mainly in the form of growing payroll and sales taxes.

Public spending for the poor is more effective in the long run and politically more attractive when it enhances opportunities. But for such public spending to be effective, two rules must prevail: First, spending should concentrate on programs that reach everyone but benefit the poor most—in the United States, secondary education, child care, and immunizations. Second, the poor's access to opportunities should be improved not by directly providing services, but by giving them tax breaks and vouchers for school, health, and housing, which would help them become effective consumers. In Chile, public spending on universal services and on voucher-like programs ensures that more than 80 percent of all public health-care services and 60 percent of all education services go to the poorest 40 percent of households—raising the total income of the poorest one-fifth of households by nearly 50 percent.

### Strengthen Domestic Policies for Global Integration

It bears repeating that the poorest countries of the world are those least integrated into global markets; the facts are so obvious that most poor developing countries have joined the bandwagon of unilateral trade opening. Since global markets reward skilled over unskilled labor, poor countries are adjusting to their growing wage inequality by increasing spending on education and training.

Then again, industrial countries are highly integrated among themselves but still relatively closed to poor country products and services. Rich countries could significantly ease global inequality by lifting their barriers to imports of agriculture and manufactured textiles. But progress against protection often implies visible short-run costs to communities and workers. Programs to retrain those workers hurt by opening markets in rich countries, and to top up their wages if they accept a lower-paying job, would reduce income inequality at home and indirectly around the world.

### LEARNING TO LIVE WITH INEQUALITY

Any hopes for a quick fix to inequality are misplaced. Belying Marx, the biggest story of the last 150 years has been the emergence in the West of a prosperous and stable middle class. But it took time. During a long transition from agriculture to industry, changes in production and in the structure of employment caused wrenching inequality. Much inequality today may be the natural outcome of what is an analogous transition from an industrial to an information age.

Still, there is no reason to despair. Some inequality is healthy and will speed the transition. The rapidly growing wages of the educated and skilled are making education and training much more attractive personal investments. As more people get greater access to education, their relative income advantage over the unskilled will decline. Meanwhile, the high cost of skilled workers should eventually induce technological change that relies more on unskilled labor, increasing the demand for workers with less training.

More fundamentally, people may care less about their current ranking in a static picture of global income distribution than about just and fair access to a better future, especially for their children. In an unequal world, good opportunities represent fair rules and matter at least as much as current status. Greater opportunities—which can be delivered today—are a better guarantee of a socially coherent global community than improved distribution tomorrow.

The real danger is that growing inequality may become a lightning rod for populist rhetoric and self-defeating isolation. It would be unfortunate if such tempting but false remedies eclipsed the more promising policies—international and domestic—that can help the world manage the long transition to a less-divided postindustrial future.

---

# ECOLOGY AND POLITICS

---

Some years ago T. S. Eliot lamented poetically that the world would end not with a bang but a whimper. For decades the nuclear sword of Damocles hung by the slenderest of threads, threatening a fiery and shattering apocalypse. The quest for security continues, and the nuclear threat, while sharply diminished, remains. Since 1947, the *Bulletin of the Atomic Scientists* has used the hands of a clock—with the hour hand pointed toward midnight and the minute hand moving seemingly inexorably toward it—to symbolize how close humankind stands to the nuclear precipice. In 1988, for the first time in sixteen years, the minute hand of the "Doomsday Clock" was moved away from the witching hour, not toward it—from three to six minutes to midnight. The clock was reset in 1990 and again in 1991, when the editors concluded that "the world has entered a new era." The hands now stood at seventeen minutes from twelve, off the scale of danger. Later, however, the hands were moved back into the danger zone, reflecting fears that forward progress on nuclear issues had stalled. Following the nuclear weapons tests by India and Pakistan in 1998 and fears that the nuclear nonproliferation regime faced possible collapse, the hands were moved closer to midnight, now only nine minutes away.

Despite the ebb and flow of these provocative if imprecise measures, it is clear the threat of a nuclear apocalypse has receded dramatically since the height of the Cold War. Nonetheless, numerous challenges broadly conceived as *ecological* threaten that the final cataclysm may still occur. Perhaps now more by accretion or accident than by design, the consequences of an ecological

373

catastrophe would be no less fatal than a nuclear one. Whether the world's political leaders and others touched by environmental challenges will cope effectively is problematic.

Part Four of *The Global Agenda* examines the politics of the ecological agenda. *Ecology* in this context refers to the relationship between humans and their physical and biological environments. The importance of the environmental issues that populate the global ecological agenda derives from the combination of world population growth and extant consumption patterns that strain the earth's delicate life-support systems. Food and resource scarcities have plagued the ecopolitical landscape from time to time in recent years as world population continues to grow inexorably, but it is a series of other environmental challenges—including acid rain, depletion of the stratospheric ozone layer, destruction of tropical rainforests, and global climate change—that has captured worldwide attention, pushing the ecological problematique to the forefront of the twenty-first century global agenda.

Environmental stresses result from human efforts to stretch the global habitat's ability to sustain ever higher living standards for ever larger numbers of people. Technological innovations are especially important, as they permit newer and sometimes more efficient uses of existing environmental resources. But they also sometimes result in pollution and other forms of environmental degradation of waterways, landmasses, and the atmosphere that threaten the environment future generations will inherit. The global commons—resources such as the oceans, the seabed, the radio spectrum, and outer space—previously regarded as the common heritage of humankind, can now be exploited by the technologically sophisticated, who may seek to deny them to others.

Environmental issues sometimes bear directly on issues of war and peace, as scarcities of renewable and nonrenewable resources may invite the classic kinds of interstate conflict that once characterized competition over territory. Water shortages in the Middle East, for example, threaten economic and political instability in an already politically volatile region, as access to water supplies by downstream countries along the region's major rivers may be constrained by the decisions of states farther upstream. Even comparatively abundant but unevenly distributed resources may create global conflicts if they lead to a level of dependence on foreign suppliers perceived as a threat to national security. Fear that Iraq's Saddam Hussein might gain control over a significant portion of world oil supplies following his invasion of Kuwait was certainly a primary motivation underlying the 1991 Persian Gulf War. If population growth and resource scarcities also portend, as some have argued, that there are "limits to growth" and that the consumption patterns of the past necessary to support the standards of living to which at least the industrial world has become accustomed must be curtailed in the future, questions of equity and justice, already so prominent on the North-South axis of the global agenda, will be magnified. The future of all people and states is thus affected by how these issues are addressed, and the world that our children and their children inherit will be profoundly affected by the choices made today.

States, acting alone, may be the appropriate vehicles for dealing with some environmental issues. Indeed, the United States and many European Union countries have made great strides in recent decades in managing ecological issues, often reversing destructive environmental trends set in motion years earlier. In many cases, however, multilateral cooperation, not unilateralism, will be required. Acid rain and other transboundary pollutants know no limits. Nuclear contamination of the atmosphere poses threats far beyond its origins. Climatological changes induced by fossil fuel consumption and destruction of the protective ozone layer caused by other abuses imperil all. Concerted international collaborative efforts are required to deal with these and many of the other ecological issues that populate the global agenda.

The Earth Summit, which took place in June 1992 in Rio de Janeiro, Brazil, was an important milestone in the development of public consciousness of environmental issues and the need for transnational cooperation to deal with them. Formally known as the United Nations Conference on Environment and Development (UNCED), the summit brought together more than 150 governments, one thousand four hundred nongovernmental organizations, and some eight thousand journalists. UNCED Secretary-General Maurice F. Strong characterized the work of the summit as "a new beginning," the "first steps on a new pathway to our common future." Earth Summit participants agreed on statements of principles relating to the environment and development and to the management of the earth's forests, conventions on climate change and biodiversity, and a program of action—*Agenda 21*—which embodied a political commitment to the realization of a broad range of environmental and development goals.

Prior to the Earth Summit the environment and development had been treated separately—and often regarded as in conflict with one another, as development frequently imperils and degrades the environment. During the Earth Summit itself the concept *sustainable development* was used to galvanize a simultaneous treatment of environmental and development issues. The concept was first articulated in *Our Common Future,* the 1987 report of the World Commission on Environment and Development, popularly known as the Brundtland Commission after the Norwegian Prime Minister who was its chair. The commission defined a sustainable society in timeless fashion: It is one that "meets the needs of the present without compromising the ability of future generations to meet their own needs."

Because "sustainability" means living off the earth's interest without encroaching on its capital, it draws attention to problems of intra- and intergenerational equity. At issue is how current needs can be met without depriving future generations of the resources necessary for their own prosperity and survival. It is unlikely that sustainability can be achieved without dramatic changes in the social, economic, and political fabric of the world as we now know it.

The sustainability concept and its underlying logic continue to color nearly all discussions of global ecological issues, including those in the many international conferences on environment and development that have been held since the Earth Summit. Many of the issues that first stimulated concern for sustainable development also remain. But rapid technological change and a rapidly globalizing world have also affected the debate, as we will see in the chapters comprising Part Four of *The Global Agenda*.

Our first essay on ecology and politics, titled "Entering the 21st Century," casts long-standing ecopolitical concerns within a new millennial context. Author John L. Petersen asks the simple question "What does a new millennium mean?" During much of the 1990s, commercial firms sought to profit from the thousand-year calendar turning as they promoted their visions of the future. Persistent concerns about the "Y2K problem"—the fact that most computers built during the last century might not roll over to recognize the year 2000, with potentially catastrophic effects on financial and transportation systems and the delivery of health care, among others—dominated headlines, as computer software companies, political pundits, and policy makers all speculated about the prospects of failed computer systems in a globalized world critically dependent on information technologies.

The Y2K problem posed potentially serious challenges. But Petersen suggests that historical changes typically take place over long periods, and that most events that have moved life in new directions are not recognized until long after they have occurred. Are impending developments in the twenty-first century likely to be any different? Petersen thinks the answer is yes.

Information technologies, which we have highlighted in previous chapters in *The Global Agenda*, figure prominently in making this century potentially different. Petersen also draws attention to issues at center stage in this section of the book. "The population explosion is an unequaled event in human history," he writes. "The tripling of the world's denizens within one lifetime . . . is clearly a big enough deal to send humanity off in a new direction." The inequality issue Birdsall addresses in the last chapter of Part Three also figures prominently. "The rich very rapidly are getting richer and the poor are becoming more disenfranchised. This trend cannot continue without dire implications for everyone on the planet." And the potential for dramatic environmental changes cannot be minimized. "Any number of events—rapid climate change, the Antarctic ice sheet breaking loose and sliding like a huge ice cube into the ocean, . . . a significant opening of the ozone hole—would be devastating and produce a world that clearly looked and behaved in numerous new ways."

Others have also noted these and other potential changes and challenges, and they, too, have speculated about their impact. Petersen adds the important insight that these prospective events are unfamiliar in the human experience. "Each is of a scale that humanity never has dealt with before. We have no experience to draw on in solving them. There is nothing in our social or governmental tool kit for responding. In fact, each of these potential events share a unique set of characteristics—they are at the same time global in scope, potentially disastrous, and intrinsically out of control." Thus "humanity well may be at a millennial crossroads."

Which path will humanity follow? Certainly there are reasons to be pessimistic about the ability of societies, governments, and international institutions to cope with today's challenges. But Petersen also observes that "history tells us we are at a moment of opportunity—a time of potential transition to a new era of human development." Science and technology will figure prominently as we "position ourselves with new knowledge to deal with the potential problems that are arrayed on our horizon."

Well-known human ecologists Paul and Anne Ehrlich are decidedly less optimistic. In their essay, "Ecological Myths: One Planet, One Experiment," they address a range of what they call "fables" about global environmental deterioration they believe others have promoted in the name of "sound science" and "balance" in the environmental debate. The "fables" deal with issues of population and food, the atmosphere and climate, toxic substances, and economics and the environment. In all four areas, and in the more detailed analyses of the questions subsumed under them, the Ehrlichs are highly critical of those who believe that current environmental trends pose no serious threat to humanity.

The Ehrlichs' prescriptions are as stark as their analyses. "Civilization's highest priority must be lowering the pressure on . . . vital ecosystems," they write. "Achieving this will require humanely reducing the size of populations worldwide by lowering birthrates to below death rates, reducing per capita consumption among the rich to make room for needed growth in consumption among the poor, and adopting more environmentally benign technologies." And they warn that "global society is running a vast and dangerous experiment. If the experiment goes wrong, there will be no way to rerun it."

Among ecological and environmental analysts the Ehrlichs are regarded as *neo-Malthusians.* The term harkens back to the Reverend Thomas Malthus, an early "growth pessimist" who in 1798 wrote a classic, the *Essay on the Principle of Population,* in which he predicted that world population growth would eventually outstrip humankind's ability to feed itself. Today, neo-Malthusians believe that world population is pushing against the earth's resources, straining its ability to meet the needs of this generation and the next. Indeed, the Ehrlichs argue that "humanity has already overshot earth's carrying capacity by a simple measure: no nation is supporting its present population on a sustainable flow of renewable resources."

Counterpoised to the neo-Malthusians are "growth optimists." Often called *cornucopians,* they place greater faith in the ability of humankind to cope with ecopolitical challenges. For them, the magic of the marketplace is the adjustment mechanism that ultimately will balance the size and distribution of the human population and the sustaining capabilities of the physical, social, and economic environments. Economists steeped in the tradition of economic liberalism are often among the chief advocates of the cornucopian viewpoint. Though not beyond challenge, their perspective is a useful antidote to the pessimism of neo-Malthusians, who too often leave us with the impression that little can be done to ameliorate the global environmental adversities that humankind now faces.

In our next selection, by Mark Sagoff, the author asks simply "Do We Consume Too Much?" Reflecting cornucopian logic, he concludes that "the idea that increasing consumption will inevitably lead to depletion and scarcity, as plausible as it may seem, is mistaken both in principle and in fact."

Sagoff argues that four "misconceptions" lead us to this erroneous conclusion: that we are running out of raw materials; that we are running out of food and timber; that we are running out of energy; and that the Global North exploits the Global South. In each case Sagoff provides credible evidence to counter the "misconception."

So what is wrong with consumption? Here Sagoff departs from the usual cornucopian viewpoint. He notes that "the imposition of a market economy on traditional cultures in the name of development—for example, the insistence that everyone produce and consume more—can dissolve the ties to family, land, community, and place on which indigenous peoples traditionally rely for their security." Instead, and drawing on long-standing religious and philosophical traditions and values, Sagoff argues that "well-being depends upon health, membership in a community in which one feels secure, friends, faith, family, love, and virtues that money cannot buy." From this perspective, the differences between growth optimists and growth pessimists are often misdirected: "As long as the debate over sustainability is framed in terms of the physical limits to growth rather than the moral purpose of it, mainstream economic theory will have the better of the argument. If the debate were framed in moral or social terms, the result might well be otherwise."

Sagoff prefers to frame the ecological debate in the latter terms. "In defending old-growth forests, wetlands, or species," he writes, "we make our best arguments when we think of nature chiefly in aesthetic and moral terms." Thus the world has enough resources "to provide everyone the opportunity to live a decent life." But "we consume too much when market relationships displace the bonds of community, compassion, culture, and place. We consume too much when consumption becomes an end in itself and makes us lose affection and reverence for the natural world."

In the tradition of Malthus's classic essay on population principles, neo-Malthusians often direct attention to the relationship between population growth and food production and consumption. In Chapter 35, "Dietary Implications of the Globalization of Food Trade," Tim Lang takes a slightly different tact, focusing instead on how globalization has encouraged the worldwide spread of the "Northern diet," one highly dependent on processed foods and "replete with saturated fats and lower than desirable in anti-oxidants."

Lang describes how a confluence of interests among government agencies, transnational corporations, and food retailers has promoted the globalization of the food industry, which permits many countries to consume foodstuffs far in excess of what they produce domestically. He also notes some of the environmental costs incurred in creating and selling processed foods, particularly energy consumption. One study, for example, found that the production of one truckload of strawberry yogurt in Europe required burning some 10,000 liters of diesel fuel.

The globalization of food trade has also affected what farmers grow and how they grow it. Today wholesalers and retailers require that products be "unblemished, of a certain size, uniformity, and so on, which only a narrow form of farming can produce." Similarly, the global food system has impacted local systems, as reliance on a few foreign suppliers has increased. "An export orientation imposed on its farmers means a dislocation in food culture: produce is sold that is not consumed locally, and products are consumed that are produced elsewhere. This new economic regime undermines the policies of those developing countries that were previously committed to policies of national food self-reliance."

As the global food system becomes more homogenized, Lang asks—almost rhetorically—"Is it beyond the realm of possibility that, over the next decades, we shall witness a spread of so-called Western diseases of affluence, such as coronary heart disease and some of the food-related cancers?"

Laurie Garrett, author of our next chapter titled "Encroaching Plagues: The Return of Infectious Disease," also worries about the impact of globalization on people's health. Garrett explains how, surprisingly, humans have become vulnerable to threats from microorganisms once thought to have largely been conquered. Microbes have proven to be remarkably adaptable, thus challenging the belief widespread since World War II that the world's public health community could leave "the age of infectious disease permanently behind."

The mobility of people in a world undergoing rapid globalization sharpens the threat of encroaching plagues: "Every week one million people cross an international border. One million a week travel between the industrial and developing worlds. And as people move, unwanted microbial hitchhikers tag along. . . . In the age of jet travel . . . a person incubating a disease such as Ebola can board a plane, travel 12,000 miles, pass unnoticed through customs and immigration, take a domestic carrier to a remote destination, and still not develop symptoms for several days, infecting many other people before his condition is noticeable."

Rapid urbanization throughout the world, much of it related to overpopulation in the Global South as people migrant from rural areas to cities in search of economic opportunity, is also a major contributing factor. "These new centers of urbanization typically lack sewage systems, paved roads, housing, safe drinking water, medical facilities, and schools adequate to serve even the most affluent residents. They are squalid sites of destitution where hundreds of thousands live much as they would in poor villages, yet so jammed together as to ensure astronomical transmission rates for airborne, waterborne, sexually transmitted, and contact-transmission microbes."

Garrett worries about the national security implications of the return of infectious diseases, including what she sees as the threat of biological warfare. In a larger sense, however, the microbial threat grows out of the complex human-millieu relationships which intertwine humankind with its biological and physical environments without regard to the political borders that separate peoples. If Garrett's analysis is correct, political leaders and public health officials alike will be tested as they seek to cope with the epidemiological challenges of a borderless world.

The prospect of global climate change also promises to challenge political leaders. The issue figured prominently at the 1992 Earth Summit. At that time negotiators reached agreement on a Framework Convention on Climate Change whose purpose was to address the human causes of climate change by reducing emissions of carbon dioxide and other "greenhouse" gases. The agreement imposed few obligations on the signatory parties, reducing their incentives to comply with agreed-upon targets and complicating the politics of climate change policy in a global context.

For years scientists had warned that global warming—the gradual rise in world temperatures—would cause dramatic changes in world climatological patterns, stimulating widespread changes in the world's political and economic systems and relationships. Many also believed that an increase in human-made gases released into the atmosphere—principally carbon dioxide caused by burning fossil fuels—was the primary climate change culprit, altering the natural "greenhouse" effect of the atmosphere when it traps heat from the earth that would otherwise escape into outer space.

Critics of the thesis that human activity causes global warming countered that the observable rise in global temperature during the past century is part of the cyclical pattern of temperature changes the world has experienced for tens of thousands of years. That view is increasingly discredited, however. Since 1988, hundreds of scientists from around the world have been organized as a team, known as the Intergovernmental Panel on Climate Change (IPCC), whose purpose is to assess the evidence of climate change and its causes. In 1995, the IPCC for the first time stated conclusively its belief that global climate trends are "unlikely to be entirely due to natural causes." Instead, "the balance of evidence. . . . suggests a discernible human influence on global climate." Without significant efforts to reduce the emission of greenhouse gases, the IPCC concluded, dramatic global temperature rises during the twenty-first century could exceed those which ended the last ice age. Already the world has entered a period of climatic instability likely to cause, as the IPCC put it, "widespread economic, social and environmental dislocation."

If the scientific community is now comparatively united in its assessments of the causes and consequences of global climate change, the world's political leaders remain in disarray as they assess policy choices for dealing with it. Differences between the Global North and South are especially acute, reflecting in part the vast differences in their economies and the role of energy resources, past, present, and future, in fueling economic advancement. These differences were cast in sharp relief when many of the signatories of Earth Summit's Framework Convention on Climate Change met in Kyoto, Japan, in 1997 to hammer out a new agreement (now known as the Kyoto Protocol) that would move the world community toward enforceable standards designed to reduce harmful emissions.

Seth Dunn assesses the sources of contention between North and South—and often within the South itself—in the next chapter, "Climate Change: Can the North and South Get In Step?" A primary source of North-South differences turns on present and projected estimates of harmful emissions. "With only a fifth of the world's population, industrial and former Eastern Bloc nations account for 74 percent of the carbon emitted since 1950. These countries produce 60 percent of today's annual emissions." Against this background, Southern states see Northern efforts to establish rigorous emission standards as attempts to perpetuate their underdevelopment.

The North responds by pointing out that "developing countries . . . are quickly becoming major emitters in their own right. Today, the South produces 40 percent of the world's carbon total—2.5 billion tons. And . . . booming population and economic growth is fueling an explosive increase in carbon emissions."

Southern states are themselves also divided. A group of countries known as "small island states" are especially worried that the interests of oil-producing countries in extracting and marketing fossil fuels literally endangers their very existence. Most predictions of the consequences of global warming portend a dramatic rise in sea levels, which could engulf these low-lying island states, threatening their peoples and destroying their habitats and cultures.

Dunn assesses the prospects for bridging North-South differences and moving the world community toward a climate change agreement acceptable to all. He suggests the 1987 Montreal Protocol on protecting the earth's ozone layer may provide "a helpful map" to climate change negotiators. He also points to the Clean Development Mechanism in the Kyoto Protocol as potentially useful. But he finally concludes that the best way to bridge the North-South gap on this critical environmental issue is to convince governments that "tangible development benefits"—"cleaner air, greater energy self-reliance, added government revenue, more jobs, leadership in new industries"—can flow from efforts to address climate change issues, particularly as they affect the Global South. Simply put, governments must do more to "utilize these connections in far more opportunistic fashion than they have to date." He adds that "the challenge of resolving the 'developing country issue' is mainly a conceptual one: to transcend today's fractious finger pointing and fixation on costs, and envision the Kyoto Protocol as a valuable and vital stepping-stone toward sustainability."

Demographic issues and concerns underlay virtually all of the issues that address the intersection of ecology and politics. We address these issues and concerns directly in our next two chapters. The first focuses on a long-standing concern—rapid population growth in the Global South—the second on a more recent attention-getter—rapid aging in the Global North.

In "The Next Doubling: Understanding Global Population Growth," Jennifer D. Mitchell begins by examining the sheer magnitude of projected population growth, which in the lifetime of most readers of this book is likely to result in a world not of 6 billion people, as today, but of 9 billion or more. Mitchell notes that the effects of this dramatic increase will "ripple out" from the "frontline" states—those countries that will experience "the greatest immediate burdens" because they have the highest population growth rates—"to encompass the world as a whole."

Three factors explain this startling reality: unmet demand for family planning in much of the most rapidly growing regions of the world; a desire for large families among couples even when family planning services are available; and population momentum—the often poorly understood fact that "nearly one-half of the [population] increase projected for the next fifty years will occur simply because the next reproductive generation . . . is so much larger than the current reproductive generation." Indeed, population momentum is the single most important explanation of current and projected population growth.

Having identified the three dimensions of the population explosion, Mitchell turns her attention to remedies. She describes obstacles to the provision of family planning services but concludes optimistically that if a wide range of family planning alternatives are available, couples are likely to use them. She also describes the obstacles—economic, religious, and cultural—to encouraging smaller families, but again ends on an optimistic note, saying "even deeply rooted beliefs are subject to reinterpretation." Beyond this, reducing child mortality, enhancing the economic situation of women, and improving education and educational opportunities all hold out the promise of encouraging smaller families and reaping the benefits that implies.

Population momentum poses the biggest threat of all, but even here some helpful steps can be taken. One is to delay new births. "To understand why delay works," Mitchell writes, "it's helpful to think of momentum as a kind of human accounting problem, in which a large number of births in the near term won't be balanced by a corresponding number of deaths over the same period of time. One side of the population ledger will contain . . . 130 million annual births. . . , while the other side will contain only about 50 million annual deaths. So to put the matter in a morbid light, the longer a substantial number of those births can be delayed, the longer the death side of the balance sheet will be when births eventually occur." Strategies designed to delay marriage and hence childbirth thus promise to slow the momentum of population growth.

Governments have a role to play in much of this. In 1994, they met in Cairo at the International Conference on Population and Development (ICPD), where they designed a strategy to address population stabilization issues and promote sustainable economic growth. The Programme of Action agreed to at the conference took a historic step toward global recognition of the critical role that women play in both development and population stabilization. It also set out specific goals to be achieved by 2015 that deal with access to primary school education, family-planning services, reproductive health, infant and underfive mortality, maternal mortality, and life expectancy. Developed and developing countries alike were expected to contribute resources to realization of these ambitious goals.

Mitchell reports that states' commitments toward realization of these goals have fallen short of expectations. Furthermore, she notes that while many of the ICPD objectives are now imbedded in population planning programs, "global population growth has gathered so much momentum that it could simply overwhelm a development agenda." The imperative of curbing population growth remains nonetheless. "Whether we realize it or not," Mitchell writes, "our attempts to stabilize population—or our failure to act—will likely have consequences that far outweigh the implications of the military or commercial crisis of the moment." She adds that "slowing population growth is one of the greatest gifts we can offer future generations."

Population growth has already slowed in the Global North—so dramatically, in fact, that many Northern countries now face negative growth and the prospect of a long-term decline and eventual extinction of their national population base. Peter G. Peterson, chair of the prestigious New York–based Council on Foreign Relations, addresses this startling prospect in "Gray Dawn: The Global Aging Crisis."

Peterson begins with the observation that, "unlike global warming, there can be little debate over whether or when global aging will manifest itself. And unlike with other challenges, even the struggle to preserve and strengthen unsteady new democracies, the costs of global aging will be far beyond the means of even the wealthiest nations—unless retirement benefit systems are radically reformed." These stark projections flow from two simple facts: life expectancy has grown dramatically over the past several decades, and the working-age population necessary to support the gray generation is declining.

As developed countries face the daunting task of caring for their aging populations, they inevitably will confront questions with global implications. Peterson poses them: "Will the developed world be able to maintain its security commitments?" "Will Young/Old become the next North/South fault line?" His answers are tentative but hardly encouraging.

Peterson concludes that the "leaders of major economies . . . are well briefed on the stunning demographic trends that lie ahead" but quickly adds that "so far they have responded with paralysis rather than action." He briefly outlines an agenda states might pursue "to overcome the economic and political challenges of an aging society." In the end, however, he acknowledges that "all of the proposed strategies unfortunately touch raw nerves—by amending existing social contracts, by violating cultural expectations, or by offending entrenched ideologies."

As changing demographic patterns and lifestyle preferences test political wills and the ability of the earth's delicate life-support systems to support the world's six-plus billion people, the obvious question to ask is whether these developments are caldrons brewing violent international conflicts.

War inflicts human suffering that is often difficult to comprehend. But it also sometimes precipitates enormous desecration of the environment. Rome sowed salt on a defeated Carthage to prevent its resurgence. The Dutch breached their own dikes to allow ocean saltwater to flood fertile farmlands in an effort to stop the advancing Germans during World War II. The United States used defoliants on the dense jungles in Vietnam in an effort to expose enemy guerrillas. And Iraq engaged in acts of "environmental terrorism" when it released millions of gallons of oil into the Persian Gulf during the war over Kuwait. But is the reverse true? Does desecration of the environment precipitate violent conflict?

On the surface the answer would appear to be yes, but this may be too facile a conclusion. Systematic inquiry by Thomas F. Homer-Dixon and his associates into the relationship between scarcities of critical environmental resources and violent conflict in Africa, Asia, and elsewhere leads to the conclusion that environmental scarcities "do not cause wars between countries, but they can generate severe social stresses within countries, helping to stimulate subnational insurgencies, ethnic clashes, and urban unrest." These dynamics are especially acute in the Global South, whose societies are generally "highly dependent on environmental resources and less able to buffer themselves from the social crises that environmental scarcities cause."

Scarcity takes various forms, as Homer-Dixon explains in "Environmental, Scarcity, and Violence." How differences in scarcities interact with one another complicates our understanding of the relationship between environmental factors and violent conflict and lead us to be cautious in predicting the outcome of potential environmental conflicts.

Homer-Dixon acknowledges that many of the violent conflicts the world has witnessed in the past decade cannot be attributed to environmental scarcities, but he predicts pessimistically that "we can expect [scarcity] to become a more important influence in coming decades because of larger populations and higher per capita resource consumption rates." He adds that if a group of states he calls "pivotal" fall on the wrong side of the "ingenuity gap"—the ability to adapt to environmental scarcity and avoid violent conflict—humanity's overall prospects will dramatically worsen. "Such a world will be neither environmentally sustainable nor politically stable. The rich will be unable to fully isolate themselves from the crises of the poor, and there will be little prospect of building the sense of global community needed to address the array of grave problems—economic, political, as well as ecological—that humanity faces."

The environmental scarcities of concern to Homer-Dixon are primarily those that fall within states' borders. Common property resources are different. When resources are held in common, individual actors have an incentive to exploit them to their maximum, because the collectivity must bear the costs of exploitation but they alone realize the benefits. The metaphor of the tragedy of the commons, a stock concept in environmental politics, helps explain this typical national response to the global commons. Marvin S. Soroos examines the applicability of the metaphor in our final selection, "The Tragedy of the Commons in Global Perspective," and uses it as a springboard to probe several environmental issues and strategies for avoiding environmental tragedies. Importantly, he relates these strategies to values (conservation, production, equity, and freedom), the realization of which necessarily often entails tough political choices as states seek to cope with ecological exigencies.

Soroos concludes that "remarkable progress has been made in establishing the institutional infrastructure needed to preserve the natural environment." And even as he wonders about the ability of sovereign states to cooperate effectively to cope with their common environmental challenges, his analysis of the many areas in which states have already proven an ability to strike bargains to protect their mutual interests makes us optimistic that a global tragedy of the commons may be averted. Thus the future is replete with opportunities as well as challenges.

# 32

# ENTERING THE 21ST CENTURY

JOHN L. PETERSEN

**John L. Petersen speculates about the issues and challenges that will shape the new millennium. They range broadly over technological innovations and patterns of human behavior and development whose consequences are difficult to predict but which portend that "we have come to a historical moment of change." Petersen is founder and president of The Arlington Institute, which specializes in studying the future.**

What does a new millennium mean? That's like asking what a birthday means. Most of them don't *mean* anything; they are just another year passing—except for a few particular ones. If it is your sixteenth birthday and you can get a driver's license, that's special. On your eighteenth, you can vote, and you come of age legally at twenty-one. Fifty probably signifies a particular transition to most people, and sixty-five is often time for retirement. It is not so much that the day has significance, but, rather, what happens to one on that day that makes it memorable. As often as not, a birthday is important when it represents a transition from one distinct time of life to another.

Years are momentous to individual people as decades, centuries, and millennia are to societies and civilizations. Past millennial shifts are particularly significant if they are coincident with major cultural change. On December 31, 999, for example, most places in the world were pretty grim and, unless you were educated (and probably living in Europe), that day was not much different than the one before it. January 1, 000, didn't exist until after the fact, so no one (except

387

the shepherds and wise men perhaps) celebrated that particular day. (The year 2000 [is] different.)

Unlike birthdays, social transitions happen over time, usually years. Historical evolutions from one era to another have taken hundreds or thousands of years. Nevertheless, as life has moved into its most recent periods, key events—such as the invention of movable type by Johannes Gutenberg and the invention of the transistor—can be identified as signals of the beginning of a new era. Usually, major social or economic shifts are obvious only in hindsight, but, in the present case, history gives substantive clues about what may be happening now that can be coupled with present and potential events which easily could be early indicators of great change.

Life on this planet has evolved in a fascinatingly regular way. Starting with single cellular life and marching through multiple cellular life, vertebrates, mammals, early man, and homo sapiens, the length of dominance of each era turns out to be about one-tenth of the previous one. That relationship holds to the recent past, continuing with the transition from hunter-gatherers to organized agriculture, the move into towns and cities, and the beginning of the industrial age. Nomadic hunter-gatherers lasted about fifty thousand years, for instance, while the period of time dominated by the development of towns and cities was around five thousand years, and the era begun by Gutenberg's movable type ran somewhat less than five hundred years.

If that spiraling sequence of development, which roughly goes back to the beginning of life as we know it, holds into the recent past and near future, one could posit that the present computer or information age will be about fifty years long. Its beginning could be marked arbitrarily with the development of the transistor in the early 1950s, possibly to end shortly after 2000. That is but one of a number of indicators that raise the possibility that the beginning of the new millennium also could be the beginning of an important new period in the evolution of humanity.

The other characteristic of each era is a significant increase in knowledge compared to its predecessor. Multiple cellular life is more complex than single cellular life. Living in cities and towns represents a higher level of information content than simple living centered on early agriculture. Each subsequent age is organized around far more intelligence than the previous one, perhaps by an order of magnitude.

So, the key to a new human era is the development of new knowledge that becomes the fundamental attribute of the succeeding years. This historical relationship of time and knowledge suggests that humans will (must) develop a great deal of knowledge in a short period of time in order to enter the next era of life.

What kind of knowledge will that be? There is no shortage of candidates, for this is a time of an explosion in knowledge. It has been suggested, for example, that more than 85 percent of the scientists who ever have lived are alive today, and that humans have learned more about science in the last fifty years than in the five thousand preceding years. It is hard, if not impossible, therefore, to know before the fact which of the many big changes that appear on the horizon might be the seminal one that establishes humanity on a new trajectory. Clearly, the world is experiencing exponential advances in computer capability. Within the next decade, the planet with be circled by approximately seventeen hundred new communication satellites, weaving an information web around the globe that could be a profound stage-setter for the future. The advent of this "global brain" certainly is of a level of significance that would qualify as a new era.

The population explosion is an unequaled event in human history. The tripling of the world's denizens within one lifetime—with all of the attendant problems that are likely to ensue from the invariable concentrations of impoverished people—is clearly a big enough deal to send humanity off in a new direction. A companion issue is that of the haves and have-nots. The rich very rapidly are getting richer and the poor are becoming more disenfranchised. This trend cannot continue without dire implications for everyone on the planet.

Although it is not yet known generally, it appears that the Earth is on the verge of an energy revolution that would make fossil fuels obsolete. Quantum mechanics say almost all of the energy in the universe exists in the open space around us. If we could convert that electromagnetic energy into heat or electricity, we clearly would enter a new era that would befit being named after that event. A breakthrough could come within two or three years, so the timing would be about right for a new epoch.

Of course, the world's environmental concerns could turn into something that might describe a new historical era. Any number of events—rapid climate change, the Antarctic ice sheet breaking loose and sliding like a huge ice cube into the ocean (and flooding many coastal cities), a significant opening of the ozone hole—would be devastating and produce a world that clearly looked and behaved in numerous new ways. Something as amazing as the unambiguous discovery of extraterrestrial life certainly would produce unprecedented change. There are a variety of potential events of this magnitude arrayed upon the horizon. . . .

Variations on these and other potentially extraordinary events are cataloged by Eugene Linden in *The Future in Plain Sight: Nine Clues to the Coming Instability.* Linden carefully details how erratic global financial markets, the urbanization of the Third World, human migration patterns, the have/have-not situation, unusual environment and weather indicators, biospheric degradation, worldwide food shortages, resurgent infectious diseases, and the increase in groups of "true believers" all point toward a coming period of global instability. He suggests that any of these nine indicators could result in major change, with the possibility of two or more of them happening concurrently or in sequence, producing exponential effects.

He outlines the grand problem in stark terms: "Humanity has proliferated to the point where we now have the capacity to destabilize global systems that were beyond the reach of our ancestors. The spiderweb of links connecting peoples and economies around the world can spread ill as well as good. Even in the limited sphere of finance, the scale and connectedness of global markets make a return to instability a frightening prospect. Stability has produced a situation in which we can no longer afford instability."

There is a problem with these scenarios—they are not familiar events. Each is of a scale that humanity never has dealt with before. We have no experience to draw on in solving them. There is nothing in our social or governmental tool kit for responding. In fact, each of these potential events share a unique set of characteristics—they are at the same time global in scope, potentially disastrous, and intrinsically out of control. What that means is that no one government or other institution can solve these quandaries. Our social and economic systems are not designed to deal effectively with issues of this character.

The potential solutions for these global issues run counter to many of the fundamentals upon which advanced human society is built. Financial investor and philanthropist George Soros makes the case most articulately in *The Crisis of Global Capitalism: Open Society Endangered.* After showing that financial markets are intrinsically unstable, he cites a basic mismatch between the ideal values of the financial and political worlds. Open societies (like that in the U.S.) balance on the perilous pyramid point between the extremes of closed, authoritative societies on one side and Russian-like economic and social collapse on the other. Significant shock to an open society—particularly one with the value set of a competitive, materialistic economy—has the distinct possibility of pushing a previously open society down one of the steep precipices to either authoritarian control or large-scale instability. His is an argument for collective, rather than individual, decision-making. When people act only for themselves, no one does so for the common good. In the end, the exclusive focus on competition must give way to a balanced approach that embraces both competition and cooperation.

Garrett Hardin's celebrated 1968 article in *Science.* "The Tragedy of the Commons," expanded the notion which already was implicit in the mathematical game called "Prisoners' Dilemma"—that there are circumstances where individuals following what for each of them would rationally appear to be their own personal best interests will, as a group, suffer more than if they had adopted a more modest strategy of cooperation. Others are making these points as well. There is a need for fundamental change in our systems and outlook if we are to advance (let alone survive) in the coming few years. Our industrial-age society and economy exist in an era of post-industrial-age problems; there is a serious mismatch.

This, by the way, is not millennial madness. It is coincidental that the confluence of these trends converges on the beginning of the millennium. None of this has anything intrinsically to do with the year 2000.

## A MILLENNIAL CROSSROADS

There are grounds, then, to suggest that humanity well may be at a millennial crossroads. We have come to a historical moment of change. On one hand, we are confronted by a series of potentially extraordinary events that are incompatible with fundamental systemic weaknesses within our political and economic processes. There are clear indicators suggesting that, if we continue as we have, there is likely to be large-scale instability that has the possibility of plunging advanced, open societies backward into authoritarian or chaotic situations, wiping out decades of advancement. In the face of large-scale chaos, reasonable people will opt for stability, however it is obtained.

On the other hand, history tells us we are at a moment of opportunity—a time of potential transition to a new era of human development. That evolution, though, comes with lots of new knowledge and rapid change. We can move swiftly ahead in a new direction, developing fresh perspectives around common institutions like politics and economics, or continue as we have and risk the possibility of what, in the worst case, could be disaster.

I believe the choice is ours, and with this choice we have been given the resources—in fact, the vehicle—with which to transit this era and, in the process, position ourselves with new knowledge to deal with the potential problems that are arrayed on our horizon. A common thread has emerged out of many areas of science, technology, and society in the last few years—the fact that all of life coexists in a huge system of systems. We live among relationships, tied and linked inextricably to millions of dependencies, most of which we are not aware of. The clear connections between sciences like physics, chemistry, and biology, in the past discounted or unobserved, have spawned an explosion of disciplines which exist on the borders between the fundamentals. Anyone who—along with dozens, if not thousands, of others—has been at the mercy of an erratic computer network clearly understands the notion of interdependency. Ecologists finally have come to the conclusion that a combination of technological, economic, and attitudinal changes must evolve concurrently if there is to be any significant change in the world's pollution habits. When there are financial crises in Asia, they ripple throughout the rest of the world's economies.

This relationship was not obvious in the past. We generally thought of ourselves as independent, able as individuals, corporations, and countries to pursue our own interests, giving little thought of what the implications might be for others located somewhere else. We embraced what we thought naturalist Charles Darwin said and took it as gospel. It was okay that there would be big winners and losers, attributing it to natural selection. We didn't know that these ideas would produce pollution and large-scale poverty, to name two current problems. The issue wasn't shortage of basic supplies. There clearly is enough (food, for example) for everyone; it just isn't distributed equitably.

During the industrial age, value was measured in physical goods called capital: land, machinery, buildings, and money. Those commodities were considered to be limited. Therefore, an economic system came into being based upon scarcity, assigning value for something based upon one's perception of its relative availability. Because what was valued was physical, it was clear who possessed it.

This was a zero-sum relationship: if one party owned it, another didn't. It was natural that a philosophy should evolve that pitted people against each other in competition, vying for scarce capital goods.

The world is changing, however. Systems theory—and common sense—tell us that, when a part of a system is not working well, because of the interconnections with the rest of it, the larger system is affected as well. If the problem is big enough, the entire system ceases to function effectively. It is axiomatic that a failure in part of the system affects the whole system. What we now are looking at is a series of very big problems that could drag down the entire system if they are not effectively dealt with. It is becoming clearer that, in one way or another, we all are dependent upon everyone else.

This presents a new principle for approaching the problems of the future. If there are enough resources within the system for everyone and if serious system failure is possible and plausible, it is obvious that it is in all of our best interests that we should cooperate to maintain the health of the system. In writing about the political implications of such a policy, Soros suggests: "Suppose that people came to recognize that global competition has become too fierce and there is greater need for cooperation; suppose further that they learned to distinguish between individual decision-making and collective decision-making. The representatives they elected would then advocate different policies and they would be held to different standards of behavior."

It also is clear that capital will be much less valued in the future, compared to information and knowledge. One merely has to look at the success of Microsoft, which, in traditional terms, manufacturers nothing, to see this trend. That information is the capital commodity of the future introduces quite a different element to the human economic process, for information is unlimited, not scarce. Because it is not zero-sum, many people can have the same information without it losing value. As it is distributed (perhaps at no cost), information may increase in value, as in the case of Internet browsers. Or it can be stolen off a hard drive and one never will know that it has been copied. Furthermore, there is one characteristic of information that is key—in general, it has value only if communicated.

As connectivity explodes and contextual change continues unabated, these two ideas—cooperation and communication—form the underpinnings of a new framework for future human activity. In the short term, they could provide the fundamental structure for dealing with the big problems on the horizon. In the long term, they could catapult us into a new era of human development.

# 33

# ECOLOGICAL MYTHS: ONE PLANET, ONE EXPERIMENT

## PAUL R. EHRLICH AND ANNE H. EHRLICH

**Human ecologists Paul R. and Anne H. Ehrlich seek to balance cornucopians' optimism about global environmental trends. They address what they call "myths" or "fables" about "issues relating to population and food, the atmosphere and climate, toxic substances, and economics and the environment." Paul R. Ehrlich, author of several books including *The Population Bomb*, is Bing Professor of Population Studies, and Anne H. Ehrlich is senior research associate, in the Department of Biological Sciences at Stanford University.**

When polled, 65 percent of U.S. citizens say they are willing to pay good money for better environmental protection, but at the same time most do not believe that environmental deterioration is a crucial issue in their own lives. This seeming contradiction may stem from the fact that it is difficult to recognize subtle and gradual environmental change. But it may also stem from another fact: that various sources, including conservative think tanks such as the Cato Institute and the Heritage Foundation, have been disseminating erroneous information regarding the true state of the environment. Adam Myerson, editor of the Heritage Foundation's *Policy Review,* pretty much summed up this viewpoint in the journal when he maintained that "leading scientists have done major work disputing the current henny-pennyism about global warming, acid rain, and other purported environmental catastrophes."

A flood of recent books and articles has also advanced the notion that all is well with the environment after giving undue prominence to the opinions of one or a handful of contrarian scientists in the name of "sound science" and "balance." With strong and appealing messages, these authors have successfully sowed the seeds of doubt among policy makers and the public about the reality and importance of phenomena such as overpopulation, global climate change, ozone depletion, and loss of biodiversity. . . .

What follows is a sampling of the myths, or fables, that the promoters of "sound science" and "balance" are promulgating about issues relating to population and food, the atmosphere and climate, toxic substances, and economics and the environment. By looking at them through the lens of the present scientific consensus, we aim to reveal the gross errors on which they are founded. Thus we may return to higher ground and engage in a crucial dialogue about how to sustain the environment.

## FABLES ABOUT POPULATION AND FOOD

*There is no overpopulation today because the earth has plenty of room for more people.* In fact, humanity has already overshot earth's carrying capacity by a simple measure: no nation is supporting its present population on a sustainable flow of renewable resources. Rich agricultural soils are being eroded in many areas at rates of inches per decade, though such soils are normally formed at rates of inches per millennium. Accumulations of "fossil" fresh water, stored underground over thousands of years during glacial periods, are being mined as if they were metals—and often for low-value uses such as irrigating forage crops like alfalfa, for grazing animals. Water from those aquifers, which are recharged at rates measured in inches per year, is being pumped out in feet per year. And species and populations of microorganisms, plants, and other animals are being exterminated at a rate unprecedented in 65 million years—on the order of ten thousand times faster than they can be replaced by the evolution of new ones.

*We needn't worry about population growth in the United States, because it's not nearly as densely populated as other countries.* The idea that the number of people per square mile is a key determinant of population pressure is as widespread and persistent as it is wrong. In *Apocalypse Not,* published by the Cato Institute, economist Ben Bolch and chemist Harold Lyons point out that if the 1990 world population were placed in Texas, less than half of 1 percent of earth's land surface, "each person would have an area equal to the floor space of a typical U.S. home." They also say: "Anyone who has looked out an airplane window while traveling across the country knows how empty the United States really is."

But the key issue in judging overpopulation is not how many people can fit into any given space but whether the earth can supply the population's long-term requirements for food, water, and other resources. Most of the "empty" land in the United States either grows the food essential to the well-being of Americans and much of the world (as in Iowa), supplies us with forestry products (as in northern Maine), or, lacking water, good soil, and a suitable climate, cannot contribute directly to the support of civilization (as in much of Nevada). The point is that densely populated countries such as the Netherlands, Bermuda, and Monaco and cities such as Singapore, São Paulo, Mexico City, Tokyo, and New York *can* be crowded with people only because the rest of the world is not.

*We should have a bigger population for no other reason than that "people like to be alive."* One can respond to such statements by asking, "Would people like to be alive if they had to live like chickens in factory farms?" But such retorts are unnecessary. The best way to maximize the number of Americans (or Chinese or Nigerians) who live wouldn't be to cram as many of them as possible into these countries in the next few decades until they self-destruct. Rather, it is to have permanently sustainable populations in those nations for tens of thousands, perhaps millions, of years.

*We need a larger population so we will have more geniuses to solve our environmental problems.* Having additional people to work on problems does not necessarily lead to solutions. Consider what happened to the people of Easter Island after this lush, sixty-four-square-mile subtropical Pacific island, some two thousand miles west of Chile, was colonized by Polynesians some fifteen hundred years ago. Even as the population soared to around twenty thousand, all those minds couldn't solve the tiny island's resource problems. The large forest of towering palm trees that graced the land was harvested more rapidly than it regenerated. Once they were gone, there was no way to build canoes for porpoise hunting, and without the forest to absorb and meter out rainfall, streams and springs dried up, unprotected soil eroded away, crop yields dropped, and famine struck the once-rich island. Unlike most premodern peoples, the islanders apparently didn't limit their fertility. Instead, as food supplies became short they switched to cannibalism, which turned out to be an effective—if not very attractive—method of population control. A common curse became, "The flesh of your mother sticks between my teeth."

Can't today's population, with its knowledge of the histories of past civilizations and billions of working minds, help us avoid the fate of the Easter Islanders, and the Henderson Islanders (who completely died out on one of the Pitcairn islands in the South Pacific), the classic Mayans, the Anasazi (Native Americans who built the vast pueblos of Chaco Canyon), and others who destroyed the environmental supports of their societies? We wish the answer were yes. Yet the billions of human minds we have today are not stopping society from destroying its resources even faster than earlier civilizations destroyed theirs.

But that aside, perhaps the larger point is that environmental rather than genetic differences determine what proportion of a population will display genius. It's very hard to become the next Mozart if one is starving to death on the outskirts of Port-au-Prince. Having more people today is not the solution for generating more geniuses. Creating environments in which the inherent talents of people now disadvantaged—by race or gender discrimination, poverty, or malnutrition—can be fully expressed, is.

*Feeding the world's population is a problem of distribution, not supply.* Of course, if everyone shared food resources equally and no grain were fed to animals, all of humanity could be adequately nourished today. Unfortunately, such scenarios are irrelevant. Although people in developed countries could eat lower on the food chain—that is, by consuming less meat and more grain—and might be willing to make such sacrifices to improve the environment, it is as unrealistic to think we will all suddenly become vegetarian saints as it is to think we will suddenly trade in our cars for bicycles or go to bed at sunset to save energy.

But even if everyone *were* willing to eat a largely vegetarian diet today, with only a small supplement from fish and range-fed animals, and food were equitably distributed to everyone, today's harvests could feed about 7 billion such altruistic vegetarians, according to calculations by the Alan Shawn Feinstein World Hunger Program at Brown University and . . . the Center for Conservation Biology, at Stanford. Since the world's population is nearly 6 billion already, that is hardly a comforting number.

*We needn't worry about future food supplies because scientific breakthroughs (as yet unimagined) will boost grain yields around the world.* Analyses of food-production trends over the past few decades suggest that there certainly *is* cause to worry about maintaining food supplies. While it is true that the most important indicator of human nutrition, world grain production, has roughly tripled since 1950, what food optimists overlook is that the Green Revolution has already been put in place in most suitable areas, and most of the expected yield gains have been achieved. Consequently, grain production increases have failed to keep up with population growth since 1985, and we've seen no productivity gains in absolute terms since 1990. Meanwhile, grain reserves have shrunk severely. A new kit of tools to expand food production is required to carry us into the future, yet no such kit appears to be on the horizon. And even if some unanticipated breakthrough were to be made, it would take years if not decades to develop and deploy new crop varieties—years during which demand would continue rising as the population expanded.

## FABLES ABOUT THE ATMOSPHERE AND CLIMATE

*There is no evidence that global warming is real.* The climatic system is exceedingly complex and not entirely understood, but some facts are indisputable. First, scientists have known for more than a century that releasing carbon dioxide could add to the greenhouse effect caused by the gaseous composition of earth's atmosphere. The atmosphere contains an array of natural greenhouse gases—including water vapor, carbon dioxide, and methane—that are relatively transparent to the incoming short-wavelength energy of sunlight but relatively opaque to the long-wavelength infrared energy radiated upward by the sunlight-warmed earth. The greenhouse gases and clouds together absorb most of this outgoing infrared energy and reradiate some of it back toward earth, thus functioning as a heat-trapping blanket over the planet. The naturally occurring concentrations of these gases are enough to raise earth's average surface temperature to about 59 degrees F. Without greenhouse gases, it would be about 0 degrees, the oceans would be frozen to the bottom, and life as we know it would be impossible.

Second, scientists also know that humanity is adding to the greenhouse effect—that the atmospheric concentration of carbon dioxide in 1992 was some 30 percent above preindustrial levels, and the concentration of methane has increased by 145 percent. Both gases are natural atmospheric constituents whose concentrations have fluctuated substantially in geologic history. But analyses of air trapped in ice cores from the Antarctic and Greenland ice caps show that today's levels are by far the highest concentrations of these greenhouse gases in at least the past one hundred sixty thousand years. Moreover, nitrous oxide, another greenhouse gas, has increased about 15 percent over its preindustrial level. And chlorofluorocarbons (CFCs)—the ozone-destroying chemicals—also contribute to the greenhouse effect.

Thermometers worldwide have documented nearly a full 1-degree rise since the nineteenth century. Furthermore, a consensus has formed in the climatological community that a "discernible signal" of anthropogenic warming is beginning to emerge from the "noise" of natural climatic variation. In fact, the 1995 report of the scientific committee of the Intergovernmental Panel on Climate Change (IPCC) stated that based on the warming recorded over the past century, and especially in recent decades, "the balance of evidence suggests that there is a discernible human influence on global climate."

*Global warming exists only in computer simulations.* The IPCC's conclusion was, indeed, based primarily on a new generation of computer simulations. But the results were also based on detailed comparisons with actual temperature records. Moreover, the total body of evidence that the planet is warming is now overwhelming. For example, surface-temperature records, even when corrected for the effects of urban "heat islands" (areas artificially heated by structures such as buildings and parking lots), show that the 10 warmest years in the past 140 years have all occurred since 1980. And the most recent satellite measurements show that shrinkage in Arctic sea ice, another expected result of global warming, accelerated significantly between 1987 and 1994.

*Even if the concentration of carbon dioxide doubled, since it is responsible for only 1 percent of the greenhouse effect it wouldn't contribute to global warming.*

By itself, a doubling of $CO_2$ (which, incidentally, accounts for some 10 to 25 percent of the natural greenhouse effect, not 1 percent) would warm earth by less than 2 degrees F. But therein lies the power of positive feedback. A 2-degree rise in temperature would cause more water to evaporate from the oceans and thus contribute additional water vapor to the greenhouse effect, resulting in a final warming most climatologists project to be a little less than 4 degrees. But if the complicating ice and cloud feedbacks are added in, models suggest that anywhere from 3 to 9 degrees of warming would result from a doubling in $CO_2$ levels. Scientists cannot make more accurate predictions at the moment because of uncertainties surrounding the feedback processes, yet most think the upper limit represents ecological disaster. For example, 9 degrees is about the difference in global average temperature that separates today's climate from that of the last ice age, when the present site of New York City was visited by a mile-thick glacier.

*If the average mean temperature of the world were to rise a few degrees in [this] century, we could simply wear lighter clothes and use more air-conditioning.* The idea that the primary reason to be concerned about global warming is that our backyards will be a little hotter during the summer barbecue season is as pervasive as it is wrong. The larger problem is that climate change could seriously disrupt a food-production system that already is showing signs of stress. Other potential problems include sea-level rise, which would result in coastal flooding and salinization of groundwater, as well as more intense storms. Finally, natural ecosystems—our life-support systems—will have great difficulty adjusting to rapid climate change. The trees in southern forests can't just fly up to New England or put on a lighter shirt when the heat becomes too much for them.

*CFCs can't rise 18 miles into the atmosphere to deplete the ozone layer because they are made from molecules that are 4 to 8 times heavier than air.* This statement reveals an outrageous misconception about the dynamics of the atmosphere. Gases of the atmosphere are not layered like a lasagna. If they were, the lowest few feet of atmosphere would consist of krypton, ozone, nitrous oxide, carbon dioxide, and argon. Above that would be a thick layer of pure oxygen, and above that an even thicker layer of pure nitrogen followed by water vapor, methane, neon, helium, and hydrogen. In fact, the atmosphere undergoes dynamic mixing, dominated by motions of large air masses, which thoroughly mixes light and heavy gas molecules. Because of this mixing, CFCs have been detected in literally thousands of stratospheric air samples by dozens of research groups all over the world.

*The chlorine in CFCs is not likely to deplete the ozone layer because volcanoes pump out 50 times more chlorine annually than an entire year's production of CFCs.* Mount Erebus *does* pump out 50 times more chlorine per year in the form of hydrogen chloride (HCl) than humanity adds in CFCs. But the statement is irrelevant to depletion of the ozone layer because much of the HCl released by volcanoes is dissolved in the abundant steam that is also emitted and is thus quickly rained out. Unfortunately, unlike HCl, CFCs are not water soluble and thus cannot be washed out of the atmosphere until they have been broken down. And by then, they will already have done their damage to the ozone layer.

*If there were, in fact, some reduction in the ozone layer, we could simply wear more hats and sunscreen lotion to avoid skin cancer.* The direct effects of a thinning of the ozone layer—which include not only increased rates of skin cancer (including lethal melanomas) but also disruptions of the immune system—could, of course, be partially avoided by increased use of hats and sunscreen. But rubbing lotions on earth's plants and animals would be required as well, since the most important threat from ozone depletion is to natural and agricultural ecosystems. Increases of ultraviolet-B radiation could significantly reduce yields of major crops and has been shown to have other significant adverse effects—such as mutation and immune-system impairment—in a wide variety of plants, animals, and microorganisms.

## FABLES ABOUT TOXIC SUBSTANCES

*Without the use of massive quantities of pesticides, starvation would stalk the planet.* The truth is that we are already using far too great a tonnage of pesticides for the results achieved. Humanity now applies about 2.5 million tons of synthetic pesticides worldwide each year, and pesticide production is a multi-billion dollar industry. Yet pests and spoilage still destroy about 25 to 50 percent of crops before and after harvest. That proportion, if anything, is higher than average crop losses before synthetic pesticides were widely introduced after World War II.

The strategy of large-scale broadcast spraying of pesticides has proven a poor one—except from the standpoint of petrochemical-company profits. An important reason for this lack of success is the rapidity with which pest populations evolve resistance: aided by short generation times and large populations, more than 500 species of insects and mites no longer respond to pesticides, and resistance to herbicides has been noted in more than 100 species of weeds and 150 species of plant pathogens.

Moreover, only a small proportion of the pesticides applied to fields ever actually reaches the target pest. For instance, of those delivered by aerial crop dusters, some 50 to 75 percent miss the target area and less than 0.1 percent may actually reach the pest. The remainder by definition is an environmental contaminant that can injure people and non-target species and in some cases migrate to the far reaches of the globe.

Yet in most cases, pests can be effectively controlled without heavy application of pesticides by using more biologically based methods. Known as integrated pest management (IPM), this approach involves various strategies such as encouraging natural enemies of pests, developing and planting pest-resistant strains of crops, fallowing, mixed cropping, destroying crop wastes where pests shelter, as well as some use of pesticides. IPM is generally vastly superior to chemical-based pest-control methods from both economic and environmental perspectives.

Indonesia, for example, has had remarkable success with IPM. In 1986, responding to the failure to chemically control the brown planthopper, a presidential decree banned fifty-seven of sixty-six pesticides used on rice. Pesticide subsidies, which were as high as 80 percent, were phased out over two years, and some of the resources saved were diverted into IPM. Since then, more than two hundred fifty thousand farmers have been trained in IPM techniques, insecticide use has plunged by 60 percent, the rice harvest has risen more than 15 percent, and farmers and the Indonesian treasury have saved more than $1 billion.

Pesticide use no doubt could be greatly reduced everywhere by wider adoption of IPM, which relies on synthetic pesticides as a scalpel only when needed rather than a bludgeon. Relaxing cosmetic standards on foods (such as allowing signs of minor insect damage) might also lead to reductions in pesticide use, as could the recent shift in public preferences toward "organically grown" foods. In fact, Americans increasingly distrust toxic chemicals, as is indicated by soaring sales of organically grown fruits and vegetables, which doubled to $7.6 billion from 1989 to 1994.

Overall, pesticide use in the United States could be reduced by 50 percent for a negligible increase (less than 1 percent) in food prices, according to calculations made in 1991 by the authors of the *Handbook of Pest Management in Agriculture.* Such a reduction could prove to be a great bargain if, as some scientists think, exposure to pesticide residues can impair the human immune system. And in view of today's deteriorating epidemiological environment, in which new diseases are emerging and drug-resistant strains of bacteria are causing resurgences of diseases once believed conquered, any loss of immune function should be taken seriously . . .

## FABLES ABOUT ECONOMICS AND THE ENVIRONMENT

*The United States can't afford stronger environmental protection; it would interfere with growth of the gross national product.* In 1990, William K. Reilly, then head of the U.S. Environmental Protection Agency, reported that the direct cost of compliance with federal environmental regulations was more than $90 billion per year—about 1.7 percent of the nation's GNP. But Reilly also pointed out that, during the two decades when the United States made substantial environmental progress, "the GNP increased by more than 70 percent." Thus, at worst, it seems that environmental regulation may slightly slow growth in the most commonly used measure of economic progress.

But that said, it should be noted that there is a growing distrust of the ability of GNP to mirror such progress, or more specifically, the enhancement of social well-being assumed to go along with it. In fact, between 1957 and 1992, although

U.S. per-capita income doubled, the percentage of people considering themselves "very happy" declined from 35 to 32 percent.

One of the most prominent critics of GNP as an indicator of well-being has been economist Herman E. Daly of the University of Maryland, formerly with the World Bank. Daly has suggested a new measure of economic well-being, the index of sustainable economic welfare (ISEW), which attempts to incorporate environmental factors including depreciation of "natural capital," such as soil lost to erosion, in its calculation. Between 1951 and 1990, the U.S. per-capita GNP in inflation-adjusted dollars more than doubled, whereas the ISEW grew considerably less than 20 percent and actually declined slightly between 1980 and 1990. "Economic welfare has been deteriorating," Daly says, largely because of "the exhaustion of resources and unsustainable reliance on capital from overseas to pay for domestic consumption and investment."

Other nations are also actively seeking better indicators of human satisfaction, especially those that include the critical factor of depreciation of natural capital, from the microbes that maintain soil fertility to fresh water stored in aquifers. Norway has started accounting for its remaining balances of mineral and living resources. France now has "natural patrimony accounts" that track the status of all resources influenced by human activity. And the Dutch government has instituted an accounting system that includes environmental damage and the costs of repairing it. Sweden, Germany, and the United States are all moving in the same direction, with the U.S. Department of Commerce developing a "green gross domestic product." In short, recognition is growing that once a nation has attained a certain level of individual material comfort, boosting the GNP alone is no longer a sufficient aim.

*Stricter environmental regulations will cost American jobs by forcing industries to relocate in nations with weaker standards.* Certainly environmental regulations can cost some jobs, especially in extractive industries or when outdated factories are forced to close because the costs of installing emissions controls exceed the value of the plants. It should be noted, though, that some of the industries (such as mining and logging) that complain the loudest about jobs lost to environmental regulation are of the boom-and-bust variety—set to move on anyway when local resources are depleted.

Other companies pressed by regulations may indeed choose to relocate to nations with weaker environmental laws (and cheaper labor). But as they do, other new jobs are often created, such as in high-tech businesses that favor areas where environmental quality is high, both because clean air and water are essential for their operations and because a healthy local environment helps them attract skilled labor. Moreover, even if factories required to install pollution-control equipment close down and throw their employees out of work, others will purchase smokestack scrubbers, thus creating jobs in firms that make such equipment. Overall, environmental protection is not a major cause of job losses and can be a significant source of new jobs.

*Economics, not ecology, should guide policy decisions.* A politician who says something like, "The time has come to put the economy ahead of the environment," clearly doesn't understand that the economy is a wholly owned subsidiary of natural ecosystems, and that the natural environment supplies humanity with an indispensable array of goods and services. In fact, expressed in standard economic terms, the value of ecosystem services is enormous. For example, the ability of the ecosystem to control pests could be worth $1.4 trillion annually, since without natural pest control there could be no production of agricultural crops. Ecosystem services might be valued at a total of about $20 trillion per year—almost equal to the gross global product. But these valuations only hint at the actual value of the services, for without them there would be no human society to enjoy their unsung benefits.

All economists understand that economics is supposed to seek wise ways to allocate resources to meet human needs. As traditionally practiced, however, economics has often considered only the delivery of conventional material goods and services while ignoring environmental goods and services. That economics is not a wise guide for environmental policy decisions is underlined by economists themselves, who say they detect few "signals" indicating serious environmental problems. They are, of course, waiting for price signals reflecting shortages of resources while remaining ignorant of the depletion of many of the most critical resources such as biodiversity, water quality, and the atmosphere's capacity to absorb greenhouse gases without catastrophic consequences, which are not priced by markets.

## ONE PLANET, ONE EXPERIMENT

A quick review of some compelling statistics reveals how wrong—and indeed how threatening to humanity's future—proponents of the notion that we have nothing to worry about can be. The roughly five-fold increase in the number of human beings over the past century and a half is the most dramatic terrestrial event since the retreat of ice-age glaciers thousands of years ago. That explosion of human numbers has been combined with a four-fold increase in consumption per person and the adoption of a wide array of technologies that needlessly damage the environment. The result is a twenty-fold escalation since 1850 of the pressure humanity places on its environment, as indexed by energy use, the best single measure of a society's environmental impact. Despite such ominous trends, the antienvironmental proponents continue to hammer away in print and over the airwaves, sowing confusion and doubt in the minds of many citizens about the seriousness—if not the very existence—of environmental deterioration. Thus efforts on behalf of the environment have been limited mainly to grassroots initiatives such as curbside recycling, ecotourism, and enthusiasm for anything "organic." While we applaud such endeavors, they are utterly insufficient steps that may divert attention from much more basic issues. Instead, society needs to take a longer view and recognize that to be sustainable, the economy must operate in harmony with earth's ecosystems.

Civilization's highest priority must be lowering the pressure on those vital ecosystems, seeking a sustainable food-population balance, and safeguarding human health against global toxification and emerging pathogens alike. Achieving this will require humanely reducing the size of populations worldwide by lowering birthrates to below death rates, reducing per capita consumption among the rich to make room for needed growth in consumption among the poor, and adopting more environmentally benign technologies.

Global society is running a vast and dangerous experiment. If the experiment goes wrong, there will be no way to rerun it. In the end, we can only hope that science and reason will prevail and that the public and political leaders will heed its warnings.

# 34

---

# DO WE CONSUME
# TOO MUCH?

---

MARK SAGOFF

**Growth pessimists worry that humans' consumption of renewable and non-renewable resources exceeds sustainable levels. Mark Sagoff challenges that viewpoint in "Do We Consume Too Much?" Still, he concludes there are reasons that go beyond economics to curb consumption: "We consume too much when market relationships displace the bonds of community, compassion, culture, and place ... [and when] consumption becomes an end in itself." Sagoff is senior research scholar in the School of Public Affairs at the University of Maryland. With Eric Katz he is author of *Nature as Subject: Human Obligation and Natural Community* (1996).**

In 1994, when delegates from around the world gathered in Cairo for the International Conference on Population and Development, representatives from developing countries protested that a baby born in the United States will consume during its lifetime twenty times as much of the world's resources as an African or an Indian baby. The problem for the world's environment, they argued, is overconsumption in the North, not overpopulation in the South.

Consumption in industrialized nations "has led to overexploitation of the resources of developing countries," a speaker from Kenya declared. A delegate from Antigua reproached the wealthiest 20 percent of the world's population for consuming 80 percent of the goods and services produced from the earth's resources.

Do we consume too much? To some, the answer is self-evident. If there is only so much food, timber, petroleum, and other material to go around, the more we consume, the less must be available for others. The global economy cannot grow indefinitely on a finite planet. As populations increase and economies expand, natural resources must be depleted; prices will rise, and humanity—especially the poor and future generations at all income levels—will suffer as a result.

Other reasons to suppose we consume too much are less often stated though also widely believed. Of these the simplest—a lesson we learn from our parents and from literature since the Old Testament—may be the best: although we must satisfy basic needs, a good life is not one devoted to amassing material possessions; what we own comes to own us, keeping us from fulfilling commitments that give meaning to life, such as those to family, friends, and faith. The appreciation of nature also deepens our lives. As we consume more, however, we are more likely to transform the natural world, so that less of it will remain for us to appreciate. . . . Today those who wish to protect the natural environment rarely offer ethical or spiritual reasons for the policies they favor. Instead they say we are running out of resources or causing the collapse of ecosystems on which we depend. Predictions of resource scarcity appear objective and scientific, whereas pronouncements that nature is sacred or that greed is bad appear judgmental or even embarrassing in a secular society. Prudential and economic arguments, moreover, have succeeded better than moral or spiritual ones in swaying public policy.

These prudential and economic arguments are not likely to succeed much longer. It is simply wrong to believe that nature sets physical limits to economic growth—that is, to prosperity and the production and consumption of goods and services on which it is based. The idea that increasing consumption will inevitably lead to depletion and scarcity, as plausible as it may seem, is mistaken both in principle and in fact. It is based on four misconceptions.

## MISCONCEPTION NO. 1:
## WE ARE RUNNING OUT OF RAW MATERIALS

In the 1970s Paul Ehrlich, a biologist at Stanford University, predicted that global shortages would soon send prices for food, fresh water, energy, metals, paper, and other materials sharply higher. "It seems certain," Paul and Anne Ehrlich wrote in *The End of Affluence* (1974), "that energy shortages will be with us for the rest of the century, and that before 1985 mankind will enter a genuine age of scarcity in which many things besides energy will be in short supply." Crucial materials would near depletion during the 1980s, Ehrlich predicted, pushing prices out of reach. "Starvation among people will be accompanied by starvation of industries for the materials they require."

Things have not turned out as Ehrlich expected. In the early 1990s real prices for food overall fell. Raw materials—including energy resources—are generally more abundant and less expensive today than they were twenty years ago. When

Ehrlich wrote, economically recoverable world reserves of petroleum stood at 640 billion barrels. Since that time reserves have *increased* by more than 50 percent, reaching more than 1,000 billion barrels in 1989. They have held steady in spite of rising consumption. The pre-tax real price of gasoline was lower during [the 1990s] than at any other time since 1947. The World Energy Council announced in 1992 that "fears of imminent [resource] exhaustion that were widely held twenty years ago are now considered to have been unfounded."

The World Resources Institute, in a 1994–1995 report, referred to "the frequently expressed concern that high levels of consumption will lead to resource depletion and to physical shortages that might limit growth or development opportunity." Examining the evidence, however, the institute said that "the world is not yet running out of most nonrenewable resources and is not likely to, at least in the next few decades." A 1988 report from the Office of Technology Assessment concluded, "The nation's future has probably never been less constrained by the cost of natural resources."

It is reasonable to expect that as raw materials become less expensive, they will be more rapidly depleted. This expectation is also mistaken. From 1980 to 1990, for example, while the prices of resource-based commodities declined (the price of rubber by 40 percent, cement by 40 percent, and coal by almost 50 percent), reserves of most raw materials increased. Economists offer three explanations.

First, with regard to subsoil resources, the world becomes ever more adept at discovering new reserves and exploiting old ones. Exploring for oil, for example, used to be a hit-or-miss proposition, resulting in a lot of dry holes. Today oil companies can use seismic waves to help them create precise computer images of the earth. New methods of extraction—for example, using bacteria to leach metals from low-grade ores—greatly increase resource recovery. Reserves of resources "are actually functions of technology," one analyst has written. "The more advanced the technology, the more reserves become known and recoverable."

Second, plentiful resources can be used in place of those that become scarce. Analysts speak of an Age of Substitutability and point, for example, to nanotubes, tiny cylinders of carbon whose molecular structure forms fibers a hundred times as strong as steel, at one sixth the weight. As technologies that use more-abundant resources substitute for those needing less-abundant ones—for example, ceramics in place of tungsten, fiber optics in place of copper wire, aluminum cans in place of tin ones—the demand for and the price of the less-abundant resources decline.

One can easily find earlier instances of substitution. During the early nineteenth century whale oil was the preferred fuel for household illumination. A dwindling supply prompted innovations in the lighting industry, including the invention of gas and kerosene lamps and Edison's carbon-filament electric bulb. Whale oil has substitutes, such as electricity and petroleum-based lubricants. Whales are irreplaceable.

Third, the more we learn about materials, the more efficiently we use them. The progress from candles to carbon-filament to tungsten incandescent lamps, for example, decreased the energy required for and the cost of a unit of household lighting by many times. Compact fluorescent lights are four times as efficient as today's incandescent bulbs and last ten to twenty times as long. Comparable energy savings are available in other appliances: for example, refrigerators sold in 1993 were 23 percent more efficient than those sold in 1990 and 65 percent more efficient than those sold in 1980, saving consumers billions in electric bills.

Amory Lovins, the director of the Rocky Mountain Institute, has described . . . a new generation of ultralight automobiles that could deliver the safety and muscle of today's cars but with far better mileage—four times as much in prototypes and ten times as much in projected models (see "Reinventing the Wheels," January 1995, *Atlantic*). Since in today's cars only 15 to 20 percent of the fuel's energy reaches the wheels (the rest is lost in the engine and the transmission), and since materials lighter and stronger than steel are available or on the way, no expert questions the feasibility of the high-mileage vehicles Lovins describes.

Computers and cameras are examples of consumer goods getting lighter and smaller as they get better. The game-maker Sega is marketing a hand-held children's game, called Saturn, that has more computing power than the 1976 Cray supercomputer, which the United States tried to keep out of the hands of the Soviets. Improvements that extend the useful life of objects also save resources. Platinum spark plugs in today's cars last for 100,000 miles, as do "fill-for-life" transmission fluids. On average, cars bought in 1993 have a useful life more than 40 percent longer than those bought in 1970.

As lighter materials replace heavier ones, the U.S. economy continues to shed weight. [U.S.] per capita consumption of raw materials such as forestry products and metals has, measured by weight, declined steadily over the past twenty years. A recent World Resources Institute study measured the "materials intensity" of [the U.S.] economy—that is, "the total material input and the hidden or indirect material flows, including deliberate landscape alterations" required for each dollar's worth of economic output. "The result shows a clearly declining pattern of materials intensity, supporting the conclusion that economic activity is growing somewhat more rapidly than natural resource use." . . .

Communications also illustrates the trend toward lighter, smaller, less materials-intensive technology. Just as telegraph cables replaced frigates in transmitting messages across the Atlantic and carried more information faster, glass fibers and microwaves have replaced cables—each new technology using less materials but providing greater capacity for sending and receiving information. Areas not yet wired for telephones (in the former Soviet Union, for example) are expected to leapfrog directly into cellular communications. Robert Solow, a Nobel laureate in economics, says that if the future is like the past, "there will be prolonged and substantial reductions in natural-resource requirements per unit of real output." He asks, "Why shouldn't the productivity of most natural resources rise more or less steadily through time, like the productivity of labor?"

## MISCONCEPTION NO. 2:
## WE ARE RUNNING OUT OF FOOD AND TIMBER

The United Nations projects that the global population, currently 5.7 billion, will peak at about 10 billion in . . . [this] century and then stabilize or even decline. Can the earth feed that many people? Even if food crops increase sufficiently, other renewable resources, including many fisheries and forests, are already under pressure. Should we expect fish stocks to collapse or forests to disappear?

The world already produces enough cereals and oilseeds to feed 10 billion people a vegetarian diet adequate in protein and calories. If, however, the idea is to feed 10 billion people not healthful vegetarian diets but the kind of meatladen meals that Americans eat, the production of grains and oilseeds may have to triple—primarily to feed livestock. Is anything like this kind of productivity in the cards?

Maybe. From 1961 to 1994 global production of food doubled. Global output of grain rose from about 630 million tons in 1950 to about 1.8 billion tons in 1992, largely as a result of greater yields. Developing countries from 1974 to 1994 increased wheat yields per acre by almost 100 percent, corn yields by 72 percent, and rice yields by 52 percent. "The generation of farmers on the land in 1950 was the first in history to double the production of food," the Worldwatch Institute has reported. "By 1984, they had outstripped population growth enough to raise per capita grain output an unprecedented 40 percent." From a two-year period ending in 1981 to a two-year period ending in 1990 the real prices of basic foods fell 38 percent on world markets, according to a 1992 United Nations report. Prices for food have continually decreased since the end of the eighteenth century, when Thomas Malthus argued that rapid population growth must lead to mass starvation by exceeding the carrying capacity of the earth.

Farmers worldwide could double the acreage in production, but this should not be necessary. Better seeds, more irrigation, multi-cropping, and additional use of fertilizer could greatly increase agricultural yields in the developing world, which are now generally only half those in the industrialized countries. It is biologically possible to raise yields of rice to about seven tons per acre—about four times the current average in the developing world. Super strains of cassava, a potato-like root crop eaten by millions of Africans, promise to increase yields tenfold. American farmers can also do better. In a good year, such as 1994, Iowa corn growers average about 3.5 tons per acre, but farmers more than double that yield in National Corn Growers Association competitions.

In drier parts of the world the scarcity of fresh water presents the greatest challenge to agriculture. But the problem is regional, not global. Fortunately, as Lester Brown, of the Worldwatch Institute, points out, "there are vast opportunities for increasing water efficiency" in arid regions, ranging from installing better water-delivery systems to planting drought-resistant crops. He adds, "Scientists can help push back the physical frontiers of cropping by developing varieties that are more drought resistant, salt tolerant, and early maturing. The payoff on the first two could be particularly high."

As if in response, Novartis Seeds has announced a program to develop water-efficient and salt-tolerant crops, including genetically engineered varieties of wheat. Researchers in Mexico have announced the development of drought-resistant corn that can boost yields by a third. Biotechnologists are converting annual crops into perennial ones, eliminating the need for yearly planting. They also hope to enable cereal crops to fix their own nitrogen, as legumes do, mini-mizing the need for fertilizer (genetically engineered nitrogen-fixing bacteria have already been test-marketed to farmers). Commercial varieties of crops such as corn, tomatoes, and potatoes which have been genetically engineered to be re-sistant to pests and diseases have been approved for field testing in the United States; several are now being sold and planted. A new breed of rice, 25 percent more productive than any currently in use, suggests that the Gene Revolution can take over where the Green Revolution left off. Biotechnology, as the historian Paul Kennedy has written, introduces "an entirely new stage in humankind's at-tempts to produce more crops and plants."

Biotechnology cannot, however, address the major causes of famine: poverty, trade barriers, corruption, mismanagement, ethnic antagonism, anarchy, war, and male-dominated societies that deprive women of food. Local land depletion, it-self a consequence of poverty and institutional failure, is also a factor. Those who are too poor to use sound farming practices are compelled to overexploit the re-sources on which they depend. As the economist Partha Dasgupta has written, "Population growth, poverty and degradation of local resources often fuel one another." The amount of food in world trade is constrained less by the resource base than by the maldistribution of wealth.

Analysts who believe that the world is running out of resources often argue that famines occur not as a result of political or economic conditions but because there are "too many people." Unfortunately, as the economist Amartya Sen has pointed out, public officials who think in Malthusian terms assume that when ab-solute levels of food supplies are adequate, famine will not occur. This convic-tion diverts attention from the actual causes of famine, which has occurred in places where food output kept pace with population growth but people were too destitute to buy it.

We would have run out of food long ago had we tried to supply ourselves en-tirely by hunting and gathering. Likewise, if we depend on nature's gifts, we will exhaust many of the world's important fisheries. Fortunately, we are learning to cultivate fish as we do other crops. Genetic engineers have designed fish for bet-ter flavor and color as well as for faster growth, improved disease resistance, and other traits. Two farmed species—silver carp and grass carp—already rank among the ten most-consumed fish worldwide. A specially bred tilapia, known as the "aquatic chicken," takes six months to grow to a harvestable size of about one and a half pounds.

Aquaculture produced more than 16 million tons of fish in 1993; capacity has expanded over the past decade at an annual rate of 10 percent by quantity and 14 percent by value. In 1993 fish farms produced 22 percent of all food fish consumed in the world and 90 percent of all oysters sold. The World Bank reports that aquaculture could provide 40 percent of all fish consumed and more than half the value of fish harvested within the next fifteen years. . . .

For those who lament the decline of natural fisheries and the human communities that grew up with them, the successes of aquaculture may offer no consolation. In the Pacific Northwest, for example, overfishing in combination with dams and habitat destruction has reduced the wild salmon population by 80 percent. Wild salmon—but not their bio-engineered aquacultural cousins—contribute to the cultural identity and sense of place of the Northwest. When wild salmon disappear, so will some of the region's history, character, and pride. What is true of wild salmon is also true of whales, dolphins, and other magnificent creatures—as they lose their economic importance, their aesthetic and moral worth becomes all the more evident. Economic considerations pull in one direction, moral considerations in the other. This conflict colors all our battles over the environment.

The transition from hunting and gathering to farming, which is changing the fishing industry, has taken place more slowly in forestry. Still there is no sign of a timber famine. In the United States forests now provide the largest harvests in history, and there is more forested U.S. area today than there was in 1920. Bill McKibben has observed . . . that the eastern United States, which loggers and farmers in the eighteenth and nineteenth centuries nearly denuded of trees, has become reforested during [the twentieth] century (see "An Explosion of Green," April 1995, *Atlantic*). One reason is that farms reverted to woods. Another is that machinery replaced animals; each draft animal required two or three cleared acres for pasture.

Natural reforestation is likely to continue as biotechnology makes areas used for logging more productive. According to Roger Sedjo, a respected forestry expert, advances in tree farming, if implemented widely, would permit the world to meet its entire demand for industrial wood using just 200 million acres of plantations—an area equal to only five percent of current forest land. As less land is required for commercial tree production, more natural forests may be protected—as they should be, for aesthetic, ethical, and spiritual reasons.

Often natural resources are so plentiful and therefore inexpensive that they undercut the necessary transition to technological alternatives. If the U.S. government did not protect wild forests from commercial exploitation, the timber industry would have little incentive to invest in tree plantations, where it can multiply yields by a factor of ten and take advantage of the results of genetic research.

Only by investing in plantation silviculture can North American forestry fend off price competition from rapidly developing tree plantations in the Southern Hemisphere. Biotechnology-based silviculture can in the near future be expected to underprice "extractive" forestry worldwide. In this decade [the 1990s], China will plant about 150 million acres of trees; India now plants four times the area it harvests commercially.

The expansion of fish and tree farming confirms the belief held by Peter Drucker and other management experts that our economy depends far more on the progress of technology than on the exploitation of nature. Although raw materials will always be necessary, knowledge has become the essential factor in the production of goods and services. "Where there is effective management," Drucker has written, "that is, application of knowledge to knowledge, we can always obtain the other resources." If we assume, along with Drucker and others, that resource scarcities do not exist or are easily averted, it is hard to see how economic theory, which after all concerns scarcity, provides the conceptual basis for valuing the environment. The reasons to preserve nature are ethical more often than they are economic.

## MISCONCEPTION NO. 3:
## WE ARE RUNNING OUT OF ENERGY

Probably the most persistent worries about resource scarcity concern energy. "The supply of fuels and other natural resources is becoming the limiting factor constraining the rate of economic growth," a group of experts proclaimed in 1986. They predicted the exhaustion of domestic oil and gas supplies by 2020 and, within a few decades, "major energy shortages as well as food shortages in the world."

Contrary to these expectations, no global shortages of hydrocarbon fuels are in sight. "One sees no immediate danger of 'running out' of energy in a global sense," writes John P. Holdren, a professor of environmental policy at Harvard University. According to Holdren, reserves of oil and natural gas will last seventy to a hundred years if exploited at 1990 rates. (This does not take into account huge deposits of oil shale, heavy oils, and gas from unconventional sources.) He concludes that "running out of energy resources in any global sense is not what the energy problem is all about."

The global energy problem has less to do with depleting resources than with controlling pollutants. Scientists generally agree that gases, principally carbon dioxide, emitted in the combustion of hydrocarbon fuels can build up in and warm the atmosphere by trapping sunlight. Since carbon dioxide enhances photosynthetic activity, plants to some extent absorb the carbon dioxide we produce. In 1995 researchers reported in *Science* that vegetation in the Northern Hemisphere in 1992 and 1993 converted into trees and other plant tissue 3.5 billion tons of carbon—more than half the carbon produced by the burning of hydrocarbon fuels worldwide.

However successful this and other feedback mechanisms may be in slowing the processes of global warming, a broad scientific consensus, reflected in a 1992 international treaty, has emerged for stabilizing and then decreasing emissions of carbon dioxide and other "greenhouse" gases. This goal is well within the technological reach of the United States and other industrialized countries. Amory Lovins, among others, has described commercially available technologies that can "support present or greatly expanded worldwide economic activity while stabilizing global climate—and saving money." He observes that "even very large expansions in population and industrial activity need not be energy-constrained."

Lovins and other environmentalists contend that pollution-free energy from largely untapped sources is available in amounts exceeding our needs. Geothermal energy—which makes use of heat from the earth's core—is theoretically accessible through drilling technology in the United States in amounts thousands of times as great as the amount of energy contained in domestic coal reserves. Tidal energy is also promising. Analysts who study solar power generally agree with Lester Brown, of the Worldwatch Institute, that "technologies are ready to begin building a world energy system largely powered by solar resources." In the future these and other renewable energy sources may be harnessed to the nation's system of storing and delivering electricity.

[In 1996] Joseph Romm and Charles Curtis described . . . advances in photovoltaic cells (which convert sunlight into electricity), fuel cells (which convert the hydrogen in fuels directly to electricity and heat, producing virtually no pollution), and wind power ("Mideast Oil Forever?" April 1996, *Atlantic*). According to these authors, genetically engineered organisms used to ferment organic matter could, with further research and development, bring down the costs of ethanol and other environmentally friendly "biofuels" to make them competitive with gasoline.

Environmentalists who, like Amory Lovins, believe that our economy can grow and still reduce greenhouse gases emphasize not only that we should be able to move to renewable forms of energy but also that we can use fossil fuels more efficiently. Some improvements are already evident. In developed countries the energy intensity of production—the amount of fuel burned per dollar of economic output—has been decreasing by about two percent a year.

From 1973 to 1986, for example, energy consumption in the United States remained virtually flat while economic production grew by almost 40 percent. Compared with Germany or Japan, this is a poor showing. The Japanese, who tax fuel more heavily . . . , use only half as much energy as the United States per unit of economic output. (Japanese environmental regulations are also generally stricter . . . ; if anything, this has improved the competitiveness of Japanese industry.) . . .

If so many opportunities exist for saving energy and curtailing pollution, why have we not seized them? . . . "Lemon socialism," a vast array of subsidies and barriers to trade, protects politically favored technologies, however inefficient, dangerous, filthy, or obsolete. "At heart, the major obstacles standing in the way [of a renewable-energy economy] are not technical in nature," the energy consultant Michael Brower has written, "but concern the laws, regulations, incentives, public attitudes, and other factors that make up the energy market."

In response to problems of climate change, the World Bank and other international organizations have recognized the importance of transferring advanced energy technologies to the developing world. Plainly, this will take a large investment of capital, particularly in education. Yet the "alternative for developing countries," according to José Goldemberg, a former Environment Minister of Brazil, "would be to remain at a dismally low level of development which . . . would aggravate the problems of sustainability."

Technology transfer can hasten sound economic development worldwide. Many environmentalists, however, argue that economies cannot expand without exceeding the physical limits nature sets—for example, with respect to energy. These environmentalists, who regard increasing affluence as a principal cause of environmental degradation, call for economic retrenchment and retraction—a small economy for a small earth. With Paul Ehrlich, they reject "the hope that development can greatly increase the size of the economic pie and pull many more people out of poverty." This hope is "basically a humane idea," Ehrlich has written, "made insane by the constraints nature places on human activity."

In developing countries, however, a no-growth economy "will deprive entire populations of access to better living conditions and lead to even more deforestation and land degradation," as Goldemberg warns. Moreover, citizens of developed countries are likely to resist an energy policy that they associate with poverty, discomfort, sacrifice, and pain. Technological pessimism, then, may not be the best option for environmentalists. It is certainly not the only one.

## MISCONCEPTION NO. 4:
## THE NORTH EXPLOITS THE SOUTH

William Reilly, when he served a administrator of the [U.S.] Environmental Protection Agency in the Bush Administration, encountered a persistent criticism at international meetings on the environment. "The problem for the world's environment is your consumption, not our population," delegates from the developing world told him. Some of these delegates later took Reilly aside. "The North buys too little from the South," they confided. "The real problem is too little demand for our exports."

The delegates who told Reilly that the North consumes too little of what the South produces have a point. "With a few exceptions (notably petroleum)," a report from the World Resources Institute observes, "most of the natural resources consumed in the United States are from domestic sources." Throughout the 1980s the United States and Canada were the world's leading exporters of raw materials. The United States consistently leads the world in farm exports, running huge agricultural trade surpluses. The share of raw materials used in the North that it buys from the South stands at a thirty-year low and continues to decline; industrialized nations trade largely among themselves. The World Resources Institute recently reported that "the United States is largely self-sufficient in natural resources." Again, excepting petroleum, bauxite (from which aluminum is made), "and a few other industrial minerals, its material flows are almost entirely internal."

Sugar provides an instructive example of how the North excludes—rather than exploits—the resources of the South. Since 1796 the United States has protected domestic sugar against imports. American sugar growers, in part as a reward for large contributions to political campaigns, have long enjoyed a system of quotas and prohibitive tariffs against foreign competition. American consumers paid about three times world prices for sugar in the 1980s, enriching a small cartel of U.S. growers. *Forbes* magazine has estimated that a single family, the Fanjuls, of Palm Beach, [Florida], reaps more than $65 million a year as a result of quotas for sugar.

The sugar industry in Florida, which is larger than that in any other state, makes even less sense environmentally than economically. It depends on a publicly built system of canals, levees, and pumping stations. Fertilizer from the sugarcane fields chokes the Everglades. Sugar growers, under a special exemption from labor laws, import Caribbean laborers to do the grueling and poorly paid work of cutting cane.

As the United States tightened sugar quotas (imports fell from 6.2 to 1.5 million tons annually from 1977 to 1987), the Dominican Republic and other nations with climates ideal for growing cane experienced political turmoil and economic collapse. Many farmers in Latin America, however, did well by switching from sugar to coca, which is processed into cocaine—perhaps the only high-value imported crop for which the United States is not developing a domestic substitute.

Before the Second World War the United States bought 40 percent of its vegetable oils from developing countries. After the war the United States protected its oilseed markets—for example, by establishing price supports for soybeans. Today the United States is one of the world's leading exporters of oil and oilseeds, although it still imports palm and coconut oils to obtain laurate, an ingredient in soap, shampoo, and detergents. Even this form of "exploitation" will soon cease. In 1994 farmers in Georgia planted the first commercial acreage of a high-laurate canola, genetically engineered by Calgene, a biotechnology firm.

About one hundred thousand Kenyans make a living on small plots of land growing pyrethrum flowers, the source of a comparatively environmentally safe insecticide of which the United States has been the largest importer. The U.S. Department of Commerce, however, awarded $1.2 million to a biotechnology firm to engineer pyrethrum genetically. Industrial countries will soon be able to synthesize all the pyrethrum they need and undersell Kenyan farmers.

An article in *Foreign Policy* in December of 1995 observed that the biotech-nological innovations that create "substitutes for everything from vanilla to cocoa and coffee threaten to eliminate the livelihood of millions of Third World agricultural workers." Vanilla cultured in laboratories costs a fifth as much as vanilla extracted from beans, and thus jeopardizes the livelihood of tens of thousands of vanilla farmers in Madagascar. In the past, farms produced agricultural commodities and factories processed them. In the future, factories may "grow" as well as process many of the most valuable commodities—or the two functions will become one. As one plant scientist has said, "We have to stop thinking of these things as plant cells, and start thinking of them as new microorganisms, with all the potential that implies"—meaning, for instance, that the cells could be made to grow in commercially feasible quantities in laboratories, not fields.

The North not only balks at buying sugar and other crops from developing countries; it also dumps its excess agricultural commodities, especially grain, on them. After the Second World War, American farmers, using price supports left over from the New Deal, produced vast wheat surpluses, which the United States exported at concessionary prices to Europe and then the Third World. These enormous transfers of cereals to the South, institutionalized during the 1950s and 1960s by U.S. food aid, continued during the 1970s and 1980s, as the United States and the European Community vied for markets, each outdoing the other in subsidizing agricultural exports.

Grain imports from the United States "created food dependence within two decades in countries which had been mostly self-sufficient in food at the end of World War II," the sociologist Harriet Friedmann has written. Tropical countries soon matched the grain gluts of the North with their own surpluses of cocoa, coffee, tea, bananas, and other export commodities. Accordingly, prices for these commodities collapsed as early as 1970, catching developing nations in a scissors. As Friedmann describes it, "One blade was food import dependency. The other blade was declining revenues for traditional exports of tropical crops."

It might be better for the environment if the North exchanged the crops for which it is ecologically suited—wheat, for example—for crops easily grown in the South, such as coffee, cocoa, palm oil, and tea. Contrary to common belief, these tropical export crops—which grow on trees and bushes, providing canopy and continuous root structures to protect the soil—are less damaging to the soil than are traditional staples such as cereals and root crops. Better markets for tropical crops could help developing nations to employ their rural populations and to protect their natural resources. Allen Hammond, of the World Resources Institute, points out that "if poor nations cannot export anything else, they will export their misery—in the form of drugs, diseases, terrorism, migration, and environmental degradation."

Peasants in less-developed nations often confront intractable poverty, an entrenched land-tenure system, and a lack of infrastructure; they have little access to markets, education, or employment. Many of the rural poor, according to the environmental consultant Norman Myers, "have no option but to over-exploit environmental resource stocks in order to survive"—for example, by "increasingly encroaching onto tropical forests among other low-potential lands." These poorest of the poor "are causing as much natural-resource depletion as the other three billion developing-world people put together."

Myers observes that traditional indigenous farmers in tropical forests moved from place to place without seriously damaging the ecosystem. The principal agents of tropical deforestation are refugees from civil war and rural poverty, who are forced to eke out a living on marginal lands. Activities such as road building, logging, and commercial agriculture have barely increased in tropical forests since the early 1980s, according to Myers; slash-and-burn farming by displaced peasants accounts for far more deforestation—roughly three fifths of the total. Its impact is fast expanding. Most of the wood from trees harvested in tropical forests—that is, those not cleared for farms—is used locally for fuel. The likeliest path to protecting the rain forest is through economic development that enables peasants to farm efficiently, on land better suited to farming than to forest.

Many have argued that economic activity, affluence, and growth automatically lead to resource depletion, environmental deterioration, and ecological collapse. Yet greater productivity and prosperity—which is what economists mean by growth—have become prerequisite for controlling urban pollution and protecting sensitive ecological systems such as rain forests. Otherwise, destitute people who are unable to acquire food and fuel will create pollution and destroy forests. Without economic growth, which also correlates with lower fertility, the environmental and population problems of the South will only get worse. For impoverished countries facing environmental disaster, economic growth may be the one thing that is sustainable.

## WHAT IS WRONG WITH CONSUMPTION?

. . . There is a lot of misery worldwide to relieve. But as bad as the situation is, it is improving. In 1960 nearly 70 percent of the people in the world lived at or below the subsistence level. Today less than a third do, and the number enjoying fairly satisfactory conditions (as measured by the United Nations Human Development Index) rose from 25 percent in 1960 to 60 percent in 1992. Over the twenty-five years before 1992 average per capita consumption in developing countries increased 75 percent in real terms. The pace of improvements is also increasing. In developing countries in that period, for example, power generation and the number of telephone lines per capita doubled, while the number of households with access to clean water grew by half.

What is worsening is the discrepancy in income between the wealthy and the poor. Although world income measured in real terms has increased by 700 percent since the Second World War, the wealthiest people have absorbed most of the gains. Since 1960 the richest fifth of the world's people have seen their share of the world's income increase from 70 to 85 percent. Thus one fifth of the world's population possesses much more than four fifths of the world's wealth, while the share held by all others has correspondingly fallen; that of the world's poorest 20 percent has declined from 2.3 to 1.4 percent.

. . . Benjamin Barber ("Jihad vs. McWorld," March 1992, *Atlantic*) described market forces that "mesmerize the world with fast music, fast computers, and fast food—with MTV, Macintosh, and McDonald's, pressing nations into one commercially homogeneous global network: one McWorld tied together by technology, ecology, communications, and commerce." Affluent citizens of South Korea, Thailand, India, Brazil, Mexico, and many other rapidly developing nations have joined with Americans, Europeans, Japanese, and others to form an urban and cosmopolitan international society. Those who participate in this global network are less and less beholden to local customs and traditions. Meanwhile, ethnic, tribal, and other cultural groups that do not dissolve into McWorld often define themselves in opposition to it—fiercely asserting their ethnic, religious, and territorial identities.

The imposition of a market economy on traditional cultures in the name of development—for example, the insistence that everyone produce and consume more—can dissolve the ties to family, land, community, and place on which indigenous peoples traditionally rely for their security. Thus development projects intended to relieve the poverty of indigenous peoples may, by causing the loss of cultural identity, engender the very powerlessness they aim to remedy. Pope Paul VI, in the encyclical *Populorum Progressio* (1967), described the tragic dilemma confronting indigenous peoples: "either to preserve traditional beliefs and structures and reject social progress; or to embrace foreign technology and foreign culture, and reject ancestral traditions with their wealth of humanism."

The idea that everything is for sale and nothing is sacred—that all values are subjective—undercuts our own moral and cultural commitments, not just those of tribal and traditional communities. No one has written a better critique of the assault that commerce makes on the quality of our lives than Thoreau provides in *Walden*. The cost of a thing, according to Thoreau, is not what the market will bear but what the individual must bear because of it: it is "the amount of what I will call life which is required to be exchanged for it, immediately or in the long run."

Many observers point out that as we work harder and consume more, we seem to enjoy our lives less. We are always in a rush—a "Saint Vitus' dance," as Thoreau called it. Idleness is suspect. Americans today spend less time with their families, neighbors, and friends than they did in the 1950s. Juliet B. Schor, an economist at Harvard University, argues that "Americans are literally working themselves to death." A fancy car, video equipment, or a complex computer program can exact a painful cost in the form of maintenance, upgrading, and repair. We are possessed by our possessions; they are often harder to get rid of than to acquire.

That money does not make us happier, once our basic needs are met, is a commonplace overwhelmingly confirmed by sociological evidence. Paul Wachtel, who teaches social psychology at the City University of New York, has concluded that bigger incomes "do not yield an increase in feelings of satisfaction or well-being, at least for populations who are above a poverty or subsistence level." This cannot be explained simply by the fact that people have to work harder to earn more money: even those who hit jackpots in lotteries often report that their lives are not substantially happier as a result. Well-being depends upon health, membership in a community in which one feels secure, friends, faith, family, love, and virtues that money cannot buy. Robert Lane, a political scientist at Yale University, using the concepts of economics, has written, "If 'utility' has anything to do with happiness, above the poverty line the long-term marginal utility of money is almost zero."

Economists in earlier times predicted that wealth would not matter to people once they attained a comfortable standard of living. "In ease of body and peace of mind, all the different ranks of life are nearly upon a level," wrote Adam Smith, the eighteenth century English advocate of the free market. In the 1930s the British economist John Maynard Keynes argued that after a period of great expansion further accumulation of wealth would no longer improve personal well-being. Subsequent economists, however, found that even after much of the industrial world had attained the levels of wealth Keynes thought were sufficient, people still wanted more. From this they inferred that wants are insatiable.

Perhaps this is true. But the insatiability of wants and desires poses a difficulty for standard economic theory, which posits that humanity's single goal is to increase or maximize wealth. If wants increase as fast as income grows, what purpose can wealth serve?

Critics often attack standard economic theory on the ground that economic growth is "unsustainable." We are running out of resources, they say; we court ecological disaster. Whether or not growth is sustainable, there is little reason to think that once people attain a decent standard of living, continued growth is desirable. . . . As long as the debate over sustainability is framed in terms of the physical limits to growth rather than the moral purpose of it, mainstream economic theory will have the better of the argument. If the debate were framed in moral or social terms, the result might well be otherwise.

## MAKING A PLACE FOR NATURE

According to Thoreau, "a man's relation to Nature must come very near to a personal one." For environmentalists in the tradition of Thoreau and John Muir, stewardship is a form of fellowship; although we must use nature, we do not value it primarily for the economic purposes it serves. We take our bearings from the natural world—our sense of time from its days and seasons, our sense of place from the character of a landscape and the particular plants and animals native to it. An intimacy with nature ends our isolation in the world. We know where we belong, and we can find the way home.

In defending old-growth forests, wetlands, or species we make our best arguments when we think of nature chiefly in aesthetic and moral terms. Rather than having the courage of our moral and cultural convictions, however, we too often rely on economic arguments for protecting nature, in the process attributing to natural objects more instrumental value than they have. By claiming that a threatened species may harbor lifesaving drugs, for example, we impute to that species an economic value or a price much greater than it fetches in a market. When we make the prices come out right, we rescue economic theory but not necessarily the environment.

There is no credible argument, moreover, that all or even most of the species we are concerned to protect are essential to the functioning of the ecological systems on which we depend. (If whales went extinct, for example, the seas would not fill up with krill.) Species may be profoundly important for cultural and spiritual reasons, however. Consider again the example of the wild salmon, whose habitat is being destroyed by hydroelectric dams along the Columbia River. Although this loss is unimportant to the economy overall (there is no shortage of salmon), it is of the greatest significance to the Amerindian tribes that have traditionally subsisted on wild salmon, and to the region as a whole. By viewing local flora and fauna as a sacred heritage—by recognizing their intrinsic value— we discover who we are rather than what we want. On moral and cultural grounds society might be justified in making great economic sacrifices—removing hydroelectric dams, for example—to protect remnant populations of the Snake River sockeye, even if, as critics complain, hundreds or thousands of dollars are spent for every fish that is saved.

Even those plants and animals that do not define places possess enormous intrinsic value and are worth preserving for their own sake. What gives these creatures value lies in their histories, wonderful in themselves, rather than in any use to which they can be put. In *Earth in the Balance* (1992) Al Gore, then a [U.S.] senator, wrote, "We have become so successful at controlling nature that we have lost our connection to it." It is all too easy, Gore wrote, "to regard the earth as a collection of 'resources' having an intrinsic value no larger than their usefulness at the moment." The question before us is not whether we are going to run out of resources. It is whether economics is the appropriate context for thinking about environmental policy. . . .

The world has the wealth and the resources to provide everyone the opportunity to live a decent life. We consume too much when market relationships displace the bonds of community, compassion, culture, and place. We consume too much when consumption becomes an end in itself and makes us lose affection and reverence for the natural world.

# 35

## DIETARY IMPLICATIONS OF THE GLOBALIZATION OF FOOD TRADE

TIM LANG

**Globalization is a force for homogenization, blurring the borders that separate states but which also often encompass distinctive cultures and lifestyles. Tim Lang argues that liberalization of trade in food is leading to the selling of a North American diet with its often untoward health effects. Retailers are changing the global food distribution system, affecting not only what people eat but also what farmers produce and the resources required to produce it. Lang is professor of food policy in the Wolfson School of Heath Sciences, Thames Valley University. With Yiannis Gabriel, he is author of *The Unmanageable Consumer: Contemporary Consumption and Its Fragmentation* (1995).**

With the ratification of the General Agreement on Tariffs and Trade (GATT), agriculture became, for the first time, subjected to the theory of economic liberalization, which covers so many other areas of world trade. Trade liberalization in agriculture has considerable implications for a number of goals espoused by world bodies and public health practitioners. These include food security, consumer information and choice of environmental protection.

Much has been written about the meaning of globalization, but in the case of food, we should be wary about equating the changes in the world food economy with those of personal computers or cars. The selling of a Northern (American) diet to the world is an example. The North is learning the doubtful joys of consuming a highly processed diet, replete with saturated fats and lower than

420

desirable in anti-oxidants. This diet is being exploited globally, with governments and public health agencies relatively powerless to halt the process.

Indeed, in a long-term strategy document, the U.S. Department of Agriculture positively revels in the new opportunities to sell "high-value, consumer food products" to countries in the Asia Pacific Rim, for example, which have hitherto provided epidemiologic evidence about the value of low-fat diets. This same strategy document concludes that there is a "great outlook for processed foods" from the "growth in fast food and family-style restaurants" and "growth in Western-style supermarkets." The export of Northern diets to the South is reminiscent of the process whereby tobacco sales were encouraged in the South once sales were being constrained in the North due to concerted public health measures, health education campaigns and fiscal measures.

Public health agencies are easily lampooned as "killjoys" and "health missionaries" if they try to temper the kind of food products heavily advertised in these global marketing initiatives. Consumers are said to be able to "look after themselves," but the evidence from societies where advertising is subject to few constraints is that their knowledge is limited. Dietary "burgerization" is presented as driven by youthful demand, when it is in fact brilliantly and ruthlessly marketed. The burger has become a symbol of modernity and the triumph of an American mode of eating, a metaphor of how rational, bureaucratic society orders production of any good and the fulfillment of any need.

But who in the world's financial media or elected assemblies makes the policy connections with the alarming rise in U.S. obesity? And who comments on the doubtful health, not to say ethics, of subsidizing exports of wheat grains and meat consumption to food cultures where wheat is foreign and meat a rare luxury? Who, too, spoke for the billions of small farmers, the world's majority of rural dwellers or for the case that if everyone emulated the energy and fat-rich Northern diet, the planet would be put under gross strain? Is it beyond the realm of possibility that, over the next decades, we shall witness a spread of so-called Western diseases of affluence, such as coronary heart disease and some of the food-related cancers?

Proponents of globalization argue that, without trade liberalization, the poor will starve. This argument is disarming, but erroneous. There are already worrying levels of nutritional inadequacy. The United Nations estimates that one in five persons in the developing world suffers from chronic hunger—800 million people in Africa, Asia and Latin America—and that "over 2 billion subsist on diets deficient in the vitamins and minerals essential for normal growth and development, and for preventing premature death and such disabilities as blindness and mental retardation."

Transnational corporations (TNCs) now account for 70 percent of total world trade. In the food system, high levels of concentration are common, according to research by the United Nations Center on Transnational Corporations. Cargill, a family owned commodity trader, has 60 percent of world cereal trade. 80

percent of the banana market is divided among three corporations, with similar numbers in cocoa (83 percent) and tea (85 percent).

In the food sector, no one has been more significant in revolutionizing global food economies than the food retailers. United Kingdom data suggest that the same amount of food merely travels further, up and down the motorways, thereby externalizing costs (mainly energy costs) to the environment. These costs are not reflected in the "cheaper" food prices, as no one actually pays, but every citizen experiences them, and some receive ill health from them, for example from pollution from increased traffic. A German study of strawberry yogurt found ecological absurdities in the system of processing, packaging and distribution, such that a theoretical truckload of 150 gram yogurts would travel 1,005 kilometers. The strawberries came from Poland, yogurt from north Germany, corn and wheat flour from the Netherlands, jam from West Germany and sugar beet from East Germany. The aluminum for use on the cover came 300 kilometers. Only the milk and glass jar were local to Stuttgart, where theoretically the yogurt came from. To produce one truckload of strawberry yogurt, 10,000 liters of diesel fuel had been burned.

The reality of hypermarket, or supermarket, shopping is that people have to use their cars to get food, thereby severing a connection between health-enhancing exercise and their daily lives. According to the United Kingdom government's National Travel Survey, the distance traveled during shopping trips in Britain increased by 60 percent between 1975–1976 and 1989–1991.

This change in distribution not only gives retailers power over the entire food system, but also affects what the farmer grows and how she or he grows it, by the use of contracts and specifications. Needless to say, the specifications stipu-

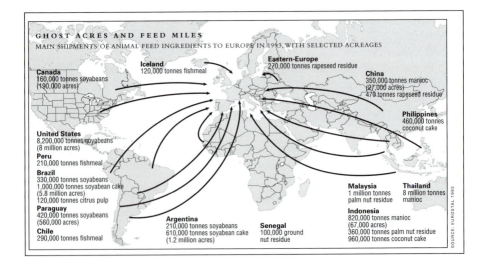

## DIFFERENT FUTURES

The left column represents the main characteristics of a global industrialized food system; the right column describes attributes of a more locally based food system.

| | | |
|---|---|---|
| *globalization* | *vs.* | *localization* |
| *urban vs. rural.* | *vs.* | *urban-rural partnership* |
| *long trade routes (food miles)* | *vs.* | *short trade routes* |
| *import/export and food-insecurity* | *vs.* | *food from local resources* |
| *fast speed, pace and scale of change* | *vs.* | *slow pace, speed, scale of change* |
| *non-renewable energy* | *vs.* | *re-usable energy* |
| *few market players (concentration)* | *vs.* | *multiple players per sector* |
| *costs externalized* | *vs.* | *costs internalized* |
| *open farming systems* | *vs.* | *closed systems* |
| *rural de-population* | *vs.* | *vibrant rural population* |
| *monoculture* | *vs.* | *biodiversity* |
| *agrochemicals* | *vs.* | *organic/sustainable farming* |
| *biotechnology* | *vs.* | *indigenous knowledge* |
| *processed (stored) food* | *vs.* | *fresh (perishable) food* |
| *food from factories* | *vs.* | *food from the land* |
| *hypermarkets* | *vs.* | *markets* |
| *de-skilling of farmers* | *vs.* | *skilled farmers* |
| *standardization* | *vs.* | *"difference"* |
| *superficial variety on shelves* | *vs.* | *real variety on field and plate* |
| *people to food* | *vs.* | *food to people* |
| *created wants (advertising)* | *vs.* | *real wants (cultural learning)* |
| *burgerization* | *vs.* | *local foods specialities* |
| *global decisions* | *vs.* | *local decisions* |
| *top-down controls* | *vs.* | *bottom-up controls* |
| *dependency culture* | *vs.* | *self-reliance* |
| *health inequalities widening* | *vs.* | *health inequalities narrowing* |
| *social polarization and exclusion* | *vs.* | *social inclusion* |
| *consumers* | *vs.* | *citizens*            —TIM LANG |

late that food is unblemished, of a certain size, uniformity, and so on, which only a narrow form of farming can produce.

Any country that participates in a deregulated global food system is likely to find its potential to create a sustainable local food system weakened by a reliance upon foreign suppliers. An export orientation imposed on its farmers means a dislocation in food culture: produce is sold that is not consumed locally, and products are consumed that are produced elsewhere. This new economic regime undermines the policies of those developing countries that were previously committed to policies of national food self-reliance.

GATT's supporters claim that the least developed countries are exempt from having to remove their agricultural import barriers and that, in the case of staple foods, no developing country has to follow GATT tariff regulations designed to reduce import barriers. But this argument ignores the fact that the International Monetary Fund (IMF) structural adjustment programs require exactly this condition, thus rendering the GATT exemption virtually meaningless.

For all its complexity, the globalization process, driven by Northern tastes and marketed everywhere in the name of Northern culture and capital, offers formidable challenges to food and public health thinking. When governments argue that they can do little but bow to market pressure and facilitate its mechanisms, the very notion of public health intervention may be troublesome. This is an ideological issue rather than a real barrier to action. The world actually needs a shift away from cheap export-led food policies to more local production for local use everywhere. This requires more people on the land, not throwing people off to make the economic audit of farming look more "efficient." The goal should be to build a better quality of life in the country, not to drive people into towns; to reduce inequalities; and to make public and environmental health part of economics, not a bolt-on extra.

# 36

# ENCROACHING PLAGUES: THE RETURN OF INFECTIOUS DISEASE

## LAURIE GARRETT

Rapid globalization has opened political borders to biological as well as economic penetration. Laurie Garrett worries that the biological evolution of microbes in combination with an increasingly borderless world exposes peoples and states to threats once thought conquered. A Pulitzer Prize winner, Garrett is a medical and science reporter for the newspaper *Newsday* and author of *The Coming Plague: Newly Emerging Diseases in a World Out of Balance* (1994).

### THE POST-ANTIBIOTIC ERA

Since World War II, public health strategy has focused on the eradication of microbes. Using powerful medical weaponry developed during the postwar period—antibiotics, antimalarials, and vaccines—political and scientific leaders in the United States and around the world pursued a military-style campaign to obliterate viral, bacterial, and parasitic enemies. The goal was nothing less than pushing humanity through what was termed the "health transition," leaving the age of infectious disease permanently behind. By the turn of the century, it was thought, most of the world's population would live long lives ended only by the "chronics"—cancer, heart disease, and Alzheimer's.

The optimism culminated in 1978 when the member states of the United Nations signed the "Health for All, 2000" accord. The agreement set ambitious goals

425

for the eradication of disease, predicting that even the poorest nations would undergo a health transition before the millennium, with life expectancies rising markedly. It was certainly reasonable in 1978 to take a rosy view of Homo sapiens' ancient struggle with the microbes; antibiotics, pesticides, chloroquine and other powerful antimicrobials, vaccines, and striking improvements in water treatment and food preparation technologies had provided what seemed an imposing armamentarium. The year before, the World Health Organization (WHO) had announced that the last known case of smallpox had been tracked down in Ethiopia and cured.

The grandiose optimism rested on two false assumptions: that microbes were biologically stationary targets and that diseases could be geographically sequestered. Each contributed to the smug sense of immunity from infectious diseases that characterized health professionals in North America and Europe.

Anything but stationary, microbes and the insects, rodents, and other animals that transmit them are in a constant state of biological flux and evolution. Darwin noted that certain genetic mutations allow plants and animals to better adapt to environmental conditions and so produce more offspring; this process of natural selection, he argued, was the mechanism of evolution. Less than a decade after the U.S. military first supplied penicillin to its field physicians in the Pacific theater, geneticist Joshua Lederberg demonstrated that natural selection was operating in the bacterial world. Strains of staphylococcus and streptococcus that happened to carry genes for resistance to the drugs arose and flourished where drug-susceptible strains had been driven out. Use of antibiotics was selecting for ever-more-resistant bugs.

More recently scientists have witnessed an alarming mechanism of microbial adaptation and change—one less dependent on random inherited genetic advantage. The genetic blueprints of some microbes contain DNA and RNA codes that command mutation under stress, offer escapes from antibiotics and other drugs, marshal collective behaviors conductive to group survival, and allow the microbes and their progeny to scour their environments for potentially useful genetic material. Such material is present in stable rings or pieces of DNA and RNA, known as plasmids and transposons, that move freely among microorganisms, even jumping between species of bacteria, fungi, and parasites. Some plasmids carry the genes for resistance to five or more different families of antibiotics, or dozens of individual drugs. Others confer greater powers of infectivity, virulence, resistance to disinfectants or chlorine, even such subtly important characteristics as the ability to tolerate higher temperatures or more acidic conditions. Microbes have appeared that can grow on a bar of soap, swim unabashed in bleach, and ignore doses of penicillin logarithmically larger than those effective in 1950.

In the microbial soup, then, is a vast, constantly changing lending library of genetic material that offers humanity's minute predators myriad ways to outmaneuver the drug arsenal. And the arsenal, large as it might seem, is limited. In 1994, the [U.S.] Food and Drug Administration licensed only three new antimicrobial drugs, two of them for the treatment of AIDS and one an antibacterial. Research and development has ground to a near halt now that the easy approaches to killing viruses, bacteria, fungi, and parasites—those that mimic the ways competing microbes kill one another in their endless tiny battles throughout the human gastrointestinal tract—have been exploited. Researchers have run out of ideas for countering many microbial scourges, and the lack of profitability has stifled the development of drugs to combat organisms that are currently found predominantly in poor countries. "The pipeline is dry. We really have a global crisis," James Hughes, director of the [U.S.] National Center for Infectious Diseases at the Centers for Disease Control and Prevention (CDC) in Atlanta, said recently.

## DISEASES WITHOUT BORDERS

During the 1960s, 1970s, and 1980s, the World Bank and the International Monetary Fund devised investment policies based on the assumption that economic modernization should come first and improved health would naturally follow. Today the World Bank recognizes that a nation in which more than 10 percent of the working-age population is chronically ill cannot be expected to reach higher levels of development without investment in health infrastructure. Furthermore, the bank acknowledges that few societies spend health care dollars effectively for the poor, among whom the potential for the outbreak of infectious disease is greatest. Most of the achievements in infectious disease control have resulted from grand international efforts such as the expanded program for childhood immunization mounted by the United Nations Children's Emergency Fund and WHO's smallpox eradication drive. At the local level, particularly in politically unstable poor countries, few genuine successes can be cited.

Geographic sequestration was crucial in all postwar health planning, but diseases can no longer be expected to remain in their country or region of origin. Even before commercial air travel, swine flu in 1918–1919 managed to circumnavigate the planet five times in eighteen months, killing 22 million people, five hundred thousand in the United States. How many more victims could a similarly lethal strain of influenza claim [now] when some half a billion passengers will board airline flights?

Every day 1 million people cross an international border. One million a week travel between the industrial and developing worlds. And as people move, unwanted microbial hitchhikers tag along. In the nineteenth century most diseases and infections that travelers carried manifested themselves during the long sea voyages that were the primary means of covering great distances. Recognizing the symptoms, the authorities at ports of entry could quarantine contagious individuals or take other action. In the age of jet travel, however, a person incubating a disease such as Ebola can board a plane, travel twelve thousand miles, pass unnoticed through customs and immigration, take a domestic carrier to a remote destination, and still not develop symptoms for several days, infecting many other people before his condition is noticeable.

Surveillance at airports has proved grossly inadequate and is often biologically irrational, given that incubation periods for many incurable contagious diseases may exceed twenty-one days. And when a recent traveler's symptoms become apparent, days or weeks after his journey, the task of identifying fellow passengers, locating them, and bringing them to the authorities for medical examination is costly and sometimes impossible. The British and U.S. governments both spent millions of dollars in 1976 trying to track down five hundred twenty-two people exposed during a flight from Sierra Leone to Washington, D.C., to a Peace Corps volunteer infected with the Lassa virus, an organism that produces gruesome hemorrhagic disease in its victims. . . .

In the fall of 1994 the New York City Department of Health and the U.S. Immigration and Naturalization Service took steps to prevent plague-infected passengers from India from disembarking at New York's John F. Kennedy International Airport. All airport and federal personnel who had direct contact with passengers were trained to recognize symptoms of *Yersinia pestis* infection. Potential plague carriers were, if possible, to be identified while still on the tarmac, so fellow passengers could be examined. Of ten putative carriers identified in New York, only two were discovered at the airport; the majority had long since entered the community. Fortunately, none of the ten proved to have the plague. Health authorities came away with the lesson that airport-based screening is expensive and does not work.

Humanity is on the move worldwide, fleeing impoverishment, religious and ethnic intolerance, and high-intensity localized warfare that targets civilians. People are abandoning their homes for new destinations on an unprecedented scale, both in terms of absolute numbers and as a percentage of population. In 1994 at least 110 million people immigrated, another 30 million moved from rural to urban areas within their own country, and 23 million more were displaced by war or social unrest, according to the U.N. High Commissioner for Refugees and the Worldwatch Institute. This human mobility affords microbes greatly increased opportunities for movement.

### THE CITY AS VECTOR

Population expansion raises the statistical probability that pathogens will be transmitted, whether from person to person or vector—insect, rodent, or other—to person. Human density is rising rapidly worldwide. Seven countries now have overall population densities exceeding two thousand people per square mile, and forty-three have densities greater than five hundred people per square mile. (The U.S. average, by contrast, is seventy-four.)

High density need not doom a nation to epidemics and unusual outbreaks of disease if sewage and water systems, housing, and public health provisions are adequate. The Netherlands, for example, with eleven hundred eighty people per square mile, ranks among the top twenty countries for good health and life expectancy. But the areas in which density is increasing most are not those capable of providing such infrastructural support. They are, rather, the poorest on earth. Even countries with low overall density may have cities that have become focuses for extraordinary overpopulation, from the point of view of public health. Some of these urban agglomerations have only one toilet for every seven hundred fifty or more people.

Most people on the move around the world come to burgeoning metropolises like India's Surat (where pneumonic plague struck in 1994) and Zaire's Kikwit (site of the 1995 Ebola epidemic) that offer few fundamental amenities. These new centers of urbanization typically lack sewage systems, paved roads, housing, safe drinking water, medical facilities, and schools adequate to serve even the most affluent residents. They are squalid sites of destitution where hundreds of thousands live much as they would in poor villages, yet so jammed together as to ensure astronomical transmission rates for airborne, waterborne, sexually transmitted, and contact-transmission microbes.

But such centers are often only staging areas for the waves of impoverished people that are drawn there. The next stop is a megacity with a population of 10 million or more. In the nineteenth century only two cities on earth—London and New York—even approached that size. Five years from now there will be twenty-four megacities, most in poor developing countries: São Paulo, Calcutta, Bombay, Istanbul, Bangkok, Tehran, Jakarta, Cairo, Mexico City, Karachi, and the like. There the woes of cities like Surat are magnified many times over. Yet even the developing world's megacities are way stations for those who most aggressively seek a better life. All paths ultimately lead these people—and the microbes they may carry—to the United States, Canada, and Western Europe.

Urbanization and global migration propel radical changes in human behavior as well as in the ecological relationship between microbes and humans. Almost invariably in large cities, sex industries arise and multiple-partner sex becomes more common, prompting rapid increases in sexually transmitted diseases. Black market access to antimicrobials is greater in urban centers, leading to overuse or outright misuse of the precious drugs and the emergence of resistant bacteria and parasites. Intravenous drug abusers' practice of sharing syringes is a ready vehicle for the transmission of microbes. Underfunded urban health facilities often become unhygienic centers for the dissemination of disease rather than its control.

## THE EMBLEMATIC NEW DISEASE

All these factors played out dramatically during the 1980s, allowing an obscure organism to amplify and spread to the point that WHO estimates it has infected a cumulative total of 30 million people and become endemic to every country in the world. Genetic studies of the human immunodeficiency virus that causes AIDS indicate that it is probably more than a century old, yet HIV infected perhaps less than .001 percent of the world population until the mid-1970s. Then the virus surged because of sweeping social changes: African urbanization; American and European intravenous drug use and homosexual bathhouse activity; the Uganda-Tanzania war of 1977–1979, in which rape was used as a tool of ethnic cleansing; and the growth of the American blood products industry and the international marketing of its contaminated goods. Government denial and societal prejudice everywhere in the world led to inappropriate public health interventions or plain inaction, further abetting HIV transmission and slowing research for treatment or a cure.

The estimated direct (medical) and indirect (loss of productive labor force and family-impact) costs of the disease [were] expected to top $500 billion by the year 2000, according to the Global AIDS Policy Coalition at Harvard University. The U.S. Agency for International Development [predicted] that by then some 11 percent of children under fifteen in sub-Saharan Africa [would] be AIDS orphans and that infant mortality [would] soar fivefold in some African and Asian nations, due to the loss of parental care among children orphaned by AIDS and its most common opportunistic infection, tuberculosis. Life expectancy in the African and Asian nations hit hardest by AIDS will plummet to an astonishing low of twenty-five years by 2010, the agency forecasts.

Medical experts now recognize that any microbe, including ones previously unknown to science, can take similar advantage of conditions in human society, going from isolated cases camouflaged by generally high levels of disease to become a global threat. Furthermore, old organisms, aided by mankind's misuse of disinfectants and drugs, can take on new, more lethal forms. . . .

## THE REAL THREAT OF BIOWARFARE

The world was lucky in the September 1994 pneumonic plague epidemic in Surat. Independent studies in the United States, France, and Russia revealed that the bacterial strain that caused the outbreak was unusually weak, and although the precise figures for plague cases and deaths remain a matter of debate, the numbers certainly fall below two hundred. Yet the epidemic vividly illustrated three crucial national security issues in disease emergence: human mobility, transparency, and tensions between states up to and including the threat of biological warfare.

When word got out that an airborne disease was loose in the city, some five hundred thousand residents of Surat boarded trains and within forty-eight hours dispersed to every corner of the subcontinent. Had the microbe that caused the plague been a virus or drug-resistant bacterium, the world would have witnessed an immediate Asian pandemic. As it was, the epidemic sparked a global panic that cost the Indian economy a minimum of $2 billion in lost sales and losses on the Bombay stock market, predominantly the result of international boycotts of Indian goods and travelers.

As the number of countries banning trade with India mounted that fall, the Hindi-language press insisted that there was no plague, accusing Pakistan of a smear campaign aimed at bringing India's economy to its knees. After international scientific investigations concluded that *Yersinia pestis* had indeed been the culprit in this bona fide epidemic, attention turned to the bacteria's origin. . . . Several Indian scientists claimed to have evidence that the bacteria in Surat had been genetically engineered for biowarfare purposes. Though no credible evidence [existed] to support it, and Indian government authorities vigorously [denied] such claims, the charge is almost impossible to disprove, particularly in a region rife with military and political tensions of long standing.

Even when allegations of biological warfare are not flying, it is often exceedingly difficult to obtain accurate information about outbreaks of disease, particularly from countries dependent on foreign investment or tourism or both. Transparency is a common problem; though there is usually no suggestion of covert action or malevolent intent, many countries are reluctant to disclose complete information about contagious illness. For example, nearly every country initially denied or covered up the presence of the HIV virus within its borders. . . . Similarly, Egypt denies the existence of cholera bacteria in the Nile's waters; Saudi Arabia has asked WHO not to warn that travelers to Mecca may be bitten by mosquitoes carrying viruses that cause the new, superlethal dengue hemorrhagic fever; few countries report the appearance of antibiotic-resistant strains of deadly bacteria; and central authorities in Serbia . . . rescinded an international epidemic alert when they learned that all the scientists WHO planned to send to the tense Kosovo region to halt a large outbreak of Crimean-Congo hemorrhagic fever were from the United States, a nation Serbia viewed with hostility.

The specter of biological warfare having raised its head, Brad Roberts of the Center for Strategic and International Studies is particularly concerned that the New Tier nations—developing states such as China, Iran, and Iraq that possess technological know-how but lack an organized civil society that might put some restraints on its use—might be tempted to employ bioweapons. The Federation of American Scientists has sought, so far in vain, a scientific solution to the acute weaknesses of verification and enforcement provisions in the 1972 Biological Weapons Convention, which most of the world's nations have signed.

That treaty's flaws, and the very real possibility of bioweapons use, stand in sharp focus today. Iraq's threat in 1990–1991 to use biological weapons in the Persian Gulf conflict found allied forces in the region virtually powerless to respond: the weapons' existence was not verified in a timely manner, the only available countermeasure was a vaccine against one type of organism, and protective gear and equipment failed to stand up to windblown sand. [In] June [1996] the U.N. Security Council concluded that Iraqi stocks of bioweaponry might have been replenished after the Gulf War settlement.

More alarming were the actions of the Aum Shinrikyo cult in Japan in early 1995. In addition to releasing toxic sarin gas in the Tokyo subway on March 18, cult members were preparing vast quantities of *Clostridium difficile* bacterial spores for terrorist use. Though rarely fatal, clostridium infections often worsen as a result of improper antibiotic use, and long bouts of bloody diarrhea can lead to dangerous colon inflammations. Clostridium was a good choice for biological terrorism: the spores can survive for months and may be spread with any aerosol device, and even slight exposure can make vulnerable people (particularly children and the elderly) sick enough to cost a crowded society like Japan hundreds of millions of dollars for hospitalizations and lost productivity.

The U.S. Office of Technology Assessment has calculated what it would take to produce a spectacular terrorist bioweapon: one hundred kilograms of a lethal sporulating organism such as anthrax spread over Washington, D.C., by a crop duster could cause well over 2 million deaths. Enough anthrax spores to kill 5 or 6 million people could be loaded into a taxi and pumped out its tailpipe as it meandered through Manhattan. Vulnerability to terrorist attacks, as well as to the natural emergence of disease, increases with population density.

## A WORLD AT RISK

A 1995 WHO survey of global capacity to identify and respond to threats from emerging disease reached troubling conclusions. Only six laboratories in the world, the study found, met security and safety standards that would make them suitable sites for research on the world's deadliest microbes, including those that cause Ebola, Marburg, and Lassa fever. Local political instability threatens to compromise the security of the two labs in Russia, and budget cuts threaten to do the same . . . in the United States . . . and . . . in Britain. . . .

Bolstering research capacity, enhancing disease surveillance capabilities, revitalizing sagging basic public health systems, rationing powerful drugs to avoid the emergence of drug-resistant organisms, and improving infection control practices at hospitals are only stopgap measures. National security warrants bolder steps.

One priority is finding scientifically valid ways to use polymerase chain reaction (popularly known as DNA fingerprinting), field investigations, chemical and biological export records, and local legal instruments to track the development of new or reemergent lethal organisms, whether natural or bioweapons. The effort should focus not only on microbes directly dangerous to humans but also on those that could pose major threats to crops or livestock. . . .

Only three diseases—cholera, plague, and yellow fever—are subject to international regulation, permitting U.N. and national authorities to interfere as necessary in the global traffic of goods and persons to stave off cross-border epidemics. The World Health Assembly, the legislative arm of WHO, recommended at its 1995 annual meeting in Geneva that the United Nations consider both expanding the list of regulated diseases and finding new ways to monitor the broad movement of disease. The Ebola outbreak in Kikwit demonstrated that a team of international scientists can be mobilized to swiftly contain a remote, localized epidemic caused by known nonairborne agents. . . .

Nobel laureate Joshua Lederberg of Rockefeller University has characterized the solutions to the threat of disease emergence as multitudinous, largely straightforward and commonsensical, and international in scope; "the bad news," he says, "is they will cost money."

Budgets, particularly for health care, are being cut at all levels of government. Dustin Hoffman made more money . . . playing a disease control scientist in the movie *Outbreak* than the combined annual budgets for the U.S. National Center for Infectious Diseases and the U.N. Programme on AIDS/HIV.

# 37

## CLIMATE CHANGE: CAN THE NORTH AND SOUTH GET IN STEP?

SETH DUNN

**At the 1992 "Earth Summit" in Rio de Janeiro the world community agreed to limit the emission of carbon dioxide and other gases thought to contribute to the gradual warming of the earth's atmosphere, which many scientists predict will dramatically alter the global environment. Contention between the Global North and South over their responsibilities for global climate change and coping with its uncertain effects has impeded efforts to devise cooperative strategies for dealing with them. Seth Dunn explores the causes of disunity on this issue within the North and South as well as between them. Seth is a research associate at the Worldwatch Institute and a contributor to its annual series on the *State of the World*.**

Climate diplomacy took a David-and-Goliath twist in the closing days of the Kyoto summit [in] December [1997]. With the protocol negotiations teetering on the verge of collapse, [then] U.S. Vice President Al Gore flew to Japan to address the historic gathering. Expectations were high that Gore, among the first to bring climate change into the political arena, would break the deadlock.

But Kinza Clodumar, president of the Republic of Nauru, outranked the vice president and was to speak first. His colorful robe bobbing in a sea of surrounding dark suits, Clodumar described a frightening future for his homeland—a tiny coral atoll island in the South Pacific that scientists believe is one of the nations most vulnerable to rising seas in a changing climate. Without immediate action by the industrial countries to curb their carbon output, he warned, Nauru will face "a terrifying, rising flood of biblical proportions." To allow the "willful destruction of entire countries and cultures," he argued, "would represent an unspeakable crime against humanity."

The Pacific Islander reserved special criticism for the world's top greenhouse gas emitter, urging Gore to abandon his government's hard-line position in the talks. "No nation has the right to place its own, misconstrued national interest before the physical and cultural survival of whole countries. The crime is cultural genocide; it must not be tolerated by the family of nations."

Clodumar's confrontation with Gore underscores an important trend in the climate debate over the last decade: Southern countries are growing increasingly assertive in challenging the sluggish steps of their more industrial neighbors in the North. While public attention has to date focused on the actions—and inaction—of industrial nations, developing countries have taken prominent roles in climate negotiations. Representing four-fifths of humanity, developing nations today comprise more than 80 percent of the signatories to the first international accord on climate change, the 1992 Rio treaty, and more than half of those to the 1997 Kyoto Protocol.

However, this greater Southern involvement in efforts to stave off global warming has been endangered . . . by aggressive U.S. posturing and demands for additional commitments from developing countries to address their emissions. In July 1997, the U.S. Senate passed a resolution threatening to withhold support for any treaty that did not require developing countries to agree to legally binding commitments within the same time period as industrial nations. This resolution isolated the United States from the rest of the world, and made for strained North-South relations before and during the Kyoto negotiations. A subsequent U.S. State Department "diplomatic full court press" to achieve the "meaningful participation of key developing countries" [did] little but draw fouls.

Despite their questionable intentions and poor timing, the awkward U.S. overtures to the South have illuminated a major challenge of the post-Kyoto debate: that of enabling both developing and industrial nations to play fair and equitable roles in the global effort to reduce greenhouse gas emissions. This challenge need not be framed in the antagonistic manner of the moment. Instead, the now-contentious "developing country issue" can be reframed and worked out in ways that will provide economic and environmental benefits for both North and South, and help stabilize the Earth's climate as well.

## THE LOW END OF THE BOAT

For small island inhabitants, paradise is being stolen away by the ocean swelling of the last century, which scientists estimate has raised sea levels more than eighteen centimeters. Between Tuvalu and the Bahamas, island elders speak of shrinking shorelines while scientists document other sea-level rise manifestations—erosion, inundation, salinization of freshwater supplies, property damages, lost

A THIRD-WORLD PERSPECTIVE ...

Per Capita Carbon Emissions, 1997
(tons per person)

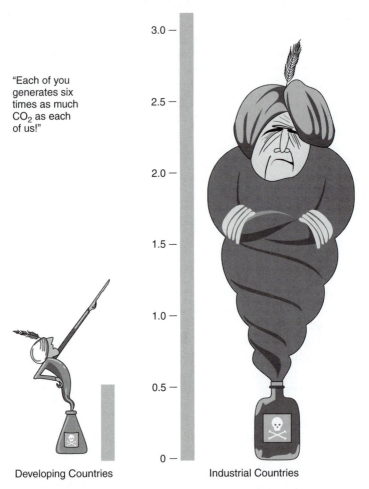

"Each of you generates six times as much $CO_2$ as each of us!"

3.0 —

2.5 —

2.0 —

1.5 —

1.0 —

0.5 —

0 —

Developing Countries          Industrial Countries

tourism—with unusual frequency. Explained a Fiji hotel manager to the *Christian Science Monitor* in [1997], "I never believed in global warming before. Now I do because the tides flood the land not twice a year as before, but at any time." Should sea level rise another meter over the next century, as scientists project, several of these islands could be literally erased from world maps. Island cultures, bound to their homes for centuries, face the devastating prospect of forced migration as their land vanishes. Jorelik Tibon, the environment agency manager of the Marshall Islands, says that the country—a scattering of low-lying coral atolls—is at risk of completely disappearing: "Sea-level rise is something so horrible here that people just don't want to think about it, especially since there's nothing they can do to stop it."

Mass exodus is already a grim reality for poor populations along low-lying coasts, who face rising seas in concert with another signature of climate change: more frequent and extreme weather events. [September 1997's] submersion of two-thirds of Bangladesh—the worst deluge in the country's history, resulting from record-long monsoon rains—left 21 million homeless. Yet scientists

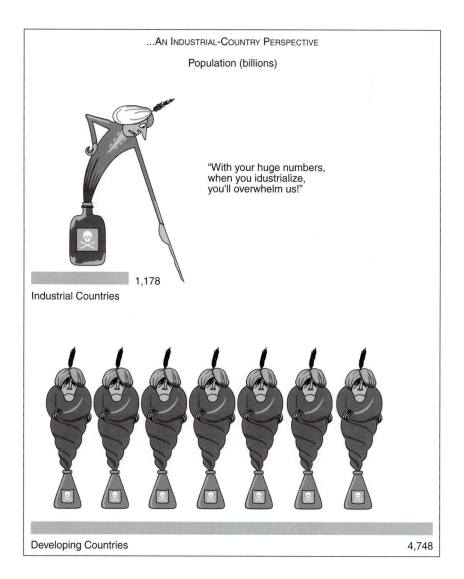

project that 70 million people will eventually be displaced as 18 percent of Bangladesh's land area is expected to be lost as the coast is further inundated. Hundreds of millions living in river basins face similar risks, like the 56 million refugees from [August 1997's] deluge in China's Yangtze River basin—that nation's worst flooding in forty-four years.

Like China, many developing nations occupy arid and semi-arid regions, making them particularly prone to experience the climate variables of drought, floods, fire, tropical disease, and heat waves. This is overwhelmingly revealed in a review of [1997's] news headlines: forest fires and drought in Indonesia, Brazil, and Mexico; floods, famine, and fevers in Africa; dry spells and torrential rains in India; heatwaves and water shortages in the Middle East; floods, drought, and cholera in Latin America. Many of these situations persisted, or even worsened, well after the highly publicized El Niño weather phenomenon ended. For example, after El Niño Mexico's prolonged drought—the worst in seventy years—was followed by the country's most severe flooding in a century.

Industrial nations also face grave impacts: several harbor densely populated and highly vulnerable coasts; the ocean currents that warm Europe could halt, ushering in a localized ice age; severe droughts could dry up agriculture in the breadbasket of the U.S. Midwest. But a hotter and more intensely wet and dry planet will be most unkind to the nearly 5 billion of its poorer inhabitants—particularly the 1.3 billion mired in extreme poverty—who are already confronted with a daunting array of environmental pressures from urban air pollution to land degradation to water pollution.

The developing South, in other words, is faced with double jeopardy in the climate gamble, being by virtue of geography and economic conditions more susceptible to the impacts and less able to adapt to them. The U.N.'s team of experts on climate change, the Intergovernmental Panel on Climate Change (IPCC), conservatively estimates climate-related damages in developing countries could reach 2 to 9 percent of their gross national product, compared with 1 to 2 percent in the industrial countries. The human dimension is more stark. Hurricane Andrew killed thirty-four in the United States in 1992, while a 1991 cyclone of the same intensity killed over two hundred thousand in Bangladesh. The [1997] summer's spate of heat waves saw one hundred deaths in Texas, but nearly thirteen hundred in India. IPCC chair Robert Watson places their plight in cool scientific language: "Developing countries would be most vulnerable to the adverse consequences of climate change in terms of human health, ecological systems, and socio-economic sectors."

## BY CAR OR BUS

Even as evidence mounts that climate instability may seriously impair their development, some Southern countries worry that industrial countries are using the climate treaty to the same end. U.S. posturing before Kyoto raised such fears

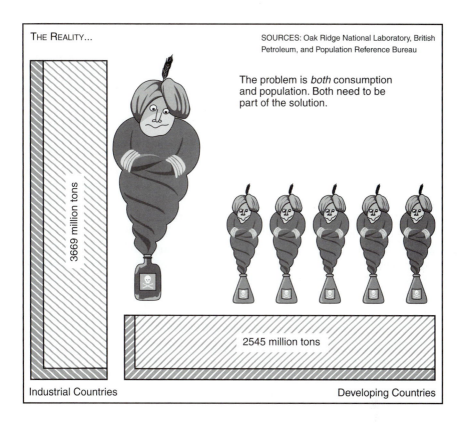

THE REALITY...

SOURCES: Oak Ridge National Laboratory, British Petroleum, and Population Reference Bureau

The problem is *both* consumption and population. Both need to be part of the solution.

3669 million tons

2545 million tons

Industrial Countries

Developing Countries

anew, forcing developing countries to become increasingly defensive toward any discussion of their future commitments—particularly in light of the difficulties industrial nations were having in taking even modest first steps. An editorial in the *China Daily* put it this way: "There are those who are unwilling to see China progress and who are trying to contain its development by pointing their fingers at the world's environmental problems."

With only a fifth of the world's population, industrial and former Eastern Bloc nations account for 74 percent of the carbon emitted since 1950. These countries produce 60 percent of today's annual emissions (see figure, page 445). From this perspective alone, a discussion of new developing country commitments could be seen as an attempt by rich countries to avoid changes in their wasteful energy habits by shifting responsibility to the poor. As China's lead negotiator put it to an American journalist: "In the developed world only two people ride in a car, and yet you want us to give up riding on a bus."

Rich nations, meanwhile, point out that developing countries, while responsible for just 26 percent of carbon emissions since 1950, are quickly becoming major emitters in their own right. Today, the South produces 40 percent of the world's carbon total—2.5 billion tons. And, as industrial countries emphasize, booming population and economic growth is fueling an explosive increase in carbon emissions in the South (see figure, page 445). The U.S. Department of Energy projects that carbon output from developing countries will, in the absence of any new policies, outgrow that of their neighbors as early as 2020, with China eclipsing the U.S. as the world's leading emitter by 2015.

Many developing nations question the fairness or relevance of this point, noting the Rio treaty's acknowledgement that "per capita emissions in developing countries are still relatively low and that the share of global emissions originating in developing countries will grow to meet their development needs." They add that most of the emissions growth in the developing world results from providing basic human needs, while that in the industrial world supports a standard of living well above the world average. And on average, the carbon released by each person in the South is less than one-fifth of that emitted by a person in an industrial country (see figure, page 438). Inter-country differences can be even greater: an average American is responsible for eight times as much polluting carbon as a Chinese citizen, and twenty times as much as an Indian. According to India's Centre for Science and Environment, even when Southern emissions equal those of the North, 20 percent of the world's population will still be releasing half of its carbon.

In reality, most countries emphasize different views of the same picture to their own advantage. Past and present emissions of the rich are critical, but so are the future emissions of the now-poor. And though the consumption patterns of those who have industrialized are a major problem, so are the population trends of the rapidly growing developing world.

## DIVERSITY OF OPINION

While the South often speaks in the climate negotiations with one voice—as the "Group of 77 (G-77) and China"—there are different perspectives among these countries themselves on how exactly to reach an equitable solution. But these differences are not hindering some Southern countries, which have begun to move beyond the stifling international political struggles and are now experimenting with possible solutions.

Southern divergences first emerged in 1990, between the members of the Organization of Petroleum Exporting Countries (OPEC) and the Alliance of Small Island States (AOSIS). The oil-rich countries, fearing lost petroleum profits, began to question the science underlying climate change and have since argued for a "go-slow" approach and special compensation for their foregone oil royalties. The coalition of small island countries, deeply concerned about sea-level rise, remains the leading voice for aggressive worldwide action and proposed far more ambitious targets than those agreed to in Kyoto.

India and China, constrained by powerful domestic interests intent on maintaining heavy fossil fuel dependence, have led resistance to calls for developing nation commitments on the grounds of equity. They define the problem as one of highly uneven per-capita emissions and argue that every person should be granted an equal "entitlement" to pollute the atmosphere. Indian negotiators stress that their people should not be limited to a few "survival emissions" while those supporting above-average standards of living in the North are consuming "luxury emissions." China has stated that it will assume no burden for reducing emissions before 2020. In earlier negotiations, one Chinese delegate declared: "The position of the G-77 and China is clear: no new commitments in whatever guise or disguise."

A handful of Asian countries have moved closer toward middle ground on the climate issue. Former "Asian tiger" South Korea has announced its intent to voluntarily assume emissions limits beginning in 2018. The Philippines, meanwhile, has brokered several North-South discussions over technological cooperation and attempted to engage a range of Asia-Pacific political leaders on the climate issue. But it remains to be seen whether the recent financial difficulties of these nations will lessen—or heighten—their commitment to these forward-looking climate efforts.

A progressive role has also been assumed by a group of Latin American countries that recognize the economic opportunities of taking part in climate protection. Costa Rica, Honduras, Nicaragua, Belize, and Panama—the Central American "emissions entrepreneurs"—are home to seventeen pilot energy and forestry "joint implementation" projects, under which countries or companies emitting excess carbon can receive partial credit for taking part in emissions-reducing projects in other nations. Further south, Brazil has brought broad Southern coalitions together, and is at the forefront of North-South dialogues over financial and technological assistance. Argentina has supported the idea of voluntary developing-country commitments. . . . These nations take a less ideological, more pragmatic approach to the issue, as seen in the exhortation of then-Costa Rican President Jose Maria Figueres in Kyoto for developing countries to "do our own part."

### "DECARBONIZING" DEVELOPMENT

Costa Rica has, in fact, done more than most nations in trying to match its call for climate protection with deeds. This small country has established a comprehensive set of policies: a goal of phasing out fossil fuel use for electricity generation by 2010; a 15 percent carbon tax (a third of the revenues support tree-planting by farmers); and an emissions-trading program to sell credits on the Chicago Board of Trade for its share of carbon reductions. It has already certified 16 million tons of carbon credits through nine joint implementation projects in clean energy and forest protection. (Forests absorb vast amounts of carbon. . . .")And in anticipation of commitments, the government is entertaining offers from industrial countries to buy them at prices of fifteen to twenty dollars per ton. . . . The government [also] announced it would protect 1.25 million acres of its tropical rainforest by selling some of these emissions offsets to companies;

the project is expected to offset more than 1 million tons over its lifetime, while generating $300 million in government revenues.

Costa Rica is quietly subverting the assumptions of many economists that slowing global warming must slow development. Indeed, while the developing world may have the most to lose in a changing climate, it will also benefit the most by finding ways to emit less. Nations from Argentina to Zimbabwe have undertaken a range of emissions-reducing initiatives—solar energy in rural areas, forest preservation, wind power installations, energy efficiency improvements—that, if multiplied and spread, could significantly rein in the future emissions trajectories of these countries. Zhong Xiang Zhang of the University of Groningen has shown, for example, that China's energy conservation programs since 1980 have lowered the country's carbon output to half of what it would have otherwise been. In removing burdensome energy subsidies, developing nations . . . clearly outperformed industrial nations during the 1990s. . . . The U.N. Development Programme (UNDP) estimates that removing all energy subsidies in the developing world would bring $35 billion in environmental, social, and economic benefits.

What is telling about these projects and policies is that few were planned with climate change in mind. Instead, most were designed to employ sustainable technologies and techniques to alleviate economic hardships—providing power to some of the 2 billion who lack it; creating jobs among the 1 billion "underemployed"; lessening urban health emergencies; and lowering reliance on oil imports. Argues Atiq Rahman of the Bangladesh Centre for Advanced Studies, "The South didn't create the problem but is responding to the challenge."

The South might also get a headstart in some of the [new] century's most promising high-technology industries, rather than relying on a one-time "parachute drop" of new technology from industrial countries. A 1997 report by the UNDP points out that "developing countries have the opportunity to become market leaders for various state-of-the-art and emerging sustainable energy technologies." A study from the U.S. Pacific Northwest National Laboratory echoes this sentiment, observing that China could become a market leader in manufacturing and commercializing energy-efficiency and renewable energy technologies—as it has with compact fluorescent light bulbs.

China is well-positioned to accomplish this: its existing use of wind, biogas, small hydro, and tidal energy already displaces 223 million tons of carbon—26 percent of its current emissions—that would have been produced by coal-fired power plants. Other developing nations are making similar early strides. The world's fourth-leading user of wind power is India; its largest energy efficient-lighting project can be found in Mexico; its biggest home solar photovoltaic program is located in Indonesia; and its largest renewable energy program, using sugarcane-derived ethanol in cars, is in Brazil.

As Jose Goldemberg of Brazil's University of São Paolo sees it, developing nations have a historic opportunity to avoid retracing the past route of industrialization, and "leapfrog" to new technologies that are not yet widely in use. Many nations in Africa, Asia, and Latin America will witness a surge in demand for energy services in the near future, and the new energy devices—small in scale and locally situated—will be an attractive alternative to the massive investments that central power plants and electric grid extensions require. Developing countries thus have a strong interest—economically and environmentally—in gaining access to the technologies that can help them cut back on carbon.

## SHARING BENEFITS

The Montreal Protocol to protect the earth's ozone layer may provide a helpful map for negotiators navigating the current climate discussions. A key step to securing stronger developing-country participation in the ozone effort was the creation of the Multilateral Fund—an innovative international body set up to direct rich nation funds and technologies toward helping developing countries curtail their chlorofluorocarbon (CFC) use. In Montreal in 1987, industrial nations alone took on specific goals for reducing CFC use, while developing countries argued for the right to use as many ozone-depleting technologies as they wished, and for as long as possible. But over the next few years, many developing nations realized that it was in their interest to move as quickly as possible to the new alternatives—and to secure help from the fund in doing so. . . . Richard Benedick, chief U.S. negotiator in the Montreal talks, believes the ozone negotiations "showed that as soon as cost-effective technologies become available, the

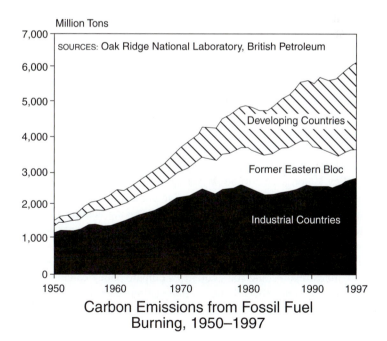

Carbon Emissions from Fossil Fuel
Burning, 1950–1997

developing countries will be eager to acquire them, mainly through the market, rather than be left behind in the march of progress."

A somewhat analogous fund, the Clean Development Mechanism (CDM), is taking shape under the Kyoto Protocol. This mechanism, a blend of both developing and industrial country proposals, has the potential to break the negotiations logjam over North-South commitments to emissions reductions. CDM has its roots in Brazil's protocol proposal, which called for a "Clean Development Fund" that would levy a fee on industrial nations that miss their targets and use the funds to support technology transfer and adaptation programs in developing countries.

In Kyoto, the Brazilian idea blended with the U.S.-pioneered concept of joint implementation, where countries can receive credit for taking part in emissions-reducing projects in other nations. Late in the Kyoto meeting, a hybrid North-South institution had emerged—offering a refreshing reminder that behind the scenes, far from the political posturing for the meeting's media circus, countries were quietly working together to achieve compromise and cooperation. . . .

## BECOMING BETTER NEIGHBORS

There is a growing consensus, in industrial and developing countries alike, that involvement in the CDM may be one of the most environmentally effective and politically constructive ways to achieve greater global participation in the climate effort. Its long-term impact, though, will depend on progress in the parallel and often paralyzing debates over U.S. ratification, emissions trading, and new developing country commitments. And it cannot alone accomplish the steep worldwide cuts necessary for avoiding dangerous climate disruption. . . .

That climate protection presents tangible development benefits—both immediate and long-term—is a critical point that most governments miss. This is unfortunate, for a better gauging of these gains is essential to engaging developing countries fairly and more fully in the climate dialogue. And focusing on the advantages of climate action is imperative for leveraging badly needed domestic policy reforms, even as details over . . . international instruments are hammered out over the coming . . . years.

Indeed, while capital and technologies are poised to flow from North to South, a useful policy lesson seems to be migrating in the opposite direction. The limited but noteworthy steps made by developing countries in cutting back on carbon suggest that greater progress will be made in taking action to reduce emissions when the policies are designed to address other development concerns. That is, taking into consideration what the IPCC calls "multiple benefits"—cleaner air, greater energy self-reliance, added government revenue, more jobs, leadership in new industries—could tilt a country's climate policy calculus away from "analysis paralysis" and toward meaningful action, even before counting the avoided damages. Whether in the special interest-dominated North or the cash-strapped South, efforts to phase out fossil fuel subsidies, enact carbon taxes, improve energy efficiency, and promote clean energy technologies are unlikely to accumulate sufficient political support unless they can be linked to this broader framework of goals.

For countries to bridge the North-South divide abroad and close the gap between reality and rhetoric at home, will depend in no small part on the ability of governments to utilize these connections in far more opportunistic fashion than they have to date. The challenge of resolving the "developing country issue," it turns out, is mainly a conceptual one: to transcend today's fractious finger pointing and fixation on costs, and envision the Kyoto Protocol as a valuable and vital stepping-stone toward sustainability. Then all nations might better recognize, and begin to reap, the rewards of taking part in the great global endeavor to help poor nations bypass the fossil-fuel era of the rich en route to a carbon-free future.

Ultimately, Benedick's words on the Montreal Protocol ring even truer for Kyoto: "The North's interests in maintaining a healthy planet can only be achieved through aggressive efforts to support national economic advancement in the South." If we are to take real steps together toward a stable climate, we must become better neighbors . . . learning to share the air and the myriad benefits of protecting it. Argentina's Estrada puts it well: "We are all adrift in the same boat. And there's no way that only half the boat is going to sink."

# 38

# THE NEXT DOUBLING: UNDERSTANDING GLOBAL POPULATION GROWTH

JENNIFER D. MITCHELL

In the next half-century, world population is projected to increase by more that 50 percent. Nearly all of the growth will occur in the Global South. Jennifer D. Mitchell identifies the three dimensions of the projected population explosion—unmet demand for family planning; a desire for large families; and population momentum—and assesses how each might be met. She concludes that "our attempts to stabilize population—or our failure to act— will likely have consequences that far outweigh the implications of the military or commercial crisis of the moment." At the time this chapter was written, Mitchell was a staff researcher at the Worldwatch Institute and a contributor to its annual series on the State of the World.

In 1971, when Bangladesh won independence from Pakistan, the two countries embarked on a kind of unintentional demographic experiment. The separation had produced two very similar populations: both contained some 66 million people and both were growing at about 3 percent a year. Both were overwhelmingly poor, rural, and Muslim. Both populations had similar views on the "ideal" family size (around four children); in both cases, that ideal was roughly two children smaller than the actual average family. And in keeping with the Islamic tendency to encourage large families, both generally disapproved of family planning.

But there was one critical difference. The Pakistani government, distracted by leadership crises and committed to conventional ideals of economic growth, wavered over the importance of family planning. The Bangladeshi government did not: as early as 1976, population growth had been declared the country's number one problem, and a national network was established to educate people about family planning and supply them with contraceptives. As a result, the proportion of couples using contraceptives rose from around 6 percent in 1976 to about 50 percent today, and fertility rates have dropped from well over six children per woman to just over three. Today, some 120 million people live in Bangladesh, while 140 million live in Pakistan—a difference of 20 million.

Bangladesh still faces enormous population pressures—by 2050, its population will probably have increased by nearly 100 million. But even so, that 20 million person "savings" is a colossal achievement, especially given local conditions. Bangladeshi officials had no hope of producing the classic "demographic transition," in which improvements in education, health care, and general living standards tend to push down the birthrate. Bangladesh was—and is—one of the poorest and most densely populated countries on earth. About the size of England and Wales, Bangladesh has twice as many people. Its per capita GDP is barely over $200. It has one doctor for every 12,500 people and nearly three-quarters of its adult population are illiterate. The national diet would be considered inadequate in any industrial country, and even at current levels of population growth, Bangladesh may be forced to rely increasingly on food imports.

All of these burdens would be substantially heavier than they already are, had it not been for the family planning program. To appreciate the Bangladeshi achievement, it's only necessary to look at Pakistan: those "additional" 20 million Pakistanis require at least 2.5 million more houses, about 4 million more tons of grain each year, millions more jobs, and significantly greater investments in health care—or a significantly greater burden of disease. Of the two nations, Pakistan has the more robust economy—its per capita GDP is twice that of Bangladesh. But the Pakistani economy is still primarily agricultural, and the size of the average farm is shrinking, in part because of the expanding population. Already, one fourth of the country's farms are under one hectare, the standard minimum size for economic viability, and Pakistan is looking increasingly towards the international grain markets to feed its people. In 1997, despite its third consecutive year of near-record harvests, Pakistan attempted to double its wheat imports but was not able to do so because it had exhausted its line of credit.

And Pakistan's extra burden will be compounded in the next generation. Pakistani women still bear an average of well over five children, so at the current birthrate, the 10 million or so extra couples would produce at least 50 million children. And these in turn could bear nearly 125 million children of their own. At its current fertility rate, Pakistan's population will double in just twenty-four years—that's more than twice as fast as Bangladesh's population is growing. H.E. Syeda Abida Hussain, Pakistan's Minister of Population Welfare, explains the problem bluntly: "If we achieve success in lowering our population growth substantially, Pakistan has a future. But if, God forbid, we should not—no future."

## THE THREE DIMENSIONS OF THE POPULATION EXPLOSION

Some version of Mrs. Abida's statement might apply to the world as a whole. About 5.9 billion people currently inhabit the earth. By the middle of [this] century, according to U.N. projections, the population will probably reach 9.4 billion—and all of the net increase is likely to occur in the developing world. [In 1998 the United Nations revised its population projections downward. Its "most likely" projection indicates that world population will reach 8.9 billion in 2050, roughly 500 million less than its 1996 estimate. This revision also anticipates that population growth will be smaller in the particular countries and regions Mitchell cites, but the revised figures do not alter the substantive arguments and conclusions that she offers in this chapter. Also noteworthy is that while fertility rates are expected to decline, nearly all of the increase in world population will occur in the Global South—eds.] (The total population of the industrial countries is expected to decline slightly over the next fifty years.) Nearly 60 percent of the increase will occur in Asia, which will grow from 3.4 billion people in 1995 to more than 5.4 billion in 2050. China's population will swell from 1.2 billion to 1.5 billion, while India's is projected to soar from 930 million to 1.53 billion. In the Middle East and North Africa, the population will probably more than double, and in sub-Saharan Africa, it will triple. By 2050, Nigeria alone is expected to have 339 million people—more than the entire continent of Africa had thirty-five years ago.

Despite the different demographic projections, no country will be immune to the effects of population growth. Of course, the countries with the highest growth rates are likely to feel the greatest immediate burdens—on their educational and public health systems, for instance, and on their forests, soils, and water as the struggle to grow more food intensifies. Already some one hundred countries must rely on grain imports to some degree, and 1.3 billion of the world's people are living on the equivalent of one dollar a day or less.

But the effects will ripple out from these "frontline" countries to encompass the world as a whole. Take the water predicament in the Middle East as an example. According to Tony Allan, a water expert at the University of London, the Middle East "ran out of water" in 1972, when its population stood at 122 million. At that point, Allan argues, the region had begun to draw more water out of its aquifers and rivers than the rains were replenishing. Yet today, the region's population is twice what it was in 1972 and still growing. To some degree, water management now determines political destiny. In Egypt, for example, President Hosni Mubarak has announced a $2 billion diversion project designed to pump water from the Nile River into an area that is now desert. The project—Mubarak calls it a "necessity imposed by population"—is designed to resettle some 3 million people outside the Nile flood plain, which is home to more than 90 percent of the country's population.

Elsewhere in the region, water demands are exacerbating international tensions; Jordan, Israel, and Syria, for instance, engage in uneasy competition for the waters of the Jordan River basin. Jordan's King Hussein once said that water was the only issue that could lead him to declare war on Israel. Of course, the United States and the western European countries are deeply involved in the region's antagonisms and have invested heavily in its fragile states. The Western nations have no realistic hope of escaping involvement in future conflicts.

Yet the future need not be so grim. The experiences of countries like Bangladesh suggest that it is possible to build population policies that are a match for the threat. The first step is to understand the causes of population growth. John Bongaarts, vice president of the Population Council, a non-profit research group in New York City, has identified three basic factors. (See figure on page 452.)

*Unmet demand for family planning.* In the developing world, at least 120 million married women—and a large but undefined number of unmarried women—want more control over their pregnancies, but cannot get family planning services. This unmet demand will cause about one-third of the projected population growth in developing countries over the next fifty years, or an increase of about 1.2 billion people.

*Desire for large families.* Another 20 percent of the projected growth over the next fifty years, or an increase of about 660 million people, will be caused by couples who may have access to family planning services, but who choose to have more than two children. (Roughly two children per family is the "replacement rate," at which a population could be expected to stabilize over the long term.)

*Population momentum.* By far the largest component of population growth is the least commonly understood. Nearly one-half of the increase projected for the next fifty years will occur simply because the next reproductive generation—the group of people currently entering puberty or younger—is so much larger than the current reproductive generation. Over the next twenty-five years, some 3 billion people—a number equal to the entire world population in 1960—will enter their reproductive years, but only about 1.8 billion will leave that phase of life. Assuming that the couples in this reproductive bulge begin to have children at a fairly early age, which is the global norm, the global population would still expand by 1.7 billion, even if all of those couples had only two children—the long-term replacement rate.

## MEETING THE DEMAND

Over the past three decades, the global percentage of couples using some form of family planning has increased dramatically—from less than ten to more than 50 percent. But due to the growing population, the absolute number of women not using family planning is greater today than it was thirty years ago. Many of these women fall into that first category above—they want the services but for one reason or another, they cannot get them.

## Population of Developing Countries, 1950–1995, with Projected Growth to 2050

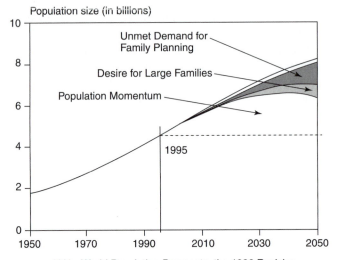

SOURCE: U.N., *World Population Prospects: the 1996 Revision* (New York: 1998); and John Bongaarts, "Population Policy Options in the Developing World," *Science*, 11 February 1994.

Sometimes the obstacle is a matter of policy: many governments ban or restrict valuable methods of contraception. In Japan, for instance, regulations discourage the use of birth control pills in favor of condoms, as a public health measure against sexually transmitted diseases. A study conducted in 1989 found that some sixty countries required a husband's permission before a woman can be sterilized; several required a husband's consent for all forms of birth control.

Elsewhere, the problems may be more logistical than legal. Many developing countries lack clinics and pharmacies in rural areas. In some rural areas of sub-Saharan Africa, it takes an average of two hours to reach the nearest contraceptive provider. And often contraceptives are too expensive for most people. Sometimes the products or services are of such poor quality that they are not simply ineffective, but dangerous. A woman who has been injured by a badly made or poorly inserted IUD may well be put off by contraception entirely.

In many countries, the best methods are simply unavailable. Sterilization is often the only available nontraditional option, or the only one that has gained wide acceptance. Globally, the procedure accounts for about 40 percent of contraceptive use and in some countries the fraction is much higher: in the Dominican Republic and India, for example, it stands at 69 percent. But women don't generally resort to sterilization until well into their childbearing years, and in some countries, the procedure isn't permitted until a woman reaches a certain age or bears a certain number of children. Sterilization is therefore no substitute for effective temporary methods like condoms, the pill, or IUDs.

There are often obstacles in the home as well. Women may be prevented from seeking family planning services by disapproving husbands or in-laws. In Pakistan, for example, 43 percent of husbands object to family planning. Frequently, such objections reflect a general social disapproval inculcated by religious or other deeply rooted cultural values. And in many places, there is a crippling burden of ignorance: women simply may not know what family planning services are available or how to obtain them.

Yet there are many proven opportunities for progress, even in conditions that would appear to offer little room for it. In Bangladesh, for instance, contraception was never explicitly illegal, but many households follow the Muslim custom of *purdah,* which largely secludes women in their communities. Since it's very difficult for such women to get to family planning clinics, the government brought family planning to them: some 30,000 female field workers go door-to-door to explain contraceptive methods and distribute supplies. Several other countries have adopted Bangladesh's approach. . . .

Reducing the price of contraceptives can also trigger a substantial increase in use. In poor countries, contraceptives can be an extremely price-sensitive commodity even when they are very cheap. Bangladesh found this out the hard way in 1990, when officials increased contraceptive prices an average of 60 percent. . . . Despite regular annual sales increases up to that point, the market slumped immediately . . . The next year, prices were rolled back; sales rebounded and have grown steadily since then.

Additional research and development can help broaden the range of contraceptive options. Not all methods work for all couples, and the lack of a suitable method may block a substantial amount of demand. Some women, for instance, have side effects to the pill; others may not be able to use IUDs because of reproductive tract infections. The wider the range of available methods, the better the chance that a couple will use one of them.

### PLANNING THE SMALL FAMILY

Simply providing family planning services to people who already want them won't be enough to arrest the population juggernaut. In many countries, large families are still the ideal. In Senegal, Cameroon, and Niger, for example, the average woman still wants six or seven children. A few countries have tried to legislate such desires away. In India, for example, the Ministry of Health and Family Welfare is interested in promoting a policy that would bar people who have more than two children from political careers, or deny them promotion if they work within the civil service bureaucracy. And China's well-known policy allows only one child per family.

But coercion is not only morally questionable—it's likely to be ineffective because of the backlash it invites. A better starting point for policy would be to try to understand why couples want large families in the first place. In many developing countries, having lots of children still seems perfectly rational: children

are a source of security in old age and may be a vital part of the family economy. Even when they're very young, children's labor can make them an asset
rather than a drain on family income. And in countries with high child mortality
rates, many births may be viewed as necessary to compensate for the possible
deaths (of course, the cumulative statistical effect of such a reaction is to *over-
compensate*).

Religious or other cultural values may contribute to the big family ideal. In
Pakistan, for instance, where 97 percent of the population is Muslim, a recent
survey of married women found that almost 60 percent of them believed that the
number of children they have is "up to God." Preference for sons is another widespread factor in the big family psychology: many large families have come about
from a perceived need to bear at least one son. In India, for instance, many Hindus believe that they need a son to perform their last rites, or their souls will not
be released from the cycle of births and rebirths. Lack of a son can mean abandonment in this life too. Many husbands desert wives who do not bear sons. Or
if a husband dies, a son is often the key to a woman's security: 60 percent of Indian women over 60 are widows, and widows tend to rely on their sons for support. In some castes, a widow has no other option since social mores forbid her
from returning to her birth village or joining a daughter's family. Understandably, the fear of abandonment prompts many Indian women to continue having
children until they have a son. It is estimated that if a son preference were eliminated in India, the fertility rate would decline by 8 percent from its current level
of 3.5 children per woman.

Yet even deeply rooted beliefs are subject to reinterpretation. In Iran, another
Muslim society, fertility rates have dropped from seven children per family to
just over four in less than three decades. The trend is due in some measure to a
change of heart among the government's religious authorities, who had become
increasingly concerned about the likely effects of a population that was growing
at more than 3 percent per year. In 1994, at the International Conference on Population and Development (ICPD) held in Cairo, the Iranian delegation released
a "National Report on Population" which argued that according to the "quota-
tions from prophet Mohammad . . . and verses of [the] holy Quran, what is standing at the top priority for the Muslims' community is the social welfare of Muslims." Family planning, therefore, "not only is not prohibited but is emphasized
by religion."

Promotional campaigns can also change people's assumptions and behavior,
if the campaigns fit into the local social context. Perhaps the most successful effort of this kind is in Thailand, where Mechai Viravidaiya, the founder of the
Thai Population and Community Development Association, started a program
that uses witty songs, demonstrations, and ads to encourage the use of contraceptives. The program has helped foster widespread awareness of family planning throughout Thai society. Teachers use population-related examples in their
math classes; cab drivers even pass out condoms. Such efforts have paid off: in
less than three decades, contraceptive use among married couples has risen from

8 to 75 percent and population growth has slowed from over 3 percent to about 1 percent—the same rate as in the United States.

Better media coverage may be another option. In Bangladesh, a recent study found that while local journalists recognize the importance of family planning, they do not understand population issues well enough to cover them effectively and objectively. The study, a collaboration between the University Research Corporation of Bangladesh and Johns Hopkins University in the United States, recommended five ways to improve coverage: develop easy-to-use information for journalists (press releases, wall charts, research summaries), offer training and workshops, present awards for population journalism, create a forum for communication between journalists and family planning professionals, and establish a population resource center or data bank.

Often, however, the demand for large families is so tightly linked to social conditions that the conditions themselves must be viewed as part of the problem. Of course, those conditions vary greatly from one society to the next, but there are some common points of leverage:

*Reducing child mortality* helps give parents more confidence in the future of the children they already have. Among the most effective ways of reducing mortality are child immunization programs, and the promotion of "birth spacing"—lengthening the time between births. (Children born less than a year and a half apart are twice as likely to die as those born two or more years apart.)

*Improving the economic situation of women* provides them with alternatives to childbearing. In some countries, officials could reconsider policies or customs that limit women's job opportunities or other economic rights, such as the right to inherit property. Encouraging "micro-lenders" such as Bangladesh's Grameen Bank can also be an effective tactic. In Bangladesh, the Bank has made loans to well over a million villagers—mostly impoverished women—to help them start or expand small businesses.

*Improving education* tends to delay the average age of marriage and to further the two goals just mentioned. Compulsory school attendance for children undercuts the economic incentive for larger families by reducing the opportunities for child labor. And in just about every society, higher levels of education correlate strongly with smaller families.

## MOMENTUM: THE BIGGEST THREAT OF ALL

The most important factor in population growth is the hardest to counter—and to understand. Population momentum can be easy to overlook because it isn't directly captured by the statistics that attract the most attention. The global growth rate, after all, is dropping: in the mid-1960s, it amounted to about a 2.2 percent annual increase; today the figure is 1.4 percent. [The 1998 United Nations data revisions indicate the current growth rate is 1.33 percent—eds.] The fertility rate is dropping too: in 1950, women bore an average of five children each; now they bear roughly three. But despite these continued declines, the absolute number of births won't taper off any time soon. According to U.S. Census Bureau estimates, some 130 million births will still occur annually for the next twenty-five years, because of the sheer number of women coming into their childbearing years.

The effects of momentum can be seen readily in a country like Bangladesh, where more than 42 percent of the population is under fifteen years old—a typical proportion for many poor countries. Some 82 percent of the population growth projected for Bangladesh over the next half century will be caused by momentum. In other words, even if from now on, every Bangladeshi couple were to have only two children, the country's population would still grow by 80 million by 2050 simply because the next reproductive generation is so enormous.

The key to reducing momentum is to delay as many births as possible. To understand why delay works, it's helpful to think of momentum as a kind of human accounting problem, in which a large number of births in the near term won't be balanced by a corresponding number of deaths over the same period of time. One side of the population ledger will contain those 130 million annual births (not all of which are due to momentum, of course), while the other side will contain only about 50 million annual deaths. So to put the matter in a morbid light, the longer a substantial number of those births can be delayed, the longer the death side of the balance sheet will be when the births eventually occur. In developing countries, according to the Population Council's Bongaarts, an average 2.5-year delay in the age when a woman bears her first child would reduce population growth by over 10 percent.

One way to delay childbearing is to postpone the age of marriage. In Bangladesh, for instance, the median age of first marriage among women rose from 14.4 in 1951 to 18 in 1989, and the age at first birth followed suit. Simply raising the legal age of marriage may be a useful tactic in countries that permit marriage among the very young. Educational improvements, as already mentioned, tend to do the same thing. A survey of twenty-three developing countries found that the median age of marriage for women with secondary education exceeded that of women with no formal education by four years.

Another fundamental strategy for encouraging later childbirth is to help women break out of the "sterilization syndrome" by providing and promoting high-quality, temporary contraceptives. Sterilization might appear to be the ideal form of contraception because it's permanent. But precisely because it is permanent, women considering sterilization tend to have their children early, and then resort to it. A family planning program that relies heavily on sterilization may therefore be working at cross purposes with itself: when offered as a primary form of contraception, sterilization tends to promote early childbirth.

## WHAT HAPPENED TO THE CAIRO PLEDGES?

At the 1994 Cairo Conference, some one hundred eighty nations agreed on a twenty-year reproductive health package to slow population growth. The agreement called for a progressive rise in annual funding over the life of the package; according to U.N. estimates, the annual price tag would come to about $17 billion by 2000 and $21.7 billion by 2015. Developing countries agreed to pay for two-thirds of the program, while the developed countries were to pay for the rest. On a global scale, the package was fairly modest: the annual funding amounts to less than two weeks' worth of global military expenditures.

Today, developing country spending is largely on track with the Cairo agreement, but the developed countries are not keeping their part of the bargain. . . .

Population funding is always vulnerable to the illusion that the falling growth rate means the problem is going away. Worldwide, the annual population increase has dropped from a high of 87 million in 1988 to 80 million today. [The 1998 United Nations data revisions indicate that currently the annual population increase is 78 million people—eds.] But dismissing the problem with that statistic is like comforting someone stuck on a railway crossing with the news that an oncoming train has slowed from eighty-seven to eighty kilometers an hour, while its weight has increased. It will now take 12.5 years instead of 11.5 years to add the next billion people to the world. But that billion will surely arrive—and so will at least one more billion. Will still more billions follow? That, in large measure, depends on what policy makers do now. Funding alone will not ensure that population stabilizes, but lack of funding will ensure that it does not.

## THE NEXT DOUBLING

In the wake of the Cairo conference, most population programs are broadening their focus to include improvements in education, women's health, and women's social status among their many goals. These goals are worthy in their own right and they will ultimately be necessary for bringing population under control. But global population growth has gathered so much momentum that it could simply overwhelm a development agenda. Many countries now have little choice but to tackle their population problem in as direct a fashion as possible—even if that means temporarily ignoring other social problems. Population growth is now a global social emergency. Even as officials in both developed and developing countries open up their program agendas, it is critical that they not neglect their single most effective tool for dealing with that emergency: direct expenditures on family planning.

The funding that is likely to be the most useful will be constant, rather than sporadic. A fluctuating level of commitment, like sporadic condom use, can end up missing its objective entirely. And wherever it's feasible, funding should be designed to develop self-sufficiency—as, for instance, with UNFPA's $1 million grant to Cuba, to build a factory for making birth control pills. The factory, which has the capacity to turn out 500 million tablets annually, might eventually even provide the country with a new export product. Self-sufficiency is likely to grow increasingly important as the fertility rate continues to decline. As Tom Merrick, senior population advisor at the World Bank explains, "while the need for contraceptives will not go away when the total fertility rate reaches two—the donors will."

Even in narrow, conventional economic terms, family planning offers one of the best development investments available. A study in Bangladesh showed that for each birth prevented, the government spends sixty-two dollars and saves six hundred fifteen dollars on social services expenditures—nearly a tenfold return. The study estimated that the Bangladesh program prevents eight hundred ninety thousand births a year, for a net annual savings of $547 million. And that figure does not include savings resulting from lessened pressure on natural resources.

Over the past forty years, the world's population has doubled. At some point in the latter half of [this] century, today's population of 5.9 billion could double again. But because of the size of the next reproductive generation, we probably have only a relatively few years to stop that next doubling. To prevent all of the damage—ecological, economic, and social—that the next doubling is likely to cause, we must begin planning the global family with the same kind of urgency that we bring to matters of trade, say, or military security. Whether we realize it or not, our attempts to stabilize population—or our failure to act—will likely have consequences that far outweigh the implications of the military or commercial crisis of the moment. Slowing population growth is one of the greatest gifts we can offer future generations.

# 39

# GRAY DAWN: THE GLOBAL AGING CRISIS

PETER G. PETERSON

Global demographic developments are often thought to have their origin in and exert their greatest impact on the Global South. Peter G. Peterson challenges that popular viewpoint. Focusing on the profound demographic transformation arising from the rapidly aging societies in the Global North, he argues that "the graying of the developed world's population may actually do more to reshape our collective future" than any of the major global hazards confronting us. Peterson is chairman of the Council of Foreign Relations and author of *Gray Dawn: How the Coming Age Will Transform America—and the World* (1999).

## DAUNTING DEMOGRAPHICS

The list of major global hazards in the next century has grown long and familiar. It includes the proliferation of nuclear, biological, and chemical weapons, other types of high-tech terrorism, deadly superviruses, extreme climate change, the financial, economic, and political aftershocks of globalization, and the violent ethnic explosions waiting to be detonated in today's unsteady new democracies. Yet there is a less-understood challenge—the graying of the developed world's population—that may actually do more to reshape our collective future than any of the above.

Over the next several decades, countries in the developed world will experience an unprecedented growth in the number of their elderly and an unprecedented

457

decline in the number of their youth. The timing and magnitude of this demographic transformation have already been determined. [This] century's elderly have already been born and can be counted—and their cost to retirement benefit systems can be projected.

Unlike with global warming, there can be little debate over whether or when global aging will manifest itself. And unlike with other challenges, even the struggle to preserve and strengthen unsteady new democracies, the costs of global aging will be far beyond the means of even the world's wealthiest nations—unless retirement benefit systems are radically reformed. Failure to do so, to prepare early and boldly enough, will spark economic crises that will dwarf the recent [economic] meltdowns in Asia and Russia.

How we confront global aging will have vast economic consequences costing quadrillions of dollars over the next century. Indeed, it will greatly influence how we manage, and can afford to manage, the other major challenges that will face us in the future.

For this and other reasons, global aging will become not just the transcendent economic issue of the twenty-first century, but the transcendent political issue as well. It will dominate and daunt the public-policy agendas of developed countries and force the renegotiation of their social contracts. It will also reshape foreign policy strategies and the geopolitical order.

The United States has a massive challenge ahead of it. The broad outlines can already be seen in the emerging debate over Social Security and Medicare reform. But ominous as the fiscal stakes are in the United States, they loom even larger in Japan and Europe, where populations are aging even faster, birthrates are lower, the influx of young immigrants from developing countries is smaller, public pension benefits are more generous, and private pension systems are weaker.

Aging has become a truly global challenge, and must therefore be given high priority on the global policy agenda. A gray dawn fast approaches. It is time to take an unflinching look at the shape of things to come.

*The Floridization of the developed world.* Been to Florida lately? You may not have realized it, but the vast concentration of seniors there—nearly 19 percent of the population—represents humanity's future. Today's Florida is a demographic benchmark that every developed nation will soon pass. Italy will hit the mark as early as 2003, followed by Japan in 2005 and Germany in 2006. France and Britain will pass present-day Florida around 2016; the United States and Canada in 2021 and 2023.

*Societies much older than any we have ever known.* Global life expectancy has grown more in the last fifty years than over the previous five thousand. Until the Industrial Revolution, people aged sixty-five and over never amounted to more than 2 or 3 percent of the population. In today's developed world, they amount to 14 percent. By the year 2030, they will reach 25 percent and be closing in on thirty in some countries.

*An unprecedented economic burden on working-age people.* Early in the next century, working-age populations in most developed countries will shrink.

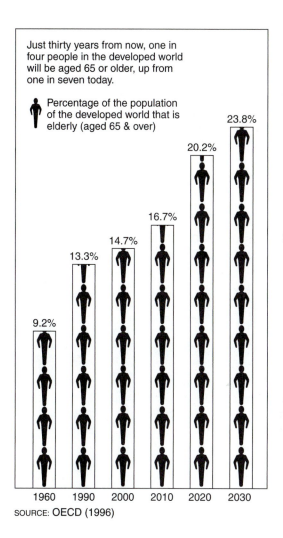

Just thirty years from now, one in four people in the developed world will be aged 65 or older, up from one in seven today.

Percentage of the population of the developed world that is elderly (aged 65 & over)

| 1960 | 1990 | 2000 | 2010 | 2020 | 2030 |

9.2% — 13.3% — 14.7% — 16.7% — 20.2% — 23.8%

SOURCE: OECD (1996)

Between 2000 and 2010, Japan, for example, will suffer a 25 percent drop in the number of workers under age thirty. Today the ratio of working taxpayers to nonworking pensioners in the developed world is around three to one. By 2030, absent reform, this ratio will fall to one and one-half to one, and in some countries, such as Germany and Italy, it will drop all the way down to one to one or even lower. While the longevity revolution represents a miraculous triumph of modern medicine and the extra years of life will surely be treasured by the elderly and their families, pension plans and other retirement benefit programs were not designed to provide these billions of extra years of payouts.

*The aging of the aged: the number of "old old" will grow much faster than the number of "young old."* The United Nations projects that by 2050, the number of people aged sixty-five to eighty-four worldwide will grow from 400 million to 1.3 billion (a threefold increase), while the number of people aged eighty-five and over will grow from 26 million to 175 million (a sixfold increase)—and the number aged one hundred and over from one hundred thirty-five thousand to 2.2 million (a sixteenfold increase). The "old old" consume far more health care than the "young old"—about two to three times as much. For nursing-home care, the ratio is roughly twenty to one. Yet little of this cost is figured in the official projections of future public expenditures.

*Falling birthrates will intensify the global aging trend.* As life spans increase, fewer babies are being born. As recently as the late 1960s, the worldwide total

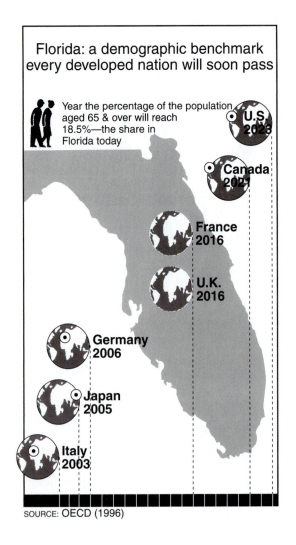

Florida: a demographic benchmark every developed nation will soon pass

Year the percentage of the population aged 65 & over will reach 18.5%—the share in Florida today

U.S. 2023
Canada 2021
France 2016
U.K. 2016
Germany 2006
Japan 2005
Italy 2003

SOURCE: OECD (1996)

fertility rate (that is, the average number of lifetime births per woman) stood at about 5.0, well within the historical range. Then came a behavioral revolution, driven by growing affluence, urbanization, feminism, rising female participation in the workforce, new birth control technologies, and legalized abortion. The result: an unprecedented and unexpected decline in the global fertility rate to about 2.7—a drop fast approaching the replacement rate of 2.1 (the rate required merely to maintain a constant population). In the developed world alone, the average fertility rate has plummeted to 1.6. Since 1995, Japan has had fewer births annually than in any year since 1899. In Germany, where the rate has fallen to 1.3, fewer babies are born each year than in Nepal, which has a population only one-quarter as large.

*A shrinking population in an aging developed world.* Unless their fertility rates rebound, the total populations of Western Europe and Japan will shrink to about one-half of their current size before the end of the next century. In 1950, seven of the twelve most populous nations were in the developed world: the United States, Russia, Japan, Germany, France, Italy, and the United Kingdom. The United Nations projects that by 2050, only the United States will remain on the list. Nigeria, Pakistan, Ethiopia, Congo, Mexico, and the Philippines will replace the others. But since developing countries are also experiencing a drop in fertility, many are now actually aging faster than the typical developed country. In France, for example, it took over a century for the elderly to grow from 7 to 14 percent of the population. South Korea, Taiwan, Singapore, and China are projected to traverse that distance in only twenty-five years.

*From worker shortage to rising immigration pressure.* Perhaps the most predictable consequence of the gap in fertility and population growth rates between developed and developing countries will be the rising demand for immigrant workers in older and wealthier societies facing labor shortages. Immigrants are typically young and tend to bring with them the family practices of their native culture—including higher fertility rates. In many European countries, non-European foreigners already make up roughly 10 percent of the population. This includes 10 million to 13 million Muslims, nearly all of whom are working-age or younger. In Germany, foreigners will make up 30 percent of the total population by 2030, and over half the population of major cities like Munich and Frankfurt. Global aging and attendant labor shortages will therefore ensure that immigration remains a major issue in developed countries for decades to come. Culture wars could erupt over the balkanization of language and religion; electorates could divide along ethnic lines; and émigré leaders could sway foreign policy.

## GRAYING MEANS PAYING

Official projections suggest that within thirty years, developed countries will have to spend at least an extra 9 to 16 percent of GDP simply to meet their old-age benefit promises. The unfunded liabilities for pensions (that is, benefits already earned by today's workers for which nothing has been saved) are already almost $35 trillion. Add in health care, and the total jumps to at least twice as much. At minimum, the global aging issue thus represents, to paraphrase the old quiz show, a $64 trillion question hanging over the developed world's future.

To pay for promised benefits through increased taxation is unfeasible. Doing so would raise the total tax burden by an unthinkable 25 to 40 percent of every worker's taxable wages—in countries where payroll tax rates sometimes already exceed 40 percent. To finance the costs of these benefits by borrowing would be just as disastrous. Governments would run unprecedented deficits that would quickly consume the savings of the developed world.

And the $64 trillion estimate is probably low. It likely underestimates future growth in longevity and health care costs and ignores the negative effects on the economy of more borrowing, higher interest rates, more taxes, less savings, and lower rates of productivity and wage growth.

There are only a handful of exceptions to these nightmarish forecasts. In Australia, total public retirement costs as a share of GDP are expected to rise only slightly, and they may even decline in Britain and Ireland. This fiscal good fortune is not due to any special demographic trend, but to timely policy reforms—including tight limits on public health spending, modest pension benefit formulas, and new personally owned savings programs that allow future public benefits to shrink as a share of average wages. This approach may yet be emulated elsewhere.

Failure to respond to the aging challenge will destabilize the global economy, straining financial and political institutions around the world. Consider Japan, which today runs a large current account surplus making up well over half the capital exports of all the surplus nations combined. Then imagine a scenario in which Japan leaves its retirement programs and fiscal policies on autopilot. Thirty years from now, under this scenario, Japan will be importing massive amounts of capital to prevent its domestic economy from collapsing under the weight of benefit outlays. This will require a huge reversal in global capital flows. To get some idea of the potential volatility, note that over the next decade, Japan's annual pension deficit is projected to grow to roughly three times the size of its recent and massive capital exports to the United States; by 2030, the annual deficit is expected to be fifteen times as large. Such reversals will cause wildly fluctuating interest and exchange rates, which may in turn short-circuit financial institutions and trigger a serious market crash.

As they age, some nations will do little to change course, while others may succeed in boosting their national savings rate, at least temporarily, through a combination of fiscal restraint and household thrift. Yet this too could result in a volatile disequilibrium in supply and demand for global capital. Such imbalance could wreak havoc with international institutions such as the European Union.

In recent years, the EU has focused on monetary union, launched a single currency (the euro), promoted cross-border labor mobility, and struggled to harmonize fiscal, monetary, and trade policies. European leaders expect to have their

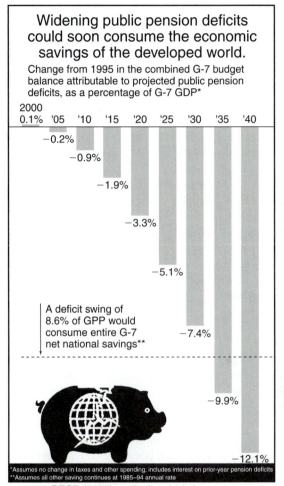

## Widening public pension deficits could soon consume the economic savings of the developed world.

Change from 1995 in the combined G-7 budget balance attributable to projected public pension deficits, as a percentage of G-7 GDP*

2000
0.1%  '05   '10   '15   '20   '25   '30   '35   '40

−0.2%

−0.9%

−1.9%

−3.3%

−5.1%

A deficit swing of 8.6% of GPP would consume entire G-7 net national savings**

−7.4%

−9.9%

−12.1%

*Assumes no change in taxes and other spending; includes interest on prior-year pension deficits
**Assumes all other saving continues at 1985–94 annual rate

SOURCE: OECD (1995), author's calculations

hands full smoothing out differences between members of the Economic and Monetary Union (EMU)—from the timing of their business cycles to the diversity of their credit institutions and political cultures. For this reason, they established official public debt and deficit criteria (three percent of GDP for EMU membership) in order to discourage maverick nations from placing undue economic burdens on fellow members. But the EU has yet to face up to the biggest challenge to its future viability: the likelihood of varying national responses to the fiscal pressures of demographic aging. Indeed, the EU does not even include unfunded pension liabilities in the official EMU debt and deficit criteria—which is like measuring icebergs without looking beneath the water line.

When these liabilities come due and move from "off the books" to "on the books," the EU will, under current constraints, be required to penalize EMU members that exceed the three percent deficit cap. As a recent IMF report concludes, "over time it will become increasingly difficult for most countries to meet the deficit ceiling without comprehensive social security reform." The EU could, of course, retain members by raising the deficit limit. But once the floodgates are opened, national differences in fiscal policy may mean that EMU members rack up deficits at different rates. The European Central Bank, the euro, and a half-century of progress toward European unity could be lost as a result.

The total projected cost of the age wave is so staggering that we might reasonably conclude it could never be paid. After all, these numbers are projections, not predictions. They tell us what is likely to happen if current policy remains unchanged, not whether it is likely or even possible for this condition to hold. In all probability, economies would implode and governments would collapse before the projections ever materialize. But this is exactly why we must focus on these projections, for they call attention to the paramount question: Will we change course sooner, when we still have time to control our destiny and reach a more sustainable path? Or later, after unsustainable economic damage and political and social trauma cause a wrenching upheaval?

## A GRAYING NEW WORLD ORDER

While the fiscal and economic consequences of global aging deserve serious discussion, other important consequences must also be examined. At the top of the list is the impact of the age wave on foreign policy and international security.

*Will the developed world be able to maintain its security commitments?* One need not be a Nobel laureate in economics to understand that a country's GDP growth is the product of workforce and productivity growth. If workforces shrink rapidly, GDP may drop as well, since labor productivity may not rise fast enough to compensate for the loss of workers. At least some developed countries are therefore likely to experience a long-term decline in total production of goods and services—that is, in real GDP.

Economists correctly focus on the developed world's GDP per capita, which can rise even as its workforce and total GDP shrink. But anything with a fixed cost becomes a national challenge when that cost has to be spread over a smaller population and funded out of shrinking revenues. National defense is the classic example. The West already faces grave threats from rogue states armed with biological and chemical arsenals, terrorists capable of hacking into vulnerable computer systems, and proliferating nuclear weapons. None of these external dangers will shrink to accommodate our declining workforce or GDP.

Leading developed countries will no doubt need to spend as much or more on defense and international investments as they do today. But the age wave will put immense pressure on governments to cut back. Falling birthrates, together with a rising demand for young workers, will also inevitably mean smaller armies. And how many parents will allow their only child to go off to war?

With fewer soldiers, total capability can be maintained only by large increases in technology and weaponry. But boosting military productivity creates a Catch-22. For how will governments get the budget resources to pay for high-tech weaponry if the senior-weighted electorate demands more money for high-tech medicine? Even if military capital is successfully substituted for military labor, the deployment options may be dangerously limited. Developed nations facing a threat may feel they have only two extreme (but relatively inexpensive) choices: a low-level response (antiterrorist strikes and cruise-missile diplomacy) or a high-level response (an all-out attack with strategic weapons).

*Will Young/Old become the next North/South fault line?* Historically, the richest industrial powers have been growing, capital-exporting, philanthropic giants that project their power and mores around the world. The richest industrial powers of the future may be none of these things. Instead, they may be demographically imploding, capital-importing, fiscally starving neutrals who twist and turn to avoid expensive international entanglements. A quarter-century from now, will the divide between today's "rich" and "poor" nations be better described as a divide between growth and decline, surplus and deficit, expansion and retreat, future and past? By the mid-2020s, will the contrast between North and South be better described as a contrast between Young and Old?

If today's largest low-income societies, especially China, set up fully funded retirement systems to prepare for their own future aging, they may well produce ever larger capital surpluses. As a result, today's great powers could someday depend on these surpluses to keep themselves financially afloat. But how should we expect these new suppliers of capital to use their newly acquired leverage? Will they turn the tables in international diplomacy? Will the Chinese, for example, someday demand that the United States shore up its Medicare system the way Americans once demanded that China reform its human rights policies as a condition for foreign assistance?

As Samuel Huntington recently put it, "the juxtaposition of a rapidly growing people of one culture and a slowly growing or stagnant people of another culture generates pressure for economic and/or political adjustments in both societies." Countries where populations are still exploding rank high on any list of potential trouble spots, whereas the countries most likely to lose population—and to see a weakening of their commitment to expensive defense and global security programs—are the staunchest friends of liberal democracy.

In many parts of the developing world, the total fertility rate remains very high (7.3 in the Gaza Strip versus 2.7 in Israel), most people are very young (49 percent under age fifteen in Uganda), and the population is growing very rapidly (doubling every twenty-six years in Iran). These areas also tend to be the poorest, most rapidly urbanizing, most institutionally unstable—and most likely to fall under the sway of rogue leadership. They are the same societies that spawned most of the military strongmen and terrorists who have bedeviled the United States and Europe in recent decades. The Pentagon's long-term planners predict that outbreaks of regional anarchy will occur more frequently early [this] century. To pinpoint when and where, they track what they call "youth bulges" in the world's poorest urban centers.

Is demography destiny, after all? Is the rapidly aging developed world fated to decline? Must it cede leadership to younger and faster-growing societies? For the answer to be no, the developed world must redefine that role around a new mission. And what better way to do so than to show the younger, yet more tradition-bound, societies—which will soon age in their turn—how a world dominated by the old can still accommodate the young.

## WHOSE WATCH IS IT, ANYWAY?

From private discussions with leaders of major economies, I can attest that they are well briefed on the stunning demographic trends that lie ahead. But so far they have responded with paralysis rather than action. Hardly any country is doing what it should to prepare. Margaret Thatcher confesses that she repeatedly tried to raise the aging issue at G-7 summit meetings. Yet her fellow leaders stalled. "Of course aging is a profound challenge," they replied, "but it doesn't hit until early in the next century—after my watch."

Americans often fault their leaders for not acknowledging long-term problems and for not facing up to silent and slow-motion challenges. But denial is not a peculiarly American syndrome. In 1995, Silvio Berlusconi's *Forza Italia* government was buffeted by a number of political storms, all of which it weathered—except for pension reform, which shattered the coalition. That same year, the Dutch parliament was forced to repeal a recent cut in retirement benefits after a strong Pension Party, backed by the elderly, emerged from nowhere to punish the reformers. In 1996, the French government's modest proposal to trim pensions triggered strikes and even riots. A year later the Socialists overturned the ruling government at the polls.

Each country's response, or nonresponse, is colored by its political and cultural institutions. In Europe, where the welfare state is more expansive, voters can hardly imagine that the promises made by previous generations of politicians can no longer be kept. They therefore support leaders, unions, and party coalitions that make generous unfunded pensions the very cornerstone of social democracy. In the United States, the problem has less to do with welfare-state dependence than the uniquely American notion that every citizen has personally earned and is therefore entitled to whatever benefits government happens to have promised.

How governments ultimately prepare for global aging will also depend on how global aging itself reshapes politics. Already some of the largest and most strident interest groups in the United States are those that claim to speak for senior citizens, such as the American Association of Retired Persons, with its 33 million members, 1,700 paid employees, ten times that many trained volunteers, and an annual budget of $5.5 billion.

Senior power is rising in Europe, where it manifests itself less through independent senior organizations than in labor unions and (often union-affiliated) political parties that formally adopt pro-retiree platforms. Could age-based political parties be the wave of the future? In Russia, although the Communist resurgence is usually ascribed to nationalism and nostalgia, a demographic bias is at work as well. The Communists have repositioned themselves as the party of retirees, who are aggrieved by how runaway inflation has slashed the real value of their pensions. In the 1995 Duma elections, over half of those aged fifty-five and older voted Communist, versus only ten percent of those under age forty.

Commenting on how the old seem to trump the young at every turn, Lee Kuan Yew once proposed that each taxpaying worker be given two votes to balance the lobbying clout of each retired elder. No nation, not even Singapore, is likely to enact Lee's suggestion. But the question must be asked: With ever more electoral power flowing into the hands of elders, what can motivate political leaders to act on behalf of the long-term future of the young?

A handful of basic strategies, all of them difficult, might enable countries to overcome the economic and political challenges of an aging society: extending work lives and postponing retirement; enlarging the workforce through immigration and increased labor force participation; encouraging higher fertility and investing more in the education and productivity of future workers; strengthening intergenerational bonds of responsibility within families; and targeting government-paid benefits to those most in need while encouraging and even requiring workers to save for their own retirements. All of these strategies unfortunately touch raw nerves—by amending existing social contracts, by violating cultural expectations, or by offending entrenched ideologies. . . .

# 40

## ENVIRONMENT, SCARCITY, AND VIOLENCE

THOMAS HOMER-DIXON

**Resource scarcities are often thought to be a potential source of violent international conflict. Thomas Homer-Dixon offers a more tempered view, concluding from research in disparate locales that "environmental scarcities usually do not cause wars among countries, but they can generate severe social stresses within countries, helping to stimulate subnational insurgencies, ethnic clashes, and urban unrest." Homer-Dixon is associate professor of political science and Director of the Peace and Conflict Studies Program at the University of Toronto. With Jessica Blitt he is editor of *Ecoviolence: Links Among Environment Population and Security* (1998) and author of *Environment, Scarcity, and Violence* (1999), from which this chapter is excerpted.**

. . . Scarcities of critical environmental resources—especially of cropland, freshwater, and forests—contribute to violence in many parts of the world. These environmental scarcities usually do not cause wars among countries, but they can generate severe social stresses within countries, helping to stimulate subnational insurgencies, ethnic clashes, and urban unrest. Such civil violence particularly affects developing societies, because they are, in general, highly dependent on environmental resources and less able to buffer themselves from the social crises that environmental scarcities cause.

---

**Note:** Most footnotes have been deleted; others have been renumbered.

Although this violence affects developing societies most, policy makers and citizens in the industrialized world ignore it at their peril. It can harm rich countries' national interests by threatening their trade and economic relations, entangling them in complex humanitarian emergencies, provoking distress migrations, and destabilizing pivotal countries in the developing world.

In South Africa, for example, severe land, water, and fuelwood scarcities in the former black homelands have helped drive millions of poor blacks into squatter settlements around the major cities. The settlements are often constructed on the worst urban land, in depressions prone to flooding, on hillsides vulnerable to slides, or near heavily polluting industries. Scarcities of land, water, and fuelwood in these settlements help provoke interethnic rivalries and violent feuds among settlement warlords and their followers. This strife jeopardizes the country's transition to democratic stability and prosperity.

In Pakistan, shortages and maldistribution of good land, water, and forests in the countryside have encouraged millions of the rural poor to migrate into major cities, such as Karachi and Hyderabad. The conjunction of this in-migration with high fertility rates is causing city populations to grow at an astonishing 4 to 5 percent a year, producing fierce competition—and often violence—among ethnic groups over land, basic services, and political and economic power. This turmoil exacts a great toll on the national economy.

In Chiapas, Mexico, Zapatista insurgents rose against land scarcity and insecure land tenure caused by ancient inequalities in land distribution, by rapid population growth among groups with the least land, and by changes in laws governing land access. The insurgency rocked Mexico to the core, helped trigger a peso crisis, and reminded the world that Mexico remains—despite the pretenses of the country's economic elites—a poor and profoundly unstable developing country.

## THE CRITICAL ROLE OF ENVIRONMENTAL RESOURCES

It is easy for the billion-odd people living in rich countries to forget that the well-being of about half of the world's population of 6.0 billion remains directly tied to local natural resources. 60 to 70 percent of the world's poor people live in rural areas, and most depend on agriculture for their main income; a large majority of these people are smallholder farmers, including many who are semi-subsistence (which means they survive mainly by eating what they grow). Over 40 percent of people on the planet—some 2.4 billion—use fuelwood, charcoal, straw, or cow dung as their main source of energy; 50 to 60 percent rely on these biomass fuels for at least some of their primary energy needs. Over 1.2 billion people lack access to clean drinking water; many are forced to walk far to get what water they can find.

The cropland, forests, and water supplies that underpin the livelihoods of these billions are renewable. Unlike nonrenewable resources such as oil and iron ore, renewables are replenished over time by natural processes. In most cases, if used prudently, they should sustain an adequate standard of living indefinitely. Unfortunately, in many regions where people rely on renewables, they are being depleted or degraded faster than they are being renewed. From Gaza to the Philippines to Honduras, the evidence is stark: aquifers are being overdrawn and salinized, coastal fisheries are disappearing, and steep uplands have been stripped of their forests leaving their thin soils to erode into the sea.

This environmental scarcity helps generate chronic, diffuse, subnational violence—exactly the kind of violence that bedevils conventional military institutions. Around the world, we see conventional armies pinned down and often utterly impotent in the face of interethnic violence or attacks by ragtag bands of lightly armed guerrillas and insurgents. As yet, environmental scarcity is not a major factor behind most of these conflicts, but we can expect it to become a more important influence in coming decades because of larger populations and higher per capita resource consumption rates. . . .

## SOURCES OF ENVIRONMENTAL SCARCITY

Environmental scarcities usually have complex causes. The depletion and degradation of a resource are a function of the physical vulnerability of the resource, the size of the resource-consuming population, and the technologies and practices this population uses in its consumption behavior. The size of the population and its technologies and practices are, in turn, a result of a wide array of other variables, from women's status to the availability of human and financial capital.

In addition, resource depletion and degradation are together only one of three sources of environmental scarcity. Depletion and degradation produce a decrease in total resource *supply* or, in other words, a decrease in the size of the total resource "pie." But population growth and changes in consumption behavior can also cause greater scarcity by boosting the *demand* for a resource. Thus, if a rapidly growing population depends on a fixed amount of cropland, the amount of cropland per person—the size of each person's slice of the resource pie—falls inexorably. In many countries, resource availability is being squeezed by both these supply and demand pressures.

Finally, scarcity is often caused by a severe imbalance in the distribution of wealth and power that results in some groups in a society getting disproportionately large slices of the resource pie, whereas, others get slices that are too small to sustain their livelihoods. Such unequal distribution—or what I call *structural scarcity*—is a key factor in virtually every case of scarcity contributing to conflict. Often the imbalance is deeply rooted in institutions and class and ethnic relations inherited from the colonial period. It is frequently sustained and reinforced by international economic relations that trap developing countries into dependence on a few raw material exports. It can also be reinforced by heavy external debts that encourage countries to use their most productive environmental resources—such as their best croplands and forests—to generate hard currency rather than to support the most impoverished segments of their populations.

In the past, analysts and policy makers have usually addressed these three sources of scarcity independently. But research shows that supply, demand, and structural scarcities interact and reinforce each other in extraordinarily pernicious ways.

One type of interaction is *resource capture.* It occurs when powerful groups within a society recognize that a key resource is becoming more scarce (due to both supply and demand pressures) and use their power to shift in their favor the laws and institutions governing resource access. This shift imposes severe structural scarcities on weaker groups. Thus, in Chiapas, worsening land scarcities, partly caused by rapid population growth, encouraged powerful landowners and ranchers to exploit weaknesses in the state's land laws in order to seize lands from campesinos and indigenous farmers. Gradually these peasants were forced deeper into the state's lowland rain forest, farther away from the state's economic heartland, and deeper into poverty.

In the Jordan River basin, Israel's critical dependence on groundwater flowing out of the West Bank—a dependence made acute by an increasing Israeli population and salinization of aquifers along the Mediterranean coast—has encouraged Israel to restrict groundwater withdrawals on the West Bank during the occupation. These restrictions have been far more severe for Palestinians than for Israeli settlers. They have contributed to the rapid decline in Palestinian agriculture in the region, to the dependence of Palestinians on day labor within Israel and, ultimately, to rising frustrations in the Palestinian community.

Another kind of interaction, *ecological marginalization,* occurs when a structural imbalance in resource distribution joins with rapid population growth to drive resource-poor people into ecologically marginal areas, such as upland hillsides, areas at risk of desertification, and tropical rain forests. Higher population densities in these vulnerable areas, along with a lack of the capital and knowledge needed to protect local resources, causes local resource depletion, poverty, and eventually further migration, often to cities.

Ecological marginalization affects hundreds of millions of people around the world, across a wide range of geographies and economic and political systems. We see the same process in the Himalayas, Indonesia, Central America, Brazil, Rajasthan, and the Sahel. For example, in the Philippines, an extreme imbalance in cropland distribution between landowners and peasants has interacted with high population growth rates to force large numbers of the landless poor into interior upland regions of the archipelago. There, the migrants use slash-and-burn agriculture to clear land for crops. As more millions arrive from the lowlands, new land becomes hard to find; and as population densities on the steep slopes increase, erosion, landslides, and flash floods become critical. During the 1970s and 1980s, the resulting poverty helped drive many peasants into the arms of the communist New People's Army insurgency that had a stranglehold on upland regions. Poverty also drove countless others into wretched squatter settlements in cities like Manila.

## THE IMPORTANCE OF CONTEXT

Of course, numerous contextual factors have combined with environmental and demographic stress to produce these outcomes. Environmental scarcity is never a sole or sufficient cause of large migrations, poverty, or violence; it always joins with other economic, political, and social factors to produce its effects. In the Filipino case, for example, the lack of clear property rights in upland areas encouraged migration into these regions and discouraged migrants from conserving the land once they arrived. And President Marcos's corrupt and authoritarian leadership reduced regime legitimacy and closed off options for democratic action by aggrieved groups.

Analysts often overlook the importance of such contextual factors and, as a result, jump from evidence of simple correlation to unwarranted conclusions about causation. Some commentators, for instance, have asserted that rapid population growth, severe land scarcity, and the resulting food shortfalls caused the 1994 Rwandan genocide. In an editorial in August 1994, the *Washington Post* argued that, while the Rwandan civil war was "military, political, and personal in its execution," a key underlying cause was "a merciless struggle for land in a peasant society whose birthrates have put an unsustainable pressure on it." Yet close analysis shows that the genocide arose mainly from a conventional struggle among elites for control of the Rwandan state. Land scarcity played at most a peripheral role by reducing regime legitimacy in the countryside and restricting alternatives for elite enrichment outside of government.

Although context is important, analysts should avoid swinging to the opposite extreme, in which the causal role of environmental scarcity is entirely subordinated to that of contextual factors. For example, some skeptics claim that environmental scarcity's contribution to conflict merits little independent attention, because scarcity is wholly a result of political, economic, and social factors, such as failed institutions and policies. Since these factors are the ultimate causes of the conflict, policy makers trying to prevent conflict should focus on them and not on the scarcity. But our research has identified three reasons why such arguments are incomplete at best.

First, environmental scarcity is not only influenced by social factors like institutions and policies, it can itself affect these institutions and policies in harmful ways. In other words, we should not assume that institutions and policies, taken together, are a completely independent and external starting point in the causal chain; it turns out that they can be shaped by environmental scarcity, sometimes negatively. For instance, during the 1970s and 1980s the prospect of chronic food shortages and a serious drought encouraged governments along the

Senegal River to build a series of irrigation and flood-control dams. Because of critical land scarcities elsewhere in the region, land values in the basin shot up. In order to profit from this change, the Mauritanian government, controlled by Moors of Arab origin, captured the resource by rewriting the laws governing land ownership and abrogating the traditional rights of black Mauritanians to farm, herd, and fish along the Mauritanian side of the river. Thus, regional land and water scarcity influenced Mauritania's institutions and laws of land ownership in a way that harmed the interests of a substantial fraction of the country's population.

Second, the degree of environmental scarcity a society experiences is not, as it turns out, wholly a result of economic, political, and social factors, such as failed institutions and policies; it is also partly a function of the particular physical characteristics of the society's surrounding environment. These characteristics are, in some respects, independent of human activities. For instance, the depth of soils in the Filipino uplands prior to land-clearing and the features that make Israel's aquifers vulnerable to salt intrusion are physical "givens" of these environmental resources. Third, once environmental scarcity becomes irreversible (as, for example, when Haiti's vital topsoil washes into the sea), then the scarcity is, almost by definition, an external influence on society. Even if enlightened reform of institutions and policies removes the underlying political and economic causes of the scarcity, because the scarcity itself is irreversible, it will remain a continuing burden on society.

Policy makers will neither adequately understand nor respond to many important cases of civil violence around the world—cases such as the Filipino insurgency or the chronic instability in Haiti—if they do not take into account the independent causal role of environmental scarcity.

## PIVOTAL COUNTRIES

Scarcity-induced resource capture by Moors in Mauritania helped ignite violence over water and cropland in the Senegal River basin, producing tens of thousands of refugees. Expanding populations, land degradation, and drought spurred the rise of the Sendero Luminoso guerrillas in the southern highlands of Peru. In Haiti, forest and soil loss has worsened a persistent economic crisis that generates strife and periodic waves of boat people. And land shortages in Bangladesh, exacerbated by fast population growth, have prompted millions of people to migrate to India—an influx that has, in turn, caused ethnic strife in the state of Assam.

Close study of such cases shows that severe environmental scarcity can constrain local food production, aggravate poverty of marginal groups, spur large migrations, enrich elites that capture resources, deepen divisions among social groups, and undermine a state's moral authority and capacity to govern. Marginal groups that are highly dependent on increasingly scarce resources find themselves trapped in a vise between rising scarcity on one side and institutional and policy failures on the other. These long-term, tectonic stresses can slowly tear apart a poor society's social fabric, causing chronic popular unrest and violence by boosting grievances and changing the balance of power among contending social groups and the state. . . .

Thus, environmental scarcity is mainly an *indirect* cause of violence, and this violence is mainly *internal* to countries. It is not the type of violence that analysts commonly assume will occur when critical resources are scarce—that is, "resource wars" among countries, in which scarcity directly stimulates one country to try to seize the resources of another.

Although this internal violence may not be as conspicuous or dramatic as wars among countries, it may nonetheless have broad implications. Some of the countries worst affected by internal environmental scarcity are *pivotal;* in other words, their stability and well-being profoundly affect broader regional and world security.[1] These countries include South Africa, Mexico, Pakistan, India, and China. India and China deserve particular attention because of their size and importance; together they make up nearly 40 percent of the world's population. Although neither currently exhibits widespread violence in which environmental factors play a role, in both cases, there are clear reasons to believe that environmentally induced violence may be widespread in the future.

### India

Since independence, India has often seemed on the brink of disintegration. But it has endured, despite enormous difficulties, and by many measures the country has made real progress in bettering its citizens' lives. Recent economic liberalization has produced a surge of growth and a booming middle class (often estimated at 150 million strong). However, the country's prospects remain uncertain at best.

Although India has reduced its fertility rates significantly, the rate of population growth in 1998 is still high, at about 1.5 percent a year. India's population in 1998 [was] 975 million, and it expands by some 15 million people annually, which means it adds the equivalent of Indonesia to its population every fourteen years. About 700 million of these people live in the countryside, and one-third still lack the income to buy a nutritionally adequate number of calories. The U.N.'s latest low and medium projections for India's population in 2025 are 1.22 and 1.33 billion, respectively.

Already, water scarcities and cropland fragmentation, erosion, and salinization are widespread. Fuelwood shortages, deforestation, and desertification also affect broad tracts of countryside. Robert Repetto writes:

---

[1] For a definition, see Robert Chase, Emily Hill, and Paul Kennedy, "Pivotal States and U.S. Strategy," *Foreign Affairs* 75, no. 1 (1996), pp. 33–51.

In most respects, India's environment has deteriorated markedly since [1970]. In canal-irrigated areas, dams are rapidly silting up because of deforestation upstream, and millions of hectares of farmland have become waterlogged or salinized because water has been applied improperly. In large areas where tubewell development has been intensive, water tables are falling; in coastal areas, salt water is invading and ruining the aquifers, depriving tens of millions of people of drinking and irrigation water. In areas of intensive farming, deficiencies in organic matter and micronutrients have emerged and limit crop yields.

In the uncultivated parts of rural India, two thirds of the total area, overharvesting of fuelwood and overgrazing of livestock—combined with unsustainable rates of commercial exploitation—have devegetated the landscape. . . . Large-scale soil erosion and disruption of hydrological flows have resulted. Increasing shortages of fuelwood, fodder, and other useful products of India's commons have added to the deprivations of the rural poor, especially women, who are most dependent on those resources.[2]

Rural resource scarcities and population growth have combined with an inadequate supply of rural jobs and economic liberalization in cities to widen wealth differentials between countryside and urban areas. These differentials propel waves of rural-urban migration. The growth rates of many of India's cities are nearly twice that of the country's population, which means that cities like Delhi, Mumbai, and Bangalore double in size every twenty years. Their infrastructures are overtaxed: Delhi has among the worst urban air pollution in the world, power and water are regularly unavailable, garbage is left in the streets, and the sewage system can handle only a fraction of the city's wastewater.

India's growing population has sometimes impeded the loosening of the state's grip on the economy: as the country's workforce expands by 6.5 million a year, and as resentment among the poor rises against those castes and classes that have benefited most from economic liberalization, left-wing politicians have been able to exert strong pressure to maintain subsidies of fertilizers, irrigation, and inefficient industries and to retain statutory restrictions on corporate layoffs. Rapid population growth has also led to fierce competition for limited status and job opportunities in government and education. Attempts to hold a certain percentage of such positions for lower castes have caused bitter intercaste conflict. The right-wing Bharatiya Janata Party has often capitalized on upper- and middle-caste resentment of encroachment on their privileges, mobilizing this resentment against minorities like Muslims.

These pressures are largely beyond the control of India's increasingly corrupt and debilitated political institutions. At the district and state levels, politicians routinely hire local gang leaders or thugs to act as political enforcers. At the national level, kickbacks and bribes have become common in an economic system

<hr/>

[2] Robert Repetto, *The "Second India" Revisited: Population, Poverty, and Environmental Stress over Two Decades* (Washington, D.C.: World Resources Institute, 1994), p. 6.

still constrained by bureaucracy and quotas. The central government in Delhi and many state governments are widely seen as unable to manage India's rapidly changing needs and, as a result, have lost much of their legitimacy. Furthermore, the mid-1990s have seen a sharp weakening of the Congress Party, which has traditionally pulled together the interests of multiple sectors of Indian society. The parties that have gained at Congress's expense represent a profusion of narrow caste, class, religious, and regional interests.

Although in recent decades the exploding megacities of the developing world have been remarkably quiet, India shows the record may be changing: the country's widespread urban violence in early 1993, following the demolition of Babri Masid mosque, was concentrated in the poorest slums of cities like Ahmadabad and Mumbai. Gang rapes, murders, and acts of arson continued for months after the demolition. Although Western commentators usually described the unrest as strictly communal between Hindus and Muslims, in actual fact Hindus directed many of their attacks against recent Hindu migrants from rural areas. B. K. Chandrashekar, a sociology professor at the Indian Institute of Management, says that "the communal violence was quite clearly a class phenomenon. Indian cities became the main battlegrounds because of massive migrations of the rural poor in the past decades."[3]

Indian social institutions and democracy are now under extraordinary strain. The strain arises from a rapid yet incomplete economic transition, from widening gaps between the wealthy and the poor, from chronically weak political institutions, and, not least, from continued population growth and worsening environmental scarcities. Should these converging pressures cause major internal violence—or, in the worst case, should they cause the country to fragment into contending regions—the economic, migration, and security consequences for the rest of the world would be staggering.

## China

Population growth and environmental scarcities are also putting extreme pressure on China's populace and government. Most experts and commentators on China have been distracted by the phenomenal economic boom in the country's coastal areas. They have tended to project these trends onto the rest of the country and to neglect the dangers posed by demographic and environmental stresses. But, as with India, the costs of misreading the Chinese situation could be very high. The country has over a fifth of the world's population, a huge military with growing power-projection capability, and unsettled relations with some of its neighbors. The effects of Chinese civil unrest and internal disruption could spread far beyond its borders.

[3] Raj Chengappa and Ramesh Menon, "The New Battlefields," *India Today* 18, no. 2 (31 January 1993), p. 28.

In recent years, China has embarked on an economic and social transition that is almost unimaginably complicated. Countless urgent problems, some small and some very large, must be addressed immediately as the country develops at breakneck speed. Given China's vast population, this transition will be far harder than that of South Korea or Taiwan, two countries that optimistic commentators often consider exemplars. The management demands on the central, provincial, and local Chinese governments are without precedent in human history.

Chinese leaders recognize that unchecked expansion of the country's already huge population—now around 1.25 billion—will make economic development far more difficult. Fertility rates peaked during the Cultural Revolution between 1969 and 1972. Population growth peaked at about 13 million per year in the mid-1990s, as the babies born during the Cultural Revolution reached their reproductive years.

In the late 1980s and early 1990s, specialists tempered their optimism about Chinese ability to bring population growth down to replacement rate. Market liberalization in the countryside had undermined the one-child policy. In rural areas, state coercion seemed less effective, and peasants enriched by market reforms could more easily pay fines levied for having too many children. In some provinces, therefore, it became common for mothers to bear two or more children. More recent evidence, however, suggests that Chinese authorities have renewed their commitment to limiting population growth. In response to often extremely coercive measures by low-level officials, fertility rates have fallen below two children per woman for the first time. But experts are not sure that this accomplishment can be sustained for long, and even if it is, China's population will continue to grow well into the [current] century. The U.N.'s current low and medium projections for China's population in 2025 are 1.37 and 1.48 billion, respectively.

Larger populations and higher per capita resource consumption (resulting from economic growth) aggravate regional scarcities of water and land. Water shortages in much of northern and western China are now critical and constrain development. In 1995, the great Yellow River, still referred to as the "sorrow of China" because of its catastrophic floods in years passed, was dry at its mouth for over one hundred days because of upstream withdrawals. The aquifers under Beijing supply 50 percent of the city's water, but their water levels are falling by a meter a year, causing the ground to sink throughout the region as groundwater is extracted. The central government has responded by announcing plans to build a giant canal to move 15 billion metric tons of water annually from a tributary of the Yangtze River in the south to northern regions, including Beijing, a distance of almost fourteen hundred kilometers. If built, this canal will be one of the great engineering feats of human history, cutting across hundreds of geological formations, streams, and rivers; the current plan is to construct an eight-kilometer siphon to suck the water under and past the Yellow River. . . .

Water scarcity is only one of a host of evermore tangled resource problems in China. At about a tenth of a hectare per capita, cropland availability is among the lowest in the developing world. Several hundred thousand hectares of farmland are lost every year to erosion, salinization, and urban expansion. Tracts of villas and suburban-style homes are gobbling up rich rice fields around major cities. Near many towns and cities, new Special Economic Zones—industrial parks that offer tax and service advantages to foreign investors—sprawl across good farmland. Each new auto-assembly plant, poultry-processing site, or paint factory takes a further chunk of valuable farmland. When these losses are combined with population growth, the amount of cropland per person is falling steadily by 1.5 percent a year.

Continued population growth and worsening environmental scarcities make China's rapid economic and social transition harder in many ways. First of all, they increase wealth gaps between the cosmopolitan coast, which is linked to the Pacific economy, and the more conservative interior and northern regions where water and fuelwood are desperately scarce and the land often badly damaged. Although economic growth in many interior regions has been fast, it has tended to lag far behind growth in regions closer to the coast. This widening gap has spurred a circular migration of people in search of economic opportunity—a huge flow, often estimated at 100 million people, moving back and forth between rural areas and coastal cities.

One of human history's great migrations, this movement has gone largely unremarked in the West, yet a visitor sees its evidence everywhere. The halls, corridors, and stairwells of major train stations teem with weathered and disheveled peasants from the countryside on their way to the city. In big cities, construction sites are lined with the tents and shacks of workers from rural areas; in Shanghai alone, over a million newcomers live on construction sites, moving from one to another as work demands. This flood of rural migrants has produced a jump in crime and a widely remarked drop in cleanliness and hygiene in the big cities.

Resource shortages increase wealth gaps not only between regions, but also between rich and poor people within regions. Shortages of land and water increase opportunities for powerful members of China's elite—often well-connected members of the Communist Party or their family members—to gain windfall profits through speculation.

In addition, environmental problems and population growth boost the already huge capital demands faced by the state and the economy. New dams and canals have to be built to store scarce water and move it around, cheap housing is needed for rural-urban migrants, and agricultural stations and research laboratories need funding to increase food output. Yet between 1978 and 1994, central and local government revenues as a percentage of gross domestic product (GDP) fell by almost two-thirds; the figure for central government revenue alone (at a mere 3.9 percent in 1994) was among the lowest in the world. As a result, one sees rooms full of advanced equipment sitting idle in leading research labs—including labs dedicated to solving China's critical water and agricultural problems—while scientists read novels for lack of research funds. Meanwhile, in the private sector, too much capital is being channeled into high-margin luxury shopping centers, villas, and office buildings in cities like Shanghai.

Finally, resource and environmental stresses increase the susceptibility of the Chinese economy and society to sudden shocks like droughts, floods, and sharp changes in the international economy. A visitor gets the overriding impression that the country has a razor-thin margin for error when it comes to basics such as energy, food, and water. The leadership, media, and general public are acutely aware, for instance, of national food production. A slight shortfall in grain production in 1994 pushed up inflation sharply; in each June, the whole country seems to breath a sigh of relief if a good wheat harvest is announced. Serious environmental scarcities and population pressures mean there is little slack in the system to keep the effects of sudden, unanticipated shocks from propagating through the economy and society.

These three problems—rising wealth differentials, capital shortfalls, and susceptibility to shocks—are not unmanageable, but they demand consistently strong, competent, and resilient government at all levels of society. Unfortunately, the Chinese national government today lacks robust moral authority among the Chinese public. A high degree of moral authority—or *legitimacy* as political scientists like to call it—is key to the country's long-term stability.

It is true that the Communist Party has a deep reservoir of support among the Chinese, because it unified China, made the country respected around the world, and guaranteed the basics of life to its people. Yet communist ideology no longer serves as a moral glue; in the wake of the Cultural Revolution, it attracts virtually no support. Moreover, the crackdown following the 1989 Tiananmen Square massacre halted the evolution of alternative political ideas and institutions that might have formed the foundation for a newly legitimized Chinese state. Debate over central political questions—the rate of democratization, the nature of political representation, and the like—has been largely suspended. In this vacuum, the legitimacy of China's national government now mainly rests on two pillars: continued economic growth and nationalism. The nationalism, in turn, centers on a cluster of issues, including Chinese dominion over Taiwan, Tibet, and several groups of tiny islands in the South China Sea.

Even a brief slackening of economic growth would accentuate the underlying stresses posed by increasing wealth differentials and capital shortfalls. During this delicate period of economic transition, marginal groups—such as poor farmers, rural-urban migrants, and workers in state industries that are being streamlined—are especially vulnerable. The Chinese state no longer guarantees an "iron rice bowl," or bottom-line social security, for the weakest members of its population. Yet the labor force grows relentlessly by 6 million people a year. If the economy falters, the potential for urban and rural unrest could encourage a regime struggling for legitimacy to retreat to evermore aggressive nationalism.

We all have a stake in the success of the grand Chinese experiment with economic liberalization. In a land of scarce environmental resources and a still-expanding population, rapid economic growth is essential to provide capital, jobs, and know-how. But this rapid growth itself often worsens the country's underlying resource scarcities and environmental problems, and these problems, in turn, threaten growth. Whether and how China breaks out of this vicious cycle will shape much of human history for decades, if not centuries, to come.

## INGENUITY AND ADAPTATION

Some people reading the preceding accounts of India and China will say "nonsense!" They will argue that market reforms and adequate economic growth will enable these countries to manage their problems of population growth, environmental stress, and poverty relatively easily.

These optimists, who are often economists, generally claim that few if any societies face strict limits to population or consumption. Many intervening factors—physical, technological, economic, and social—permit great resilience, variability, and adaptability in human-environmental systems. In particular, they claim, properly functioning economic institutions, especially markets, can provide incentives to encourage conservation, resource substitution, the development of new sources of scarce resources, and technological innovation. Increased global trade allows resource-rich areas to specialize in production of goods (like grain) that are derived from environmental resources, while other areas specialize in nonresource-intensive production, such as services and high technology. These economic optimists are commonly opposed by neo-Malthusians—often biologists and ecologists—who claim that finite natural resources place strict limits on the growth of human population and consumption both regionally and globally; if these limits are exceeded, poverty and social breakdown result.

The debate between these two camps is now largely sterile. Nevertheless, although neither camp tells the whole story, each grasps a portion of the truth. The economic optimists are right to stress the extraordinary ability of human beings to surmount scarcity and improve their lot. The dominant trend over the past two centuries, they point out, has not been rising scarcity but increasing aggregate wealth. In other words, most important resources have become *less* scarce, at least in economic terms.

The optimists also provide a key insight that we should focus on the supply of human ingenuity in response to increasing resource scarcity rather than on strict resource limits. Many societies adapt well to scarcity without undue hardship to their populations; in fact, they often end up better off than they were before. In these societies, necessity is the mother of invention; they supply enough ingenuity in the form of new technologies and new and reformed social institutions—like efficient markets, clear and enforced property rights, and effective government—to alleviate the effects of scarcity.

The critical question then is, What determines a society's ability to supply this ingenuity? The answer is complex: different countries—depending on their social, economic, political, and cultural characteristics—will respond to scarcity in different ways and, as a result, they will supply varying amounts and kinds of ingenuity.

In the next decades, growing populations, rising per capita resource consumption, and persistent inequalities in resource access guarantee that scarcities of renewables will affect many poor countries with unprecedented severity, speed, and scale. As a result, resource substitution and conservation tasks will be more urgent, complex, and unpredictable, boosting the need for many kinds of ingenuity. In other words, these societies will have to be smarter—technically and socially—in order to maintain or increase their well-being in the face of rising scarcities.

Optimists often make the mistake of assuming that an adequate supply of the right kinds of ingenuity is always assured. But supply will be constrained by a number of factors, including the brain drain out of many poor societies, limited access to capital, and often incompetent bureaucracies, corrupt judicial systems, and weak states. Moreover, markets in developing countries frequently do not work well: property rights are unclear; prices for water, forests, and other common resources do not adjust accurately to reflect rising scarcity; and thus incentives for entrepreneurs to respond to scarcity are inadequate. Most importantly, however, the supply of ingenuity can be restricted by stresses generated by the very resource crises the ingenuity is needed to solve. Scarcity can engender intense rivalries among interest groups and elite factions that impede the development and delivery of solutions to resource problems. It changes the behavior of subgroups within societies by changing their profit and loss calculations in ways that can exacerbate political conflict.

It turns out that we cannot leave to economists the task of predicting the social consequences of severe environmental scarcity. Politics—the sometimes nasty struggle for relative advantage and power among narrow groups—is a key factor affecting whether or not societies adapt successfully to environmental scarcity.

In Haiti, for example, shortages of forests and soil have inflamed competition among social groups; this competition, in turn, obstructs technical and institutional reform. In some cases, powerful groups that profit from high fuel-wood prices have ripped up the seedlings of reforestation projects to keep the supply of fuelwood limited. In the Indian state of Bihar, which has some of the highest population growth rates and rural densities in the country, land scarcity has deepened divisions between landholding and peasant castes, promoting intransigence on both sides that has helped bring land reform to a halt. In South Africa, scarcity-driven migrations into urban areas, and the resulting conflicts over urban environmental resources (such as land and water), have encouraged communities to segment along lines of ethnicity or residential status. This segmentation has shredded networks of trust and eviscerated local institutions. Powerful warlords, linked to Inkatha or the African National Congress, have taken advantage of these dislocations to manipulate group divisions within communities, often producing horrific violence and further institutional breakdown.

Societies like these face a widening "ingenuity gap" as their requirement for ingenuity to deal with environmental scarcity rises while their supply of ingenuity stagnates or drops. A persistent and serious ingenuity gap raises grievances and erodes the moral and coercive authority of government, which boosts the probability of serious civil turmoil and violence. This violence further undermines the society's ability to supply ingenuity. If these processes continue unchecked, the country may fragment as the government becomes enfeebled and peripheral regions come under the control of renegade authorities. Countries with a critical ingenuity gap therefore risk becoming trapped in a vicious cycle, in which severe scarcity further undermines their capacity to mitigate or adapt to scarcity.

In coming decades, we can expect an increasing division of the world into those societies that can keep the ingenuity gap closed—thus adapting to environmental scarcity and avoiding turmoil—and those that cannot. If several pivotal countries fall on the wrong side of this divide, humanity's overall prospects will dramatically worsen. Such a world will be neither environmentally sustainable nor politically stable. The rich will be unable to fully isolate themselves from the crises of the poor, and there will be little prospect of building the sense of global community needed to address the array of grave problems—economic, political, as well as ecological—that humanity faces.

# 41

# THE TRAGEDY OF THE COMMONS IN GLOBAL PERSPECTIVE

MARVIN S. SOROOS

The "tragedy of the commons" is a key concept in ecological analysis. Marvin S. Soroos describes the metaphor, relates it to many of the specific issues on the global agenda of environmental issues, and suggests strategies for averting environmental tragedies. Noteworthy is his observation that "remarkable progress has been made in establishing the international institutional infrastructure needed to preserve the natural environment." Soroos is professor of political science and public administration at North Carolina State University and author of *The Endangered Atmosphere: Preserving a Global Commons* (1997).

## THE ENVIRONMENT ON THE GLOBAL AGENDA

The convergence of 118 heads of state on Rio de Janeiro in June 1992 for the United Nations Conference on the Environment and Development, otherwise known as the Earth Summit, confirmed the rise of the deteriorating state of the global environment to a prominent position on international agendas. The environment is a relatively new issue, having received substantial attention from policy makers and publics for only about three decades. While certain specific ecological problems were addressed considerably earlier, they were not viewed as part of a much larger crisis in the relationship between a rapidly growing and industrializing world population and the natural order upon which it depends for its survival and economic well-being.

Two events took place in 1972 that were especially important in the emergence of the environment as a global issue. One was the publication of the Club of Rome's influential and controversial report entitled *The Limits to Growth.*[1] The book warned of an uncontrollable collapse of modern civilization within a century if bold steps were not taken promptly to restrain exponential growth trends in population and industrial production that would otherwise overshoot the availability of food, deplete the planet's one-time endowment of nonrenewable reserves of fossil fuels and minerals, and seriously degrade the environment with pollutants. The other event was the United Nations Conference on the Human Environment, held in Stockholm in June 1972, which focused world attention on a wide range of interrelated environmental problems and led to the creation of the United Nations Environment Programme (UNEP) that has done much to stimulate national and international efforts to preserve the natural environment.

Numerous problems appear on the global environmental agenda, each of which has serious consequences in its own right. On the land areas, tropical forests are being burned or logged at an alarming rate with little concern for the resulting extinction of untold numbers of species of plants and animals, many of which remain to be recorded. Deserts are expanding in numerous parts of Africa and Asia, largely due to human activities—in particular the stripping of wooded areas for firewood, the overgrazing of livestock, and improper irrigation. Overuse and misuse of land has reduced its fertility and led to substantial erosion of topsoil; aquifers are rapidly being drawn down to provide irrigation water for expanding agricultural operations. A legacy of toxic waste dumps threatens the health of millions of people, especially in the industrialized regions of the world.

The marine environment has been badly contaminated by pollutants, especially in largely self-contained areas such as the Mediterranean Sea, the Baltic Sea, the Caribbean Sea, the Red Sea, and the Persian Gulf. The most spectacular cause of ocean pollution has been accidents involving supertankers, the best known being the groundings of the *Torrey Canyon* in 1967, the *Amoco Cadiz* in 1978, and the *Exxon Valdez* in 1989. Larger quantities of pollutants enter the oceans and seas from land-based sources, such as river systems laden with sewage, industrial effluents, and runoff from agricultural areas containing fertilizers and pesticides. The oceans have also been a repository for toxic substances ranging from chemical weapons and radioactive wastes to sludge from sewage treatment plants.

Atmospheric pollutants became the leading environmental concern during the 1980s. In the heavily industrialized regions of Europe and North America, the severe consequences of the transboundary flow of pollutants, in particular sulfur

---

[1] Donnella H. Meadows, Dennis L. Meadows, Jørgen Randers, and William H. Behrens, *The Limits to Growth* (New York: Signet, 1972).

and nitrogen oxides responsible for acid precipitation, became all too apparent as aquatic life disappeared in numerous freshwater lakes and a phenomenon known as "forest death syndrome," or *waldsterben* in German, spread rapidly through forested areas. Transboundary air pollution has become a problem in other regions, such as East Asia where Japan is victimized by acid-forming pollutants from China and Korea. Massive clouds of smoke from forest fires land-clearing operations in Indonesia have endangered health and disrupted commerce over large areas of Southeast Asia.

Even more alarming are the warnings of the scientific community about the loss of ozone in the stratosphere and the apparent trend toward a general warming of the atmosphere. These two problems are central to what has become known during the past decade as the "global change" problematique, which refers to a number of complex and interrelated alterations of the natural environment resulting from the growing scale of human activities.

Concern about ozone depletion rose sharply in the mid-1980s following revelations of a recurring "ozone hole" over Antarctica during the southern spring seasons and a lesser amount of ozone loss at other latitudes. Scientists have linked most of the loss of stratospheric ozone to a family of synthetic chemical compounds known as CFCs, which have been widely used in aerosol sprays, refrigerants, foam packaging and insulation, and cleaning solutions, as well as to halons used primarily in fire extinguishers. Increased exposure to the sun's intense ultraviolet (UV) radiation may contribute to human health problems including the deadly melanoma variety of skin cancer, weakened immune systems, and eye disorders such as cataracts. Scientists have linked increased amounts of UV radiation to leaf damage, lessened photosynthesis, mutations, and stunted growth in approximately half of the agricultural crops that have been studied. There is also widespread concern that ecosystems will be seriously disrupted if UV radiation kills microorganisms such as phytoplankton and zooplankton, which are the bases of food chains.

Forecasts of a general warming of the atmosphere take into account the increased concentrations of "greenhouse gases" such as carbon dioxide, methane, CFCs, and nitrous oxides. The Intergovernmental Panel on Climate Change attributes a rise of 0.3 and 0.6° C in global temperatures over the past century in part to human pollutants and projects a further increase of 0.8 to 3.5° C by 2100 if significant mitigating actions are not taken.[2] Many questions remain on the potential consequences of a warming of this magnitude. Coastal cities, lowlying agricultural areas, and even entire small island nations may become uninhabitable if a continued warming trend causes ocean levels to rise by an anticipated fifty centimeters by 2100 and triggers a significant increase in the number and

---

[2] J.T. Houghton, L.G. Meira Filho, B.A. Callander, N. Harris, A. Kattenberg, and K. Maskell, *Climate Change 1995: The Science of Climate Change* (Cambridge: Cambridge University Press, 1996), pp. 4–7.

intensity of tropical storms.[3] Farming elsewhere may be disrupted by changing temperatures and rainfall patterns, and numerous ecosystems such as forests may be unable to adapt to rapidly migrating climatic zones. A weakening of ocean currents caused by a reduction of temperature contrasts between equatorial and polar regions could lead to even more fundamental changes in the planet's weather patterns.

The international community has been very active over the past three decades in addressing many of these environmental problems. The Stockholm conference of 1972 was the first of a series of major world conferences sponsored by the United Nations, sometimes referred to as "global town meetings," that keyed on specific global problems. Among these were world conferences on population (1974 and 1984), food (1974), human settlements (1976), water (1977), desertification (1977), new and renewable sources of energy (1981), and outer space (1982). The Third United Nations Law of the Sea Conference (UNCLOS III), which was convened twelve times between 1973 and 1982, took up several environmental problems, most notably the depletion of marine fisheries and pollution of the oceans. The World Meteorological Organization (WMO) sponsored World Climate Conferences in 1979 and 1990. More recent gatherings include the Earth Summit in Rio in 1992, the International Conference on Population and Development in Cairo in 1994, and two 1996 gatherings—the Second U.N. Conference on Human Settlements, in Istanbul, and the World Food Summit in Rome.

A more significant development, however, has been the establishment of a network of international institutions that address environmental issues. The United Nations Environment Programme (UNEP), which is headquartered in Nairobi, Kenya, plays a central role in stimulating and coordinating action on environmental problems both by other international agencies and by nations. The organization has taken a leading role in identifying and investigating ecological problems and in monitoring the state of many aspects of the environment through its Global Environmental Monitoring System (GEMS). Several specialized agencies affiliated with the United Nations have a longer history of concern with environmentally related problems, including the International Maritime Organization (IMO) on pollution from oceangoing vessels, the WMO on the effects of atmospheric pollutants on the weather, the World Health Organization (WHO) on the impact of pollutants on human health, the International Atomic Energy Agency (IAEA) on the dangers of radioactive substances, the Food and Agricultural Organization (FAO) on the condition of ocean fisheries and the effects of environmental degradation on food production, and the International Labor Organization (ILO) on environmental hazards in work places. Environmental problems have also occupied a prominent place on the agendas of numerous regional organizations, most notably those of the European Union.

[3] Ibid., p. 6.

Nongovernmental organizations (NGOs) have been active participants in efforts to address global environmental problems at both national and international levels. The Stockholm conference drew participation from 237 NGOs, and more than six thousand are registered with the Environmental Liaison Center in Nairobi. Upwards of seven thousand NGOs participated in the official meetings of the Earth Summit or the informal, and more boisterous, Environmental Forum that took place simultaneously in the parks of downtown Rio. The World Conservation Union (formerly the International Union for the Conservation of Nature and Natural Resources) and the World Wildlife Fund (WWF) have been collaborating with UNEP on the World Conservation Strategy that was launched in 1980. The International Council of Scientific Unions (ICSU) has been called upon for much of the scientific information that has guided the formulation of international policies and regulations on environmental matters. In the mid-1980s, ICSU launched the International Geosphere-Biosphere Program, an international scientific project that has mobilized the world's scientists to conduct research on the relationships between atmospheric, marine, and terrestrial components of the earth system and the impact of human activities on them. Numerous public advocacy groups such as Greenpeace, Friends of the Earth, the International Institute for Sustainable Development, and the Worldwatch Institute publicize environmental problems and prod national governments and international bodies to take action on them.

Despite the relative newness of the environment as a global policy problem, remarkable progress has been made in establishing the international institutional infrastructure needed to preserve the natural environment. There is certainly reason to wonder, however, whether sovereign states, which now number nearly two hundred, can achieve the level of international cooperation needed to effectively address problems of the magnitude and complexity of climate change.

## GLOBAL TRAGEDIES OF THE COMMONS

Garrett Hardin's well-known parable of the "tragedy of the commons" is a useful model for analyzing the human sources of many environmental problems and the strategies by which they might be addressed.[4] The parable has applicability to all levels of political organization ranging from the smallest village to the global community of states. Let us first review Hardin's story and then consider how it applies to several of the global environmental problems mentioned in the previous section. Potential strategies for averting a "tragedy" are taken up in the next section.

We are asked to imagine an old English village that has a community pasture on which the resident herders are freely permitted to graze their individually owned cattle for their own profit. Such an arrangement, known as a "commons,"

---

[4] "The Tragedy of the Commons," *Science* 162 (1968), pp. 1241–1248.

works well as long as the number of cattle is small relative to the size of the pasture. But once the combined herd of the villagers reaches and exceeds the "carrying capacity" of the pasture, the grasses are gradually depleted and the undernourished cattle produce less meat and milk for their owners. If more and more cattle are added to an already overcrowded pasture, the eventual outcome is its total destruction as a resource and the villagers can no longer derive a profit from grazing cattle on it. Such an unfortunate eventuality is what Hardin refers to as a "tragedy."

Hardin contends that a tragedy is virtually inevitable when there is no legal limit on the number of cattle the villagers may graze on the pasture. Each villager can be expected to calculate that the profits derived from adding a cow to the pasture will accrue to himself exclusively. Alternatively, whatever costs arise due to what this cow contributes to an overgrazing of the pasture will be divided among all the herders of the village. Therefore, the individual villager figures that there is more to gain personally from adding a cow to the pasture than to lose from the resulting damage from overgrazing. Moreover, the logic that leads the villager to add a single cow to an already overused pasture also holds for even further additions by him. And what is rational behavior for one villager is also rational for others. Thus, if the villagers pursue their rational self-interest, the pasture will be destroyed by the ever-increasing herd.

Why do the village herders, upon seeing the earlier signs of the unfolding tragedy, fail to exercise restraint in adding cattle, realizing that they will all pay a heavy price if the pasture becomes badly overgrazed? The answer lies in the possibility that at least one among them will not act responsibly, but rather will continue to add cattle to the pasture. This so-called "free rider" not only takes advantage of the restraint of the other villagers for his own financial benefit but may also bring about the very tragedy they were attempting to avert. Thus, unless the villagers are confident that all will limit their herds, they become resigned to the inevitability of a tragedy and continue adding cattle to the overcrowded pasture in order to maximize their personal share of what the pasture has to offer before it is rendered useless.

Global environmental problems are obviously much more complex than the story of destruction of the common pasture in the English village. Nevertheless, distinct parallels exist between the causes of some global problems and the reasons for the tragedy in Hardin's parable. The similarity is especially notable in the case of the living resources of the ocean. Coastal populations have harvested fish in the oceans for millennia, in most cases at sustainable levels. The situation has changed dramatically in recent decades, however, both because of a rapidly growing world population that is looking more to the oceans for a source of protein and because of technological advancements that made it possible to greatly increase the catch. Schools of fish can now be located more efficiently using helicopters, radar, and sonar, while strong synthetic fibers and mechanical hauling devices allow for the use of larger nets that will hold much greater quantities of fish. Drift nets up to thirty miles in length have been widely used with a devastating impact on marine life. Perhaps the biggest change in the modern fishing industry has been the use of gigantic stern-ramped trawlers and factory ships with the capacity for on-board processing of the catch, which are often accompanied by numerous specialized support vessels. Such "fishing armadas" can stay away from their home ports for many months while intensively harvesting fisheries in distant reaches of the oceans.

Traditionally, international law has treated the oceans as a commons, the only exception being a three-mile zone of territorial waters that for centuries was recognized as being within the jurisdiction of coastal states. Beyond this narrow coastal zone, fishing boats from all lands could help themselves to the ocean's bounty for their private gain because fish became their property upon being caught. Under these rules the total world catch tripled between 1950 and 1975. "Tragedies" were apparent in some regions for species such as cod, halibut, herring, anchovy, swordfish, haddock, and the California sardine, as evidenced by a dramatic drop in catches as not enough fish were left to regenerate the stock for the future. These stocks were overfished for essentially the same reasons that the herders added cattle to an already overgrazed pasture in Hardin's village. The operators of fishing fleets received all the profits from the sale of their catch while dividing the costs associated with overfishing with all others harvesting the same fishery. Furthermore, fugitives that they are, fish passed up by one fleet in the interests of conservation are likely to turn up in the nets of others, who as free riders continue to deplete the fishery.

Pollution of the oceans and atmosphere also fits the pattern of Hardin's tragedy of the commons. But rather than taking something out of an area that is beyond the jurisdictions of nations, pollution involves its use for the disposal of unwanted substances. Few problems arose as long as the amount of pollution generated by human activities was small relative to the vastness of the mediums into which they were introduced. But as with other resources, there are limits to the amount of pollutants that can be absorbed and dispersed by the oceans and atmosphere before serious problems begin to emerge, as is now apparent in the case of the ozone-depleting and greenhouse pollutants. The task of determining harmful levels of pollution is complicated by the delay between the time that substances are introduced into the environment and the point at which the consequences become apparent.

As sinks for pollutants, the oceans and the atmosphere have also traditionally been treated as international commons. All countries have been free to make use of them for getting rid of wastes whose disposal would otherwise be expensive or inconvenient. Introducing pollution into these mediums can have considerable offsetting costs, but from the perspective of the polluters, these costs are shared very widely while the benefits of having a cheap way of discarding wastes accrue to them exclusively. Thus, strong financial incentives are present for continuing the polluting activity. Moreover, any restraint that is exercised out of concern for the quality of the environment is likely to be futile and self-defeating if other polluters, including one's competitors, do not exercise similar responsibility.

Population can also be looked upon as a "tragedy of the commons" type of problem, as Hardin does in his original essay and his later theory of "lifeboat ethics."[5] In this formulation, food and other resources correspond to the pasture of the English village, births to the addition of cattle to the pasture, and the parents of the new arrivals to the herders. Parents, it could be argued, derive significant private benefits from children, such as companionship and affection, a source of labor, and security in old age. The environmental costs associated with what their children contribute to the overpopulating of their country or the world as a whole are shared with the rest of the population. Couples may also calculate that any restraint they exercise in limiting the size of their families will have little or no beneficial impact, because others who are less ecologically responsible will continue to have large numbers of offspring. The parallel is strained by the fact that most people do not have free access to the food and resources they need for their children, but must pay for them. Hardin suggests that free access to necessities, as through welfare payments or international food assistance, in effect creates a commons and the subsequent behavior that brings about its destruction.

## AVERTING ENVIRONMENTAL TRAGEDIES

Several strategies hold some promise for avoiding the tragedy that Hardin forecasts will occur if all villagers have open access to the community pasture. One is to encourage *voluntary restraint,* possibly through education about the ecological consequences of irresponsible actions and by bringing social pressures to bear on members of the community who have not moderated their actions. Hardin has little faith in voluntary restraints because of the prospect that free riders will take advantage of the situation. A second option is to adopt enforceable *regulations* that limit the number of cattle each villager can graze on the pasture. Such rules—which can take the form of limits, quotas, prohibitions, and rules on equipment—are restrictive enough to keep the total use of a resource from exceeding its carrying capacity. A third possibility is *financial incentives,* such as in the form of taxes or fees on cattle added to the pasture, that are sufficiently high to make it unprofitable to overuse a commons.

Two additional strategies for averting a tragedy would discard the commons arrangement. The pasture could be *partitioned* into fenced-in plots that would be assigned to individual villagers. Under this setup, the villagers would not only receive all the profits from grazing cattle on their sections, but would also absorb all the costs if they allow them to become overgrazed. Thus, a built-in

---

[5] See "Living on a Lifeboat," *Bioscience* (1974), pp. 561–568.

incentive exists for the villagers to conserve their plots, or what Hardin refers to as "intrinsic responsibility." *Community ownership* of the herd is the final alternative. Rather than allowing privately owned cattle to graze the pasture, as under the other arrangements, access would be limited to a publicly owned herd, with the profits being distributed among the villagers. Under such an arrangement, the community as a whole would not only receive all the profits, but also absorb all the costs of overgrazing. Thus, the managers of the community herd would have little incentive for allowing the pasture to become overgrazed.[6]

These strategies have been used to differing degrees by the international community in its efforts to address environmental problems. Because nations are reluctant to sacrifice any part of their sovereignty to a higher authority, it is sometimes impossible to do more than encourage them to act responsibly to minimize damage to the environment beyond their borders. In this regard, one of the most commonly cited articles of the Stockholm Declaration of 1972 sets forth the principle that "States have . . . the responsibility to ensure that activities within their jurisdiction or control do not cause damage to the environment of other States or of areas beyond the limits of national jurisdiction."

Appeals to states to act voluntarily in an ecologically responsible manner have generally not been auspicious successes. However, there has been an encouraging tendency in recent years for a number of European countries to act unilaterally in setting target years for ambitious reductions of emissions of pollutants responsible for acid precipitation. In the mid-1980s, countries declared goals of reducing their sulphur dioxide emissions well beyond the 30 percent cutback (from 1980 levels) mandated by an international protocol adopted in 1985. Sweden, for example, set the ambitious target of an 80 percent reduction by 2000, which it had largely achieved by 1991. These unilateral commitments to deep reductions in air pollution set an example that other countries will hopefully follow.[7]

More is accomplished to ameliorate environmental problems when specific obligations are written into regulations that are negotiated and adopted in international institutions. Approximately twenty international fishery commissions, the equivalent of the village government in Hardin's story, were created by fishing nations to conserve the fisheries that they harvest in common. Some of these commissions established rules that limited the annual catch at or below a scientifically determined "maximum sustainable yield" (MSY) for the fishery. One strategy was to limit fishing to a prescribed season, which would be abruptly closed when the combined efforts of the fishing operators approached the MSY.

---

[6] See Natalia Mirovitskaya and Marvin S. Soroos, "Socialism and the Tragedy of the Commons: Reflections on Environmental Practice in the Soviet Union and Russia," *Journal of Environment & Development,* Vol. 4, No. 1, pp. 77–109.

[7] See Marvin S. Soroos, *The Endangered Atmosphere: Preserving a Global Commons* (Columbia: University of South Carolina Press, 1997), chapter 5.

Other commissions assigned a share of the MSY to countries based on their historical proportion of the catch from a fishery.

International restrictions have also been adopted to reduce pollution of the marine environment. The landmark Convention for the Prevention of Pollution by Oil was adopted in 1954 and amended several times in the International Maritime Organization (IMO). Among the provisions of the treaty was a prohibition on discharges of crude and heavy fuel oils in the seas within fifty miles of coastlines. In 1973, the IMO adopted another convention, known as MARPOL '73, that covered a broader range of pollutants and extended the prohibition to the discharge of oily substances to areas deemed especially vulnerable to damage from pollution. The disposal of toxic substances in the seas is the subject of other international treaties, the most important one being the London Dumping Convention of 1972. It establishes a "black list" of highly toxic chemicals—such as mercury, DDT, PCBs, persistent plastics, high-level radioactive wastes, and agents of chemical or biological warfare that may not be disposed of in the oceans— and a "gray list" of less harmful wastes that may be dumped under controlled conditions. In 1993 the parties to the London Convention adopted a permanent ban on the dumping of all radioactive wastes at sea.

Compared to the oceans, the atmosphere is still a relatively underdeveloped subject of international law. The Economic Commission for Europe (ECE), which includes Eastern and Western European countries in addition to the United States and Canada, adopted a protocol in 1985 that committed ratifiers to a 30 percent reduction of their sulfur dioxide emissions by 1993 (based on 1980 levels). A 1988 protocol freezes nitrogen oxide emissions at 1987 levels by 1994, while a 1991 protocol limits the release of volatile organic compounds. A revised and more sophisticated sulfur protocol was adopted in 1994; it is based on the concept of "critical loads," the amount of acidic deposition that areas can absorb without serious environmental damages. Similarly, the 1987 Montreal Protocol mandated a 30 percent reduction in the production of CFCs by 1993 and a 50 percent cutback by 1998. Subsequent amendments to the protocol were adopted in London in 1990 and Copenhagen in 1992 that provided for the complete phasing out of CFCs and most other ozone-depleting chemicals by 1996. Under terms of the 1997 Kyoto Protocol that addresses climate change, the European countries are committed to reducing their greenhouse gas emissions by 8 percent from 1990 levels by 2008–2012, the United States by 7 percent, and Japan by 6 percent.

For international regulations to be effective, mechanisms may be needed both for detecting violations and for sanctioning the violators. Few international agencies are well equipped to perform these tasks. Certain international fishery commissions have had programs for monitoring compliance with their rules through independent onboard inspections of fishing vessels. Likewise, the ECE sponsors a network of stations known as EMEP that monitors the transboundary flow of air pollutants between its members. Sanctions are generally left to other states that have an interest in seeing to it that international rules are being followed. For example, a United States law provides that countries which violate international agreements on the protection of marine mammals will lose 50 percent of the quota of fish they would otherwise be permitted to harvest in the coastal fishery zone of the United States.

While financial incentives have been used extensively within countries to discourage environmentally harmful behaviors under the guise of principles such as the "polluter pays," the international community has yet to make significant use of the potentially powerful strategy for preserving commons. The members of the European Union have considered, but have not been able to agree upon, a community-wide carbon tax to achieve emission reduction targets for greenhouse gas emissions.

The partitioning of resources used by large numbers of states is a feasible strategy for avoiding some but not all environmental problems. Pollutants introduced into the atmosphere cannot be confined within the boundaries of states because air circulates with prevailing wind currents. Likewise, ocean currents widely disperse many of the pollutants introduced into the marine environment. Ocean fisheries, most of which are located near coastlines, are more susceptible to partitioning. The Convention on the Law of the Sea, which was adopted in 1982 but did not come into force until 1994 upon receiving its sixtieth ratification, gives coastal states jurisdiction over the resources of the oceans and seabed out to a distance of two hundred nautical miles off shorelines, in what is called an "exclusive economic zone" (EEZ). Coastal states are empowered to determine the maximum catch within their EEZs and to decide who will be allowed to harvest fish up to this limit. They may reserve the fisheries for their own nationals or allow foreign operators to take part of the catch, possibly for a negotiated fee.

Such an arrangement can be an effective way of conserving fisheries consisting of localized or sedentary species provided the coastal state is diligent in managing them and has the means of enforcing the limits that it has set. Unfortunately, the experience so far has been that most coastal states exercise too little restraint on their nationals, who have been quick to increase the intensity of their harvesting, thus provoking a tragedy on their own making. As a consequence, the United States and Canada have been forced to indefinitely close the once highly productive Georges Banks and Grand Bank fisheries off their east coasts, throwing tens of thousands of fishermen and processors out of work. Migratory species, such as the skipjack tuna and some species of whales, which move through the EEZs of two or more countries and the high seas as well, pose a more complicated problem because cooperation among several states is needed to prevent overharvesting. A similar problem occurs with andromous species, most notably salmon, which live most of their life spans in the high seas, where they can be harvested legally by any country, but migrate to freshwater streams to spawn. Coastal states are reluctant to invest heavily to conserve spawning habitats if the stock is likely to be overfished by other countries on the high seas. Here again, cooperative arrangements among several states are necessary if the fishery is to be conserved.

Community ownership of the means of using a resource is rare at the international level. The primary stumbling block to an international consensus on the 1982 Convention on the Law of the Sea was the provision for a commercial arm of an International Seabed Authority, to be known as the Enterprise. This international public corporation would mine the mineral-rich nodules lying on the floor of the deep seas in competition with private seabed-mining firms. The private firms would be required to assist the Enterprise both by sharing the fruits of their prospecting efforts and by making mining technologies available at reasonable commercial rates. The objective behind the creation of the Enterprise would not, however, be to conserve the nodules, which are in bounteous supply. Rather it is designed to ensure that less technologically advanced countries will have an opportunity to participate in the development of a resource declared to be the "common heritage of mankind" by the U.N. General Assembly in 1970.

Of the four principal types of strategies that can be adopted to avert a tragedy, regulations appear to have the broadest applicability and the greatest potential for success for preserving global commons. Appeals for voluntary restraint too often go unheeded and some of the most critical natural resources cannot physically be divided into self-contained sections. Moreover, a community in which sovereign states are the predominant actors is poorly equipped to impose taxes internationally or to set up international public enterprises to play a major role in exploitation of natural resources. The governments of most nations, however, recognize the need for rules to preserve those aspects of the global environment that are beyond the jurisdiction of any state. This is not to say, however, that they don't often balk at agreeing to specific regulations and complying with them.

## RECONCILING ALTERNATIVE VALUES

Each of the five strategies for averting an environmental tragedy that were outlined in the previous section has certain advantages and disadvantages. Which is the most appropriate in a specific context depends in part on the relative priority that is given to values such as conservation, production, equity, and freedom.

*Conservation* implies that the resource is neither overused or misused, so that its future value is not substantially diminished. In the analogy of the English village, conservation means that the pasture is sustainably grazed so that there is no noticeable decline in the grass cover, which reduces the number of cattle that can be sustained. In the case of ocean fisheries, conservation implies that enough of the stock of the fish remains after the harvest to allow for a regeneration of the fishery up to its optimal levels. In regard to pollution, conservation can be interpreted to mean not allowing pollutants to reach a level at which serious harm to the environment begins to take place. For example, acid-forming precipitants would not be allowed to exceed the critical load above which there would be significant damage to forests and freshwater aquatic life.

*Maximizing production* is often a strong competing priority. The villagers depended upon their cattle for a livelihood and, therefore, could not accept sharp cutbacks on their herds. Their interests would be best served by an arrangement that allows them to graze as many cattle as possible without bringing about an environmentally destructive overshoot. Thus, international fishery commissions limit the catch of fish on the basis of the MSY. Requiring costly equipment for preventing pollution can have a substantial effect on industrial production, especially if a total cleanup is the objective. It should be noted that the dictates of short-term production and profit may be at odds with the same values over the longer run. Short-term gain may be achieved by ravaging the resource until it is totally destroyed, while long-term profitability depends upon careful stewardship of the resource to preserve its future value.

*Equity* implies fairness in whatever management strategy is adopted. What is fair, however, is subject to divergent interpretations. For example, in the village setting, does the principle of equity dictate that all the herders be allowed to graze the same number of cattle on the pasture regardless of size of family or the number of cattle they owned before limits were imposed? Likewise, if the pasture is partitioned, would it be necessary for all to have equally sized plots? If the pasture is to be used by a community-owned herd, should all households receive an equal share of the profits? Similar issues of equity have complicated the task faced by fishery commissions in dividing up the total allowable catch among member countries. To what extent should the national shares be based on factors such as geographical proximity, population size, investments in fishing fleets, and distribution of the catch historically? The fairness of the provisions for EEZs under the new ocean law has been criticized on grounds that most of the productive fisheries will come under the control of a few states.

In the case of measures to control pollution, the fairness question arises over whether the percentage reductions in emissions should be required of all countries. Less developed countries, which historically are responsible for a small share of the pollutants causing problems such as ozone depletion and global warming, may contend that it is their "turn to pollute" to achieve their aspirations for economic development and a higher standard of living for their populations. Thus, international efforts to address the threat of climate change have proceeded on the principle of "common but differentiated responsibilities" which thus far have excused developing countries from binding limitations on greenhouse gas emissions. Financial incentives, such as taxes on smokestack emissions or carbon taxes, are widely considered a just way of implementing the "polluter pays" principle.

From one perspective, equity is a matter of all being equally free to exploit a resource even though some, by virtue of their capital and advanced technologies, may be better able to take advantage of available opportunities. From another perspective, equity is an outcome that is equally favorable to all members of the community, including the poorer, less advantaged ones. At UNCLOS III a sharp dispute arose over rules for developing the seabed between a small group of advanced states whose companies possessed technologies for mining the mineral-rich nodules and the large majority of countries that would be left out of the potential mineral bonanza unless they could participate in an international enterprise.

*Freedom* suggests flexibility in the types of activities that are permitted. Most actors—be they states, corporations, or individuals—value freedom and are reluctant to submit to limitations on their behavior. Freedom for states is embodied in the principle of sovereignty; for corporations, in the doctrine of free enterprise; and for individuals, in the principle of human rights as expressed in documents such as the Universal Declaration of Rights of 1948. In a frontier situation, where population is sparse, a greater amount of freedom of action can be tolerated without the prospect of severe environmental degradation. As a population becomes more dense and puts heavier demands on the environment, as it has done globally in recent decades, maintaining the quality of the environment becomes a more pressing problem. It should also be kept in mind that the freedom of one party to act often impinges on the freedom of others. For example, the freedom to emit sulfur dioxide indiscriminately may negate the freedom of others to fish in freshwater lakes and enjoy healthy forests.

No single strategy can be expected to maximize the achievement all four of these values. The steps necessary to conserve the resources of commons may require substantial compromises on freedom. Thus, preserving the ozone layer has required relinquishing the prerogative of producing and using CFCs and other chemicals that threaten atmospheric ozone. Maximizing commercial use of commons is also often at odds with the dictates of equity. For example, assigning quotas equally to all members of community, regardless of their capacity to make use of their shares, may lead to unexploited opportunities to exploit a commons, unless the quotas can be freely traded. Achieving equity may also be at odds with the goal of conservation. Allowing the developing countries to increase their emissions of greenhouse gases to the much higher levels that have prevailed in the industrial countries would thwart any prospect of minimizing climate change. Thus, developing countries have bargained for substantial amounts of technical and economic assistance as a quid pro quo for their acceptance of international rules that prevent them from substantially increasing their use of the atmosphere as a sink for these pollutants.

## CONCLUSIONS

Having taken note of the emergence of the environment as a major global issue and the initiation of an international response, this essay demonstrates some ways the story of the overgrazing of the pasture of the English village parallels several of the most serious environmental problems appearing on the agendas of international institutions. Hardin's story is helpful for understanding the motivation behind a variety of environmentally destructive behaviors, even by those who are well aware of the consequences of their actions. It is also useful for identifying courses of action that have potential for averting an environmental tragedy and the problems inherent in reconciling the objective of conservation with other values, such as maximizing production, achieving equity, and allowing freedom of action.

The parable fits some environmental contexts much better than others. It is especially applicable to the exploitation of limited resources in international commons, such as the oceans, atmosphere, radio waves, and outer space. It is of less value in analyzing the use of resources that lie entirely within the boundaries of states, notably fossil fuels, minerals, forests, and agricultural land, which have not been freely accessible to users from other countries. It has been proposed, however, that some of these latter resources be considered parts of the common heritage of humankind. For example, the millions of species of plants and animals that exist on the planet have been described as the "genetic heritage of mankind," even though the specimens of many are geographically concentrated within the borders of a single state.[8] Likewise, unique human artifacts from ancient civilizations, such as temples, sculptures, and paintings, have been designated by UNESCO as the "cultural heritage of mankind." Identifying them as such confers on the states in which they are located a responsibility to preserve them for present and future generations of the world's population.

[8] See Norman Myers, *The Primary Resource: Tropical Forests and Our Future* (New York: Norton, 1984).

# CREDITS

**CHAPTER 1**

K. J. Holsti, *International Politics: A Framework for Analysis,* 4th ed. (Englewood Cliffs, N.J.: Prentice-Hall) pp. 114–59. © 1983. Reprinted by permission of the author. Some footnotes have been deleted.

**CHAPTER 2**

Robert O. Keohane & Joseph S. Nye, Jr., "Power and Interdependence in the Information Age" from the Sept/Oct 1998 *Foreign Affairs,* 7, NO. 5 pp. 81–94. Copyright © 1998 by the council on Foreign Relations, Inc. Reprinted with permission.

**CHAPTER 3**

Bjorn Moller (original)

**CHAPTER 4**

Jack S. Levy (edited original)

**CHAPTER 5**

John Mueller, "The Obsolescence of Major War" from *Bulletin of Peace Proposals,* Vol. 21, No. 3, 1990, pp. 321–328. Copyright © 1990 Sage Publications, Ltd. Reprinted with permission.

**CHAPTER 6**

Paul H. Nitze, "The Threat Mostly to Ourselves," from the Op/Ed page of *The New York Times* October 28, 1999, p. A25. Copyright © 1999 The New York Times. Reprinted with permission.

## CHAPTER 7

Richard K. Betts, "The New Threat of Mass Destruction" from *Foreign Affairs,* Jan/Feb 1998, pp. 26–41. Copyright © 1998 by the Council on Foreign Relations, Inc. Reprinted with permission.

## CHAPTER 8

Walter Laqueur, "Terror's New Face: The Radicalization and Escalation of Modern Terrorism: From *Harvard International Review,* Vol. 20, No. 4, pp. 48–51. Reprinted with permission.

## CHAPTER 9

Robert A. Sirico, "The Trouble with Sanctions," *USA Today* magazine, Vol. 128, September 1999, pp. 14–15. Reprinted by permission of the Society for the Advancement of Education.

## CHAPTER 10

Joseph S. Nye, Jr., "The Changing Nature of World Power" from *Political Science Quarterly,* Vol. 105, No. 2, 1990, pp. 177–192. Reprinted by permission of The Academy of Political Science.

## CHAPTER 11

Ole R. Holsti (original)

## CHAPTER 12

David Held & Anthony McGraw, with David Goldblatt & Jonathan Perraton "Governing Globalization: Managing the Globalization of Organized Violence" in Global Governance, October 1999.

## CHAPTER 13

Richard N. Haas, "What to Do with American Primacy" from *Foreign Affairs,* Sept/Oct 1999, pp. 37–49. Copyright © 1999 by the council on Foreign Relations, Inc. Reprinted with permission.

## CHAPTER 14

Donald J. Puchala (original)

## CHAPTER 15

Ted Robert Gurr (original)

## CHAPTER 16

Richard Falk, "The New Interventionism and the Third World" from *Current History,* November 1999, pp. 370–375. Copyright © 1999 Current History, Inc. Reprinted with permission.

## CHAPTER 17

Samuel P. Huntington, "The Coming Clash of Civilizations or, The West Against the Rest," from *The New York Times,* June 6, 1993, p. E19.

## CHAPTER 18

David P. Forsythe (original)

## CHAPTER 19

Harvey Starr (original)

## CHAPTER 20

Bruce Russett (original)

## CHAPTER 21

Christopher C. Joyner (original)

## CHAPTER 22

Robert Gilpin in *The Political Economy of International Relations,* pp. 227–295. Copyright © 1987 Princeton University Press. Reprinted by permission of Princeton University Press.

## CHAPTER 23

Linda Y. C. Lim (original)

## CHAPTER 24

Thomas L. Friedman, "The World is Ten Years Old: The New Era of Globalization" in *The Lexus and the Olive Tree: Understanding Globalization,* 1999, pp. ix–x, xiii–xvi, xviii, 7–13. Copyright © 1999 Thomas L. Friedman. Reprinted by permission of International Creative Management, Inc.

## CHAPTER 25

Kathleen Newland, "Workers of the World, Now what?" from *Foreign Policy,* 114, Spring 1999, pp. 52–64. Copyright © 1999 by the Carnegie Endowment for International Peace. Reprinted with permission.

## CHAPTER 26

Paul Krugman, "Competitiveness: A Dangerous Obsession" from March/April 1994 *Foreign Affairs,* 73, pp. 28–44. Copyright © 1999 by the Council on Foreign Relations, Inc. Reprinted with permission.

## CHAPTER 27

Jeffrey Sachs & Felipe Larrain, "Dollarization is More Straightjacket than Salvation" from *Foreign Policy,* 116 Fall 1999, pp. 80–91. Copyright © 1999 by the Carnegie Endowment for International Peace. Reprinted with permission.

## CHAPTER 28

Ethan B. Kapstein, "Global Rules for Global Finance" from *Current History,* November 1998, pp. 355–360. Copyright © 1999 Current History, Inc. Reprinted with permission.

## CHAPTER 29

Greg Mastel (original)

## CHAPTER 30

Daniel J. Burton, Jr., "The Brave New Wired World" from *Foreign Policy*, 106, Spring 1997, pp. 23–37. Copyright © 1997 by the Carnegie Endowment for International Peace. Reprinted with permission.

## CHAPTER 31

Nancy Birdsall, "Life is Unfair: Inequality in the World" from *Foreign Policy,* 101, Spring 1998, pp. 76–92. Copyright © 1998 by the Carnegie Endowment for International Peace. Reprinted with permission.

## CHAPTER 32

John L. Peterson, "Getting Ready for the 21st Century," *USA Today* magazine, Vol. 127, May 1999, pp. 56–58. Reprinted by permission of the Society for the Advancement of Education.